# Database-Driven Web Sites, Second Edition

## Mike Morrison

## Joline Morrison

### University of Wisconsin - Eau Claire

THOMSON

COURSE TECHNOLOGY

Australia • Canada • Mexico • Singapore • Spain • United Kingdom • United States

## Database-Driven Web Sites, Second Edition

by Mike Morrison and Joline Morrison

**Senior Vice President, Publisher:**
Kristen Duerr

**Executive Editor:**
Jennifer Locke

**Product Manager:**
Barrie Tysko

**Developmental Editor:**
Marilyn Freedman

**Production Editor:**
Aimee Poirier

**Associate Product Manager:**
Janet Aras

**Editorial Assistant:**
Christy Urban

**Marketing Manager:**
Angie Laughlin

**Cover Designer:**
Joseph Lee
Black Fish Design

**Manufacturing Coordinator:**
Denise Powers

**Compositor:**
GEX Publishing Services

# BRIEF
# Contents

# TABLE OF
# Contents

# Preface

**W**eb development tools have changed dramatically since publication of the first edition of *Database-Driven Web Sites* in 2000. Today, Microsoft Visual Studio .NET and ASP.NET make it far easier to create and maintain complex Web applications than ever before. Naturally, Visual Studio .NET and ASP.NET are extensively covered in this book and represent a major change in what was covered in the first edition. Like the first edition, this book pulls together all of the Web technologies needed to create sophisticated Web sites. This includes expanded coverage of HTML, JavaScript, Web server administration, and database concepts, along with new and extensive coverage of VB .NET programming, ASP.NET, and Web application projects.

At the same time, the Personal Oracle9*i* database is now covered, along with the Microsoft Access database. You can use either Oracle or Access with this book. However, using the Personal Oracle 9*i* database (or even just reading about it) gives you experience with the types of client/server databases used to power commercial Web sites. The Personal Oracle9*i* database is identical in almost all ways to the Oracle Enterprise client/server database used in corporate and commercial settings.

Although we have dropped coverage of the older ASP, CGI, and ActiveX Web technologies, once you see what you can do with ASP.NET, we don't think you will miss these older technologies.

Creating ASP.NET applications calls for a clean break with the older ASP way of doing things. If you create ASP.NET applications outside of a Visual Studio .NET Web application project you lose many of the features that make Visual Studio .NET and ASP.NET so exciting. These features include drag and drop graphic page design, separate code files automatically synchronized with files containing HTML interface content, pop-up code completion lists, reliable, easy to use integrated page to page debugging, and project file management. Used within the context of a Web application project, Visual Studio .NET and ASP.NET provide all of this and thereby solve the complaints we have had with earlier generations of Web development technologies. All of this (and more than we can cover in the preface) makes it far easier to create and maintain complex Web applications than ever before.

## THE INTENDED AUDIENCE

*Database-Driven Web Sites, Second Edition* is intended for the individual who wants to create dynamic Web pages that interact with a database. Although substantial coverage of JavaScript and VB .NET is provided in this book, we recommend that you take **two programming**

**courses before working through this book**. The language(s) used in these prerequisite courses does not matter. These programming courses could be taught using Visual Basic, C++, Java, Perl, JavaScript, or any other language. What this book requires is a level of programming maturity and experience, not a specific language. Although it helps to have prior experience in Web programming, HTML, and/or database programming, this book provides enough information in all of these areas to enable you to complete the tutorials, projects, and cases in the book.

## THE APPROACH

This book integrates content and theory with tutorial exercises that help you put into practice what you are reading about. As you progress through the book you will study code examples, look at sample Web pages, and create a series of Web pages that bring together a number of techniques for creating dynamic Web pages. Data about two fictitious organizations, Clearwater Traders and Northwoods University, are used throughout the book to illustrate concepts and develop techniques. Each chapter concludes with a summary and review questions that highlight and reinforce the major concepts of each chapter. Hands-on Projects are included at the end of each chapter to let you practice and reinforce the techniques presented in the chapter. Additionally, four Case Projects are included with each chapter to let you create database-driven Web pages based entirely on your own design. Two of these Case Projects are ongoing—they build on previous chapters—and should be completed in sequence as you work through the chapters. The other two Case Projects do not require completing cases from previous chapters.

As you work through this book, you will use Visual Studio .NET as the development environment for the tutorials, projects, and cases. In the process, you will become familiar with Visual Studio .NET's capabilities as an HTML editor, script editor, VB .NET development environment, and Web form development environment.

## OVERVIEW OF THIS BOOK

The examples, tutorials, Hands-on Projects, and Cases in this book will help you achieve the following objectives:

- Understand the architecture of the World Wide Web.
- Create HTML pages using the XHTML standard.
- Use JavaScript to enhance Web pages.
- Use the Internet Information Services (IIS) Web server administration utility to configure virtual directories.
- Learn how to configure and work with ASP.NET Web application projects.
- Understand how to use VB .NET in a Web application project.

- Create and process Web forms using Server Controls.
- Become familiar with relational database concepts and learn how to create queries using SQL.
- Learn how to retrieve and display data in a Web form.
- Create integrated Web database applications.

In **Chapter 1**, you will become familiar with the architecture of the World Wide Web and learn about communication protocols and Web addressing. You will also learn how multiple server processes can run on the same Web server and examine different technologies that you can use to create Web pages that interact with a database. In **Chapter 2**, you will become acquainted with Clearwater Traders and Northwoods University, two fictitious organizations that the book uses to illustrate database-driven Web sites. You will learn about the Visual Studio .NET integrated development environment and use it to become familiar with HTML documents and basic HTML commands. In **Chapter 3**, you will learn how to reference objects in HTML documents using the HTML Document Object Model and dot syntax. You will create and debug client-side scripts that use JavaScript variables, decision control and looping structures, methods, event handlers, and custom functions. In **Chapter 4**, you will learn how to create JavaScript programs to validate HTML form inputs and create and read cookies. In addition, you will use arrays to structure data and reference form elements. You will also learn how to use the Script Debugger to locate and correct errors in client-side scripts. In **Chapter 5**, you will become familiar with the components of a Web server and learn how to specify the Web server's home directory and default document. You will use IIS to create and configure Web server physical directories, virtual directories, and applications. In **Chapter 6**, you will learn about the .NET framework, ASP.NET, and .NET server controls. You will learn how to use the Visual Studio .NET integrated development environment to create and manage Web application projects, and you will learn how to access and reference Web Forms. In **Chapter 7**, you will learn about the VB .NET programming language. You will declare and assign values to variables, create user-defined procedures, work with complex numeric and string expressions, create decision and repetition (looping) structures, and create and reference object classes. You will learn about the VB .NET collection class and use the VB .NET Debugger to monitor program execution. In **Chapter 8**, you will learn how Web servers use server-side processing to create dynamic Web pages. You will create event handlers for ASP.NET server controls. In addition, you will create HTML elements in Web forms; HTML server controls; list, radio button, check box, and calendar rich server controls; and validation controls. In **Chapter 9**, you will become familiar with client/server relational database concepts and terms and become familiar with the Oracle9i client/server database. You will learn how Web forms communicate with databases and learn how to create a data connection in Visual Studio .NET. In addition, you will write SQL queries to retrieve records from a single database table, join multiple database tables, perform operations on groups of data values, and insert, update, and delete data records. You will also learn how to sort and filter retrieved values. In **Chapter 10**, you will write VB .NET commands to create data components and retrieve and display database data on Web forms. You will create DataList and DataGrid rich server controls that allow users to display, update, and delete database data. You will learn how to validate user inputs in DataList and DataGrid controls. In addition, you will create a Web form that allows users to insert data into a database, and create a Web form that displays data that has master/detail relationships. In **Chapter 11**, you will become familiar with an integrated Web application that contains multiple Web forms. You will transfer processing from one Web form to another, share data values across multiple Web forms, simultaneously insert records in master and detail tables, add template columns to a DataGrid control, and implement security using forms-based authentication. Finally, you will deploy a completed Web application on a production Web server.

## Features

Each chapter in *Database-Driven Web Sites, Second Edition* includes the following elements to enhance the learning experience:

- **Chapter Objectives:** Each chapter in this book begins with a list of the important concepts to be mastered within the chapter. This list provides you with a quick reference to the contents of the chapter as well as a useful study aid.

- **Running Cases:** Beginning with Chapter 2, data from the fictitious Clearwater Traders company is used throughout the book for in-chapter tutorials, and data from the fictitious Northwoods University is used in end of chapter Hands-on Projects.

- **Step-By-Step Methodology:** As new concepts are presented in each chapter, step-by-step instructions allow you to actively apply the concepts you are learning.

- **Tips:** Chapters contain Tips designed to provide you with practical advice and proven strategies related to the concept being discussed. Tips also provide suggestions for resolving problems you might encounter while proceeding through the chapters.

- **Coverage of both Oracle9*i* and Microsoft Access 2002:** Beginning in Chapter 9 and continuing through Chapter 11, database concepts and programming techniques are presented for both Oracle9*i* and Access 2002.

- **Chapter Summaries:** Each chapter's text is followed by a summary of chapter concepts. These summaries provide a helpful way to recap and revisit the ideas covered in each chapter.

- **Review Questions:** End-of-chapter assessment begins with a set of review questions that reinforce the main ideas introduced in each chapter. These questions ensure that you have mastered the concepts and understand the information you have learned.

 **Hands-on Projects:** Along with conceptual explanations and tutorials, each chapter provides Hands-on Projects related to each major topic aimed at providing you with practical experience. Some of these involve enhancing or extending the exercises in the chapter tutorials, and some involve creating new applications. Some of the Hands-on Projects provide detailed instructions, whereas others provide less detailed instructions that require you to apply the materials presented in the current chapter and previous chapters with less guidance. As a result, the Hands-on Projects provide you with practice implementing Web programming in real-world situations.

**Case Projects:** Starting with Chapter 2 and continuing through the remaining chapters, four cases are presented at the end of each chapter. These cases are designed to help you apply what you have learned in the chapter to real-world situations. They give you the opportunity to independently synthesize and evaluate information, examine potential solutions, and make recommendations, much as you would in an actual business situation. These cases are based on four fictitious organizations: Ashland Valley Soccer League, Al's Body Shop, Sun Ray Videos, and Learning Technologies, Inc. The first two cases in each chapter, Ashland Valley Soccer League and Al's Body Shop, are independent from chapter to chapter. The Sun Ray Videos and Learning Technologies, Inc. are running cases that require completing cases from previous chapters.

In addition to these book-based features, *Database-Driven Web Sites, Second Edition* includes two software components:

- The Course Technology Kit for Oracle9*i* Software is available when purchased as a bundle with this book. It provides the Oracle9*i* database software, Release 2 (Version 9.2.0.1.0), on three CDs, so users can install this software on their own computers. The software included in the kit can be used with Microsoft Windows NT, Windows 2000 Professional, and Windows XP Professional operating systems. The installation instructions for Oracle9*i* and the log in procedures are available at *www.course.com/cdkit* on the Web page for this book's title.

- A DVD of Microsoft Visual Studio .NET Professional 60-day trial software is located in the back of this book. Please note that 60 days after installation this trial software will no longer function.

## TEACHING TOOLS

The following supplemental materials are available when this book is used in a classroom setting. All of the teaching tools available with this book are provided to the instructor on a single CD-ROM.

**Electronic Instructor's Manual.** The Instructor's Manual that accompanies this textbook includes:

- Additional instructional material to assist in class preparation, including suggestions for lecture topics.

- Solutions to all of the in-chapter tutorials and end-of-chapter materials, including the Review Questions, Hands-on Projects, and Case Projects.

- Installation and configuration troubleshooting techniques.

- Tips for correcting common errors.

**ExamView**. ExamView®—the ultimate tool for your objective-based testing needs. ExamView® is a powerful objective-based test generator that enables instructors to create paper, LAN, or Web-based tests from testbanks designed specifically for their Course Technology text. Instructors can utilize the ultra-efficient QuickTest Wizard to create tests in less than five minutes by taking advantage of Course Technology's question banks, or customize their own exams from scratch.

**PowerPoint Presentations**. This book comes with Microsoft PowerPoint slides for each chapter. These are included as a teaching aid for classroom presentation, to make available to students on the network for chapter review, or to be printed for classroom distribution. Instructors can add their own slides for additional topics they introduce to the class.

**Data Files**. Data Files, containing all of the data necessary for steps within the chapters, Hands-on Projects, and Case Projects, are provided through the Course Technology Web site at *www.course.com*, and are also available on the Instructor's Resources CD-ROM.

**Solution Files**. Solutions to the in-chapter tutorials, end-of chapter review questions, Hands-on Projects, and Case Projects are provided on the Instructor's Resources CD-ROM and may also be found on the Course Technology Web site at *www.course.com*. The solutions are password protected.

# ACKNOWLEDGMENTS

We would like to thank all of the people who helped to make this book possible. Thanks are due to our editor, Marilyn Freedman, who continues to be a pleasure to work with and who works as late at night as we do. We would also like to thank Barrie Tysko and Jennifer Locke from Course Technology for providing us with the support for developing this book with the latest Web development tools.

We are grateful to our reviewers for providing lots of comments and positive direction during the development of this book. They include David Barrentine, Johnson Community College; Gary Hackbarth, Iowa State University; A. Michael Hearn, Community College of Philadelphia; Jim Kattke, Augsburg College; Edward Kowalski, Briarcliffe College; Angela Mattia, J. Sargeant Reynolds Community College; Margaret McCoey, La Salle University; George M. Parsons, High Point University; Don Smith, Microsoft; and Dr. Kenneth D. Weeks, University of Wisconsin-Superior.

Finally, we thank our students and colleagues at the University of Wisconsin-Eau Claire who continue to teach us how to be better teachers and authors.

# Read This Before You Begin

## TO THE USER

If you are working in a computer laboratory, you must be able to start Visual Studio .NET and Internet Information Services (IIS) with local administration privileges. Your instructor or technical support person will provide instructions for starting and using these applications with the necessary privileges.

## Data Files

To complete the steps and projects in this book, you will need data files that have been created for this book. Your instructor will provide the data files to you. You also can obtain the files electronically from the Course Technology Web site by connecting to *www.course.com*, and then searching for this book title. Each chapter in the book has its own set of data files. These include files used in the Tutorials and also include any files that may be needed for end-of-chapter Hands-on Projects and Case Projects.

In the book, you are usually asked to run scripts and programs from the A: drive. You are usually reminded that your drive letter (and path) may be different. Throughout, keep in mind that it is always possible to use a different drive. You are free to save files wherever it is convenient for you. However, you must be sure to appropriately configure Visual Studio .NET and the Web server for the actual drive and paths you are using while working through the exercises. Instructions on how to configure Visual Studio .NET and the Web server are included in the relevant chapters. When you see instructions referring to the A: drive keep in mind that your drive letter and path may be different.

Once you begin working with Web application projects in Chapter 8, you will find that performance will improve dramatically if you store your project on and run your projects from a hard disk rather than a floppy disk. In Chapter 11, the files required for the integrated Web application are too large to fit on a floppy disk, so you will have to save your work on a hard disk at that point. We recommend saving your work on a hard disk for all of your Web application projects, beginning with Chapter 8.

## Solution Files

### Floppy Disk Solution Folders

Throughout this book you will be instructed to save files to your Solution Disk (for example, "save the file as logon_VALIDATE.htm in the Chapter4\Tutorials folder on your Solution Disk"). Therefore, it is important to make sure you are using the correct Solution Disk when you begin working on each chapter.

To create your Solution Disk folders, you will need 11 blank, formatted high-density disks. You will use one floppy disk for each chapter in the book, so label each disk accordingly (for example, Chapter1 Solutions, Chapter2 Solutions, and so on). On each disk, create an empty Solution folder, then create an empty folder for the chapter. In each chapter folder, create empty Projects, Tutorials, and Cases subfolders. For example, if your Solution folder is in the root folder of your A: drive, the subfolders will be:

- A:\Solution\Chapter1\Projects
  (Note: Chapter 1 doesn't have any tutorial exercises or cases)

- A:\Solution\Chapter2\Cases

- A:\Solution\Chapter2\Cases\Als

- A:\Solution\Chapter2\Cases\Ashland

- A:\Solution\Chapter2\Cases\LTI

- A:\Solution\Chapter2\Cases\Sunray

- A:\Solution\Chapter2\Projects

- A:\Solution\Chapter2\Tutorials

- A:\Solution\Chapter3\Cases

- A:\Solution\Chapter3\Cases\Als

- A:\Solution\Chapter3\Cases\Ashland

- A:\Solution\Chapter3\Cases\LTI

- A:\Solution\Chapter3\Cases\Sunray

- A:\Solution\Chapter3\Projects

- A:\Solution\Chapter3\Tutorials

- --- and so on for the rest of the chapters

Chapter 11 solution files will not fit on a floppy disk if you are using the Access database and must be stored on a hard disk. If you are using Access, and you need to turn in files from Chapter 11 for a class assignment, you must submit the files online or by copying files onto two floppy disks. Be aware, however, that to work with the completed Chapter 11 tutorial files, the files will need to be on a hard disk, not two floppy disks.

## Hard Disk Solution Folders

We recommend working with solution files stored on a hard disk, if possible, and, if needed, copying the solutions as needed to floppy disks when you need to turn in assignments.

The folder structure on a hard disk will be the same as that used on each floppy disk. If you follow the floppy disk Solution folder example in the preceding section, substitute the C: drive for the A: drive.

## Using Your Own Computer

To use your own computer to complete the chapters, Hands-on Projects, and Case Projects in this book, you will need the following:

- **350MHz Pentium II or faster computer**. This computer must have at least 256 MB of RAM and at least 3 GB of free hard disk space. You will need 6 GB of free hard disk space if you plan to install the Personal Oracle 9*i* database rather than Access.

- **Microsoft Windows 2000 Professional or Windows XP Professional**. Visual Studio .NET cannot be installed on Windows XP Home edition, Windows NT, Windows ME, or Windows 98.

- **Internet Information Server (IIS)**. The IIS Web server is included on the Windows 2000 Professional and Windows XP Professional installation CD. However, it is not automatically installed. To install IIS, go to the control panel (select Start, then Control Panel) and select Add or Remove Programs. Next, select Add/Remove Windows Components. Check the Internet Information Services (IIS) box in the Components list. Click the Details button, then clear the SMTP Service box (this is an unneeded security risk), and then click OK. Click the Next button. If you are prompted for the Windows installation CD, put it in your CD drive, and then let the installation complete.

- **Microsoft Visual Studio .NET Professional**. Be sure to install IIS before installing Visual Studio .NET. If you accidentally reverse the sequence, you will need to reinstall Visual Studio .NET (after installing IIS) to allow it to add server extensions to IIS that are needed for Web application projects. Visual Studio .NET requires approximately 2 GB of disk space.

- **Microsoft Access 2000 or Access XP**. You will need to install either an Access database or a Personal Oracle 9*i* database. Access 2000 and Access XP come with their respective Microsoft Office software suites, and you can install them from the Microsoft Office installation CDs.

- **Personal Oracle 9*i***. You will need to install either an Oracle 9*i* database (version 9.2.0.1.0 or later) or an Access database to complete the exercises in this book. If your computer has Internet access, a third option might be to access an Oracle 9*i* database server that has been set up for you by your instructor. In this case, you instructor will provide instructions on how to access the Oracle9*i* database server. The Course Technology Kit for Oracle9*i* Software contains the database software necessary to perform all the Oracle database tasks shown in this textbook. Detailed installation, configuration, and log on information are provided at *www.course.com/cdkit*. Look for this book's listing and front cover, and click on the link to access information specific to this book.

- **Microsoft Internet Explorer 6.0.2 or higher**. Microsoft Internet Explorer, Version 6, is installed during the Visual Studio .NET installation process. However, you can also download a copy of Internet Explorer 6.0.2 or higher from the Internet Explorer home page at no cost. Connect to *www.microsoft.com/windows/ie/*, and then click the Download link on the menu on the left side of the Web page.

## A Note on Syntax

This book contains many examples of code statements. Sometimes these statements are too long to fit on a single line in this book. A single line of code that must appear on two lines in the book due to its length will appear with an arrow in the right margin as follows:

```
lblMsg.Text = row.Cells(1).Text & " " & row.Cells(2).Text ⤶
                & " " & row.Cells(3).Text & " was added to your cart"
```

## Visit Our World Wide Web Site

Additional materials designed especially for you might be available for your course on the World Wide Web. Go to *www.course.com*. Periodically search this site for more details.

---

## TO THE INSTRUCTOR

If your users are working in a computer laboratory, they must be able to start Visual Studio .NET and Internet Information Services (IIS) with local administration privileges. The Instructor's Manual provides strategies and instructions for configuring your computer laboratory to provide these privileges, as well as configuration troubleshooting techniques and tips for correcting common errors.

To complete the chapters in this book, your users must use a set of data files. These files are included in the Instructor's Resources. The Instructor's Resources also contains solutions to all of the Tutorials, Hands-on Projects, and Case Projects used in the book. The data and solution files may also be obtained electronically through the Course Technology Web site at *www.course.com*. Follow the instructions in the Help file to copy the data files to your server or standalone computer. You can view the Help file using a text editor such as WordPad or Notepad. Once the files are copied, you should instruct your users how to copy the files to their own computers or workstations. The Tutorials, Hands-on Projects, and Case Projects in this book were tested using Windows 2000 Professional; Windows XP Professional; Access XP; Personal and Enterprise editions of Oracle 9*i*, Release 9.2.0.1.0; IIS 5.0 (Windows 2000 version); IIS 5.1 (Windows XP Professional version); and Internet Explorer 6.0.2.

## Course Technology Data Files

You are granted a license to copy the data files to any computer or computer network used by individuals who have purchased this book.

# 1

# INTRODUCTION TO WEB DATABASE PROGRAMMING

**In this chapter, you will:**

♦ Become familiar with the architecture of the World Wide Web

♦ Learn about communication protocols and Web addressing

♦ Learn how multiple server processes can run on the same Web server

♦ Become familiar with data-based Web pages, and examine different technologies that you can use to create data-based Web pages that interact with a database

♦ Understand the role that the eXtensible Markup Language (XML) plays in data-based Web applications

♦ Understand the role that client-side scripts play in validating user inputs in data-based Web pages

The e-commerce boom is fueling the demand for data-intensive Web sites that merge Web and database technologies. Customers need to be able to get information about a vendor's products and services, submit inquiries, select items for purchase, and submit payment information. Companies need to be able to track customer inquiries and preferences and process customer orders. In addition, companies are widely using intranets to provide managers and employees with a readily accessible interface to internal databases. This demand for data-intensive Web sites is the driving force behind the merger of Web sites and database technologies. As commerce on the Web expands, Web developers are experimenting with a variety of technologies that promise to increase the utility and speed up the development and maintenance of Web sites.

A **Web application** consists of one or more files that developers create to solve a problem or provide a service through a Web site. A complex Web application may consist of multiple Web pages that perform many different functions within the application. One page might display information about a vendor's products, a second page might gather inputs about a user's selections, and a third page might summarize the user's order and provide delivery information. Developers may create each of these pages using a different technology, so a Web application often integrates many different technologies.

This chapter describes the architecture of the World Wide Web, explores Web page addressing and processing, and describes different technologies that are currently available for creating Web applications that derive information from a database. The chapter also presents an overview of how you can use XML to enhance Web applications.

## THE ARCHITECTURE OF THE WORLD WIDE WEB

The Web consists of computers on the Internet that are interconnected in a specific way, making those computers and their contents easily accessible to each other. When computers are interconnected, some computers act as servers, and other computers act as clients. People generally think of a **server** as a computer that shares its resources with other computers. A **client** is a computer that requests and uses server resources. Today, almost any computer can be a server and can run more than one server process. Therefore, it is more accurate to refer to a server as a particular process that enables other computers to share the resources of the computer on which the server process is running.

Examples of server resources include data, such as files; hardware, such as printers; or shared server-based programs, such as databases and e-mail programs. A **server process** is a program that listens for and responds to requests from clients. For example, when you start an e-mail program and connect to an e-mail server, the e-mail server process notifies you if you have new messages, sends you your new messages when you request them, and forwards your messages to the recipient's e-mail server.

 The same computer can act as both a client and a server. For example, your workstation could share files with other users, and it could also request files from other servers.

The Web has a **client/server architecture**, which means that programs on servers communicate and share files with client workstations over a network. Users at home or in offices work on client-side computers that are connected to the Internet, and use programs called **Web browsers**, or simply **browsers**, to access the information on the Internet. Two popular browsers are Netscape Navigator and Microsoft Internet Explorer. **Web servers** are computers, often located at businesses, that are connected to the Internet and run special Web server software. Web servers store the files that people can access via the Internet.

A **Web page** is usually a file with an .htm or .html extension. The file contains **HyperText Markup Language (HTML)** tags and content in the form of text, numbers, images, video, and audio. Most Web page files today use the shorter .htm extension, so the .htm extension will be used in this book. HTML is a document-layout language that defines the content and appearance of Web pages. HTML is not a programming language, although it can contain embedded programming commands. The primary task of HTML is to define the structure and appearance of Web pages and to allow Web pages to embed hyperlinks that enable you to easily move to a different, related Web page.

HTML allows you to specify how text will appear in a Web browser by bracketing the text with **tags**, which are formatting commands enclosed in angle brackets. For example, the tag <b> specifies that text within a Web page appears in boldface type. You can make the word *hello* appear in boldface in a Web browser by placing it within an opening bold tag (<b>) and a closing bold tag (</b>), as follows: <b>hello</b>. The tags don't appear on the Web page display, but their effect, the word *hello* in boldface, appears.

The special software that runs Web servers includes a component called a listener. The **listener** is a server process that "listens" for messages that are sent to the server from the client browsers. When a Web server's listener receives a message from a browser requesting a Web page, the listener forwards the request to the Web server. The Web server then reads and sends, or downloads, the requested HTML file, which specifies the content and appearance of the Web page, back across the Internet to the user's browser.

When a file is sent from a server to a client, it is said to be **downloaded**. When a file is sent from a client to a server, it is said to be **uploaded**.

After the client downloads the HTML file, it appears in the user's browser as a Web page formatted according to the HTML tags the file contains. Figure 1-1 illustrates the Web architecture.

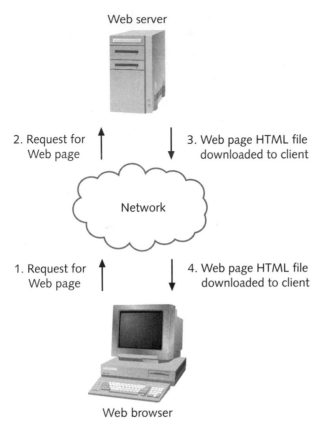

Web server

2. Request for Web page

3. Web page HTML file downloaded to client

Network

1. Request for Web page

4. Web page HTML file downloaded to client

Web browser

**Figure 1-1**   Web architecture

## COMMUNICATION PROTOCOLS AND WEB ADDRESSES

Communication protocols are agreements between a sender and a receiver regarding how to send and interpret data. Two important protocols that are used to send data over the Internet are the Transmission Control Protocol and the Internet Protocol. All data transported over the Internet—such as e-mail messages, files, and Web pages—is broken into **packets**, or small chunks of data that can be routed independently through the Internet over different transmission lines. The **Transmission Control Protocol (TCP)** defines how the sending computer breaks down long messages into packets and how the receiving computer reassembles them into complete messages. The **Internet Protocol (IP)** specifies how the sending computer formats message addresses. Both protocols are typically used to transfer data on the Internet, so people commonly abbreviate and refer to them as **TCP/IP**.

When users configure their computers to connect to a TCP/IP network, they install and configure TCP/IP networking software on the computer's hard drive and in its internal configuration files. When they boot the computer, this software is loaded into memory to process TCP/IP network traffic. Users can then use the computer to send e-mail, browse the Web, or act as a Web server.

Every computer that is connected to the Internet has a unique **IP address** that specifies the computer's network location. IP addresses are generally expressed as four numbers (ranging in value from 0 to 255) separated by periods (or decimal points). An example of an IP address is 137.28.23.210. Numbers of this type are difficult to remember, so an IP address can also be represented by a **domain name**, which is a name that has meaning to people and is easier to remember. Examples of domain names are msdn.microsoft.com and nytimes.com.

A **domain name server (DNS)** is a computer that maintains tables with domain names matched to their corresponding IP addresses. Domain name servers are maintained by **Internet service providers (ISPs)** that provide commercial Internet access for customers and by organizations with many users connected to the Internet. Examples of popular ISPs are America Online (AOL) and Prodigy. There are many other ISPs throughout the world that offer Internet service to local and regional customers.

 Many domain names have a *www* prefix, such as *www.amazon.com*. Others, such as *msdn.microsoft.com*, do not. Suppose you enter a domain name that has two words that are separated by periods, such as amazon.com, in your browser's Address field. The browser first tries to find the Web site represented by the domain name as entered. If it does not find a Web site associated with the domain name as entered, the browser will automatically prefix the domain name with *www* and try to find the Web site represented by the *www*-prefixed domain name.

Information on the World Wide Web is usually transferred using a communication protocol called the **HyperText Transfer Protocol (HTTP)**. HTTP coordinates communications between Web servers and browsers for sending Web pages across the Internet. Web browsers also support older Internet protocols such as the File Transfer Protocol (FTP). FTP is an underlying protocol often used to transfer data files such as word processing documents and spreadsheets.

Users request a Web page from a Web server by entering the Web page's Web address in their browser. A **Web address**, also called a **Uniform Resource Locator (URL)**, is a string of characters, numbers, and symbols that specify the communications protocol (such as HTTP or FTP) and the domain name or IP address of a Web server. Optionally, the string may also specify the folder path for the HTML file that specifies the contents of the Web page, as well as the name of the HTML Web page file. Figure 1-2 illustrates the components of a URL.

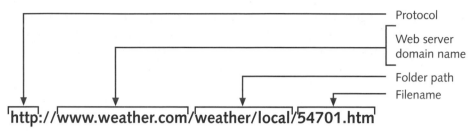

Protocol

Web server
domain name

Folder path

Filename

`http://www.weather.com/weather/local/54701.htm`

**Figure 1-2**    URL components

If the URL does not specify a communication protocol, Web browsers assume the HTTP protocol by default. If the URL does not specify a folder path, the Web server assumes that the default starting location is the Web server's home directory. This directory provides the starting point for all of the files that are available to client browsers from the Web server. The Web administrator specifies the actual physical path to the Web server's home directory while configuring the Web server. This folder can be any folder on the Web server's hard drive.

After the domain name, a URL can contain a series of folder names, separated by front slashes (/), which specify a location in the Web server's file system. The filename extension determines whether the Web server processes the request by running a program or by simply downloading a file. If the filename extension specifies a program file, the Web server runs the program, which generates the HTML code that ultimately appears in the user's browser. Figure 1-3 shows an example of a URL in which the filename specifies a program with a .pl extension, which specifies a program file written using the PERL programming language.

Filename is a
program

**Figure 1-3**    URL that specifies a program filename

If the filename specifies a known file type that isn't a program, the Web server downloads the file to the client browser without performing any processing. A **known file type** is a file with an extension that the Web server recognizes. If the document has an .html or .htm extension, the client browser displays the document directly as a Web page. If the document has a recognized file extension, such as .doc for Microsoft Word documents or .ppt for Microsoft Powerpoint documents, the browser gives the user the option of opening the file directly in the browser or saving the document in the file system of the client workstation. Figure 1-4 illustrates a URL with a known document file type, as well as the dialog box that appears to allow the user either to open or save the document.

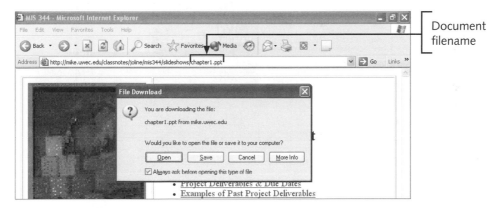

**Figure 1-4**   URL that specifies a document filename

If the user enters the Web server domain name in his or her browser and does not specify the name of an HTML file, then the Web server downloads its default home page to the user's browser. Therefore, the Web administrator must also specify the Web server's default home page filename when configuring the Web server. Typical default home page filenames used by administrators are default.htm, index.htm, and home.htm. Figure 1-5 shows an example of a URL (*http://www.uwec.edu/*) that does not specify a folder path or HTML file, and displays the Web server's default home page.

When a user specifies a domain name as part of a Web address, the Web browser sends a message to a domain name server requesting the IP numeric address corresponding to the domain name. After receiving the IP address, the browser tries to contact the server listening on that address. If the user knows the desired IP address, he or she can slightly reduce the time needed to download a Web page by entering the numeric IP address directly, rather than using the domain name. You should use domain names if they exist, however. Although looking up an IP address from a domain name stored in a domain name server can slow response time, a Web administrator might change the IP address assigned to a server while retaining the same domain name. URLs that specify a Web server address or domain name are called **Internet URLs**, because they specify a communications protocol, such as HTTP or FTP, in the first part of the URL.

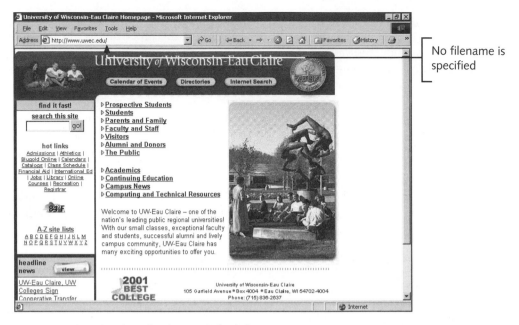

**Figure 1-5**   URL that displays a default home page

A URL can also be a **file URL**, which is a reference to an HTML file stored on the user's hard drive. A file URL is usually used by programmers only when they are developing new Web pages and want to see how the pages appear in a browser. For example, if you are developing a Web page that is stored in a file named index.htm that is stored on drive C in the \Webdocs folder of your workstation, you would enter the following file URL: file:///c:\Webdocs\index.htm.

In a file URL, three front slashes (/) follow the *file* keyword.

Although *file:///* is the standard file URL notation, Microsoft browsers allow a shorthand form of this notation. You can shorten the file URL file:///c:\Webdocs\index.htm to c:\Webdocs\index.htm.

## RUNNING MULTIPLE SERVER PROCESSES ON THE SAME WEB SERVER

**1**

Recall that a server process listens for and responds to requests from clients. A single server can host many different server processes. For example, a small company might run its e-mail server and Web server on the same computer. Servers using Internet protocols manage multiple listener processes through the concept of ports.

A **port** corresponds to a memory location on a server. A port is identified by a number, and is associated with a TCP/IP-based server process. Every request that is sent from a client to a server must specify the server's IP address, and the port number of the server process to which the message is directed. For example, when you use an e-mail program to request your new e-mail messages, the e-mail program automatically formats the request to include the e-mail server's IP address and the correct port number for the server process that responds to these requests.

TCP/IP software is loaded when a server is booted. When the TCP/IP software is loaded, a TCP/IP table that lists port numbers and associated server programs is also loaded. Table 1-1 lists common TCP/IP server processes and their default port numbers.

**Table 1-1**    Default port numbers for common TCP/IP server processes

| TCP/IP Server Process | Port Number |
|---|---|
| FTP server control | 21 |
| Telnet | 23 |
| SMTP e-mail server (sending messages) | 25 |
| Web server | 80 |
| POP3 e-mail server (receiving and managing messages) | 110 |

A message addressed to a specific IP address must always specify the port to which the message is directed. The port for messages addressed to Web servers is port 80. When a browser sends a request to a Web server for a Web page, the Web server listener process sees the message is addressed to its IP address and to port 80. Because both necessary conditions (the IP address and port corresponding to the Web server process) are met, the Web server processes the request.

If the Web server administrator chooses to change or reassign the Web server process port to a value other than 80, the URL must indicate the assigned port by placing the alternate port value after the Web server IP address or domain name, separated by a colon, using the following format:

```
http://web_server_address:port_number/
```

For example, the following URL specifies port 81:

```
http://137.28.224.5:81/examples/example1.htm
```

## DATA-BASED WEB PAGES

In a **static Web page**, the developer determines the content when creating the page. When any user accesses a static Web page, it always displays the same information. Figure 1-6 shows an example of a static Web page. It always appears with the same basic elements, regardless of when or how the user retrieves it.

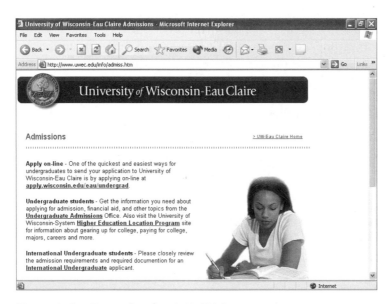

**Figure 1-6**    Example of a static Web page

In a **dynamic Web page**, the content varies based on user inputs or data retrieved from external sources. Figure 1-7 shows an example of a dynamic Web page based on user inputs, where the user used the Google search engine to find images based on motorcycles.

Figure 1-8 shows an example of a dynamic Web page based on retrieved data values. On this page, the user retrieves data about soccer teams from a database.

Regardless of whether a dynamic Web page is created based on user inputs or retrieved data, the Web server program must format the dynamic content in an HTML document, then send the HTML document to the client's browser as a Web page. In this book, **data-based Web pages** refer to dynamic Web pages that derive some or all of their content from data files or databases, and may be based on user inputs.

You can create data-based Web pages using data stored in data files or data stored in a database. Data-based Web pages can use data retrieved from XML files, which are text files that store data using a standardized structure. In this book, you will create data-based Web pages using data retrieved directly from databases and using data stored in XML files. The following sections provide an overview of how developers create data-based Web pages using these two approaches.

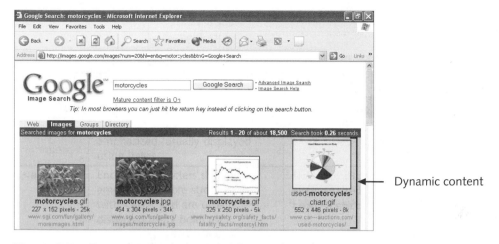

**Figure 1-7**    Example of a dynamic Web page based on user inputs

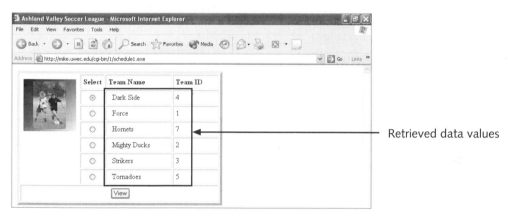

**Figure 1-8**    Example of a dynamic Web page based on retrieved data

## CREATING DATA-BASED WEB PAGES USING DIRECT DATABASE RETRIEVALS

You can create data-based Web pages using data that is retrieved from a database and then placed in the Web page. You can use either server-side processing or client-side processing to retrieve the data. With server-side processing, a Web server receives a request from a user's browser, performs the processing tasks and database queries necessary to create the dynamic Web page, and sends the finished Web page back to the user's browser. Client-side processing queries the database directly from a program running in the client browser and bypasses the Web server. Figure 1-9 shows some of the primary server-side and client-side processing technology choices available to Web programmers for creating data-based Web pages using direct database retrievals.

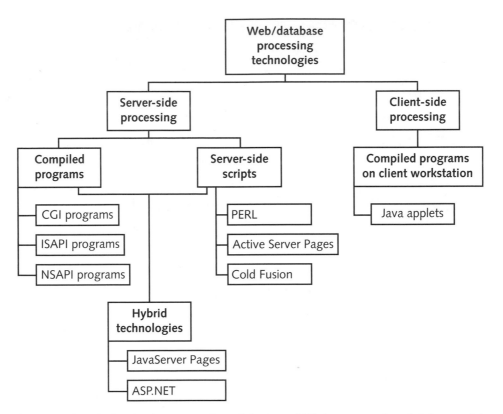

**Figure 1-9**    Technologies supporting data-based Web pages using database retrievals

The following subsections explore these technologies in more detail.

## Server-Side Processing

Recall that dynamic Web pages can be based on user inputs. Most server-side data-based Web page technologies use **HTML forms**, which are enhanced HTML documents that, like paper forms, collect user inputs and send them to the Web server for processing. HTML forms allow users to input data using text boxes, option buttons, and lists. Figure 1-10 shows an example of an HTML form used to gather input about student projects. It contains option buttons, text boxes, and command buttons.

When the user clicks the Submit Form button, the HTML form is submitted to the Web server, and a program running on the Web server processes the form inputs and dynamically composes a Web page reply. This program, called the **servicing program**, can use a variety of approaches to process inputs and create dynamic Web page outputs. Form servicing programs can be compiled executable programs, uncompiled programs (scripts) that are interpreted and processed when they are run, or a hybrid of both.

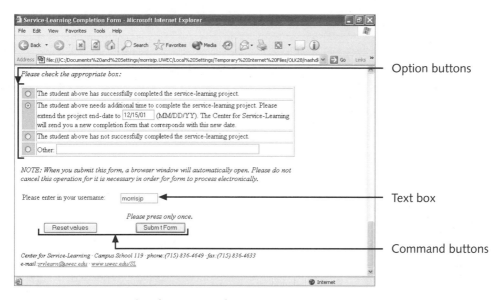

Option buttons

Text box

Command buttons

**Figure 1-10**    Example of an HTML form

## Server-Side Compiled Programs

**Compiled programs** are written in a text-based programming language, and then translated into the machine language understood by a computer's processor. The original text program is referred to as the **source code**. The translated version is referred to as the **compiled code**. When you create a compiled program, the computer's hard drive stores the compiled code, and this compiled code does not need to be recompiled each time it is run. Figure 1-11 shows the processing steps that occur when you use a server-side compiled program to create a data-based Web page.

When a user submits an HTML form to a server program for processing, the Web server receives the form inputs and starts the servicing program. The program is not part of the Web server listener or administration utilities, but is an independent program that runs on the Web server. The servicing program retrieves the form input variables, processes them, queries the database as needed, stores the output values formatted with HTML tags in a server memory location, and then terminates. The Web server then reads the output values and sends them back to the user's browser, where they appear as a Web page.

You can create server-side programs using almost any language that can create programs, provided the language supports commands used by one of the communication protocols that establish guidelines for communication between Web servers and servicing programs. The first communication protocol established for use with HTML forms was the **Common Gateway Interface (CGI)**. Today, many servicing programs on Web sites still use CGI-based programs. Most CGI programs are written in C, Java, or PERL.

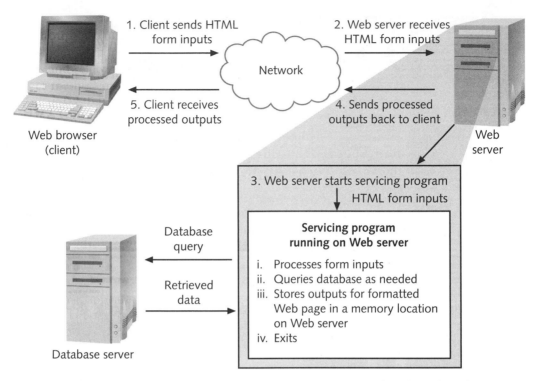

**Figure 1-11** Using a server-side compiled program to create a data-based Web page

A disadvantage of using CGI–based servicing programs is that each form that is submitted to a Web server starts its own copy of the servicing program on the Web server. In Figure 1-12, you can see that when three different browsers submit form inputs from the same Web page to a Web server, the Web server simultaneously starts and runs the same CGI program three times. The Web server starts a new copy of the CGI program for each browser request.

A busy Web server is likely to run out of memory when it services many forms simultaneously, so as interactive Web sites have gained popularity, Web server vendors have developed new technologies to process form inputs without starting a new copy of the servicing program for each browser's inputs. These technologies for communicating with Web servers include Netscape's Netscape Service Application Programming Interface (NSAPI) and Microsoft's Internet Server Application Programming Interface (ISAPI). These technologies rely on procedures residing in dynamic–link libraries (DLLs). The DLL allows a single set of procedures stored in the DLL to service multiple users without starting multiple instances of the procedures.

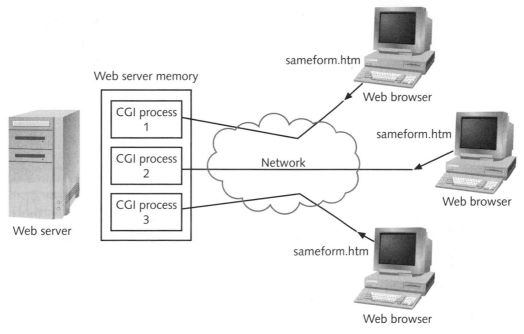

**Figure 1-12** Web server running the same CGI process three times to service inputs from multiple browsers

A **dynamic-link library (DLL)** is a compiled code module that other programs can call. A DLL is not a stand-alone program, but it contains code that can be *linked* to, and simultaneously used by, many different programs. An example of a DLL is cards.dll, which is stored in your \Windows\System32 folder. This DLL contains the graphic images and programs for a deck of playing cards, and is used in many card games.

NSAPI and ISAPI programs are usually written in C or C++. Figure 1-13 shows how a single ISAPI or NSAPI process can service form inputs from multiple client browsers.

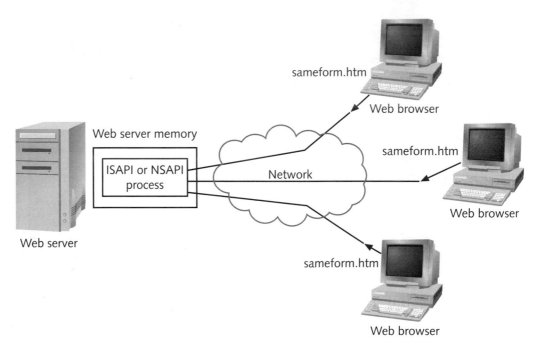

**Figure 1-13**   Web server running a single ISAPI or NSAPI process to service inputs from multiple browsers

## Server-Side Script Processing

A **script** is a computer program that is translated into a machine-readable format and executed one line at a time. Every time you run a script, it must be translated to machine-readable format, so in general, scripts execute more slowly than compiled programs. **Server-side scripts** execute on the Web server, process HTML form inputs that change database values, create dynamic Web pages that show data, and generally do everything compiled programs do.

One approach for creating server-side scripts is to use the CGI communication protocol and write the script using the PERL (*Practical Extraction and Report Language*) scripting language. PERL contains features derived from UNIX, C, and BASIC. The current version of PERL, version 6, handles binary and text file processing on a variety of operating systems and Web server platforms. The language itself is terse, and programmers specify many operations with one- or two-character commands. Special characters such as $, #, %, and / are heavily used to indicate data types and operations. Figure 1-14 shows an example of a PERL script that interacts with an HTML form.

The HTML form allows a user to enter a name in a text box referenced as T1, and select an option button in a radio button group referenced as R1. When the user clicks Submit, the PERL script executes, and creates and returns the HTML document shown in Figure 1-15. This document displays the name that the user entered, along with text displaying the label of the selected option button.

PERL has built-in functions for manipulating text strings and processing files, and for making the code easier to understand and work with. Although it is possible to write well-documented and maintainable PERL scripts, the language encourages cryptic shortcuts, so PERL scripts are often difficult to understand and maintain.

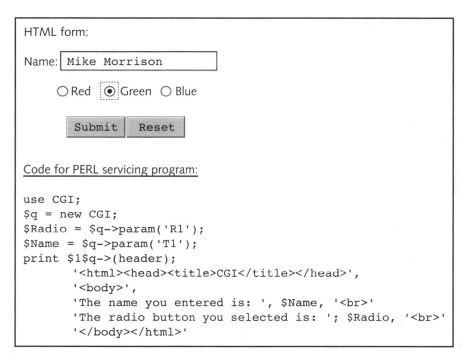

Figure 1-14    PERL server-side script example

Figure 1-15    Web page output from a PERL script

Microsoft's **Active Server Page (ASP)** technology provides an approach for creating server-side scripts that do not use the CGI protocol. When a user enters input values into an HTML form and clicks the Submit button, the form can call a server-side ASP file. By default, the commands in an ASP file, which has an .asp extension, are in the VBScript programming language, which is similar to Visual Basic. Programmers can also create ASPs using the JavaScript language, which is similar to VBScript, but has a different syntax. Figure 1-16 shows the code for an ASP servicing program that performs the same processing tasks as those in the PERL script in Figure 1-14. The VBScript commands are enclosed within <% %> tags. The output would look the same as the Web page output shown in Figure 1-15.

```
<SCRIPT LANGUAGE='VBSCRIPT'>
<HTML><HEAD><TITLE>CGI</TITLE></HEAD>
<BODY>
The name you entered is:
<%= request.querystring ('R1') %>
The radio button you selected is:
<%= request.querystring ('T1') %>
</BODY></HTML>
```
— VBScript commands

**Figure 1-16**    ASP server-side script example

 ASP scripts usually execute on Microsoft Web servers, although some third-party add-on programs enable ASPs to execute on other Web servers.

When an ASP file is submitted to a Microsoft Web server, the file's .asp extension signals the server to process the file as an ASP script and then return the output to the user as a formatted Web page. Script delimiter tags (<% … %>) indicate to the browser which commands to process as code rather than display as Web page text and tags. As processing proceeds, retrieved data values might appear on the current Web page or might be passed as parameters to a different Web page that the script code calls. ASP scripts have an advantage over CGI programs in that a single ASP script started in the Web server's main memory can service multiple forms submitted to the Web server.

## Server-Side Hybrid Processing

The advantage of using compiled server-side programs is that after they are developed, they are compiled and stored in a machine-readable format. They do not need to be translated into machine-readable format each time they execute, so they usually run faster than scripts. Also, programmers usually create compiled programs in integrated development environments that often provide debugging utilities that make it easy to locate and correct errors. The advantage of using scripts is that you can modify them using a text editor; you do not have to install an associated development environment to modify them. Hybrid server-side programming strives to combine the advantages of compiled server-side programs and server-side scripts: You create a server-side script, and you do not have to compile it explicitly. The first time a user accesses a Web page that calls the script, the script is compiled into machine-readable format and stored as an executable file. This way, you can always work with an ordinary text file and need not install an integrated programming development environment to modify the script. The program does not need to be translated into machine language each time it runs, which improves performance.

Shortly after Microsoft introduced ASP technology, Sun Microsystems introduced JavaServer Page (JSP) technology. JSPs are similar to ASPs, with one major difference: ASPs use server-side script processing, and code within an ASP must be interpreted from source code text into machine-readable format each time it runs. JSPs use server-side hybrid processing. JSP source code is automatically compiled into machine-readable format the first time a user accesses it. The Web server saves the compiled JSP program and uses this rather than the source code the next time anyone else tries to access this particular JSP. This reduces the Web server's processing, and shortens the time the user has to wait to view a response from the Web server. If a programmer modifies the JSP source code, the Web server notes that the source code file has been modified since the compiled version was created, and compiles and saves the compiled program the next time a user accesses the page.

Microsoft has released a new version of ASP called ASP.NET. ASP.NET uses the server-side hybrid processing model and adds features that simplify database access. ASP scripts created using ASP.NET are not backward-compatible with ASP scripts created using the original ASP server-side scripting technology, and upgrading older ASP scripts to ASP.NET requires substantial revisions. Most new Web programming projects that use ASP technology will probably use ASP.NET pages rather than the older ASP technology. ASP.NET pages can run alongside ASP pages on the same Web server because ASP.NET pages use an .aspx file extension to tell the Web server to process them as ASP.NET rather than as ASP.

 ASP.NET is sometimes called ASP+, which is the name that Microsoft originally gave the product.

## Client-Side Processing

You can create data-based Web pages that perform direct database retrievals using compiled programs that are downloaded and subsequently installed and executed on the client workstation. Figure 1-17 illustrates one way that client browsers install and interact with client-side compiled programs to create data-based Web pages.

When a user clicks a hyperlink on a Web page that is associated with a compiled client-side program, the Web server processes the request and sends the code for the compiled client-side program to the user's workstation. The user's workstation must be able to install and run the executable program file. When installed and running, this program sends data directly to and retrieves data directly from the database server as needed, bypassing the Web server.

Before a client-side program is installed on your workstation, a security warning such as the one shown in Figure 1-18 appears on your screen.

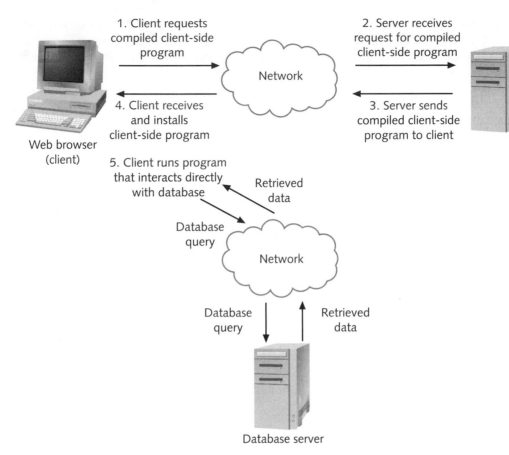

1. Client requests compiled client-side program

2. Server receives request for compiled client-side program

Network

4. Client receives and installs client-side program

3. Server sends compiled client-side program to client

Web browser (client)

5. Client runs program that interacts directly with database

Retrieved data

Database query

Network

Database query

Retrieved data

Database server

**Figure 1-17**    Using a compiled client-side program to create data-based Web pages

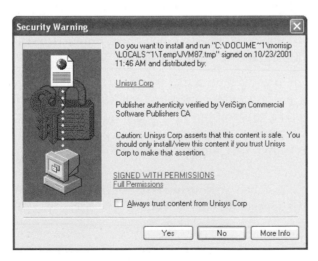

**Figure 1-18**    Security warning that appears prior to installing a client-side program

This warning informs you that an application is about to be installed on your workstation, and specifies the source of the application. You should download and install applications only from reputable sources. After you click Yes on the security warning dialog box, the application is downloaded, installed, and started on your workstation.

A second approach to running compiled programs in a browser relies on using Java applets. **Java applets** are self-contained Java programs designed to run in a generic Java runtime environment supplied by most Web browsers. Figure 1-19 shows an example of a Java applet running in a Web browser.

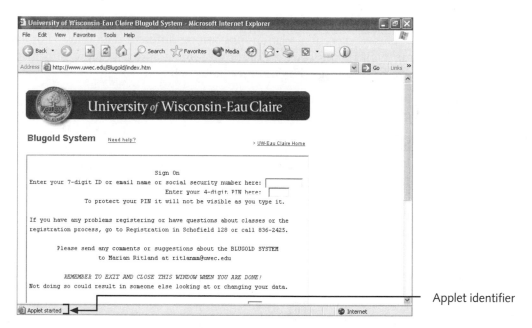

Applet identifier

**Figure 1-19**    Example Java applet

You can identify an applet by the "Applet started" text that appears in the browser status line. For security reasons, Java applets can send data to and receive data only from a database server process running on the same computer as the Web server process. A Java applet cannot read data from or write data to any files on the user's workstation. Java applets are intended to run uniformly on any operating system and with any Web browser. Unfortunately, the Java runtime environment is implemented inconsistently in different browsers, and even within different versions of the same browser. This makes it difficult to create a Java applet that runs identically within all browsers.

## Creating Data-Based Web Pages Using Data Stored in XML Files

Different applications often use different database and file formats for storing data. This causes problems when these applications need to share data. For example, suppose a company wants to send purchase orders to a vendor electronically. If the company's purchase order information is stored in a different format than the vendor's, the purchase information must be translated to a format that is compatible with the vendor's program or be reentered manually. This problem also occurs within the same organization: A sales database in the marketing department may not be able to use information about customers from the company's accounting system, because the data is not in a compatible format.

One way to overcome this dilemma is to translate data into a standard format that is compatible with a variety of applications. **XML (eXtensible Markup Language)** provides rules, guidelines, and conventions for representing data in a text file format. The developer must structure the data in a specific and unambiguous format. XML also allows developers to represent relationships among different data values. For example, an XML file can contain information about customers and also show information about the different products that each customer has purchased.

In an HTML document, the HTML tags primarily define the appearance of the data, and HTML standards define the exact meaning of each tag. For example, the <b> tag defines that the text that follows appears in boldface font. In an XML file, custom tags define the *meaning* of the data (rather than its appearance), and developers define and create these custom tags. For example, a custom <customer> tag might indicate that the text that follows is about a customer and that it is divided into name, address, and telephone number sections. In addition to providing the tags that define the data structure, the XML file also contains the actual data values. Figure 1-20 shows an example of an XML-formatted text file.

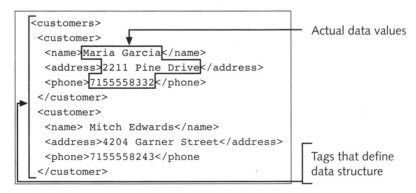

**Figure 1-20**    Example XML-formatted text file

You can create XML-formatted files that contain data values that you want to appear in Web pages and then display these XML files directly in a Web browser. You can also create XML-based Web pages using a variety of technologies to format and manipulate the data stored in XML files. Two approaches are available for formatting and manipulating data stored in XML files: server-side XML processing and client-side XML processing.

In **server-side XML processing**, a conversion program runs on the Web server that extracts the data from the database and converts the retrieved data to an XML format. You then use an XML/HTML conversion program to translate the XML data into a formatted HTML file. (The processes that translate the data to XML format and the XML to HTML can be combined into a single program.) The HTML file is then transmitted across the network to the user's browser. Figure 1-21 illustrates server-side XML processing.

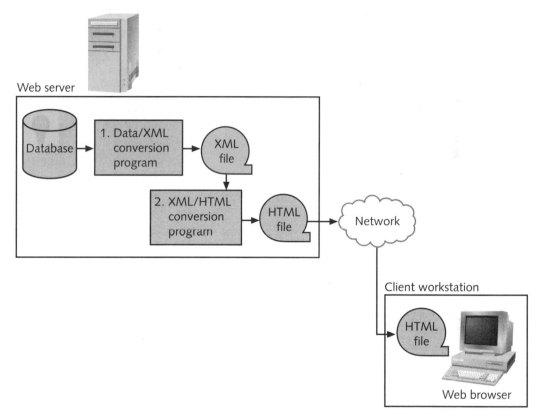

**Figure 1-21**   Server-side XML processing

**Client-side XML processing** converts the database data to an XML-formatted file on the Web server and then downloads the XML file to the client workstation. Figure 1-22 illustrates this approach. The server downloads the XML file through the network to the client workstation, where it is processed by an XML parser running on the client. An **XML parser**, which is also called an **XML processor**, interprets and translates the XML tags so that a browser presents them as a formatted Web page. Microsoft provides an XML parser through the **MSXML dynamic-link library (MSXML.DLL)**. The client-side technologies used in this book to transform XML files to formatted Web pages include cascading stylesheets, eXtensible Stylesheet Language Transformations (XSLTs), and data binding. Of these three technologies, cascading stylesheets and data binding are client-side only. XSLTs can be processed either on the client or on the server.

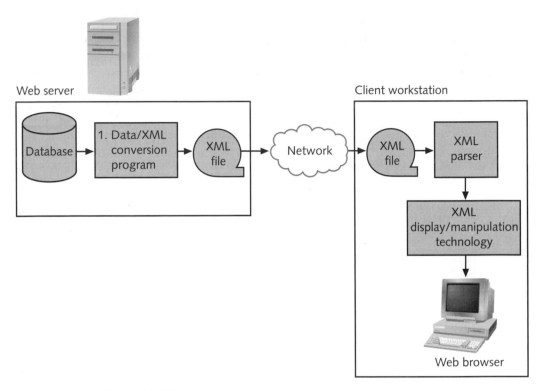

**Figure 1-22**    Client-side XML processing

## Client-Side Scripts

Developers who create data-based Web pages using server- and client-side direct data access and XML technologies often use client-side scripts to add functionality to their Web pages. **Client-side scripts** consist of text commands that are embedded in an HTML document, along with the HTML tags and the Web page content. Developers place the script code within delimiter tags to indicate to the user's browser that this text is code rather than Web page text. If capable of recognizing and interpreting the script code, the user's browser processes the code. If the browser cannot recognize and interpret the code, the script code appears as text on the Web page unless the script author has enclosed the code in an HTML comment. An HTML comment is text within an HTML file that does not appear on the Web page, but is used to internally document or describe the HTML file's contents.

Client-side scripts support tasks such as verifying data, opening new browser windows, providing animated graphics, and performing other programming tasks that do not require interaction with the Web server. Client-side scripts differ from server-side scripts in that they do not directly support interaction with traditional files or databases. The most popular languages for creating client-side scripts are JavaScript and VBScript.

Client-side scripts are often used to validate user inputs entered on HTML forms that Web browsers submit to server-side programs for processing. This approach avoids transmitting inputs to the Web server that are incomplete or have errors, and offloads error checking and handling from the Web server program to the client workstation. Figure 1-23 shows an example of the output of a client-side script program that verifies whether or not an online shopper entered all required fields in the shipping address.

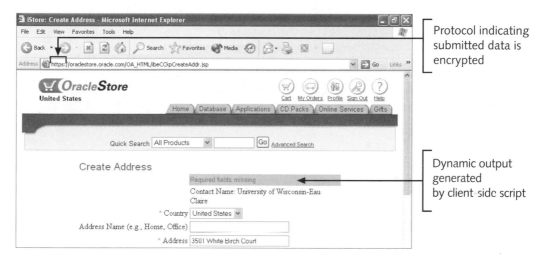

**Figure 1-23**    Client-side script output for data verification

In Figure 1-23, the "Required fields missing" message appears after the user tries to submit the form to the Web server. After checking the values in the form fields and determining that the user did not enter some of the required field values, a client-side script displayed the message.

In Figure 1-23, the https:// protocol identifier indicates that the Web server uses the **secure socket protocol**, which means that the data is **encrypted**, or translated into a secret code. Most Web servers that process online transactions use the HyperText Transfer Protocol over Secure Socket Layer (*https*) protocol.

Developers can also use client-side scripts to create advanced Web page features, such as an image map that allows the user to move the mouse pointer over a graphic image and click to access different Web page links, or to open a new browser window to display an alternate Web page. Client-side scripts can create timers that display graphics or play sounds, or can create "cookies" that store data on a user's computer about his or her actions while browsing a Web page.

In this book, you will learn how to create client-side scripts using JavaScript. JavaScript's syntax is similar to that of C, C++, and Java. Developers can add JavaScript client-side scripts to otherwise standard HTML Web pages using special HTML delimiter tags. Figure 1-24 shows an HTML document that contains code for a JavaScript procedure that ensures that a user entered his or her name in a form input box.

```
<html><head><title>Clearwater Traders - Order Tracking</title></head>
<body>
<h2>Clearwater Traders - Order Tracking</h2>

<script language = "JavaScript">
  <!-- hide this script from old browsers
  function validate(){
    if (document.login.StudentName.value == "") {
      alert ("Please enter your name!")
          return
    }
    alert ("Thanks for entering your name, " +
           document.login.StudentName.value + "!")
    document.login.submit()
  }
  //-->
</script>

<form name="login" onsubmit="validate()">
  Please enter your name:
  <input type="text" name="StudentName" size="20">
  <input type="submit">
</form></body></html>
```

**Figure 1-24**   JavaScript client-side script

When the user enters his or her name in the name input box and then clicks the Submit Query button, the script runs and the dialog box shown in Figure 1-25 appears.

**Figure 1-25**   Output from an example client-side script when the user enters her name

If the user does not enter his or her name before clicking the Submit Query button, the dialog box shown in Figure 1-26 appears.

1

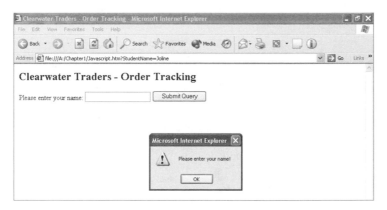

**Figure 1-26**    Output from an example client-side script when the user does not enter her name

Developers can also use JavaScript for server-side processing. This process requires using Web server–specific language derivatives. Developers can use a version of JavaScript called LiveWire on Netscape Web servers for server-side processing of form inputs. Alternatively, developers can use a Microsoft-specific version of JavaScript called Jscript in Active Server Pages on Microsoft Web servers.

VBScript is the default scripting language for ASPs, and its syntax is similar to that of Visual Basic. Only Microsoft Web browsers can interpret client-side scripts written in VBScript. JavaScript is the most commonly used and supported client-side scripting language, and can be interpreted by Netscape, Microsoft Internet Explorer, and most other browsers.

## CREATING DATABASE-DRIVEN WEB SITES

You can use many different technologies to create programs that generate data-based Web pages. These technologies differ based on whether the programs run on the server or on the client workstation, and whether the programs are stored in a text (script) format or in a machine language (compiled) format. The technologies are similar because all of them enable the user to interact with a database using his or her browser. Figure 1-27 illustrates the technologies you will use in this book to create database-driven Web sites.

Figure 1-27 shows the client workstation, Web server, and database server processes running on different computers connected by a network, but you will probably run all three of these processes on your computer. On the client side, you will use the Internet Explorer Web browser to display Web pages. In Chapter 2 you will learn how to create Web pages using HTML, and in Chapters 3 and 4 you will learn how to create client-side scripts using JavaScript. You will use the Internet Information Services (IIS) as the Web server process. In Chapter 5, you will learn how to configure a Web server using IIS.

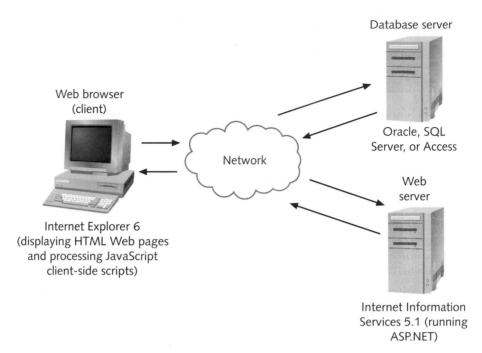

**Figure 1-27**    Database-driven Web site technologies

You will use the ASP.NET hybrid technology to create server-side scripts, which the Web server stores as compiled programs. In Chapters 6, 7, and 8 you will become familiar with ASP.NET. In Chapter 9, you will learn about databases, and you will learn how to interact with a database in the ASP.NET environment. In Chapters 10 and 11, you will learn how to create dynamic data-based Web pages in which an ASP.NET script interacts with the database process.

## CHAPTER SUMMARY

- ❐ The Web has a client/server architecture consisting of Web servers that communicate with client workstations running Web browsers. A Web server is a computer that is connected to the Internet and runs a software process called a listener that receives and processes users' requests for Web pages. A Web browser is a program that users run to request and display Web pages on their computers.

- ❐ A Web page is a file with an .htm or .html extension. The file contains HTML tags and text that define the appearance and content of a Web page display.

❏ A communication protocol is an agreement between a sender and a receiver that specifies how to send and interpret data. Two of the main Internet protocols are the Transmission Control Protocol, which defines how to break down and reassemble long messages, and the Internet Protocol, which specifies how to address messages. Together, these protocols are called TCP/IP.

❏ Every computer that is connected to the Internet has a unique IP address that specifies the computer's network location. An IP address can be represented by a domain name, which is a descriptive name that is associated with a specific IP address.

❏ You can request a Web page by specifying a Web address URL. A URL is a string of characters, numbers, and symbols that specify the communications protocol, the domain name or IP address of a Web server, the folder path where the Web page HTML is located, and the name of an HTML Web page file.

❏ A single computer can host many different server processes. Servers using Internet protocols manage multiple server processes using ports, which are memory locations that specify which server process will receive incoming network messages.

❏ By default, Web server processes run on port 80. If a Web server process is running on another port, the URL for Web page requests to that server must specify the port number.

❏ A static Web page is a Web page file that always displays the same information. A dynamic Web page has content that varies based on user requests. Data-based Web pages are dynamic Web pages that derive some or all of their content from data files or databases.

❏ You can create data-based Web pages using data stored in data files or using data retrieved directly from a database. Many data-based Web pages use data retrieved from XML (eXtensible Markup Language) files, which are text files that store data using a standard structure.

❏ You can create data-based Web pages that derive their data directly from a database using either server-side or client-side processing. With server-side processing, a Web server receives a request from a user's browser, performs processing and database queries necessary to create the dynamic Web page, and sends the finished Web page back to the user's browser. With client-side processing, the user's workstation downloads the processing program and performs all processing; the processing bypasses the Web server.

❏ Server-side processing usually involves HTML forms, which are enhanced HTML documents that collect user inputs and send them to the Web server. A servicing program on the Web server then processes these inputs.

❏ Server-side servicing programs can be compiled programs, scripts, or hybrids that combine the advantages of both compiled programs and scripts. You can use the CGI protocol to create server-side compiled programs. You can create server-side scripts using PERL or Active Server Pages. To create hybrid programs, you can use JavaServer Pages and ASP.NET.

◻ You can create data-based Web pages using client-side processing by creating programs that are downloaded and subsequently installed and executed on the client workstation. Most compiled client-side programs use Java applets.

◻ XML provides rules, guidelines, and conventions for representing data in a text file format. XML uses tags to specify the data's structure in a specific and unambiguous format. You can display XML files directly in a Web browser, or you can use a variety of technologies that format and manipulate the data stored in XML files and create Web pages.

◻ In server-side XML processing, you write a conversion program, which runs on the Web server, to extract the data from the database and convert the retrieved data to an XML format. You then use an XML/HTML conversion program to translate the XML data to an HTML file representing a formatted Web page.

◻ Client-side XML processing converts the database data to an XML-formatted file on the Web server, then downloads the file to the client workstation. The client workstation can then translate or transform the XML file data so it appears in a Web page.

◻ Client-side scripts contain text commands, which are embedded in an HTML document, along with the HTML tags and the Web page content, and perform tasks such as verifying data and opening new browser windows on data-based Web pages.

## REVIEW QUESTIONS

1. A(n) _____ is a computer process that enables a computer to share its resources with other computers on the network.

2. True or false: A workstation can act as both a client and a server in a client/server architecture.

3. A(n) _____ is a computer at a business location that is connected to the Internet and runs special software that includes a component called a _____, which monitors incoming messages.

   a. Web server, port

   b. Web browser, listener

   c. Web server, listener

   d. Web browser, port

4. What is a Web browser?

5. _____ is a page layout language that formats text and graphics to appear as Web pages.

6. What are the possible file extensions for a Web page file?

7. What is a port? Describe how ports are used to process client requests.

1

8. A _____ is an agreement between a sender and receiver about how messages are communicated.

   a. Port

   b. Process

   c. Protocol

   d. Packet

9. Describe the TCP and IP Internet communication protocols.

10. How are domain names associated with IP addresses?

11. The main Web communication protocol is _____.

12. What is a URL? What are the possible components of a URL?

13. When is a Web server's default home page displayed?

14. Why should you normally use a domain name rather than an IP address within a URL?

15. What is a file URL?

16. When do you need to specify a port number in a URL?

17. Describe two approaches that use server-side processing to create data-based Web pages.

18. How do you use client-side processing to create data-based Web pages?

19. Explain how hybrid server-side processing differs from other types of server-side processing.

20. Why do JSPs perform better than ASPs?

21. What is the difference between applications created using ASP and using ASP.NET?

22. _____ provides a set of rules that allow developers to create text files that define the content and structure of data.

   a. XML

   b. HTML

   c. HTTP

   d. HTTPS

23. What is the difference between server-side XML processing and client-side XML processing?

24. What are client-side scripts? List two uses for client-side scripts.

25. True or false: You can use client-side scripts to retrieve data directly from databases.

# HANDS-ON PROJECTS

The following projects ask you to find examples of Web sites or Web pages that have certain characteristics. You will be asked to create a screenshot of the Web page. To create a screenshot, display the image on your screen and then press Print Screen, which places a copy of the current screen display image on the Windows Clipboard. You can then paste the image into Microsoft Word. Save all screenshot images in the Chapter1\Projects folder on your Solution Disk.

## Project 1-1 Finding a Default Home Page

Find an example of a Web site that displays a default home page when you specify the domain name or IP address in the Address field of your browser. Save the screenshot of the default home page in a file named 1Project1.doc.

## Project 1-2 Finding a Web Page that Displays a Known File Type

Find an example of a Web page that displays a known file type (such as a word processor document) when you type or select a filename in the Address field of your browser. Save the screenshot of the Web page in a file named 1Project2.doc.

## Project 1-3 Finding a Dynamic Web Page that Displays Values based on User Inputs

Find an example of a dynamic Web page that contains data values based on user inputs. Save the screenshot of the Web page in a file named 1Project3.doc.

## Project 1-4 Finding a Dynamic Web Page that Retrieves Data Values

Find an example of a dynamic Web page that contains data that is retrieved from a data file or database. Save the screenshot of the Web page in a file named 1Project4.doc.

## Project 1-5 Finding a Web Page with a Client-Side Validation Script

Find an example of a Web page that contains a client-side script that validates user inputs. Create a screenshot of the output from the client-side script that appears on the Web page and save the file as 1Project5a.doc. Also create a screenshot of the script code, and save the file as 1Project5b.doc. (*Hint:* To view the script code, click View on the Internet Explorer menu bar, and then click Source. Scroll down the Web page source code until you see the script specification, which will look something like Figure 1-24.)

# 2

# INTRODUCTION TO HTML

**In this chapter, you will:**

◆ Become acquainted with Clearwater Traders and Northwoods University, two fictitious organizations that illustrate database-driven Web sites

◆ Learn about the Visual Studio .NET integrated development environment

◆ Become familiar with HTML documents and basic HTML commands

◆ Use the Visual Studio .NET HTML Designer to create static Web pages

◆ Create HTML tables

◆ Use HTML commands to create hyperlinks in HTML documents

◆ Create HTML forms that accept user inputs

**W**hen you create data-based Web pages, you write programs that send queries to a database based on user inputs. These programs then create dynamic Web pages that display query results in the user's browser. To write these programs, you must be familiar with HyperText Markup Language (HTML), which specifies the appearance and contents of Web pages. In this chapter, you will learn about HTML and become familiar with the structure of an HTML document. You will learn basic HTML commands, and use these commands in the Visual Studio .NET environment to create static Web pages. You will also learn how to create HTML tables, which display data values in a tabular format. (You will use tables to display database data in later chapters.) And, you will learn how to create HTML forms. Web developers use HTML forms to collect user inputs, which Web server programs then use to create and process database queries. This chapter is not a comprehensive overview of HTML; instead, it describes the HTML commands you will use in later chapters to create data-based Web pages.

This book follows the eXtensible HyperText Markup Language (XHTML) 1.0 standards for HTML Web page formatting. **XHTML** is a set of standards for HTML that that was established in 1999 by the World Wide Web Consortium (W3C) working group of the International Standards Organization. These standards seek to make HTML tags and syntax work well with XML documents. (Recall that XML provides a way to format data that appears in Web pages.) Specific XHTML standards for HTML formatting will be highlighted throughout the chapter.

For some commands, XHTML standards are not yet supported by Internet Explorer Version 6.0 or Visual Studio .NET. In these cases, we will emphasize the disparity and use the HTML 4.01 standard command.

The next section will acquaint you with Clearwater Traders and Northwoods University, which are two fictitious organizations that you will encounter throughout the tutorials and end-of-chapter projects in this book. Then you will learn how to use HTML to create static Web pages for these organizations.

# Case Study Organizations Illustrating Database-Driven Web Sites

In this book, you will encounter tutorial exercises and end-of-chapter projects that illustrate Web sites and data-based Web pages for Clearwater Traders and Northwoods University. These two fictional organizations have Web site and database requirements that demonstrate the concepts and tasks that this book presents. The following subsections describe the Web site requirements for these fictional organizations.

## The Clearwater Traders Sales Order Web Site

Clearwater Traders markets a line of clothing and sporting goods via mail-order catalogs. Clearwater Traders accepts customer orders via telephone, mail, and fax, and wants to begin accepting orders using its Web site. Currently the company stores information about products, customers, and customer orders in its relational database. Figure 2-1 shows the proposed home page for the Clearwater Traders Web site.

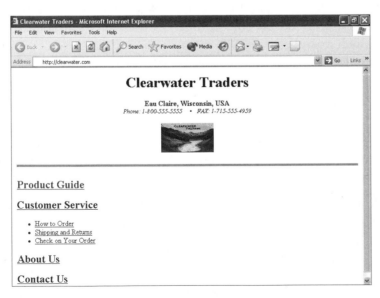

**Figure 2-1** Clearwater Traders home page

When the user clicks the Product Guide hyperlink, the Web site displays information about available merchandise, including item descriptions, photo images, sizes, prices, and whether or not an item is available. When the user clicks the How to Order hyperlink, a Web page appears that allows the user to specify the desired quantity of each item, and enter shipping and billing information. When the user clicks the Check on Your Order hyperlink, the user can select one of his or her orders, and view its current status. To support these operations, the Web site must be able to translate user inputs into queries that it sends to the organization's database.

## The Northwoods University Student Registration Web Site

Northwoods University has decided to replace its aging mainframe-based student registration system with a more modern database system that includes a Web-based interface. Figure 2-2 shows the proposed Web site's home page.

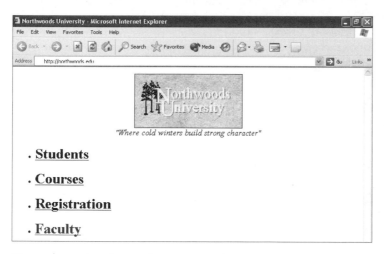

**Figure 2-2**   Northwoods University home page

Because security is a prime concern on this Web site, when the user clicks any of the hyperlinks on the home page, a dialog box appears asking the user to log on using a user ID and personal identification number (PIN). When users click the Students hyperlink, they will be able to view information about current students. When users click the Courses hyperlink, the site gives them the option of viewing current course listings or viewing information on courses they have completed. They can also request transcripts using the Web site. When users click the Registration hyperlink, they can view which courses are available during the current term, and can enroll in open courses. Users can click the Faculty link to view information about the faculty.

Faculty members log on to the system by entering their faculty IDs and PINs. Then they can select from a list of the courses they are teaching in the current term and retrieve a list of students enrolled in the selected course. A faculty member also could retrieve a list of his or her student advisees, select one, and then retrieve that student's past and current course enrollment information.

# THE VISUAL STUDIO .NET INTEGRATED DEVELOPMENT ENVIRONMENT

Visual Studio .NET is an integrated development environment for creating Windows and Web-based applications. An **integrated development environment (IDE)** is an environment for developing programs that displays multiple windows for performing different tasks. An IDE usually has an integrated debugging environment that enables you to step through your program commands, and observe how the program executes and how variable values change during execution. In this chapter, you will become familiar with HTML commands by creating static Web pages using the HTML editor provided in the Visual Studio .NET integrated development environment. Now you will start Visual Studio .NET and examine its environment.

To start Visual Studio .NET and examine its environment:

1. Click **Start** on the taskbar, point to **All Programs**, point to **Microsoft Visual Studio .NET**, and then click **Microsoft Visual Studio .NET**. (Windows NT users will point to Programs instead of All Programs.) The Visual Studio .NET integrated development environment opens, as shown in Figure 2-3. Maximize the window if necessary.

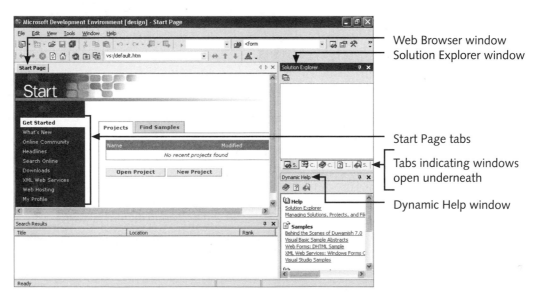

**Figure 2-3**    Visual Studio .NET integrated development environment

Your Visual Studio .NET window may look different from Figure 2-3 because your IDE has different windows open. To open all of the windows shown in Figure 2-3, perform the following steps:  Click View on the menu bar, and then click Solution Explorer; click View on the menu bar, and then click Class View; click Help on the menu bar, and then click Contents; click Help on the menu bar, and then click Index; click Help on the menu bar, and then click Search; click Help on the menu bar, and then click Dynamic Help; click Help on the menu bar, and then click Search results; click Help on the menu bar, and then click Show Start Page.

In the Visual Studio .NET IDE in Figure 2-3, the Web Browser, Solution Explorer, Search Results, and Dynamic Help windows are currently open. Note that tabs appear at the bottom of the Solution Explorer window. These tabs indicate that other IDE windows are open underneath the Solution Explorer window. To view the name of the window associated with each tab, place the mouse pointer on the tab. A ScreenTip appears, showing the window name. To move one of these windows so it is visible on top of the Solution Explorer window, you click the tab associated with the window.

In the Visual Studio .NET IDE, you can open or close windows as needed. To close a window that is currently open, click the Close button on the window title bar. To open a new window, click View or Help on the menu bar, and then click the name of the window that you want to open. You use the windows listed under the View menu to create and manage applications, and you use the windows listed under the Help menu to search for and view online help topics.

The **Web Browser window** displays the built-in Web browser within the IDE. Currently, the Web Browser window displays the Visual Studio **Start Page**, which is the default home page for the Web browser within the Visual Studio .NET IDE. The tabs that appear on the left side of the Start Page enable you to access different Web pages within the default home page. (You may have to scroll down in the Web Browser window to view all of its contents.)  In Visual Studio .NET, a **project** is a set of related files—such as code, images, HTML documents, and so forth—that comprise an application. The Get Started page enables you to create new projects or to access existing ones. You use the What's New, Online Community, Headlines, Search Online, and Downloads pages to access Web links that contain information or to communicate with other Visual Studio users. The Web Hosting page enables you to configure the Web server within Visual Studio. Finally, you use the My Profile page to set your user preferences for how the Visual Studio .NET IDE appears and behaves by changing IDE properties such as the keyboard mapping, the window layout, and the Help system configuration.

 To display the Start Page at any time in Visual Studio, click Help on the menu bar and then click Show Start Page.

The **Solution Explorer window** lists all solutions that are currently open in the IDE. A **solution** consists of one or more projects. For small applications, a solution might contain only a single project. For large applications, a solution can contain multiple projects. When you create a new project on the Start Page, the Visual Studio .NET IDE automatically creates a new solution. You can add new projects to an existing solution.

The Visual Studio .NET IDE is a complex environment with many features. If you encounter problems when using a feature, your first source of information is the Visual Studio .NET Help system. In this system, you use the **Search window** and the **Search Results window** to search for and retrieve online help information. When you type a search condition in the Search window, the results appear in the Search Results window. You can **filter** searches, which limits the search to a specific product in the Visual Studio environment, such as Visual Basic or Visual C++. Now you will make the Search window visible and retrieve information about the Solution Explorer window.

To make the Search window visible and retrieve online help information:

1. Move the mouse pointer onto the fifth tab from the left edge of the Solution Explorer window. The Search ScreenTip appears. Click the **Search** tab. The Search window appears as the top window.

You can also open the Search window by clicking Help on the menu bar and then clicking Search.

2. Type **solution explorer window** in the Look for text box, open the **Filtered by list**, select **.NET Framework SDK**, and then click **Search**. The Help Search In Progress dialog box appears briefly, and then the search results appear as a list in the Search Results window.

3. Double-click the first item in the Search Results window list. Detailed information for the item appears in the Web Browser window.

If a dialog box opens that states that the local disk does not contain the required files, you probably did not install the online Help system when you installed Visual Studio .NET. You can exit Visual Studio .NET and install the online Help system, and then repeat this set of steps. Or you can place the required CD in your CD-ROM drive, click Browse, navigate to your CD-ROM drive, and then view the online Help information.

4. Double-click the second item in the Search Results window to view the item's detailed Help information.

5. Close the Search Results window.

The **Dynamic Help window** displays context-sensitive Help topics for the object that is currently selected and active in the IDE. In Figure 2-3, the Solution Explorer is currently selected, so the Dynamic Help window displays Help topics for the Solution Explorer. Now you will make the Solution Explorer window visible and active in your IDE and then retrieve information about this window using the Dynamic Help window. Then you will make the Class View window visible and active and observe how the Dynamic Help window changes.

To use the Dynamic Help window to retrieve information about the Solution Explorer window and the Class View window:

1. Click the **Solution Explorer** tab, which is the first tab on the bottom edge of the upper-right window. This makes the Solution Explorer window visible and active. Note that the Dynamic Help window topics appear as shown in Figure 2-3.

To make the Solution Explorer window visible and active, you could also click View on the menu bar and then click Solution Explorer.

2. Click the **Solution Explorer** link in the Dynamic Help window. A description of the Solution Explorer appears in the Web Browser window.

3. Click the **Class View** tab, which is the second tab on the bottom edge of the upper-right window. Note that the Dynamic Help window topics change to show topics about the Class View window.

The Class View window allows you to view the components of a solution based on hierarchical relationships among projects and the objects they contain.

You will use the Visual Studio .NET IDE throughout the book to create data-based Web applications. In this chapter, you will use it to create HTML documents that define static Web pages. When you use the Visual Studio .NET IDE to create static Web pages, you mainly work in the Web Browser window. Because you will not work with projects or solutions, you will now close the Solution Explorer and Class View window. You will also close the Help system windows, so that only the Web Browser window remains open.

To close all windows in the IDE except the Web browser window:

1. Switch to the Solution Explorer window, then click the **Close** button on the Solution Explorer window.

2. Close all other open windows except for the Web Browser window.

3. Click **Help** on the menu bar, then click **Show Start Page** to redisplay the Start Page.

If you accidentally close the Web Browser window, click Help on the menu bar and then click Show Start Page to reopen the Web Browser window.

## HTML DOCUMENTS AND BASIC HTML COMMANDS

HTML is a document layout language with hypertext-specification capabilities. A **document layout language** is a language consisting of special formatting symbols that developers use within a text document to specify the document's appearance. These symbols specify the position, size, style, and formatting for objects such as text, tables, lists, and graphic images. Users can view or print the document using a Web browser that interprets the codes and formats the output. **Hypertext** is a way to navigate through a document or series of documents by following links represented by keywords or images. HTML is not a programming language, although it can contain embedded programming language commands. The primary task of HTML is to define the structure and appearance of Web pages and to allow Web pages to contain embedded hypertext links to other documents or to other Web pages.

An **HTML document** is a text file with an .htm or .html extension that contains formatting symbols, called *tags*, which define how a Web page appears in a Web browser, and text, which presents the content that appears on the Web page. In this book, you will use the .htm extension for HTML document files, because that is the default extension that Visual Studio .NET gives to HTML files.

Because HTML files are text files, you can create them using a text editor such as Notepad. You can also create HTML documents using an **HTML converter**, which converts Web page content from a non-HTML format, such as a word processor file to an HTML document. For example, you can convert a Microsoft Word source document into an HTML document that can appear as a Web page in a user's browser. Or, you can use an **HTML editor**, such as the one in Visual Studio .NET, which allows you to specify the Web page's visual appearance and automatically inserts the HTML tags required to format the document. In this book, you will use the Visual Studio .NET HTML editor to create Web pages.

When you create an HTML document using an HTML converter or HTML editor, the converter or editor usually adds a lot of extra and often extraneous tags to the HTML document.

As a Web developer, you must be familiar with the underlying HTML tags that specify the appearance of a Web page, because you often need to modify these tags to control the appearance and functionality of the Web page. In the following sections, you will learn how to use basic HTML tags to create a Web page using the Visual Studio .NET HTML editor. Initially, you will enter the HTML commands directly, rather than specifying the

Web page appearance visually and allowing Visual Studio .NET to generate the HTML commands automatically.

The first step in creating a Web page is to visualize how the page will look when it appears in a browser. Figure 2-4 shows a design diagram for the Clearwater Traders home page. The home page contains many basic Web page elements, including different heading levels, a bulleted list, a numbered list, a graphic, a horizontal rule, and formatted text. To create the HTML document for this home page, you must understand HTML tags, the structure of an HTML document, and how to use tags and other HTML components to format the page content.

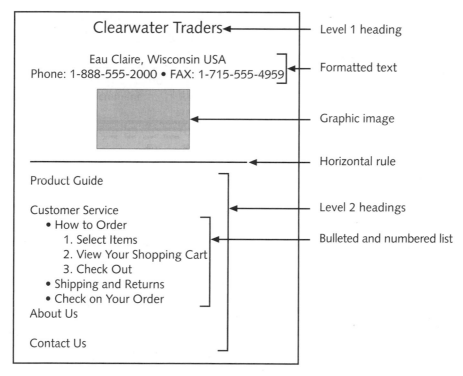

**Figure 2-4**   Design diagram for Clearwater Traders home page

## HTML Tags

An HTML document that defines a Web page consists of the Web page **elements**, which are the text and images that appear on the Web page, and HTML tags, which are codes that define Web page elements, such as graphics or hyperlinks. Tags also define the format of Web page elements, such as text.

You enclose tags in angle brackets (< >) using the following general syntax:

```
<tag_name>element</tag_name>.
```

The first tag is the **opening tag**, and the second tag, in which a front slash (/) precedes the *tag_name*, is the **closing tag**. The *tag_name* specifies a particular formatting symbol, and the *element* specifies the item, such as text or a graphic object, that the tag formats. Although most browsers currently accept HTML tag names in uppercase, lowercase, or mixed-case letters, the XHMTL standard specifies that you must enter all tags in lower-case letters. The XHTML standard also specifies that all HTML tags must appear in opening/closing tag pairs.

Some tags are **empty tags**, which means that they do not enclose any elements such as text or graphics. The XHTML standard states that empty tags do not require a closing tag, but that you should express the tag using the **minimized tag syntax**, which combines the opening and closing tags into a single tag as follows: `<tag_name />`. Note that there is always a blank space between the *tag_name* and the following slash (/).

 In some cases, the XHTML recommendation for always including closing tags conflicts with the HTML 4.01 standard, which forbids certain closing tags. In this book, we will highlight the conflict, but code examples will conform to the HTML 4.01 standard when a conflict occurs, because that is the standard that most browsers support.

An example of a tag is `<b>`, which specifies that the text that the tag encloses appears in boldface type. The following syntax specifies that the text "Clearwater Traders" appears in boldface type:

```
<b>Clearwater Traders</b>
```

If a browser encounters an unrecognized or misspelled tag, the browser treats the tag as part of the Web page text and displays the text of the tag.

You can enclose elements in multiple tag pairs to specify multiple formatting instructions. For example, you could enclose a text element in a tag pair to specify that it appears in boldface type, and in a second tag pair to specify that the text element also appears in italic type. The tag to format a text element in italic type is `<i>`. The following syntax specifies that the text "Clearwater Traders" appears in boldface and italic type:

```
<b><i>Clearwater Traders</i></b>
```

Note that the opening and closing tags are nested: The `<i>` opening and closing tags are the inner tags, and the `<b>` opening and closing tags are the outer tags. The XHTML standard states that when you enclose text in multiple tag pairs, the closing tags have to be nested. However, in current browsers, including Internet Explorer Version 6, when you enclose an element in multiple tags, the opening and closing tags can be in any order.

You can modify tags with **attributes**, which instruct the tag to display its enclosed element in a certain way. The general syntax for a tag attribute is `attribute_name="attribute_value"`. Attributes always appear in attribute name/value pairs, and the XHTML standard specifies that the attribute value is always enclosed in double quotation marks. Current browsers, including Internet Explorer Version 6, do not require attribute values to be enclosed in double quotation marks. To adhere to the XHMTL standard, however, we will always enclose attribute values in double quotation marks.

Some attributes represent Boolean values in which the attribute value is either true or false. In the HTML 4.01 standard, if you include the name of a Boolean attribute in a tag, the attribute value is true. If you omit the name of a Boolean attribute in a tag, the attribute value is false. Setting a Boolean attribute value to true by including it or setting its value to false by omitting the attribute is called **attribute minimization**.

The XHTML standard does not support attribute minimization and states that you must always include both the attribute name as well as its value. For example, you can create a table in an HTML document using the `<table>` tag. If you want the table to display border lines, you use the *border* attribute, which is a Boolean attribute. To create a table and set its border attribute to "true," you would theoretically use the following tag: `<table border="true">`. Unfortunately, no current browsers support the XHTML standard for Boolean attributes, so we will display Boolean attributes using their minimized format. For the table border attribute, the syntax is as follows: `<table border>`.

You can use multiple attributes to modify a tag by listing the attributes and their associated values within the opening tag, using a blank space to separate each attribute/value pair. For example, to create a table on a Web page, you use the `<table>` tag. To specify that the table will occupy 50 percent of the total Web page width, you can use the *width* attribute. To specify that the table will occupy 50 percent of the total Web page height, you can use the height attribute. The modified table tag would appear as follows: `<table width="50%" height="50%">`.

## HTML Document Structure

The code in Figure 2-5 shows the basic structure of an HTML document.

```
<!DOCTYPE document_type_specification>
<html>
 <head>
  <title>Web_page_title</title>
 </head>
 <body>
  Web_page_body_elements
 </body>
</html>
```

**Figure 2-5**    Basic HTML document structure

The first line of the document contains the **document type declaration tag**, or **DOCTYPE tag**, which specifies the HTML version that the developer used to create the Web page. The XHTML standard specifies that every HTML document must have a DOCTYPE tag, although current browsers do not require the DOCTYPE tag. The DOCTYPE tag specifies the kind of tags that the page contains and describes what they do. The `<html>` opening and closing tags specify that the interpreter process the enclosed text as an HTML document. The `<head>` opening and closing tags enclose the document's header section. The **header section** contains information about the Web page. The Web browser uses this information, but it does not appear on the Web page. The header section often contains **meta tags**, which are tags that enclose information about the Web page that the Web page does not display. The meta tag information is visible to the browser in which the Web page appears and to search engines such as Google and Yahoo!. Meta tag information helps the browser display the Web page correctly, and enables Web page developers to define keywords to describe their Web pages. The header section defines the *Web_page_title,* which is the text that appears in the title bar of the user's browser window when the page appears. You enclose the *Web_page_title* text in the opening and closing `<title>` tags.

The *Web_page_title* text is saved as the Web page's description when a user saves a link to the Web page using a Netscape bookmark, or saves the page as a favorite using Microsoft Internet Explorer.

The *Web_page_body_elements* are the text, graphics, and other elements that comprise the content of the Web page, as well as the HTML tags that format the Web page content. You enclose these elements in the opening and closing `<body>` tags.

## Using Visual Studio .NET to Create an HTML Document

Now that you understand the basic structure of an HTML document, you are ready to use the Visual Studio .NET IDE to create an HTML document for a static Web page. You will create the Clearwater Traders home page shown in the design diagram in Figure 2-4. First you will create a new blank HTML document file, then view the document in HTML Designer, which is the Visual Studio HTML editor.

To create a new blank HTML document:

1. In Visual Studio .NET, click **File** on the menu bar, point to **New**, and then click **File**. The New File dialog box opens.

2. Make sure that the General category folder is selected, click the **HTML Page template** icon, and then click **Open**. The HTML Designer opens in the Web browser window, as shown in Figure 2-6. If necessary, click the Design tab in the bottom-left corner of the window.

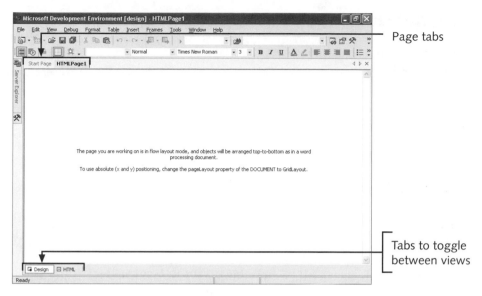

**Figure 2-6**   HTML Designer in Design view

Note that the tabs at the top of the page allow you to navigate among different Web pages in the Web browser window. Currently, there are tabs representing the Start Page and your new Web page, which has the default name HTMLPage1.

The HTML Designer provides two views of the document: Design view and HTML view. **Design view** allows you to specify the Web page content as it will appear in the user's browser. You can add Web page text and graphics, drag and drop them into position on the Web page, and edit their appearance. **HTML view** allows you to view and edit the underlying HTML tags and Web page content. To view an HTML document in Design view, you click the Design tab at the bottom of the HTML Designer window. To view the document in HTML view, you click the HTML tab. Because you are learning to become a Web page developer, you will enter most of the Web page content and formatting in HTML view, so you can become familiar with the tags you use to format Web pages.

HTML Designer has automatically created the HTML tags that define the structure of the HTML document, but currently the document does not have a title or any content. Now you will view the new HTML document in HTML view.

To view the HTML document in HTML view:

1. In the HTML Designer in Design view, click the **HTML** tab the bottom-left corner of the browser window. The HTML commands for the blank Web page appear, as shown in Figure 2-7.

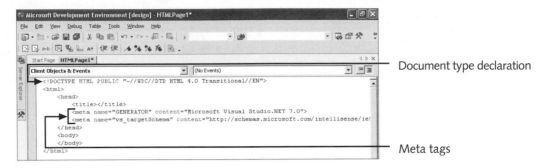

**Figure 2-7**   HTML tags for a blank Web page

2. If necessary, modify the document so the tags are indented as shown in Figure 2-7, and remove the blank lines between the opening and closing **<body>** tags.

When you switch to HTML view, your Web page's document name on the page tab appears with an asterisk (*) beside its name. This indicates that you have changed the document, but have not yet saved the changes.

In Figure 2-7, note that the **<html>** tag aligns with the left edge of the HTML view window, which indicates that the **<html>** tag is the first tag in the document. Also note that the **<head>** and **<body>** tags are indented, which shows that they are nested within the **<html>** tag. Similarly, the **<title>** tag is indented again, which indicates that it is nested within the **<head>** tag. Using this nested tag indenting style makes it easier to understand the structure of an HTML document. In this book, you will format HTML documents so that each opening/closing tag pair appears on the same line, and you will indent tags that are nested within other tags. As you become a more experienced HTML developer, you will probably develop your own preferences for formatting HTML documents.

Sometimes the Visual Studio .NET text editor is configured to format your HTML code automatically. Because this formatting may not be what you want, it is a good idea to configure your Visual Studio .NET environment so that it does not apply automatic formatting. You will do this next.

To configure the Visual Studio .NET text editor so it does not automatically format your code:

1. Click **Tools** on the menu bar, and then click **Options**.

2. Select the **Text Editor** folder in the list in the left window pane, select the **HTML/XML** folder, and then click **Format**.

3. Under the Apply Automatic Formatting heading, clear the **When saving document**, **When switching from Design to HTML/XML view**, and **Apply line breaks** check boxes.

4. Make sure that the *Insert attribute value quotes* check box is checked, then click **OK** to save your changes.

2

The first line of the document contains the following tag:

```
<!DOCTYPE HTML PUBLIC ↵
"-//W3C//DTD HTML 4.0 Transitional//EN">
```

 This book uses the line continuation character ( ↵ ) to indicate that a command should appear all on one line when you type it in the Visual Studio .NET IDE.

This is the DOCTYPE tag, which specifies the kind of tags the page contains and describes what they do. HTML 4.0 comes in three flavors: Strict, Transitional, and Frameset. HTML 4.0 Strict is a concise version of HTML 4.0 that emphasizes structure over presentation. HTML 4.0 Transitional includes all tags and attributes of HTML 4.0 Strict, but adds items to provide more flexibility in usage and presentation. HTML Frameset supports HTML frames, which enable you to divide your Web page into different sections. The DOCTYPE tag in Figure 2-7 specifies that this Web page uses HTML 4.0 Transitional.

Most current Web programmers omit the document type declaration from their Web pages, because current browsers use a default standard interpretation of tags. For instance, if you omit the closing `</html>` tag from an HTML document, browsers still display the page. Suppose you mistype an HTML tag, thus creating a tag that the HTML 4.0 standard does not define. For example, suppose that you want to format some Web page text using a large font. You have forgotten which exact tag you use to do this, so you make a guess, and try to use a `<bigger>` tag, as shown in the following example: `<bigger>Is this Big?</bigger>`. (The HTML 4.0 standard does not define the `<bigger>` tag.) Browsers will ignore the mistyped tag and display the text "Is this Big?" as unformatted.

Your blank HTML document also contains the following meta tags within the document heading:

```
<meta name="GENERATOR" content="Microsoft Visual Studio
.NET 7.0"> ↵
<meta name="vs_targetSchema" ↵
content="http://schemas.microsoft.com/intellisense/ie5">
```

Recall that a meta tag is an HTML tag that does not affect the appearance of the Web page, but is visible to and read only by search engines. Visual Studio .NET automatically inserts this tag whenever you create a Web page in its HTML editor. The first meta tag, which sets the name attribute to "GENERATOR," specifies that the Web page was developed using Visual Studio .NET Version 7.0. The second meta tag, which sets the name attribute to "vs_targetSchema," specifies the Web browser for which the developer is designing the HTML page. Note that the content attribute value of this tag is "http://schemas.microsoft.com/intellisense/ie5." As you enter tags and text in the Visual Studio HTML Designer, ScreenTips automatically appear to provide you with choices for HTML tag attributes. In Visual Studio .NET, Microsoft calls this feature

**IntelliSense**. This feature provides intelligent selections based on the commands you have entered so far. The vs_targetSchema meta tag specifies that the Visual Studio .NET IDE bases its IntelliSense commands on tags that the Internet Explorer 5.0 (IE5) Web browser supports.

On your screen, the HTML Designer color-codes the text in HTML view. The HTML tag names appear in brown. The tag angle brackets and front slashes for closing tags appear in blue, and the Web page content that you enter (such as the Web page title) appears in black. Now you will add the Web page title, which will be "Clearwater Traders." Then you will save your HTML document file.

To add the Web page title and save the file:

1. In HTML view, place the insertion point after the closing angle bracket in the `<title>` tag and type **Clearwater Traders**, so the line that contains the `<title>` tag appears as follows:

   `<title>Clearwater Traders</title>`

   Note that the Web page filename on the page tab at the top of the window appears as HTMLPage1*. Whenever you change a Visual Studio .NET file, the page tab displays the filename followed by an asterisk. This signals that your file has unsaved changes. After you save the file, the asterisk will appear again the next time you change the file.

2. To save your file, click the **Save** button on the toolbar, navigate to the Chapter2\Tutorials folder on your Solution Disk, and save the file as **clearwater.htm**. Note that the document title on the page tab now appears as "clearwater.htm."

Now you will view the HTML document as a Web page in the Internet Explorer Web browser. Recall that when you are developing new Web pages, you can view a Web page by specifying a file URL, which consists of the system drive letter, the folder path, and the name of the HTML file that you want to view.

To view the HTML document in a Web browser:

1. Start Internet Explorer, click **File** on the menu bar, click **Open**, click **Browse**, and then navigate to the Chapter2\Tutorials folder on your Solutions Disk. Select **clearwater.htm**, click **Open**, and then click **OK**. The current Clearwater Traders home page appears as shown in Figure 2-8.

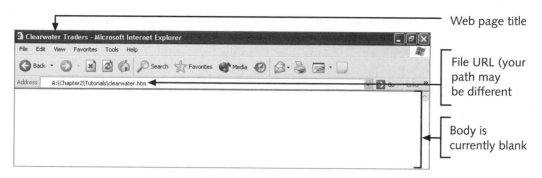

**Figure 2-8**   Current Clearwater Traders home page

In this book, the workstation's A drive references all solution files. If your solution files were stored in a different location, your path would be different.

> 2. Close Internet Explorer.

Note that the Web page title appears in the window title bar. The Web page is currently blank, because you have not yet defined the Web page content in the body section of the HTML document.

If you want to take a break, you can close your HTML document file in Visual Studio .NET, and then open it later to continue working. Now, you will close your file.

To close your HTML document file:

> 1. Return to Visual Studio .NET if necessary. Click **File** on the menu bar, and then click **Close**. The Start Page appears again in Visual Studio .NET.

To close the HTML document, you could also click the document close button on the right edge of the screen across from the page tabs.

> 2. Click **File** on the menu bar, and then click **Exit** to close Visual Studio .NET.

To close Visual Studio .NET, you could also click the window close button on the Visual Studio .NET window.

## HTML Headings

The first step in developing the Clearwater Traders home page in Figure 2-4 is to create the HTML headings. You use **HTML headings** to create page headings that consist of text that appears in a larger font than the other text on a Web page. To create a heading, you use a **heading tag**, which has the following general format: `<hlevel_number>heading_text</hlevel_number>`. HTML supports six levels of headings, numbered from 1 to 6. The heading level indicates the amount of emphasis that the designer places on the enclosed text. Level 1 headings use a very large font size, and level 6 headings use a very small font size. Figure 2-9 shows the relative sizes of HTML headings, as well as the size of regular text that is not within a heading tag. Actual font sizes might appear differently in different Web browsers.

# H1 Heading

## H2 Heading

### H3 Heading

H4 Heading

H5 Heading

H6 Heading

Regular Text

**Figure 2-9**     Relative sizes of HTML headings

You always place headings in the body section of the Web page. You can combine headings with other tags to create hyperlinks and provide additional text formatting. As you type HTML commands in HTML view in the HTML Designer, the editor automatically displays IntelliSense lists of tags and attributes. If you select an item from a list and press the Tab key, the item appears in the HTML view editing area. Now you will reopen your HTML document and add the level 1 and level 2 headings to the Clearwater Traders home page. Then, you will view your headings in Design view.

To reopen your document and add and then view the level 1 and level 2 headings:

1. If necessary, start Visual Studio .NET, click the **Open File** button on the toolbar, navigate to the Chapter2\Tutorials folder on your Solution Disk, select **clearwater.htm**, and click **Open**. The Clearwater Traders home page appears in the HTML Designer in Design view.

2. Click the **HTML** tab to switch to HTML view, place the insertion point after the closing angle bracket of the opening `<body>` tag, and if necessary, press **Enter** to create a new blank line. The insertion point appears on a blank line beneath the `<body>` tag.

3. Press **Tab** to indent the tag, and then type **<**. An IntelliSense list of available tags appears. Scroll down the list, select **h1**, and press **Tab**. The **<h1** tag appears in the editor.

To move automatically to the first item in the list that begins with a specific letter, type the letter.

4. Type **>** to close the **<h1>** tag. The closing **</h1>** tag appears.

If the closing tag does not appear, click Tools on the menu bar, click Options, click the Text Editor folder, click the HTML/XML subfolder, select HTML Specific, select the Close tag check box, and then click OK.

5. Type **Clearwater Traders** as the text for the level 1 heading. Be sure that the text is between the **<h1>** and **</h1>** tags, as shown in the shaded code in Figure 2-10.

```
<!DOCTYPE HTML PUBLIC "-//W3C//DTD HTML 4.0 Transitional//EN">
<html>
  <head>
    <title>Clearwater Traders</title>
    <meta name="GENERATOR" content="Microsoft Visual Studio.NET 7.0">
    <meta name="vs_targetSchema" ↵
    content="http://schemas.microsoft.com/intellisense/ie5">
  </head>
  <body>
    <h1>Clearwater Traders</h1>
    <h2>Product Guide</h2></h2>
    <h2>Customer Service</h2>
    <h2>About Us</h2>
    <h2>Contact Us</h2>
  </body>
</html>
```

**Figure 2-10**   HTML commands to specify Web page headings

6. Move the insertion point so it follows the closing angle bracket in the **</h1>** tag, and press **Enter** to create a new blank line.

7. Add the four level 2 headings as shown in the shaded code in Figure 2-10. If necessary, delete any blank lines between the final **</h2>** tag and the closing **</body>** tag so your code looks like Figure 2-10, then click the **Save** button to save your file.

8. To view the formatted headings, click the **Design** tab to switch to Design view. Your Web page headings should appear as shown in Figure 2-11.

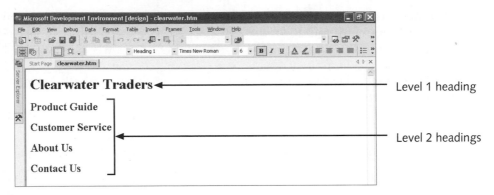

**Figure 2-11**    Formatted Web page headings

## Modifying the Alignment of Web Page Text

In Figure 2-4, the Clearwater Traders level 1 heading appears centered on the Web page. Remember that by default, headings are always left-justified, but you can specify a different alignment using the HTML **align attribute** within the opening heading tag.

> The HTML 4.01 standard has deprecated the align attribute, which means that future releases of browsers and HTML editors may not recognize this attribute. We will describe and use the align attribute because it is so widely used in current HMTL documents.

The basic syntax of an opening level 1 heading tag with the align attribute is `<h1 align="desired_alignment">`. Alignment values are *center*, *right*, and *left*. For example, to create the level 1 "Clearwater Traders" heading shown in Figure 2-4 and center the heading on the Web page, you would use the following heading tag: `<h1 align="center">Clearwater Traders</h1>`.

Now you will modify the tag for this heading to include the align attribute, which centers the text.

To add the align attribute and center the heading text:

1. Switch to HTML view, place the insertion point just after the *1* in the opening `<h1>` tag and then press the **space bar**. A list of tag attributes appears.

2. Select **align**, and then press **Tab**. The align attribute appears in the tag. Note that the tag attribute appears in red in the editor.

3. Type `="`. A list of possible alignment values appears. Select **center**, press **Tab**, then type `"` to close the attribute definition. The completed tag should appear as follows: `<h1 align="center">`.

4. Save the file and then view the document in Design view to confirm that the "Clearwater Traders" heading is now centered on the page.

Another way to change the alignment of Web page text is to use the style attribute. You can use the **style attribute** to define many properties of Web page elements, such as text alignment, font style and size, color, and so on. The basic syntax of the style attribute is: `style="style_name: style_value"`. The *style_name* parameter identifies the style that you are specifying, such as the font size or background color. The *style_value* parameter specifies the corresponding style value.

A convenient way to specify style attributes and values is to use the Style Builder utility within the HTML Designer. Now you will use Style Builder to modify the Clearwater Traders heading so it appears right-justified on the Web page. Then you will switch to HTML view to examine the style attribute and value that the utility added to the `<h1>` tag for the associated text.

To change the alignment of the heading text and examine the associated tag in HTML view:

1. If necessary, switch to Design view and select the **Clearwater Traders** text so it appears highlighted.

2. Click **Format** on the menu bar and then click **Build Style**. The Style Builder dialog box opens.

 If Build Style is disabled, right-click in the Design view window, click Properties, open the Target Schema list, select Internet Explorer 5.0, then click OK.

3. Select **Text** in the left pane, open the **Horizontal Alignment** list, select **Right**, and then click **OK** to apply the change. The Clearwater Traders heading now appears right-justified instead of centered in Design view.

4. Switch to HTML view and note that the level 1 heading tag appears as follows:

```
<h1 align="center" style="TEXT-ALIGN: right">
Clearwater Traders</h1>
```

Note that the style attribute overrides the align attribute.

5. In HTML view, delete the style attribute and associated value, so that the `<h1>` tag appears as `<h1 align="center">`, and so the text is centered. Save the file.

You can use the style attribute to modify many other properties of text, including the font size and style, and the text foreground and background color.

## Text Formatting Commands

Next you will add the formatted text under the Clearwater Traders level 1 heading. You will type the company location text ("Eau Claire, Wisconsin, USA") and the text for the telephone numbers in your HTML document and view the result. For now, you will insert an asterisk (*) in place of the bullet between the telephone numbers. You will learn how to insert special characters such as bullets in a later section in this chapter.

To add the location and telephone number text:

1. If necessary, switch back to HTML view. Place the insertion point after the closing `</h1>` tag, press **Enter** to move to a new blank line, and then add the following location and telephone number text. You should insert five blank spaces before and after the asterisk (*).

```
Eau Claire, Wisconsin, USA
Phone:  1-800-555-5555      *      FAX: 1-715-555-4959
```

 You could also enter this text in Visual view, but doing so causes the HTML Designer to add extra tags that you may not want, and makes it harder to customize the document's appearance.

2. Switch to Design view to view your changes. Your Web page should appear as shown in Figure 2-12.

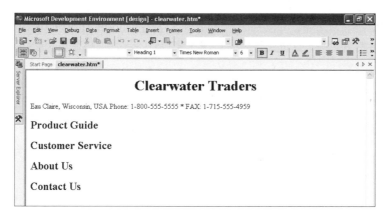

**Figure 2-12**    Web page with location and phone number text

Note that the new text appears left-justified and all on one line, even though you typed the text on two separate lines in the HTML editor. Also note that all of the extra blank spaces that you entered before and after the asterisk appear as a single blank space. Browsers ignore blank spaces and line breaks within HTML code. You must add tags and special characters to display blank spaces within document text and to create line breaks. You can also use special formatting characters to add non-keyboard elements such as bullets. The following sections describe how to format text line spacing and justification, insert special characters, and enhance text appearance.

## Text Line Spacing and Justification

When you include text in an HTML document, the text appears as a continuous paragraph with no line breaks unless you add tags to create new paragraphs and line breaks. You enclose text that is in a new paragraph in the **paragraph tag** (<p>). The Web browser displays a blank line between any previous text and the text that follows the <p> tag. Text within the paragraph tags automatically wraps to the next line, based on the size of the browser window. Current browsers do not require you to place a closing tag (</p>) at the end of the paragraph, but the XHTML standard states that all tags must have a matching closing tag, so it is a good practice always to include the closing paragraph tag.

You can use the **line break tag** (<br>) to insert a line break, which is also called a hard return. The text immediately following the line break tag appears on the line immediately below the previous text. The line break tag is an **empty tag**, which means that it does not enclose any Web page elements. Therefore, to conform to the XHTML standard, you will always express it using the minimized tag syntax, which is **<br />**.

The line break tag does not require a closing (</br>) tag, and you should not include one, because it causes some browsers to create an additional line break.

Figure 2-13 illustrates Web page body text coded as a new paragraph and including a line break.

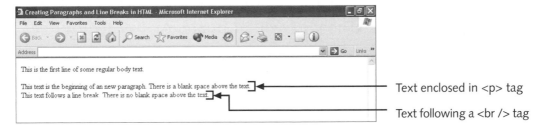

**Figure 2-13**    Web page body text with paragraph and line breaks

You would use the code in Figure 2-14 to create the Web page shown in Figure 2-13. Note that the regular Web page text appears on the first line of the Web page. Blank space appears above the text enclosed in the <p> tag, and the text following the <br /> tag appears on the next line, with no blank space above it.

By default, Web page body text, like Web page heading text, is left-justified. You can use the align attribute within the paragraph tag to specify the paragraph alignment. The basic syntax of the paragraph tag with the align attribute is **<p align="*desired_alignment*">**. Table 2-1 summarizes the tags to specify line breaks and justified paragraph text.

```
<html>
  <head>
    <title>Creating Paragraphs and Line Breaks in HTML</title>
  </head>
  <body>
    This is the first line of some regular body text.
    <p>
      This text is the beginning of a new paragraph.
      There is a blank space above the text.
      <br />This text follows a line break.  There is no
      blank space above the text.
    </p>
  </body>
</html>
```

**Figure 2-14**    Code to create Web page with paragraph and line breaks

**Table 2-1**    Tags to specify line breaks, paragraphs, and paragraph alignment

| Tag | Description | Example |
|---|---|---|
| `<br />` | Creates a line break | `<br />Text following a line break` |
| `<p>` or `<p align="left">` | Creates a new left-justified paragraph | `<p>Text within a left-justified paragraph</p>` |
| `<p align="center">` | Creates a new centered paragraph | `<p align="center">Text within a centered paragraph</p>` |
| `<p align="right">` | Creates a new right-justified paragraph | `<p align="right">Text within a right-justified paragraph</p>` |

Now you will add the tags to place the location and phone number text in a centered paragraph and to create a line break between the location and the phone numbers.

To add the paragraph and line break tags:

1. Switch to HTML view, and add paragraph and line break tags to the location and phone number text as follows:

```
<p align="center">Eau Claire, Wisconsin, USA
<br />Phone: 1-888-555-2000      *            ↵
FAX: 1-715-555-4959</p>
```

The HTML editor will automatically place the closing paragraph tag (</p>) immediately after the opening tag, so you will need to move the closing tag from its current position so it appears after the FAX phone number text.

Sometimes when you select an attribute value from a list, the editor deletes the text that immediately follows the attribute list. If this happens, retype the deleted text.

2. Save the file and then switch to Design view to view your changes. Your Web page text should appear with the location and phone number text centered and on separate lines.

## HTML Character Entities

Sometimes you need to include special characters in a Web page that are not on your computer keyboard. For example, you separate the Clearwater Traders telephone numbers with a bullet and extra blank spaces that you cannot represent directly in the text, but must display using special character codes called character entities. **Character entities** are numbers or character strings that you insert directly within the Web page body text. You always precede character entity codes with an ampersand (&) and follow them with a semicolon (;). You can assign some character entities using either a number code or a character code. Character codes are usually case-sensitive, and you enter them in lowercase letters. Table 2-2 lists some of the commonly used HTML character entities and their corresponding number or character codes.

**Table 2-2** Common HTML character entity codes

| Character | Description | Number Code | Character Code |
|---|---|---|---|
| • | Bullet | &#149; | |
| • | Middle dot | &#183; | &middot; |
| © | Copyright symbol | &#169; | &copy; |
| ® | Registered trademark | &#174; | &reg; |
| < | Left-pointing angle bracket (less than symbol) | &#60; | &lt; |
| > | Right-pointing angle bracket (greater than symbol) | &#62; | &gt; |
| | Non-breaking space, used to add blank spaces within text |   |   |

Character entities sometimes look different in different browsers, so it is a good idea to preview your Web pages in a variety of browsers to confirm that the character entities appear correctly.

You can combine character entity codes by listing them one after another. For example, you write the codes to create a bullet followed by two blank spaces as &#149;  . Now you will modify the Clearwater Traders Web page to include the bullet between the two telephone numbers and the five extra blank spaces.

Design view works well for adding blank spaces, so you will add the blank spaces in Design view. Then, you will switch to HTML view to add the bullet character code.

To add the bullet and blank spaces between the telephone numbers:

1. If necessary, switch to Design view, then place the insertion point just before the asterisk that separates the phone numbers, and press the **space bar** four times to add four additional blank spaces before the asterisk. (There should now be a total of five blank spaces, because there was already one blank space between the telephone number and the asterisk.)

2. Place the insertion point just after the asterisk that separates the telephone numbers, and press the **space bar** four times to add four additional blank spaces after the asterisk. (There is already one blank space between the asterisk and the second phone number.)

3. Switch to HTML view, delete the asterisk between the telephone numbers, and type **&#149;** in its place to add the bullet special character. Note the ** ** character codes that the HTML editor has added to represent the blank spaces that you added in Steps 1 and 2 in Design view.

4. If necessary, remove any blank spaces between the character entity codes to format your HTML code. Note that the character entity codes appear in red text.

5. Save the file, then switch to Design view. Your Web page text should appear with the blank spaces and the bullet between the telephone numbers, as shown in Figure 2-15.

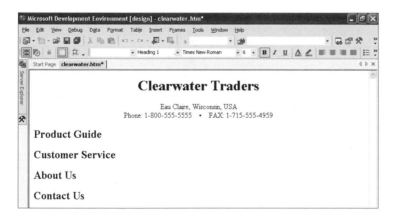

**Figure 2-15**    Web page with character entities

## Character Tags

The location text on the Clearwater Traders home page ("Eau Claire, Wisconsin, USA") should appear in a larger font than the telephone numbers, and in a bold font style. The telephone numbers should appear in an italic font style. To format these items, you can use HTML **character tags**, which allow Web page developers to specify exact text properties, such as boldface, superscript, or italic font styles. Table 2–3 summarizes some commonly used character tags.

**Table 2-3**    Character tags

| Tag | Description | Usage | Display Style |
|---|---|---|---|
| `<em>` | Enclosed characters should be emphasized, usually displayed using italics | `<em>Emphasized text</em>` | *Emphasized text* |
| `<strong>` | Enclosed characters should be emphasized more strongly than with `<em>`, and are usually displayed using boldface | `<strong>Strongly emphasized text</strong>` | **Strongly emphasized text** |
| `<code>` | Enclosed characters are computer code, and are usually displayed in a fixed-width font such as Courier | `<code>N = N + 1</code>` | `N = N + 1` |
| `<cite>` | Enclosed characters are a bibliographic citation, and are usually displayed using italics | `<cite>EnhancedGuide to Oracle8i, Course Technology, 2001, pp. 1-12</cite>` | *Enhanced Guide to Oracle8i, Course Technology, 2001, pp. 1-12* |
| `<b>` | Bold font | `<b>Bold text</b>` | **Bold text** |
| `<i>` | Italic font | `<i>Italic text</i>` | *Italic text* |
| `<u>` | Underlined font | `<u>Underlined text</u>` | <u>Underlined text</u> |
| `<big>` | Increased font size | `<big>Bigger text</big>` | Bigger text |
| `<small>` | Smaller font size | `<small>Smaller text</small>` | Smaller text |
| `<sub>` | Subscript text | `<sub>Sub</sub> script text` | Sub script text |
| `<sup>` | Superscript text | `<sup>Super</sup>script text` | Super script text |
| `<blink>` | Alternating foreground and background colors | `<blink>Blinking text</blink>` | Blinking text |
| `<s>` or `<strike>` | Strike-through text | `<strike>Strike-through text</strike>` | ~~Strike-through text~~ |
| `<tt>` | Teletype style (fixed-width font) | `<tt>Fixed-width text</tt>` | `Fixed-width text` |

Recall that you can enclose text in multiple character tags to specify multiple formatting instructions. For example, you would use the following HTML code to display a bold italic font: `<i><b>Bold italic text</b></i>`. Recall that to comply with the XHTML standard, you must nest the tags so the closing tags appear in the reverse order of the opening tags.

Now you will add character tags to the location and telephone number text. To specify that the location text appears with emphasis, you will use the `<strong>` tag, and to specify that it appears in a larger font, you will use the `<big>` tag. You will specify that the telephone numbers appear in a small italic font using the `<i>` and `<small>` character tags.

To add character tags to the location and telephone number text:

1. Switch back to HTML view and add the following character formatting tags:

```
<p align="center">  ↵
<strong>Eau Claire, Wisconsin, USA</strong>
<br /><small><i>Phone: 1-800-555-5555
    
&#149;    
FAX: 1-715-555-4959</i></small></p>
```

HTML Designer automatically places the closing character tags immediately after the opening tag, so you need to move the closing tag into the proper position.

2. Save the file and then switch to Design view to view the Web page text with the text style changes.

## Graphic Images

Web pages usually contain graphic images and other graphics objects to make them more appealing or to convey visual information. In Figure 2-4, the Clearwater Traders home page contains a graphic image of the Clearwater Traders logo, and a horizontal rule to divide the page into sections. In this book, you will display images as inline images. **Inline images** appear directly on the Web page, and the user's browser loads them while loading the Web page.

To display an inline graphic image in a Web page, you use the **image tag**, which specifies the filename of the graphic image. The basic syntax of the image tag is `<img src="image_filename" />`. The `<img>` tag is an empty tag, so you configure this tag using the minimized tag syntax in which a slash (/) appears just before the tag's closing angle bracket. The src attribute specifies the image source file, so the *image_filename* value is the name of a graphics file with a .gif or .jpg extension.

Most Web browsers that can display graphics support two types of graphic images: GIF (Graphics Interchange Format) and JPEG (Joint Photographic Experts Group). Before you can display an image on a Web page, you must convert the image to one of these file types using a graphics software application.

You can specify the *image_filename* value using an absolute file path, a relative file path, or an absolute URL location. An **absolute file path** specifies the exact location of a file in the browser's file system, including the drive letter, complete folder path, and filename. The only time you use an absolute file path is when you display a Web page using a file URL on your local workstation. In an absolute file path, you separate the names of different folders within the folder path using a front slash (/). An example of an absolute path to the clearlogo.jpg file that is stored in the Chapter2 folder on your Data Disk is `a:/Chapter2/clearlogo.jpg`.

In DOS or Windows file system commands, you separate each folder name in a path using a back slash (\). In HTML commands, however, you usually separate folder names using front slashes (/). Microsoft Internet Explorer Version 6 accepts either front slashes or back slashes in HTML folder path specifications. Because some browsers accept only front slashes, in this book you will use front slashes to separate folder names.

A **relative file path** specifies a file location relative to the location of the current HTML file. The location of the current HTML file is called the **current working directory**. In this chapter, you will always store image files in the current working directory. An **absolute URL location** specifies the location of a graphics file on a Web server. You will learn more about relative file paths and absolute URL locations in Chapter 5 when you learn how to configure your Web server.

By default, images appear on the left edge of a Web page. One way to change the image alignment is to place the image in a new paragraph and specify the paragraph alignment using the align attribute within the paragraph tag. An advantage of using the new paragraph approach is that it adds blank space above and below the image. Another way is to place the image in an HTML table. (You will learn how to create HTML tables that contain images later in this chapter.)

Now you will add the Clearwater Traders logo to the Clearwater Traders home page. You will place the image in a new paragraph and center the paragraph on your Web page. The logo source file is named clearlogo.jpg, and is stored in the Chapter2 folder on your Data Disk. You will copy this file to the Chapter2\Tutorials folder on your Solution Disk, which stores your clearwater.htm file. Because the image file is in the same folder as the HTML document file, it is in the current working directory, so you can specify the image source file using a relative path that includes just the filename.

To add the clearlog.jpg image to the Web page:

1. Start Windows Explorer, copy **clearlogo.jpg** from the Chapter2 folder on your Data Disk to the Chapter2\Tutorials folder on your Solution Disk, then close Windows Explorer.

2. Switch to Visual Studio .NET, switch to HTML view if necessary, create a blank line just above the <h2> tag for the "Product Guide" level 2 heading, and add the following tags:

```
<p align="center"><img src="clearlogo.jpg"  /></p>
```

3. Save the file, then switch to Design view to view your changes. Your Web page text appears with the Clearwater Traders logo immediately below the telephone numbers, as shown in Figure 2-16.

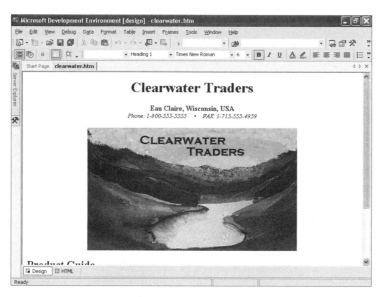

**Figure 2-16**    Web page with a graphic image

If your graphic image appears as a picture icon ⊠ instead of the actual image, you might have made an error either in the image tag command or the path to the source filename. Check your code, make sure it exactly matches the code specified in Step 2, and make sure that the clearlogo.jpg file is in the same folder as the clearwater.htm Web page file.

You might need to close your HTML document and open it again to display the graphic image in Visual Studio .NET in Design view.

Currently, the Web browser determines the display size of the graphic image based on the size of the Web page, the position of the image on the page, and the surrounding Web page items. You can specify an exact size for the image directly within the image tag. You should always specify an exact size. Otherwise, the Web browser has to open the image source file, determine the image size, and then format the page and display the image. If you specify the image size directly in the image tag, the Web browser simply formats the page and displays the image as specified in the HTML code. There are two ways to specify the width and height of an image. You can use the **width attribute** and the **height attribute** within the image tag using the following syntax: `<img  src="`*`image_filename`*`" width="`*`desired_width`*`" height="`*`desired_height`*`" />`. You can specify the desired display width and height either as a numerical value in pixels or as a percentage of the Web page width and height. The following commands specify the size of an image file named sample.jpg using both methods:

```
<img src="sample.jpg" width="100" height="75" />
<img src="sample.jpg" width="40%" height="15%" />
```

 A pixel, or picture element, is the smallest addressable unit on a screen. You can specify the size of graphic images using pixels.

An alternate way to specify the size of an image is to use the style attribute and values for the WIDTH and HEIGHT style names. (Recall that you use the style attribute to specify a variety of formatting specifications for Web page elements.) To use the style attribute to specify WIDTH and HEIGHT styles, the general syntax is as follows: `style="WIDTH: `*`N`*`px"`. In this syntax, *N* represents the width of the column, in pixels. An example of a style attribute that specifies an image's width and height is as follows:

```
style="WIDTH: 193px; HEIGHT: 114px"
```

Determining the correct image size on a Web page is usually a trial-and-error process. When you are using HTML Designer, you can visually resize the image in Design view. Currently, the Clearwater Traders logo is larger than the logo in the design diagram in Figure 2-4. Now you will adjust the image size in Design view and then examine the modified image tag in HTML view.

To resize the image:

1. In Design view, select the graphic image so that selection handles appear around its perimeter. Click the bottom-right selection handle and drag toward the top-left corner of your screen so that the image appears as shown in Figure 2-17.

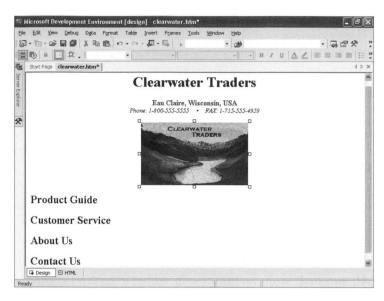

**Figure 2-17**    Web page with a resized graphic image

2. Save the file, switch to HTML view, and examine the modified image tag. Your tag should look similar to the following tag, although your values for the image height and width may differ:

```
<img style="WIDTH: 197px; HEIGHT: 116px"
src="clearlogo.jpg" height=116 width=197 />
```

Note that the HTML editor specified the image size using both the style attribute and the height and width attributes. Visual Studio .NET does this to ensure compatibility with browsers that do not yet recognize the style attribute. Also, the HTML editor may have placed the height and width attribute definitions in different positions before or after the image filename. The height and width attribute definitions can appear anywhere within the image tag and in any order, as long as `img` is the first item within the tag.

3. Because the XHTML standard states that all attribute values must be enclosed in quotation marks, type quotation marks around the height and width attribute values. These attribute values should appear as follows, although your actual values may be different:

```
height="116" width="197"
```

4. Save the file.

## Horizontal Rules

In the design for the Clearwater Traders home page in Figure 2-4, a horizontal rule appears between the logo and level 2 headings. A **horizontal rule** is a horizontal line that visually separates a Web page into sections to make the page easier to read and interpret. To create a horizontal rule, you use the **horizontal rule tag**, which has the following syntax: `<hr />`. The horizontal rule tag is another empty tag, so you specify the tag using the minimized tag syntax. A horizontal rule creates a simple line break and appears directly below the text that precedes it, with no extra space added above or below. You can include attributes within the horizontal rule tag to specify the line's thickness, shading, width, and alignment. Figure 2-18 shows examples of how horizontal rules with different attribute values appear in Web pages.

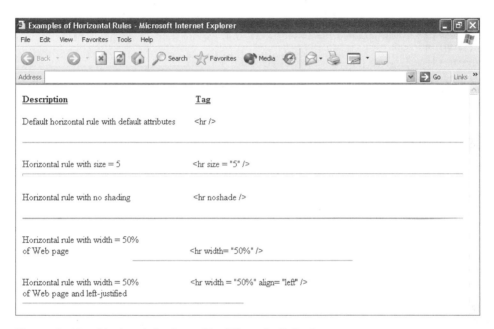

**Figure 2-18**    Horizontal rules with different attributes

By default, horizontal rules are 3 pixels high, appear centered across the width of the entire Web page, and are shaded so they appear to be inset within the Web page. You can modify the rule height, remove the shading so the rule appears as a two-dimensional flat line on the Web page, change the width to a specific pixel length or so that the rule extends across a specific percentage of the Web page, and change the rule alignment. Table 2-4 summarizes the attributes of horizontal rules. Note that you can list multiple attributes within the tag, as long as `hr` is the first tag element. The order in which the attributes appear in the tag does not matter.

**Table 2-4**    Horizontal rule attributes

| Property | Attribute | Example |
|----------|-----------|---------|
| Line height | `size="number_of_pixels"` | `<hr size="5" />` |
| No shading | `noshade` | `<hr size="5" noshade />` |

**Table 2-4**    Horizontal rule attributes (continued)

| Property | Attribute | Example |
|----------|-----------|---------|
| Width | width="*number_of_pixels*"<br>WIDTH="*percent_of_ page_width*" | `<hr size="5" width="32" />`<br>`<hr noshade width="50%" />` |
| Alignment | align="*desired_alignment*" | `<hr align="center" size="5" />` |

The noshade attribute is an example of a Boolean attribute. By including noshade within the `<hr />` tag, you specify that the noshade attribute value is true. By omitting noshade within the tag, you specify that the noshade attribute value is false.

Now you will create the horizontal rule in the Clearwater Traders Web page. The rule will be 5 pixels thick, have no shading, and be centered across the width of the entire Web page.

To create the horizontal rule:

1. If necessary, switch to HTML view. Create a new blank line after the closing `</p>` tag for the paragraph that contains the image tag, and before the line that contains the opening `<h2>` tag for the "Product Guide" level 2 heading. Then type the following command:

   `<hr size="5" noshade />`

2. Save the file, then switch to Design view. Your Web page should now include a horizontal rule below the Clearwater Traders logo.

# HTML Lists

HTML allows you to create formatted lists for grouping and formatting related text items. You can create **unordered lists**, in which the list items have no particular order. You usually use unordered lists for bulleted items or items that have no specific sequence, such as links to other Web pages. You can also create **ordered lists** for list items that have a definite sequential order. In an ordered list, a number appears automatically before each list item. You would use an ordered list for sequential items such as a table of contents or an instruction sequence.

## Unordered Lists

You define an unordered list using the **unordered list tag** (`<ul>`). Within the `<ul>` tag, you define each individual list item using the **list item tag** (`<li>`). An unordered list has the following general syntax:

```
<ul>
    <li>first_item_text</li>
    <li>second_item_text</li>
    . . .
</ul>
```

By default, Web browsers add a leading bullet to each unordered list item and place each item on a new line. Remember that it is a good practice to indent the individual list items within the HTML code so that the code is easier to understand. Now on your Clearwater Traders Web page, you will add the unordered list that appears under the Customer Service level 2 heading.

To add the unordered list:

1. Switch to HTML view, create a new blank line directly below the closing `</h2>` tag that encloses the "Customer Service" level 2 heading, press **Tab** to indent the insertion point, and then add the following tags and text:

```
<ul>
    <li>How to Order</li>
    <li>Shipping and Returns</li>
    <li>Check on Your Order</li>
</ul>
```

2. Save the file, then switch to Design view to view your changes. Your bulleted list should appear as shown in Figure 2-19.

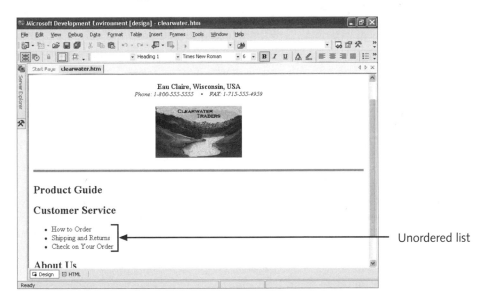

**Figure 2-19**   Web page with an unordered list

## Ordered Lists

You define an ordered list using the **ordered list tag** (`<ol>`). As with an unordered list, you include each individual list item within the opening and closing ordered list tag using the list item tag. By default, ordered lists use Arabic (standard English-style) numbers and start with the number 1. You can define an alternative numbering style using the **numbering type attribute**, which has the following syntax: `type="desired_numbering_type"`. Usually, the *desired_numbering_type* value is the first value in the sequence. For example, for a list that starts with uppercase letters, the *desired_numbering_type* value is "A." You can specify a different start value for the first list item using the **start attribute**, which has the following format: `start="desired_start_value"`.

Table 2-5 shows the different ordered list numbering styles, list definitions specifying different type and start attributes, and the resulting numbering sequence. For example, to define an ordered list that uses lowercase Roman numerals with a start value of vi, you would use the following ordered list tag: `<ol type="i" start="6">`.

**Table 2-5**    Ordered list styles

| Numbering Style | Type Definition | Sample Sequence |
|---|---|---|
| Arabic numerals | `<ol start="3">` | 3, 4, 5, 6, … |
| Capital letters | `<ol type="A" start="3">` | C, D, E, F, … |
| Lowercase letters | `<ol type="a" start="3">` | c, d, e, f, … |
| Roman numerals | `<ol type="I" start="3">` | III, IV, V, VI, … |
| Lowercase Roman numerals | `<ol type="i" start="3">` | iii, iv, v, vi, … |

Now you will create the ordered list shown in Figure 2-4 that appears under the "How to Order" bulleted item. This list specifies the sequence for placing an order. It uses the default numbering type and the default start value, which is 1. You will use the `<small>` character formatting tag to place the ordered list items in a smaller font than the unordered list items.

To create an ordered list:

1. Switch to HTML view, create a new blank line directly below the "How to Order" unordered list item, press **Tab** to indent the insertion point, and add the following commands:

```
<ol>
    <small><li>Select Items</li></small>
    <small><li>View Your Shopping Cart</li></small>
    <small><li>Check Out</li></small>
</ol>
```

2. Save the file, then switch to Design view to view your changes. Your ordered list should appear as shown in Figure 2-20. Note that because you enclosed the `<li>` tags within the `<small>` tags, the ordered list numbers appear in the smaller font along with the list text.

## Comments in HTML Documents

HTML code for even a simple Web page can become complex. It is a good practice to add comment tags to label different Web page sections internally. Comments are not visible when the Web page appears in a Web browser, but users can view the HTML source code for the page and view the comments.

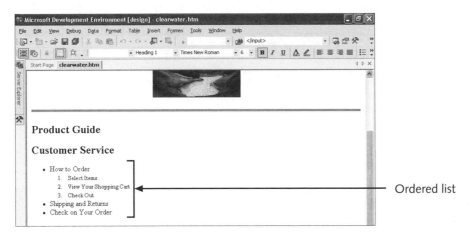

**Figure 2-20**    HTML ordered list

 You can view the HTML source code for any Web page by clicking View on the browser menu bar and then clicking Source. You might want to view the source code of a Web page to see how a developer achieved a certain formatting layout.

An **opening comment tag** uses the syntax **<!--**, which is an opening angle bracket, then an exclamation point, followed by two hyphens. A **closing comment tag** uses the syntax **-->**, which is two hyphens followed by a closing angle bracket. Now you will add comment tags to your HTML document to make it more readable.

To add comments to your HTML document:

1. Switch to HTML view and add the shaded comments and blank line shown in Figure 2-21 to complete the Clearwater Traders home page. The comments appear in green text in the HTML editor.

2. Save the file, and then switch to Design view to confirm that your Web page display has not changed.

3. Click **File** on the menu bar, and then click **Close** to close the completed Clearwater Traders home page.

```
<body>
  <!-- CT location and telephone numbers -->
  <h1 align=center>Clearwater Traders</h1>
  <p align=center><strong>Eau Claire, Wisconsin, USA</strong> ↵
  <br /><small><i>Phone: 1-800-555-5555   ↵
         ↵
  FAX: 1-715-555-4959</i></small></p>

  <!-- CT logo and horizontal rule -->
  <p align=center><img style="WIDTH: 197px; HEIGHT: 116px" ↵
  src="clearlogo.jpg"   height="116" width="197" /></p>
  <hr size="5" noshade />
  <h2>Product Guide</h2>
  <h2>Customer Service</h2>
    <ul>
      <li>How to Order</li>
        <ol>
        <small><li>Select Items</small></li>
        <small><li>View Your Shopping Cart</small></li>
        <small><li>Check Out</small></li></ol>
      <li>Shipping and Returns</li>
      <li>Check on Your Order</li>
    </ul>
  <h2>About Us</h2>
  <h2>Contact Us</h2>
</body>
```

**Figure 2-21**    Completed HTML document body with comments

## TABLES IN WEB PAGES

Sometimes it is difficult to control the exact placement of elements on a Web page. One way to gain more control over element placement is to place elements in HTML tables. **HTML tables** display Web page elements in columns and rows and allow you to control the relative position of elements. HTML tables are useful for displaying data that Web pages retrieve from relational databases. HTML tables are also useful for displaying text next to graphic images instead of above or below them, and for displaying graphic images beside each other.

Figure 2-22 illustrates a design diagram for the Clearwater Traders Product Guide Web page, which shows data about Clearwater Traders products. This Web page contains two tables. The first table displays the page's heading objects. It has one row and two columns and does not display row or column lines. (In Figure 2-22, the lines appear as dashes to illustrate the table structure.)  The first column contains the Clearwater Traders logo, and the second column contains the text "Product Guide." The heading objects were placed in a table rather than as separate objects on the Web page because tables provide an easy way to display text next to graphic images. The second table displays the data for each product, which includes the Item ID, the Item Description, and a graphic image showing a picture of each product. Now you will learn how to create and format HTML tables.

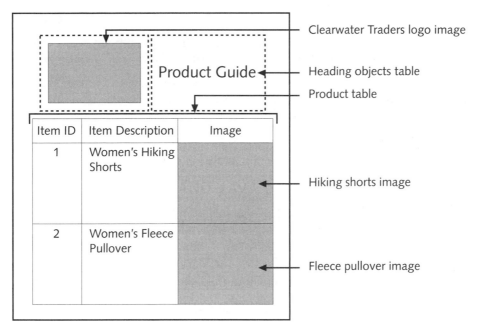

**Figure 2-22**    Design diagram for the Clearwater Traders Product Guide Web page

## HTML Table Definition Tags

You define an HTML table using the **table tag**, which has the following syntax: `<table>`*table_contents*`</table>`. Within the *table_contents*, you define individual rows using the **table row tag** (`<tr>`), and individual elements within each row using the **table data tag** (`<td>`). The number of `<td>` tags that appear in the first table row specifies the number of columns that the table contains. The following code illustrates the general syntax for defining a table that contains two columns and two rows:

```
<table>
    <tr><td>element</td><td>element</td></tr>
    <tr><td>element</td><td>element</td></tr>
</table>
```

The elements within table data tags can be text, graphic images, lists, other tables, or most other types of Web page elements. It is a good practice to indent the tags for each table row as shown so you can easily identify the individual table rows and data items.

To insert a graphic image into a table item, you place the image tag directly between the `<td>` opening and closing tags. You can specify image properties and format text within a table just as you can within any other part of a Web page. Now you will create a new HTML document, and create the heading objects table that contains the Clearwater Traders logo and the "Product Guide" level 2 heading text, as shown in Figure 2-22.

To create the Product Guide Web page:

1. In Visual Studio .NET, create a new HTML document file, and save the file as **products.htm** in the Chapter2\Tutorials folder on your Solution Disk.

2. Switch to HTML view and type the shaded code shown in Figure 2-23 to define the Product Guide Web page title and the table for the logo and heading text. Adjust the indenting of the code as necessary so nested tags appear indented.

```
<!DOCTYPE HTML PUBLIC "-//W3C//DTD HTML 4.0 Transitional//EN">
<html>
  <head>
    <title>Clearwater Traders</title>
     <meta name="GENERATOR" content="Microsoft Visual Studio .NET 7.0">
     <meta name="vs_targetSchema"
     content="http://schemas.microsoft.com/intellisense/ie5"></head>
     <body>
      <!-- table to display logo and page heading -->
      <table>
      <tr><td><img src="clearlogo.jpg" /></td>
          <td><h2>Product Guide</h2></td></tr>
      </table>
     </body>
</html>
```

**Figure 2-23**    HTML tags and elements to create Product Guide Web page title and table

3. Save the file, then switch to Design view.

4. Resize the image so your heading table looks like Figure 2-24, switch back to HTML view, place the height and width attribute values in quotation marks, and then save the file.

**Figure 2-24**    Heading table

2

## Table Size and Alignment

Web browsers determine the width of a table based on the widths of the data values in the individual table columns, and the table height based on the number of data rows. You can also specify a particular table size using the width and height attributes within the table tag. You used these attributes earlier to specify the sizes of inline graphic images. You can specify the width or height attribute value either as a percentage of the overall Web page size or in pixels. Usually when you create tables that contain database values, you omit the height attribute value and specify only a value for the table's width attribute. This allows the table to grow vertically depending on the number of records that appear.

In Visual Studio .NET, you can also modify the table size by displaying the table in Design view, selecting the table so selection handles appear on its perimeter, and then dragging the selection handles to change the table to the desired size. When you do this, the HTML editor automatically enters the style attribute in the table tag and specifies the WIDTH and HEIGHT values in pixels.

By default, browser tables align on the left edge of the Web page. You can use the align attribute (`align="desired_alignment"`) within the table tag to change the table alignment. Now you will modify your table specification so that the table is centered on the Web page and spans 60 percent of the available Web page width.

To modify the table size and alignment:

1. In HTML view, modify the table tag by adding the following align and width attribute values:

   ```
   <table align="center" width="60%">
   ```

2. Save the file, then switch to Design view to view the centered and resized table.

By default, gridlines always appear around the table columns in Design view in Visual Studio .NET. These gridlines assist you while you design and configure the table, but do not appear when the Web page appears in a Web browser unless you explicitly add attributes to the table tag to display the gridlines. You will learn how to display and configure gridlines later in this chapter. It is a good idea always to preview Web pages that contain HTML tables in Internet Explorer to see how the tables will actually look to users. Now you will open the Web page in Internet Explorer and display the Product Guide Web page to confirm that the table gridlines are not visible.

To view the Web page in Internet Explorer:

1. Start Internet Explorer, click **File** on the menu bar, click **Open**, click **Browse**, and navigate to the Chapter2\Tutorials folder on your Solution Disk.

2. Select **products.htm**, click **Open**, and then click **OK**. The current Product Guide Web page appears as shown in Figure 2-25. Note that the gridlines do not appear in the heading table.

**Figure 2-25**    Heading table in Internet Explorer

## Column Headings

You can create a heading row in a table that displays the column heading text in a larger, boldface font. To create column headings, you use the **table heading tag** (`<th>`) in place of the table data tag for the first column row. By default, table headings appear centered within table columns. A table can have multiple heading rows.

Now you will create the product table in Figure 2-22. For now, you will enter the table values directly into the table. In later chapters, you will learn how to write programs to retrieve this data from a database and display it in a Web page table. You will place this table in a new paragraph using the paragraph tag (`<p>`), so there is a blank space between the heading objects table and the product table. Then you will enter the HTML code to create the row for the column headings and the rows containing the first two Clearwater Traders products. Because the table contains graphic images of Clearwater Traders products, you will first need to copy the image files to the Tutorials folder on your Chapter2 Solution Disk.

To create the product table:

1. If necessary, start Windows Explorer, and copy **shorts.jpg** and **fleece.jpg** from the Chapter2 folder on your Data Disk to the Chapter2\Tutorials folder on your Solution Disk.

2. In Visual Studio .NET, switch to HTML view, place the insertion point after the `</table>` closing tag, and add the shaded HTML code shown in Figure 2-26 to create the product table. (The figure shows only the body section of the HTML document.)

3. Save the file, then switch to Design view to view the product table.

Recall that by default, gridlines do not appear between table columns and rows. Now you will view the Product Guide Web page in Internet Explorer to preview how the product table will look in a browser.

To preview the Product Guide Web page in Internet Explorer:

1. Switch to Internet Explorer.

2. Press **F5** to refresh your Web page display. The product table appears as shown in Figure 2-27.

```
<body>
  <!-- table to display logo and page heading -->
  <table align="center" width="60%">
    tr><td><img src="clearlogo.jpg" style="WIDTH: 159px; HEIGHT:
    101px" height="101" width="159" /></td><td><h2>Product Guide</h2></td></tr>
  </table>
   <p><table width="100%" align="center">
    <tr><th>Item ID</th><th>Item Description</th><th>Image</th></tr>
    <tr><td>1</td><td>Women's Hiking Shorts</td><td>
       <img src="shorts.jpg" /></td></tr>
    <tr><td>2</td><td>Women's Fleece Pullover</td><td>
       <img src="fleece.jpg" /></td></tr>
   </table></p>
</body>
```

**Figure 2-26**    HTML code to create the product table

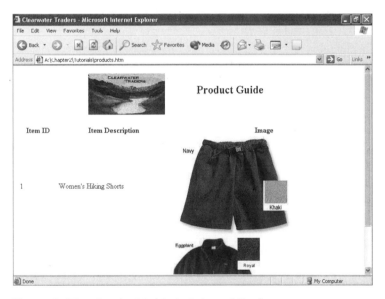

**Figure 2-27**    Product table in Internet Explorer

Currently the current product table is hard to read because it does not have borders to define the table columns and rows. The next section introduces the table attributes that control table borders and border spacing.

## Table Borders and Cell Spacing

The border, cellspacing, and cellpadding attributes control the appearance of a table's border and gridlines. The **border attribute** instructs the browser to display a border around the table and gridlines around the table columns and rows, and has the following syntax: `border="thickness"`. By default, tables appear as three-dimensional objects, and the *thickness* value, specified in pixels, controls the depth of the border that surrounds the table. The gridlines that define individual columns and rows are always one pixel thick. If you omit the border *thickness* value and simply enter `border` in the table tag, the outside border size will be the default value of one pixel.

The **cellspacing attribute** determines the amount of space, in pixels, between the inside border lines of adjacent table cells. The attribute uses the following syntax: `cellspacing="spacing"`. To remove the space between the inside cell border lines, you set the *spacing* attribute value equal to zero. The **cellpadding attribute** determines the amount of space, in pixels, between the inside cell border and the object or text within the cell, depending on the justification of the text within the cell. The syntax of the cellpadding attribute is `cellpadding="padding"`, where the *padding* attribute value specifies the number of pixels between the cell border and its contents. Figure 2-28 illustrates these attributes.

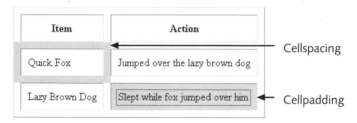

**Figure 2-28**    Table cellspacing and cellpadding

 For an object that is left-justified within a table cell and does not fill the cell, the cellpadding attribute specifies the space between the object and the top and left edges of the cell. For right-justified objects that do not fill the cell, the cellpadding attribute specifies the space between the object and the top and right edges of the cell. For objects that fill the cell, the cellpadding attribute specifies the space between the object and all of the cell edges.

Now you will add a border and modify the cellspacing and cellpadding attributes of the product table. You will specify the border as 5 pixels, the cellspacing as 3 pixels, and the cellpadding as 5 pixels.

To modify the table border, cellspacing, and cellpadding:

1. Switch back to Visual Studio .NET, switch to HTML view, and add the following attributes to the table tag for the product table:

```
<table width="100%" align="center" border="5"
cellspacing="3" cellpadding="5">
```

2. Save the file, switch to Internet Explorer, and press **F5** to refresh the display. The table now appears with a border, gridlines, and modified cell spacing, as shown in Figure 2-29.

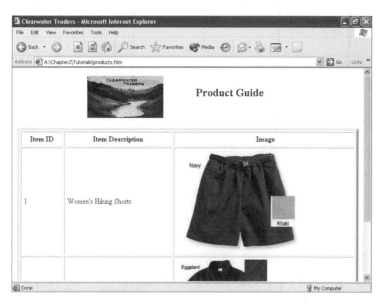

**Figure 2-29**     Table with border, gridlines, and modified cell spacing

## Specifying Table Column Widths

Web browsers automatically size the width of table columns based on the data values they contain. For example, in Figure 2-29, the first column is wide enough to accommodate the longest data value, which is the Item ID column title, without wrapping its text to two lines. The browser uses this approach for all of the other columns. The last table column has extra space on its right edge because the images do not require the entire column width. As before, when you do not specify an item's size, the Web browser has to perform extra processing to determine the size, and this causes the Web page to load more slowly. You should always specify the width of table columns to speed up displaying a table.

To specify the widths of table columns explicitly, you add the width attribute to the table heading tag for each column in the row that contains the table headings, which is usually the first row of the table. (If a table does not have table headings in the first row, you can add the width attribute to the table data tag for each column in the first row.) When you specify the widths for the columns in the first row, you set the width for all table rows. You can specify the width attribute in pixels or as a percentage of the table display width. If you specify the column width as a percentage of the table display width, the sum of the width attribute values for all of the columns must equal 100 percent.

In Visual Studio .NET, you can visually resize the columns. To do this, you place the mouse pointer on the gridline to the right edge of the column you want to resize, so the pointer appears as the **column divide pointer** ↔. You can then drag the column to the desired width. When you do so, the HTML editor specifies the column width using the style attribute and the WIDTH style name. When you resize a table column in Design view, the HTML editor adds a style attribute to the table heading tag and to every table data tag for that column. Now you will specify the column widths in the product table visually in Design view.

To specify the column widths in the product table visually in Design view:

1. Switch back to Visual Studio .NET, switch to Design view if necessary, and place the mouse pointer on the division line between the Item ID and Item Description columns in the product table. The mouse pointer changes to the column divide pointer ✛.

2. Drag the mouse pointer toward the left edge of the screen to make the Item ID column narrower. Size the column so that it is just wide enough that the Item ID heading text appears on one line, as shown in Figure 2-30.

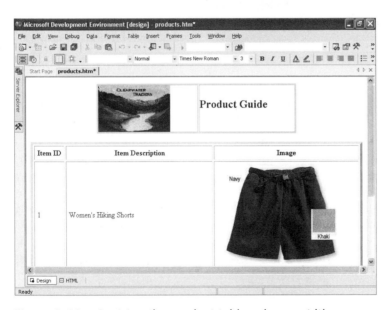

**Figure 2-30**     Resizing the product table column widths

3. Place the mouse pointer on the division line between the Item Description and Image columns, and make the Item Description column wider, so your table looks like Figure 2-30.

4. Switch to HTML view and examine the style tags that the HTML Designer has added to the column heading and cell tags. Note that because you did not resize the Image column, the HTML Designer did not add any style tags to this column's tags. The Image column's width will automatically occupy the remaining table width.

5. Save the file, then switch to Internet Explorer and press **F5** to refresh your display of the product table. The Item ID and Image columns are now narrower, and the Item Description column is wider.

# Aligning Table Objects

By default, table data items appear left-justified and vertically centered within table cells. You can control the alignment of individual table objects using the align and vertical align attributes. You have already used the align attribute to control text alignment in headings and paragraphs. The **vertical align attribute** controls vertical text placement. The general syntax of the vertical align attribute is `valign="vertical_alignment"`. The vertical alignment value can be *top*, *middle* (which is the default value), or *bottom*. You must place the align and valign attributes in the table heading or table data tags for each table item.

Now you will modify the alignments of some of your table objects. You will specify that the Item ID values appear horizontally centered and vertically aligned at the top of their cells. You will align the Item Description heading cell text on the left side of its cell, and the Item Description values at the top of their cells.

To modify the table object alignments:

1. Switch back to Visual Studio .NET. In HTML view, add the following align attribute to the Item Description table heading tag. Do not modify the WIDTH attribute value for the style attribute.

```
<th style="WIDTH: npx" align="left">Item Description</th>
```

 Because your value for the column width may be different, this code example uses *n* instead of the exact column width. You should not change the column width.

2. Add the following valign attributes to the tags for the first row of product table data items. Do not modify the WIDTH value for the style tags.

```
<td style="WIDTH: npx" valign="top">1</td>
<td style="WIDTH: npx" valign="top"> ↵
Women's Hiking Shorts</td>
```

3. Add the following valign attributes to the tags for the second row of product table data items. Do not modify the WIDTH value for the style tags.

```
<td style="WIDTH: npx" valign="top">2</td>
<td style="WIDTH: npx" valign="top"> ↵
Women's Fleece Pullover</td>
```

4. Save the file, and then switch to Design view to view your modified column alignments. The table data items should appear vertically aligned at the top of the data cells.

# HYPERLINKS

A hyperlink is a reference in an HTML document that enables a user to jump to another location. The hyperlink can be associated with a single keyword, a group of words, or a graphic object.

When you associate a hyperlink with a single keyword or phrase, the browser underlines the keyword or phrase on the Web page and displays the keyword or phrase in a color different from the rest of the Web page text. When you move the mouse pointer onto text or a graphic associated with a hyperlink, the pointer changes to the link select pointer , and the location that the link references, which is called the **link anchor**, appears on the status line of the browser display. Figure 2-31 shows a Web page that contains examples of these three types of hyperlinks.

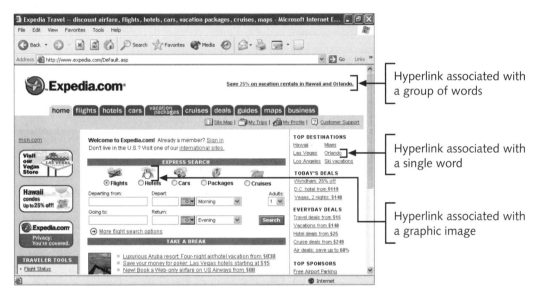

**Figure 2-31**    Examples of Web page elements associated with hyperlinks

The link anchor might reference an object on the same Web page, or it might reference a separate HTML document. The hyperlink could also be associated with a Web processing program that creates a dynamic Web page. In this section, you will learn how to create hyperlinks that reference different Web pages. These hyperlinks use the same syntax as hyperlinks that are associated with programming code that creates dynamic Web pages, which you will create and use in later chapters.

To create a hyperlink to a different Web page, you use the link tag. The opening **link tag** has the following syntax: `<a href="marker">`. The *marker* value can be the filename of a processing program or the URL of a second Web page's HTML file. The closing link tag is `</a>`. For example, to create a hyperlink to an HTML file named referencedfilename.htm in which the link anchor consists of the keywords "View File," you would use

2

the following link tag: `<a href="referencedfilename.htm">View File</a>`. As with graphic image references, if the referenced Web page file is in the current working directory, which is the same folder as the Web page file that contains the hyperlink, you simply list the filename without any drive letter or folder path information. If the referenced Web page file is in another folder on the workstation running the Web browser, you must list the path to the referenced file, including the drive letter and folder path. If the referenced Web page is on a different Web server, you reference the page's complete URL.

Now you will open an HTML file named clearwater_done.htm that contains the elements and tags for the Clearwater Traders home page that you created earlier in the chapter. You will create a link anchor from the Product Guide level 2 heading to the Product Guide page you just created. Because both the clearwater_done.htm and products.htm Web page files are in the same folder, which is the Chapter2\Tutorials folder on your Solution Disk, you do not need to specify any path information; the hyperlink will just reference the filename. Hyperlinks are not activated in Design view or the HTML editor, so after you create the hyperlink, you will test it in your browser.

To create and test a hyperlink to a different Web page:

1. In Visual Studio .NET, click **File** on the menu bar, point to **Open**, and then click **File**. Navigate to the Chapter2 folder on your Data Disk, select **clearwater_done.htm**, and then click **Open**. The Clearwater Traders home page appears in Design view.

2. Click **File** on the menu bar, click **Save clearwater_done.htm As**, navigate to the Chapter2\Tutorials folder on your Solution Disk, and then click **Save**.

3. Switch to HTML view, then modify the Product Guide level 2 heading specification to reference the products.htm file by adding a link tag, using the following code:

   ```
   <a href="products.htm"><h2>Product Guide</h2></a>
   ```

4. Save the file, then switch to Internet Explorer, click **File** on the menu bar, click **Open**, navigate to the Chapter2\Tutorials folder on your Solution Disk, select **clearwater_done.htm**, click **Open**, and then click **OK**. The Clearwater Traders home page appears, and the Product Guide heading is highlighted and underlined to indicate it contains a hyperlink reference.

5. Move the mouse pointer so it is on the Product Guide hyperlink. Note that the hyperlink reference appears in the browser status line as shown in Figure 2-32.

6. Click the **Product Guide hyperlink**. The Product Guide Web page appears.

7. Switch back to Visual Studio .NET and close the **products.htm** and **clearwater_done.htm** Web page files.

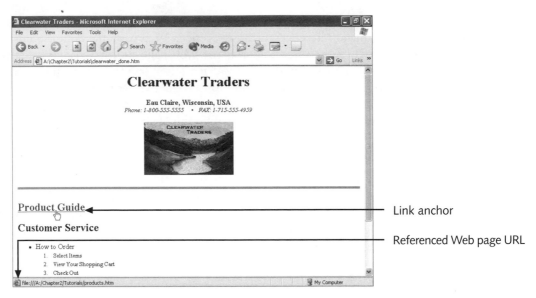

**Figure 2-32**     Viewing a link anchor to a different Web page

# HTML Forms

To do business on the Web, a company needs to be able to interact with customers and get customer inputs using Web pages. One way you can acquire user inputs is by using HTML forms, which are enhanced HTML documents that look like paper forms. When a user submits a form to a Web server, a program running on the Web server processes the form inputs and dynamically composes a Web page reply. HTML forms allow users to input data using interface items called **form elements**. These interface items are very similar to the items that you interact with in most Windows-based programs, such as text boxes, command buttons, and selection lists.

When a user submits a form to the Web server, the browser submits the value of each form element to the Web server as a parameter. A **parameter** is a variable value that is passed from one program to another program. The browser submits the form element values in a **parameter list**, which consists of the name of every form element along with its current value. You can create a form anywhere within an HTML document using the **form tag**, which has the following syntax:

```
<form name="frmForm_Name"  ↵
action="processing_program_filename">
form_element_tags
</form>
```

The *Form_Name* value identifies the form internally within the Web page. In this book, you will preface form names with the prefix *frm*. The **action attribute** specifies the action the Web server performs when the user submits the form. Usually the action

2

involves calling a program or script that acts on the form input data and returns a dynamic Web page response. The *processing_program_filename* value specifies the URL or path to the program or script. You will learn how to create programs that process form values later in this book.

The *form_element_tags* define the individual form elements that the user uses to input data values. You use the **input tag** to create a new input box, radio button, check box, or command button. (You use other tags to define selection lists and text area input boxes, which you will learn about later.) The input tag has the following general syntax: `<input type="type" name="attribute_name" />` . (The input tag is an empty tag, so the last element in the tag is a front slash (/).) You use the **input type attribute** within the input tag to specify the type of input element that you wish to create. Every form element should have a **name attribute**, which is a text string that identifies the element internally within the form. The *attribute_name* can be any text string, and is enclosed in double quotation marks.

Table 2-6 summarizes the most common types of HTML form elements. The table also shows the elements' associated input tag type attribute value and the prefix that you use for the *attribute_name*, which helps to identify the element type based on its name.

**Table 2-6**    HTML form elements

| HTML Form Element | Element Function | Input Type Attribute Value | *Attribute_name* Prefix |
|---|---|---|---|
| Input box | Entering a single line of text into a form | text | txt |
| Password input box | Entering a single line of text in which the values are masked as asterisks (*), such as for entering passwords | password | txt |
| Command button | Starting an action such as executing a client-side or server-side program | button | cmd |
| Submit command button | Submitting the form to the processing program | submit | cmd |
| Reset command button | Returning the form to its original state (clearing all user inputs or returning them to their original values) | reset | cmd |
| Radio button (or option button) | Selecting a single option from a predefined group of items | radio | opt |
| Check box | Selecting whether an option is checked or unchecked, or true or false | checkbox | chk |

**Table 2-6**    HTML form elements (continued)

| HTML Form Element | Element Function | Input Type Attribute Value | Attribute_name Prefix |
|---|---|---|---|
| Text area | Entering multiple lines of text into a form, such as a paragraph of text | Not used with `<input>` tag | txt |
| Selection list | Selecting a single item from a predefined list of items | Not used with `<input>` tag | lst |
| Hidden element | Storing a data item that is not visible to the user | `hidden` | hdn |

You can alternately use the **ID attribute** to identify a form element. You can use an ID attribute to uniquely identify every Web page element, including elements such as paragraphs, tables, and table data tags. Microsoft introduced the ID attribute in Internet Explorer Version 4, and made it optional for every HTML document element. In 1998, the ID attribute became part of the HTML 4.0 standard. Netscape Version 6 was the first Netscape browser to implement the ID attribute. To assign an ID attribute value, you use the following syntax: `ID="id_value"`.

The XHTML standard requires every Web page element to have an ID attribute identifier. We do not follow this convention in this book because the presence of an ID attribute sometimes causes client-side and server-side programs to work incorrectly in current browsers.

Whenever you copy and paste the tag for a Web page element in HTML Designer, the HTML Designer automatically creates an ID attribute and assigns a default value to it.

In this book, you will assign the *attribute_name* using a descriptive name with mixed-case letters in which the first letter of each word is capitalized. You will use the element name prefixes shown in Table 2-6 at the beginning of element names. You will always type the element name prefixes in all lowercase letters. For example, an input box that customers use to enter their first names would be named `txtFirstName`.

After you create a form in an HTML document, you add tags to create the form elements. Figure 2-33 illustrates the form element tags in Table 2-7 and the appearance of the corresponding form element.

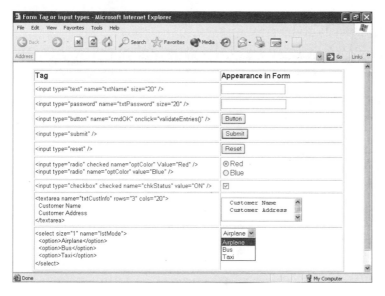

**Figure 2-33**    HTML form elements and tags

The following sections describe how to define different form elements.

## Input Boxes

Web page developers use input boxes to gather text inputs. The general syntax for a tag that defines an input box is:

```
<input type="input_type" name="txtBoxName"
size="max_characters" />
```

The *input_type* attribute value can be either text or password. The *text* value defines an input box in which the input appears exactly as the user types it. The *password* value defines an input box that masks the characters that the user types by inserting an asterisk (*) in place of each typed character. An input box can have an optional size attribute, *max_characters*, which defines the maximum number of characters that the text box can hold. The following tags define input boxes that can hold a maximum of 20 characters into which the user can type a user name and password:

```
<input type="text" name="txtUsername" size="20" />
<input type="password" name="txtPassword" size="20" />
```

## Command Buttons

A command button is a form element that a user clicks to perform an action. On Web forms, command buttons usually call scripts to validate form inputs, submit form values to the Web server, or clear form elements and reset them to their initial values. To define a command button, you use the following syntax:

```
<input type="button" name="cmdButton_Name" ↵
onclick="button_action" value="button_label" />
```

The **onclick attribute** specifies the name of a program that executes or another action that occurs when the user clicks the button. The default label that appears on a command button is "Button," but you can specify a different label using the **value attribute**. The following code creates a command button named cmdOK with the label "OK." When the user clicks this command button, a client-side script function named validateEntries() executes.

```
<input type="button" name="cmdOK" ↵
onclick="validateEntries()" value="OK" />
```

You can create a special kind of command button called a **submit button** by setting the type attribute value to *submit*. When the user clicks a submit button, the form submits the values of the form elements as parameters to a form processing program that the action attribute defines in the form definition tag. The default button caption is "Submit Query," but you can add an optional value attribute to specify a different button caption. The following code defines a form named frmProcessOrder that contains a submit button with the label "Process Order." When the user clicks the button, the form passes the form field values to a script named process.aspx.

```
<form name="frmProcessOrder" action="process.aspx">
    <input type="submit" value="Process Order" />
</form>
```

You can also create a reset button in a Web form. When the user clicks a **reset button**, the form clears all form element values or resets them to their initial values. The form does not submit the values of the form elements to the Web server. To create a reset button, you set the input type attribute value to *reset*. Although the default button caption is "Reset," as with the submit button, you can add an optional value attribute to specify a different button caption. The following code creates a reset button with the caption "Clear":

```
<input type="reset" value="Clear" />
```

## Radio Buttons

Radio buttons allow the user to select a single value from a group of related values. You define related radio buttons as a **radio button group**, which allows the user to select only one button in the group at one time. To define a radio button group, you create a series of individual radio buttons using the following syntax:

```
<input type="radio" name="optRadioButtonName" ↵
value="radio_button_value" />radio_button_label
```

Each radio button in a radio button group has the same name attribute value. For example, in Figure 2-33, the name attribute value for both radio buttons is *optColor*. The *radio_button_value* attribute indicates the value of the specific radio button. For example, in Figure 2-33, the value of the first radio button is Red and the value of the second radio button is Blue. Usually the value of a radio button is the same as the label beside the radio button, but it does not have to be. The entire radio button group assumes the value of the selected radio button. For example, if the user selects the first radio button in Figure 2-33, the value of the optColor radio button group is Red, and the program passes the value Red as a parameter to the Web server when the user submits the form.

If a radio button's input tag contains the **checked attribute**, then the radio button appears selected when the form first opens. The checked attribute is a Boolean attribute, so when you place the checked attribute in the input tag, the attribute value is true and the button appears checked. The *radio_button_label* text specifies the label that appears next to the radio button, and you place it just after the radio button's <input> tag. In Figure 2-33, the label beside the first radio button is "Red," and the label beside the second radio button is "Blue."

## Check Boxes

A check box defines an element that can have one of two opposite values, such as true or false, or on or off. You use the following syntax to define a check box element:

```
<input type="checkbox" name="chkBoxName" ↵
value="check_box_value">
```

The value attribute specifies the value of the check box when the box is checked. Some examples of values might be true, false, on, or off. If the check box's input tag contains the **checked** attribute, then the check box appears checked when the form first opens. The following tag defines a check box named chkRushDelivery that appears checked when the form first opens. When the check box is checked, its value corresponds to the text string "ON." A form might use this check box to indicate whether or not an order will have rush delivery.

```
<input type="checkbox" name="chkRushDelivery" ↵
value="ON" checked>
```

## Text Areas

A **text area** is an input box that can contain multiple lines of text. To define a text area input box, you use the **textarea tag**, which has the following syntax:

```
<textarea name="txtAreaName" ↵
rows="max_rows" cols="max_characters">
    current_text
</textarea>
```

The **rows attribute** value specifies the maximum number of rows that can appear in the text area, and the **cols (columns) attribute** value specifies the maximum number of characters that can appear in a single row. The *current_text* value can optionally define text that appears in the text area when the form first opens. The following code defines a blank text area named txtCustomerInfo that contains three rows and can contain a maximum of 20 characters per row:

```
<textarea name="txtCustomerInfo" ⤶
rows="3" cols="20"></textarea>
```

## Selection Lists

A **selection list** defines a list from which the user can select specified values. The Web developer can populate the list using static values or using values retrieved from a database. To create a selection list, you use the **select tag**, which has the following syntax:

```
<select name="lstList_Name" size="max_items_displayed">
        <option>first_list_item</option>
        <option>second_list_item</option>
        …
</select>
```

Within this tag, the size attribute's *max_items_displayed* value specifies how many list items appear in the list. When the size attribute is 1, the list is a drop-down list that displays only the selected item. If the user wants to view the rest of the list selections, he or she must open the list. When the *items_displayed* value is greater than 1, then the list appears as a list box with vertical scroll bars, from which the user can select the list item. If the list contains more elements than the size value specifies, then the user can scroll to view all list items. To define the individual list items, you use the **option tag**, which encloses the text that defines each list item. The following code defines a selection list that displays one selection and allows the user to select from the static values Airplane, Train, and Bus:

```
<select name = "lstMode" size="1">
        <option>Airplane</option>
        <option>Train</option>
        <option>Bus</option>
</select>
```

## Hidden Form Elements

A **hidden form element** is an element that is not visible to the user. Developers use hidden form elements to submit data values to the Web server that are not currently visible on the form. These data values might be for internal programming documentation, such as showing the date that the form HTML code was last modified or the date the form was submitted to the Web server. Or, the developer might use these elements to store data values that the user entered in a form on a previous Web page and that need to be submitted with the current form. The general syntax to create a hidden form element is as follows:

```
<input type="hidden" name="hdnName" ↵
value="initial_value" />
```

An example of a hidden form element tag that specifies the date that the current form was last modified is as follows:

```
<input type="hidden" name="hdnDateModified" ↵
value="11/15/2006" />
```

## Creating a Web Form

Now you will create the Web page shown in Figure 2-34. This Web page contains a form that Clearwater Traders customers would use to enter order information. At this time, you will only learn how to create the form input elements. You will learn how to create scripts to process the form later in the book.

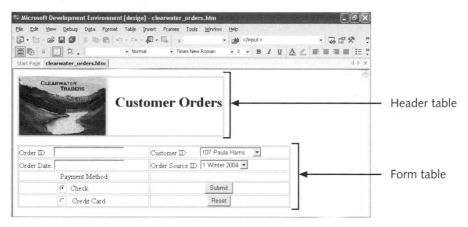

**Figure 2-34**    Clearwater Traders Customer Orders Web page

On this Web page, the Clearwater Traders logo and the Web page heading appear in the header table at the top of the Web page, just as it does on the Product Guide page. The form elements appear in the form table under the header table. The form elements are in a table so that they will appear side by side on the Web page. The user will specify the Order ID and Order Date values using input boxes, the Payment Method value using radio buttons, and the Customer ID and Order Source ID values using selection lists. After entering values for the customer order form elements, the user can click the Submit button to submit the form element values to a processing program, or click the Reset button to reset the form element values to their original values.

Normally the Web server would generate a form like this one as a dynamic Web page, and would automatically insert the Order ID value before displaying the page to the user. You will learn how to write programs to do this later in this book. In this chapter, you will insert the Order ID value manually.

To create this Web page, you will first open a Web page file named clearwater_orders.htm that is stored in the Chapter2 folder on your Data Disk. This file contains the HTML elements and tags to define the header table that displays the Clearwater Traders logo and the Customer Orders heading. After you open the file, you will save the file on your Solution Disk.

To open and then save the Web page file:

1. In Visual Studio .NET, click the **Open** button on the toolbar, navigate to the Chapter2 folder on your Data Disk, select **clearwater_orders.htm**, then click **Open**. The Clearwater Traders Customer Orders Web page opens.

2. Click **File** on the menu bar, click **Save clearwater_orders.htm As**, navigate to the Chapter2\Tutorials folder on your Solution Disk, and click **Save**.

Now you will create the form table and form elements in Figure 2-34. First you will enter the form tag. You will name the form frmCustomerOrders, and for now, you will specify the form action attribute value using the placeholder "action marker." You will learn how to create and use form action attributes in later chapters.

To create the form tag:

1. Switch to HTML view, create a new blank line just above the closing `</body>` tag, press **Tab** as many times as necessary to indent the line so it begins directly below the closing `</table>` tag, and then type the following code to define the form tag:

```
<form name="frmCustomerOrders" ⤸
action="action marker"></form>
```

Next you will define the form table that encloses the form elements. The form table will occupy 80 percent of the Web page width. You will enter the tags to define the form elements in the first row of the form table. The first cell in the first row will contain the Order ID input box, and the second cell will contain the Customer ID selection list. You will enter the text for the labels of the form elements first, and then enter the tags to define the form elements, so that the labels appear on the left side of the form elements, as shown in Figure 2-34. You will populate the selection list using sample data values for Clearwater Traders customers.

To define the form table and first table row:

1. In HTML view, add a new blank line after the opening `<form>` tag, press **Tab** to indent the line, and then type the shaded code shown in Figure 2-35 to define the form table and create the form elements in the first table row.

(Figure 2-35 shows only the HTML commands for the body section for the Web page, and omits the header section tags.)

```
<body>
  <table><tr><td><img src="clearlogo.jpg" height="128" width="190"></td>
    <td><h1 align="center">  Customer Orders</h1></td></tr>
  </table>
  <form name="frmCustomerOrders" action="action marker">
    <table width="80%">
    <!-- first row to add Order ID and Customer ID inputs -->
     <tr><td>Order ID:   
        <input type="text" name="txtOrderID" size="20" /></td>
        <td>Customer ID:      
         <select name="lstCustomer" size="1">
           <option>107 Paula Harris</option>
           <option>232 Mitch Edwards</option>
         </select>
        </td>
     </tr>
    </table>
  </form>
</body>
```

**Figure 2-35**    Code to define form table and create first table row

2. Save the file, then switch to Design view to view your table and form elements. Note that the form items are not operational: You cannot type a value into the Order ID input box or open the Customer ID selection list. To test the form items, you must view the Web page in a browser.

3. Switch to Internet Explorer, click **File** on the menu bar, click **Open**, click **Browse**, and if necessary, navigate to the Chapter2\Tutorials folder on your Solution Disk. Select **clearwater_orders.htm**, click **Open**, and then click **OK**. The current Customer Orders Web page appears as shown in Figure 2-36.

**Figure 2-36**    Customer Orders Web page with elements in the first form table row

4. To test the form elements, place the insertion point in the Order ID input box and type **1060**. Then open the Customer ID selection list and select **Customer ID 107**, which is the ID for Paula Harris.

Now you will add the elements for the second and third rows in the form table. The second row contains an input box for the Order Date and a selection list for the Order Source ID, which indicates the Clearwater Traders catalog in which the items appear. The third row contains the "Payment Method" label in the first column, and does not contain anything in the second column. As before, you will enter the labels for the form elements, followed by the tags to define the elements. For the Order Source ID selection list values, you will enter sample data values for Clearwater Traders order sources.

1. Switch back to Visual Studio .NET, switch to HTML view, and create a new blank line just above the closing `</table>` tag for the form table. (This is the tag that is just above the closing `</form>` tag in the editor.)

2. Type the shaded code shown in Figure 2-37 to define the elements in the second and third rows of the form table. (Figure 2-37 shows only the HTML tags and text for the Web page form elements.)

3. Save the file and then switch to Design view. Your Web page should now display the first three rows of the form table shown in Figure 2-34.

4. Switch to Internet Explorer and press **F5** to refresh the Web page display. Confirm that the new form elements are operational by typing a value in the Order Date input box and then opening the Order Source ID list.

 If your form elements do not appear aligned as shown in Figure 2-34, open the form in Design view in the HTML Designer. Place the insertion point in front of the element and press the space bar to add blank spaces or press Delete to remove blank spaces as needed to make the alignment of the form elements approximately match that of Figure 2-34.

To complete the Customer Orders Web page, you need to create the radio buttons and command buttons that appear in the fourth and fifth rows of the form table. Recall that radio buttons enable users to select a single value from a set of related values, and that related radio button selections exist in a radio button group. When you create the Check and Credit Card radio buttons, you will specify that the name attribute for both buttons is optPmtMethod. This way, the radio buttons are in the same radio button group and work together by allowing only one button to appear selected at one time. For the radio button value attribute, you will assign the Check radio button to have the value "CHECK," and the Credit Card radio button to have the value "CC" (for credit card). When the user selects the Check radio button, the value for the optPmtMethod radio group will be "CHECK." When the user selects the Credit Card radio button, the value for the radio group will be "CC." You will include the checked attribute in the tag for the Check radio button, so this button appears selected when the form first opens. You will also specify a custom label for the submit button by assigning "Submit" as its value attribute.

```
<form name="frmCustomerOrders" action="action marker">
  <table width="80%">
  <!-- first row to add Order ID and Customer ID inputs -->
    <tr><td>Order ID:   
      <input type="text" name="txtOrderID" size="20" /></td>
      <td>Customer ID:      
        <select name="lstCustomer" size="1">
          <option>107 Paula Harris</option>
          <option>232 Mitch Edwards</option>
        </select>
      </td>
    </tr>
    <!-- second row to add Order Date and Order Source ID inputs -->
    <tr>
      <td>Order Date: <input type="text" size="20"  ↵
      name="txtOrderDate" /></td>
      <td>Order Source ID:
        <select name="lstOrderSourceID" size="1">
          <option>1 Winter 2004</option>
          <option>2 Spring 2005</option>
        </select>
      </td>
    </tr>
    <!-- third row to add Payment Method label and blank cell -->
    <tr>
      <td align="center">Payment Method:</td>
      <!--blank cell in third row, second column -->
      <td></td>
    </tr>
  </table>
  </form>
</body>
</html>
```

**Figure 2-37**    HTML commands to define the second and third table rows

To create the form radio and command buttons:

1. Switch back to Visual Studio .NET, switch to HTML view, create a new blank line just above the final closing `</table>` tag, and then type the shaded code shown in Figure 2-38 to add the form radio and command buttons in the fourth and fifth table rows.

2. Save the file, then switch to Design view to preview the new form elements. Your screen should look like Figure 2-34. If necessary, add or delete blank spaces so the form elements appear aligned as shown in Figure 2-34.

3. Switch to Internet Explorer and press **F5** to refresh your browser display.

4. Place the insertion point in the Order ID input box and type **1060**.

5. Press **Tab**, open the Customer ID list, and select Customer ID **232 Mitch Edwards**.

```
<!-- fourth row to add Check radio button and Submit button -->
  <tr>
    <td>    
          
             
      <input type="radio" name="optPmtMethod" ↵
      checked VALUE="CHECK" />
        Check
    </td>
    <td align="center"><input type="submit" ↵
    value="Submit" name="cmdSubmit" /></td>
  </tr>
<!-- fifth row to add Credit Card radio button and Reset button -->
  <tr>
    <td>     
         
         
        
      <input type="radio" name="optPmtMethod" value="CC" />
        Credit Card
    </td>
    <td align="center"><input type="reset" ↵
    value="Reset" name="cmdReset" /></td>
  </tr>
```

**Figure 2-38**    HTML commands to add radio and command buttons in the fourth and fifth table rows

6. Press **Tab** and type **2/15/2004** for the Order Date.

7. Press **Tab** and confirm that Order Source ID 1 Winter 2004 is selected.

8. Click the **Credit Card** radio button.

9. You cannot click Submit, because you have not yet created a processing program. Click **Reset**. The form clears the input boxes, and the default Check radio button is selected.

10. Close Internet Explorer and Visual Studio .NET.

## CHAPTER SUMMARY

❑ In this book, you will create Web pages for Clearwater Traders, which is a fictitious organization that markets clothing and sporting goods, and for Northwoods University, which is a fictitious university that has a Web-based student registration system.

❑ Visual Studio .NET is an integrated development environment for creating Windows and Web-based applications. It displays multiple windows that the user can open or close as needed to perform different tasks.

**2**

❐ You can use the HTML Designer to develop Web pages within the Visual Studio .NET IDE. As you do this, the Web browser window displays the Web page under development.

❐ HTML is a document layout language that you use to define the structure and appearance of Web pages and to enable Web pages to contain embedded hypertext links to other documents or Web pages. An HTML document contains Web page elements, which include the text and images that appear on the Web page, and HTML tags, which are codes that define how the Web page elements appear.

❐ An HTML document consists of a header section, which contains information about the Web page that the Web browser uses, and a body section, which contains the text that appears in the Web browser.

❐ In Visual Studio .NET, you can develop Web pages in Design view, in which you specify the Web page elements as they will appear in the user's browser by adding Web page text and graphics, moving them into position on the Web page, and editing their appearance. You can also develop Web pages in HTML view, in which you can directly view and edit the underlying HTML tags and Web page content.

❐ You can create headings in a Web page using heading tags that automatically format the text enclosed within the headings. Level 1 headings use the largest font size, whereas level 6 headings use a very small font size. You always place heading tags in the body section of a Web page, and by default, headings appear left-justified. You can modify the alignment of headings using the align attribute.

❐ Paragraph and line break tags add line breaks and white space to a Web page. Character entity tags display special symbols, such as blank spaces and bullets. Character tags specify characteristics of individual characters such as character font style or size.

❐ Web pages contain images and other graphic objects to make the pages appealing and to convey visual information. You can display graphic images as inline images that load when the user's browser loads the Web page. To create an inline image, you use the image tag, which specifies the image's source file, as well as properties such as image size and alignment.

❐ Horizontal rules provide a way to separate a Web page visually into different sections and make it easier to read.

❐ HTML documents can contain unordered lists, in which the items do not appear in a definite sequential order, and ordered lists, which preface list items with numbers or other ordering characters.

❐ HTML documents can contain tables to display Web page content in a matrix format. Tables are useful for displaying database data and for displaying graphic objects next to text. You can specify the table's size, alignment, border style, cellpadding, and cellspacing properties. You can also specify the width and height of individual cells within a table, and the horizontal and vertical alignment of text within cells.

❑ A hyperlink is a reference in an HTML document that allows you to jump to an alternate location on a different Web page. A hyperlink can be associated with one or more text keywords or with a graphic object.

❑ HTML forms collect user inputs using form elements, such as input boxes, radio buttons, command buttons, check boxes, selection lists, and text areas. You can also create hidden form elements that are not visible to the user and are often used to store information.

❑ A form has a name attribute, which internally references the form, and an action attribute, which specifies the action to perform when the user submits the form to the Web server. Usually, the action involves executing a script or program.

❑ When you create a radio button in an HTML form, you specify values for the button's name and value attributes. You always place related radio buttons in a radio button group, which allows the user to select only one of the grouped buttons at one time. To place multiple radio buttons in a radio button group, you set the name attribute of the related buttons to the same value. The selected button's value then becomes the value for the radio button group.

❑ An HTML form can contain submit and reset command buttons. A submit button submits form values to the Web server, and a reset button resets form elements to their original states. When the user clicks a submit button to submit form values to the Web server, the form passes to the Web server a parameter list containing the values of all form elements.

❑ You can place form elements within a table to format the elements so they appear side by side on a Web page. To do this, you first create the form. Then you create the table and enclose the table and table formatting tags within the form tags.

## REVIEW QUESTIONS

1. A(n) _____ is an application development environment with many different windows that the user can open and close as needed.

2. What is the difference between a file with an .htm extension and a file with an .html extension?

3. A(n) _____ is a code that defines a Web page element or defines the formatting of items on a Web page.

   a. Form

   b. Script

   c. Tag

   d. HTML document

4. The _____ and _____ are the two main sections of an HTML document.

**2**

5. Write the HTML tag and text that defines the title of a Web page as "My Home Page."

6. Describe the difference between a Web page title and a Web page heading.

7. The _____ tag places the text within the tag in a new paragraph that is formatted with a blank line above and below it. The _____ tag defines a line break, which places the text that follows on a new blank line.

8. If a picture icon ⊠ appears instead of an image, what probably happened?

9. Write the code to create a tag for a horizontal rule that is 4 pixels high, occupies 25 percent of the Web page width, is right-justified, and has no shading.

10. Write the code to create an unordered list that contains the elements Spring, Summer, Fall, and Winter.

11. Write the code to create an ordered list that contains the following elements: Tiberius, Gaius, Claudius, and Nero. Start the list with the Roman numeral II.

12. You use the `<!-- -->` tag to create a:

   a. Table

   b. Form

   c. Comment

   d. Note

13. The _____ tag specifies column headings, which appear centered and in a bolder font than normal table data items. The _____ tag formats normal table data items.

14. _____ defines the number of pixels between the gridlines that outline each individual table cell, and _____ specifies the number of pixels between the cell contents and the gridlines.

15. What happens when you move the mouse pointer over a Web page item associated with a hyperlink?

16. A form element's _____ attribute specifies how the element is internally referenced.

   a. Name

   b. Action

   c. ID

   d. Both a and c

17. A(n) _____ form element can accept only one line of input text, whereas a(n) _____ form element can accept multiple lines of input text.

18. What is the relationship between a radio button and a radio button group?

19. What does a radio button's value attribute specify?

20. A command button's _____ attribute specifies the name of a script or program that executes when the user clicks the button.

21. What is a hidden form element, and for what purpose do you use it?

---

## HANDS-ON PROJECTS

### Project 2-1  Completing the Clearwater Traders Product Guide Web Page

In this project, you will complete the Product Guide Web page that you created in the chapter so that it displays the values shown in Figure 2–39.

1. Open the products_DONE.htm file from the Chapter2 folder on your Data Disk and save the file as 2Project1.htm in the Chapter2\Projects folder on your Solution Disk.

2. Copy the following files from the Chapter2 folder on your Data Disk to the Chapter2\Projects folder on your Solution Disk:  clearlogo.jpg, shorts.jpg, fleece.jpg, sandals.jpg, parka.jpg, and tents.jpg.

3. Add rows to the products table to display the data and images shown in Figure 2–39.

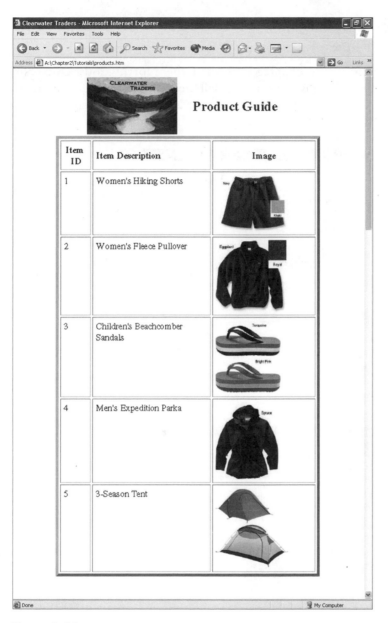

Figure 2-39

## Project 2-2  Creating the Northwoods University Home Page and Faculty Page

In an earlier section, this chapter described the Northwoods University Student Registration Web site. In this project, you will create the Northwoods University home page, shown in Figure 2-40, and the Northwoods University Faculty Web page shown in Figure 2-41.

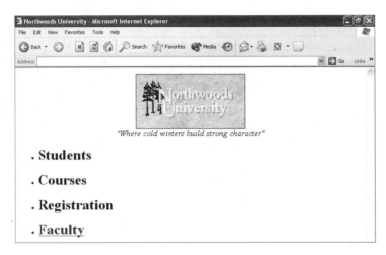

**Figure 2-40**

**Figure 2-41**

1. Copy nwlogo.jpg, which contains the image for the Northwoods University logo shown in Figure 2-40, from the Chapter2 folder on your Data Disk to the Chapter2\Projects folder on your Solution Disk.

2. Create a new HTML document and save it as 2Project2_HOME.htm in the Chapter2\Projects folder on your Solution Disk. Specify the Web page title as "Northwoods University." Create the graphic image tag and place the image and its adjacent text in a table. Use the unordered list tag to create the bulleted list. Format the Web page so it appears as shown in Figure 2-40. (You will create the hyperlink for the Faculty list item in Step f of this project.)

3. Create a new HTML document, and save it as 2Project2_FACULTY.htm in the Chapter2\Projects folder on your Solution Disk. Specify the Web page title as "Northwoods University." Create a table to format the graphic image and heading so they appear as shown in Figure 2-41.

4. Copy the following files that contain the images of Northwoods University faculty members from the Chapter2 folder on your Data Disk into the Chapter2\Projects folder on your Solution Disk: blanchard.jpg, brown.jpg, cox.jpg, and williams.jpg.

5. Create a table that contains two columns and two rows. The first row will contain the data for Northwoods University faculty members John Blanchard and Kim Cox, and the second row will contain the data for Phillip Brown and Jerry Williams. Within each individual cell, create a second table with two columns and one row. The first column will contain the faculty member's photograph, and the second column will contain the faculty member's name, location, telephone number, and rank. The graphic image's filename is the same as the associated faculty member's last name.

6. Create a hyperlink in the 2Project2_HOME.htm file so that when the user clicks the "Faculty" heading on the Northwoods University home page, the Faculty Web page appears.

## Project 2-3  Creating the Northwoods University Student Registration System Logon Page

In this project, you will create a Web page that displays the form elements shown in Figure 2-42 to allow a student at Northwoods University to log on to the student registration system.

1. If necessary, copy the nwlogo.jpg file, which contains the image for the Northwoods University logo, from the Chapter2 folder on your Data Disk to the Chapter2\Projects folder on your Solution Disk.

2. Create a new HTML document, and save it as 2Project3.htm in the Chapter2\Projects folder on your Solution Disk. Specify the Web page title as "Northwoods University." Add the commands to display the Northwoods University logo as an inline graphic image and to display the heading text "Student Registration System."

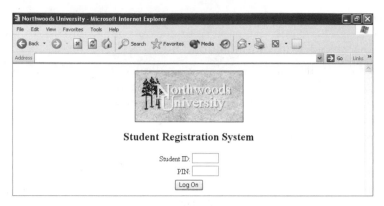

**Figure 2-42**

3. Create an HTML form with input boxes to allow the user to enter his or her student ID and PIN. Name the form frmStudentLogin and set the form action attribute as "action marker." Name the user ID input box txtStudentID, and the PIN input box txtPIN. Create a submit command button. Name the command button cmdSubmit and change its label to "Log On." Place the form elements in a table to align them as shown in Figure 2-42.

## Project 2-4   Creating the Northwoods University Student Information Page

In this project, you will create a Web page that displays the HTML form elements shown in Figure 2-43.

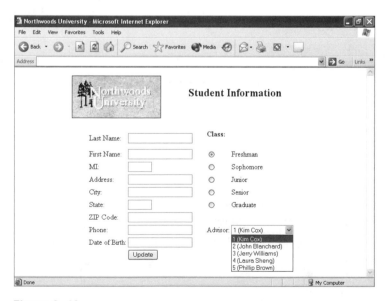

**Figure 2-43**

1. If necessary, copy the nwlogo.jpg file, which contains the image for the Northwoods University logo, from the Chapter2 folder on your Data Disk to the Chapter2\Projects folder on your Solution Disk.

2. Create a new HTML document and save it as 2Project4.htm in the Chapter2\Projects folder on your Solution Disk. Specify the Web page title as Northwoods University. Create a table to display the Northwoods University logo as an inline graphic image and to display the heading text "Student Information" as shown in Figure 2-43.

3. Create a table that displays all of the form elements shown. Provide each form element name attribute with an appropriate prefix and a descriptive name. For example, the code to specify the name of the "Last Name" text input would be `name="txtLastName"`.

4. Specify that only the first radio button (Freshman) is selected when the Web page first appears. Name the radio button group optS_Class, and set the value of each individual radio button equal to the corresponding label value. For example, the value for the Freshman radio button would be "Freshman."

5. For the Advisor list, enter the values for each faculty member as shown in Figure 2-43.

6. Create a button input element as shown, and change its name attribute to cmdUpdate. Specify its onclick attribute value as cmdUpdate_Click.

## CASE PROJECTS

### Case Project 2-1  Ashland Valley Soccer League

The Ashland Valley Soccer League would like to create a Web site to allow players and coaches to access information about league teams, soccer fields, and game schedules. Each team is identified by a team ID and team name (such as "The Force" or "Tornadoes"). Each field is identified by a field ID, description, and address. Each game has a date and a start time, the names of the two teams that are playing, the field ID, and the game status (pending, played, or canceled). In this project, you will create a series of Web pages for this Web site. Include one or more graphic images on each Web page. The Chapter2\Ashland folder on your Data Disk includes graphic images you can use, or you can select your own images. Save the Web pages in the Chapter2\Cases\Ashland folder on your Solution Disk.

1. Design and create a home page for the Ashland Valley Soccer League. Create a heading objects table that is similar to the one in Figure 2-24 to format a graphic and the home page title text. Below the heading table, create an unordered list that includes the following bulleted items:  Games, Teams, and Fields. Save the Web page file as Ashland.htm.

2. Create a Web page with the heading "Fields." On this Web page, create a table that contains data values describing Ashland Valley Soccer League fields. Make up data values for at least five different field IDs, descriptions, and addresses. Save the Web page file as Fields.htm.

3. Create a Web page with the heading "Teams." On this Web page, create a table that contains the fields and data values for the Ashland Valley Soccer League teams. Make up data values for at least five different team ID and team name values. Save the Web page file as Teams.htm.

4. Create a Web page with the heading "Games." On this Web page, create a form that contains form elements that allow users to enter values for game information. Include selection lists for field names and team names. Use radio buttons to specify the game status (Pending, Played, or Cancelled). Create a submit button to allow the user to submit the values to the database. Format the form elements using a table to place the items in two columns. Save the Web page file as Games.htm.

5. On the home page, create hyperlinks from the Games, Fields, and Teams bulleted items to the associated Web pages that you created in Steps 2, 3, and 4.

## Case Project 2-2  Al's Body Shop

Al's Body Shop provides a variety of automotive and body shop services. Al would like to create a Web site to allow customers to use their Web browsers to access information about the shop's services. He would also like customers to be able to use a Web-based interface to view information about their work orders, and he would like to enable employees to enter information about work orders online. In this case project, you will create a series of Web pages for Al's Body Shop. Include one or more graphic images on each Web page. The Chapter2\Als folder on your Data Disk includes a graphic image you can use, or you can select your own images. Save the Web pages in the Chapter2\Cases\Als folder on your Solution Disk.

1. Design and create a home page for Al's Body Shop. On the home page, include the following items:  Customers, Services, and Work Orders. Include a table on the home page to format text and graphics so they appear next to each other. Save the Web page file as Als.htm.

2. Create a Web page with the heading "Customers." On this Web page, create a table that contains name, address, and telephone number values for at least five customers. Save the Web page file as Customers.htm.

3. Create a Web page with the heading "Services." On this Web page, create a table that contains an ID value, description, and charge for at least five different body shop services. Save the Web page file as Services.htm.

4. Create a Web page with the heading "Work Orders." On this Web page, create a form that contains form text input elements that allow users to enter a work order ID, work order date, and vehicle identification number. Include a selection list for the service description, and specify at least three different service options.

(Assume that each work order has only one service.) Create a check box to indicate whether or not the customer has paid for the work order. Create a submit button to allow the user to submit the values to the database. Format the form elements using a table to place items in two columns. Save the Web page file as Workorders.htm.

5. On the home page, create hyperlinks from the Customers, Services, and Work Orders items to the associated Web pages that you created in Steps 2, 3, and 4.

## Case Project 2-3:  Sun-Ray Videos

Sun-Ray Videos is a video rental store that wants to create a Web-based system to allow its customers to select video recordings or game cartridges online, check out items, and then specify whether they will pick up the item or wish to have it delivered. The Web site needs to display each video or game title, its format (VCR, DVD, PlayStation, and so on), and its rental cost. Each video has an associated category (New Release, Action, Horror, Comedy, Sci-Fi, Children's, or Games). When a customer selects a video, rental information must be recorded, including the date rented, date due, date returned, delivery mode (delivery or pick up), rental cost, and late fee. (A $1.00 delivery charge is added for each item that is delivered. A late fee of $2.00 per day is charged for each late item.) In this case project, you will create a series of Web pages for Sun-Ray Videos. Include one or more graphic images on each Web page. The Chapter2\Sunray folder on your Data Disk includes graphic images that you can use, or you can select your own images. Save the Web pages in the Chapter2\Cases\Sunray folder on your Solution Disk.

1. Design and create a home page for Sun-Ray Videos. On the home page, include the following items: "View Titles" and "Rent a Video." Include a table on the home page to format text and graphics so they appear next to each other. Save the Web page file as Sunray.htm.

2. Create a Web page with the heading "Videos." On this Web page, create a table that contains at least five data values for videos, including the title, category, and rental cost. Save the Web page file as Videos.htm.

3. Create a Web page with the heading "Rent a Video." On this Web page, create a form that contains form elements to allow users to select a video title, a format, and the delivery mode (Pick Up or Delivery). Create selection lists for the video title and format, and create radio buttons to allow the user to select the delivery mode. Make up your own video title selections. Create a submit button to allow the user to submit the values to the database. Format the form elements using a table to place the form elements in two columns. Save the Web page file as Rentals.htm.

4. On the home page, create hyperlinks from the "View Titles" and "Rent a Video" items to the associated Web pages that you created in Steps 2 and 3.

## Case Project 2-4  Learning Technologies, Incorporated

Learning Technologies, Incorporated (LTI), is a leading publisher of college textbooks on information technology topics. It would like to have a Web-based interface to allow company representatives to access information about books online, including book titles, warehouse locations, and author information. It would also like to enable company representatives to update the quantity of a specific book title that is on hand at a specific warehouse. In this case project, you will create a series of Web pages for Learning Technologies, Inc. Include one or more graphic images on each Web page. The Chapter2\LTI folder on your Data Disk includes some graphic images you can use, or you can select your own images. Save the Web pages in the Chapter2\Cases\LTI folder on your Solution Disk.

1. Design and create a home page for LTI. Create a heading objects table like the one shown in Figure 2-22 to format a graphic and the home page title text. Below the heading table, create an unordered list that includes the following bulleted items: Authors, Books, Warehouses, and Update Warehouse QOH. Save the Web page file as Lti.htm.

2. Create a Web page with the heading "Authors." On this Web page, create a table that contains values for at least five author names, addresses, and telephone numbers. Save the Web page file as Authors.htm.

3. Create a Web page with the heading "Books." On this Web page, create a table that contains values for at least five books, including the book's international standard book number (ISBN), title, publication date, and price. Save the Web page file as Books.htm.

4. Create a Web page with the heading "Warehouses." On this Web page, create a table that contains at least five data values for LTI warehouses, including the warehouse ID, address, city, and state. Save the Web page file as Warehouses.htm.

5. Create a Web page with the heading "Update Warehouse QOH." On this Web page, create a form that contains form elements that allow users to select a warehouse, select a book title, and update the quantity on hand for the selected book at the selected warehouse. Include selection lists for warehouse locations and book titles. Create at least three different warehouse location options, and at least five different book titles. Use an input box to allow the user to enter the updated quantity on hand. Create a submit button to allow the user to submit the values to the database, and change the button label to "Update." Format the form elements using a table to place the items in two columns. Save the Web page file as UpdateQOH.htm.

6. On the home page, create hyperlinks from the Authors, Books, Warehouses, and Update Warehouse QOH bulleted items to the associated Web pages that you created in Steps 2, 3, 4, and 5.

# 3

# INTRODUCTION TO CLIENT-SIDE SCRIPTS

**In this chapter, you will:**

♦ Learn how to reference objects in HTML documents using the HTML Document Object Model and dot syntax

♦ Learn how to create and debug client-side scripts that use JavaScript methods, event handlers, and custom functions

♦ Create and manipulate JavaScript variables

♦ Create and use JavaScript built-in objects

♦ Learn how to use JavaScript global functions to perform data type conversions

♦ Become familiar with JavaScript decision control and looping structures

♦ Understand the differences between JavaScript and Java

Recall from Chapter 1 that a script is a text file that contains source code that a script interpreter translates into machine language one line at a time each time the script runs. (Recall that machine language is the binary language understood by your computer's processor.) Web applications often use client-side scripts, which are embedded in HTML files that run in the user's Web browser on the user's workstation. Client-side scripts do not interact with the Web server.

People use the term *script* to describe hybrid JSP and ASP.NET server-side scripts, even though these server-side scripts do not follow the traditional scripting model of interpreting source code one line at a time. JSP and ASP.NET scripts are compiled rather than interpreted, and therefore run faster and more efficiently than other types of scripts.

Client-side scripts are usually small programs that use less than 100 lines of code and perform the following types of tasks within Web pages:

- Validate and enhance HTML forms

- Manipulate and display XML data that the Web page developer embeds in an HTML document

- Link to, manipulate, and display XML data sent in a separate file to the client

- Create and read cookies that store user preferences and selections on the client workstation

- Display new Web pages in the current browser window or in new browser windows

- Control Web page content and appearance

Scripts are usually short because you create them using text editors or HTML development environments such as Microsoft FrontPage. These environments do not have the extensive project management and debugging features that integrated development environments such as Visual Studio .NET provide for languages such as Java or C++. The most popular client-side scripting languages are JavaScript and VBScript. Most browsers support JavaScript, whereas only Internet Explorer supports VBScript. Because more developers use JavaScript and more Web browsers support JavaScript, in this book you will learn how to write client-side scripts using JavaScript.

Netscape developed JavaScript in 1995 as a server-side scripting language that was originally called LiveScript. Shortly thereafter, Netscape and Sun Microsystems formed an alliance to develop LiveScript into a client-side scripting language. At the same time, they decided to change the name of LiveScript to JavaScript. For security reasons, client-side JavaScript programs cannot start new applications on the client computer, and, with the exception of cookies, they cannot read from or write to files on the client or server computer.

Both Microsoft and Netscape are working with the European Computer Manufacturers Association (ECMA) to develop a standardized JavaScript that is called ECMAScript. Current Microsoft and Netscape JavaScript versions conform closely to the ECMAScript standards.

In this chapter, you will learn how to reference HTML document objects within scripts using the document object model and dot syntax. You will learn about object events, and learn how to call methods that perform tasks such as manipulating number and character values. You will also become familiar with manipulating JavaScript variables and creating decision control and looping structures. In Chapter 4, you will learn how to use JavaScript for tasks such as validating form inputs, creating cookies, and opening new browser windows.

**3**

## REFERENCING HTML DOCUMENT OBJECTS

To enhance Web pages, JavaScript program commands must be able to reference objects on a Web page. JavaScript commands reference Web page objects using the HTML document object model (DOM). The following subsections review object-oriented concepts and describe how to reference HTML document objects using the HTML DOM and dot syntax.

### Object-Oriented Concepts

An **object** is an abstract representation of something in the real world that has specific properties and actions. An example of an object is an HTML form, which looks like a paper form, and which you use to gather user inputs. The Web contains many different HTML forms, and all of these forms have similar characteristics. In the object-oriented world, an **object class** defines the properties and actions of similar objects. Because all forms have similar characteristics, it makes sense to create a form object class, and then create individual objects within the class to represent each individual form. A **class instance** is an object that belongs to a class. Each individual form is a class instance of the form object class. Objects can also contain other objects, which are called **child objects**. For example, every form contains child objects such as text inputs, radio buttons, and command buttons.

Every object has **properties** that define the object's structure. In HTML documents, properties are usually element attributes. For example, all HTML form object instances have a name attribute as an object property. An **event** is an action that occurs within an object as a result of a user action. For example, clicking a form command button triggers an onclick event for the button. Suppose you create an HTML document that contains a form, and the form contains a command button that you create using the following tag: `<input type="button" name="cmdMyButton" onclick="myJavaScriptFunction()">`. This button has an onclick event whose value is "myJavaScriptFunction()." When a user clicks the button, the browser executes an event handler that you have associated with the button's onclick event. An **event handler** is a block of program commands that you embed within the HTML document. These program commands execute when the event occurs. If the button does not have an associated event handler, the button ignores the event.

HTML document objects that JavaScript programs reference also have methods. A **method** performs a specific action on an object, or uses the object in a way that affects the document or script. For example, an HTML form text input has methods named focus and select. The focus method moves the insertion point to the text input, and the select method moves the insertion point to the text input and selects the current text. (You will learn how to call these methods later in the chapter.) Object methods are always available to JavaScript programs, whereas an event must have an associated event handler to perform an action.

## The HTML Document Object Model

The **HTML document object model (DOM)** is a hierarchical naming system that enables you to reference and access HTML document objects and their associated properties, methods, and events within JavaScript commands. Netscape Navigator Version 2 was the first browser to support JavaScript client-side scripts. To enable these scripts to reference objects within a Web page, Netscape developed the first DOM. To enable Internet Explorer to support JavaScript programs, Microsoft created its own DOM, which first appeared with Internet Explorer Version 3. Compatibility problems exist between latest versions of the Netscape DOM and the Internet Explorer DOM, and as a result, scripts that developers create using the Netscape DOM may not run correctly in Internet Explorer and vice versa.

In this book, you will use the Internet Explorer browser. If you try to run your scripts using a Netscape browser, they may not run correctly.

The DOM specifies HTML document objects, object relationships, and properties. HTML objects have child objects and properties, and child objects have child objects and properties, and so on. Figure 3-1 shows the basic HTML document object model that Netscape first introduced in Netscape Navigator 2, and that Microsoft subsequently supported in Internet Explorer Version 3. Current Netscape and Internet Explorer browsers still support this basic model, and this is the DOM that provides the greatest level of compatibility between all browsers. Therefore, you will use this DOM to reference HTML objects in the JavaScript code in this book.

In this DOM, the top-level object class is window, which represents a browser window. The basic child object classes within a window are history, document, and location. The document object contains all of the elements, or child objects, on a Web page. The primary child objects are link, form, and anchor. A form object can contain all of the child objects shown. In JavaScript commands, you reference HTML DOM objects using dot syntax.

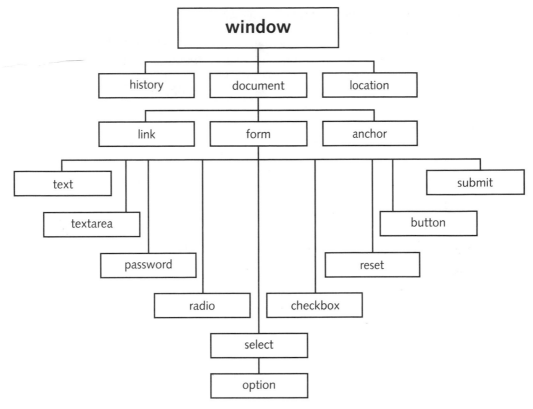

**Figure 3-1**   Basic HTML document object model

## Referencing HTML Objects Using Dot Syntax

You use **dot syntax** to reference an object in an HTML document based on its hierar-chical location among the DOM HTML objects in Figure 3-1. You reference objects by moving down the object tree hierarchy and separating individual object names with dots (periods). This hierarchy is called the **object path**. This style of referencing objects is compatible with most browsers.

Because window is the top DOM object, the first object in the object path is always window. Then you follow window with a dot and the name of the window object or property you wish to reference. For example, to reference the history property of an HTML document, you use the following dot syntax: `window.history`. To reference the HTML document object in a window, you use the following dot syntax: `window.document`.

## Dot Syntax Using Object Names

Recall from Chapter 2 that you assign a name to an HTML element by specifying a value for its name attribute in the element's opening tag. You can reference an HTML link, form, or anchor object using its object name in dot syntax as follows: `window.document.object_name`. The root of the reference begins with window, which references the current browser window, followed by a dot. The reference then moves to document, which references the document in the window, followed by another dot. From there, the reference specifies the object name of the link, form, or anchor.

To reference a child element within a document form, you place a dot after the form's *object_name* and then specify the name of the form element. For example, suppose that you create a Web page that contains a form named frmCustomer, and that this form contains a text input named txtLastName. You would reference txtLastName using dot syntax and object names as follows: `window.document.frmCustomer.txtLastName`. Note that the dot syntax follows the hierarchical order of the DOM.

Because a browser window never displays more than one document object at one time, you can shorten references to objects contained within a document by omitting *window* from the object path. For example, you can shorten `window.document.frmCustomer.txtLastName` to `document.frmCustomer.txtLastName`.

Once you specify the object path, you can then reference an object's properties and call its methods. To reference the current value of a text input, you use the **value property**. For example, to reference the current value in the txtLastName text input, you use the following dot syntax: `document.frmCustomer.txtLastName.value`. Similarly, to select the text in the text input, you would call the **select method** as follows: `document.frmCustomer.txtLastName.select()`.

## Dot Syntax Using Object IDs

Another way to reference HTML objects in dot syntax is to use the object ID attribute. Recall from Chapter 2 that the ID attribute uniquely identifies an element within an HTML document. Any HTML tag can have an ID attribute value. For example, you can assign an ID value to a paragraph tag (`<p>`) or to a table data element tag (`<td>`). You would use the following syntax to define the ID attribute to identify a paragraph in an HTML document: `<p id="first_paragraph">My first paragraph.</p>`.

You can use the ID attribute value instead of the name attribute value when specifying the path to an object using dot syntax. For example, suppose you have a form in which the ID attribute value is frmCustomer1, and this form contains a radio button group with the ID attribute value optRadio1. The dot syntax notation to reference this radio button group would be `window.document.frmCustomer1.optRadio1`. As with object names, you can omit *window* from the object path.

The XHTML standard states that you should use the ID attribute in dot syntax rather than the name attribute. However, the name attribute has been in use longer and is more widely used, and older browsers support the name attribute. Furthermore, the ID attribute does not always work correctly when you reference HTML objects in JavaScript programs. In this book, you will use both the ID attribute and the name attribute in dot syntax to reference HTML objects. Because the ID attribute does not always work correctly when you reference objects in JavaScript programs, you will use the name attribute to reference objects in the JavaScript programs you write in this chapter and in Chapter 4.

In two circumstances, you should use the ID attribute rather than the name attribute in dot syntax. The first circumstance is when you want to reference an HTML object that does not have an associated name attribute. For example, a table data element tag (<td>) cannot have an associated name attribute. You can, however, assign an ID attribute value to a table data element, and then reference the table data element using dot syntax.

The other circumstance in which you should use the ID attribute rather than the name attribute in dot syntax is in server-side programs, which you will learn how to create starting in Chapter 6. You must always use the ID attribute in dot syntax in ASP.NET server-side scripts, because ASP.NET does not support the name attribute.

If an object has both a name attribute value and an ID attribute value, you cannot reference the object in Internet Explorer using the name attribute value in dot syntax. Internet Explorer always gives the ID attribute precedence over the name attribute. Therefore, you should never use both the name attribute and the ID attribute to identify the same element. When you copy and paste the tag for an element in the Visual Studio .NET IDE, the IDE automatically assigns a default ID attribute value to the pasted element tag. You must be careful always to delete these default ID attribute values when you are using name attributes to reference objects.

## CREATING A CLIENT-SIDE SCRIPT

Now you will learn how to use the Visual Studio .NET IDE to add JavaScript commands to an HTML document and reference document objects using dot syntax. You will create the Web page shown in Figure 3-2, which contains an HTML form with a text input and a command button. (You would not create this application for a production Web site, because it does not do anything useful. However, creating this Web page will help you learn some introductory concepts about client-side scripts.)

When the Web page first appears, it executes a client-side script that displays a dialog box that shows the current text in the text input. Currently, this text is "Sample Text." Clicking the Select Text command button executes a client-side script that moves the insertion point to the text input and selects the existing text. Now you will create the HTML document and add the form inputs. Then you will learn how to create the tags that define a client-side script.

**Figure 3-2** HTML document containing form elements to illustrate client-side scripts

## Using the Visual Studio .NET IDE to Create a Client-Side Script

When you created HTML documents in the Visual Studio .NET IDE in Chapter 2, you used IntelliSense lists to provide choices for HTML tag attributes. You can also use IntelliSense lists to provide choices in JavaScript commands. This IntelliSense information lists available child objects, methods, properties, and events that you can use to complete HTML, dot syntax, and program statements.

Items within the IntelliSense lists have visual icons to specify the item type. The IntelliSense lists preface HTML tags with the tag icon , object properties with the property icon , form object events with the event icon , and form object methods with the method icon . Now you will start Visual Studio .NET, create a new HTML document that contains the form elements shown in Figure 3-2, and examine the tags and properties that the IntelliSense lists provide.

To create the form and examine tags and properties in the IntelliSense lists:

1. Start Visual Studio .NET, create a new HTML file, and save the file as **script1.htm** in the Chapter3\Tutorials folder on your Solution Disk.

2. Click the **HTML** tab to switch to HTML view, then place the insertion point on the line below the opening **<body>** tag. Type **<**. An IntelliSense list appears that shows allowable element names.

3. Type **f**. The list moves to the first selection that begins with the letter *f*. Note that the IntelliSense list prefaces HTML tag selections with the tag icon .

4. Press the **down arrow** two times to select **form**, and then press **Tab** to complete the tag.

5. Press the **space bar** to open the IntelliSense list of attributes for the form element. The list prefaces the form attributes with the property icon .

6. Type **n** to move to the first value that begins with the letter *n*, and then press **Tab** to select the name attribute.

7. Type **= "frmForm1">** to specify the name attribute and close the opening form tag.

Next you will add the text input and command button elements to the form. For now, you will associate the command button's onclick event with the text "action marker." Later you will replace "action marker" with an event handler that calls a client-side script function.

To add the form text input and command button:

1. If necessary, press **Enter** two times to move the closing **</form>** tag down two lines. Place the insertion point on the blank line between the opening and closing form tags.

2. Press **Tab** to indent your code, and then type the following tags:

```
<p><input type="text" name="txtInput"
 value="Sample Text" size="30"></p>
<p><input type="button" name="cmdSelect"
 value = "Select Text" onclick="action marker"></p>
```

Notice that each time you press the space bar after typing an attribute entry, a list of available properties and events appears. Also notice that the IntelliSense list prefaces the onclick event with the event icon 𝄢 .

3. Save the file, then click the **Design** tab to view the Web page in Design view. Your Web page should look similar to Figure 3-2.

## Adding Script Tags to an HTML Document

In an HTML file, you create a client-side script by enclosing JavaScript commands within the **script tag**, which has the syntax shown in Figure 3-3.

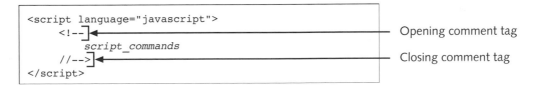

```
<script language="javascript">
    <!--                          ———————— Opening comment tag
        script_commands
    //-->                         ———————— Closing comment tag
</script>
```

**Figure 3-3**   Script tag syntax

In the script tag, the language attribute specifies the scripting language. Because older Web browsers cannot interpret JavaScript commands, you usually enclose JavaScript commands in HTML comment tags, as shown in Figure 3-3. If you do not enclose the JavaScript commands in HTML comment tags, older browsers display the JavaScript code as text in the body of the Web page. JavaScript commands are case-sensitive, and can span multiple lines in a text editor and HTML file. You designate the end of each separate command with a semicolon (;).

The client-side scripts you create in this book will always specify the language attribute. Some developers use the type attribute to specify the scripting language, using the following syntax: `type="text/javascript"`. The type attribute was introduced with Internet Explorer 5 and Netscape 6.

Recall that in HTML documents, you create HTML comments to explain and clarify what a particular line or lines of code are doing. You can also include comment statements within a JavaScript script by placing two forward slashes (//) at the beginning of a line of comment text. The JavaScript interpreter ignores comment statements as it processes the script. If a comment consists of more than one line of text, you can denote the beginning of the comment with the /* character, and denote the end of the comment with the */ character. The following code shows an example of a comment that spans two lines:

```
/* This is the first line of a comment and
this is the second line of the comment. */
```

Note in Figure 3-3 that you must preface the line signaling the end of the script by typing the JavaScript comment indicator (//) followed by the closing HTML comment tag (-->). This signals to the JavaScript interpreter that it has reached the end of the script commands.

The JavaScript interpreter processes script commands in an HTML document sequentially from the beginning to the end of the document. You can place script tags almost anywhere in an HTML document, depending on when you want the script to execute. An opening script tag can be the first tag in the document, before the opening `<html>` tag. It can also be the last tag in the document, after the closing `</html>` tag. You can place script tags within the heading tags, within the body tags, or within form tags in the HTML body. However, you should not place script tags within document title tags or within a style tag. The script interpreter does not look for script tags in these locations, so scripts placed within these tags effectively disappear.

When you place the `<script>` tags within the HTML document body the script executes when the browser encounters the `<script>` tags. If you have a script that references elements within the Web page, such as form elements, you should place the script within the HTML document body tags, after the tags that create the form elements. Otherwise, the form elements do not yet exist, and the script cannot reference them. You should avoid nesting scripts within additional elements, such as within a table.

A document can contain multiple sets of script tags. However, it is a good practice to enclose all script commands within a single script tag, because this makes the document easier to understand and maintain. Now you will add script tags to your HTML document.

To add the script tags to the document:

1. In Visual Studio .NET, click the **HTML** tab to open the editor in HTML view. Place the insertion point after the closing `</form>` tag, and if necessary, press **Enter** to create a new blank line.

2. Press **Tab** to indent the insertion point, and type the following script opening tag:

```
<script language="javascript">
```

3. Press **Enter** to move to the next line. The Visual Studio .NET IDE automatically inserts the closing **</script>** tag. Press **Tab** to indent the insertion point, type **<!--** for the opening comment tag, and then press **Enter**. For now, you will not enter any script commands, so you will just finish the script specification.

4. Type **//-->** to finish the script specification, and then save the file. Your script tags should look like the tags in Figure 3-3.

## JAVASCRIPT METHODS, FUNCTIONS, AND EVENT HANDLERS

When you write JavaScript programs, you use methods, functions, and event handlers to process data and display outputs. The following subsections explore these topics.

### JavaScript Methods

Recall that an object has associated methods that perform specific actions on the object or use the object in a way that affects the document or script. Many of the objects in Figure 3-1 have associated methods that you can call within JavaScript commands. In this section, you will become familiar with some of the most common object methods for the window object and the document object. You will learn how to use other HTML object methods in Chapter 4.

### JavaScript Window Methods

Table 3-1 summarizes some common methods for the window object.

**Table 3-1**    Common JavaScript window object methods

| Window Method | Description | Syntax | Example |
|---|---|---|---|
| Alert | Opens a dialog box in the window that displays a short message | `window.alert ("alert_text");` | `window.alert("This can be any message.");` |
| Close | Closes the current window | `window.close();` | `window.close();` |
| Focus | Sets the application's focus to the window | `window.focus (window_name);` | `window.focus ("course_books");` |
| Open | Opens a new window | `new_window = window.open("URL", "window_name", "properties");` | `new_window = window.open ("http://www.course .com","good_books", "height=150 width=150");` |

To call a method, you use the following dot syntax: `document.object_name.method_name(parameter1, parameter2, …)`. In this syntax, *parameter1* and *parameter2* specify data values that you pass to the method. For example, for the alert method, you would pass as a parameter the text string that appears in the alert. The examples in Table 3-1 show that if the method has associated parameters, you place the parameter values in the parentheses following the method name. If the method has no associated parameters, you place empty parentheses after the method name.

You use the alert method to open a message box that displays a short message, as shown in Figure 3-4  To call the alert method and display the alert shown in Figure 3-4, you use the following command: `window.alert("This is an alert message that can say whatever you want!");`.

**Figure 3-4**   JavaScript alert

For methods that JavaScript associates with the current window object, you can omit the window portion of the syntax and simply list the method name. You can omit *window* from the syntax because the default object is the current window. For example, you could display the alert in Figure 3-4 using the command `alert("This is an alert message that can say whatever you want!");`. In this book, you will omit *window* when calling methods associated with the current window.

The text in an alert can reference and display properties of HTML form elements. To reference an HTML form element, you use dot syntax to specify the path to the object. Recall that for the form you created earlier, the form name was frmForm1, and the text input name was txtInput. Recall that to reference the current value of a text input, you use the value property. The following dot syntax references the value of the text input on the form: `document.frmForm1.txtInput.value`. For example, to display the value that appears in a text input in an alert, you would use the following command:

```
alert(document.frmForm1.txtInput.value);
```

Now you will add a JavaScript command to your Web page to display an alert that shows the current contents of the txtInput form element. As you specify the object path to the txtInput form element, you will use IntelliSense lists to navigate down the DOM and then select the value property.

To add the command to display an alert that shows the current contents of the form text input:

1. In Visual Studio .NET, place the insertion point after the opening HTML comment tag (**<!--**), and then press **Enter** to create a new blank line in the document.

2. Press **Tab** to indent the insertion point, then type the following: **alert(document..** After you type the final dot (.), an IntelliSense list opens, showing a list of all available document properties, events, and methods for the document. The IntelliSense list also shows additional objects that are within the document. These objects include the form child object classes shown in Figure 3-1.

Note that the list prefaces methods with the method icon ⚞⬥.

3. Type **f** to move to the selections that begin with the letter *f*, scroll down the list, select **frmForm1**, and press **Tab** to select the form name.

4. Type **.** (dot). Another IntelliSense list opens, showing a list of all available form properties, events, and methods. Type **t** to move to the selections that begin with the letter *t*, scroll down the list, select **txtInput**, and press **Tab** to select the text input.

5. Type **.** (dot). An IntelliSense list opens, showing a list of all available object properties, events, and methods. Type **v** to move to the selections that begin with the letter *v*, and press **Tab** to select the value property.

6. Type **.** (dot). Note that an IntelliSense list does not appear this time. No IntelliSense list appears because this is the lowest-level object in the DOM. There are no properties, methods, or events below the value property.

7. Delete the ending **.** (dot), type **);** to complete the command, and then save the file. The code for the body of your HTML document should appear as shown in Figure 3-5.

Recall that JavaScript commands are case-sensitive. In your script code, you must type *alert*, *document*, and *value* in lowercase letters. You must type *frmForm1* and *txtInput* using mixed-case letters exactly as specified in the name attribute values associated with the input tags that define the text inputs. (The text in the script opening and closing tags is not case-sensitive, but the XHTML standard encourages using lowercase letters for all HTML tags.)

Now you will test your script. You cannot run a client-side script directly in the Visual Studio .NET IDE. You must open the Web page in your browser and test the script there.

```
<body>
   <form name="frmForm1">
     <p><input type="text" name="txtInput"
     value="Sample Text" size="30"></p>
     <p><input type="button" name="cmdSelect"
     value = "Select Text" onclick="action marker"></p>
   </form>
   <script language="javascript">
     <!--
         //command to display alert
         alert(document.frmForm1.txtInput.value);
     //-->
   </script>
</body>
```

Script tags and comments

**Figure 3-5**    HTML code calling the alert method

To test the script in your browser:

1. Start Internet Explorer and then open **script1.htm** from the
   Chapter3\Tutorials folder on your Solution Disk. The Web page opens, and
   the client-side script generates the alert, as shown in Figure 3-6.

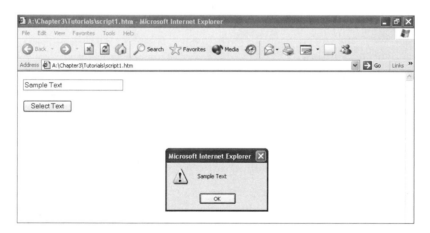

**Figure 3-6**    Alert generated by a script

If your script does not run correctly, or if a dialog box with the message "A Runtime Error has occurred. Do you wish to Debug?" appears, click No. Then switch back to Visual Studio .NET, make sure your script code exactly matches the code shown in Figure 3-5, and that your document form name and text input name are correct. Remember that JavaScript commands are case-sensitive. Also, make sure that the form name and form element names do not contain values for the ID attribute, because the ID attribute takes precedence over the name element in Internet Explorer. After correcting any errors, delete the cached Web pages in your browser. If after correcting your errors and deleting your cached Web pages the script still does not run correctly, proceed to the section in this chapter titled "Displaying Script Error Information in Internet Explorer." From now on, perform these steps if your scripts do not run correctly.

2. Click **OK** to close the alert.

Recall that when you place a script tag within an HTML document, the script tag's position in the document affects when the script runs. For example, if you move the script to the Web page heading section, it will not run correctly. This is because the form's txtInput element, which the script references, does not yet exist. You cannot write a command that references the value of the form's txtInput element until after the command that creates the form element executes.

## JavaScript Document Methods

Table 3-2 summarizes common JavaScript document object methods.

**Table 3-2** Common JavaScript document object methods

| Document Method | Description | Syntax |
|---|---|---|
| Clear | Clears the current contents of the document | `document.clear();` |
| Close | Closes the document | `document.close();` |
| Open | Opens the document, and makes it available to be written to | `document.open();` |
| Write | Writes elements to the document | `document.write(tags_and_elements);` |

The document methods enable you to create dynamic Web pages using client-side scripts. For example, you could use the document.clear method to clear the contents of the current document, and then use the document.write method to add new HTML tags and elements dynamically. If you call the document.write method using a command within the Web page `<body>` tags, the method will write its text directly on the Web page below the existing elements. If you call the document.write method using a command with the Web page's `<head>` tags, the method will clear the current Web page text and write the text on a new blank page.

Now you will use the document.write method within your script1.htm Web page to write the current contents of the text input directly onto the Web page below the existing Web page text.

To use the document.write method to write new text on the current Web page:

1. Switch to Visual Studio .NET and switch to HTML view if necessary. Place the insertion point at the end of the line that calls the alert method, and then press **Enter** to create a new blank line.

2. Type the following code to write the current value of the txtInput form element onto the Web page:

```
document.write(document.frmForm1.txtInput.value);
```

Note that after you type *document.w*, the write method appears in an IntelliSense list.

3. Save the file, then switch to Internet Explorer, and press **F5** to reload the file. When the alert appears, click **OK**. The document.write method executes and writes the current input text on the Web page, as shown in Figure 3-7.

**Figure 3-7**    Using the document.write method to write text directly on a Web page

## JavaScript Functions

To make programs easier to understand and work with, programmers create functions. A **function** is a self-contained group of program commands that you can call within a larger program. Most programming languages have **built-in functions**, which are functions that are part of the programming language and perform common tasks. JavaScript has built-in functions called **global functions** that you can call from any JavaScript command. You will learn how to use JavaScript's global functions later in this chapter. In this section, you will learn how to create **custom functions**, which are functions that programmers create to perform program-specific tasks.

Usually, you create a custom function and specify its commands in one part of an HTML document. You then create a command in another part of the document that **calls** the function and causes the function commands to execute. The command that calls the function may pass one or more parameters to the function. The function commands may perform an action or return a data value to the command that called the function.

 Some languages make a distinction between a subroutine and a function. A subroutine is a self-contained group of program commands, just like a function. However, a subroutine does not return a value, whereas a function usually returns a value. In languages that derive their commands from the C programming language, such as Java and JavaScript, there is no distinction between a subroutine and function. You can write a JavaScript function to return a value or just to perform actions and not return a value.

You learned in the previous section that you can place script tags anywhere in an HTML document. To make your HTML documents and script code easier to understand and maintain, it is a good practice to identify the tasks that you want a client-side script to perform in an HTML document, and then create a separate JavaScript function for each task. You should place all of the function code in the heading section of your HTML document. You can then place the commands that call the functions where you want them to execute in the document body. Figure 3-8 illustrates the structure of an HTML document that contains function definitions and function calls.

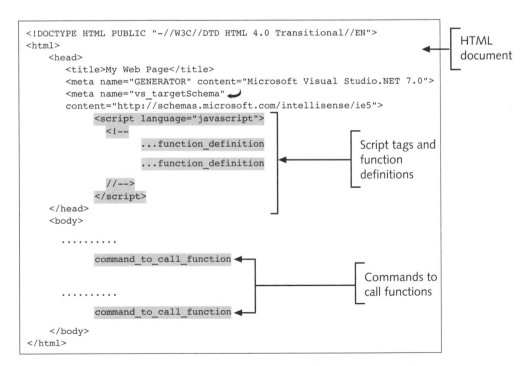

**Figure 3-8**    HTML document structure with script functions

In an HTML document, the function definition, which comprises the commands in a JavaScript function, does not execute until a command in the document body calls the function. When a command calls the function, the browser loads the function program code into the memory of the client workstation and interprets and executes the function commands. Commands within the document body can call the same function multiple times, and a function can call other functions. The following subsections describe how to create a custom function, and how to write commands to call custom functions.

## Creating a Custom Function

Figure 3-9 shows the general syntax to create a JavaScript function.

The first line of a function contains the **function declaration**, which defines the function name and specifies the parameters that the function receives from the calling program or command. A function declaration must begin with the reserved word `function`, which must appear in lowercase letters. Capitalizing the *f* in function, as in *Function*, will generate an error. (Recall that all JavaScript commands are case-sensitive, so always enter code using upper- and lowercase letters exactly as shown in the examples.) After the word *function*, you specify the name of the function and an optional parameter list. You enclose the parameter list in parentheses and use commas to separate the individual parameter values. The function name must begin with a letter, and can contain numbers, letters, and underscores (_). Function names cannot contain any other special characters, such as hyphens (-) or pound signs (#). Letters within function names are case-sensitive.

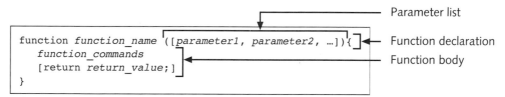

**Figure 3-9**  General syntax for a JavaScript function

Parameters can be **literal values**, which are actual data values, such as the number 50 or the text string "John." When a parameter literal value is a text string, you enclose the text letters in quotation marks. Parameters can also be variable values. (You will learn how to declare variables and assign values to variables in JavaScript later in this chapter.) You can include any number of parameters in a function's parameter list, or you can include no parameters in the list. If you include no parameters, the empty opening and closing parentheses must still follow the function name.

After the function declaration, an opening curly brace ({) marks the beginning of the **function body**, which contains the function's program commands. The opening curly brace must be on the same line as the function declaration. The closing curly brace (}) marks the end of the function body. The function body can optionally include a `return` command, which specifies the value that the function returns to the calling command.

The *return_value* can be any data value, including the logical values true or false, text strings, numbers, and objects. After the `return` command executes, program execution immediately exits the function, and program control returns to the command that called the function. If the `return` command is not present, execution exits the function at the end of the function body, after the closing curly brace.

The HTML document that you are working with contains a command button labeled "Select Text." When the user clicks this button, the current text in the form's text input is selected. To implement this functionality, you will call the select method for the text input. (Recall that the select method for a text input places the insertion point in the text input and selects the current text.) To call the select method for the text input named txtInput in the frmForm1 form, you use the following command: `document.frmForm1.txtInput.select()`. Note that because the select method has no parameters, an empty set of parentheses follows the method name.

Now you will create a custom function named SelectText in your script1.htm document. You will add the script tags and the function within the document heading, because this is where programmers usually place JavaScript commands that define custom functions.

To add the function to the script:

1. Switch back to Visual Studio .NET, switch to HTML view if necessary, and create a new blank line just above the closing `</head>` tag.

2. Type the following code to create a script in the document heading to define the function:

```
<script language="javascript">
<!--
    //function to select text in text input
    function SelectText() {
        document.frmForm1.txtInput.select();
        }
//-->
</script>
```

3. Save the file.

## Calling a Function

You can call a JavaScript function directly within a JavaScript command by specifying the name of the function followed by the list of parameter values that you want to pass to the function, using the following syntax:

```
function_name(parameter1_value, parameter2_value, ...)
```

The *function_name* in the function call must exactly match the *function_name* in the function declaration. You enclose the parameter list in parentheses, and separate each parameter value with a comma. If a function has no parameters, you call the function by specifying the function name followed by an empty parameter list ( ).

Now you will add a command in the script1.htm HTML document to call the SelectText() function. Then you will switch to Internet Explorer to confirm that the function executes correctly and selects the text in the text input.

To add a command to call the function in the document body and then test the function:

1. In Visual Studio .NET, delete the command that calls the document.write method, add the shaded code in Figure 3-10 to call the function, and then save the file.

```
<head>
   <title></title>
   <meta name="GENERATOR"  _  ↵
   content="Microsoft Visual Studio.NET 7.0">
   <meta name="vs_targetSchema" ↵
   content="http://schemas.microsoft.com/intellisense/ie5">
   <script language="javascript">
   <!--
      //function to select text in text input
      function SelectText()  {                         ◄─── Function
         document.frmForm1.txtInput.select();               definition
      }
   //-->
   </script>
</head>
<body>
   [commands to define form elements]
   <script language="javascript">
      <!--
         //command to display alert
         alert(document.frmForm1.txtInput.value);
         //command to call function to select text
         SelectText(); ◄──────────────────────────── Function call
      //-->
   </script>
</body>
```

**Figure 3-10**   JavaScript function and function call

2. Switch to Internet Explorer and press **F5** to reload the script1.htm HTML document. The alert showing the sample text appears. Click **OK**. When the function executes, the text in the text input appears selected.

## Event Handlers

Recall that HTML objects have events that occur as a result of user actions. Also recall that you can create event handlers that contain program commands that execute when an event occurs. In general, you place the command to create an event handler within the HTML tag that creates the object that you associate with the event. You create an event handler using the following syntax:

```
<element attributes ↵
event_handler_name="JavaScript_command">
```

In this syntax, *element* defines the HTML tag, and *attributes* includes all attributes you use to specify that object's properties. For example, to create an event handler for a command button object, *element* would be `input`, and *attributes* would be `type="button"`. The *event_handler_name* identifies the event handler. In general, to create an event handler name, you preface the name of the event with the word *on*. For example, for the click event for a command button, the *event_handler_name* value is onclick. The *JavaScript_command* specifies the JavaScript command that you want to execute as a result of the event. Often, this code calls a function.

Table 3-3 summarizes common HTML object events; their associated elements; the action that **triggers**, or causes, the event to occur; and the standard name of the associated event handler.

**Table 3-3**    Common HTML object events

| Event | Associated Element | Tags Containing Event Handler | Triggering Action | Event Handler Name |
|-------|--------------------|-------------------------------|-------------------|--------------------|
| Abort | Inline images | `<img>` | User aborts loading an image | onabort |
| Change | Text inputs, text areas, selection lists | `<input>` | User changes the object's value | onchange |
| Click | Command buttons, radio buttons, check boxes, hyperlinks | `<input>` `<a>` | User clicks the object | onclick |
| Focus | Windows and form elements | `<body>` `<form>` | User selects the window or form element | onfocus |
| Load | Documents | `<body>` | Browser loads the document | onload |
| Select | Text inputs, text areas | `<input>` | User selects the element's text | onselect |
| Submit | Forms | `<form>` | User submits a form to the Web server | onsubmit |
| Unload | Documents | `<body>` | User exits the Web page | onunload |

Two of the most common event handlers that programmers use in client-side scripts are onclick and onload. In the following subsections, you will learn how to create an onclick and an onload event handler.

## Creating an Onclick Event Handler

Recall that when you created the command button in the script1.htm document, you specified the onclick attribute value for the form's command button as "action marker." This attribute really was a template for an event handler. Now you will create this event handler, and specify that it calls the SelectText() function using the following function call: `SelectText()`. Then, you will switch to Internet Explorer, reload your Web page, and confirm that the event handler successfully calls the function.

To create and test an onclick event handler:

1. In Visual Studio .NET, modify the onclick attribute value in the command button's **<input>** tag so it looks like the shaded text in Figure 3-11, and then save the file.

Function call in event handler

```
<form name="frmForm1">
   <p><input type="text" name="txtInput" value="Sample Text" size="30"></p>
   <p><input type="button" name="cmdSelect"
   value = "Select Text" onclick="SelectText()"></p>
</form>
```

**Figure 3-11**    Function call in an onclick event handler

2. Switch to Internet Explorer, and press **F5** to reload the script1.htm HTML document. The alert showing the sample text appears. Click **OK**. The text in the text input appears selected, indicating that the command in the document body called the function. Click anywhere in the text input to cancel the selection.

3. Click the **Select Text** button to select the text using the button's event handler. The text appears selected again.

## Creating an Onload Event Handler

Earlier, you placed a set of script tags at the end of the HTML document's body section in the script1.htm document. These commands execute when the browser loads the HTML document and after it creates the form elements. Usually, however, it is not a good practice to place JavaScript tags and commands at the end of the body section of an HTML document. Recall from Chapter 2 that Web pages that display inline graphic images require a separate Web server connection for each graphic image. It usually takes longer to load graphic images than to load the text of the document, so a script placed at the end of the body section may execute before all of the images load. If the script references a graphic image or other element that has not yet appeared on the Web page, the script may fail and an error message will appear.

If you should not place a script at the end of an HTML document's body section, how can you create a script that executes when a browser first loads the document? To execute a script when a browser first loads, you create an onload event handler associated with the HTML document, and have this event handler call a function or execute a command. When you create an event handler that you associate with a document, such as an onload event handler, you place the code for the event handler in the document's `<body>` tag. The JavaScript commands that you associate with the onload event handler execute immediately after the browser finishes loading all the Web page elements, including the inline graphic images. You might use an onload event handler to write a value in a text input or to place the insertion point in a text input.

Now you will save your current script1.htm file as script2.htm, and delete the script tags at the end of the document's body section. Then you will create and test an onload event handler that displays the alert showing the text in the text input when the form first loads.

To create and test an onload event handler:

1. Return to Visual Studio .NET and save script1.htm as **script2.htm** in the Chapter3\Tutorials folder on your Solution Disk.

2. Delete the opening and closing `<script>` tags in the document body, along with all script commands and comments.

3. Modify the document's `<body>` tag by adding the following code, and then save the file:

   ```
   <body onload=alert(document.frmForm1.txtInput.value)>
   ```

4. Switch to Internet Explorer and open **script2.htm**. As soon as the page loads, the alert shown in Figure 3-6 appears. This time, you are displaying the alert using the document's onload event handler.

5. Click **OK** to close the alert, then switch back to Visual Studio .NET and close the script2.htm file.

## DISPLAYING SCRIPT ERROR INFORMATION IN INTERNET EXPLORER

In the JavaScript programs that you have written so far, you may have made typing errors that caused your scripts to run incorrectly. When an error occurs in a client-side script, Internet Explorer displays a default error notification message such as the one in Figure 3-12. (The error message is slightly different for different versions of Internet Explorer.)

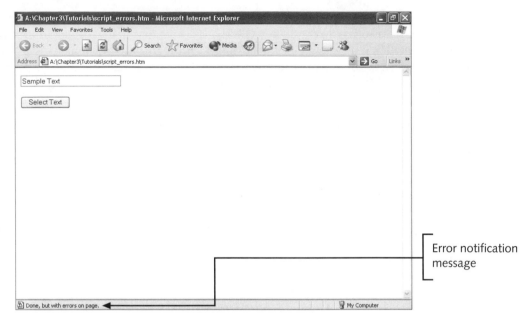

Figure 3-12    Internet Explorer default error notification message

Many times, Web page users do not notice when a script fails and this message appears. This is appropriate because most users are not capable of or interested in debugging the failed script commands. To help in debugging client-side scripts, however, script developers usually configure Internet Explorer to display the Script Debugger Error dialog box in Figure 3-13, which provides information about script errors.

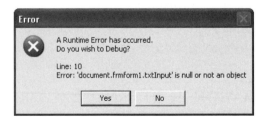

Figure 3-13    Script Debugger Error dialog box

The Script Debugger Error dialog box shows the line number on which the error occurs and provides a short description of the error. The dialog box also gives the user the option of opening the Script Debugger and finding the error. The **Script Debugger** is an application that allows you to step through individual script commands, locate the exact line on which an error occurs, and view how script variable values change during execution. (You will learn how to create and use variables in JavaScript programs in the next section.)

For the short, simple scripts you create in this chapter, you can usually find and correct your errors based on the line number and error description that Internet Explorer provides in the Script Debugger Error dialog box. You will learn how to use the Script Debugger in Chapter 4. The next section describes how to configure Internet Explorer so it displays or suppresses the error notification message shown in Figure 3-12 and explains how to retrieve and interpret additional Internet Explorer script error information. The final section describes how to configure your workstation to display the Script Debugger Error dialog box shown in Figure 3-13.

## Configuring Internet Explorer to Display or Suppress Default Script Error Notification Messages

To configure Internet Explorer to display or suppress default script error messages, you use the Advanced properties page in the Internet Options dialog box shown in Figure 3-14.

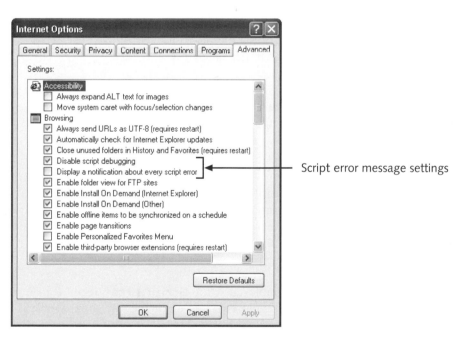

**Figure 3-14**    Internet Options Advanced properties page

The Advanced properties page has two check boxes that allow you to configure how Internet Explorer handles client-side script errors. When the *Disable script debugging* check box is checked and the *Display a notification about every script error* check box is cleared, the browser displays the error notification message shown in Figure 3-12 and allows you to retrieve additional information if you desire. By default, the *Disable script debugging* check box is checked and the *Display a notification about every script error* check box is cleared.

Now you will configure your browser to use the default script error settings. Then you will open a Web page file named script_errors.htm that contains a client-side script with errors, and explore how the default settings work. Whenever you change the script debugging settings in Internet Explorer, you must exit and then restart Internet Explorer to apply the changes to take effect.

To configure your browser to use the default script error settings:

1. Switch to Internet Explorer, click **Tools** on the menu bar, click **Internet Options**, and then click the **Advanced** tab. The Advanced properties page appears as shown in Figure 3-14. Your current properties may be different.

2. If necessary, check the **Disable script debugging** check box and clear the **Display a notification about every script error** check box. Then click **OK**.

3. Exit Internet Explorer, then restart it, and open **script_errors.htm** from the Chapter3 folder on your Data Disk. The Web page appears in your browser as shown in Figure 3-12. (The error notification message does not appear yet.)

4. Click **Select Text** to select the current text in the text input. The error notification message in Figure 3-12 appears, indicating that the script for the command button event handler failed.

 The error notification message may disappear when you move your mouse pointer. If the error notification message is not visible, click Select Text again and do not move your mouse pointer.

The default error notification message enables observant Web page users to note when a script error occurs, but does not force them to click a button or make a choice about debugging. Although users can easily miss the error notification message after a script error occurs, the icon on the browser window's status bar changes from the Internet Explorer icon 🖅 to the Script Error icon 📄. Next, you will double-click the Script Error icon 📄 and view more information about the error.

To view more information about the script error:

1. In Internet Explorer, double-click the **Script Error icon** 📄 on the browser status bar. The Internet Explorer script error message box opens, as shown in Figure 3-15. If necessary, click **Show Details** to display the detailed error information.

 If the script error icon is not visible, make sure that you have opened script_errors.htm from the Chapter3 folder on your Data Disk, and have clicked Select Text.

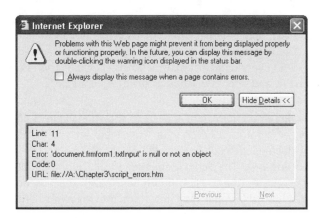

**Figure 3-15**    Default detailed script error information

    2. Click **OK** to close the script error message box.

The script error message box shows the script line number that is causing the error and describes the error. In this case, the error occurs on line 11, and the message description is "Error: 'document.frmform1.txtInput' is null or not an object." This means that the referenced object (document.frmform1.txtInput) either is not defined in the Web page or is not correctly referenced in the JavaScript command.

## Configuring Your Workstation to Display the Script Debugger Error Message Box

If you check the *Display a notification about every script error* check box on the Internet Options Advanced properties page in Figure 3-14, Internet Explorer displays the Script Debugger message box in Figure 3-13 only if the Script Debugger is installed on your workstation. (If the Script Debugger is not installed on your workstation, the detailed script information shown in Figure 3-15 appears instead.) Now you will check the *Display a notification about every script error* check box on the Internet Options Advanced properties page in your browser, run the script again, and view the Script Debugger message box.

To configure your browser always to show script error messages:

    1. In Internet Explorer, click **Tools** on the menu bar, click **Internet Options**, and then click the **Advanced** tab.

    2. Check the **Display a notification about every script error** check box, clear the **Disable script debugging** check box, and then click **OK**.

    3. Exit Internet Explorer, restart it, and then reopen the script_errors.htm file in the Chapter3 folder on your Data Disk. Click **Select Text**. The Script Debugger Error message box shown in Figure 3-13 appears. Click **No** to close the message box.

If the Script Debugger Error message box does not appear, click Tools on the Internet Explorer menu bar, click Internet Options, click the Advanced tab, and confirm that the Disable script debugging check box is cleared and the Display a notification about every script error check box is checked. Then exit Internet Explorer, restart it, and open the script_errors.htm file again.

 If the default detailed script error information appears as shown in Figure 3-15, either the Script Debugger is not installed on your workstation or you do not have the Disable script debugging check box cleared on the Advanced tab in the Internet Options dialog box. The Script Debugger should automatically install when you install Visual Studio .NET. If the Script Debugger is not installed, you can download the application file from the following URL: *http://msdn.microsoft.com/downloads/default.asp?url=/downloads/sample.asp?url=/msdn-files/027/001/733/msdncompositedoc.xml*. Click the Windows Script Debugger link in the left pane of the window, and then click the Download for Windows XP, 2000, NT 4.0 link to download the file. After the file downloads, double-click the downloaded file in Windows Explorer to install the Script Debugger.

 If the preceding URL does not work correctly, open *http://msdn.microsoft.com*, and search using the phrase "Microsoft Windows Script Debugger." Be sure to include the quotation marks around the search phrase. This search should return the correct URL. If it does not, search again using the same phrase but omitting the quotation marks around the search phrase. This search is likely to return many results; choose the search result for the Windows Script Debugger, not the Windows Script Host.

The message in the Error message box reports the line of the script where the error is occurring (line 10), and describes the error ("'document.frmform1.txtInput' is null or not an object"). Note that the line number reported by the Script Debugger (line 10) is not the same as the line number reported by the default error message, which was line 11. Because the default error message sometimes provides different information than the Script Debugger message, it is a good practice to use the messages from both sources when you are debugging a script.

A common source of script errors is referencing form objects incorrectly in JavaScript commands. This error, in which the Script Debugger reports that a document object (document.frmform1.txtInput) is not an object, indicates that the JavaScript command references the object incorrectly. This error may result from failing to use the correct object name in the dot syntax reference or from a capitalization error.

For the simple scripts that you create in this chapter, the error messages that appear in the default error messages are usually sufficient to enable you to locate the program line that is causing the error. When you create more complex scripts in Chapter 4, you will learn how to use the Script Debugger to find errors.

# USING VARIABLES IN JAVASCRIPT COMMANDS

Programs use variables to store numbers, text, dates, and other types of data that the browser can display and that client-side script commands can manipulate. Every variable has a data type that specifies the kind of data that the variable stores. Programs use data types for error checking. For example, you cannot add a text string such as "New York" to the number 10. Data types also enable a computer to optimize how it uses main memory storage space to store data values. Table 3-4 summarizes some of the JavaScript data types.

**Table 3-4**    JavaScript data types

| Data Type | Description | Example Values |
|-----------|-------------|----------------|
| Boolean | Logical values that can be true or false | true, false |
| Number | Number values | 10, –3.1, 22.78 |
| Object | Objects in the DOM, such as windows, documents, forms, and form elements | document.frmForm1.txtInput |
| String | Character strings | "This is the time" |

Boolean data types store variables that you test to determine whether the variable value is true or false. You use number data types to store values that are used in arithmetic calculations. Object values reference HTML document objects, and string data types store character strings.

Some programming languages are strongly typed. A **strongly typed programming language** requires that the programmer always declare a variable and specify the type of data that the variable will store before he or she assigns a value to the variable or references the variable in a program command. In a strongly typed programming language, the programmer cannot perform operations that manipulate variables that store different types of data without first explicitly converting the data values to the correct data type. For example, in a strongly typed programming language, you cannot add the number 3 to the text string "6" without first converting the text string "6" to a number.

In contrast, languages such as JavaScript are **loosely typed**, which means that the programmer does not need to specify the type of data that a variable will store when the programmer declares the variable. The language automatically adjusts the variable's storage space to conform to the data values that the programmer assigns to it. A loosely typed language automatically converts variables to the correct data type within commands that perform operations, such as adding two values.

The following subsections describe how to declare JavaScript variables and assign values to variables. They also discuss how to use the JavaScript arithmetic operators to manipulate variable values.

## Declaring JavaScript Variables and Assigning Values to Variables

To declare a variable in a JavaScript program, you use the following syntax:

```
var variable_name;
```

The keyword **var** signifies that the program line declares a variable. Variable names must begin with a letter, and can contain numbers, letters, and underscores (_). Letters within variable names are case-sensitive. Many JavaScript programmers use the **interCap convention** for naming variables, in which the variable name begins with a lowercase letter, and the first letter of subsequent words within the variable name begin with an uppercase letter. For example, the following JavaScript code declares a variable named storeNumber:

```
var storeNumber;
```

To assign a value to a variable, you specify the variable name, followed by an equals sign (=), followed by the value you wish to assign to the variable. For example, the following command assigns the value 10 to the storeNumber variable:

```
storeNumber = 10;
```

Once you assign a value to a variable, the variable assumes the appropriate data type. Although the name chosen for the storeNumber variable implies that the variable will store a number value, you do not specify the type of data that the variable will store when you declare the variable. The following code declares the storeNumber variable, and then assigns the text data value "Hello" to the variable:

```
var storeNumber;
storeNumber = "Hello";
```

You can declare a variable and assign its initial value in a single command using the following syntax: `var variable_name = initial_value;`. For example, you use the following command to declare the variable storeNumber and assign 10 as its initial value:

```
var storeNumber = 10;
```

## Using JavaScript Operators to Manipulate Variables

JavaScript has operators that allow you to perform arithmetic and string operations on literal and variable values. JavaScript also has operators that allow you to combine operators and assignment statements in a single command. The following subsections describe the arithmetic operators, the string operators, and the operators that combine operations and assignments. The final subsections describe using the overloaded plus sign operator (+), discuss the order in which the JavaScript interpreter evaluates operators, and show how to format output values.

## JavaScript Arithmetic Operators

Table 3-5 summarizes common arithmetic operators that you can use to perform operations on numeric data in JavaScript commands.

**Table 3-5**    Common JavaScript arithmetic operators

| Operator | Name | Description | Example |
|---|---|---|---|
| + | Addition | Adds two numbers | `storeNumber = storeNumber + 10;` |
| ++ | Increment | Adds the number 1 to the current value of a variable | `newStoreNumber = StoreNumber++;` |
| - | Subtraction | Returns the difference of two numbers | `storeNumber = storeNumber - 10;` |
| - | Unary negation | Returns the negative value of a variable | `negStoreNumber = -storeNumber;` |
| -- | Decrement | Returns the value of a variable minus 1 | `lessStoreNumber = storeNumber--;` |
| * | Multiplication | Multiplies two numbers | `storeNumberProduct = storeNumber * 10;` |
| / | Division | Divides two numbers | `storeNumberDivide = storeNumber/10;` |
| % | Modulus | Returns the integer remainder of two numbers | `modStoreNumber = storeNumber%10;` |

## The JavaScript String Concatenation Operator

Often you need to join, or **concatenate**, two separate string elements into a single string element. For example, suppose you declare a variable named firstName that stores the value "Sarah" and a second variable named lastName that stores the value "Miller," and that you want to combine the strings into a single variable named fullName that stores the value "Sarah Miller." To do this, you use the JavaScript concatenation operator (+) in the following command:

```
fullName = firstName + lastName;
```

The JavaScript concatenation operator (+) is also sometimes called the string addition operator.

To display string values on multiple lines, you concatenate the text string "\n" at the position in the string where you want the text that follows to appear on the next line. For example, the following code creates a text string that places the first name (Sarah) on one line, and the last name (Miller) on a second line:

```
fullName = firstName + "\n" + lastName;
```

The value stored in the fullName variable would appear on a Web page as follows:

Sarah

Miller

## Combining Operators and Assignment Statements

In addition to providing the equals sign (=) assignment operator, JavaScript has assignment operators that allow you to perform operations and assignments in a single command. Table 3-6 summarizes the combined arithmetic assignment operators.

**Table 3-6** JavaScript arithmetic assignment operators

| Operator | Description | Example | Equivalent Assignment |
|---|---|---|---|
| += | Adds a value to a variable and assigns the sum to the variable | `storeNumber += 2;` | `storeNumber = storeNumber + 2;` |
| -= | Subtracts a value from a variable and assigns the difference to the variable | `storeNumber -= 2;` | `storeNumber = storeNumber - 2;` |
| *= | Multiplies a value and a variable and assigns the product to the variable | `storeNumber *= 2;` | `storeNumber = storeNumber * 2;` |
| /= | Divides a variable by a value and assigns the result to the variable | `storeNumber /= 2;` | `storeNumber = storeNumber/2;` |

## Using the Overloaded Plus Sign (+) Operator

In the previous sections, you learned that you can use the plus sign (+) for numeric addition, such as in the command `storeNumber = storeNumber + 2;`. You can also use the plus sign for string concatenation, such as in the command `fullName = "Sarah" + "Miller";`. In JavaScript, the plus sign is **overloaded**, which means that you can use it for two different operations. How does the JavaScript interpreter know when to use the plus sign for addition and when to use the plus sign for string concatenation? The interpreter decides based on the data types of the variables or literal values that the programmer includes in the command.

When the variables or literals on both sides of the plus sign are strings, the plus sign will always concatenate the strings. When the variables or literals on both sides of the plus sign are numbers, the plus sign will always add the numbers. When the value on one side of the plus sign is a number, and the value on the other side of the plus sign is a string, the interpreter always performs a concatenation operation.

Figure 3-16 shows a series of variable declarations and associated assignment statements that use the overloaded plus sign to perform both addition and concatenation operations. In this example, the program code initially assigns numeric literal values (1 and 2) to the first two variables (number1 and number2), and the variables assume the number data type. The code assigns string literal values to the next four variables (string1, string2, string3, and string4), so these variables assume the string data type.

```
//declare variables and assign initial values
var number1 = 1;
var number2 = 2;
var string1 = "ABC";
var string2 = "def";
var string3 = "3";
var string4 = "4";
var result;

//perform assignments
result = number1 + number2;   // result is 3
result = string1 + string2    // result is "ABCdef"
result = string3 + string4    // result is "34"
result = number1 + string3    // result is "13"
```

**Figure 3-16**    Assignment statements using the overloaded plus sign operator

The first assignment statement demonstrates adding two numeric values. Recall that adding two numbers is always a numeric operation, and the result is always a number. The second assignment statement demonstrates concatenating two string values, which always joins two strings to create a third string.

The third assignment statement is slightly different from the second, because both string3 and string4 contain numbers. However, the programmer initially assigned these numbers as string values by enclosing the numerals in quotation marks ("3" and "4"). It makes no difference that the strings are numeric characters. The operation concatenates the values as strings rather than adding them as numbers. The fourth example attempts to perform an addition operation between a number data type and a string data type. The JavaScript interpreter must make a choice. Recall that the interpreter always performs the string concatenation operation when one variable is a string variable and the other is a number variable. The interpreter automatically converts the number data value (1) to a string ("1"), and then concatenates it with the value of string3 ("3"). The result is the string "13."

## Specifying the Order of Operations

As with most programming languages, JavaScript evaluates operations in a specific order, and, by default, the interpreter evaluates some operators before other operators. Table 3-7 illustrates the order that the JavaScript interpreter uses to evaluate arithmetic operators in program commands.

**Table 3-7**    JavaScript order of arithmetic operations

| Operator | Symbol | Order |
|---|---|---|
| Parentheses | (), [] | Evaluated first |
| Unary negation | - | |
| Multiplication, division, modulus | *, /, % | |
| Addition, subtraction | +, - | |
| Assignment | =, +=, -=, *=, /= | Evaluated last |

The interpreter evaluates operations in parentheses or square brackets first, and then evaluates additional operations in the order listed. The interpreter evaluates assignment operations last. For operations at the same level, such as addition and subtraction, the JavaScript interpreter evaluates the operations from left to right.

For concatenation operations, the JavaScript interpreter evaluates the operations from left to right, and evaluates operations in parentheses first. Recall that when you attempt to add a string value to a number value, the JavaScript interpreter converts the number to a string and performs a concatenation operation. Figure 3-17 illustrates how the order-of-precedence rules apply, with the JavaScript interpreter evaluating operations from left to right.

```
//declare variables and assign initial values
var number1 = 1;
var number2 = 2;
var string3 = "3";
var string4 = "4";
var result;

//perform assignments mixing concatenation and addition
result = number1 + number2 + string3; // result is "33"
result = string3 + number1 + number2  // result is "312"

/* perform assignments mixing concatenation and
addition using parentheses to force ordering precedence */
result = number1 + (number2 + string3) // result is "123"
result = string4 + (number1 + number2) // result is "43"
```

**Figure 3-17**    Operation order for combining concatenation and addition operations

In the first operation, the interpreter first adds number1 (which has the value "1") to number2 (which has the value "2"), which results in a numeric value of 3. The interpreter then concatenates the resulting numeric value of 3 with the string3 value of "3," and the result is "33."   In the second operation, the interpreter concatenates string3 (which has the value "3") with number1 (which has the value "1"). The JavaScript interpreter first converts the number1 value to a string, and evaluates the operation as the string value "31." The interpreter then concatenates the value "31" with the value of number2 (which has the value "2") to generate the string "312."

The second set of operations uses parentheses to change the order of processing. In the first assignment statement, the parentheses instruct the JavaScript interpreter first to concatenate number2 (which has the value "2") and string3 (which has the value "3") to create the string "23." The interpreter then concatenates the value of number1 (which has the value "1") on the left side of the string to create the string "123." In the second assignment statement, the parentheses instruct the JavaScript interpreter first to add number1 (which has the value "1") and number2 (which has the value "2") to produce the numeric value 3. The interpreter then concatenates the value of string4 (which has the value "4") on the left side of the resulting string to create the string "43."

To gain experience with declaring variables and performing arithmetic and concatenation operations, you will write a script for the Clearwater Traders Web page shown in Figure 3-18.

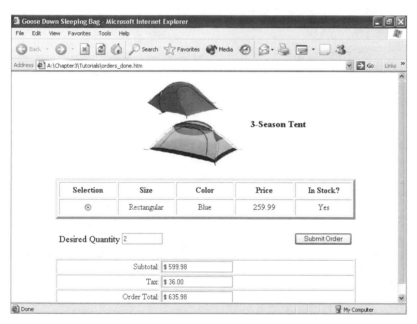

**Figure 3-18**    Web page with a script that performs arithmetic calculations

This Web page summarizes order information for 3-Season Tents on the Clearwater Traders Web site. After the user specifies a value in the Desired Quantity text input and clicks the Submit Order button, a script executes that calculates the order subtotal, sales tax, and final order total. The script then displays the values on the Web page. Now you will open the HTML document and add a function named WriteSummary(), which calculates and displays the order information.

To add the function:

1. Switch to Windows Explorer, and copy **tents.jpg** from the Chapter3 folder on your Data Disk to the Chapter3\Tutorials folder on your Solution Disk so the graphic image will appear on the Web page.

2. Switch to Visual Studio .NET, open **orders.htm** from the Chapter3 folder on your Data Disk, and save the file as **orders_done.htm** in the Chapter3\Tutorials folder on your Solution Disk.

3. Switch to HTML view, place the insertion point after the closing `</title>` tag, which is on line 4, and press **Enter** to create a new blank line in the file.

4. Type the following code to create the script tags and the function declaration, and then save the file:

```
<script language="javascript">
   <!--
       //function to summarize order
       function WriteSummary()    {
       }
   //-->
</script>
```

To create and display the order summary information, you need to declare the variables shown in Table 3-8. You will write commands that perform calculations with and assign values to these variables, and then display the calculated values in form elements on the Web page. Table 3-8 shows the dot syntax for the form element that will display the value of each variable. These form elements already exist in the HTML document.

**Table 3-8**    Variables to calculate and display order summary information

| Variable Name | Description | Form Element That Displays a Variable |
|---|---|---|
| subTotal | Order subtotal, calculated as desired quantity times price | `document.frmOrderItem.txtsubTotal` |
| salesTax | Order sales tax, calculated as subtotal amount times 6 percent `(subTotal * .06)` | `document.frmOrderItem.txtTax` |
| orderTotal | Order subtotal plus sales tax `(subTotal + salesTax)` | `document.frmOrderItem.txtOrderTotal` |

Now you will add the commands to declare these variables, perform the specified calculations, and display the results in the text inputs on the Web page. You will concatenate a dollar sign followed by a blank space ("$ ") to the left edge of the outputs to indicate that the values are currency. (Recall that when you perform a concatenation operation between a string and a number value, the JavaScript interpreter converts the number to a string.)

To add the commands to create and manipulate the variables:

1. In Visual Studio .NET, place the insertion point after the opening curly brace { in the function heading, and press **Enter** to create a new blank line.

2. Press **Tab** to indent the first line of the script, then type the shaded commands shown in Figure 3-19 to declare the variables, perform the calculations, and assign the results to the form elements.

```
<script language="javascript">
  <!--
  //function to summarize order
  function WriteSummary()    {
     var subTotal;
     var salesTax;
     var orderTotal;
     subTotal = document.frmOrderItem.txtQuantity.value * 299.99;
     document.frmOrderItem.txtSubTotal.value = "$ " + subTotal;
     salesTax = subTotal * .06;
     document.frmOrderItem.txtTax.value = "$ " + salesTax;
     orderTotal = subTotal + salesTax;
     document.frmOrderItem.txtOrderTotal.value =
     "$ " + orderTotal;
  }
  //-->
</script>
```

**Figure 3-19**    JavaScript code to calculate the order summary

Next, you must create an event handler for the Submit Order button that calls the new function. Recall that to create an event handler for a button, you create an onclick attribute in the button's input tag and set the onclick attribute value to the command that calls the function. After creating the event handler, you will view and test the Web page in your browser.

To create the event handler and test the script:

1. In Visual Studio .NET, scroll down to the tag that defines the Submit Order button. (This tag is approximately 12 lines above the last line of code in the file.)

2. Modify the button input tag by adding the onclick attribute value as follows:

```
<input type="button" value="Submit Order" ↵
onclick="WriteSummary()">
```

3. Save the file, then switch to Internet Explorer and open **orders_done.htm** from the Chapter3\Tutorials folder on your Solution Disk.

4. To test the script, type **2** in the Desired Quantity text box and then click **Submit Order**. The script executes and the values shown in Figure 3-18 appear.

The values for sales tax and the order total are not formatted as currency with two decimal places. You will learn how to format number values using JavaScript built-in objects in the next section.

## USING JAVASCRIPT BUILT-IN OBJECT CLASSES

Recall that most programming languages have built-in functions, which perform common tasks such as manipulating text strings and formatting output. To perform similar operations in JavaScript, you use **built-in object classes** that have specific properties, events, and methods. To use a built-in object, you create an instance of the built-in object class and then assign a data value to the new object's value property. You can then use the object's methods to perform tasks on the associated value. For example, you could create a new object to represent the value in the Tax text input in Figure 3-18. You could then apply a method to this object to format it as currency with two decimal places.

The most commonly used JavaScript built-in object classes are String, Math, Date, and Number. For example, the String object has a method named toUpperString that converts the current string value to uppercase letters. If you need to convert a string value to uppercase letters, you would create a string object, assign the value to the String object's value property, and then use the object's toUpperString method to perform the conversion.

To create a new object, you use the following syntax:

```
var variable_name = new object_type();
```

In this syntax, *variable_name* can be any legal JavaScript variable name. The keyword **new** creates a new object, and must start with a lowercase *n*. The *object_type* parameter is one of the built-in JavaScript object types. The built-in object types you will use in this book include String, Math, Date, and Number. The following subsections describe the String, Math, Date, and Number object types in more detail.

### String Objects

You use the following code to create a new String object named currentItem and assign "3-Season Tents" to its value property:

```
var currentItem = new String();
currentItem.value = "3-Season Tents";
```

Table 3-9 summarizes important properties and methods of the String object, and shows examples of the resulting values for the string object whose value is "3-Season Tents."

**Table 3-9**    String object properties and methods

| Property or Method | Description | Example | Result |
|---|---|---|---|
| *string_object*.length | Property that describes the string length | `currentItem.length` | 14 (length includes blank spaces within the string) |
| *string_object*.toLowerString | Method to convert the string to all lowercase letters | `currentItem.toLowerString` | "3-season tents" |
| *string_object*.toUpperString | Method to convert the string to all uppercase letters | `currentItem.toUpperString` | "3-SEASON TENTS" |

## Math Objects

You use the Math object class to expand the usefulness of the JavaScript arithmetic operators. The Math object class has methods to perform trigonometric functions and math functions for scientific applications. You do not create object instances of the Math class. Rather, you apply the class's methods to variables or other objects. Table 3-10 describes some useful Math object methods and provides examples for their use.

**Table 3-10**    Math object methods

| Method | Description | Example | Result |
|---|---|---|---|
| Math.abs(*number*) | Returns the absolute value of *number* | `Math.abs(-3.14)` | 3.14 |
| Math.pow(*number1, number2*) | Raises *number1* to the *number2* power | `Math.pow(3,2)` | 9 |
| Math.max(*number1, number2*) | Returns the greater of *number1* or *number2* | `Math.max(5, 7)` | 7 |
| Math.min(*number1, number2*) | Returns the lesser of *number1* or *number2* | `Math.min(5, 7)` | 5 |

## Date Objects

You use Date objects to format and manipulate date and time values, and to retrieve the date and time on the current workstation. In JavaScript, a date value is divided into individual year, month, day, current hour, minute, and second components. You use the following code to create a new Date object named currentDate:

```
var currentDate = new Date();
```

Table 3-11 summarizes some useful Date object methods. The examples assume that the current date is February 28, 2005, 10:35:22 A.M.

**Table 3-11**    Useful Date object methods

| Method | Description | Example | Result |
|--------|-------------|---------|--------|
| *date_object*.getFullYear() | Returns the current year, in a four-digit format | `currentDate.getFullYear()` | 2005 |
| *date_object*.getMonth() | Returns the current month (1–12) | `currentDate.getMonth()` | 2 |
| *date_object*.getDate() | Returns the current day of the month (1–31) | `currentDate.getDate()` | 28 |
| *date_object*.getHours() | Returns the current hour, using a 24-hour clock and starting with 0 (0–23) | `currentDate.getHours()` | 10 |
| *date_object*.getMinutes() | Returns the current minute, starting with 0 (0–59) | `currentDate.getMinutes()` | 35 |
| *date_object*.getSeconds() | Returns the current second, starting with 0 (0–59) | `currentDate.getSeconds()` | 22 |

## Number Objects

You use Number objects to format numeric values. For example, you would use the following code to create a new Number object named currentPrice and assign its value as 299.99:

```
var currentPrice = new Number();
currentPrice = 299.99;
```

An important Number object method is toFixed, which returns a number value rounded to a specific number of decimal places. You will use the toFixed method to format currency values to two decimal places. The toFixed method has the following general syntax: *number_object*.toFixed(*decimal_places*);. For example, you use the following code to format the currentPrice number object to two decimal places: `currentPrice.toFixed(2);`.

The script that you created to summarize the order on the Web page in Figure 3-18 shows currency values that contain four decimal places. To format the currency using two decimal places, you will declare the variables that store the subtotal, tax, and order total values as built-in Number objects. Then you will use the toFixed method to display the output as currency values with two decimal places. Finally, you will test your changes to confirm that your Number objects appear with two decimal places.

To display the order summary values as currency using built-in Number objects:

1. Switch back to Visual Studio .NET and modify the WriteSummary function code by changing the shaded lines as shown in Figure 3-20.

```
<!--
    //function to summarize order
    function WriteSummary()  {
        var subTotal = new Number();
        var salesTax = new Number();
        var orderTotal = new Number();
        subTotal =
        document.frmOrderItem.txtQuantity.value * 299.99;
        document.frmOrderItem.txtSubTotal.value =
        "$ " + subTotal.toFixed(2);
        salesTax = subTotal * .06;
        document.frmOrderItem.txtTax.value =
        "$ " + salesTax.toFixed(2);
        orderTotal = subTotal + salesTax;
        document.frmOrderItem.txtOrderTotal.value =
        "$ " + orderTotal.toFixed(2);
    }
//-->
```

**Figure 3-20**    Code to create built-in Number objects and format number values

2. Save the file, then switch to Internet Explorer and press **F5** to reload the file.

3. Type **2** in the Desired Quantity text input and then click **Submit Order**. The order summary information appears formatted to two decimal places as shown in Figure 3-18.

4. Switch back to Visual Studio .NET and close **orders_done.htm**.

# USING GLOBAL FUNCTIONS TO PERFORM EXPLICIT DATA TYPE CONVERSIONS

By default, all data values that users enter into Web page forms are text strings. For example, when you entered the value 2 in the txtQuantity text input on the Order Summary Web page, JavaScript interpreted the value as the text string "2." This is true for all form elements, including radio button and check box values, selection list values, and text area form element values. Often you write scripts that use user input values in arithmetic calculations. In the Order Summary Web page, the user enters "2" in the Quantity text input. In the command that multiplied the Quantity value times the price to calculate the subtotal, the JavaScript interpreter automatically converts the text string "2" to a number before it performs the multiplication operation. These automatic data type conversions work well except when you perform an addition operation on a text string.

Suppose you write a script that contains a command to add the number 1 to the current value in the txtQuantity text input. Also suppose that the user types *2* into the form input. When the script executes, the command will add the number 1 to the text string "2," and the result will be the string "21." (Recall that JavaScript always performs a concatenation operation when you use the plus sign operator with a string variable and a number variable.) To process number data values that users enter into text inputs as numbers rather than as text strings, you need to convert the values so JavaScript interprets them as numbers. To convert text strings to numbers, you must perform an explicit data type conversion.

To perform an explicit data type conversion, you write a program command to convert a value from one data type to another. This command changes the way the program represents the data internally in memory. JavaScript provides global functions to perform explicit data type conversions. (Recall that a global function is a built-in function that you can reference in any JavaScript command). The main explicit data type conversions involve converting strings to numbers and converting numbers to strings.

## Converting Strings to Numbers

In JavaScript, you can convert text strings to numbers using the parseInt() and parseFloat() global functions. The **parseInt()** global function converts a string representation of a number into a number representation and removes any decimal or fractional parts. The **parseFloat()** global function converts a string representation of a number into a number representation and retains the decimal or fractional parts. To add a string value to a numeric value, you must first use the parseInt() or parseFloat() function to convert the string value to a number, and then add the two numbers. The general syntax for these functions is as follows:

```
number_variable = parseInt("string_number");
number_variable = parseFloat("string_number");
```

In this syntax, *number_variable* represents an existing number variable. The *string_number* parameter represents a text string that is a numeric character. The code in Figure 3-21 shows examples of how to use the parseInt() and parseFloat() functions.

```
var number1 = 12;
var string1 = "42.5";
var result;

//assign values
result = number1 + string1              // result is "1242.5"
result = number1 + parseInt(string1)    // result is 54
result = number1 + parseFloat(string1)  // result is 54.5
```

**Figure 3-21**    Using the parseInt() and ParseFloat() functions

The first command declares a number variable named number1 and assigns the value 12 to it. The second command declares a string variable named string1 and assigns the value "42.5" to it. The first assignment command adds the two values without performing any data type conversions. Because adding a string value to a number results in a concatenation operation, the two values are joined as text strings, resulting in the text string "1242.5."

In the second assignment command, the parseInt() function converts the string1 variable to a number. Because the parseInt() function removes the decimal fraction, the function returns the value 42, which the command then adds to the value of number1 (12), resulting in the value 54. In the third assignment command, the parseFloat() function converts the value of string1 to a number and retains the decimal fraction. The resulting addition operation adds the number 42.5 to the number 12, and results in the value 54.5.

## Converting Numbers to Strings

The easiest way to convert a date or number variable to a string data type is to concatenate the date or number variable to an empty string literal. An **empty string literal** is a string value that does not contain any characters, and consists of two double quotation marks, with no characters inserted in between: `""`. Consider the following code sample:

```
var number1 = 13;
newString = number1 + "";      //value of newString is "13"
```

The first command declares a number variable named number1 and assigns the value 13 to it. The second command concatenates the variable with an empty string literal, which converts the number to a string, and assigns the new string value to a string variable named newString. The value stored in the newString variable is the string value "13."

You will use the Web page in Figure 3-22 to gain experience with using these explicit data type conversion functions. This Web page contains three form input elements. The first two elements (txtInput1 and txtInput2) store input values that the user enters. When the user clicks Add, a user-defined function named AddValues() executes. The AddValues() function converts the two input values to numbers using the parseFloat() function, adds them, and displays the result in the third form input element (txtResult). When the user clicks Concatenate, a user-defined function named ConcatenateValues() executes. This function adds the two values, but does not perform a conversion. Because the values in form inputs are always text strings, the script concatenates the values. When the user clicks Add & Truncate, a user-defined function named AddTruncateValues() executes. This function first converts the two values to numbers using the parseInt() function, which truncates (removes) the decimal fractions of the numbers. If the user clicks Clear, a user-defined function named ClearValues executes and clears all of the form inputs.

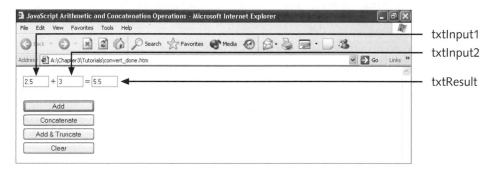

**Figure 3-22**    Web page with functions that use explicit type conversions

You will add these functions to a Web page file named convert.htm that is stored in the Chapter3 folder on your Data Disk. This Web page contains a form named frmFormAdd. The form contains the text inputs shown in Figure 3-22. The Web page already contains the script tags, function declarations, and event handlers for the command buttons. You will add the code for the AddValues() function. This function contains commands that declare variables to represent the two input values, converts the variable values to numbers using the parseFloat() global function, and then adds the values. After you create the function, you will open the Web page in your browser and test the function.

To add the code for the AddValues() function and test the function:

1. In Visual Studio .NET, open **convert.htm** from the Chapter3 folder on your Data Disk and save the file as **convert_done.htm** in the Chapter3\Tutorials folder on your Solution Disk.

2. Switch to HMTL view, place the insertion point after the opening curly brace ({) in the AddValues() function declaration, and press **Enter** to create a new blank line.

3. Press **Tab** to indent your function code, then type the following commands:

```
var input1 = document.frmFormAdd.txtInput1.value;
var input2 = document.frmFormAdd.txtInput2.value;
document.frmFormAdd.txtResult.value =
parseFloat(input1) + parseFloat(input2);
```

4. Save the file, then switch to Internet Explorer and open the file.

5. Place the insertion point in the first text input and type **2.5**, press **Tab** to move the insertion point to the second text input, and type **3**.

6. Click **Add**. The sum of the numbers appears as 5.5 as shown in Figure 3-22, indicating that the values were added as numbers. Note that because you used the parseFloat() function, the decimal fraction appears in the sum of the values.

Now you will add the code to create the other functions. For the ConcatenateValues() function, your code will not perform any data type conversions, but will just add the values. For the AddTruncateValues() function, you will use the same code as for the AddValues() function, but use the parseInt() global function instead of the parseFloat() function. For the ClearValues() function, you will set all of the form input values equal to empty string literals.

To create and test the AddTruncateValues() and ClearValues() functions:

1. Switch back to Visual Studio .NET and add the shaded code in Figure 3-23 to create the remaining functions.

```
function AddValues() {
   var input1 = document.frmFormAdd.txtInput1.value;
   var input2 = document.frmFormAdd.txtInput2.value;
   document.frmFormAdd.txtResult.value = parseFloat(input1)+ parseFloat(input2);
}
function ConcatenateValues()  {
   var input1 = document.frmFormAdd.txtInput1.value;
   var input2 = document.frmFormAdd.txtInput2.value;
   document.frmFormAdd.txtResult.value = input1 + input2;
}
function AddTruncateValues()  {
   var input1 = document.frmFormAdd.txtInput1.value;
   var input2 = document.frmFormAdd.txtInput2.value;
   document.frmFormAdd.txtResult.value = parseInt(input1)+ parseInt(input2);
}
function ClearValues()         {
   document.frmFormAdd.txtInput1.value = "";
   document.frmFormAdd.txtInput2.value = "";
   document.frmFormAdd.txtResult.value = "";
}
```

**Figure 3-23**   Code to create functions containing explicit data type conversions

2. Save the file, then switch to Internet Explorer and press **F5** to reload the Web page.

3. Place the insertion point in the first text input, type **2.5**, press **Tab** to move the insertion point to the second text input, and type **3**.

4. Click **Concatenate**. The concatenated text string appears as "2.53."

5. Click **Clear** to clear the form text inputs.

6. Place the insertion point in the first text input, type **2.5**, press **Tab** to move the insertion point to the second text input, type **3**, and then click **Add & Truncate**. The parseInt() function truncates the decimal fraction of the first value, and the sum of the values appears as 5.

7. Switch back to Visual Studio .NET and close the file.

# Decision Control Structures

Almost every minute of every day, you make decisions. Will you walk to the corner grocery store, or will you drive? If you walk, will you wear a coat or bring an umbrella? Program commands often have to make decisions also. So far, all of the JavaScript commands that you have written execute sequentially, one after another. However, sometimes you need to write programs with **decision control structures** that execute alternate statements based on conditions that the interpreter evaluates as true or false. In JavaScript, you create decision control structures using `if`, `if/else`, `if/else if`, and `switch` control structures. The following subsections describe these control structures. The final subsection describes how to evaluate multiple conditions in a control structure using the AND and OR logical operators.

## The `if` Control Structure

An **if control structure** tests whether a condition is true or false. If the condition is true, the interpreter executes a set of program statements. If the condition is false, the interpreter skips the program statements. The general syntax of the `if` control structure in JavaScript is as follows:

```
if (condition) {
program_statements
}
```

Recall that JavaScript commands are case-sensitive, so the `if` command must be in lowercase letters, and you enclose the *condition* in parentheses. If the *condition* is true, the JavaScript interpreter executes the program statements between the curly braces. If the condition is false, the interpreter skips these statements.

The general syntax of a *condition* is as follows: *expression1 comparison_operator expression2*. In this syntax, *expression1* is usually a variable or an object such as a form text input. *Expression2* can be a variable, object value, or a literal value whose value is being compared to *expression1*. The *comparison_operator* is a symbol that defines the type of comparison that is being made between *expression1* and *expression2*. Table 3-11 summarizes the JavaScript comparison operators and shows examples of JavaScript *condition* statements.

**Table 3-12**     JavaScript comparison operators

| Operator | Description | Example | Explanation |
|---|---|---|---|
| == | Compares two expressions to determine whether they are equal | `intCounter == 10` | Returns true if intCounter is equal to 10, and false if intCounter is not equal to 10 |
| != | Compares two expressions to determine whether they are not equal | `intCounter != 10` | Returns true if intCounter is not equal to 10, and returns false if intCounter is equal to 10 |
| > | Compares two expressions to determine whether the first is greater than the second | `intCounter > 10` | Returns true if intCounter is greater than 10, and false if intCounter is less than or equal to 10 |
| < | Compares two expressions to determine whether the first is less than the second | `intCounter < 10` | Returns true if intCounter is less than 10, and false if intCounter is greater than or equal to 10 |
| >= | Compares two expressions to determine whether the first is greater than or equal to the second | `intCounter >= 10` | Returns true if intCounter is greater than or equal to 10, and false if intCounter is less than 10 |
| <= | Compares two expressions to determine whether the first is less than or equal to the second | `intCounter <= 10` | Returns true if intCounter is less than or equal to 10, and false if intCounter is greater than 10 |

Now you will create a JavaScript function that contains an `if` control structure. You will use the completed Clearwater Traders Order Summary Web page that appears in Figure 3–18. (If you did not modify this file earlier in the tutorial, a completed copy exists in a file named orders_if.htm in the Chapter3 folder on your Data Disk.) You will modify this Web page so that the function validates that the user entered a legal value in the Desired Quantity text input before it displays the order summary information. To do this, you will add an `if` control structure in which the *condition* tests whether the user entered a legal value in the Desired Quantity text input by confirming that the value is not equal to an empty string literal (" "). If the value is not an empty string, the code calculates and displays the order summary information and displays an alert to thank the user for his or her order. If the value is an empty string, the interpreter skips the program steps and the alert and order summary information will not appear.

To add the `if` control structure to the Clearwater Traders Order Summary Web page and test the script:

1. In Visual Studio .NET, open **orders_done.htm** from the Chapter3\Tutorials folder on your Solution Disk; and save the file as **orders_if_done.htm** in

the Chapter3\Tutorials folder on your Solution Disk. (If you did not complete the orders_done.htm Web page, open the orders_if.htm file from the Chapter3 folder on your Data Disk instead.)

2. Add the shaded code in Figure 3-24 to declare a variable to reference the value in the Desired Quantity text input, create the `if` control structure, and display the alert.

```
function WriteSummary() {
    var currQuantity = document.frmOrderItem.txtQuantity.value;
    if (currQuantity != "") {
        var subTotal = new Number();
        var salesTax = new Number();
        var orderTotal = new Number();
        subTotal = currQuantity * 299.99;
        document.frmOrderItem.txtSubTotal.value = "$ " + subTotal.toFixed(2);
        salesTax = subTotal * .06;
        document.frmOrderItem.txtTax.value =
        "$ " + salesTax.toFixed(2);
        orderTotal = subTotal + salesTax;
        document.frmOrderItem.txtOrderTotal.value = "$ " + orderTotal.toFixed(2);
        alert("Thank you for your order!");
    }
}
```

**Figure 3-24**    Code for the `if` control structure

3. Save the file, then switch to Internet Explorer and open **orders_if_ done.htm** from the Chapter3\Tutorials folder on your Solution Disk.

4. Do not type a value in the Desired Quantity text input. Click **Submit Order**. The Web page does not change. This result indicates that the `if` control structure evaluated the condition that the value in the Desired Quantity text input is not an empty string literal as false, and skipped the program statements to display the order summary information and the alert.

5. Type **2** in the Desired Quantity text input, and then click **Submit Order**. The order summary information and alert appear. This result indicates that the `if` control structure evaluates the condition as true, and executes the program statements to display the order summary information and the alert.

6. Click **OK** to close the alert.

## The `if/else` Control Structure

In the current Order Summary Web page script, nothing happens when you click the Submit Order button after not entering a value in the Desired Quantity text input. This may seem confusing to users, and the program should provide feedback advising users that they had made an error. To implement this type of feedback, you can use an `if/else` control structure. An **if/else control structure** tests a condition, and executes one set of program statements if the condition is true, and an alternate set of program statements if the condition is false.

The general syntax for an `if/else` control structure is as follows:

```
if (condition) {
    program_statements
} else {
    alternate_program_statements
}
```

When the *condition* is true, the *program_statements* execute. When the *condition* is false, the *alternate_program_statements* execute. Now you will modify the `if` control structure in the Order Summary Web page so that it uses an `if/else` control structure. If the user enters a value, the order summary information and the "thank you" alert appear. If the user does not enter a value in the Desired Quantity text input, an alert appears advising the user to enter a value.

To change the control structure in the Web page to an `if/else` control structure:

1. Switch back to Visual Studio .NET, and save the orders_if_done.htm file as **orders_if_else_done.htm** in the Chapter3\Tutorials folder on your Solution Disk.

2. Add the shaded code in Figure 3-25.

```
function WriteSummary() {
    var currQuantity = document.frmOrderItem.txtQuantity.value;
    if (currQuantity != "") {
        var subTotal = new Number();
        var salesTax = new Number();
        var orderTotal = new Number();
        subTotal = currQuantity * 299.99;
        document.frmOrderItem.txtSubTotal.value = "$ " + subTotal.toFixed(2);
        salesTax = subTotal * .06;
        document.frmOrderItem.txtTax.value = "$ " + salesTax.toFixed(2);
        orderTotal = subTotal + salesTax;
        document.frmOrderItem.txtOrderTotal.value = "$ " + orderTotal.toFixed(2);
        alert("Thank you for your order!");
    } else {
        alert("Please enter a value for Desired Quantity.");
    }
}
```

**Figure 3-25**    Code for an `if/else` control structure

3. Save the file, then switch to Internet Explorer and open **orders_if_else_done.htm** from the Chapter3\Tutorials folder on your Solution Disk.

4. Do not type a value in the Desired Quantity text input. Click **Submit Order**. The alert appears prompting you to enter a value for Desired Quantity. Click **OK** to close the alert.

5. Type **2** for Desired Quantity, then click **Submit Order**. The order summary values and "thank you" alert appear. Click **OK** to close the alert.

## The `if`/`else if` Control Structure

The `if`/`else` control structure allows you to execute one set of program statements if a condition is true and an alternate set of program statements if the condition is false. What can you do if you want to test for different and unrelated conditions in a single decision control statement, and execute a different set of program instructions for each true condition?  For example, in the Order Summary Web page, you may first want to test to confirm that the user entered a value in the Desired Quantity text input. If the user did not enter a value, you want to display an alert advising him or her to enter a value. Next, you may want to test to confirm that the value was greater than zero. If the value was not greater than zero, you want to display an alternate alert advising the user to enter a non-zero value. If the user entered a valid non-zero value, you want to display the order summary information and the "thank you" alert. To create this type of structure, you can use an `if/else  if` control structure. An `if/else if` **control structure** allows you to test for many unrelated conditions, and execute specific program statements for each true condition.

The general syntax of the `if/else if` control structure is:

```
if (condition1) {
    program_statements1
} else if (condition2) {
    program_statements2
} else if (condition3) {
    program_statements3
...
} else {
    alternate_program_statements
}
```

In this syntax, the interpreter first evaluates *condition1*. If *condition1* is true, the interpreter executes *program_statements1* and then exits the control structure. If *condition1* is false, the interpreter evaluates *condition2*. If *condition2* is true, the interpreter executes *program_statements2* and then exits the control structure. The interpreter continues to evaluate each condition, one after another, until it finds a true condition. If the interpreter does not find a true condition, it executes the *alternate_program_statements* following the `else` command.

Now you will modify the WriteSummary() function in the Order Summary Web page to use an `if/else if` control structure. The first condition will test whether the value in the Desired Quantity text input is an empty string literal. If it is, an alert will appear advising the user to enter a value. The second condition will test whether the entered value is less than or equal to zero. If the value is less than or equal to zero, an alert will appear advising the user to enter a value greater than zero. The **else** portion of the control structure, which executes if all other conditions are false and confirms that the user entered a valid non-zero value, displays the order summary information and the "thank you" alert.

Recall that all values that users enter in Web page text inputs are text strings. Before you can test to confirm that the value in the Desired Quantity text input is greater than zero, you must convert the value to a number using the parseFloat() function.

To modify the WriteSummary() function to use an **if/else if** control structure:

1. Switch back to Visual Studio .NET and save the file as **orders_if_else_if_done.htm** in the Chapter3\Tutorials folder on your Solution Disk.

2. Modify the code in the WriteSummary() function so it looks like the code in Figure 3-26.

```
function WriteSummary() {
   var currQuantity = document.frmOrderItem.txtQuantity.value;
   if (currQuantity == "") {
      alert("Please enter a value for Desired Quantity.");
   } else if (parseFloat(currQuantity) <= 0) {
      alert("Please enter a value for Desired " +
      "Quantity that is greater than 0.");
   } else {
      var subTotal = new Number();
      var salesTax = new Number();
      var orderTotal = new Number();
      subTotal = document.frmOrderItem.txtQuantity.value * 299.99;
      document.frmOrderItem.txtSubTotal.value = "$ " + subTotal.toFixed(2);
      salesTax = subTotal * .06;
      document.frmOrderItem.txtTax.value = "$ " + salesTax.toFixed(2);
      orderTotal = subTotal + salesTax;
      document.frmOrderItem.txtOrderTotal.value = "$ " + orderTotal.toFixed(2);
      alert("Thank you for your order!");
   }
}
```

**Figure 3-26**    Code for if/else if control structure

3. Save the file, then switch to Internet Explorer and open **orders_if_else_if_done.htm** from the Chapter3\Tutorials folder on your Solution Disk.

4. Do not type a value in the Desired Quantity text input. Click **Submit Order**. The alert appears, prompting you to enter a value for Desired Quantity. Click **OK** to close the alert.

5. Type **0** for Desired Quantity, then click **Submit Order**. The alert appears, prompting you to enter a value greater than zero. Click **OK** to close the alert.

6. Type **2** for Desired Quantity, then click **Submit Order**. The order summary and "thank you" alert appear. Click **OK** to close the alert.

## The `switch` Control Structure

The `if/else if` control structure tests for multiple conditions and then executes the program statements associated with the first true condition. In the preceding example, both of the condition statements compare a value to the value in the Desired Quantity text input. When you create an `if/else if` control structure in which all of the condition statements compare the value of the same variable or object, you can use the `switch` control structure instead. The **switch control structure** allows you to test multiple conditions that compare the same variable value. The `switch` control structure executes faster than the equivalent `if/else if` structure, and requires fewer program lines. However, a limitation of the `switch` structure is that you can use it only when the condition evaluates whether an expression is equal to another expression. You cannot use the `switch` structure to evaluate whether an expression is greater than or less than another value, or whether an expression is not equal to another value.

The general syntax for the `switch` control structure is as follows:

```
switch (expression) {
case value1 :
      program_statements1;
      break;
case value2 :
      program_statements2;
      break;
case value3 :
      program_statements3;
      break;
...
default :
      alternate_program_statements;
}
```

In this syntax, the `switch` structure begins with the keyword `switch`. The *expression* denotes the variable or object whose value the `switch` structure tests. To use the `switch` structure in place of the `if/else if` structure in the preceding example, the *expression* references the value in the Desired Quantity text input.

Each `case` statement evaluates whether the *expression* is equal to an associated value that is denoted by *value1*, *value2*, and so forth. If the *expression* is equal to a value in a `case` statement, the associated program statements execute. For the Order Summary Web page, in the first `case` statement, *value1* would be the empty string literal (`""`), and the program statement would display the alert advising the user to enter a value for the

**3**

Desired Quantity. The `default:` statement has program statements that execute if *expression* does not match any of the values in the `case` statements.

The `break` command within each `case` statement is optional, and instructs the program to exit the `switch` structure. Sometimes in a `switch` structure, you want to continue to evaluate case expressions even after a matching expression is found. By omitting the `break` command in a `case` statement, program execution will continue to evaluate the other `case` statements even after a `case` statement evaluates as true.

Now you will modify the Order Summary Web page to use a `switch` control structure in place of the `if/else if` control structure. The *expression* will reference the value in the Desired Quantity text input, using the code `(document.frmOrderItem.txtQuantity.value)`. The `case` statements will test whether the text input contains the empty string literal (`""`) or the value "0." (Recall that a `switch` structure can test only whether the expression is equal to a value, so you cannot test whether the value in the text input is greater than zero.) You will include a `break` command within each `case` statement because you want to exit the `switch` structure each time the interpreter finds an error.

To modify the WriteSummary() function to use a `switch` control structure:

1. Switch back to Visual Studio .NET, and save the file as **orders_switch_ done.htm** in the Chapter3\Tutorials folder on your Solution Disk.

2. Modify the code in the WriteSummary() function so it looks like the code in Figure 3-27. Note that for the `case` statement that tests whether the text input is equal to the number zero, you enclose the number "0" in double quotation marks. This is because the value that the user enters into the text input is actually a text string containing the number zero.

3. Save the file, then switch to Internet Explorer and open **orders_switch_ done.htm** from the Chapter3\Tutorials folder on your Solution Disk.

4. Do not type a value in the Desired Quantity text input. Click **Submit Order**. The alert appears prompting you to enter a value for Desired Quantity. Click **OK** to close the alert.

5. Type **0** for Desired Quantity, then click **Submit Order**. The alert appears prompting you to enter a value greater than zero. Click **OK** to close the alert.

6. Type **2** for Desired Quantity, then click **Submit Order**. The order summary values and the "thank you" alert appear. Click **OK** to close the alert.

7. Switch back to Visual Studio .NET and close the orders_switch_done.htm file.

```
function WriteSummary() {
    switch (document.frmOrderItem.txtQuantity.value) {
      case "" :
        alert("Please enter a value for Desired Quantity.");
        break;
      case "0" :
        alert("Please enter a value for Desired Quantity that is greater ↵
        than 0.");
        break;
      default :
        var subTotal = new Number();
        var salesTax = new Number();
        var orderTotal = new Number();
        subTotal = document.frmOrderItem.txtQuantity.value * 299.99;
        document.frmOrderItem.txtSubTotal.value = "$ " + subTotal.toFixed(2);
        salesTax = subTotal * .06;
        document.frmOrderItem.txtTax.value = "$ " + salesTax.toFixed(2);
        orderTotal = subTotal + salesTax;
        document.frmOrderItem.txtOrderTotal.value = "$ " + orderTotal.toFixed
(2);
        alert("Thank you for your order!");
    }
}
```

**Figure 3-27** Code for `switch` control structure

## Using the AND and OR Logical Operators in Control Structure Conditions

Sometimes you need to test multiple conditions in a single condition statement. For example, it would simplify the data validation process on the Order Summary Web page if you could use a *single* condition statement to evaluate whether the value that the user enters in the Desired Quantity text input is not an empty string and is also greater than zero. Then you could display a single alert advising the user to enter a quantity value greater than zero.

You can test two separate conditions at the same time using the AND logical operator. With the AND operator, both conditions must be true for the overall condition to be true. In JavaScript, `&&` represents the AND logical operator. The general syntax for joining two conditions in a comparison is as follows:

```
((condition1) && (condition2))
```

You can use this condition in any of the `if` control structures. Note that you must enclose each individual *condition* in parentheses, and you must enclose the entire joined condition in parentheses.

You can also join two separate conditions using the OR operator. With the OR operator, if either condition is true, the overall condition is true. In JavaScript, you represent the OR operator using a double bar (||). (On most keyboards, you type the bar character (|) by pressing Shift plus the key directly above the Enter key.) The general syntax for joining two conditions using the OR operator is as follows:

```
((condition1) || (condition2))
```

Table 3-12 illustrates the JavaScript logical operators.

**3**

**Table 3-12**   JavaScript logical operators

| Logical Operator | JavaScript Operator | Example Expressions | Result |
|---|---|---|---|
| AND | && | ((5 > 2) && (34 > 5))<br>((5 > 2) && (34 < 5)) | True<br>False |
| OR | \|\| | ((5 > 2) \|\| (34 > 5))<br>((5 > 2) \|\| (34 < 5))<br>((5 < 2) \|\| (34 < 5)) | True<br>True<br>False |

Recall that if you join two conditions using the JavaScript AND operator (&&), both conditions must be true for the condition to be true. In the first AND example, both expressions are true, so the condition is true. In the second AND example, the second expression (34 < 5) is not true, so the overall condition is false. With the OR operator ||, if either condition is true, the overall condition is true. In the first OR example, both conditions are true, so the overall condition is true. In the second OR example, the first condition is true and the second condition is not true, so the overall condition is true. In the third OR example, neither condition is true, so the overall condition is false.

To gain experience using the AND logical operator in a control structure, you will open a Web page file that contains the **if/else** logical structure for validating the form inputs for the Order Summary Web page in Figure 3-18. You will modify the file so the condition uses the AND logical operator (&&) to confirm that the value that the user enters is not an empty string literal ("") and is also greater than zero. Because the value the user enters in the text input is a text string, you will use the parseFloat() function within the condition to convert the string to a number. If the combined condition is true, the order summary and "thank you" alert appear. If the condition is false, an alert appears that advises the user to enter a value that is greater than zero.

To use the AND logical operator in a condition:

1. In Visual Studio .NET, open the **orders_AND.htm** file from the Chapter3 folder on your Data Disk, and save the file as **orders_AND_done.htm** in the Chapter3\Tutorials folder on your Solution Disk.

2. Switch to HTML view, then modify the condition in the **if** control structure code as follows:

```
if ((currQuantity != "") && ↵
(parseFloat(currQuantity))> 0){
```

3. Modify the command that creates the second alert as follows:

```
alert("Please enter a value for " +
"Desired Quantity that is greater than 0.");
```

4. Save the file, then switch to Internet Explorer and open **orders_AND_ done.htm** from the Chapter3\Tutorials folder on your Solution Disk.

5. Do not type a value in the Desired Quantity text input. Click **Submit Order**. The alert appears prompting you to enter a value for Desired Quantity that is greater than zero. Click **OK** to close the alert.

6. Type **0** for Desired Quantity, then click **Submit Order**. The alert appears again, prompting you to enter a value greater than zero. Click **OK** to close the alert.

7. Type **2** for Desired Quantity, then click **Submit Order**. The order summary values and the "thank you" alert appear. Click **OK** to close the alert.

8. Switch back to Visual Studio .NET and close the file.

## CREATING REPETITION (LOOPING) STRUCTURES

Sometimes a program needs to process multiple items or data values the same way. For example, you might want to check the value of every radio button on a Web page form to see whether the user has selected a specific radio button. Or you might write a math function that checks all numbers between 1 and 50 and identifies each number that is a prime number. On a more practical note, you could write a program that calculates the net present value of a series of payments that you will receive each year for the next 20 years.

To process multiple values the same way, you use a repetition structure called a loop. A **loop** repeatedly executes a series of program statements and periodically evaluates an exit condition. If the exit condition is false, the loop repeats the program statements and then reevaluates the exit condition. If the exit condition is true, the loop terminates. A loop can be a **pretest loop**, in which the loop evaluates the exit condition before any program commands execute. If the exit condition is true, none of the loop's program statements execute. Alternatively, a loop can be a **posttest loop**, in which one or more program commands execute before the loop evaluates the exit condition the first time. The following subsections describe how to create `while` loops, `do while` loops, and `for` loops in JavaScript programs.

### while Loops

A `while` loop is a pretest loop that you use to evaluate the exit condition before executing any of the loop program statements. If the exit condition is initially false, none of the loop program statements execute. As long as the exit condition is true, the loop program statements execute. The general JavaScript syntax for a `while` loop is:

```
while (condition) {
      program_statements
}
```

You structure a `while` loop's *condition* using the same syntax as a decision control structure condition. The *program_statements* can include any legal JavaScript commands. In a `while` loop, the *program_statements* must contain an assignment statement that controls loop execution. For example, you might increment a counter variable value by one using the `++` increment operator, and use this variable in the *condition* to control how many times the loop executes. During program execution, the JavaScript interpreter first evaluates the *condition*. If the *condition* is true, the interpreter executes the *program_statements*. The interpreter then evaluates the *condition* again, and exits the loop if the *condition* has become false. If the *condition* is initially false, the JavaScript interpreter exits the loop without executing any of the *program_statements*.

Now you will create the HTML document shown in Figure 3-28. This document has a script that uses a `while` loop to display the number values on the Web page.

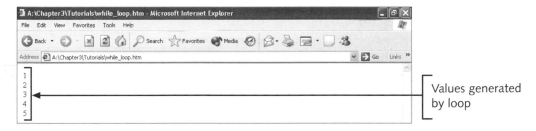

**Figure 3-28**    Web page created using a `while` loop

This Web page uses the document onload event handler to call a function when the Web page loads. The function first assigns 1 as the initial value of a variable named counter. The function contains a `while` loop. The loop *condition* is true when counter is 5. The loop uses the document.write method to write the current value of counter to the Web page, and then uses the `++` operator to increment counter by one each time the loop executes. The loop will execute five times before the *condition* `counter = 5` becomes false. Note that the text string within the document.write method concatenates the value of the counter variable with the line break tag `<br>`, expressed as a text string, so each counter value appears on a separate line on the Web page.

To create the Web page that uses a `while` loop:

1. In Visual Studio .NET, create a new HTML file. Save the file as
   **WHILE_loop.htm** in the Chapter3\Tutorials folder on your Solution Disk.

2. Add the shaded code in Figure 3-29 to modify the Web page title, create the function, and create the onload event handler.

3. Save the file, switch to Internet Explorer, and open **WHILE_loop.htm** from the Chapter3\Tutorials folder on your Solution Disk. Your Web page output should look like Figure 3-28.

```
<!DOCTYPE HTML PUBLIC "-//W3C//DTD HTML 4.0 Transitional//EN">
<html>
    <head>
    <title>Web Page To Display Loop Results</title>
    <meta name="GENERATOR"
    content="Microsoft Visual Studio.NET 7.0">
        <meta name="vs_targetSchema"
        content="http://schemas.microsoft.com/intellisense/ie5">
        <script language="javascript">
            <!--
                function runLoop() {
                    var counter = 1;
                    while (counter<=5) {
                        document.write(counter + "<br>");
                        counter++;
                    }
                }
            //-->
        </script>
    </head>
    <body onload="runLoop()">
    </body>
</html>
```

**Figure 3-29**    Code for a Web page script that uses a `while` loop

Recall that the `while` loop is a pretest loop, which always tests the exit condition before executing any loop program statements. This allows program execution to bypass the loop program statements entirely. For example, in the Web page you just created using the `while` loop, if you specify the exit condition as `while counter < 1`, the exit condition is initially false, so the JavaScript interpreter bypasses the loop program statements and no text will appear on the Web page.

## do while Loops

Sometimes you need to structure a loop so that the loop program statements always execute at least one time before the interpreter evaluates the exit condition. To do this, you use a posttest loop. In JavaScript, you can use the `do while` loop as a posttest loop. The general syntax of a `do while` loop is:

```
do {
        program_statements
} while (condition)
```

In this loop, the JavaScript interpreter executes the *program_statements* once and then evaluates the *condition*. If the *condition* is false, the interpreter exits the loop. If the *condition* is true, the interpreter executes the *program_statements* again and then reevaluates the *condition*. Now you will create the Web page in Figure 3-28 using a `do while` loop.

To create a Web page using a `do while` loop:

1. In Visual Studio .NET, save your file as **DO_WHILE_loop.htm** in the Chapter3\Tutorials folder on your Solution Disk.

2. Modify the code within the **<script>** tags as shown in Figure 3-30.

```
<script language="javascript">
   <!--
      function runLoop() {
         var counter = 1;
         do {
            document.write(counter + "<br>");
            counter++;
         } while (counter<=5)
      }
   //-->
</script>
```

**Figure 3-30**    Code for a Web page script that uses a `do while` loop

3. Save the file, then switch to Internet Explorer and open **DO_WHILE_loop.htm** from the Chapter3\Tutorials folder on your Solution Disk. Your Web page output should look like Figure 3-28.

## `for` Loops

When you create `while` and `do while` loops, you must explicitly declare and increment the counter variable that controls the number of times the loop executes. In a `for` loop, you declare and control the counter variable within the loop structure. The general syntax for a JavaScript `for` loop is:

```
for (initial_expression; condition;
update_expression) {
        program_statements
}
```

In this syntax, *initial_expression* is a JavaScript command that executes once at the beginning of the loop, declares a variable, and assigns a starting value to it. An example of *initial_expression* is `var i=1;`.

 In JavaScript programs, many programmers use *i* to represent a counter variable within a loop. The letter *i* stands for *index*. You can also use more descriptive names, such as *counter*, or any other variable name.

The *condition* evaluates the value of the *initial_expression* to determine when the loop terminates. As long as the *condition* is true, the loop continues to execute. The *update_expression* specifies how the counter increments. The following code creates a `for` loop that executes five times, and uses the `++` operator to increment the counter by one:

```
for (var i = 1; i < 6; i++) {
        program_statements
}
```

Now you will create the Web page in Figure 3-28 using a `for` loop.

To create the Web page using a `for` loop:

1. Switch to Visual Studio .NET and save your file as **FOR_loop.htm** in the Chapter3\Tutorials folder on your Solution Disk.

2. Modify the function code so it looks like the code in Figure 3-31.

```
<script language="javascript">
   <!--
      function runLoop() {
         for (var i=1; i<6; i++) {
            document.write(i + "<br>");
         }
      }
   //-->
</script>
```

**Figure 3-31**    Code for a Web page script that uses a `for` loop

3. Save the file, then switch to Internet Explorer and open **FOR_loop.htm** from the Chapter3\Tutorials folder on your Solution Disk. Your Web page should look like Figure 3-28.

## Selecting a Loop Structure

The `while`, `do while`, and `for` loops provide you with a variety of loop structures. Which loop structure should you use?  Many times you can use any one of the three structures to achieve the same result. Occasionally, you must select a pretest (`while`) loop over a posttest (do while) loop to have the option of skipping the loop program statements. Some people prefer the for loop because it allows them to quickly and easily specify the starting and ending counter values and the loop increment value. Other people are just more comfortable with the while loop because that is what they always use. If you are writing scripts that must be compatible with older browsers, you should avoid the do while loop, because browsers earlier than Internet Explorer 4 and Netscape Navigator 4 don't support it. In most cases, however, you should use the loop structure that seems easiest and best to you.

## CONTRASTING JAVASCRIPT AND JAVA

Students are often curious about how the JavaScript programming language compares to the Java programming language. After deciding to release JavaScript into the public domain, Netscape collaborated with Sun Microsystems, and the companies jointly decided to name the product JavaScript. (The product was formerly called LiveScript.) Recall that although JavaScript is a unique programming language, much of its syntax is similar to that of C, C++, and Java.

Even though both JavaScript and Java use a C-style syntax for common programming tasks, their underlying structures and purposes are very different. You include JavaScript code within HTML documents, it interacts with Web page objects using the DOM, and the Web browser interprets the program commands at run time. In contrast, Java is a full-featured programming language that you use to write compiled programs. Programmers use Java to create Java applets, which are compiled programs that Web servers download to client workstations. Programmers can create links from HTML documents to Java applets, but the Java applet executes on the client workstation, independently of the Web browser and Web page. Once the Java applet begins execution, it cannot interact with Web page elements.

Another significant difference between the two languages is how they use objects. Java is a full-featured object-oriented programming language that enables programmers to create custom objects that can inherit properties and methods belonging to parent objects. As a result, Java enables programmers to create user interfaces that are independent of the Web browser. Java also supports file and database operations. In contrast, JavaScript does not allow programmers to create their own custom objects. In JavaScript, programmers can use only predefined objects, such as String(), Number(), Date(), or Math(). For security reasons, JavaScript programmers cannot perform operations using files and databases. JavaScript interfaces appear only in a Web browser, so you can use only interface elements that are available within a Web page, such as form elements and tables.

Both JavaScript and Java use a similar dot syntax to reference and manipulate language objects, such as text strings, numeric variables, and math and date variables. For example, the following Math object methods are the same in both JavaScript and Java:

```
Math.abs(val)          // absolute value of val
Math.max(val1, val2)   // greater of val1 and val2
Math.round(val)        //rounded to next lower or higher integer
```

The following example shows how to manipulate a previously declared string variable named string1. This code will work identically in JavaScript and Java.

```
string1.length // number of characters in the string
string1.substring(start, end)  /* string of characters ⤸
between the start and end values */
string1.charAt(index)     // character at the index position
```

If you are planning to learn how to program with Java, learning JavaScript first will help you get started with Java. If you already know how to program with Java, you have a head start on learning JavaScript.

## CHAPTER SUMMARY

- ❏ Programmers use client-side scripts for tasks such as validating user inputs entered on HTML forms, opening new browser windows, and creating cookies.

- ❏ The HTML document object model (DOM) is a hierarchical naming system that enables scripts to reference browser objects. You can access and manipulate DOM objects using dot syntax containing either object name or id attribute values.

- ❏ Properties define an object's structure, and are usually element attributes in HTML documents. Events are actions that take place in a document as a result of a user action. An event can have an associated event handler, which is a series of program commands that execute when the event occurs. Methods perform actions on objects.

- ❏ The Visual Studio .NET IDE displays IntelliSense lists that provide selections for available child objects, methods, properties, and events.

- ❏ In an HTML file, you enclose JavaScript commands within **<script>** tags. It is a good practice to place all the script commands in the document header within a single set of script tags.

- ❏ You can use the window.alert method to display a short message. You can use the document.write method to write text directly on a Web page.

- ❏ Functions are self-contained groups of program commands that you can call within a script. JavaScript has built-in global functions that are included with the language. You can create user-defined functions that perform specific tasks.

- ❏ You can create an onclick event handler that executes when a user clicks a command button, and an onload event handler that executes when an HTML document loads in a browser.

- ❏ When you place a script within an HTML document, its position in the document affects when the script runs. JavaScript code that is not within a function executes as the document loads, at the moment that the browser reads the lines of code. Code within a function executes when it is called by an event handler or by a function call within another code block.

❑ JavaScript is a loosely typed language, so the JavaScript interpreter does not assign a data type to a variable until a program statement assigns a value to the variable. JavaScript data types include boolean, function, number, object, and string.

❑ The JavaScript language has operators to perform arithmetic operations and string concatenation operations. Although these operators have a specific order of precedence, you can use parentheses or square brackets to specify the order for arithmetic operations in a command explicitly.

❑ The plus sign operator (+) is an overloaded operator, and you can use it both to add numbers and concatenate strings. JavaScript automatically converts numbers to strings when you use both strings and numbers in an expression with the + operator.

❑ You can use JavaScript built-in objects to perform common actions for formatting and manipulating Number, String, Date, and Math variable values.

❑ You can use the JavaScript parseFloat() and parseInt() global functions to convert string variable values to number data types.

❑ In a JavaScript program, you create decision control structures using `if`, `if/else`, `if/else if`, and `switch` statements.

❑ If you join two condition expressions using the AND operator (`&&`), both conditions must be true for the overall expression to be true. If you join two conditions using the OR operator (`||`), only one condition must be true for the overall expression to be true.

❑ JavaScript provides `while`, `do while`, and `for` loops. You should not use the `do while` loop if you want your scripts to be compatible with older browsers.

❑ Although JavaScript is a unique programming language, much of its syntax is similar to that of C, C++, and Java. Java is a full-featured object-oriented programming language, while JavaScript is more limited and runs within HTML documents.

# REVIEW QUESTIONS

1. What is a script?

2. Web database developers use client-side scripts to:

   a. Create and read cookies

   b. Create JavaScript applets

   c. Validate user inputs

   d. Both a and c

3. A(n) _____ defines the structure and properties of similar objects, and a(n) _____ is an object that belongs to a class.

4. A(n) _____ is an action that occurs as a result of a user action, and a(n) _____ performs an action on an object.

   a. Event handler, function

   b. Method, event

   c. Function, subroutine

   d. Event, method

5. What is the HTML document object model?

6. Explain why scripts written for Internet Explorer might not work with Netscape Navigator.

7. What is the top-level object in the HTML DOM?

8. Use dot syntax to write a statement that references the current value of a text input named txtPassword in a form named frmLogin.

9. When should you use the id attribute in dot syntax to reference objects, and when should you use the name attribute?

10. Use Visual Studio .NET's IntelliSense lists to find examples of two events, two methods, and two properties for an HTML text input element.

11. Use Visual Studio .NET's IntelliSense lists to find examples of one property and three methods for a string object. (*Hint*: In a JavaScript line of code, declare `var myString = new String();` . In the next line, type `myString.` to open an IntelliSense list.)

12. Why do you place JavaScript commands within HTML comment tags?

13. In JavaScript, you normally place the code to define functions in the _____ section of an HTML document.

14. Write the JavaScript command to display a message box containing the text "Hello."

15. Write an HTML tag to create a command button with the label "Process Data" that contains an event handler that calls a JavaScript function named "ProcessData()" when the user clicks the button.

16. What is the difference between a language that is strongly typed and a language that is loosely typed?

17. Write a single JavaScript command to declare a variable named myNumber that has an initial value of 100.

18. Describe two ways to indicate that JavaScript lines are comments.

19. In a JavaScript function, the `return` command:

   a. Specifies the value that a function returns to the calling program

   b. Signals the JavaScript interpreter to resume execution in the calling program

   c. Returns the memory space used in the function back to the shared memory pool

   d. Both a and b

20. Where can you place script tags in an HTML document?

21. What is the result of each JavaScript operation, and what is the resulting data type?

    a. 3 + '4'

    b. '3' + '4'

    c. '3' + 4 + 5

    d. 3 + 4

    e. 3 + 4 + '5'

22. What is the result of each JavaScript operation, and what is the resulting data type?

    a. 3 + (4 + '5')

    b. (3 + 4) + '5'

    c. '3' + (4 + 5)

    d. ('3' + 4) + 5

23. Write a JavaScript command to add (not concatenate) the following variables and assign the result to a variable named result:

    ```
    var number1 = 4;
    var string1 = '5';
    ```

24. Write a decision control structure that tests whether a variable named age is between 0 and 120. If age is between these values, display an alert stating "Value is valid." Otherwise, display an alert stating "Value is invalid."

25. Write a decision control structure that uses the **switch** structure to evaluate the value of a variable named userChoice. The **switch** structure should display a message stating "Red" if userChoice has the value "Red," "Yellow" if userChoice has the value "Yellow," and "Green" if userChoice has the value "Green."

26. Write a series of JavaScript commands that declare a variable named sum and assigns the numeric literal 1 to it. Create a **for** loop that displays an alert showing the current value of sum 10 times.

27. Describe two major differences between Java and JavaScript.

## HANDS-ON PROJECTS

### Project 3-1 Creating a Script to Validate Order Data

In this project, you will create a function in the HTML document in Figure 3-32 that confirms that the value the user enters in the Desired Quantity text input is greater than zero, and then displays an alert showing the total order amount. You will create a second function that clears all form inputs when the user clicks the Clear button.

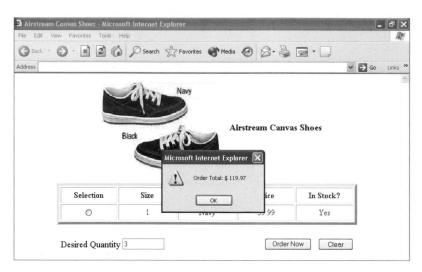

**Figure 3-32**

1. Open shoes.htm from the Chapter3 folder on your Data Disk and save the file as 3Project1.htm in the Chapter3\Projects folder on your Solution Disk. Copy the shoes.jpg file from the Chapter3 folder on your Data Disk to the Chapter3\Projects folder on your Solution Disk so the inline graphic image appears on the Web page.

2. Create a function named validateQuantity() that ensures that the number in the Desired Quantity text input is greater than or equal to 1 and less than 100. If the entry is incorrect, the function should display an alert stating "Desired Quantity value must be between 1 and 100." After the user clicks OK, select txtOrderQuantity. When a user makes a valid entry, the function should display an alert showing the order total, which is price times quantity, formatted as currency. For example, if the user types the number *1* in the Desired Quantity text input and clicks Submit Order, the alert should display "Order Total:  $39.99."

3. Create a function named clearEntry() that sets the value of the Desired Quantity text input to an empty string literal.

4. Create event handlers to associate each button with the function it calls.

## Project 3-2 Creating a Script to Validate Logon Data

In this project, you will write a script that validates the data that the user enters in the HTML document in Figure 3-33 to log on to the Northwoods University student registration system. You will create a function that confirms that the user entered a value for the User ID and PIN values.

3

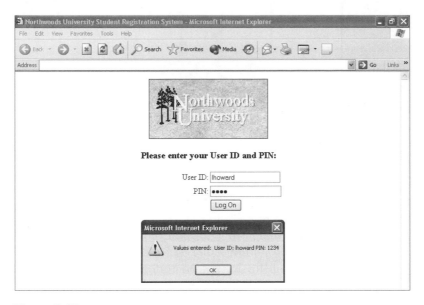

**Figure 3-33**

1. Open logon.htm from the Chapter3 folder on your Data Disk and save the file as 3Project2.htm in the Chapter3\Projects folder on your Solution Disk. Copy the nwlogo.jpg file from the Chapter3 folder on your Data Disk to the Chapter3\Projects folder on your Solution Disk so the graphic image displays correctly.

2. Create a function named submitClick() that determines whether the user entered values for User ID and PIN. If the user entered both values, display the alert showing the values for User ID and PIN as shown. (The alert will appear in the middle of the browser window.) If the user did not enter a value in the User ID input, display an alert stating "User ID not entered," and then set the focus to the txtUserid. If the user did not enter the PIN value, display an alert stating "PIN not entered," and then set the focus to txtPIN. Use an `if/else if` control structure.

3. Create an event handler for the button that calls the submitClick() function.

## Project 3-3   Creating a Script to Display Student Data

In this project, you will add a script to the HTML document in Figure 3-34 that displays an alert that summarizes the values that the user enters in the form inputs.

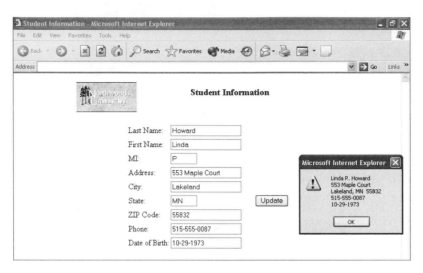

**Figure 3-34**

1. Open student.htm from the Chapter3 folder on your Data Disk and save it as 3Project3.htm in the Chapter3\Projects folder on your Solution Disk. If necessary, copy the nwlogo.jpg file from the Chapter3 folder on your Data Disk to the Chapter3\Projects folder on your Solution Disk so the graphic image displays correctly.

2. Create a function named displayEntries() that summarizes the user entries and displays them in an alert as shown. (*Hint:* Make sure that none of the form elements have an id attribute value, because the id attribute overrides the name attribute when you reference it in a script. Use the \n character to display text output on separate lines.)

3. Create an event handler for the Update button that calls the displayEntries() function.

## Project 3-4 Creating a Script to Display Fibonacci Numbers

You create a series of Fibonacci numbers by starting with 0 and 1 as the first two values. You add these values to determine the third number, which is 1. You then add the two values that are currently the last two values in the series (1 and 1) to determine the next value in the series, which is 2. You then again add the last two numbers in the series (1 and 2) to identify the next value in the series, which is 3. A list of the first 10 Fibonacci numbers is as follows: (0, 1, 1, 2, 3, 5, 8, 13, 21, 34). In this project, you will modify the Web page shown in Figure 3-35. This Web page contains a form that allows the user to enter the number of Fibonacci numbers that he or she wishes to generate. When the user clicks Generate, an alert opens showing the generated numbers.

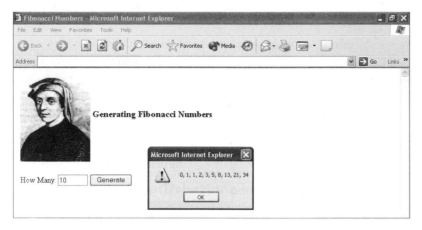

**Figure 3-35**

1. Open fibonacci.htm from the Chapter3 folder on your Data Disk and save the file as 3Project4.htm in the Chapter3\Projects folder on your Solution Disk. Copy the Fibonacci.gif graphic image file to the Chapter3\Projects folder on your Solution Disk so the graphic image appears correctly.

2. Create a function named generateNumbers() that generates the number of Fibonacci numbers that the user specifies in the How Many text input. Use a loop to generate the numbers and then display the resulting numbers in an alert as shown. When the user clicks OK on the alert, the script should clear the How Many text input value and place the insertion point in the How Many text input.

3. Create an event handler associated with the Generate command button that calls the function.

## Project 3-5 Creating a Web Page to Convert English and Metric Measurements

In this project, you will write the JavaScript code to convert distance, volume, weight, and temperature values expressed in U.S./English measurements to their equivalent metric values and vice versa using the Web page in Figure 3-36. A user can type values in either the U.S./English or the Metric column inputs on the form. When the user clicks Convert, the Web page displays the converted value in the opposite column. For example, if the user types *3* in the Metric Volume input and *60* in the U.S./English Temperature input and then clicks Convert, the associated metric values appear as shown in Figure 3-36. Similarly, if the user types values in the Metric Volume and Metric Temperature inputs and then clicks Convert, the associated U.S./English values appear. The user can type values in any or all of the inputs in either the U.S./English or Metric column, or type some values in the U.S./English column and some values in the Metric column. If the user types a value in both inputs in the same category, an error alert appears.

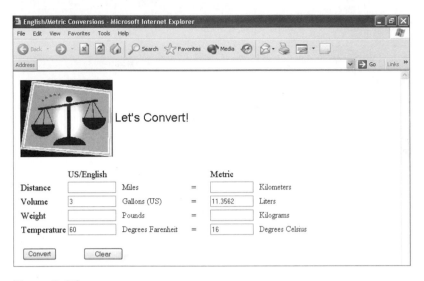

**Figure 3-36**

1. Open the measures.htm file from the Chapter3 folder on your Data Disk and save the file as 3Project5.htm in the Chapter3\Projects folder on your Solution Disk. Copy the scales.jpg file from the Chapter3 folder on your Data Disk to the Chapter3\Projects folder on your Solution Disk so the graphic image displays correctly.

2. Create a JavaScript function named convertValues() that evaluates whether the user entered a value in either the U.S./English or Metric input for each measure type and then performs and displays the appropriate conversion. Use the following conversion factors: 1 mile = 1.609347 kilometers; 1 gallon = 3.7854 liters; 1 pound = .4536 kilograms; Temperature_Celsius = (Temperature_Fahrenheit − 32)/1.8; Temperature_Fahrenheit = 1.8*Temperature_Celsius + 32. Format the values so that the distance, volume, and weight values truncate to four decimal places, and the temperature values truncate to whole numbers.

3. In the convertValues() function, evaluate whether the user enters a value in both the U.S./English and the Metric input for the same measurement category. For example, if the user types a value for both the U.S./English value and the Metric value for Distance and then clicks Convert, the alert in Figure 3-37 appears. When the user clicks OK on the alert, the text in the U.S./English measurement input appears selected.

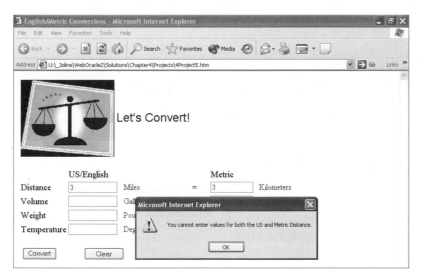

**Figure 3-37**

4. Create a JavaScript function named clearValues() that clears all of the form inputs.

5. Create event handlers so that when the user clicks Convert, the convertValues() function executes, and so that when the user clicks Clear, the clearValues() function executes.

## CASE PROJECTS

### Case 3-1 Ashland Valley Soccer League

In this case, you will work with Web pages that have been created for the Ashland Valley Soccer League, which is a fictitious organization that Case 2-1 in Chapter 2 describes. Copy the .htm and graphic image files from the Chapter3\Cases\Ashland folder on your Data Disk to the Chapter3\Cases\Ashland folder on your Solution Disk. Add a script to the Games.htm page that displays an alert that summarizes the values the user enters in the Game ID, Game Date, Home Team, Visiting Team, and Status text inputs. Display each input value on a separate line in the alert.

### Case 3-2 Al's Body Shop

In this case, you will work with Web pages that have been created for Al's Body Shop, which is a fictitious organization that Case 2-2 in Chapter 2 describes. Copy the .htm and graphic image files from the Chapter3\Cases\Als folder on your Data Disk to the

Chapter3\Cases\Als folder on your Solution Disk. Add a script to the Workorders.htm page that displays an alert that summarizes the user input values in the Work Order ID, Date, VIN , and Service text inputs. Display each input value on a separate line in the alert.

Before you can complete Case 3-3, you must have completed Case 2-3 in Chapter 2.

## Case 3-3 Sun Ray Videos

Copy the .htm and graphic image files for the Web pages that you created in Case 2-3 in Chapter 2 from the Chapter2\Cases folder on your Solution Disk to the Chapter3\Cases folder on your Solution Disk. Add a script to the Rentals.htm Web page in the SunrayPages folder so that when the user clicks the Submit button, the script displays an alert thanking the user for his or her rental order.

Before you can complete Case 3-4, you must have completed Case 2-4 in Chapter 2.

## Case 3-4 Learning Technologies, Incorporated

Copy the .htm and graphic image files for the Web pages that you created in Case 2-4 in Chapter 2 from the Chapter2\Cases folder on your Solution Disk to the Chapter3\Cases folder on your Solution Disk. Add a script that summarizes the user inputs. (Do not display the values for selection lists in the alert. You will learn how to do this in Chapter 4.) Display each input value on a separate line in the alert.

# USING CLIENT-SIDE SCRIPTS TO ENHANCE WEB APPLICATIONS

**In this chapter, you will:**

♦ Learn how to create JavaScript programs to validate HTML form inputs
♦ Use arrays to structure data and reference form elements
♦ Use JavaScript commands to validate values represented by HTML form option buttons, check boxes, and selection lists
♦ Learn how to use the Script Debugger to locate and correct errors in client-side scripts
♦ Learn different ways to display messages in JavaScript programs
♦ Use JavaScript commands to create and read cookies
♦ Use JavaScript commands to change the page that appears in an existing browser window and open a new browser window

In the previous chapter, you learned how to write JavaScript commands to perform basic programming tasks in Web pages. This chapter describes more advanced JavaScript programming techniques. First you will learn how to create JavaScript programs that validate HTML form inputs, and you will learn how to reference and validate values that HTML forms represent using option buttons, check boxes, and selection lists. Then you will learn more advanced techniques for debugging client-side scripts, including how to use the Script Debugger. After you are familiar with the Script Debugger, you will use JavaScript commands to create and read cookies that store information on the user's workstation, and you will create JavaScript commands that display new Web pages in the current browser window and open new browser windows.

## USING CLIENT-SIDE SCRIPTS TO VALIDATE HTML FORM INPUTS

When a user submits a Web page that contains an HTML form to a Web server, the Web page often contains a **form validation function**, which is a client-side script function that validates the HTML form values before sending them to the server. When a script **validates** HTML form values, it confirms that the user has entered all of the required values in the form, and that the entered values are legal or reasonable. For example, if a customer uses an HTML form to submit an order to the Clearwater Traders Web server, the form validation function should confirm that the customer entered required delivery information, such as the customer's name, address, and telephone number. The function should also confirm that the customer selected an item, entered a desired order quantity, and entered a credit card number using the correct format for the card type. By validating form inputs in a client-side script, the browser avoids sending incomplete or incorrect inputs to the Web server. This speeds up Web page processing because the user does not have to wait for the incorrect inputs to arrive at the Web server and then wait for the Web server to return an error message to his or her browser.

In Chapter 3, you learned how to write and call simple JavaScript form validation functions by creating an onclick event handler for a command button's onclick event. In this section, you will learn how to use the onsubmit event handler to call a form validation function, and how to structure a form validation function that the onsubmit event handler calls. You will also learn how to use built-in functions within form validation functions to evaluate whether users enter numerical or date values in form inputs.

## Creating and Calling a Form Validation Function

The Web browser executes a client-side form validation function before the browser submits the form values to the Web server. (Recall that when a browser submits a Web page form to the Web server, the browser passes all of the form input values as parameters to the Web server.) The best way to call a form validation function is to place the function call in an event handler associated with the form's onsubmit event, which executes just before the browser submits the form to the Web server. The following subsections describe how to create an onsubmit event handler to call a form validation function, and how to create the corresponding form validation function.

 Another way to call a form validation function is to place the function call in the onclick event handler of the form's submit button. However, this is not a good practice. In Internet Explorer 6, if a form contains a single text input and a submit button, when the user presses the Enter key, the browser bypasses the submit button's onclick event handler and automatically submits the form to the Web server. The browser thus bypasses the call to the form validation function.

## Creating an Onsubmit Event Handler

To create an onsubmit event handler, which calls a form validation function from within the `<form>` tag, you use the following general syntax:

```
<form onsubmit="return form_validation_function ()">
```

In the onsubmit event handler syntax, the keyword `return` should always be used. If you include `return` in the event handler, the form validation function must return a value of either true or false. If the form validation function returns the value true, the browser submits the form to the Web server. If the function returns the value false, the browser does not submit the form to the Web server. If you omit `return` from the onsubmit event handler, the event handler calls the form validation function and then always submits the form to the Web server regardless of the value that the function returns.

The following code shows an example of the onsubmit event handler for a form named frmExample. The event handler calls a form validation function named validEntries().

```
<form name="frmExample" action="process.aspx"
onsubmit="return validEntries()">
```

If the validEntries() function returns the value true, the browser submits the form to the Web server, and the Web server processes the form inputs using an ASP.NET server-side script named process.aspx. If the validEntries() function returns the value false, the browser does not submit the form to the Web server. Prior to terminating, the validEntries() function will display an error message that describes the problem with the form inputs.

## Structuring a Form Validation Function

When you use the onsubmit event handler to call a form validation function, you must structure the function so that it tests whether multiple different error conditions exist. You use an `if/else if` decision control structure to test for multiple different error conditions. Figure 4-1 shows the general syntax of a form validation function.

In this syntax, each condition tests to determine whether a specific error condition is true. When an error condition is true, the form validation function displays an alert advising the user of the nature of the error, calls the focus method to place the insertion point in the input that contains the error, and returns the value false. The function then terminates. If none of the error conditions are true, the function returns the value true, and the browser submits the form to the Web server. You can test for multiple error conditions in the same condition statement only if the alert message adequately describes all of the errors.

```
function validation_function_name {
   if (error_condition_1) {
      alert("error_condition_1 description");
      set_focus_to_input_with_error;
      return false;
   } else if (error_condition_2) {
      alert("error_condition_2 description");
      set_focus_to_input_with_error;
      return false;
   } else if (error_condition_3) {
      alert("error_condition_3 description");
      set_focus_to_input_with_error;
      return false;
   …
   } else {
      return true;
   }
}
```

**Figure 4-1**    General syntax for a form validation function

In general, you should test for error conditions in form text inputs in a left-to-right, top-to-bottom fashion. In other words, test for errors in the order in which you would read these inputs on the Web page.

Now you will add a form validation function to the Northwoods University Log On Web page shown in Figure 4-2. This Web page allows users to log on to the Northwoods University student registration system. The user types his or her user ID, PIN (personal identification number), and date of birth, and then clicks Submit Query. The Submit Query button calls a form validation function and then submits the form to the Web server. The form validation function confirms that the PIN value is a four-digit number and that the date value is in the correct format.

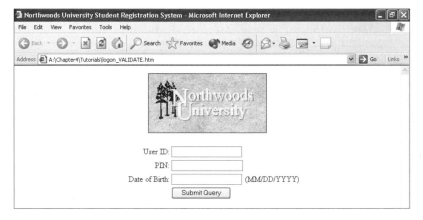

**Figure 4-2**    Northwoods University Log On page

First you will open the Northwoods University Log On Web page file, which is saved in the logon.htm file in the Chapter4 folder on your Data Disk, and save the file as logon_VALIDATE.htm in the Chapter4\Tutorials folder on your Solution Disk. You will create a form validation function named validEntries() that evaluates whether an error condition exists for the PIN text input. Recall that user input values in form text inputs are always text strings, so you will first use the parseFloat() function to convert the text string to a number. Then you will create an **if/else** decision structure in which the condition evaluates whether or not the value in the PIN text input is less than 1 or greater than 9999. (You will learn how to validate the date entry later.) If the number is not valid, the function displays an alert describing the error and returns the value false. If the number is valid, the function displays an alert advising the user that the PIN value is valid, and returns the value true. (In an actual system, the browser would submit the Web page directly to the Web server without displaying an alert saying it is valid.) You will add an onsubmit event handler to the form to call the function.

To add the validation function and event handler to the Log On page:

1. Start Visual Studio .NET, open **logon.htm** from the Chapter4 folder on your Data Disk, and save the file as **logon_VALIDATE.htm** in the Chapter4\Tutorials folder on your Solution Disk. Copy the **nwlogo.jpg** file from the Chapter4 folder on your Data Disk to the Chapter4\Tutorials folder on your Solution Disk so the inline graphic image appears on the Web page.

2. Click the **HTML** tab to switch to HTML view, and if necessary, add a new blank line just above the closing **</head>** tag, and then add the code in Figure 4-3 to create the form validation function.

```
<script language="javascript">
<!--
   function validEntries() {
      var pinValue = parseFloat(document.frmLogin.txtPIN.value);
      //evaluate PIN value to determine if it is valid
      if ((pinValue < 1) || (pinValue > 9999)) {
         alert("Please enter a four-digit PIN number.");
         document.frmLogin.txtPIN.select();
         return false;
      } else {
         alert("PIN value is valid.");
         return true;
      }
   }
//-->
</script>
```

**Figure 4-3**    Code to create the form validation function

3. Add the following code to the `<form>` tag to create the onsubmit event handler to call the function and then save the file:

```
<form name=frmLogin action="action marker" onsubmit=
"return validEntries()">
```

Now you will open Internet Explorer and test your form validation function. You will enter a valid PIN value in the form, and confirm that an alert appears saying that the value is valid. Then you will enter some invalid values and confirm that the error message alert appears.

To test the form validation function:

1. Start Internet Explorer and open **logon_VALIDATE.htm** from the Chapter4\Tutorials folder on your Solution Disk.

2. Do not enter a value for User ID. Type **1234** in the PIN text input. (Because the PIN text input is a Password style input, the values appear as asterisks [*].) (Your values may appear as bullets, depending on your browser configuration.)

3. Click **Submit Query**. An alert appears confirming that the PIN value is valid. Click **OK** to close the alert. A Web page appears displaying the message "The page cannot be displayed," which confirms that the validation function returned the value true. (Remember that if the form validation function returns the value true, the browser will try to submit the form to the Web server. Because the form tag is calling an invalid program (`action="action marker"`), an error appears stating the page cannot be displayed. Don't worry about this error for now. You will learn how to create server-side programs to process forms in Chapter 6.)

 If the alert does not appear, use the debugging techniques you learned in Chapter 3 to find and correct the script command that is causing the error.

4. Click the **Back** button on your browser toolbar to redisplay the Log On Web page.

5. Type **12345** in the PIN text input, and then click **Submit Query**. Because this is a five-digit number rather than a four-digit number, the alert appears asking you to enter a four-digit PIN number. Click **OK** to close the alert. The current PIN text appears selected.

## Validating Numeric and Date Input Values

Form validation functions often need to confirm that the user enters number values in a text input that requires numbers. Similarly, validation functions need to confirm that the user enters a valid date in a text input that requires a date input. To validate numeric inputs, you use the JavaScript isNaN() function. To evaluate date variable values, you create a JavaScript Date object.

## Using the isNaN() function to Validate Numeric Inputs

To convert the value that the user enters in the PIN text input to a number, the Log On Web page form validation function uses the parseFloat() function and then evaluates whether or not the value is less than 1 or greater than 9999. What happens when the user enters in the PIN text input a text string that does not contain numeric characters? Does the parseFloat() function successfully perform the conversion, or does it return an error? To answer this question, you will add an alert to the form validation function so you can view the value that the parseFloat() function returns when it receives a non-numeric text string.

To modify the form validation function to show the value that the parseFloat() function returns when it receives non-numeric inputs:

1. Switch to Visual Studio .NET and add the following command to display the value that the parseFloat() function returns. Add the command just after the command that uses the parseFloat() function, as shown.

   ```
   var pinValue = parseFloat(document.frmLogin.txtPIN.value);
   alert("PIN value: " + pinValue);
   ```

2. Save the file, then switch to Internet Explorer and press **F5** to refresh the display.

3. Type **asdf** in the PIN text input, and then click **Submit Query**. An alert appears with the message "PIN value: NaN."

4. Click **OK** to close the alert. An alert appears advising that the PIN value is valid. Click **OK** to close the second alert, and then click the **Back** button on your browser toolbar to redisplay the Log On Web page.

The alert showed that the value of pinValue was "NaN." In JavaScript, "NaN" is a symbolic constant that stands for "not a number." (In programming, a **symbolic constant** is an English-like text string that is associated with a numerical value. For example, you might create a symbolic constant named "pi" that is associated with the value 3.14157.) The JavaScript interpreter returns "NaN" when the parseFloat() and parseInt() functions receive a parameter that is not a number. However, because the first error condition (that the PIN value was less than 1 or greater than 9999) was not true, the `else` part of the decision structure executed, and displayed the message confirming that the PIN value was valid. Therefore, you need some way to explicitly test whether the user enters a non-numeric value in the PIN text input.

To verify that the value the user enters in a text input is numeric, you use the built-in isNaN() function. The **isNaN() function** returns a value of true if the parameter you pass to it is not a number, and returns a value of false if the parameter you pass to it is a number. When you use the isNaN() function within a form validation function, you place the isNaN() function call directly within a condition comparison in an `if` decision structure using the following syntax:

```
if (isNaN(input_string) == true) {
    //commands to execute if input_value is not a number
}
```

In this syntax, the *input_string* parameter is the value that the function evaluates as numeric or non-numeric.

Suppose you have a form named frmExample that contains a text input named txtInput1. You would use the following code to evaluate whether the current value of txtInput1 is a number and display an alert advising the user to enter a number if the current value is not a number:

```
if (isNaN(document.frmExample.txtInput1.value) == true) {
    alert("Please enter a number.");
}
```

Now you will modify the Log On Web page form validation function by adding a condition that calls the isNaN() function and evaluates whether or not the value that the user enters in the PIN text input is a number. If the value is not a number, the isNaN() function returns the value true. Then, the form validation function displays an alert advising the user to enter a number for the PIN value, selects the current PIN text using the select() method, and returns the value false. If the PIN value is a number, the isNaN() function returns the value false. Program execution moves to the `else` part of the structure and displays the alert advising the user that the PIN value is valid.

To modify the form validation function to use the isNaN() function to test for numeric values:

1. Switch back to Visual Studio .NET and modify the form validation function so your function looks like Figure 4-4. (Note that you delete the command that creates the alert that displays the PIN value.)

2. Save the file, then switch to Internet Explorer and press **F5** to refresh your display.

3. Type **asdf** in the PIN text input and click **Submit Query**. An alert appears displaying the message "PIN value must be a number," which is the message that appears when the isNaN() function evaluates that the PIN value is not numeric. Click **OK** to close the alert.

4. Type **12345** in the PIN text input and click **Submit Query**. An alert appears displaying the message "Please enter a four-digit PIN number," confirming that the code that validates the range of numbers is working correctly. Click **OK** to close the alert.

```
function validEntries() {
     var pinValue = parseFloat(document.frmLogin.txtPIN.value);
     //evaluate PIN value to determine if it is valid
     if (isNaN(pinValue) == true) {
          alert("PIN value must be a number.");
          document.frmLogin.txtPIN.select();
          return false;
     } else if ((pinValue < 1) || (pinValue > 9999)) {
          alert("Please enter a four-digit PIN number.");
          document.frmLogin.txtPIN.select();
          return false;
     } else {
          alert("PIN value is valid.");
          return true;
     }
}
```

Add/modify
this code

**Figure 4-4**    Using the isNaN() function in the form validation function

5. Type **1234** in the PIN text input and click **Submit Query**. Because this is a valid PIN value, an alert appears displaying the message "PIN value is valid." Click **OK** to close the alert. A Web page appears displaying the message "The page cannot be displayed," which confirms that the validation function returned the value true, and the browser attempted to submit the form to the Web server.

6. Click the **Back** button on the browser toolbar to redisplay the previous Web page.

## Using Date Objects to Validate Date Inputs

Recall that JavaScript has built-in objects that have associated properties, events, and methods. For example, in Chapter 3 when you needed to display HTML form text input values as currency values with two decimal places, you created a Number object and assigned its value as the value in a form text input. Then you used the Number object's toFixed() method to format the value so it had two decimal places. To test whether or not a text input contains a valid date value, you create a Date object, then assign its value property as either a text string or a value represented by a variable, using the following syntax:

```
var date_object_name = new Date(date_value)
```

If *date_value* is a string literal, you must enclose the value in quotation marks. For example, the following code creates a new date object named testDate and sets its value as 12/14/2005: `var testDate = new Date("12/14/2005");`. If *date_value* references a variable or a form element, you do not enclose the name in quotation marks. When you pass an empty string literal ("") to the Date object, the Date object assumes the value of the current client workstation date.

When you create a new date object and assign its value, if *date_value* is not a valid date, the JavaScript interpreter returns the "NaN" symbolic constant. You use the following general syntax to create a new date object, evaluate whether a date object is a valid date value, and then execute commands if the date value is not valid:

```
var date_object_name = new Date(value);
if (date_object_name == "NaN") {
    //commands to execute if value is not a date
}
```

Suppose you have a form named frmExample that contains a text input named txtDateInput. You would use the following code to evaluate whether the current value of txtDateInput is a date and display an alert advising the user to enter a date in the correct format if the current value is not a date:

```
var dateObject = ↵
    new Date(document.frmExample.txtDateInput);
    if (dateObject == "NaN") {
    alert("Please enter a date in the format MM/DD/YYYY.");
}
```

JavaScript supports many valid date formats. A date can consist of a combination of numbers and formatting characters, as in "12/04/1984" or "12-04-1984." A date can also be a combination of the month name along with the day number, year number, and formatting characters, as in "12 December 1984" or "December 4, 1984." You can represent a month or date number with or without leading zeroes. For example, you can represent a date as "02/07/1970" or as "2/7/1970." If you represent a year using only the last two digits, as in "02/07/70," JavaScript assumes the century digits are 19, so the year would be 1970.

You represent different date formats using a lowercase *m* to specify each digit in the month number, a lowercase *d* to specify each digit in the day number, and a lowercase *y* to specify each digit in a year. You use the word *month* to specify that the month name is spelled out, as in "January." Table 4-1 summarizes some commonly used JavaScript date formats.

**Table 4-1**    Common JavaScript date formats

| Format | Example |
|---|---|
| mm/dd/yyyy (American)<br>dd/mm/yyyy (European)<br>mm/dd/yy<br><br>m/d/yyyy | 12/04/1984<br>04/12/1984<br>12/04/84 (in a two-digit year representation, the century defaults to 1900)<br>12/4/1984 (leading zero does not appear in days or months with only one digit) |
| mm-dd-yyyy<br>mm-dd-yy<br>m-d-yyyy | 12-04-1984<br>12-04-84<br>12-4-1984 |
| month d, yyyy | December 4, 1984 |
| d month yyyy | 4 December 1984 |

To make HTML forms that contain dates easier to use, you should always provide a visual cue to enable the user to enter date values in the correct format. For example, Figure 4-2 shows the date format for the Date of Birth text input as MM/DD/YYYY.

Now you will create a new date object and assign its value as the value in the Date of Birth text input on the Log On Web page. Then you will add a condition to the form validation function to evaluate whether the date object is a valid date.

To validate the date value and display an alert if the value is not valid:

1. Switch back to Visual Studio .NET and add or modify the shaded code, as shown in Figure 4-5, to create the date object, evaluate whether it contains a valid date value, and modify the alert message.

```
function validEntries() {
   var pinValue = parseFloat(document.frmLogin.txtPIN.value);
   var sdobValue = new Date(document.frmLogin.txtDOB.value);
   //evaluate PIN value to determine if it is valid
   if (isNaN(pinValue) == true) {
      alert("PIN value must be a number.");
      document.frmLogin.txtPIN.select();
      return false;
   } else if ((pinValue < 1) || (pinValue > 9999)) {
      alert("Please enter a four-digit PIN number.");
      document.frmLogin.txtPIN.select();
      return false;
   } else if (sdobValue == "NaN") {
      alert("Please enter a date in the format MM/DD/YYYY.");
      document.frmLogin.txtDOB.select();
      return false;
   } else {
      alert("Input values are valid.");
      return true;
   }
}
```

Add this code

Modify this code

**Figure 4-5**   Code to validate the date value

2. Save the file, then switch to Internet Explorer and press **F5** to reload the file.

3. Type **1234** in the PIN text input and **12/04/1984** in the Date of Birth text input, and then click **Submit Query**. Because these are both valid values, an alert appears reporting that the input values are valid.

4. Click **OK** to close the alert, then click the **Back** button on the browser toolbar to redisplay the Log On Web page. Because the PIN text input is a password input, its value is cleared. The date value still appears in the Date of Birth text input.

5. Type **1234** in the PIN text input, change the Date of Birth text input value to **12041984**, then click **Submit Query**. Because the Date of Birth input value is not a valid date, an alert appears advising you to enter a date in the correct format. Click **OK** to close the alert. The current date value appears selected.

Although you can use the Date object to evaluate whether an input string is formatted as a date, you cannot use the Date object to validate that the month or day numbers represent valid date values, as you will see next. To see how JavaScript interprets invalid month and day values, you will add to your data validation function an alert that displays the entered date value after the user clicks the Submit Query button.

To enter and display invalid date values:

1. Switch back to Visual Studio .NET and add the following command just below the `else` portion of the `if/else if` decision structure:

```
} else {
    alert("Date value:" + sdobValue);
    alert("Input values are valid.");
    return true;
}
```

2. Save the file, then switch to Internet Explorer and press **F5** to reload the file.

3. Type **1234** for the PIN value, change the Date of Birth value to **13/04/1984**, and then click **Submit Query**. Note that this is not a valid date, because there are only 12 months in a year.

4. The alert displays the message "Date value: Fri Jan 4 00:00:00 CST 1985." (Your time zone may be different.) Note that this date is one month beyond the date of 12/04/1984. Because you specified the month number as 13, the JavaScript interpreter added one month to the last legal month value, which is 12.

5. Click **OK** to close the alert displaying the date. The alert appears advising that the input values are valid, confirming that the JavaScript interpreter did not flag the invalid month number.

6. Click **OK** to close the alert advising that the values are valid, then click the **Back** button on the browser toolbar to redisplay the Web page.

7. Type **1234** for the PIN value and **12/32/1984** for the Date of Birth value, then click **Submit Query**. This is not a valid date, because December has only 31 days. The alert displays the message "Date value: Tue Jan 1 00:00:00 CST 1985." Note that this date is one day beyond the date of 12/31/1984, so the JavaScript interpreter added one day to the last legal day value, which is 31.

8. Click **OK** to close the alert displaying the date. The alert appears advising that the input values are valid, confirming that the JavaScript interpreter did not flag the invalid day number.

9. Click **OK** to close the alert advising that the values are valid, then click the **Back** button on the browser toolbar to redisplay the Web page.

10. Switch back to Visual Studio .NET and close **logon_VALIDATE.htm**.

The JavaScript interpreter does not flag invalid numeric date values, but instead converts them to future dates. Table 3-11 describes the getMonth() and getDate() Date object methods, which extract the month number and the day number of a date object. However, you cannot use these methods in a form validation function, because of the way the getMonth() and getDate() methods work.

The getMonth() method always returns a value between 0 and 11. If the user enters a month value from 1 to 12, the getMonth() method returns the actual value minus 1. If the user enters a month value between 13 and 24, the getMonth() method returns the actual value minus 13. If the user enters a month value that is greater than 24, the getMonth() method divides the month number by 12, subtracts 1 from the remainder, and then returns the resulting value. For example, if the user enters 30 for the month value, the getMonth() method divides 30 by 12, which results in 2 with a remainder of 6. It subtracts 1 from the remainder of 6, and returns the value 5.

Similarly, the getDate() method always returns a value between 1 and 31. If the user enters a value between 1 and 31, the method returns the actual value. If the user enters a value between 32 and 62, the method returns the value minus 31. If the user enters a value greater than 62, the method divides the value by 31, then returns the remainder. For example, if the user enters the value 75, the method divides 75 by 31, which results in 2 with a remainder of 13, so the method returns the value 13.

To explicitly evaluate whether or not month and day values fall within a range of allowed values, you either create separate text inputs on the form for entering the month, day, and year values or parse the month, day, and year from the single text input using string parsing methods. After separating the date components (using either approach), you can then construct the form validation function to evaluate them individually.

## USING ARRAYS TO REFERENCE FORM ELEMENTS

An **array** is a data structure that you use to store and process similar data items. You can visualize an array as a single-column spreadsheet. In a spreadsheet, each row has a number that appears on the left side of the first column. In an array, the row number is called the array **index**. Each row also has an associated data value in the first column, which is called an array element or item. This kind of an array is called a **one-dimensional array**.

Arrays can be particularly useful when you want to validate several inputs having the same data type. Suppose an HTML form contains several text inputs in which users enter date values. To validate these date values, you could create a Date object for each text input and pass it to the validation function multiple times. Or, you could create multiple Date objects and place the object names in an array. You could then use a loop within a form validation function to validate each Date object in the array.

In this section, you will learn how to create and process an array. You will also learn how to use arrays to reference HTML document objects.

## Creating and Processing an Array

To create an array, you create an instance of the JavaScript built-in Array object using the following syntax:

```
var arrayName = new Array([size]);
```

In this syntax, *arrayName* is the name of the new array, and must follow the rules for naming all JavaScript variables. The *size* parameter is optional. If you specify a *size* value, the JavaScript interpreter allocates the memory for storing this number of rows in the array. If you omit the *size* parameter, the interpreter automatically creates a new array row when you assign a value to a row. Even when you specify the size of the array with the *size* parameter, if you increment the array index past the initial *size* value and assign a value to the new array item, you will increase the size of the array. If you try to reference an array item that is beyond the maximum array size, an error will occur.

In most cases, it is probably best to omit the *size* parameter. If you select a *size* value that is too small, the JavaScript interpreter will automatically create new rows as they are needed. If you select a *size* value that is too large, however, the unused rows will remain idle and waste memory space.

You would use the following code to create a new array named northwoodsCourses:

```
var northwoodsCourses = new Array();
```

To create a new array item and assign a value to it, you use the following syntax:

```
arrayName[index] = value;
```

In this syntax, *index* references the row number to which you are assigning the associated *value*. In JavaScript, the first index value in an array starts with 0. You would use the following command to assign the first value in the northwoodsCourses array as "Intro. to Information Systems":

```
northwoodsCourses[0] = "Intro. to Information Systems";
```

To reference a specific array value, you use the following syntax:

```
value = arrayName[index];
```

For example, to assign the value that is in the first row of the northwoodsCourses array to a variable named courseCurrent, you would use the following command:

```
courseCurrent = northwoodsCourses[0];
```

Because arrays contain multiple values, you usually use loops to process array values. The starting index value is always 0. To determine the final array index value, you use the Array object's length property. The **length property** returns the number of elements in the array, which is a value that is one greater than the largest index value in the array. For example, if an array contains five elements, its length value is 5, and its index values are numbered 0 through 4. You would use the following syntax to assign the length of the northwoodsCourses array to a variable named numberCourses:

```
numberCourses = northwoodsCourses.length;
```

To gain experience using an array, you will work with the Web page shown in Figure 4-6, which displays the names of courses offered at Northwoods University.

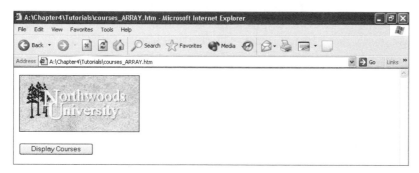

**Figure 4-6**   Web page to display courses using array processing

When the user clicks Display Courses, a JavaScript function dynamically writes the course names on the Web page. You will write a JavaScript function to create an array for this Web page, populate the array with five course names, and then create a loop in the function that steps through the array and writes the value of each array item on the Web page using the document.write() method.

To write a function to create and display an array of course names:

1. In Visual Studio .NET, open **courses.htm** from the Chapter4 folder on your Data Disk, and save the file as **courses_ARRAY.htm** in the Chapter4\Tutorials folder on your Solution Disk.

2. Create a new blank line just above the closing **</head>** tag, then add the code in Figure 4-7 to create, populate, and process the array.

```
<script language="javascript">
     <!--
     function displayCourses() {
          //create array and add items
          var northwoodsCourses = new Array();
          northwoodsCourses[0] = "Intro. to Information Systems";
          northwoodsCourses[1] = "Systems Analysis";
          northwoodsCourses[2] = "Database Management";
          northwoodsCourses[3] = "Programming in C++";
          northwoodsCourses[4] = "Web-Based Systems";
          for (var i=0; i < northwoodsCourses.length; i++) {
               document.write (northwoodsCourses[i] + "<br>");
          }
     }
     //-->
</script>
```

**Figure 4-7**    JavaScript code to create and process an array

3. Modify the tag for the Display Courses button by adding the following code to create an event handler that calls the function:

   ```
   <input type="button" value="Display Courses"
   onclick="displayCourses();">
   ```

4. Save the file, then switch to Internet Explorer and open **courses_ARRAY.htm** from the Chapter4\Tutorials folder on your Solution Disk. The Web page appears as shown in Figure 4-6.

5. Click **Display Courses**. The course listing created by the array processing function appears on the Web page as shown in Figure 4-8. (The Northwoods logo and Display Courses button no longer appear because they are overwritten by the function output.)

**Figure 4-8**    Course listing created by array processing

6. Switch back to Visual Studio .NET and close **courses_ARRAY.htm**.

## Using Arrays That Reference Document Objects

Recall from Chapter 3 that JavaScript commands reference Web page objects using the HTML document object model (DOM). When your browser loads an HTML document, it creates arrays to reference DOM objects. For example, if an HTML document contains two separate sets of <form> tags, the browser creates an array named *forms* to reference the document's form objects. You could reference these forms using the following dot syntax:

```
document.forms[0]
document.forms[1]
```

The dot syntax `document.forms[0]` references the form that the first form tag in the document defines, and `document.forms[1]` references the form that the second form tag in the document defines. You can use similar dot syntax to reference form attribute values. For example, you would use the following dot syntax to reference the name attribute value of the first document form: `document.forms[0].name`.

Similarly, the browser maintains an array named *elements* to reference all the elements in each form. Suppose that the first form in a document contains two text inputs. You could reference these text inputs using the following dot syntax:

```
document.forms[0].elements[0]
document.forms[0].elements[1]
```

As with forms, `document.forms[0].elements[0]` references the first element in the form, and `document.forms[0].elements[1]` corresponds to the second element within the form. You can use dot syntax to reference element attribute values, such as the element name, type, and value. For example, you would use the following dot syntax to reference the value that is currently stored in the first element in the first form: `document.forms[0].elements[0].value`.

These document arrays are useful when you need to write JavaScript commands to systematically examine all of the objects in a document or a form. For example, you might want to examine all of the text inputs in a form to determine whether any of them have been left blank, or you might want to examine all of the radio buttons in a form to determine which one the user has selected.

Now you will write a JavaScript function that uses the elements array and dot syntax to reference form element property values in the completed Northwoods University Log On form that you created earlier in the chapter. (A copy of the completed file is stored as logon_DONE.htm in the Chapter4 folder on your Data Disk.) You will modify the validation function so it displays a series of alerts that report the form element index numbers and values.

To use the elements array in a JavaScript function:

1. In Visual Studio .NET, open **logon_DONE.htm** from the Chapter4 folder on your Data Disk, and save the file as **logon_ARRAY.htm** in the Chapter4\Tutorials folder on your Solution Disk.

2. Modify the final `else` condition within the form validation function so it appears as follows:

```
} else {
  for (var i=0; i < document.forms[0].elements.length; ↵
  i++) {
     alert("Element: " + i + " Value: " + ↵
     document.forms[0].elements[i].value);
  }
  return true;
}
```

3. Save the file, then switch to Internet Explorer and open **logon_ARRAY.htm** from the Chapter4\Tutorials folder on your Solution Disk. The Log On Web page appears.

4. Type **Miller** for the User ID, **1234** for the PIN, and **12/04/1984** for the Date of Birth, then click **Submit Query**. An alert appears with the message "Element: 0 Value: Miller," which reports the element number (0) and value ("Miller") for the first form element, which is the User ID text input. Click **OK** to close the alert.

5. A second alert appears with the message "Element: 1 Value: 1234," which reports the element number (1) and value ("1234") for the second form element, which is the PIN text input. Click **OK** to close the alert.

6. A third alert appears with the message "Element: 2 Value: 12/04/1984," which reports the element number (2) and value ("12/04/1984") for the third form element, which is the Date of Birth text input. Click **OK** to close the alert.

7. A fourth alert appears with the message "Element: 3 Value: Submit Query," which reports the element number (3) and value ("Submit Query") for the fourth form element, which is the Submit Query button. Click **OK** to close the alert. Click the **Back** button on your browser toolbar to redisplay the Web page.

8. Switch to Visual Studio .NET and close the **logon_ARRAY.htm** file.

# VALIDATING RADIO BUTTON, CHECK BOX, AND SELECTION LIST VALUES

The form validation functions you have created so far evaluate values that users enter into form text inputs. Recall that HTML forms also allow users to specify input values using form controls such as radio buttons, check boxes, and selection lists. Referencing the values that these controls represent in JavaScript commands requires different programming approaches from those used for form text inputs. The following sections describe how to use JavaScript commands to reference and validate values that HTML forms represent as radio buttons, check boxes, and selection lists.

## Validating Values Represented by Radio Buttons

Recall that a radio button group allows the user to select a value from a predefined group of related values. Figure 4-9 shows the tags and associated radio buttons for a radio button group that allows the user to select a color from a predefined list of colors.

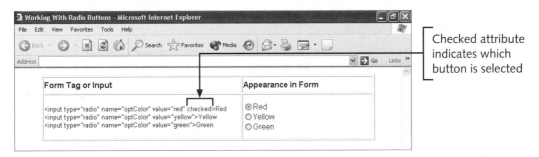

**Figure 4-9**    Example radio button group

Recall that you define a radio button group by specifying that multiple radio buttons have the same name attribute. In the tags in Figure 4-9, the name attribute value ("optColor") is the same for each radio button. The first radio button in the group contains the checked attribute, which indicates that the button is currently selected. Only one button in a radio button group can be checked at a time.

When a form contains radio buttons, you often need to verify that the user has selected (checked) one of the radio group buttons. To do this, the form validation function must examine each radio button in the radio group and evaluate whether its checked property value is true. To support this process, the browser maintains an array for every radio button group. You use the following syntax to reference an individual radio button within an HTML form radio button group array:

> document.*form_name*.*radio_group_name*[*i*]

In this syntax, *form_name* is the name of the form that contains the radio buttons, and *radio_group_name* is the value of the name attribute of each radio button in the group. The array index value *i* references the number of the radio button within the group, and corresponds to the order in which you define the buttons in the form. For example, suppose the form in Figure 4-9 is named frmInput. You would reference the first (Red) radio button as `document.frmInput.optColor[0]`, the second (Yellow) radio button as `document.frmInput.optColor[1]`, and the third (Green) radio button as `document.frmInput.optColor[2]`.

As with other document objects, you can use dot syntax to reference radio button properties. For example, you would use the following dot syntax to reference the value attribute of the third radio button: `document.frmInput.optColor[2].value`. To evaluate whether a radio button is currently checked and then execute some commands if the button is checked, you use the following syntax:

```
if (document.form_name.radio_group_name[i].checked) {
    commands to execute if the button is checked
}
```

You would use the following code to determine whether the first button in the optColor radio button group is selected and then display the button's value property:

```
if (document.frmInput.optColor[0].checked) {
    alert("Color value is: " +
    document.frmInput.optColor[0].value);
}
```

To gain experience evaluating and displaying radio button properties, you will use the Northwoods University Faculty Web page shown in Figure 4-10. This Web page enables users to enter data about Northwoods University faculty members into the organizational database. Faculty information includes the faculty member's ID number, last name, first name, office location, and telephone number. Faculty members can have one of four different ranks: Full, Associate, Assistant, or Instructor. The form represents these values as a radio button group named optRank.

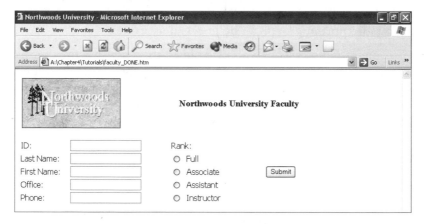

**Figure 4-10**    Northwoods University Faculty Web page

You will add a form validation function to this Web page that confirms that the user selected one of the radio buttons, and then displays the value of the selected radio button. If the user does not select a radio button, an alert will appear advising the user to select a faculty rank. Recall that a form validation function uses an `if/else if` structure to validate form input values. When an input value has an error, its associated validation condition structure evaluates as false, and an alert appears advising the user how to correct the invalid input.

To validate that the user selects a radio button, you will declare a variable named rankChecked and initially set the variable value as false. You will then use a `for` loop to evaluate the checked attribute for each radio button in the radio button group array. If the loop finds a radio button for which the checked attribute value is true, the function sets the value of rankChecked to true and displays an alert showing the value of the selected radio button. If the loop does not find a radio button in which the checked attribute is true, the rankChecked value remains false. The function's `if/else if` structure will then evaluate the value of rankChecked. If the value is true, the radio group passes its validation test. If the value is false, the function displays an alert advising the user to select a radio button.

To add the radio button validation function to the Faculty Web page:

1. In Visual Studio .NET, open **faculty.htm** from the Chapter4 folder on your Data Disk and then save the file as **faculty_DONE.htm** in the Chapter4\Tutorials folder on your Solution Disk.

2. Click the **HTML** tab to switch to HTML view, create a new blank line just above the closing `</head>` tag in the file, then add the script code in Figure 4-11.

```
<script language="javascript">
  <!--
    function validateRank() {
       //variable to evaluate if radio button is checked
       var rankChecked = false;
       //loop to check if user checked a radio button
       for (var i=0; i < document.frmFaculty.optRank.length; i++) {
          if (document.frmFaculty.optRank[i].checked) {
             rankChecked = true;
             alert ("Current faculty rank is " +
             document.frmFaculty.optRank[i].value);
          }
       }
       //data validation conditions
       if (rankChecked == false) {
          alert("Please select a faculty rank.");
          return false;
       } else {
          alert ("Form values are valid.");
          return true;
       }
    }
  //-->
</script>
```

**Figure 4-11**    Script to validate and display form radio button values

3. Add the following onsubmit event handler to the `<form>` tag:

```
<form name="frmFaculty" action="ignore"
    onsubmit="return validateRank()">
```

4. Save the file, then switch to Internet Explorer and open **faculty_DONE.htm** from the Chapter4\Tutorials folder on your Solution Disk. The form appears as shown in Figure 4-10.

5. Do not select a radio button. Click **Submit**. The alert asking you to select a faculty rank appears. Click **OK** to close the alert.

6. Select the **Full** radio button, then click **Submit**. An alert appears advising you that the current rank is FULL (which is the value associated with the first radio button). Click **OK** to close the alert.

7. An alert appears advising you that the form values are valid. Click **OK** to close the alert. The Web page appears displaying the message "The page cannot be displayed," which confirms that the validation function returned the value true, and the browser attempted to submit the form to the Web server. Click the **Back** button on the browser toolbar to redisplay the Faculty Web page.

8. Switch back to Visual Studio .NET and close **faculty_DONE.htm**.

## Validating Values Represented by Check Boxes

Recall that you can use a check box on a Web form to define an element that can have one of two opposite values, such as true or false, or on or off. Figure 4-12 shows the tag for a check box that specifies whether an order should be delivered using the Rush Delivery option. Note that if the checked attribute is present, the check box appears checked.

**Figure 4-12**   Example check box

Unlike radio buttons, check boxes do not exist in groups, so in many situations you do not need to use an array or a loop to determine whether a check box is checked. Instead, you directly evaluate whether or not the check box is checked in the condition of an if decision structure, using the following syntax:

```
if (document.form_name.checkbox_name.checked == true) {
   commands to execute if the check box is checked
} else {
   commands to execute if the check box is cleared
}
```

To gain experience working with check boxes, you will use the Terms Web page in Figure 4-13, which allows users to enter into the organizational database information about course terms at Northwoods University. Users can enter the term ID, enter the term description (such as "Spring 2005"), and use a check box to specify whether enrollment during the term is open or closed. If the check box is checked, enrollment is open, and if the check box is cleared, enrollment is closed. Now you will write a function that evaluates whether or not the check box is checked. If the check box is checked, the function will display an alert advising the user that enrollment for the current term is open. If the check box is cleared, the function will display an alert advising the user that enrollment for the current term is closed.

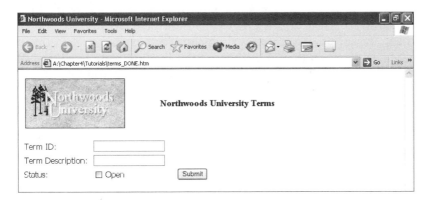

**Figure 4-13**    Northwoods University Terms Web page

To write a function to evaluate whether the check box is checked or cleared:

1. In Visual Studio .NET, open **terms.htm** from the Chapter4 folder on your Data Disk and save the file as **terms_DONE.htm** in the Chapter4\Tutorials folder on your Solution Disk.

2. Click the **HTML** tab to switch to HTML view, create a new blank line before the closing **</head>** tag in the file, then add the script code in Figure 4-14.

```
<script language="javascript">
    <!--
        function evaluateCheckBox() {
            if (document.frmTerms.chkStatus.checked == true) {
                alert("Current term status = Open");
            } else {
                alert("Current term status = Closed");
            }
        }
    //-->
</script>
```

**Figure 4-14**    Script to evaluate a form check box value

3. Add the following onsubmit event handler to the **<form>** tag:

```
<form name="frmTerms" action="action marker"
onsubmit="evaluateCheckBox()">
```

Note that because you will submit the form to the Web server whether the check box is checked or cleared, you can omit the **return** keyword in the onsubmit event handler.

4. Save the file, then switch to Internet Explorer and open **terms_DONE.htm** from the Chapter4\Tutorials folder on your Solution Disk. The form appears as shown in Figure 4-13.

5. Do not check the check box. Click **Submit**. An alert appears advising "Current term status = Closed." Click **OK** to close the alert. Because the browser cannot perform the specified form action, which is "action marker," an error message appears advising you that "The page cannot be displayed." Click the **Back** button on the browser toolbar to redisplay the Terms Web page.

6. Check the **Status** check box, then click **Submit**. An alert appears advising "Current term status = Open." Click **OK** to close the alert, then click the **Back** button on the browser toolbar to redisplay the Terms Web page.

7. Switch back to Visual Studio .NET and close **terms_DONE.htm**.

## Validating Values from Selection Lists

Recall that you can create a selection list in a Web page form from which the user can select predefined values. You use a selection list rather than radio buttons when there are more than five or six choices or when the choices change frequently. By allowing the user to select from a list rather than requiring the user to type a value explicitly, you save the user time and effort. A selection list also ensures that the selected value is valid. In contrast, when a user types a value, there is a chance that the value may contain spelling or formatting errors. Figure 4-15 shows an example of a Web page form selection list.

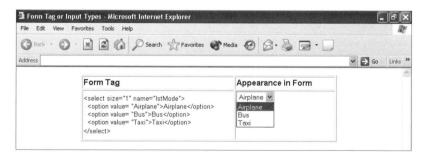

**Figure 4-15**    Example selection list

Recall that you define the list using the **<select>** tag, and that you define the individual list elements using the **<option>** tag. Also recall that when the size attribute is 1, the list is a drop-down list that displays only the selected item. To view the rest of the list selections, the user must open the list.

When a form contains a selection list, the browser maintains an array named *options* to reference the list's elements. You can reference each list element using the following syntax:

```
document.form_name.list_name.options[i]
```

In this syntax, the index *i* references each individual list element. If the Web page form name in Figure 4-15 is frmInputs and the selection list name is lstMode, you would reference the value of the first list option ("Airplane") as `document.frmInputs. lstMode.options[0]`, the second list option value ("Bus") as `document.frmInputs. lstMode.options[1]`, and the third list option value ("Taxi") as `document. frmInputs.lstMode.options[2]`. You could reference the text associated with the first list element as `document.frmInputs.lstMode[0].text`.

A selection list has a **selectedIndex property**, which specifies the index value of the list element that is currently selected. If the selectedIndex property value is 0 or greater, a list item is selected. For a list in which no list item is selected, the selectedIndex property value is the default value, −1.

 If a selection list's size attribute value is 1, the selectedIndex property value is always 0 when the form first opens. If you want to ensure that the user explicitly selects a value from a list, you cannot use a drop-down list, so you should set the list's size attribute equal to 2 or greater.

In the list in Figure 4-15, if the user selects the first list item ("Airplane"), the selectedIndex value is 0. To reference the selectedIndex property of this selection list, you would use the following command: `document.frmInputs.lstMode.selectedIndex`. You would use the following code to declare a variable named currentSelection, assign to it the current selectedIndex value, and then display an alert showing the value of the selected list item:

```
var currentSelection = ⤸
document.frmInputs.lstMode.selectedIndex;
alert("Current mode is " + ⤸
document.frmInputs.lstMode.⤸
options[currentSelection].text);
```

To gain experience working with selection lists, you will use the Northwoods University Locations Web page shown in Figure 4-16. This Web page allows users to enter information about classrooms, offices, and other locations on the Northwoods University campus into the organizational database. Users enter the location ID, building code, room number, and room capacity. They can select the building code values from a selection list, which has the following values: CR (Classroom), BUS (Business), LIB (Library), SCI (Science), and GYM (Gymnasium). When the form first opens, no building code value is selected, so the user must explicitly select a value from the list.

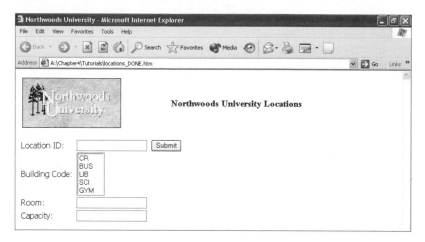

**Figure 4-16**    Northwoods University Locations Web page

Now you will write a form validation function that confirms that the user selected a value from the building codes list and then displays an alert showing the selected value. The function will first confirm that the user selected a building code value by declaring a variable to reference the list's selectedIndex property and then evaluating the variable's value. If the selectedIndex value is −1, which indicates that the user did not select a list value, an alert will appear asking the user to select a value. The form validation function will then return the value false. If the user has selected a value from the list, an alert will appear displaying the selected list item text, and the function will return the value true and submit the form to the Web server.

To write the function to validate and display the list selection:

1. In Visual Studio .NET, open **locations.htm** from the Chapter4 folder on your Data Disk, then save the file as **locations_DONE.htm** in the Chapter4\Tutorials folder on your Solution Disk.

2. Click the **HTML** tab to switch to HTML view, create a new blank line just above the closing **</head>** tag in the file, then add the script code in Figure 4-17.

3. Add the following onsubmit event handler to the **<form>** tag:

```
<form name="frmLocations" action="action marker"
onsubmit="return validateList()">
```

4. Save the file, then switch to Internet Explorer and open **locations_DONE.htm** from the Chapter4\Tutorials folder on your Solution Disk. The form appears as shown in Figure 4-16.

```
<script language="javascript">
  <!--
    function validateList() {
       var selectedValue = document.frmLocations.lstBuilding.selectedIndex;
       if (selectedValue == -1) {
          alert("Please select a building code.");
          return false;
       } else {
          alert("Current building code is " +
          document.frmLocations.lstBuilding.options[selectedValue].text);
          return true;
       }
    }
  //-->
</script>
```

**Figure 4-17**    Script to evaluate selection list values

5. Do not select a value from the Building Codes list. Click **Submit**. An alert appears asking you to select a building code. Click **OK** to close the alert.

6. Select **CR** from the Building Code selection list, then click **Submit**. An alert appears showing the current building value as "CR." Click **OK** to close the alert. A Web page appears displaying the message "The page cannot be displayed," which confirms that the validation function returned the value true, and the browser attempted to submit the form to the Web server. Click the **Back** button on the browser toolbar to redisplay the Locations Web page.

7. Switch back to Visual Studio .NET and close **locations_DONE.htm**.

## USING THE SCRIPT DEBUGGER TO DEBUG CLIENT-SIDE SCRIPTS

In Chapter 3 you learned how to configure Internet Explorer to display script error messages, and you learned how to retrieve information about script errors by double-clicking the script error icon 🔼 on the Internet Explorer status bar. As you create more complex client-side scripts, you need to learn more sophisticated debugging approaches. Recall that the Script Debugger is an application that allows you to step through individual script commands, locate the exact line on which an error occurs, and view how script variable values change during execution. When you install Visual Studio .NET on your workstation and configure Internet Explorer to use the default script error settings, a Script Debugger error message box similar to the one in Figure 4-18 appears when a script error occurs.

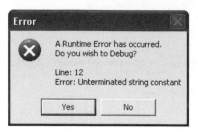

**Figure 4-18**    Script Debugger error message

This message provides two choices: You can click No to ignore the error and open the document in Internet Explorer, or click Yes to open the document in the Script Debugger. The following subsections explore techniques for finding script errors using Script Debugger messages and describe how to use the Script Debugger environment in Visual Studio .NET.

## Finding Errors Using Script Debugger Messages

If Visual Studio .NET is installed on your computer, the Script Debugger should be installed also. If the Script Debugger is not installed, you can download the Script Debugger from Microsoft's Web site and install it. Instructions for downloading and installing the Script Debugger are presented in Chapter 3 in the section titled "Configuring Your Workstation to Display the Script Debugger Error Message Box."

To find errors using Script Debugger error messages, you note the line number on which the error occurred, then click No on the default error message dialog box to ignore the error and open the Web page in Internet Explorer. Then you examine the associated script command line in Visual Studio .NET and try to locate the error. Now you will use a Web page file named error1.htm to view the default Script Debugger error messages and examine the corresponding script code lines in Visual Studio .NET.

To view the default Script Debugger error messages and corresponding script code lines:

1. In Visual Studio .NET, open **error1.htm** from the Chapter4 folder on your Data Disk, and save the file as **error1_DONE.htm** in the Chapter4\ Tutorials folder on your Solution Disk. The Northwoods University Faculty Web page appears in Design view. Click the **HTML** tab to view the document in HTML view.

2. Switch to Internet Explorer and open **error1_DONE.htm** from the Chapter4\Tutorials folder on your Solution Disk. The error message in Figure 4-18 appears, which reports that the error is on line 12. (Your line number may be different.) Click **No** to close the error message. The Web page appears in the browser window.

If the error message in Figure 4-18 does not appear, click Tools on the menu bar, click Internet Options, click the Advanced tab, clear the *Disable script debugging* check box, and check the *Display a notification about every script error* check box. Then close and reopen Internet Explorer and repeat Step 2. If you still do not see the error message in Figure 4-18, you probably need to install the Script Debugger on your workstation. The "Configuring Your Workstation to Display the Script Debugger Error Message Box" section in Chapter 3 provides instructions for downloading and installing the Script Debugger.

3. Select the **Full** radio button, then click **Submit**. Another error message appears that reports that an error is on line 33. (Your line number may be different.) Do not click any buttons on the error message.

The first error message, which reports that the error is on line 12, appears when the browser initially loads the Web page. The second error message, which reports that the error occurs on line 33, appears when the JavaScript interpreter executes the script associated with the Submit button's onclick event handler. You will often find that the error is not on exactly the same line of code that the error message reports. This discrepancy between source code line numbers and Script Debugger error messages exists because the JavaScript interpreter interprets line numbers differently than the Visual Studio .NET editor. However, the error message usually provides an idea of the approximate line on which the error occurs. Now you will switch to Visual Studio .NET and examine the code lines that appear in the error messages.

To examine the code lines that generate the error messages:

1. Switch to Visual Studio .NET and move the insertion point to **line 12** in error1_DONE.htm. (If your first error message displayed a different line number, move to that line number instead.)

The Visual Studio .NET editor displays the current line number, column number, and character position in the bottom status bar. The line number is preceded by the text "Ln," the column number by the text "Col," and the character number by the text "Ch." The column number indicates how many spaces the insertion point is from the left edge of the window. The character number indicates how many characters the insertion point is from the first character in the line.

2. Examine the code on line 12 (or the line number that your error message indicates). This is a command in the validateRank() function that creates an `if` decision structure to evaluate whether the current radio button is checked. This command does not seem to have any errors.

3. Examine the code on the next line, which displays an alert showing the value of the selected radio button. Note that the alert message is not formed correctly: It is missing the closing double quotation mark in the alert message. Don't fix this error.

4. Move the insertion point to **line 33**, which is the line number that appeared on the second error message. This line consists of a paragraph tag (<p>) and appears to be correct.

5. Examine the next code line, which is the <form> tag. This tag contains the onsubmit event handler that calls the validateRank() function. Recall that the validateRank() function contains the missing double quotation mark. When an error line number refers to an HTML element that calls a JavaScript function, it is a good bet that the error is actually in the JavaScript function.

Use the following guidelines when you are finding JavaScript command errors based on the line numbers listed in Script Debugger error messages:

- Command errors may not be on the exact line that the default error message reports, but are often a few lines before or after the reported error line.

- When an error line number refers to an HTML element that calls a JavaScript function, the error is probably in the JavaScript function.

# Finding Errors Using the Script Debugger in Visual Studio .NET

The Script Debugger enables you to step through individual script commands, view how script variable values change during execution, and identify the command line on which errors occur. The following subsections show how to start the Script Debugger from a Script Debugger error message. They also describe the Script Debugger environment in Visual Studio .NET. Additional subsections describe how to view variable values during execution and how to set breakpoints in the Script Debugger.

### Starting the Script Debugger from a Script Debugger Error Message

To start the Script Debugger from a Script Debugger error message, you click Yes on the Script Debugger error message, then make selections on a series of dialog boxes to select the script debugging environment and connect the debugger to the browser execution process. Now you will select Yes on the Script Debugger error message and start the Script Debugger.

To make selections to start the Script Debugger:

1. Switch back to Internet Explorer, where the Script Debugger error message currently appears.

If the Script Debugger error message does not appear, open error1_DONE.htm in Internet Explorer, click No on the error message, select the Full radio button, then click Submit. If an Internet Explorer error message appears rather than the Script Debugger error message, close Internet Explorer, restart it, open error1_DONE.htm, click No on the error message, select the Full radio button, then click Submit.

2. Click **Yes** to start the Script Debugger. The Just-In-Time Debugging window opens as shown in Figure 4-19.

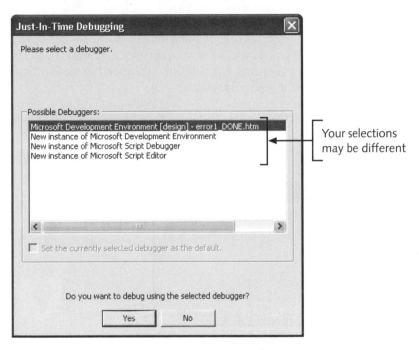

Figure 4-19     Just-In-Time Debugging window

The Just-In-Time Debugging window displays the Possible Debuggers list, which allows you to select from different debugging applications that are installed on your workstation. (Your selections may be different from the ones in Figure 4-19.) The first debugger in the list is "Microsoft Development Environment [design] – error1_DONE.htm," which is the default selection. This selection appears when Visual Studio .NET is installed on your workstation and the Web page file that generated the error, which is error1_DONE.htm, is currently open in Visual Studio .NET. The "New instance of Microsoft Development Environment" selection starts a new Visual Studio .NET session and loads the Web page file that generated the error. Other selections in the Possible Debuggers list represent other script debugging environments that are on your workstation. In this chapter, you will learn how to use the Script Debugger in Visual Studio .NET because it provides the best script debugging support currently available. Now you will select the "Microsoft Development Environment [design] – error1_DONE.htm" list item and start the Visual Studio .NET debugger.

To start the Script Debugger in Visual Studio .NET:

1. Make sure that *Microsoft Development Environment [design] – error1_DONE.htm* is selected in the Possible Debuggers list, then click **Yes**. The Attach to Process window opens. (You may need to click the Visual Studio .NET button on the taskbar to view this window.) This window specifies the type of program that

you are debugging and attaches the Script Debugger to the appropriate execution process. Because you are executing a client-side script, make sure that the *Script* check box is checked, then click **OK**.

You attach to the Common Language Runtime process if you are debugging VB .NET programs, and you attach to the Microsoft T-SQL process if you are debugging T_SQL programs that run with a SQL Server Database. These choices will not be used in this textbook.

2. The Visual Studio .NET environment opens in debugging mode. The Microsoft Development Environment window appears and displays a message stating "Microsoft JScript runtime error: Object expected," as shown in Figure 4-20.

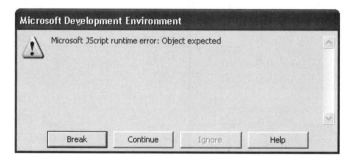

**Figure 4-20** JScript runtime error message indicating a syntax error

This error message references JScript because Microsoft refers to its version of JavaScript as JScript.

There are two basic types of program errors: syntax errors and logic errors. A **syntax error** occurs when you write a command that does not follow the rules of the programming language. Examples of JavaScript syntax errors are omitting the closing curly brace in the command that creates a function, not spelling a reserved word such as `function` correctly, or not referencing a form object name correctly using dot syntax.

A **logic error** occurs when you write a command that follows the rules of the language, but does not perform the operation as intended. For example, a logic error occurs when a loop executes too many times or too few times because you did not specify its exit condition correctly. Another logic error might occur when you create an `if/else` condition that evaluates whether a number that a user enters in a Web page form text input falls within a given range. The logic error occurs if the `if/else` condition does not evaluate correctly because you forgot to convert the text input character representation to a number using either the parseInt() or parseFloat() function.

The JScript runtime error message in Figure 4-20 usually appears when your program has a syntax error. This error dialog box contains a Break button and a Continue button.

If you click Continue, a dialog box will appear stating that no source code is available for the current location. If you click Continue on this second dialog box, the same message will appear again. If you click Break, execution will **break**, or pause temporarily. Execution will not start again until you issue a command instructing it to resume. Now you will click Continue to view the error message again. Then you will click Break to pause execution and view the Script Debugger environment.

To click Continue to view the syntax error message again, then click Break to pause execution:

1. Click **Continue** on the error message. The same error message appears again.

2. Click **Break**. The script appears in the Script Debugger environment as shown in Figure 4-21.

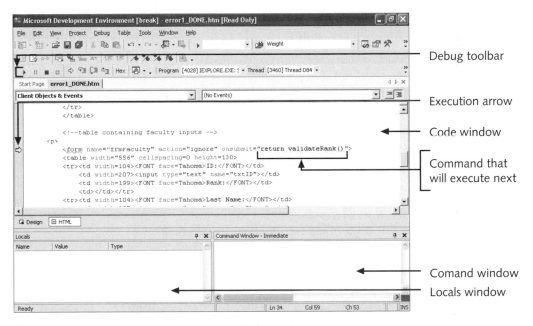

**Figure 4-21**    Visual Studio .NET Script Debugger environment

Your Script Debugger environment may display different windows. Figure 4-21 shows the debugging windows that you will learn to use in this chapter. If your environment contains extra windows, close the extra windows. If your environment does not display the Locals window in the lower area of the screen display, click Debug on the menu bar, point to Windows, then click Locals. If your environment does not display the Command window, click Debug on the menu bar, point to Windows, then click Immediate.

## The Script Debugger Environment

Figure 4-21 shows some of the basic components of the Script Debugger in the Visual Studio .NET environment. The **code window** displays the source code that is executing.

The **execution arrow** points to the program command line that will execute next. If a program command line contains multiple commands separated by semicolons, the specific command that will execute next is shaded yellow. The Locals and Immediate windows are in the bottom section of the environment, and appear only when you are debugging code. You use the **Locals window** to show the values of **local variables**, which are variables that you declare in the program using the **var** keyword. You use the **Command window** to display variable values and change variable values during execution.

 The Command window was called the Immediate window in previous versions of Visual Studio, so the terms *Command window* and *Immediate window* refer to the same window.

When you use the Script Debugger, you can create breakpoints on script commands. A **breakpoint** pauses execution on a specific command. This allows you to examine the current values of variables. It also allows you to step through subsequent commands, one line at a time, and view how execution proceeds through control structures and how variable values change.

The Debug toolbar contains buttons to control the debugging process. The first four buttons control execution. The **Continue** button ▶ restarts execution after a break. The **Break All** button ‖ breaks execution on all programs running in the Debugger environment. (The Break All button ‖ is disabled in Figure 4-21.) The **Stop Debugging** button ■ halts program execution, usually detaches the program from its execution environment, and exits the Script Debugger. The **Restart** button 🔄 restarts the program from the beginning. The environment enables the Restart button 🔄 only when execution halts, so this button appears disabled in Figure 4-21.

The next four toolbar buttons allow you to control execution during debugging. The **Show Next Statement** button ⇨ places the insertion point on the statement that will execute next. The Step Into button and Step Over button both instruct the Script Debugger to execute the next statement, but the two buttons behave differently if the next statement is a function. If the next statement is a function, the **Step Into** button steps into the first command line in the function and then pauses. The **Step Over** button executes the entire function, and then pauses on the first command after the function call. You use the **Step Out** button when execution pauses on a command line within a function, and you want to resume execution on the first command after the function call.

## Using the Script Debugger to Identify Syntax Errors

Recall that the following command causes the error in the error1_DONE.htm file:

```
alert("Current faculty rank is + document.frmFaculty.
optRank[i].value);
```

In this command, the text string "Current faculty rank is" should be enclosed in double quotation marks because it is part of a concatenation operation. The missing closing double quotation mark is a syntax error. Recall that when your script has syntax errors, the JScript runtime error message in Figure 4-20 usually appears. Visual Studio .NET does not offer additional support beyond the initial Script Debugger error message that appears in Figure 4-18, reports a line number in the vicinity of the error, and reports a brief error description. If you start the Script Debugger when this message appears, the program will break on the code line that contains the syntax error or the code line that calls the function that contains the syntax error. If you try to restart the program by clicking the Continue button ▶ on the Debug toolbar, the JScript runtime error message reappears. When you determine that your program contains a syntax error, you need to stop execution by clicking the Stop Debugging button ■. The file then appears in the Visual Studio .NET development environment, where you can correct the error. You will do this next.

To stop execution and correct the syntax error:

1. In the Script Debugger, click the **Continue** button ▶ on the Debug toolbar to resume execution. The JScript runtime error message appears.

> Another way to resume execution is to click Debug on the menu bar, then click Continue. Or, you can press F5.

2. Click **Break**. The script appears in the Script Debugger again.

3. Click the **Stop Debugging** button ■ on the toolbar. The error1_DONE.htm file appears in the Visual Studio .NET development environment.

> Another way to stop execution is to click Debug on the menu bar, then click Stop Debugging. Or, you can press Shift + F5.

4. Move the insertion point to **line 13** (or the command in your file that displays the alert showing the value of the selected radio button) and add the following double quotation mark to correct the error:

```
alert("Current faculty rank is " + document.frmFaculty.
optRank[i].value);
```

5. Save the file, then switch to Internet Explorer, where the error message in Figure 4-18 appears. Click **No** so the Script Debugger does not start, then click the **Back** button on the browser toolbar to redisplay the Web page. If necessary, click **OK** on the Internet Explorer error message.

6. Press **F5** to reload the Web page, select the **Full** radio button, and then click **Submit**. An alert appears reporting that the current faculty rank is FULL,

indicating that you have corrected the syntax error. Click **OK** to close the alert, and then click the **Back** button on the browser toolbar to redisplay the Web page.

## Viewing Variable Values in the Script Debugger

The Script Debugger helps you locate errors by enabling you to step through commands one at a time and see how variable values change during program execution. There are three different ways to view variable values in the Script Debugger: You can use ScreenTips, watches, and the Command window.

### Viewing Variable Values Using ScreenTips

One way to view variable values in the Script Debugger is to move the mouse pointer over the variable in a command in the code window and then view the variable's current value in a ScreenTip, as shown in Figure 4-22.

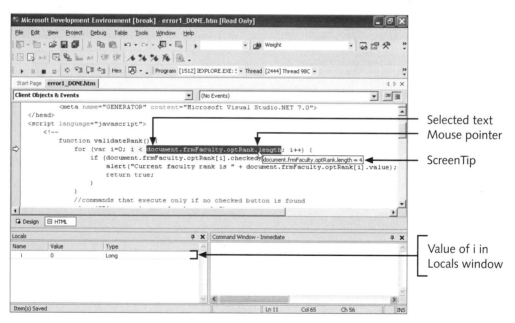

**Figure 4-22**    Using a ScreenTip to display a variable value

If a variable is a local variable, such as the loop counter *i*, you can simply place the mouse pointer onto the variable value. If the variable value is a form item, you must first select the dot syntax reference to the form item as shown in Figure 4-22, then place the mouse pointer over the selected dot syntax reference.

Now you will run the script in the error1_DONE.htm Web page, step through the program commands in the Script Debugger, and view program variable values using ScreenTips. Because you corrected the script error, the script does not generate any Script

Debugger messages. Therefore, you must start the Script Debugger in Internet Explorer and instruct it to break execution at the first JavaScript program command it encounters. You can then step through the program commands one at a time and view program variable values.

To step through the program commands and view variable values using ScreenTips:

1. In Internet Explorer, click **View** on the menu bar, point to **Script Debugger**, then click **Break at Next Statement**. The Faculty Web page still appears in the browser window.

 If the Script Debugger does not appear under View on the menu bar, click Tools on the menu bar, click Internet Options, click the Advanced tab, and then make sure that the *Disable script debugging* check box is cleared. Close Internet Explorer, then start it again and open error1_DONE.htm from the Chapter4\Tutorials folder on your Solution Disk.

2. Click the **Associate** radio button, and then click **Submit**. The Script Debugger window opens with the execution arrow on the opening `<form>` tag, and the onsubmit event handler shaded in yellow. This is the first script command in the Web page.

 If the Just-In-Time Debugging dialog box opens, click Yes, click the Microsoft Visual Studio .NET button on the taskbar if necessary, and then click OK on the Attach to Process dialog box to open the Script Debugger window. Repeat this process as necessary whenever you start a debugging session from Internet Explorer.

3. Click the **Step Into** button 与≣ to execute the next command. The execution arrow jumps to the first command in the validateRank() function, which is the command that initializes the `for` loop that evaluates which radio button is checked. The insertion point and yellow shading indicate that the first item in the `for` loop specification (`var i = 0;`) will execute next.

 You can also press F11 to execute the next command.

Three separate items are in the `for` loop specification: `var i = 0;` declares and initializes the loop counter variable; `i < document.frmFaculty.optRank.length;` specifies the loop exit condition; and `i++` specifies how the loop increments the loop counter. As you step through the script commands, the first item executes once, when the loop initializes. The second and third items execute every time the loop repeats. Now you will step through the loop.

To step through the loop:

1. Click the **Step Into** button ⟱≣. The insertion point and yellow shading jump to the second item in the `for` loop specification (`i < document.frmFaculty.optRank.length;`), which will execute next. Note that the value of `i` appears as 0 in the Locals window. (Recall that the Locals window displays the current values of all local variables.)

2. Select the **document.frmFaculty.optRank.length** text in the shaded code, then move the mouse pointer over the selected code, as shown in Figure 4-22. The ScreenTip "document.frmFaculty.optRank.length=4" appears, which shows the current value of the dot syntax expression.

3. Click the **Step Into** button ⟱≣ again. The execution arrow jumps to the next command, which is the `if` condition within the `for` loop.

4. Move the mouse pointer over the `i` in the `if` condition statement. The ScreenTip "i=0" appears, which shows that the current value of `i` is 0. Because this is the first time the loop executes, it makes sense that the value of `i` is 0.

5. Click the **Step Into** button ⟱≣ again. The execution arrow and shading jumps to the `i++` item in the `for` loop specification, which indicates that the loop will now increment the loop counter value by 1.

6. Click the **Step Into** button ⟱≣ again. The insertion point and yellow shading jump to the second item in the `for` loop specification, and the interpreter evaluates the loop exit condition again. Note that the value of `i` in the Locals window now is 1, and the value appears colored red, because it has changed.

7. Click the **Step Into** button ⟱≣ again. The execution arrow jumps to the next command, which is the `if` condition within the `for` loop.

8. Select the **document.frmFaculty.optRank[i].checked** text in the shaded code, then move the mouse pointer over the selected text. The ScreenTip "document.frmFaculty.optRank[i].checked=true" appears, indicating that the `if` condition is true.

9. Click the **Step Into** button ⟱≣ again. The execution arrow jumps to the next command, which displays the alert that appears when the code finds the checked radio button.

When the interpreter executes the alert() method, execution switches to the browser window, because the user must respond to the alert by clicking the OK button. Now you will execute the command that displays the alert.

To execute the command that displays the alert:

1. Click the **Step Into** button ⟱≣. The alert message stating that the faculty rank value is "ASSO" appears in the browser window.

If necessary, click the Internet Explorer button on your taskbar to switch to Internet Explorer.

2. In Internet Explorer, click **OK** to close the alert. The Script Debugger window appears again, and the execution arrow points to the command that returns the value true to the event handler.

3. Click the **Step Into** button ⤓ again. The execution arrow jumps to the `<body>` tag in a new Web page file named dnserror.htm.

This new Web page appears because the Faculty Web page does not have a valid onsubmit event handler in its `<form>` tag. This causes the browser to generate an error and display the dnserror.htm Web page, which is the Web page that displays the message "The page cannot be displayed." Now you will stop the current debugging session.

To stop debugging:

1. Click the **Stop Debugging** button ■ on the Debug toolbar. The error1_DONE.htm Web page HTML code appears in Visual Studio .NET.

2. Switch back to Internet Explorer, then click the **Back** button on the browser toolbar to redisplay the Faculty Web page.

### Creating a Watch to View Variable Values

In the Script Debugger, you create a **watch** to observe how a variable value changes during execution. You create a watch when you want to observe how a variable value changes during execution without constantly having to move the mouse pointer onto the variable in the code. When you create a watch, the variable value appears in a Watch window in the Script Debugger environment as shown in Figure 4-23.

The watch updates the variable value as it changes during program execution. You can create watches on multiple variables during execution. Now you will run the Faculty form script in the Script Debugger again, and create watches so you can monitor the value property of the radio button that the loop code is evaluating and monitor the current radio button's checked property value.

To create watches to monitor variable values:

1. In Internet Explorer, press **F5** to reload the Web page, click **View** on the menu bar, point to **Script Debugger**, then click **Break at Next Statement**. The Faculty Web page appears in the browser window. (If one of the radio buttons appears selected after refreshing the Web page, exit Internet Explorer, then start it again and reopen error1_DONE.htm.)

2. Do not select any of the radio buttons. Click **Submit**. If the Just-In-Time Debugging window opens, click **Yes**, switch to Visual Studio .NET if necessary, and then click **OK** in the Attach to Process window. The Script Debugger window opens with the execution arrow on the opening `<form>` tag.

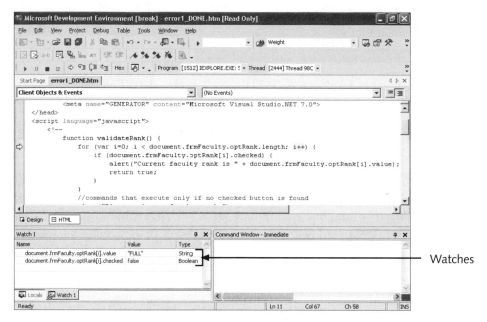

**Figure 4-23**  Using watches to display variable values

3. Click the **Step Into** button ⬇. The execution arrow jumps to the first command in the validateRank() function. Click the **Step Into** button ⬇ again. The shading jumps to the second item in the **for** loop, which is the command that checks the loop exit condition.

4. Click the **Step Into** button ⬇ again. The execution arrow jumps to the **if** condition.

5. To create the watch that tracks the current radio button value property, select the text **document.frmFaculty.optRank[i].value** in the command that displays the alert, right-click, then click **Add Watch**. The Watch 1 window opens and displays the current radio button value, as shown in Figure 4-23. If necessary, adjust the column widths in the Watch 1 window.

6. To create the watch that tracks whether the current radio button is selected, select the text **document.frmFaculty.optRank[i].checked** in the **if** condition, right-click, then click **Add Watch**. The Script Debugger adds this value to the Watch 1 window and shows whether or not the current radio button is checked. (Recall that if a radio button is checked, its checked property value is true; if the radio button is cleared, its checked property value is false.)

7. Click the **Step Into** button ⬇ again. The execution arrow jumps to the command that increments the loop counter.

8. Click the **Step Into** button ⬇ again. The shading jumps to the command that checks the loop exit condition. Note that the value in the first watch changes to "ASSO" and the new value appears red to signal that the value has

**4**

changed. Because the Associate radio button is not checked, the second watch value is still false and does not change.

9. Click the **Step Into** button $_v$ several times until the execution arrow appears on the command that displays the alert with the message "Please select a faculty value." Note when the radio button value changes to "ASST" and to "INST."

10. Click the **Step Into** button again. Execution switches to Internet Explorer, and an alert appears asking you to select a faculty value.

11. Click **OK** to close the alert. Execution switches back to the Script Debugger.

12. Click the **Stop Debugging** button ■.

Once you create a watch, the watch appears in the Script Debugger every time you run your script. To remove a watch, you must explicitly delete it by selecting the watch in the Watch 1 window, right-clicking, and then clicking Delete Watch. You can delete a watch only while you are debugging. Now you will delete the watches you just created.

To delete the watches:

1. In Internet Explorer, click **View** on the menu bar, point to **Script Debugger**, then click **Break at Next Statement**. The Faculty Web page still appears in the browser window. Select the **Instructor** radio button, then click **Submit**, click **Yes** on the Just-in-Time Debugging window, switch to Visual Studio .NET if necessary, and click **OK** on the Attach to Process Window. The Script Debugger window opens with the execution arrow on the opening <form> tag. Note that the watches you created in the previous debugging session still appear.

2. Select the **document.frmFaculty.optRank[i].value** row in the Watch 1 window, right-click, then click **Delete Watch**. The watch no longer appears.

3. Select the **document.frmFaculty.optRank[i].checked** row in the Watch 1 window, right-click, then click **Delete Watch**. The watch no longer appears.

4. Close the Watch 1 window.

5. Click the **Stop Debugging** button ■ to stop the debugging session, switch back to Internet Explorer, click **OK** to close the alert, and then click the **Back** button on the browser toolbar to redisplay the Faculty Web page.

## Using the Script Debugger Command Window

Recall that you can use the Command window to display variable values, change variable values during execution, and call functions during execution. To view a variable value in the Command window, you type a question mark in the window, followed by the variable name. The combination of the question mark and variable name is called a query. To execute the query, you press Enter. The variable's current value then appears in the Command window. To redisplay previous queries in the Command window, you press the

Up arrow key. For example, to view the current value of the `document.frmFaculty.optRank[i].value` property, you would type the following query in the Command window and then press Enter: `?document.frmFaculty.optRank[i].value`. If you press the Up arrow, the same query appears again in the Command window. You can then press Enter to execute the query again and see whether the value has changed.

You can use the Command window to view values of variables that are not in the script code. For example, the current script does not reference the value that is in the Faculty ID text input, but you could view this value in the Command window. Now you will run the Faculty Web page in the Script Debugger, enter a value for the Faculty ID, and then view the value in the Command window.

To view a variable value in the Command window:

1. In Internet Explorer, click **View** on the menu bar, point to **Script Debugger**, then click **Break at Next Statement**.

2. Type **1** in the ID text input, if necessary select the **Instructor** radio button, and then click **Submit**. If the Just-In-Time Debugging window opens, click **Yes**, switch to Visual Studio .NET if necessary, and then click **OK** in the Attach to Process window. The Script Debugger window opens with the execution arrow on the opening `<form>` tag.

3. Place the insertion point in the Command window, type **?document.frmFaculty.txtID.value**, and then press **Enter**. The value "1" appears in the Command window, as shown in Figure 4-24.

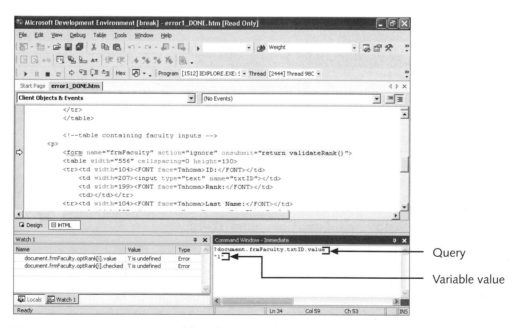

**Figure 4-24**    Viewing a variable value in the Command window

4. Press the **Up arrow**. The query appears again in the Command window. Press **Enter** to execute the query, and note that the value appears again in the Command window.

It is probably faster and easier to view variable values using ScreenTips or watches than to create a query and view a variable using the Command window. However, in addition to using the Command window to view values that are not in the script code, you can use the Command window to change variable values during program execution. To use the Command window to change variable values, you write the command to assign the new variable value using the same syntax you would use to assign the value in the program code. To execute the command in the Command window, you press Enter.

Recall that you selected the Instructor radio button before you clicked Submit in the current debugging session. Now you will execute a command in the Command window to change the selected radio button to the Full radio button. Because the Full radio button is the first radio button in the radio group, you will use the following command to specify that the first (Full) radio button is checked: `document.frmFaculty.optRadio[0]` `.checked=true`. Then you will step through the script, view the alert that shows the value of the selected radio button, and confirm that the command changed the radio button selection.

To use the Command window to change a variable value during execution:

1. If necessary, click within the Command window to set the insertion point under the current text, type the following command to assign the value true to the checked property of the first (Full) radio button, and then press **Enter**:

   `document.frmFaculty.optRank[0].checked=true`

   The value "true" appears in the Command window, confirming the property assignment operation.

2. Click the **Step Into** button ⌄≣. The execution arrow jumps to the first command in the validateRank() function. Click the **Step Into** button ⌄≣ again. The shading jumps to the command that checks the loop exit condition.

3. Click the **Step Into** button ⌄≣ again. The execution arrow jumps to the `if` condition. Click the **Step Into** button ⌄≣ again. The execution arrow jumps to the command that displays the alert.

4. Click the **Step Into** button ⌄≣ again. Execution switches to the Internet Explorer window and displays the alert advising that the current faculty rank is "FULL". This confirms that you successfully changed the variable value during program execution.

5. Click **OK** to close the alert.

6. In Visual Studio .NET, click the **Stop Debugging** button ■.

If you place the mouse pointer on the name of a function or a form object in the code window during program execution, the following ScreenTip appears: "*object_name* = { … }." You can use the Command window to evaluate the values of objects such as built-in and user-defined functions during program execution. This is useful when you want to see the value that the function returns without actually stepping through the function code. You can call both built-in (global) functions, such as isNaN(), as well as user-defined functions. To call a function in the Command window, you execute the following command: *?function_name(parameter_list)*. Now you will start the script in the Script Debugger, execute the validateRank() function from the Command window, and view the function return value in the Command window.

To execute a function from the Command window:

1. Switch to Internet Explorer, click the **Back** button to redisplay the Web page, then press **F5** to refresh the display. If the browser still displays values, or a radio button is still selected, close Internet Explorer, start it again, and open error1_DONE.htm from the Chapter4\Tutorials folder on your Solution Disk.

2. Click **View** on the menu bar, point to **Script Debugger**, then click **Break at Next Statement**.

3. Make sure that no inputs are entered on the Web page and that no radio button is selected, and then click **Submit**. If the Just-In-Time Debugging window opens, click **Yes**, switch to Visual Studio .NET if necessary, then click **OK** in the Attach to Process window. The Script Debugger window opens with the execution arrow on the opening `<form>` tag.

4. Scroll up in the code window to the command that declares the validateRank() function. Place the mouse pointer over the validateRank() function name. The ScreenTip "validateRank{…}" appears. This indicates that validateRank() is an object, so you cannot display its value in a ScreenTip.

5. To call the validateRank() function from the Command window, type **?validateRank()** in the Command window and then press **Enter**. Because the function displays an alert, execution switches to Internet Explorer.

 If execution does not switch to Internet Explorer, click the Internet Explorer button on your taskbar.

6. An alert appears asking you to select a Faculty rank. Click **OK** to close the alert. (You may need to click OK two times.)

7. Execution switches back to Visual Studio .NET, where the value false appears in the Command window. Because the user did not select a radio button, the validateRank() function returns the value false.

As you use the Command window, you may notice that it saves all previous commands that you enter. This is handy when you want to execute the same command many times. However, sometimes the Command window becomes cluttered with old commands. To clear the Command window, you place the insertion point in the window, right-click, then click Clear All. You will do this next.

To clear the Command window:

1. In Visual Studio .NET, make sure that the insertion point is in the Command window, right-click, then click **Clear All**. The commands in the Command window are cleared.

2. Click the **Stop Debugging** button ■ on the Debugging toolbar.

3. Close **error1_DONE.htm** in Visual Studio .NET.

## Using the Script Debugger to Set Breakpoints and Find Logic Errors

So far, you have used the Script Debugger to step through scripts one command at a time. For scripts with many commands, this makes debugging a slow process, because you must step through commands that are already working correctly. To debug scripts with many commands, it is useful to create a breakpoint to pause program execution on a specific command. To gain practice creating and working with breakpoints, you will use the Northwoods University Faculty Web page, which includes a form validation function named validateInputs(). This function contains commands that declare variables that represent the values that the user enters in the form's Faculty ID, Last Name, and First Name text inputs. The function also declares a variable named rankChecked that determines whether the user selected a faculty rank, and initially assigns its value as false.

The function then uses a loop to determine whether the user has selected a radio button to specify the faculty member's rank. If the user has selected a radio button, a command sets rankChecked to true. The function then uses an `if/else if` structure that evaluates whether rankChecked is true to validate that the user has selected a rank radio button. The `if/else if` structure also evaluates whether or not the user has entered values into the ID, Last Name, and First Name text inputs, and evaluates whether or not the ID value is a number between 0 and 9999 inclusive. Now you will open in Internet Explorer a file named error2.htm, which contains the Northwoods University Faculty Web page, and test the Web page's validation function. This script contains a program logic error, as you will see next.

To open the error2.htm file in Visual Studio .NET and Internet Explorer and view the program logic error:

1. In Visual Studio .NET, open **error2.htm** from the Chapter4 folder on your Data Disk and save the file as **error2_DONE.htm** in the Chapter4\Tutorials folder on your Solution Disk.

4

2. Switch to Internet Explorer and open **error2_DONE.htm** from the Chapter4\Tutorials folder on your Solution Disk. The Faculty Web page appears in the browser window.

3. In the Faculty Web page, type **asdf** for the faculty ID value, which is not a four-digit number.

4. Type **Cox** in the Last Name text input, type **Kim** in the First Name text input, select the **Full** radio button, and then click **Submit**. An alert appears stating that the form input values are valid. This is an error, because "asdf" is not a four-digit number.

5. Click **OK** to close the alert, then click the **Back** button on the browser toolbar to redisplay the Web page.

This is a program logic error. Even though the code does not display any error messages, the program isn't doing what the programmer intended it to do: It allows the user to enter character values in the ID text input. Sometimes logic errors are easy to find once you have run a script and seen the results. Other times you will see the incorrect results, but no matter how hard you scan the code, you won't be able to see why the output is incorrect.

For this error, you could step through all of the script commands until you reach the commands that evaluate the value in the ID text input. If you step through all of the script commands, you will have to step through several code lines before you reach the ones that contain the error. A better alternative is to set a breakpoint that pauses execution and lets you step through just the commands that evaluate the value in the ID text input.

To create a breakpoint, you click the mouse pointer in the gray area on the left edge of the code window where the execution arrow appears. When you create a breakpoint, a breakpoint icon ● appears beside the code line in the gray area on the left edge of the code window. To remove a breakpoint, you click the breakpoint icon ● . Now you will run the script in the Script Debugger. Then you will set a breakpoint on the command that evaluates whether the ID input value is a number.

To set a breakpoint on a command in the Script Debugger:

1. In Internet Explorer, click **View** on the menu bar, point to **Script Debugger**, then click **Break at Next Statement**.

2. Make sure that "asdf" is the value in the ID text input, "Cox" is the value in the Last Name text input, "Kim" is the value in the First Name text input, and that the Full radio button is selected. Then click **Submit**. If the Just-In-Time Debugging window opens, click Yes, switch to Visual Studio .NET if necessary, then click OK in the Attach to Process window. The Script Debugger window opens with the execution arrow on the opening <form> tag.

3. Scroll up in the code window and find the code line shown in Figure 4-25 that evaluates whether the ID value is a number. (This command should appear approximately on line 29.)

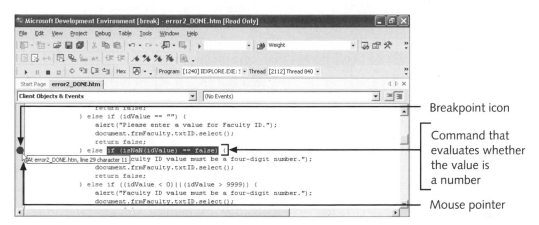

**Figure 4-25**    Setting a breakpoint on a program command

4. Move the mouse pointer onto the gray area on the left edge of the screen display, as shown in Figure 4-25, and click the gray area beside the command. The breakpoint icon ● appears in the gray area beside the program line. After you create the breakpoint, a ScreenTip appears showing the line number and starting character position of the program command on this line.

Now you will click the Continue button ▶ on the Debug toolbar to resume execution until the interpreter gets to the program line with the breakpoint. At that point, execution will pause, and you can step through the commands that evaluate whether the ID value is a number. As you do this, you will view the program variables and determine the cause of the error.

To resume execution to the breakpoint, then step through the commands that contain the error:

1. Click the **Continue** button ▶ on the Debug toolbar. The execution arrow jumps to the command with the breakpoint. Note that the values for the local variables that represent the form text inputs and the loop counter **i** appear in the Locals window.

2. Place the mouse pointer on the isNaN() function. The ScreenTip "isNaN{...}" appears, which indicates that the value of isNaN() is an object. Recall that you can use the Command window to view object values in the Script Debugger.

3. Type **?isNaN(idValue)** in the Command window, then press **Enter**. The value "true" appears, indicating that the value for the isNaN() function for the current value of idValue is true.

Because the condition in the current command compares the isNaN() function value to false, the condition evaluates to false, and the statements associated with this condition will not execute. However, you know that the current value of ID is "asdf," which is not a number, so the condition *should* evaluate to true, and the error message *should* appear. You have found the logic error: If the output of the isNaN() function is true, then the value is not a number, and the error message should appear. Now you will step to the next command to confirm that the error message does not appear.

To confirm that the error message does not appear when it should:

1. Click the **Step Into** button 👣. The execution arrow jumps to the next `else if` condition, which confirms that the error message does not appear when it should. This statement evaluates whether the ID value is less than 1 or greater than 9999.

2. Move the mouse pointer onto one of the idValue expressions in the shaded condition command. The ScreenTip "idValue=asdf" appears. Is "asdf" less than 0 or greater than 9999? It's hard to say, because you are comparing a text string value to a number value. You've found another logic error: The programmer needed to use the parseFloat() function to convert the ID value to a number before comparing its value.

3. Click the **Step Into** button 👣 again. The execution arrow jumps to the next `else if` condition, which evaluates the value in the Last Name text input.

To correct these errors, you must stop debugging, change the code in Visual Studio .NET, and then rerun the script. (In the Script Debugger in the Visual Studio .NET environment, you cannot change commands while you are debugging because the code is read-only.) Now you will stop the Script Debugger, correct the errors, then run the script again and confirm that it is working correctly.

To stop debugging, correct the errors, then test the script again:

1. Click the **Stop Debugging** button ■ on the Debug toolbar. The code appears in the Visual Studio .NET HTML editor. Note that the breakpoint icon ● still appears in the code window. Breakpoints exist across debugging sessions until you explicitly remove them.

2. Change the command that evaluates whether or not the ID value is a number, as follows. (This command is approximately on line 29.)

```
} else if (isNaN(idValue) == true) {
```

3. Change the command that assigns the value in the ID text input to the idValue variable. The command then converts the value to a number by using the parseFloat() function and adding the following characters to the assignment command. (This command is on approximately line 11.)

```
var idValue = parseFloat(document.frmFaculty.txtID.value);
```

4. Save the file, then switch back to Internet Explorer, which currently displays the alert advising you that the input values are valid. Click **OK** to close the alert, then click the **Back** button to reload the Web page. If the form inputs are not cleared, close Internet Explorer, then open it again and reopen error2_DONE.htm from the Chapter4\Tutorials folder on your Solution Disk.

5. To test the condition that evaluates whether or not the value in the ID input is a number, type **asdf** in the ID input, **Cox** in the Last Name input, and **Kim** in the First Name input. Then select the **Full** radio button, and then click **Submit**. An alert appears advising you that the ID value must be a four-digit number. Click **OK** to close the alert.

6. To test the condition that validates the number range, change the ID value to **11111**, which is a five-digit number. Do not change any of the other inputs. Click **Submit**. An alert reappears advising you that the ID value must be a four-digit number. Click **OK** to close the alert.

7. Change the ID value to **1111**, which is a legal value, but do not change any of the other inputs. Then click **Submit**. An alert appears confirming that the input values are valid. Click **OK** to close the alert, then click the **Back** button to redisplay the Web page.

8. Switch to Visual Studio .NET, and close **error2_DONE.htm**.

## DISPLAYING MESSAGES IN JAVASCRIPT PROGRAMS

You have used JavaScript's window.alert() method in many programs to display brief informational messages. An alert contains only a brief message and an OK button, so you normally use it to convey information such as why an input is incorrect or to display current data values. However, sometimes you need to display a confirm message, which allows the user to select among different options, or a prompt message, which allows the user to enter text data. The following subsections describe how to create and process confirm and prompt messages.

### Displaying a Confirm Message

When working with database-driven Web sites, it is standard to create server-side scripts that enable users to open a connection to a database and modify the database's contents. (You will learn how to implement this technique later in the book.) When a user's actions will change the database's contents, you usually ask the user to confirm the changes before proceeding. If the user clicks OK, the program commands would submit the form to the Web server and its data values would be inserted into the database. If the user clicks Cancel, the program commands would not submit the form to the database. You use JavaScript's window.confirm() method to create this type of confirm message. A **confirm message** displays a message similar to an alert, but also displays two buttons: OK and Cancel. You create a confirm message using the JavaScript window.confirm() method. You then write an `if/else` control structure to evaluate whether the user clicks OK or Cancel and execute different commands for each case.

Figure 4-26 shows an example of a confirm message.

**Figure 4-26**    Confirm message

You use the following general syntax to create a confirm message:

```
var return_value = window.confirm("message");
```

In this syntax, *return_value* references the value that the window.confirm() method returns, which can be true or false. If the user clicks OK, *return_value* is true. If the user clicks Cancel, *return_value* is false. The *message* usually poses a question and advises the user what will happen if he or she clicks OK or Cancel. You would use the following command to create a confirm message that displays the text "Simple message" and returns the value to a variable named confirmInsert:

```
var confirmInsert = window.confirm("Simple message");
```

Recall that a single JavaScript command can span two or more lines in the HTML editor because the semicolon signals the end of the code line. However, if you create a command that contains a text string that you enclose in double quotation marks, and you break the text string across multiple program lines, an error will occur. Nevertheless, sometimes you need to separate the text that appears in the *message* onto multiple editor lines, because a long text message scrolls off the right edge of your screen, which makes the command hard to read and maintain. You cannot split a text string onto multiple editor lines by simply pressing Enter and wrapping the rest of the text to the next line. For example, suppose you want to display the confirm message shown in Figure 4-26, and you created the message in the HTML editor using the following command:

```
var confirmInsert = window.confirm("You are
about to insert a new record into the database.
Click OK to continue or Cancel to abort.");
```

This command will generate an error, because the text string is not properly formed. To break the command across multiple editor lines, you would need to specify each individual code line as a separate text string and then concatenate the strings. The following code correctly splits the message text onto three editor lines:

```
var confirmInsert = window.confirm("You are " +
" about to insert a new record into the database. " +
"Click OK to continue or Cancel to abort.");
```

To evaluate which button on a confirm message the user has clicked and then execute appropriate commands, you use the following `if/else` control structure:

```
if (return_value == true) {
  commands to execute if the user clicks OK
} else {
  commands to execute if the user clicks Cancel
}
```

You can create a shorter version of this `if` control structure if you recall that the interpreter evaluates the *condition* in an `if` statement as true or false. Because the window.confirm() method always returns true or false, you can skip the intermediate step of saving the window.confirm() method return value to a *return_value* variable. Instead, you can call the window.confirm() method directly in the condition of the `if` structure using the following syntax:

```
if (window.confirm(message)) {
  commands to execute if the user clicks OK
} else {
  commands to execute if the user clicks Cancel
}
```

Recall from Chapter 3 that you can omit `window.` from all DOM references because JavaScript automatically assumes it is there.

If the user clicks OK, the window.confirm() method evaluates as true and the first set of commands execute. If the user clicks Cancel, the window.confirm() method evaluates as false and the second set of commands executes. The following code shows the shorter version of the window.confirm() method code that displays the message in Figure 4-26:

```
if (window.confirm("You are about to " +
"insert a new record into the database. " +
"Click OK to continue or Cancel to abort.")) {
    commands to execute if the user clicks OK
} else {
    commands to execute if the user clicks Cancel
}
```

Note that this example splits the *message* text literal among multiple lines in the text editor by concatenating the individual text strings together.

Now you will add a function named confirmInsert() to the Northwoods University Terms Web page in Figure 4-13. When the user clicks Submit, the function displays the confirm message in Figure 4-26, which allows the user to confirm inserting a new record or to cancel the operation. If the user confirms the insertion, an alert appears advising the user that the record has been inserted. If the user cancels the operation, an alert appears advising the user that the record was not inserted.

To add the confirm message to the Terms Web page:

1. In Visual Studio .NET, open **terms.htm** from the Chapter4 folder on your Data Disk and save the file as **terms_CONFIRM.htm** in the Chapter4\Tutorials folder on your Solution Disk.

2. Click the **HTML** tab to display the Web page in HTML view, create a new blank line just above the closing **</head>** tag in the file, and then add the code in Figure 4-27 to create the confirm message.

```
<script language="javascript">
    <!--
        function insertConfirm() {
            if (confirm("You are about to " +
                "insert a new record into the database. " +
                "Click OK to continue or Cancel to abort.")) {
                    alert("Record successfully inserted.");
                    return true;
            } else {
                    alert("Record not inserted.")
                    return false;
            }
        }
    //-->
</script>
```

**Figure 4-27**    Code to create the confirm message

3. Add the following onsubmit event handler in the **<form>** tag:

```
<form name=frmTerms action="action marker"
onsubmit="return insertConfirm()">
```

4. Save the file, then switch to Internet Explorer and open **terms_ CONFIRM.htm** from the Chapter4\Tutorials folder on your Solution Disk. The Terms Web page opens as shown in Figure 4-13.

5. Click **Submit**. (You do not need to enter any data values, because the Web page is not really inserting any data values into a database.) The confirm message in Figure 4-26 appears. Click **OK** to confirm inserting the record. The "Record successfully inserted" alert appears.

6. Click **OK** to close the alert. Because the browser cannot perform the specified form action, which is "action marker," an error message appears advising you that "The page cannot be displayed." Click the **Back** button on the browser toolbar to redisplay the Terms Web page.

7. Click **Submit** again to redisplay the confirm message, then click **Cancel**. The "Record not inserted" alert appears.

8. Click **OK** to close the alert.

## Displaying a Prompt Message

Sometimes it is useful to create a message that allows the user to enter a text value and click an OK or Cancel button to select between two different actions. For example, for security reasons, you might want to have users enter an access code before you allow them to insert a new record into a database. To do this, you create a **prompt message** like the one in Figure 4-28, which displays a message, a text input, and OK and Cancel buttons.

**Figure 4-28**    Prompt message

You use the window.prompt() method to create a prompt message. If the user clicks OK, the window.prompt() method returns the text value that the user entered into the prompt's text input. If the user clicks Cancel, the window.prompt() method returns the JavaScript value **null**, which means the value is undefined.

The general syntax for creating a prompt message is:

```
var return_value = window.prompt
("message", ["initial_value"]);
```

In this syntax, *return_value* references the value that the window.prompt() method returns, which is the text that the user types into the prompt's text input. If the user clicks Cancel, *return_value* is null. The *message* is the text that appears in the prompt message. The *initial_value* optionally defines the text string that appears in the prompt text input when the prompt message first appears. If you omit the *initial_value* from the method call, the text input is blank when the prompt message first appears.

For example, in Figure 4-28, the initial value appears as the text string "1234," and the return value is referenced by a variable named securityCode. You would use the following code to create the prompt message in Figure 4-28:

```
var securityCode = prompt("Please enter
your security code.", "1234");
```

To evaluate the value that the user enters in the prompt text input, you can use an if/else, if/else  if, or switch control structure. Now you will modify the confirmInsert() function that you created earlier in the Terms Web page to use a prompt message. When the user clicks Submit, the prompt message in Figure 4-28 appears and prompts the user to enter a security code. If the user enters a valid security code, which is either 0001 or 9999, the confirm message in Figure 4-26 appears. If the user does not enter a valid security code, a message appears advising the user that the security code is not valid. The function uses a **switch** control structure to evaluate the value that the user enters in the prompt text input.

To modify the function to display a prompt message:

1. Switch to Visual Studio .NET, and save the terms_CONFIRM.htm file as **terms_PROMPT.htm** in the Chapter4\Tutorials folder on your Solution Disk.

2. Modify the insertConfirm() function code as shown in Figure 4-29, and then save the file.

```
<script language="javascript">
     <!--
          function insertConfirm() {
            var securityCode = prompt("Please enter " +
            "your security code.", "1234");
               switch (securityCode) {
                    case "0001":
                         alert("Security code is valid.");
                         return true;
                         break;
                    case "9999":
                         alert("Security code is valid.");
                         return true;
                         break;
                    default:
                         alert("Security code is not valid.");
                         return false;
               }
          }
     //-->
</script>
```

**Figure 4-29**     Code to create and evaluate a prompt message

3. Switch to Internet Explorer and open **terms_PROMPT.htm** from the Chapter4\Tutorials folder on your Solution Disk.

4. Click **Submit**. (You do not need to enter any data values, because the Web page is not really inserting any data values into a database.) The prompt message in Figure 4-28 appears.

5. Type **0001** in the prompt text input, then click **OK**. Because this is a valid security code value, the "Security code is valid" alert appears. Click **OK** to

close the alert. Because the browser cannot perform the specified form action, which is "action marker," an error message appears advising you that "The page cannot be displayed." Click the **Back** button on the browser toolbar to redisplay the Terms Web page.

6. Click **Submit** again, then type **9999** in the prompt text input, and click **OK**. Because this is another valid security code value, the "Security code is valid" alert appears. Click **OK** to close the alert. Because the browser cannot perform the specified form action, which is "action marker," an error message appears advising you that "The page cannot be displayed." Click the **Back** button on the browser toolbar to redisplay the Terms Web page.

7. Click **Submit** again, then accept the default prompt value ("1234"), which appears in the prompt text input, and click **OK**. Because "1234" is not a valid security code value, the "Security code is not valid" alert appears. Click **OK** to close the alert. Because the validation function did not succeed, the browser does not submit the form to the Web server.

8. Click **Submit** again. Do not change the value in the prompt text input. Then click **Cancel**. Because clicking Cancel causes the prompt() method to return a null value, the "Security code is not valid" alert appears again. Click **OK** to close the alert.

9. Switch back to Visual Studio .NET and close **terms_PROMPT.htm**.

## USING CLIENT-SIDE SCRIPTS TO CREATE COOKIES

To make Web sites easier to use, Web developers need a way to store the information that users enter into Web pages. This information needs to be available every time the user connects to that Web site. For example, the first time you order merchandise from a Web site, the site may store information such as your shipping address and credit card number. For subsequent purchases, it is convenient if this information automatically appears when you log on to the Web site and make another purchase. To make information available every time a user connects to a Web site, Web developers need a way to make data persistent across multiple browser sessions. When data is **persistent**, it remains available after the user ends the current browser session. Making data persistent usually involves writing the data to a file or storing the data in a database. A **browser session** starts when you start your browser, and ends when you close your browser. During a browser session, you may connect to a Web site and enter information, and the Web site may run a program that records this data so it is persistent and is available the next time you connect to that Web site.

To store persistent data across multiple browser sessions, developers can store user information in an organizational database, on the Web server, or in a cookie on the client workstation. In this chapter, you will learn how to use JavaScript programs to create cookies that store user information on the client workstation. You will learn how to store user information in databases and on the Web server in later chapters.

**Cookies** are data items that are stored on the browser's computer. Cookies created by one Web page can be retrieved and used by other Web pages that are located in the same domain as the Web that creates the cookie. Web developers often use cookies to store information about what pages a user has viewed on a Web site and how many times a user has visited a site, and information that a user has entered during past visits, such as the user's name or shopping preferences. Developers also use cookies to create shopping carts that contain information about items a visitor has selected for purchase during a Web site session.

There are two types of cookies: temporary and persistent. **Temporary cookies**, which are also called **session cookies**, store information in the main memory of the user's computer. When the browser session ends, the system reclaims this memory space, and the cookie information is no longer available. **Persistent cookies** store information in text files on the user's workstation, and this information is available after the user exits the browser. Persistent cookies have an expiration date, and the client workstation's operating system deletes the cookie after a specific time interval.

Web browsers enforce security for both temporary and persistent cookies so that only programs that originate from the same Web server domain that created the cookie can subsequently read the cookie's contents. The browser enforces this security by storing the Web server domain name in the cookie along with the cookie's data values. For example, suppose you connect to *www.amazon.com*. During your visit, a program originating from the amazon.com domain creates a persistent cookie on your workstation that contains your credit card number. During subsequent Web sessions, the only programs that can read this cookie are programs that originate from the amazon.com domain. Otherwise, unscrupulous Web developers could create programs that read existing cookies and look for credit card information.

People have concerns about cookies and privacy. For example, have you ever noticed that the same advertisements seem to pop up all the time in your browser? As a result of consolidation in the Web advertising industry, a small number of Web advertisers create advertisements and deliver these advertising Web pages from their Web servers. These advertisers pay popular Web sites (such as *www.yahoo.com* and *www.weather.com*) to create links that download their advertising pages from the advertiser's Web server. Most of the advertising Web pages create cookies. Because the same advertiser's Web site creates many of these cookies, the advertiser's programs can read the cookies and then compile profiles on user Web browsing habits, which constitutes an invasion of privacy. Cookies are not really the problem, however; the real issue is marketing ethics. Advertisers can store the same information in their organizational databases or on Web servers as they store in cookies.

Most browsers can store a maximum of 300 total cookies, and a single Web server domain can create a maximum of 20 cookies on your computer. If the total number of cookies on your workstation exceeds the limit of 300, the browser deletes the oldest or least-used cookies. If every Web site writes the maximum number of 20 cookies on your computer, the maximum number of domains that could create cookies on your computer is 300 divided by 20, or 15. Because most domains create less than 20 cookies, the actual number of domains that store cookies on your computer at any time is likely to be more than 15.

Not all browsers support creating and maintaining cookies, and browsers that support cookies usually allow users to configure their browser so they do not create cookies. As a result, cookies are not a reliable way for Web developers to save information. The best way to store information is to use a database or a data file. However, most commercial Web sites use cookies, and for the most part, users who want to shop on the Web won't be able to shop if they disable cookies. As a consequence, cookies are an essential part of Web development. The following subsections describe how cookies structure information, how to create temporary and persistent cookies, how to view a listing of cookie files, and how to retrieve data values from cookies.

## Structuring Cookie Information

Although a cookie can store information in any format, the convention is to store information in ordered pairs of variable names and associated values using the following format:

```
variable_name=variable_value
```

You should always use this name/value pair format because ASP.NET and many other server-side programming environments have built-in functions that work with name/value pairs. A cookie can contain multiple name/value pairs. You separate each name/value pair using a semicolon (;). For example, a cookie that stores both the user ID and password values entered in a page for logging on to a Web site might have one cookie variable named userID that stores the value "Miller," and a second cookie variable named userPIN that stores the value "1234." A script would store this information in the following cookie name/value pair:

```
userID=Miller;userPIN=1234;
```

A single cookie can store a maximum of 20 name/value pairs or a maximum of 4,096 characters. If the browser tries to add a new name/value pair to a cookie and finds that the cookie exceeds the 20 name/value pair limit, the browser drops the oldest name/value pair from the cookie and then adds the new name/value pair.

## Creating and Referencing Temporary Cookies

A temporary cookie is a property of an HTML document. To reference a document's cookie property, you use the following dot syntax: **document.cookie**. To create a temporary cookie, you use the following general syntax:

```
document.cookie = "variable_name=" + "variable_value";
```

In this syntax, *variable_name* identifies the name of the cookie variable, and *variable_value* represents the associated value. You would use the following code to create a cookie with the *variable_name* userID that stores the value that appears in a text input named txtUserID on the frmLogin form:

```
document.cookie = "userID=" +
document.frmLogin.txtUserID.value;
```

To add an additional name/value pair to an existing cookie, you assign the new name/value pair to the existing document.cookie property. For example, the following code adds to the cookie created by the preceding code example a name/value pair that stores the *variable_name* userPIN and the value stored in the txtPIN text input:

```
document.cookie = "userPIN=" +
document.frmLogin.txtPIN.value;
```

Now the cookie contains the following name/value pairs:

```
userID=Miller;userPIN=1234;
```

 To view the current value of a cookie in the Script Debugger, select the text string document.cookie, then place the mouse pointer over the selected text. The cookie name/value pairs appear in a ScreenTip.

Recall that a temporary cookie persists until you end the current browser session. As long as a user is connected to the same Web site, each time you assign a new name/value pair to the document.cookie property, the browser appends the name/value pair to the current cookie. If you assign a name/value pair to an existing cookie where the *variable_name* value is the same as an existing *variable_name* value, the new name/value pair replaces the existing name/value pair.

To retrieve the contents of a cookie, you reference the document.cookie property to return the name of the cookie variable and the associated text string. For example, you would use the following command to display the current cookie name/value pair in an alert:

```
alert("Cookie value is: " + document.cookie);
```

Now you will create a function named createTempCookie() that records in a temporary cookie the values that the user enters in the User ID and Password text inputs on the Northwoods University Log On Web page in Figure 4-2. The function then displays an alert showing the cookie name/value pairs.

To create and display a temporary cookie to store the User ID and Password values:

1. In Visual Studio .NET, open **logon.htm** from the Chapter4 folder on your Data Disk and save the file as **logon_TEMPCOOKIE.htm** in the Chapter4\Tutorials folder on your Solution Disk.

2. Click the **HTML** tab to switch to HTML view, then if necessary, create a new blank line just above the closing **</head>** tag, and add the code in Figure 4-30 to create the createTempCookie() function. Note that the alert message uses the \n character to place the cookie name/value pairs on a new message line.

```
<script language="javascript">
    <!--
        function createTempCookie() {
            document.cookie = "userID=" +
            document.frmLogin.txtUserid.value;
            document.cookie = "userPIN=" +
            document.frmLogin.txtPIN.value;
            alert("Cookie value is:" + "\n" + document.cookie);
        }
    //-->
</script>
```

**Figure 4-30**     Code to create and display a temporary cookie

3. Add the following onsubmit event handler to the **<form>** tag:

```
<form name=frmLogin action="action marker" onsubmit=
"createTempCookie()">
```

4. Save the file, then switch to Internet Explorer. In Internet Explorer, open **logon_TEMPCOOKIE.htm** from the Chapter4\Tutorials folder on your Solution Disk. The Web page appears as shown in Figure 4-2.

5. Type **Miller** for the User ID and **1234** for the PIN, then click **Submit Query**. The alert showing the cookie name/value pairs appears as shown in Figure 4-31. Click **OK** to close the alert, then click the **Back** button on the browser toolbar to redisplay the Log On Web page.

**Figure 4-31**     Alert showing temporary cookie name/value pairs

6. Recall that if you assign a new name/value pair to a cookie in which the name portion is the same as an existing cookie name value, the new value overwrites the former value. Type **Black** for the User ID and **9999** for the PIN, then click **Submit Query**. Note that the alert shows that the cookie contains the new values (userID=Black and userPIN=9999). Click **OK** to close the alert, then click the **Back** button on the browser toolbar to redisplay the Web page.

## Creating Persistent Cookies

Recall that a Web page can retrieve information from a temporary cookie until the user exits the browser. After the user exits the browser, the temporary cookie information is no longer available. If you want your Web pages to retrieve cookie information that will be available across multiple browser sessions, you need to create a persistent cookie. To create a persistent cookie, you use the same syntax you used to create a temporary cookie, but you specify an expiration date. When a persistent cookie reaches its expiration date, the operating system deletes the cookie.

You use the following general syntax to create a persistent cookie:

```
document.cookie = "variable_name=" + "variable_value" + ";
expires=expiration_date";
```

Note that you separate the cookie name/value pair from the expiration date using the text string ";expires=. You specify the *expiration_date* as a text string using the following date format:

```
Day, dd-Mon-yyyy hh:mm:ss GMT
```

 *GMT* stands for Greenwich Mean Time. The browser converts the time to your time zone to determine when it will actually delete the cookie.

For example, to create a cookie that expires at 12:00 P.M. (GMT) on December 31, 2006, you would format the text string that specifies the expiration date as ";expires= Tuesday, 31-Dec-2006 12:00:00 GMT".

Now you will modify the Log On Web page to create a persistent cookie. You will modify the command that creates the cookie by setting the expiration date for the userID cookie variable as December 31, 2006, and the expiration date for the userPIN cookie variable as December 31, 2005. Then you will view the Web page in Internet Explorer, create the cookie, and view its contents.

To create a persistent cookie:

1. Switch to Visual Studio .NET and save logon_TEMPCOOKIE.htm as **logon_PERSCOOKIE.htm** in the Chapter4\Tutorials folder on your Solution Disk.

2. Modify the code by adding the highlighted code in Figure 4-32, then save the file.

3. Switch to Internet Explorer and open **logon_PERSCOOKIE.htm** from the Chapter4\Tutorials folder on your Solution Disk.

```
function createCookie() {
    document.cookie = "userID=" + document.frmLogin.txtUserid.value +
    ";expires=Monday, 31-Dec-2006 12:00:00 GMT;";
    document.cookie = "userPIN=" + document.frmLogin.txtPIN.value +
    ";expires=Sunday, 31-Dec-2005 12:00:00 GMT;";
    alert("Cookie value is:" + "\n" + document.cookie);
}
```

**Figure 4-32**    Code to create a persistent cookie

4. Type **Miller** for the user ID and **1234** for the PIN, then click **Submit Query**. The alert showing the cookie value appears as shown in Figure 4-31. Note that the document.cookie property does not display the expiration dates.

5. Click **OK** to close the alert, then click the **Back** button on the browser toolbar to redisplay the Log On Web page.

# Viewing a Listing of Cookie Files

Different browsers store cookies in different ways. Internet Explorer creates a file with a .txt extension for every individual cookie. By default, Windows XP and Windows 2000 store cookie files in the C:\Documents and Settings\*yourLoginName*\Local Settings\ Temporary Internet Files folder. Along with cookie files, this folder also stores recently accessed Web documents and images, which enable Internet Explorer to redisplay these items quickly without having to retrieve them across the Internet when you access them again.

 Windows XP and Windows 2000 also have a folder named C:\Documents and Settings\*yourLoginName*\Cookies that stores an alias to your cookie files. An alias is like a shortcut that represents a file that is in an alternate location. The Temporary Internet Files folder shows cookie expiration dates; the Cookies folder does not.

Now you will navigate to the folder that stores your temporary Internet files and find the file for the persistent cookie that your browser just created.

To find the persistent cookie file:

1. Start Windows Explorer and navigate to the **C:\Documents and Settings\** *yourLoginName*\**Local Settings\Temporary Internet Files** folder, which is the default directory where Internet Explorer stores persistent cookie files.

2. If necessary, switch to the Explorer Details view by clicking **View** on the menu bar, then clicking **Details**. If necessary, resize the file column widths so your Explorer display looks like Figure 4-33. Click the **Last Modified** column heading to sort your file listing by date, so the most recently created cookie file appears at the top of the list. Your cookie file should be similar to the one in Figure 4-33. (Your Internet address will be different.)

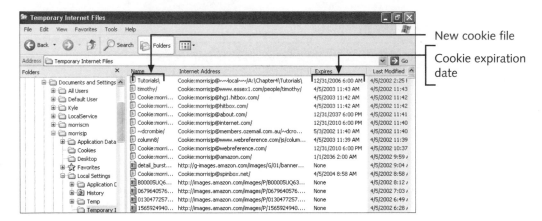

**Figure 4-33** Listing of Temporary Internet files

 If you are unable to find the folder that contains your temporary Internet files, or if the folder has no cookie files, it might be because your browser is set to save temporary files (such as cookie files) somewhere else. To find the folder where your browser saves temporary Internet files, click Tools on the Internet Explorer menu bar, click Internet Options, and then click Settings. The Settings dialog box displays the path to the Temporary Internet Files folder.

The detailed file listing shows the filenames. The Internet Address column shows how the browser associates each cookie file with a different Web server domain name. Figure 4–33 shows cookies written by the about.com and amazon.com domains, as well as many other domains. The cookie file that your Log On Web page created is named Tutorials\, and is associated with the localhost domain, which is the domain that is associated with the IP address of the local workstation. The Expires column shows the date on which specific files expire. Whenever the browser creates a new cookie or adds a new name/value pair to an existing cookie and the update specifies a new expiration date, the browser updates the cookie's expiration date. Because you can specify a new expiration date every time you add a new name/value pair to a cookie, the overall cookie expires on the date associated with the cookie name/value pair that is scheduled to persist the longest. Note that the expiration date for the cookie created by the Log On Web page is December 31, 2006, which is the expiration date you specified in your JavaScript function. The browser converted the expiration time from 12:00 P.M. GMT to the equivalent time in your time zone.

## Retrieving Individual Cookie Variable Values

So far you have learned how to display all the name/value pairs in a cookie. Because a single cookie usually stores multiple name/value pairs, you often need to extract a single value. We have written a JavaScript function named GetCookie that enables you to search a cookie. It finds a desired cookie variable name and returns the associated variable value.

An explanation of the commands and logic we use in the GetCookie() function is beyond the scope of this book. We include this function because it is easy to use for retrieving individual cookie variable values. If you want to learn more about JavaScript so you can understand how this function works, consult a comprehensive JavaScript text.

You use the following syntax to call the GetCookie() function:

```
var variableValue = GetCookie(variable_name);
```

In this syntax, when you call the GetCookie() function, you pass to it a specific *variable_name* value as an input parameter. The *variable_name* must be a valid variable name within the cookie. The GetCookie() function contains code to search all of the name/value pairs stored in the document.cookie property. The function returns the value associated with *variable_name*, and assigns its value to a variable named *variableValue*. If the function does not find the *variable_name* within the cookie's name/value pairs, it returns an empty string literal ("").

Recall that the script in the Log On Web page creates a cookie with the following name/value pairs:

```
userID=current_user_id;userPIN=current_user_PIN;
```

You would use the following command to call the GetCookie() function, pass to it the userID cookie variable name, retrieve the current value that the user entered in the User ID text input on the Log On Web page, and assign the value to a variable named currentUserID:

```
var currentUserID = GetCookie("userID");
```

The code for the GetCookie() function is stored in a file named GetCookie.txt that is in the Chapter4 folder on your Data Disk. You will copy the function code into your Web page and modify the alert that displays the cookie value so it calls the GetCookie() function. The alert will then display only the User ID value, rather than the entire cookie value.

To use the GetCookie() function in the Log On Web page file:

1. Switch back to Visual Studio .NET and save logon_PERSCOOKIE.htm as **logon_GETCOOKIE.htm** in the Chapter4\Tutorials folder on your Solution Disk.

2. In Visual Studio .NET, click **File** on the menu bar, point to **Open**, click **File**, navigate to the Chapter4 folder on your Data Disk, select **GetCookie.txt**, and then click **Open**. The text for the GetCookie() function appears in the Visual Studio .NET text editor.

3. Select all of the function text, click **Edit** on the menu bar, then click **Copy**.

4. Click the **logon_GETCOOKIE.htm** tab, place the insertion point just after the closing curly brace (**}**) for the createCookie() function, and then press **Enter** to create a new blank line in the editor.

5. Click **Edit** on the menu bar, then click **Paste as HTML**. The function code appears in the HTML editor.

6. Add to the createCookie() function the first shaded command in Figure 4-34 so that createCookie() calls the GetCookie() function. Then modify the second shaded command to display the result in the function alert.

```
function createCookie() {
    document.cookie = "userID=" + document.frmLogin.txtUserid.value +
    ";expires=Monday, 31-Dec-2006 12:00:00 GMT;";
    document.cookie = "userPIN=" + document.frmLogin.txtPIN.value +
    ";expires=Sunday, 31-Dec-2005 12:00:00 GMT;";
    var currentUserID = GetCookie("userID");
    alert("Current User ID value is:" + "\n" + currentUserID);
}
```

**Figure 4-34**     Code to call the GetCookie function to retrieve an individual cookie variable value

7. Save the file, then switch to Internet Explorer and open **logon_GETCOOKIE .htm**. Type **Miller** in the User ID text input and **1234** in the PIN text input, then click **Submit Query**. The alert showing only the userID cookie variable value appears as shown in Figure 4-35.

**Figure 4-35**     Alert showing an individual cookie variable value

8. Click **OK** to close the alert, then click the **Back** button on the browser toolbar to redisplay the Log On Web page.

9. Switch back to Visual Studio .NET and close **logon_GETCOOKIE.htm** and **GetCookie.txt**.

## USING SCRIPTS TO DISPLAY DIFFERENT WEB PAGES AND OPEN NEW BROWSER WINDOWS

Often a Web application needs to navigate to a different Web page within the current browser window. For example, the Northwoods University Registration System initially presents the Log On Web page. If the user successfully logs on to the system, the application needs to display a different Web page that presents options to allow the user to interact further with the system. You can use JavaScript commands to display a new Web page within the existing browser window.

Sometimes an application needs to open a new browser window and start a new browser session while leaving the existing session open. You use this approach when your application needs to display a new Web page, but you want to keep the current Web page available so the user can multitask between the two browser sessions. For example, a Northwoods University student may want to browse the university's course catalog while registering for classes using the registration system. You also use this approach when you want to display a message in a browser window without changing the contents of the existing browser window. For example, advertisers usually open new browser windows to hawk their wares, because users would become irate if the Web page they were browsing closed and only the advertisement remained open. The following sections describe how to use JavaScript commands to navigate to a new Web page within the existing browser window and how to open a new browser window.

## Navigating to a New Web Page in the Current Browser Window

To display a new Web page in the current browser window, you assign the window's window.location.href property to the URL of the new Web page using the following syntax:

```
window.location.href = "Web_page_URL"
```

The *Web_page_URL* specifies the new Web page using any valid URL format. In this chapter, you will use file URLs. You can use a relative or absolute folder path. (Recall from Chapter 2 that an absolute folder path specifies the path to the HTML file in the browser's file system, starting with the drive letter; a relative path specifies the path to the HTML file relative to the current working directory.)

Suppose you create a Web application that first displays the Northwoods University Log On page in Figure 4-2. If the user successfully logs on, the application displays the Registration System Menu page in Figure 4-36, which is saved in a file named nw_menu.htm.

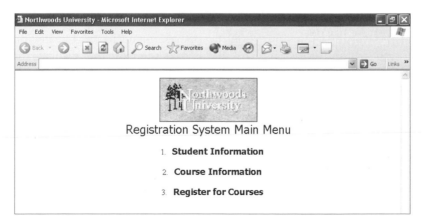

**Figure 4-36**    Registration system Main Menu Web page

You would add the following command to a script in the Log On Web page to load the nw_menu.htm Web page into the current browser window. This command uses a relative path and assumes that the nw_menu.htm file is in the same directory as the Log On Web page.

```
window.location.href = "nw_menu.htm";
```

Now you will modify the Northwoods University Log On Web page so that when the user clicks the Submit Query button, the script saves the user ID, PIN, and date of birth in a persistent cookie, displays the alert showing the current user ID value, and then displays the registration system Main Menu Web page in Figure 4-36.

To modify the Log On Web page, you will use a file named logon_NAVIGATE.htm. This file is slightly different from the Log On Web page file you have been using. In the logon_NAVIGATE.htm file, the Submit Query button is no longer a submit button that submits the form to the Web server. Instead, the Submit Query button is a regular command button that has an onclick event handler, which calls the function that creates and displays the cookie value. You need to use a command button and onclick event handler because you do not want to submit the form to the Web server before you display the Menu Web page. (In an actual system, the script would send the user ID, PIN, and date of birth values to the Web server for validation and then display the menu Web page. Because you are performing only client-side processing in this chapter, you will navigate directly to this page from the Log On Web page.)

To modify the Log On Web page function to navigate to the Menu Web page:

1. Switch to Windows Explorer and copy **nw_menu.htm** from the Chapter 4 folder on your Data Disk to the Chapter4\Tutorials folder on your Solution Disk.

2. Switch to Visual Studio .NET, open **logon_NAVIGATE.htm** from the Chapter4 folder on your Data Disk, and save the file as **logon_NAVIGATE_DONE.htm** in the Chapter4\Tutorials folder on your Solution Disk.

3. Click the **HTML** tab to switch to HTML view. Place the insertion point after the closing semicolon (;) on the last command in the CreateCookie() function, which is the command that creates the alert that displays the user ID value from the cookie. Press **Enter** to create a new blank line in the function. (This line should be just before the function's closing curly brace }.)

4. Type the following command so it is the last command in the function:

```
window.location.href = "nw_menu.htm";
```

5. Save the file, then switch to Internet Explorer and open **logon_NAVIGATE_DONE.htm** from the Chapter4\Tutorials folder on your Solution Disk. The Log On Web page opens.

6. Type **Miller** in the User ID text input, **1234** in the PIN text input, and **12/04/1984** in the Date of Birth text input, and then click **Submit Query**. An alert appears displaying the current user ID value ("Miller.") Click **OK** to close the alert. The Menu Web page appears in the current browser window.

 If the "The page cannot be displayed" error message appears, confirm that you copied nw_menu.htm into the same folder in which logon_NAVIGATE_ DONE.htm is stored.

**4**

## Opening a New Browser Window

Recall that sometimes in a Web application you need to open a new browser window to allow the user to multitask between two different Web pages, or to enable the user to view a message in a second browser window without changing or closing the first browser window. To use JavaScript to display a new Web page in a new browser window, you use the window.open() method, which has the following syntax:

```
var window_identifier = window.open(["Web_page_URL"],
["target"], ["option_list"])
```

In this syntax, *window_identifier* identifies the new window. After you open the new window, you can manipulate the window using window object methods that open, close, or move the window to a new location. You can omit the *window_identifier* in the method call if you do not need to manipulate the window using the window object methods. You pass parameters to the window.open() method by enclosing the parameter list in parentheses, and enclosing each individual parameter value in double quotation marks. Note that the general syntax for the method encloses all of the parameters in square brackets. This is because all of the window.open() method parameters are optional. To omit an individual parameter, you pass an empty string literal ("") as the parameter value. For example, the following code calls the window.open() method, and omits the *window_identifier* and all of the parameters: `window.open("", "", "")`.

The *Web_page_URL* specifies the URL of the Web page document that you want to display in the new browser window. For example, to display a Web page file named new_page.htm that is saved in the same folder as the current Web page, you would specify the *Web_page_URL* value as `"new_page.htm"`. Because this file is in the same folder as the current Web page, you can use a relative path and not specify folder path information. If you omit the *Web_page_URL* parameter value, the window displays a blank Web page.

The *target* parameter specifies the name of the new window. You use this name to reference the window if you wish to use it as a hyperlink target. Most developers omit the *target* parameter. The *option_list* parameter specifies the properties of the new browser window. Table 4-2 summarizes the new window option list parameters and their associated values.

**Table 4-2**    New window option list parameters

| Option | Description | Example Values |
|---|---|---|
| Toolbar | Displays the browser toolbar | `toolbar=yes`<br>`toolbar=no` |
| Location | Displays the Address field in the browser window to show the Web page URL | `location=yes`<br>`location=no` |
| Directories | Displays in the window title bar links to frequently used URLs | `directories=yes`<br>`directories=no` |
| Status | Shows the Web page status (loading, done loading) in the window status bar at the bottom edge of the browser window | `status=yes`<br>`status=no` |
| menubar | Displays the browser menu bar | `menubar=yes`<br>`menubar=no` |
| scrollbar | Displays scrollbars on the browser window | `scrollbar=yes`<br>`scrollbar=no` |
| resizeable | Allows the user to resize the browser window | `resizeable=yes`<br>`resizeable=no` |
| width, height | Specifies the browser window width and height, in pixels | `width=300`<br>`height=200` |

To create the *option_list*, you list the desired window options, with each option separated from the next by a comma (,). If you omit the *option_list* parameter, the new browser window opens with all options in the option list set to "yes," and the window width and height set to the same size as the user's screen display. If you specify any option value in the command, then all of the other options will be set to "no" unless you explicitly set a specific option to "yes." For example, you would use the following *option_list* to specify that the window displays a toolbar, displays a status bar, and is resizeable. All of the other window properties will be set to "no," and the window will have the default size value, which is the same size as the user's screen display.

```
"toolbar=yes, statusbar=yes, resizeable=yes"
```

You would use the following command to open a new browser window that you identify with a variable named alertWindow. This command specifies that the window displays a Web page document from a file named new_page.htm. The command omits the window *target* parameter value by passing it as an empty string literal. The window displays a toolbar and a status bar.

```
var alertWindow = window.open("new_page.htm", "",
    "toolbar=yes, statusbar=yes");
```

When a student successfully logs on to the Northwoods University Student Registration system, a second window opens to remind the student to attend a group advising session before registering. Now you will create a function named showReminder() in the Menu Web page. This function opens a second browser window that displays the Advising Reminder Web page shown in Figure 4-37.

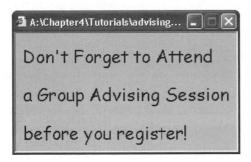

**Figure 4-37**    Advising Reminder Web page

In the showReminder() function, you will use the window.open() method to open the window and display the Advising Reminder Web page. You will omit the *target* parameter, configure the *options_list* parameter to specify the window size as 160 pixels wide and 300 pixels long, and accept the value of "no" for the other window options. You will call the window.open() method so it returns the window identifier value to a variable named winReminder.

Recall that to execute a JavaScript function when a Web page first loads, you create an event handler in the Web page's <body> tag that is associated with the Web page's onload event. Therefore, you will also create an onload event handler in the Menu Web page file to call the showReminder() function.

To create the function that opens the new browser window:

1. Switch to Windows Explorer and copy **advising_reminder.htm** from the Chapter4 folder on your Data Disk to the Chapter4\Tutorials folder on your Solution Disk.

2. Switch to Visual Studio .NET, open **nw_menu.htm** from the Chapter4\ Tutorials folder, and save the file as **nw_menu_DONE.htm** in the Chapter4\Tutorials folder on your Solution Disk.

3. Click the **HTML** tab to switch to HTML view, place the insertion point just before the closing </head> tag, and press **Enter** to create a new blank line. Then add the code in Figure 4-38 to create the script and define the function to open the new window.

```
<script language="javascript">
    <!--
        function showReminder() {
            var adWindow = window.open
            ("advising_reminder.htm","","height=160,width=300");
        }
    //-->
</script>
```

**Figure 4-38**    Code to open and configure a new browser window

4. Add the following onload event handler to the **<body>** tag to call the new function when the Web page loads:

```
<body onload="showReminder()">
```

5. Save the file, switch to Internet Explorer, and open **nw_menu_DONE.htm** from the Chapter4\Tutorials folder on your Solution Disk. The Menu Web page appears, and the Advising Reminder Web page appears in a separate browser window.

6. Close the browser window that displays the Advising Reminder Web page. Leave the Menu Web page open.

By default, the new window appears with its upper-left corner in the upper-left corner of the screen display. Recall that you can use window object methods to manipulate browser windows programmatically; Table 3-1 summarizes commonly used window object methods. For example, you could create a command button on a form that calls the window.close() method to close the current browser window. You can use the window.moveTo() method to specify the location of a window on the user's screen display. The window.moveTo() method has the following general syntax:

```
window.window_identifier.moveTo(x_position, y_position);
```

In this syntax, *window_identifier* is the variable name to which you assigned the window when you opened it using the window.open() method. For the Advising Reminder Web page, the value of *window_identifier* is winReminder. The *x_position* and *y_position* parameters specify the new x and y positions, in pixels, of the top-left corner of the current window. Now you will use the window.moveTo() method to reposition the window that displays the Advising Reminder Web page so it appears in the top-right corner of the user's screen display. To do this, you will set the *x_position* so it is equal to your screen display width resolution minus the width of the window, which is 300 pixels. For example, if your screen display resolution is $800 \times 600$, the *x_position* value will be $(800 - 300)$, or 500.

To use the window.moveTo() method to reposition the new browser window:

1. Switch to Visual Studio .NET, place the insertion point after the semicolon (;) that ends the command that uses the window.open() method, and then press **Enter** to create a new blank line.

2. Calculate the *new_x_position* of the new window by subtracting 300 from your screen width resolution, and then add the following command as the last command in the showReminder() function:

```
adWindow.moveTo(new_x_position, 0);
```

If your screen resolution is $800 \times 600$, use 500 for the *new_x_position* value.

3. Save the file, then switch back to Internet Explorer and press **F5** to refresh the browser display. The Menu Web page appears, and the Advising Reminder Web page appears in a separate window in the top-right corner of the screen

display. (You may need to switch back to Visual Studio .NET and adjust the *new_x_position* value to position the window correctly.)

4. Close the Advising Reminder Web page browser window.

5. Switch back to Visual Studio .NET and close **nw_menu_DONE.htm** and **logon_NAVIGATE_DONE.htm**.

6. Close Visual Studio .NET, Internet Explorer, and Windows Explorer.

4

## CHAPTER SUMMARY

- ❑ A form validation function is a client-side script that confirms that the user has entered all required values in an HTML form and that the values are valid.

- ❑ You structure a form validation function using an `if/else if` control structure. The function evaluates form input values in a top-down, left-to-right order, and returns the value false when an error occurs. The function returns the value true if it finds no errors.

- ❑ HTML forms have an onsubmit event that executes when a browser submits a form to the Web server. You can create an onsubmit event handler to call a form validation function.

- ❑ You use the built-in JavaScript isNaN() function to validate whether or not a user input is a number. The isNaN() function returns the value true if the entry is not a number and false if the value is a number.

- ❑ You create a Date object to validate whether or not a user input is a valid date. The Date object returns the symbolic constant NaN (not a number) when a command assigns an illegal date value to the object.

- ❑ An array is a data structure that organizes similar data items in a list structure. You can reference each array item using its index value. The first array index value is 0, and the array automatically expands as you add new items to it. You can use the length property of an array to determine the number of items the array contains.

- ❑ Web browsers create arrays to reference HTML document objects such as forms, form elements, radio buttons, and selection list options.

- ❑ To verify that a user selects a radio button within an HTML form radio group, you create a loop that evaluates the checked property value of every radio button in the radio button group.

- ❑ To determine whether or not a check box is checked or cleared, you use an `if` condition structure to evaluate whether the checked property of the check box is true or false.

- ❑ You use the options array to reference individual options in a selection list. You use the selection list's selectedIndex property to reference the list item that the user selects.

❐ The message line numbers that Script Debugger error messages report do not always correspond to the HTML editor source code lines on which the errors occur, but the error messages provide an approximate error location. When an error line number refers to an HTML element that calls a JavaScript function, the error is probably in the JavaScript function.

❐ The Script Debugger enables you to step through individual script commands, view how script variable values change during execution, and identify the command line on which errors occur.

❐ A syntax error occurs when you write a command that does not follow the rules of the programming language, and a logic error occurs when you write a command that follows the rule of the language, but does not perform the operation as intended. When a script contains a syntax error, the Script Debugger usually displays the Jscript runtime error message.

❐ In the Script Debugger, the code window displays the source code that is running, and the execution arrow marks the command that the interpreter will execute next. The Locals window shows the values of all local variables that you declare within the code block. You can use the Command window to display variable values, set variable values during execution, and issue commands to run functions.

❐ You can use ScreenTips, watches, or the Command window in the Script Debugger to view variable values during program execution. You can create breakpoints to pause program execution on a specific command.

❐ In JavaScript, you can create a confirm message—which displays a text message, an OK button, and a Cancel button—that allows the user to choose between different actions. You can create a prompt message—which displays a message, an OK button, a Cancel button, and a text input—that allows the user to enter a text value and select among different actions.

❐ A cookie contains information that a Web server stores on a user's computer. Temporary cookies store information in the main memory of the user's computer. When the user exits the browser, the system reclaims this memory, and the cookie information is no longer available. Persistent cookies store information in text files on the user's workstation, and this information is available even after the user exits the browser.

❐ Cookies store data values in name/value pairs, and you separate each name/value pair with a semicolon. A single cookie can store up to 20 name/value pairs.

❐ You use the window.open() method to start a new browser session and open a new browser window, and you use the window.location property to display the new Web page in the current browser window.

# REVIEW QUESTIONS

1. You can create a _____ event handler to call a form validation function.

   a. Form onload

   b. Form onsubmit

   c. Submit button onclick

   d. Form action

   e. Both b and c

2. In a form validation function, each `if/else if` condition should return the value _____, and the final `else` condition should return the value _____.

3. Create a `<form>` tag for a form whose name attribute value is frmSample. The form will contain an onsubmit event handler that calls a function named validateItems(). Structure the event handler so that if the function returns the value true, the browser submits the form to the Web server, and if the function returns the value false, the browser does not submit the form.

4. The JavaScript isNaN() function returns the value _____ if the value you pass to the function is a number, and returns the value _____ if the value you pass to the function is not a number.

5. Write the commands to create an `if/else` structure that determines whether a variable named myValue is a number. The structure should display an alert with the message "Value is a number" if myValue is a number, and an alert with the message "Value is not a number" if myValue is not a number.

6. Write the commands to create a new Date object named myBirthday and assign the value of a string literal corresponding to your date of birth to the object. Then write an `if` structure that displays the message "Date is not valid" if the value of myBirthday is not a valid date.

7. Write a command to declare an array named myNumberArray. Then, write the commands to create a loop that places the values 1–10 in the array. Next, write the commands to create a second loop that displays each value using an alert with the message "Current array value is: *current_value*." Use the length property to specify the exit condition for the second loop.

8. The Web browser uses an array named _____ to reference all of the items in a selection list.

9. Write an `if` decision control structure to evaluate whether the second radio button in a radio button group named optMyRadioButtons in a form named frmMyForm is currently selected. If the button is selected, write the command to display an alert with the message "The second button is selected."

10. Write an `if` decision control structure to evaluate whether a check box named chkMyCheckBox is currently checked in a form named frmMyForm. If the box is not checked, write a command to display an alert with the message "Check box is currently cleared." If the box is checked, do nothing.

11. Suppose you have a Web page with a form named frmMyForm that contains a selection list named lstMyList. Write a command to assign the value of the current selection in the selection list to a variable named currentValue.

12. Describe the differences between a syntax error and a logic error.

13. What usually appears in the Script Debugger window when a script contains a syntax error?

14. In the Script Debugger, the execution arrow points to:

    a. The code line that contains the next breakpoint

    b. The code line that just executed

    c. The code line that will execute next

    d. The code line that contains a syntax error

15. In the Script Debugger, what is the difference between the Locals window and a Watch window?

16. How do you use the Script Debugger Command window to display a variable value?

17. How do you use a ScreenTip to display an object value such as the current value in a form text input?

18. Write the commands to display a confirm message that contains the text "Sample confirm message." If the user clicks OK, display an alert with the message "User clicked OK." If the user clicks Cancel, display an alert with the message "User clicked Cancel."

19. Write the commands to display a prompt message that contains the message "Sample prompt message," and the initial text "Sample Value." If the user clicks OK, display the message the user enters in the prompt text input. If the user clicks Cancel, display an alert with the message "User clicked Cancel."

20. Describe the difference between a temporary cookie and a persistent cookie.

21. Write a command to create a temporary cookie named color with the value "brown."

22. Write a command to create a persistent cookie named height with the value "60" that expires on December 1 of this year.

23. Write a command that displays a Web page named newPage.htm that is saved in the same folder as the current working directory.

24. Write a command that opens a new browser window that displays the Web page at http://www.uwec.edu. Omit the *target* identifier, and have the window include a menu bar and nothing else. Accept the default window size.

# HANDS-ON PROJECTS

## Project 4-1 Validating the Clearwater Traders Customer Order Web Page

In this project, you will add a form validation function to the Clearwater Traders Customer Order Web page in Figure 4-39.

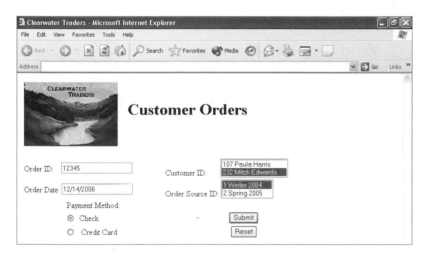

**Figure 4-39**

1. Save the clearwater_orders.htm Web page file that is in the Chapter4 folder on your Data Disk as 4Project1.htm in the Chapter4\Projects folder on your Solution Disk. Copy the clearlogo.jpg file to the Chapter4\Projects folder so the inline graphic image appears correctly on the Web page.

2. Create a form validation function that confirms that the Order ID value is a five-digit number between 1 and 99,999, the Order Date value has a valid date format, the user specifies a payment method by selecting one of the Payment Method radio buttons, and the user selects a Customer ID and Order Source ID from the form selection lists.

3. If any of the validations fail, display an alert with an appropriate message. If one of the text input values is not correct, display an alert and select the current value of the associated input.

4. Call the form validation function using a form onsubmit event handler.

5. After the form validation function validates all of the form inputs, display the alert shown in Figure 4-40 to summarize the user inputs.

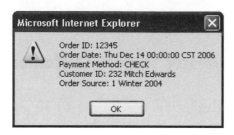

**Figure 4-40**

## Project 4-2 Validating the Northwoods University Student Information Web Page

In this project, you will add a form validation function to the Northwoods University Student Information Web page in Figure 4–41.

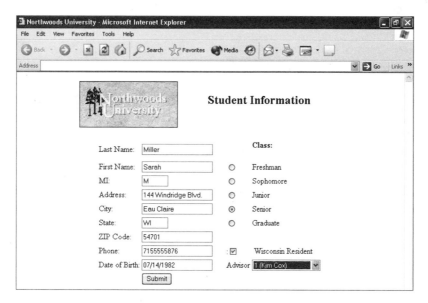

**Figure 4-41**

1. Save the student.htm Web page file that is in the Chapter4 folder on your Data Disk as 4Project2.htm in the Chapter4\Projects folder on your Solution Disk. Copy the nwlogo.jpg file to the Chapter4\Projects folder so the inline graphic image appears correctly on the Web page.

2. Create a form validation function that confirms that the user enters values in the Last Name, First Name, City, State, ZIP Code, Phone, and Date of Birth text inputs. Confirm that the Date of Birth value has a valid date format, that the user specifies a Class value by selecting one of the Class radio buttons, and that the user selects an Advisor ID from the form selection list.

3. If any of the validations fail, display an alert with an appropriate message. If one of the text input values is not entered, select the current value of the associated input.

4. Call the form validation function using a form onsubmit event handler.

5. After the form validation function validates all of the form inputs, display the alert in Figure 4-42 to summarize the user inputs. If the Wisconsin Resident check box is checked, display the message "WI Resident: YES." If the Wisconsin Resident check box is cleared, display the message "WI Resident: NO."

**Figure 4-42**

## Project 4-3 Processing a Clearwater Traders Customer Order

In this project, you will add a form validation function to the Clearwater Traders Products Web page in Figure 4-43 to confirm the user selection and prompt the user to enter a user ID.

**Figure 4-43**

1. Save the clearwater_products.htm file that is in the Chapter4 folder on your Data Disk as 4Project3.htm in the Chapter4\Projects folder on your Solution Disk. If necessary, copy the clearlogo.jpg file that is in the Chapter4 folder on your Data Disk to the Chapter4\Projects folder so the inline graphic image on the Web page appears correctly.

2. Write a form validation function to confirm that the user selects a product and enters a valid value in the Quantity text input. The Quantity value must be a number from 1 to 99 inclusive. If the user enters an invalid value, display an appropriate alert message and select the current Quantity value.

3. If the user enters valid values, display the prompt message in Figure 4-44, which asks the user to enter his or her User ID. Configure the prompt so the text string "userid" initially appears in the prompt text input and the text strings "harrispe" and "edwardsm" are valid user ID values.

**Figure 4-44**

4. If the user enters a valid User ID, display the confirm message in Figure 4-45, which asks the user to confirm the product selection. If the user does not enter a valid User ID, display an alert advising the user that the User ID value is not valid and display the Products Web page again. If the user clicks Cancel, the Products Web page appears again.

**Figure 4-45**

5. If the user clicks OK on the confirm message in Figure 4-45, the browser submits the order to the Web server. If the user clicks Cancel, the Products Web page appears again.

## Project 4-4 Saving Order Information in a Temporary Cookie

In this project, you will create a temporary cookie that stores the Order ID, Order Date, Payment Method, and Customer ID values that the user enters in the Customer Orders Web page in Figure 4-39. When the user clicks Submit, the browser displays the Products Web page in Figure 4-43. After the user selects a product and specifies a Quantity value on the Products Web page and clicks Submit, the confirm message in Figure 4-46 appears to summarize the order information.

**4**

**Figure 4-46**

1. Save the clearwater_orders.htm file that is in the Chapter4 folder on your Data Disk as 4Project4_orders.htm in the Chapter4\Projects folder on your Solution Disk. Save the clearwater_products.htm file that is in the Chapter4 folder on your Data Disk as 4Project4_products.htm in the Chapter4\Projects folder on your Solution Disk. If necessary, copy the clearlogo.jpg file that is in the Chapter4 folder on your Data Disk to the Chapter4\Projects folder so the inline graphic images appear correctly on the Web pages.

2. Create a function in the Customer Orders Web page that saves the current values of the Order ID, Order Date, Payment Method, and Customer ID in a temporary cookie and then displays the Products Web page in the same browser window. Call the function using an onclick event handler for the Submit button. (Change the Submit button type from "submit" to "button" so that when the user clicks the button, the browser does not submit the form to the Web server.)

3. Create a function in the Products Web page that displays the confirm message in Figure 4-46 when the user clicks Submit. Use the GetCookie() function to retrieve the values for the Order ID, Order Date, Payment Method, and Customer ID from the temporary cookie. If the user clicks OK on the confirm message, submit the form to the Web server. If the user clicks Cancel, display the Products Web page again.

## Project 4-5 Saving Student Information in a Persistent Cookie

In this project, you will create a persistent cookie that stores all of the values that the user enters in the Student Information Web page in Figure 4-41. When the user clicks Submit, a new browser window opens and displays the Web page in Figure 4-47, which summarizes the student information.

**Figure 4-47**

1. Save the student.htm file that is in the Chapter4 folder on your Data Disk as 4Project5_inputs.htm in the Chapter4\Projects folder on your Solution Disk. If necessary, copy the nwlogo.jpg file that is in the Chapter4 folder on your Data Disk to the Chapter4\Projects folder so the inline graphic image on the Web page appears correctly.

2. Create a new Web page file named 4Project5_summary.htm and save the new Summary Web page in the Chapter4\Projects folder on your Solution Disk.

3. In the Student Information Web page, create a function that saves the current values of the Last Name, First Name, MI, Address, City, State, ZIP Code, Phone, Date of Birth, Class, Wisconsin Resident status, and Advisor elements in a persistent cookie that expires Wednesday, December 1, 2010, at 12:00:00 GMT. The function then opens the Summary Web page in a new browser window. Call the function using an onclick event handler for the Submit button. (Change the Submit button type from "submit" to "button" so that when the user clicks the button, the browser does not submit the form to the Web server.)

4. Configure the Summary Web page browser window so it displays a toolbar, a menu bar, and the Web page status line. Do not display the location, directories, or scrollbars, and do not allow the user to resize the window. Specify the window size as 300 pixels wide and 200 pixels high, and center the window on the screen display.

5. In the Summary Web page, create an onload event handler that writes the cookie values onto the Web page using the document.write() method. Use the GetCookie() function to retrieve the individual cookie variable values, and format the Web page as shown in Figure 4-47.

# CASE PROJECTS

## Case 4-1 Ashland Valley Soccer League

In this case, you will work with Web pages that have been created for the Ashland Valley Soccer League, which is a fictitious organization that Case 2-1 in Chapter 2 describes. Copy the .htm and graphic image files in the Chapter4\Cases\Ashland folder on your Data Disk to the Chapter4\Cases\Ashland folder on your Solution Disk. The Ashland.htm Web page is the league's home page, and contains hyperlinks that call the Games, Fields, and Teams Web pages. Add a script to the Games.htm Web page for a data validation function. The data validation function should confirm that the user enters a number for the Game ID and a valid date format for the Game Date. The function should confirm that the selections for home and visiting team specify different team names, and that the user selects a value for the game status. When the script detects an error in a text input, set the focus to the text input and highlight its contents.

After the script validates the data values, write commands to create a temporary cookie to store the values of the form inputs. Then create a new Game Summary Web page named game_summary.htm. Display the Game Summary Web page in the existing browser window. Add a script to the Game Summary Web page that executes using the onload event handler, reads the cookie values, and displays a summary of the game information directly on the Game Summary Web page.

## Case 4-2 Al's Body Shop

In this case, you will work with Web pages that have been created for Al's Body Shop, which is a fictitious organization that Case 2-2 in Chapter 2 describes. Copy the .htm and graphic image files from the Chapter4\Cases\Als folder on your Data Disk to the Chapter4\Cases\Als folder on your Solution Disk. The Als.htm file is a home page that contains hyperlinks to Web pages that display information about customers, services, and work orders. Add a script in the Workorders.htm Web page so it contains a data validation function. The data validation function should confirm that the user enters values for the Work Order ID, Date, and VIN. It should validate that the Work Order ID is a number, and that the Work Order Date has a valid date format. When the script detects an error in a text input, set the focus to the text input and highlight its contents.

After the script validates the data values, display all of the input values in a confirm message. If the user clicks OK on the confirm message, submit the values to the Web server. If the user clicks Cancel, redisplay the Work Order Web page.

Before you can complete Case 4-3, you must have completed Case 3-3 in Chapter 3.

## Case 4-3 Sun-Ray Videos

Copy the Web pages that you created in Case 3 in Chapter 3 to the Chapter4\Cases\SunRay folder on your Solution Disk. Then modify the script in the Rentals Web page so it contains a data validation function. The data validation function should confirm that the user selects a video title and format and specifies a delivery mode (Pick Up or Delivery). (Make sure that the delivery mode option button is not selected when the Web page first appears.) After the script validates the data values, write commands to create a persistent cookie to store the values of the form inputs. Specify that the cookie will expire December 31, 2010, 12:00:00 GMT. Then display a prompt message asking the user to enter his or her User ID.

Create a new Web page named rental_summary.htm. If the user enters a valid user ID value and clicks OK on the prompt message, display the Rental Summary Web page in a new browser window. Configure the prompt message so that "harrispe" and "edwardsm" are valid User ID values. Add a script to the Rental Summary Web page that executes using the onload event handler. The script should read the cookie values and display a summary of the rental information directly on the Rental Summary Web page. If the user enters an invalid user ID, display an alert advising the user that the ID value was not valid and redisplay the Rentals Web page. If the user clicks the Cancel button on the prompt message, redisplay the Rentals Web page.

Before you can complete Case 4-4, you must have completed Case 3-4 in Chapter 3.

## Case 4-4 Learning Technologies, Incorporated

Copy the Web pages that you created in Case 3-4 in Chapter 3 to the Chapter4\Cases\LTI folder on your Solution Disk. Then modify the script in the Update Warehouse QOH Web page so it contains a data validation function. The function should confirm that the user selects a book title and warehouse, and enters a number value for QOH that is zero or greater. If the QOH value is not valid, the function should display an appropriate alert and then select the current value. If all of the values are valid, the function should display a confirm message that summarizes the input values. If the user clicks OK on the confirm message, submit the form to the Web server. If the user clicks Cancel, redisplay the Update Warehouse QOH Web page.

# 5

# WEB SERVERS

**In this chapter, you will:**

♦ Learn about Internet Information Services

♦ Become familiar with the components of a Web server, and specify the Web server's home directory and default document

♦ Create and configure Web server physical directories, virtual directories, and applications

♦ Learn how to organize a Web server

♦ Learn how to reference files on a Web server

♦ Understand the factors that impact Web site performance

In Chapter 1, you learned that Web servers are computers that are connected to the Internet and run Web server software. This software includes a component called a listener, which monitors requests for Web pages from client browsers. When a client browser requests a particular Web page, the Web server sends the Web page HTML document file to the browser. The Web server also processes server-side programs that create dynamic Web pages. Sometimes these programs retrieve database data by sending queries to a database server.

When you create data-based Web pages, you must test these pages on a Web server to confirm that they run correctly. The programs that you develop to run on the Web server and generate dynamic Web pages often initially contain errors. These errors can dramatically slow down the Web server. In extreme cases, an errant program can even crash the Web server process and the operating system of the computer on which the Web server process is running. It is therefore a good practice to test programs that create dynamic Web pages on a personal Web server rather than on a production Web server.

A **personal Web server** is a Web server that allows only a limited number of user connections. Usually only one person or a few people in a workgroup connect to a personal Web server and use the personal Web server to test programs that generate dynamic Web pages. A **production Web server** is a Web server that is available to anyone who connects to the Internet. Users expect production Web servers to be available all of the time. Once you demonstrate that your Web pages run correctly on a personal Web server, you move them to a production Web server and make them available to the general public.

To test dynamic Web pages on a personal Web server, you must understand how to configure a personal Web server. Configuring a Web server involves tasks such as setting up the directory structure on the Web server and designating the default home page that the Web server sends to browsers that connect to the Web server, but do not request a particular Web page. It also involves setting up directory permissions and Web site security features. Understanding Web server configuration is also crucial for troubleshooting programs that generate dynamic Web pages after you move these programs to the production Web server. In this chapter, you will learn how to configure a personal Web server using the Internet Information Services administrative utility.

 Microsoft Web server products are currently undergoing a naming transition. Microsoft sometimes refers to its Web server as the Internet Information Server, and sometimes refers to it as the Internet Information Services. The Internet Information Services administration utility is part of the Internet Information Services. Previously it was called the Internet Information Manager.

Usually, a Web server is a dedicated workstation that only services requests from Web browsers, and does not run any other server or client processes. However, to learn about Web servers in this chapter, you will run both the Web server software and the client browser software on the same workstation.

## INTERNET INFORMATION SERVICES

**Internet Information Services (IIS)** is the Web server software that comes with Windows NT, Windows 2000, and Windows XP. IIS includes the Internet Information Services administration utility, which you use to create, manage, and administer a Web server. A Web server is also called a **Web site**. If you want to set up a production Web site that can accept connections from many external users, you must purchase the server version of Windows NT, Windows 2000, or Windows XP, which includes the server version of IIS. In this book, you will use the personal version of IIS Version 5 that Microsoft includes with Windows 2000 Professional and Windows XP Professional, which will enable you to learn how to set up and administer a personal Web site.

Windows 98, Windows ME, or Windows XP Home Edition does not include the personal version of IIS Version 5.

The main difference between the personal and server versions of IIS is that the personal version can support only 10 Web server connections at one time. Each request for a Web page uses one connection for the HTML document and an additional connection for each graphic image that the HTML document references. A Web page with 10 graphic images would use a total of 11 connections, one for the HTML document and one for each graphic image. As soon as the server transfers the data that one browser connection requests, the connection terminates and becomes available to service another request. You can display a page with many graphic images using a personal Web server, but it appears in the browser window much more slowly than it would with a production Web server, because some graphic images do not download until new connections become available.

To perform Web server administrative tasks within IIS, you use the IIS administrative utility. In Windows XP, the administrative utility is part of Internet Information Services. Because IIS includes all of the Web server components, not just the administrative utility, this book will refer to the Web server software as IIS and to the administrative utility within IIS as the IIS console.

A **console** is an environment for administering a computer resource. A console makes it appear as if you are sitting in front of the screen display of the computer you are administering, even though you might be administering resources on a remote computer. A console runs in the **Microsoft Management Console (MMC)**, which is an environment for administering computer resources. Network administrators create custom consoles using **snap-ins**, which are components for computer management tasks that can be "snapped into" a generic console as needed. The **IIS console** is a custom console that contains the Internet Information Services snap-in, which includes components for administering Web servers. Windows-based computers save custom console configuration as files with .msc extensions. Now you will start the IIS console on your computer and examine the console environment.

To start the IIS console:

1. Click **Start** on the taskbar, and then click **Control Panel**. The Control Panel window opens.

If you are using Windows 2000, click Start on the taskbar, point to Settings, click Control Panel, double-click Administrative Tools, and then double-click Internet Services Manager.

2. If your Control Panel window appears in Category view, which has the heading "Pick a category," click **Performance and Maintenance**, click

**Administrative Tools**, and then double-click **Internet Information Services**. The Internet Information Services console window opens, as shown in Figure 5-1. Maximize the window.

 If your Control Panel appears in Classic view, which displays a list of Control Panel components, double-click Administrative Tools, and then double-click Internet Information Services.

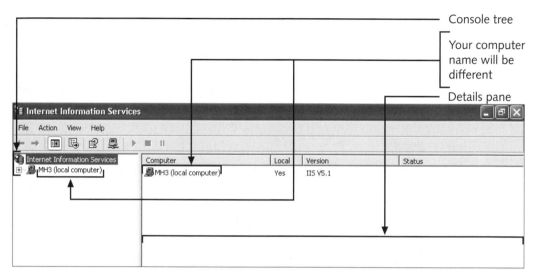

Console tree

Your computer name will be different

Details pane

**Figure 5-1**    Internet Information Services console

The left pane shows the **console tree**, which shows the items that are available in the current console. The right pane is the **details pane**, which provides details about the object that is currently selected in the console tree. Figure 5-1 shows that in the default IIS console, the top object, which is called the **console root**, is the Internet Information Services snap-in. The nodes under the IIS snap-in represent the Web servers that you can administer within your IIS console.

 If you want to administer a Web server other than the one on the local computer, you can add a Web server to your IIS console by clicking Action on the IIS menu bar, clicking Connect, and then entering the remote Web server's domain name or IP address. The remote Web server then appears as a node under the Internet Information Services snap-in. To administer a remote Web server, you must have administrative privileges for logging on to the remote computer.

The console tree consists of container objects and leaf objects. **Container objects** group related objects. Objects within a container object are called child objects. Child objects can be other container objects, or can be **leaf objects**, which are bottom–level objects that do not contain other objects. When you select a container object in the console tree, its child objects appear in the details pane. For example, in Figure 5-1, the Internet Information Services snap–in is selected, and information about its child object (the local computer) appears in the details pane.

Now you will open the local computer node and examine its child objects.

To open the local computer node:

1. Click the **plus sign** beside the name of your local computer. The Web Sites folder appears. This folder is a container object that contains objects that you use when administering a Web site. (This folder does not appear for Windows 2000 users.)

If the Default SMTP Virtual Server node or FTP Sites node appear, you are running these server processes on your computer. Unless you need to run these server processes, you should right-click these nodes and then click Stop to stop each process. (If the Stop selection is disabled, then the processes are not running.) To stop these server processes from restarting the next time you reboot your computer, Windows XP users should click Start on the taskbar, click Control Panel, click Performance and Maintenance, click Administrative Tools, double-click Services, right-click the service, click Properties, change the Startup type to Manual, and then click OK. Windows 2000 users should click Start, click Settings, click Control Panel, double-click Administrative Tools, double-click Services, right-click the process, click Properties, change the Startup type to Manual, and then click OK.

2. Click the **plus sign** beside the Web Sites folder. The Default Web Site node appears. This represents the Web site that IIS automatically creates on your local computer when you install IIS. (Windows 2000 users should skip this step.)

3. Click the **plus sign** beside the Default Web Site node. The default components of a Web site appear in the console tree, as shown in Figure 5-2. Your objects will be different if you or someone else has changed the default Web site objects on the local computer.

You can use the IIS console to start, stop, and pause your Web server, and to configure its properties. When you start a Web server, you load information about the Web site into the server workstation's memory, start the Web server listener process, and make the server available to service requests from client browsers. When you stop a Web server, you stop the Web server listener process so it can no longer service browser requests, and the system unloads the information about the Web server from memory. When you pause a Web server, the Web server listener process will no longer service new browser requests, but will still service existing connections.

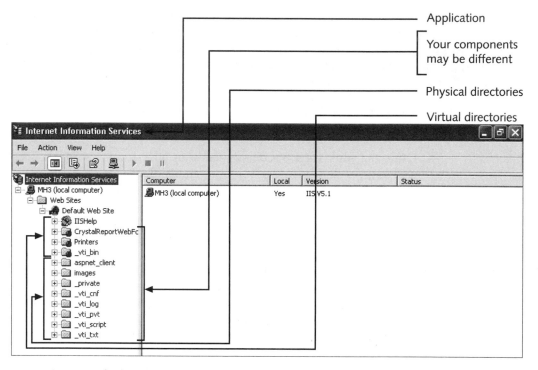

**Figure 5-2**    Default Web Site components

To start a Web server, you select the Web server in the console tree and click the Start item button ▶ on the IIS console toolbar. To stop a Web server, you select the Web server, and click the Stop Item button ■. To pause a Web server, you click the Pause Item button ‖. By default, the local Web server automatically starts when you install IIS. Now you will select the Default Web Site node and confirm that the Web site on your workstation, called the local Web server, is currently started.

To select the Default Web Site node and confirm that the local Web server is currently started:

1. In the IIS console, select the **Default Web Site** node. Its contents appear in the details pane, and the toolbar changes to show the buttons that you can use to control a Web server.

2. Confirm that the *Start item* button ▶ is selected. It should appear disabled (grayed out) if the Web server is currently started. If the Web server is not currently started, click the **Start item** button ▶ to start it.

Another way to start a Web server is to select the Web server, right-click, and then click Start.

If an error message appears when you try to start the local Web server, it may be because the Oracle Web server is running. By default, installing the personal Oracle database installs the Oracle Web server. To stop this Web server, click Start on the taskbar, click Control Panel, click Performance and Maintenance, click Administrative Tools, and then double-click Services. (Windows 2000 users should click Start, click Settings, click Control Panel, double-click Administrative Tools, then double-click Services.) Select OracleOraHome90HTTPServer, right-click, and then click Stop. To configure this service so it does not automatically restart the next time you reboot your computer, make sure that OracleOraHome90HTTPServer is still selected, right-click, click Properties, select Manual from the Startup type list, and then click OK. Close the Services window.

**5**

## WEB SERVER COMPONENTS

A Web server's **home directory** is the directory on the Web server that is the starting point for accessing the Web pages, graphic image files, programs, and other files that are available from the Web site. The home directory can be in the Web server's file system, in a shared directory on a network server to which you have mapped a drive, or on a remote Web server identified by a URL. In Figure 5-2, the Default Web Site node represents the home directory of your local Web server. Files within the home directory appear in the details pane when you select the Web Site node in the console tree.

Older Microsoft operating systems use the word *directory* instead of *folder* to describe a container for files. IIS still uses this term. In a graphical user interface, you usually refer to file containers as folders because the icon that represents the directory resembles a file folder. Therefore, this book uses the word *directory* to reference file system objects that contain files or other directories in IIS, and uses the word *folder* to describe file containers in the Windows environment. Whenever you see either term, they mean the same thing. The book uses the word *subdirectory* to reference a child directory that is within a directory.

The console tree displays the components within a Web server's home directory as physical directories, virtual directories, and applications. **Physical directories** are directories that the Web administrator creates within the Web server's home directory, or within directories that the Web administrator associates with other Web server components. The IIS console represents physical directories in the Web server console tree using the Physical Directory icon 🗀. An example of a physical directory on the Web server in Figure 5-2 is aspnet_client.

**Virtual directories** are directories that may or may not be physically within the Web server's home directory, but appear to client browsers as though they are. When you create a virtual directory, you associate it with a physical directory within the Web server's file system. You can also associate a virtual directory with a shared network directory. Virtual directories enable Web site users to access files that are in directories that are not within the home directory. This enables you to control the locations to which Web server users can navigate on your Web server, which ensures a higher level of security. The IIS console represents virtual directories using the Virtual Directory icon ☐. An example of a virtual directory on the Web server in Figure 5-2 is Printers. A virtual directory can contain physical directories.

**Applications** are virtual directories that have the permissions necessary to run server-side executable programs and scripts. Whenever you create a server-side program or script, you must store the program or script files in a physical directory that is in the Web server file system or in a shared network location. You must then create a new virtual directory that you associate with this physical directory. Finally, you must configure the virtual directory to have permissions to run server-side executable programs and scripts; this configuration converts the virtual directory to an application. The IIS console represents applications in the console tree using the Application icon ☐. An example of an application on the Web server in Figure 5-2 is IISHelp. As with a virtual directory, an application can also contain physical directories.

When a user enters a URL in his or her Web browser that contains a Web server domain name or IP address but no HTML Web page filename, the Web server returns an HTML document that the Web administrator specifies as the Web server's **default document**. If the Web server does not have a default document, users can still connect to the Web server, but they must know the path and filename of the document they wish to view and include it as part of the URL. If they do not know the path and document filename, and the Web server does not have a default document, then, depending on how the Web server is configured, the user's browser will either display a listing of the files in the home directory or an error message.

To administer a Web server, you must designate and configure the Web server's home directory and default document, and you must create and configure the Web server's physical directories, virtual directories, and applications. You perform many Web server configuration tasks using the **Web Site Properties dialog box** in the IIS console. To open the Web Site Properties dialog box for a Web server, you select the Web server in the console tree and click the Properties button ☐ on the toolbar.

Another way to open the Web Site Properties dialog box is to select the Web server, right-click, and then click Properties.

The Properties dialog box has several tab pages that allow you to specify different types of properties. The following subsections describe how to configure your Web server using the Web Site properties page, Home Directory properties page, and Document properties page.

# The Web Site Properties Page

The **Web Site properties page** enables you to configure the properties that identify the Web site, such as its IP address and port. Now you will open the Web Site Properties dialog box and examine this page.

To open the Web Site Properties dialog box and examine the Web Site properties page:

1. In the IIS console window, if necessary, select **Default Web Site** in the console tree, right-click, and then click **Properties**. The Properties dialog box opens, as shown in Figure 5-3.

2. If necessary, click the Web Site tab to view the Web Site properties page.

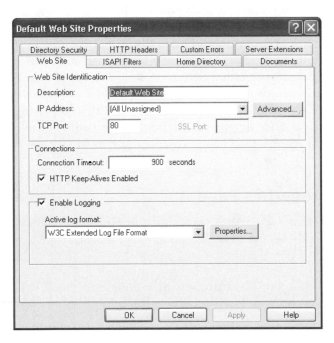

**Figure 5-3**   Web Site properties page

The Web Site properties page specifies general properties about the Web site. The *Description* field contains the Web site description that appears in the IIS console tree. Currently, the description is Default Web Site. The *IP Address* field currently appears as (All Unassigned), because you have not explicitly assigned an IP address to the Default Web Site, and the default value is the Web server on the local machine. The *TCP Port* field specifies the port on which the Web server listens for browser requests. (Recall from

Chapter 1 that a port is a memory location identified by a number that specifies which TCP/IP-based server process running on a computer will receive a message coming in from the network. Recall also that the default port for Web servers is port 80.)

Leave the Web Site properties page *IP Address* field set to (All Unassigned). This allows you to access the Web server using the *http://localhost/* URL, which is described later in this chapter.

When a browser connects to a Web server, the HTTP protocol specifies that as soon as the Web server delivers the requested Web page, the Web server terminates the connection with the browser. The *Connection Timeout* value allows you to specify a length of time, in seconds, before the server disconnects the connection. Setting a *Connection Timeout* value ensures that the Web server eventually closes all connections, even if the HTTP protocol fails to close a connection automatically. When the *HTTP Keep-Alives Enabled* check box is checked, the Web server allows a browser to maintain an ongoing open connection with the Web server, rather than reopening the client connection with each new request. This setting improves performance when you create an application that is continually sending information to a client browser and then receiving data back from the browser. When the *Enable Logging* check box is checked, it enables the Web site's logging features, which record details about user activity in the format specified in the *Active log format* list.

## The Home Directory Properties Page

You specify the home directory for a Web server on the Home Directory properties page. Now you will open and view the Home Directory properties page.

To view the Home Directory properties page:

1. If necessary, right-click the **Default Web Site** node, and then click **Properties** to open the Web Site Properties dialog box.

2. Click the **Home Directory** tab on the Properties dialog box. The Home Directory properties page appears, as shown in Figure 5-4.

The first three option buttons on the Home Directory properties page specify whether the Web site displays documents from *A directory located on this computer*, *A share located on another computer*, or *A redirection to a URL*. (A share located on another computer is a drive, directory, or folder on another server to which you map a drive.) If you select the first option button, the Home Directory properties page looks like Figure 5-4. You use the *Local Path* field to specify the path to the home directory. The remaining properties on the Home Directory properties page specify permissions that the system grants to users who connect to the Web site in the home directory. These permissions specify what users can and cannot do in the current directory. You can grant separate permissions for every Web site directory. The permissions shown in Figure 5-4 apply only to the Web site's home directory.

**Figure 5-4**  Home Directory properties page

The *Script source access* check box allows you to specify whether or not users can view the source code of scripts that are in the current directory. (Recall that scripts are programs that execute either on the Web server or client workstation and perform programming tasks.) For security reasons, you might not want users to view your script source code. Or, the script code may be proprietary, and people should not be able to use it without permission or payment. The *Read* check box allows users to download files and other contents from the current directory, and the *Write* check box allows users to upload files to the home directory. For most Web site directories, the *Read* check box is checked, and the *Write* check box is cleared.

The *Directory browsing* check box allows you to specify whether or not users can view a listing of the files and subdirectories in the current directory and access the files directly. Usually, the only time you enable directory browsing in a Web server directory is when you want to use the directory to make files available to users for reading, downloading, or printing. If you enable directory browsing, you should avoid placing sensitive files in your Web site directories, and you should carefully monitor the directory permissions so directory browsing is enabled only on the directories on which you intend it to be enabled. Normally, you disable directory browsing for the home directory, so this check box is cleared.

The *Log visits* check box enables **logging**, which creates a record in a log file when users connect to the directory. Currently, this check box is checked. The *Index this resource* check box enables Microsoft Indexing Service to include this directory in a full-text index of your Web site. When this check box is checked, users can perform full-text searches of your Web site using Microsoft's Web site search engine.

The *Application Settings* properties allow you to specify properties about applications. Because the home directory is not an application, when you configure the properties of your Web site's home directory, you remove the default application, which Microsoft creates automatically. The *Execute Permissions* list allows you to specify whether users can execute scripts, executable files, or both scripts and executable files, or not execute any files in the home directory. It is a good idea to place scripts and executable files in a separate directory from the home directory and to specify that users cannot execute any files in the home directory.

Now you will create a folder named wwwroot in the Chapter5\Tutorials folder on your Solution Disk and copy files into this new directory. These files are the Web pages and graphic images for the Clearwater Traders home page and for the Northwoods University home page.

To create the wwwroot directory and copy the files:

1. Start Windows Explorer and create a new folder named **wwwroot** in the Chapter5\Tutorials folder on your Solution Disk.

2. Copy the following files from the Chapter5 folder on your Data Disk to the new wwwroot folder on your Solution Disk: **clearlogo.jpg**, **clearwaterhome. htm**, **nwhome.htm**, and **nwlogo.jpg**.

Next, you will change the home directory of your Web site to the new wwwroot folder on your Solution Disk. When you specify the home directory, the steps are different if you are specifying a home directory that is a local drive on your computer, a share located on another computer, or a redirection to a URL. The following subsections describe the steps for specifying a home directory on a local drive and on a network share, and show how to configure the home directory and connect to the Web server using Internet Explorer.

## Specifying the Home Directory on the Local Workstation

 This section assumes your Solution Disk is on your A drive. If your Solution Disk is on a shared network drive, read the instructions, but do not perform the steps.

When you specify that the home directory is on a local drive of your Web server (such as A or C), you simply type the path to the local drive and directory in the *Local Path* field on the Home Directory properties page. Now you will specify that the home directory is on your A drive, change the properties of the home directory, and then connect to your Web site.

To change the home directory properties of your Web site:

1. On the IIS console Home Directory properties page, make sure that the *A directory located on this computer* option button is selected, and then click **Browse**.

2. Navigate to the **a:\chapter5\tutorials\wwwroot** folder on your Solution Disk, click **OK**, and then click **Apply**.

 If your Solution Disk is on a different local drive, navigate to that drive letter and path instead. If your Solution Disk is on a drive that you have mapped to a network server, skip this step and proceed to the next section.

 If you click OK on any page in the Properties dialog box, IIS saves the changes you made to the page and closes the Properties dialog box. If you click Apply, IIS saves the changes you made, but does not close the Properties dialog box.

## Specifying the Home Directory on a Network Share

 This section assumes your Solution Disk is on a drive that you have mapped to another computer. If your Solution Disk is on local drive, such as A or C, you already completed these steps in the previous section. Read the instructions, but do not perform the steps.

Today, most computers are connected to networks. If you want to make computer files available to other users on your network, you can create a network share. A **network share** is a drive or directory that network administrators configure so that users can view and manipulate its files and subdirectories from other computers on the network. Users can map a drive on their local workstation to the network share, and the network share appears as part of the local workstation's file system.

You can specify that your Web server's home directory is a network share to which you have mapped a drive. To specify that your Web server's home directory is located on a network share, you select the *A share located on another computer* option button on the Home Directory properties page and enter the network share specification. You must enter this specification using the **universal naming convention (UNC)** path to the network share. The general syntax for the UNC path is \\*server*\\*share*, in which *server* is the IP address or domain name of the server on which the network share exists, and *share* specifies the shared resource, which can be a directory name or a drive letter. Now you will specify that your Web site home directory is a network share.

To specify your Web site home directory if your Solution Disk is on a network share:

1. On the IIS console Home Directory properties page, select the **A share located on another computer** option button. Note that the Local Path label changes to "Network Directory," and the Browse button label changes to "Connect As…," as shown in Figure 5-5.

**Figure 5-5**    Specifying the home directory as a network share

2. In the Network Directory field, replace \\{server}\{share} with the UNC path to the network share to which you are connecting.

If you don't know the UNC path to the network share, but have already mapped a drive on your computer to this network share, you can use Windows Explorer to determine its UNC path. Figure 5-6 shows an example in which drive G is mapped to a network share in which server is web5, and share is c$. The complete UNC path is \\web5\c$. If you want to select a specific directory within the shared network directory, append another back slash after the share name and enter the path to the directory. For example, if the desired home directory was the _ANONFTP subdirectory that appears in Figure 5-6, the UNC would be \\web5\c$\_ANONFTP.

For security purposes, network administrators configure network shares so that only certain users have privileges to connect to them. Normally when you are performing Web server administration tasks, you log on to the Web server using a default user account that has administrative privileges for the local workstation. This local account might not have the necessary privileges to connect to the network share. If you are currently logged on to your workstation using a different user account and password than the one you use to connect to the network share, you must also specify the user account that has access to the network share. You will do this next. Then, you will save your home directory specification.

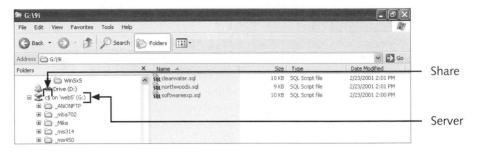

**Figure 5-6**   Determining a network share name

To specify an alternate user account and password for the network share, if necessary, and then apply your home directory specifications:

1. If you have logged on to your current workstation using a different user account than the one you use to connect to your network share, click **Connect As**, enter the user name and password for the network share, and click **OK**.

2. Reenter the password, and then click **OK**.

3. Click **Apply** to save your changes.

## Finishing the Home Directory Specifications

Now you will finish specifying your Web server's home directory. You will give users the *Read* privilege for the home directory. Because you have not yet specified the Web site's default document, you will enable directory browsing, which displays a listing of the files in the home directory to the user. You will remove the application associated with the home directory and set the execute permissions so users cannot execute any files in the home directory.

To finish the home directory specification:

1. Check the **Directory browsing** check box. Make sure that the *Read, Log visits*, and *Index this resource* check boxes are also checked, and that the other check boxes are cleared.

2. Click **Remove** to remove the application associated with the home directory. The application name no longer appears.

3. Open the *Execute Permissions* list and select **None**, and then click **OK** to save your changes and close the Properties dialog box.

In IIS, when you change permissions in a directory, you have the option of allowing subdirectories within the directory to inherit the new permissions. If the Inheritance Overrides dialog box opens, your home directory has one or more subdirectories, and these subdirectories have different permissions than the ones you are assigning to the current directory. If you would like one or more of the subdirectories to inherit the new properties, select the subdirectories that should inherit the permissions and click OK. On your Web server, you will configure the permissions of each directory separately, so you do not want any of the subdirectories to inherit the changed properties. Make sure that none of the subdirectories are selected and then click Cancel.

Note that in the IIS console, the contents of the console tree and details pane have changed. The applications and virtual directories that appeared before still appear, but the physical directories no longer appear. This is because there are no physical directories within the Web server's home directory, which is now the Chapter5\Tutorials\wwwroot folder on your Solution Disk. Note that the files that are in the home directory appear in the details pane. Now you will delete all of the applications and virtual directories that currently exist on your local Web server. (You will learn how to create new applications and virtual directories later in this chapter.) To delete an item in the console tree, select the item in the console tree and click the Delete button ✗ on the toolbar.

To delete all existing applications and virtual directories:

1. In the console tree, select an application (if one exists), click the **Delete** button ✗ on the toolbar, and then click **Yes** to confirm the deletion. (Recall that the Application icon 🌐 indicates that an item is an application.) Repeat this step for every application.

Another way to delete an application is to select the application in the console tree, right-click, and then click Delete.

2. In the console tree, select a virtual directory (if one exists), click the **Delete** button ✗, and then click **Yes** to confirm the deletion. (Recall that the Virtual Directory icon 📁 indicates that an item is a virtual directory.) Repeat this step for every virtual directory. Your IIS console should now look similar to Figure 5-7.

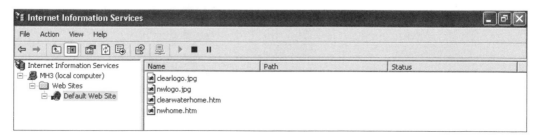

**Figure 5-7**    Current IIS console tree

## Using Internet Explorer to Connect to Your Local Web Site

Now you will start Internet Explorer, type the URL of your local Web server, and view the effects of your changes to Web site users. Before you do this, you will modify the configuration of Internet Explorer. To make Web pages appear faster, most Web browsers **cache**, or save, recently viewed Web pages on the local hard drive. This way, the Web server does not have to transmit the same file across the network if the user requests it multiple times. When you are developing new Web pages, you should configure your browser so it does not cache any Web pages, but always reloads and displays the most recent version of a Web page file. Now you will start Internet Explorer, delete all of the cached files, and change the configuration so that the browser does not cache any Web pages.

To delete the cached files and configure your browser so it does not cache Web pages:

1. Start Internet Explorer, click **Tools** on the menu bar, and then click **Internet Options**. The Internet Options dialog box opens.

2. Under Temporary Internet Files, click **Delete Files**. The Delete Files dialog box opens.

3. Check the **Delete all offline content** check box and then click **OK**.

4. Under Temporary Internet Files, click **Settings**, make sure the *Every visit to the page* option button is selected, and then click **OK**.

5. Under History, click **Clear History** and then click **Yes**.

6. If necessary, change the *Days to keep pages in history* field value to 0. Click **OK**.

Before you can connect to your local Web server, you need to understand static and dynamic IP addresses. Every computer that connects to the Internet must have a unique IP address. Some computers have **static IP addresses**, which are IP addresses that never change and always refer to a specific computer. Organizations and Internet service providers (ISPs) have blocks of static IP addresses that they assign to individual computers. Organizations and ISPs assign these static IP addresses only to computers that stay at the same physical location, or to computers that are servers, such as Web servers or database servers.

Organizations and ISPs assign static IP addresses to computers that stay in the same physical location because client programs usually look for a server at a specific IP address. Some of the values in an IP address indicate the physical network to which the computer is attached. When you move a computer with a static IP address to a new physical location, the IP address will change, so you must manually reconfigure the computer's network settings. A Web server's URL generally uses a static IP address matched to its domain name so users can always find the Web server.

New technologies are allowing organizations to use dynamic IP addresses (discussed in the next paragraph) combined with dynamic domain name server updates to allow a Web server to keep the same domain name regardless of its dynamic IP address. Although this approach may become more common in the future, most Web servers today use static addresses matched to domain names.

Computers that are connected to the Internet through large company networks or through ISPs that do not have to be at a specific IP address often have dynamic IP addresses. Special servers assign a **dynamic IP address** to a computer from a list of available addresses each time the computer is booted. A dynamic IP address might change each time the computer is booted. Dynamic IP addresses use IP addresses more efficiently than static IP addresses by reallocating idle IP addresses, thus stretching a limited pool of IP addresses to a larger pool of computers that need IP addresses. Dynamic IP addresses also allow users to attach laptop computers to different networks. When the user boots the laptop, the special server assigns the laptop an IP address that is appropriate for that network.

Recall that to request a Web page from a Web server, you type the Web server's URL in the browser's Address field. The Web server's URL is the Web server's IP address or domain name, followed by the name of the HTML document that you want to view. (Remember that if you do not specify the name of an HTML document, the Web server downloads its default document. If it does not have a default document, then it displays a file listing or an error message.) To connect to your local Web server, you need to type the IP address of your computer (which is where the local Web server's listener process is running) in your browser's Address field.

If your computer has a dynamic IP address, how can you specify the IP address of your local Web server in a URL? One way is to use a special URL called *http://localhost*. The ***http://localhost* URL** refers to the reserved IP address 127.0.0.1, which is the IP address of the local computer. Your workstation maintains this association in a file named **hosts**, which your workstation saves in the c:\Windows\System32\Drivers\Etc directory. Now you will examine this file.

To examine the contents of the hosts file:

1. Switch to Windows Explorer and navigate to the **c:\Windows\system32\ drivers\etc** directory.

Your hosts file may be in a different location, so you may need to perform a search to find the file. If you are using Windows 2000, your path will be c:\WINNT\system32\drivers\etc.

2. Right-click the hosts file, click Send To, and then click Notepad. The hosts file opens in Notepad.

If Notepad does not appear on your Send To list, right-click hosts and click Open. Select the *Select the program from a list* option button, click OK, select Notepad from the Programs list, and then click OK again. (Windows 2000 users should right-click hosts, click Open, select Notepad from the Programs list, then click OK.)

If the hosts file does not exist on your workstation, start Notepad, create a new file, and add the following line: `127.0.0.1  localhost`. Save the file as hosts in the c:\Windows\system32\drivers\etc folder. Do not add a .txt extension to the filename. Confirm that you named the file correctly by viewing the folder contents again in Windows Explorer. If you accidentally saved the file with a .txt extension, use Windows Explorer to rename the file to *hosts* (with no .txt extension). If Windows Explorer does not show file extensions, click Tools on the menu bar, click Folder Options, click the View tab, clear the *Hide extensions for known file types* check box, and then click OK. (Windows 2000 users should clear the *Hide file extensions for known file types* check box.)

The *hosts* file allows you to associate text strings with domain names or IP addresses. When you type the text string in the Internet Explorer Address field, the browser reads the *hosts* file and automatically routes your browser request to the associated Web address. The localhost identifier allows you to request Web pages from your local Web server and to create hyperlinks to other Web pages on your workstation without having to specify the actual IP address of your computer in the Web page URL.

You can also connect to your local Web server using your IP address. To determine the IP address of your workstation, click Start on the taskbar and then click Run. Type *cmd* to open a command-line window, and then type *ipconfig*. Your computer's IP address will appear. If you type *ipconfig /all*, you will see additional IP configuration information. Although you can use your IP address to access your local Web server, in this book you will use the localhost URL.

## Connecting to Your Local Web Server Using Directory Browsing

Now you will connect to your local Web server using the *http://localhost* URL. Because you enabled directory browsing on your home directory, the local Web server will display a list of your home directory files.

To connect to your local Web server:

1. In Internet Explorer, delete the current URL in the Address field, type **http://localhost**, and then press **Enter**. The Web page shown in Figure 5-8 should appear, showing a directory listing of the contents of the Web server's home directory. (The dates on your files may be different.)

**Figure 5-8**    Web server home directory listing

If this Web page does not appear, switch back to IIS and make sure that the Default Web Site is started by confirming that the Start item button ▶ is disabled. If the Default Web Site is not started, click the Start item button ▶ to start it. If an error message appears when you try to start the local Web server, it is probably because the Oracle Web server is running. By default, installing the personal Oracle database installs an Oracle Web server. To stop this Web server, click Start on the taskbar, click Control Panel, click Performance and Maintenance, click Administrative Tools, and then double-click Services. Select OracleOraHome90HTTPServer, right-click, and then click Stop. To configure this service so it does not automatically restart the next time you reboot your computer, make sure that OracleOraHome92HTTPServer is still selected, right-click, click Properties, select Manual from the Startup type list, and then click OK. Close the Services window.

If a message appears stating that the Web page cannot be found, make sure that you changed the home directory to the Chapter5\Tutorials\wwwroot folder on your Solution Disk, and make sure that you checked the *Allow directory browsing* check box. Switch back to Internet Explorer, and press F5 to reconnect to your local Web server.

If the Clearwater Traders home page appears, open the Default Web Site Properties dialog box, click the Documents tab, clear the *Enable Default Document* check box, and then click OK. If the Inheritance Overrides dialog box opens, click Cancel. Switch back to Internet Explorer, and press F5 to reconnect to your local Web server. You will learn how to specify a default document later in this chapter.

2. Click **clearwaterhome.htm**. The Clearwater Traders home page appears.

If you do not have a default document, and you do not enable directory browsing, then an error message will appear when a user tries to connect to your Web server. Now you will disable directory browsing and connect to your local Web server to confirm that an error occurs.

To disable directory browsing and then connect to your Web server:

1. Switch back to the IIS console. If necessary, open the Default Web Site Properties dialog box and select the Home Directory properties page.

2. Clear the **Directory browsing** check box and click **Apply**. If necessary, click Cancel on the Inheritance Overrides dialog box.

3. Switch back to Internet Explorer, type **http://localhost** in the Address field and then press **Enter** to reconnect to your local Web server. An error message appears stating "You are not authorized to view this page," which indicates that the Web site does not have a default document and that the home directory does not allow directory browsing.

## The Documents Properties Page

When a user enters a URL that contains a Web server domain name or IP address but no HTML Web page filename in the Address field on his or her Web browser, the Web server returns its default document, if one exists. You specify the default document filename on the Documents properties page in the Properties dialog box. Now you will open and examine the Documents properties page.

To open the Documents properties page:

1. Open the Properties dialog box for the Default Web Site.

2. Click the **Documents** tab. The Documents properties page appears, as shown in Figure 5-9.

On this page, the *Enable Default Document* check box allows you to enable or disable the default document. If this check box is checked, when a user connects to the Web server but does not specify a document filename, the Web server scans its home directory for documents that have the same name as the documents in the default document list. If the Web server finds a file with the same name as one of the files in the list, it returns the default document to the user. The Web server searches for the default documents based on the order that the documents appear in the default document list.

Suppose the *Enable Default Document* check box is cleared and directory browsing in the home directory is enabled. If a user connects to the Web server but does not specify an HTML document file, the Web server returns a listing of the documents in the home directory, as shown in Figure 5-8. If the *Enable Default Document* check box is cleared and directory browsing is disabled in the home directory, when a user connects to the Web server but does not specify an HTML document file, an error message appears in the user's browser.

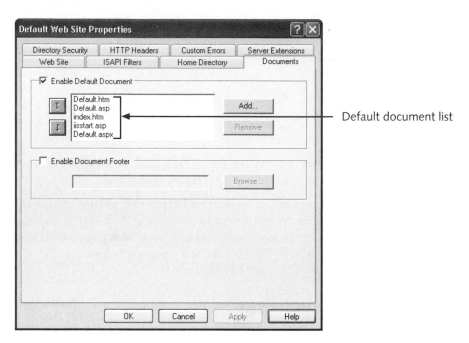

Default document list

**Figure 5-9**    Documents properties page

Now you will add the clearwaterhome.htm and nwhome.htm files to the default document list and then connect to your local Web server and view the default document.

To add the HTML documents to the default document list and view the default document:

1. On the Documents properties page, check the *Enable Default Document* check box if necessary.

2. Click **Add**. The Add Default Document dialog box opens.

3. Type **clearwaterhome.htm**, and then click **OK**. The clearwaterhome.htm file appears in the default document list. (If this file already appears in the list, someone else has already added the document to the local Web server, so you can skip this step and the next step.)

4. With clearwaterhome.htm selected in the default document list, click the **Up arrow** button **t** several times until clearwaterhome.htm appears as the first document in the list.

5. Click **Add**, type **nwhome.htm**, and then click **OK**. The nwhome.htm file appears in the default document list. With nwhome.htm selected, click the **Up arrow** button **t** several times so the file appears as the second item in the list. (If this file already appears in the list, it means that someone else already added the document to the local Web server, so you can skip this step.)

6. Click **OK** to save your changes and close the Properties dialog box. If the Inheritance Overrides dialog box opens, click Cancel.

If the Web administrator specifies a default document, and the default document exists in the home directory, then the Web server always returns the default document to the user, regardless of whether or not directory browsing is enabled in the home directory. Usually, for security reasons, you do not enable directory browsing in a Web site's home directory. Because you have specified a default document for your Default Web Site, you can now disable directory browsing on your Web site's home directory. Then you will switch back to your browser and refresh the display for your Default Web Site. This time, the Clearwater Traders home page should appear instead of the directory listing.

To disable directory browsing on the home directory of your Default Web Site:

1. Open the Properties dialog box of the Default Web Site, click the **Home Directory** tab, and make sure that the **Directory browsing** check box is cleared. Click **OK** to save your changes, and close the Properties dialog box. If the Inheritance Overrides dialog box opens, click Cancel.

2. Switch to Internet Explorer, make sure that *http://localhost* appears in the Address field, and then press **F5** to refresh the display. The clearwaterhome.htm default document, which is the first document listed in the default document list, appears.

## CREATING AND CONFIGURING WEB SERVER COMPONENTS

Recall that in the IIS console tree, the nodes under the Web server represent physical directories, virtual directories, and applications. The following subsections explain more about these components and describe how to create and modify these components on your Web server.

### Physical Directories

It is a good practice to organize computer system files by creating directories to organize files that are common to an application or task. In a Web server's file system, physical directories enable you to organize the contents of your local Web site and to control access privileges for files and applications. Recall that a physical directory is a directory that exists within the Web server's home directory, within a directory associated with a virtual directory, or within a directory associated with an application. Currently, your Web server does not contain any physical directories because your home directory, which is the Chapter5\Tutorials\wwwroot folder on your Solution Disk, does not contain any subdirectories. Now you will create some physical directories within your home directory, copy some files into these directories, and examine how these directories appear in the IIS console.

To create physical directories within the home directory:

1. In Windows Explorer, create a new folder named **Images** and a second new folder named **Pages** in the Chapter5\Tutorials\wwwroot folder on your Solution Disk.

2. Copy **clearlogo.jpg** and **nwlogo.jpg** from the Chapter5\Tutorials\ wwwroot folder to the Images folder. (You now have two copies of the clearlogo.jpg and nwlogo.jpg files on your Solution Disk.)

3. Copy **clearwaterhome.htm** and **nwhome.htm** from the Chapter5\Tutorials\wwwroot folder to the Pages folder. (You now have two copies of the clearwaterhome.htm and nwhome.htm files on your Solution Disk.)

4. Switch to the IIS console, select the **Default Web Site** node, and, if necessary, click the *Refresh* button 🔁 to refresh your console display. The new physical directories appear in the console tree, as shown in Figure 5-10.

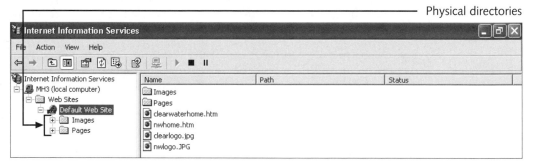

Physical directories

**Figure 5-10**    IIS console with physical directories

To access files that are in a physical directory that exists in the Web server's home directory, a user can enter the URL for a Web server, a front slash (/), the name of the physical directory, another front slash, and the filename. For example, a user would enter the following URL to access the nwhome.htm HTML file in the Pages physical directory on your Default Web Site: *http://localhost/pages/nwhome.htm*.

To control and manage physical directories, Web administrators can specify properties for each physical directory using a Properties dialog box that is similar to the one you used to set up your home directory. Now you will open the Properties dialog box for the Images physical directory and examine its contents.

To open the Images physical directory Properties dialog box:

1. Select the **Images** node in the console tree.

2. Click the **Properties** button 📰 on the toolbar. The Images Properties dialog box opens as shown in Figure 5-11. (The properties in your Properties dialog box may be different.)

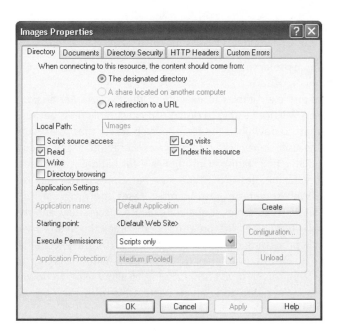

**Figure 5-11**   Physical directory Properties dialog box

A physical directory's Properties dialog box has pages that allow you to configure the directory's properties. The **Directory properties page** allows you to specify the source of the directory's content, the directory's access permissions, whether directory browsing is enabled, and the types of programs that users can execute from the directory. The Documents properties page allows you to specify a default document for the physical directory. The **Directory Security properties page** allows you to specify whether the Web server must verify the identity of the user before allowing the user to access the directory. The **HTTP Headers properties page** enables you to specify properties such as whether the directory's contents have an expiration date, whether you want all pages in the directory to display a custom header, and whether you want to specify a content rating for the directory's contents. (Web site developers can rate Web site locations in terms of their level of sexual content, violence, and strong language, and users can set their browser properties to restrict access to certain types of content.) The **Custom Errors properties page** allows you to create custom error messages that are sent to users when Web server errors occur.

It is useful to enable directory browsing on physical directories within the home directory when you want to use the Web server to distribute files to users. Now you will configure your Images and Pages physical directories so they allow directory browsing. You will disable the default document in both directories.

To change the properties of the physical directories to allow directory browsing:

1. In the Images Properties dialog box, make sure that the Directory properties page is selected and then check the **Directory browsing** check box. Make

sure that the *Read*, *Log visits*, and *Index this resource* check boxes are also checked, and that the other check boxes are cleared.

2. Make sure that *None* is selected in the *Execute Permissions* list.

If you enable scripts and executables to execute in the *Execute Permissions* list in a directory, users will not be able to download executable files, because when the user attempts to download the file, the Web server tries to execute the file instead. If the user right-clicks a script or executable file and selects Save Target As..., a dialog box stating "Getting File Information: ..." appears and stays open for several minutes as the Web server attempts to run the executable file on the Web server. Because in most cases the program isn't intended to be run on the Web server, it doesn't execute successfully, and the Web server eventually terminates the program. Sometimes the Web server uses all of its available processing capability to attempt to run the executable program. This slows down response times for other users who are trying to access pages on the Web server. If you are planning to allow users to download executable files from a directory, always select None in the *Execute Permissions* list.

3. Click the **Documents** tab at the top of the Images Properties dialog box to view the Documents properties page for the Images directory. Make sure that the *Enable Default Document* check box is cleared. Then click **OK** to close the Properties dialog box for the Images directory.

4. Select the **Pages** folder in the console tree, click the **Properties** button to open its Properties dialog box, make sure that the Directory properties page is selected, and then check the **Directory browsing** check box. Make sure that the *Read*, *Log visits*, and *Index this resource* check boxes are also checked, and that the other check boxes are cleared.

5. Confirm that *None* is selected in the *Execute Permissions* list.

6. Click the **Documents** tab to view the Documents properties page. Make sure that the *Enable Default Document* check box is cleared, then click **OK**.

Now you will view the contents of these folders in Internet Explorer. Since directory browsing is enabled, you will see a directory listing of their contents.

To view the contents of the folders in Internet Explorer:

1. Switch to Internet Explorer, type **http://localhost/Images** in the Address field, and then press **Enter**. The listing for the Images folder appears.

2. Click the **To Parent Directory** link. The Address field shows the parent directory, which is http://localhost, and the Clearwater Traders home page appears, rather than the directory listing. Recall that if a default document file exists within a directory, the default document appears rather than the directory listing, and directory browsing is disabled.

3. In your Web browser, type **http://localhost/Pages** in the *Address* field and then press **Enter**. The listing for the Pages directory appears.

After you configure the properties of a physical directory, any subdirectories that you subsequently make within the directory automatically inherit the parent directory's properties. For example, if you make a subdirectory named MoreImages within the Images directory, then the MoreImages subdirectory will have the same properties as the Images parent directory. Now you will create a subdirectory named MoreImages in the Images directory. Then, you will view its properties in the IIS console to see how the subdirectory inherits its configuration properties from its parent directory.

To make a subdirectory within a physical directory and see how it inherits its properties from its parent directory:

1. Switch to Windows Explorer and create a folder named **MoreImages** in the Images folder.

2. Switch to the IIS console and click the **plus sign** beside the Images physical directory to view its subdirectories. The MoreImages physical directory appears.

 If a plus sign does not appear beside the Images physical directory, click the Refresh button 🔄 to refresh your IIS console display. If the plus sign still does not appear, close the IIS console and then restart it.

3. Select the **MoreImages** node, right-click, and then click **Properties**. The MoreImages Properties dialog box opens. Note that the properties are the same as the ones you specified for the Images parent directory: The *Read*, *Directory browsing*, *Log visits*, and *Index this resource* check boxes are checked, and the other check boxes are cleared.

4. Select the **Documents** tab, and note that the *Enable Default Document* check box is cleared.

5. Click **Cancel** to close the Properties dialog box without saving your changes.

To use the IIS console to delete a physical directory on a Web site, you select the physical directory node in the console tree and then click the Delete button ✗ on the toolbar. When you delete a physical directory using the IIS console, the system deletes the physical directory and all of its contents from the Web server's file system. Now you will delete the Images physical directory from the home directory using the IIS console. This action will also delete the MoreImages subdirectory.

To delete a physical directory using the IIS console:

1. Select the **Images** node in the console tree, and then click the **Delete** button ✗ on the toolbar. The Confirm Folder Delete dialog box opens, asking whether you are sure you want to delete the Images folder and all of its contents.

2. Click **Yes**. The Images physical directory no longer appears in the console tree.

If an error message appears, delete the More Images physical directory first, then delete the Images physical directory.

3. Switch to Windows Explorer and confirm that the Images folder no longer exists in the Chapter5\Tutorials folder on your Solution Disk.

## Virtual Directories

Recall that a virtual directory appears to client browsers as a physical directory within the home directory. However, you can associate a virtual directory with a physical directory that is located anywhere in the Web server's file system, on a network share, or using a redirection to a URL that references a directory on another Web server.

You can create virtual directories to enable users to access Web pages and other files that are stored in directories that are not within the home directory and its subdirectories. For example, you could create a virtual directory to enable users to directly access files in the a:\Chapter5 folder on your Data Disk, or in a physical or virtual directory on an alternate Web server. Virtual directories provide flexibility for configuring your Web server. Virtual directories also provide extra security; Web site visitors cannot use directory browsing to navigate to the parent directory of a virtual directory.

A virtual directory has an associated **alias**, which is the name that client browsers use to access the virtual directory's contents. An alias is usually shorter than the original directory path specification and is more convenient for users to type. An alias is also more secure, because visitors do not need to know the actual names of the physical directories in which you store your Web server files. An alias should be a short, descriptive text string with no blank spaces.

To create a virtual directory in the IIS console, you use the Virtual Directory Creation Wizard, which presents a series of pages that prompt you to enter the specifications for the virtual directory. These pages include:

- A **Welcome page**, which welcomes you to the wizard

- An **Alias page**, which prompts you to enter the alias associated with the new virtual directory

- A **Web Site Content Directory page**, which prompts you to enter the drive letter and directory path or URL you associate with the virtual directory

- An **Access Permissions page**, which allows you to specify the virtual directory's file permissions

- A **Finish page**, which signals that the virtual directory creation process is complete

Now you will create a physical directory named Products in the Chapter5\Tutorials folder on your Solution Disk, and copy into the new folder the .htm file and graphics files for a Web page that displays information about Clearwater Traders products. Then you will use the Virtual Directory Creation Wizard to create a new virtual directory that you associate with the Products folder.

To create the folder, copy the files, and create the virtual directory:

1. In Windows Explorer, create a new folder named **Products** in the Chapter5\Tutorials folder on your Solution Disk.

2. Copy the following files from the Chapter5 folder on your Data Disk to the Products folder on your Solution Disk: **clearlogo.jpg**, **fleece.jpg**, **parka.jpg**, **products.htm**, **sandals.jpg**, **shorts.jpg**, and **tents.jpg**.

3. Switch to the IIS console, select the **Default Web Site** node in the console tree, right-click, point to **New**, and then click **Virtual Directory**. The Virtual Directory Creation Wizard Welcome page appears. Click **Next**.

4. In the *Alias* field, type **Cwproducts** and then click **Next**.

5. On the Web Site Content Directory page, click **Browse**, navigate to the Chapter5\Tutorials folder on your Solution Disk, select the **Products** folder, and then click **OK**. The full path to this folder appears in the *Directory* field. Click **Next**. The Access Permissions page appears, as shown in Figure 5-12.

 If your Solution Disk is on a network share, do not click Browse. Instead, in the Directory field, type the UNC path (\\*server*\*share*) to the Chapter5\Tutorials folder on your Solution Disk, click Next, enter the user name and password you use to connect to the network share, click Next, reenter the password, and then click OK.

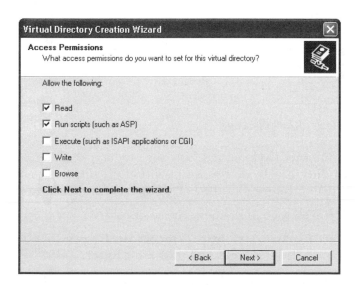

**Figure 5-12**   Virtual Directory Creation Wizard Access Permissions page

You can configure virtual directories the same way you configure physical directories. You can specify the file access permissions as *Read*, *Run scripts*, *Execute*, *Write*, and *Browse*. As with physical directories, when you create a subdirectory in the physical directory that you associate with a virtual directory, the subdirectory inherits its parent directory's access permissions.

Because the Cwproducts virtual directory contains the Products Web page and its graphic images, you will enable *Read* access to allow users to view and access the HTML document and its associated graphic images. Because you will not use the virtual directory to run scripts or programs, you will disable the other access permissions.

To configure the access permissions for the new virtual directory:

1. On the Access Permissions page, make sure that the *Read* check box is checked. Clear all of the other check boxes, click **Next**, and then click **Finish**.

2. The new virtual directory appears in your console tree and is identified by the Virtual Directory icon 📁, as shown in Figure 5-13. The files within the virtual directory appear in the details pane.

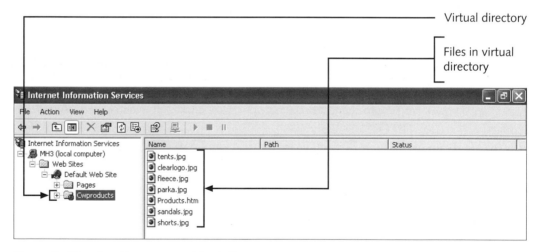

**Figure 5-13**    Creating a new virtual directory

Now you will switch to Internet Explorer and view the products.htm Web page in the new Cwproducts virtual directory. To do this, you will use the http://localhost URL, plus the name of the virtual directory, plus the HTML document filename.

To view the products.htm Web page in the new virtual directory:

1. Switch to Internet Explorer, type **http://localhost/Cwproducts/products.htm** in the Address field, and then press **Enter**.

2. The products.htm Web page, which is stored in the Chapter5\Tutorials\Products folder (physical directory) on your Solution Disk, appears using the virtual directory specification in the URL.

Virtual directories have a Properties dialog box that has essentially the same pages as the Properties dialog box for physical directories. You can use the Properties dialog box to change properties of the virtual directory or to specify additional property values, such as the virtual directory's default document. Now you will open the Properties dialog box for the Cwproducts virtual directory and specify that the products.htm file is the default document. Then, you will connect to your local Web server and type the URL to the Cwproducts virtual directory, but not specify the HTML document filename. Because products.htm is the default document in this directory, the Web page will appear automatically.

To change the virtual directory properties:

1. Select the **Cwproducts** node in the console tree and then click the **Properties** button 🗎. The Cwproducts Properties dialog box opens. Note that the tabs are the same as the tabs in the physical directory Properties dialog box, except that the Directory tab is labeled "Virtual Directory."

2. Click the **Documents** tab to display the Documents properties page. To add a new default document, click **Add**, type **products.htm** in the Add Default Document text box, and click **OK**. Click the **Up arrow** button 🔼 several times, until products.htm appears as the first item in the default document list. Then click **OK** again to save your changes and close the Properties dialog box.

3. Switch to Internet Explorer, type **http://localhost/Cwproducts** in the Address field, and then press **Enter**. The Product Guide Web page appears again, indicating that it is now the default document for the Cwproducts virtual directory.

Virtual directories allow you to change the physical location of Web page files on your Web server without changing the URLs that users specify to request Web pages. For example, suppose that you decide to move the Products folder and its contents from the Chapter5\Tutorials folder on your Solution Disk to the Chapter5 folder on your Solution Disk. Web site users usually access the products.htm Web page by connecting to your Web server and navigating to the Cwproducts virtual directory. After you move the physical location of the Products folder, you can change the Cwproducts virtual directory specification so it references the new location. Then users can still access the virtual directory and its contents using the same URL. In the next set of steps, you will move the Products folder and its contents to a new physical location, and then modify the Cwproducts virtual directory so it references the new folder location. Then you will access the Products Web page using the same URL you used when the Products folder was in its former location.

To change the folder (physical directory) location and virtual directory specification:

1. Switch to Windows Explorer and move the Products folder and its contents from the Chapter5\Tutorials folder on your Solution Disk to the Chapter5 folder on your Solution Disk.

2. Switch to the IIS console and click the **Refresh** button 🔃 to refresh the IIS console display. An Error dialog box opens that states "The system cannot find the path specified." This error message appears because the physical directory associated with the Cwproducts virtual directory is no longer in the same location as it was when you created the virtual directory. Click **OK**. Note that the Cwproducts virtual directory node changes to the Error icon 🛑 to show that the virtual directory is no longer valid.

3. Open the Properties dialog box for the Cwproducts virtual directory, and make sure that the *Virtual Directory* tab is selected.

4. Click **Browse**, navigate to the Chapter5 folder on your Solution Disk, and select the **Products** folder. Click **OK** to associate the Cwproducts virtual directory with the Products folder in its new location, and then click **OK** again to close the Properties dialog box. Note that the icon beside the Cwproducts virtual directory changes back to the Virtual Directory icon 📁, indicating that the virtual directory is again valid.

5. Switch to Internet Explorer and press **F5** to refresh your display. The products.htm Web page appears using the same URL as before, even though you moved the file to a different physical location.

Recall that to delete an item in the console tree, you select the item and then click the Delete button ✕ on the toolbar. When you remove a virtual directory on a Web server, IIS does not delete the associated physical directory or its files. It only removes the association between the virtual directory and the Web server, and makes the directory's contents unavailable to Web site users. Now you will remove the Cwproducts virtual directory. Then you will try to access its contents to see what happens.

To remove the virtual directory:

1. Switch to the IIS console, select the **Cwproducts** virtual directory node in the console tree, click the **Delete** button ✕, and then click **Yes** to confirm removing the virtual directory. The virtual directory no longer appears in the console tree.

2. Switch to Internet Explorer and press **F5** to refresh your display. A Web page appears stating that the specified Web page cannot be found.

## Applications

Recall that an application is a virtual directory that has access permissions that enable users to run server-side executable programs or scripts that you store in the physical directory that you associate with the virtual directory. The IIS console tree represents applications using the Application icon 🌐.

To create an application, you create a virtual directory using the Virtual Directory Creation Wizard and specify on the Access Permissions page that users can execute scripts or executable files within the virtual directory. To convert an existing virtual directory to an application, you open the virtual directory's Properties dialog box and click the Create button on the Virtual Directory properties page. To convert an existing application to a virtual directory, you open the application's Properties dialog box and click the Remove button on the Virtual Directory properties page.

Although a virtual directory's Virtual Directory properties page allows you to select *Scripts only* or *Scripts and Executables* in the *Execute Permissions* list, doing so will not convert the virtual directory to an application. To convert the virtual directory to an application, you must click the Create button on the Virtual Directory page.

**5**

You create an application for every server-side compiled program or script on your Web server. A server-side compiled program or script starts a **process** that runs in the Web server's memory and controls the program's execution. The memory area where a process runs is called its **process space**. The process space stores information about the process, such as its current state and the current values of its variables. You specify the location of a program's process space based on the memory model of its associated application. A **memory model** specifies how an environment stores the data for its processes in the main memory of a computer. IIS supports the following memory models for applications, and Figure 5-14 illustrates these models.

- **Low (IIS Process)**: The process runs in the same process space as the IIS and all other Web server-side script or application processes on the Web server.

- **Medium (Pooled)**: The process runs in a process space apart from the Web server, but shared by other Web server-side script and application processes.

- **High (Isolated)**: The process runs in its own isolated process space.

IIS Version 4, which is the predecessor to IIS Version 5, supports only the Low memory model.

If you configure all applications to use the Low memory model and run in the IIS process space, a poorly written application can monopolize all of the memory space or overwrite important memory items that belong to the Web server's processes. This causes the Web server to crash. Conversely, if you configure all applications to use the High memory model and run in an isolated process space, poorly written applications will not affect the Web server or other applications. However, applications may run slowly because the Web server may become short of available memory. When you configure applications to use the Medium memory model, they run in a pooled process space. If an application writes process data in a place where it shouldn't, it will only cause the other applications within the pooled process space to fail, but will not cause the Web server to crash.

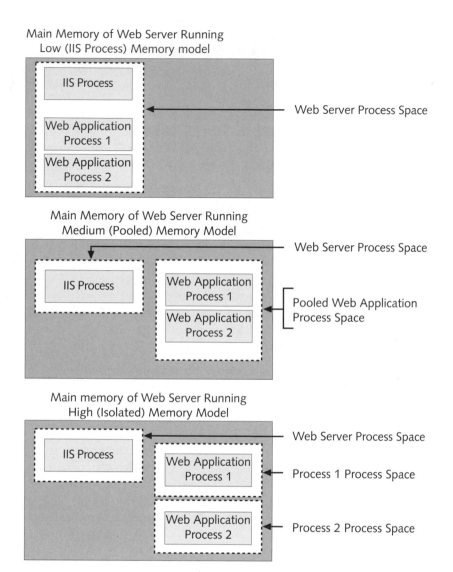

**Figure 5-14**    Web server application memory models

When you configure an application, you can select the desired memory model from the *Application Protection* list on the Virtual Directory properties page in the Properties dialog box. A good practice for assigning process spaces to Web server applications is to protect the Web server by avoiding the Low memory model. Then determine which applications are mission-critical, and configure these mission-critical applications to use the High memory model. Finally, configure all non-critical applications to run in the pooled memory space using the Medium memory model.

Sometimes a mysterious problem affects IIS Version 5 Web servers when running ASP scripts. ASP pages that used to work perfectly with the Medium memory model and haven't been reconfigured, moved, copied, or changed in any way cease to work. An internal server error message appears in the browser when the user tries to access the page; however, the message provides no insight into what is causing the problem. The only solutions for this problem are either to reconfigure the application so it uses the Low memory model, or to reinstall the server's operating system and reconfigure the Web server. This problem has been observed only on computers doing dual duty as servers and as desktop computers, and has not been observed on dedicated Web servers. Because Web developers normally run a personal Web server on their desktop/development computer, they may face this problem.

Now you will create an IIS application that you will associate with an ASP.NET server-side script that is saved on your Data Disk in a file named HitCounter.aspx. This script creates a Web page that displays a hit counter that displays the number of times that an individual user has run the script. First you will create a folder named HitCounter in the Chapter5\Tutorials folder on your Solution Disk and copy HitCounter.aspx into the HitCounter folder.

To create the application folder and copy the script file:

1. Switch to Windows Explorer and create a new folder named **HitCounter** in the Chapter5\Tutorials folder on your Solution Disk.

2. Copy **HitCounter.aspx** from the Chapter5 folder on your Data Disk to the Chapter5\Tutorials\HitCounter folder on your Solution Disk.

Now you will create an application named HitCounter that you will associate with the Chapter5\Tutorials\HitCounter folder on your Solution Disk. Because this folder contains a script rather than an executable file, you will specify that the application has the *Read* and *Run scripts* permissions shown in Figure 5-12. A Web server application must always have the *Read* permission along with one of the execute permissions. If you do not assign the *Read* permission, the application files will not execute. Users do not need the *Execute*, *Write*, or *Browse* privileges to execute this script.

To create the application:

1. Switch to the IIS console, select the **Default Web Site** node in the console tree, if necessary, right-click, point to **New**, and then click **Virtual Directory**. The Virtual Directory Creation Wizard Welcome page appears. Click **Next**.

2. On the Alias page, type **HitCounter** for the alias and then click **Next**.

3. On the Directory page, click **Browse** and navigate to the Chapter5\Tutorials\HitCounter folder on your Solution Disk. Select the **HitCounter** folder, click **OK**, and then click **Next**. (If your Solution Disk is on a network share, type the UNC path to the network share instead.)

4. On the Access Permissions page, make sure that the *Read* and *Run scripts (such as ASP)* check boxes are checked and that all of the other check boxes are cleared. Click **Next** and then click **Finish**. The new HitCounter application appears under the Default Web Site node in the console tree.

Note that the wizard creation process does not give you the opportunity to specify which memory model you want the application to use. To specify the memory model, you must open the application's Properties dialog box and choose the memory model on the Virtual Directory properties page. Now you will open the application's Properties dialog box and examine its Virtual Directory properties page.

To open the application's Properties dialog box:

1. Select the **HitCounter** node in the console tree, if necessary, and click the **Properties** button ![icon] on the toolbar. The HitCounter Properties dialog box opens, as shown in Figure 5-15.

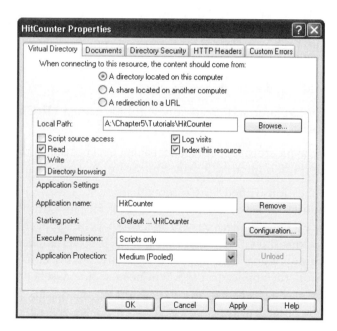

**Figure 5-15**    Application Properties dialog box

The *Application Settings* section on the Virtual Directory properties page specifies properties that are specific to the application. The *Execute Permissions* list specifies the types of processes that users can execute within the application. Possible values are *None*, which specifies that users cannot execute any applications; *Scripts only*, which specifies that users can execute only scripts; and *Scripts and Executables*, which specifies that users can execute both scripts and executable files. Because you checked the *Run scripts* check box on the Virtual Directory Creation Wizard Access Permissions page, *Scripts only* appears selected.

The *Application Protection* list specifies which memory model the application will use. The default value is the Medium (Pooled) memory model. This application is not mission-critical, so you will accept the default Medium memory model.

When you specified the *Run scripts* permission in the Virtual Directory Creation Wizard, the virtual directory became an application. If you click the Remove button, you will change the application to a virtual directory, and disable the *Application Protection* list. You can easily convert virtual directories to applications and vice versa using the Virtual Directory properties page in the Properties dialog box. Now you will click the Remove button, and convert the HitCounter application to a virtual directory.

To convert the application to a virtual directory:

1. On the Virtual Directory properties page, click **Remove**. The *Application name* field and *Application Protection* list are disabled. Note that the HitCounter node in the console tree changes to the Virtual Directory icon 🗀.

2. To restore the application, click **Create**. This converts the HitCounter virtual directory back to an application, and restores the Application specifications. Note that the HitCounter node in the console tree changes back to the Application icon 🧩.

3. Click **OK** to save your changes and close the Properties dialog box.

Users can run Web server applications by:

- Entering a URL for the application file directly in the Web browser *Address* field. An **application URL** includes the Web server name, the application name, and the name of the application file. For example, you would use the following URL to run the application you just created: *http://localhost/HitCounter/HitCounter.aspx*.

- Clicking a hyperlink that references the application URL.

- Clicking an HTML form button in which the onclick attribute calls a JavaScript function that calls the application URL.

- Submitting a form in which the form's action attribute references the application URL.

Now you will run the HitCounter application using the first approach. You will switch to Internet Explorer and specify the application's URL in the browser's *Address* field.

To run the HitCounter application:

1. Switch to Internet Explorer, type **http://localhost/hitcounter/ hitcounter.aspx** in the *Address* field and then press **Enter**. The dynamic Web page generated by the HitCounter application appears, as shown in Figure 5-16. In this URL, hitcounter is the name of the application and hitcounter.aspx is the specific application file that is in the folder associated with the application.

Application URL

Script filename

Application name

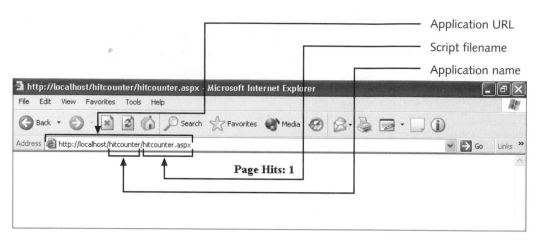

**Figure 5-16** Running an application

 If hitcounter.aspx does not run, make sure that the *Read access* check box is checked on the Virtual Directory properties page in the Properties dialog box. If an error message appears stating that you do not have the required privileges to write to the HitCounter.txt file, switch to Windows Explorer, navigate to the Chapter5\Tutorials\HitCounter folder on your Solution Disk, right-click the HitCounter.txt file, click Properties, select the Security tab, select your user name in the *Group or user names* list, check the *Allow* check box beside the *Write permission*, and then click OK.

2. Press **F5** a few times to refresh the display. This causes the application to execute again and increment the Page Hits value.

Recall that users can run scripts or executable files on an IIS Web server only if the script or file is stored in a folder (physical directory) that you associate with an application. Script or executable files will not execute from a physical directory or a virtual directory, even if the *Execute Permissions* list selection is *Scripts only* or *Scripts and Executables*. To confirm this, you will switch back to the IIS console and change the HitCounter application to a virtual directory. Then you will try to run the HitCounter.aspx script again.

To change the HitCounter application to a virtual directory and try to run the script:

1. Switch to the IIS console, select the **HitCounter** node, if necessary, in the console tree, and click the **Properties** button 📝 to open the Properties dialog box.

2. On the Virtual Directory properties page, click **Remove** to remove the application. Then click **OK** to close the Properties dialog box and save your changes. The HitCounter node appears in the console tree as a Virtual Directory icon 📁.

3. Switch to Internet Explorer and press **F5** to run the HitCounter.aspx application again. A message stating "Server Application Unavailable" appears, indicating that the application is no longer available.

4. Switch back to the IIS console, open the HitCounter Properties dialog box, and click **Create** to change the virtual directory to an application. Then click **OK** to close the Properties dialog box and save your changes.

5. Switch back to Internet Explorer and press **F5** to run the HitCounter.aspx application again. The HitCounter page appears again, indicating that the application executed successfully.

You can specify a default document for an application, just as you specified a default document for the home directory, physical directories, and virtual directories. When you specify a default document for an application, the user needs to enter only the application name in the browser *Address* field, and does not need to include the script or executable filename. Now you will specify that hitcounter.aspx is the default document for the HitCounter application. Then, you will enter only the application name in the browser *Address* field and omit the script filename.

To specify a default document for an application:

1. Select the **HitCounter** application node, and click the **Properties** button to open the Properties dialog box. Click the **Documents** tab to open the Documents properties page.

2. On the Documents properties page, click **Add**. The Add Default Document dialog box opens. Type **hitcounter.aspx** in the *Default Document Name* field, and click **OK** to save the new default document name.

3. On the Documents properties page, make sure that hitcounter.aspx is selected in the default document list. Then click the **Up arrow** button several times until hitcounter.aspx appears as the first document in the default document list. Click **OK** to close the Properties dialog box and save your changes.

4. Switch to Internet Explorer, type **http://localhost/hitcounter** in the *Address* field, and press **Enter**. The application runs again and increments the Page Hits value by one.

## ORGANIZING YOUR WEB SERVER

Web administrators organize Web server files by placing them in directories that make the files easier to locate and manage. These directories enable the administrator to control file access permissions and ensure the security of the Web site. Many Web administrators organize Web server files by creating separate directories for different types of files. Figure 5-17 shows an example of a Web site that uses this organizational approach.

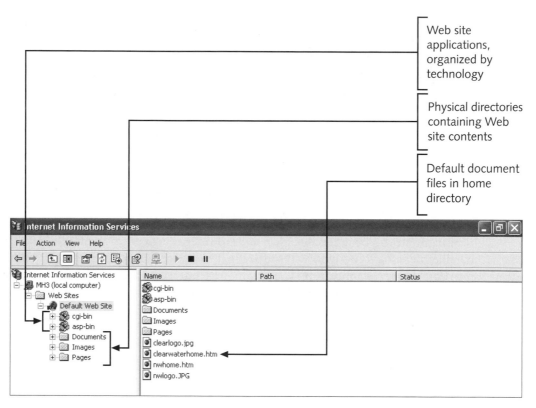

Web site applications, organized by technology

Physical directories containing Web site contents

Default document files in home directory

**Figure 5-17**    Common Web site structure

In this structure, the home directory contains the HTML files and graphic images that comprise the default document or documents. The home directory also contains physical directories that store the rest of the Web site's content, organized by file types. For example, the Web server in Figure 5-17 stores Web page HTML files in the Pages physical directory and graphic image files in the Images physical directory. The Documents physical directory stores word processor documents and spreadsheets that users can download. The Web server also has applications that it associates with server-side program files. The Web server administrator has grouped these applications based on their associated processing technologies. In this example, the cgi-bin application is associated with programs that use the Common Gateway Interface (CGI) protocol, and the asp-bin application is associated with Active Server Page scripts.

The cgi-bin and asp-bin applications derive their names from a file structure model often used on computers that run the UNIX operating system. In this structure, all executable (binary) files are stored in a directory named BIN.

The Web server configuration in Figure 5-17 enables Web administrators to store all Web page files and graphic image files in a central location. With this approach, the Web server needs to store only a single copy of all pages and images. Whenever a Web page references another Web page or a graphic image file, it references the file that is in the Pages or Images physical directory. This approach makes it easier to manage and maintain the Web page and graphic image files, and minimizes the amount of disk space required for Web page and image files, because the Web server does not store duplicate copies of the same file in different locations.

This configuration also enables Web administrators to control file access privileges based on each directory's contents. The Images, Pages, and Documents physical directories store files that users download to their browsers, so these directories require only the *Read* access permission. Directories that store CGI and Active Server Page files contain script and executable files, so these directories require the *Scripts only* or *Scripts and Executables* access permissions and must be associated with applications.

From a security standpoint, the Web site structure in Figure 5-17 is not optimal. You should not place all Web site contents in physical directories within the home directory. If you inadvertently enable directory browsing in the home directory, users can access all of the Web server directories and possibly delete files or introduce harmful files. Instead, you should place only the default document files in the home directory. Then, you should create physical directories outside of the home directory that contain all other Web site files, and associate these physical directories with virtual directories to allow users to access their contents. When users access Web site contents using a virtual directory, they can access only the files and physical directories that are within the virtual directory. They cannot navigate to any other directories on the Web site using directory browsing.

The Web structure in Figure 5-17 does not work very well for a Web site that contains many different Web applications that create dynamic Web pages. (Recall from Chapter 1 that a Web application consists of one or more files that developers create to solve a problem or provide a service through a Web site.) Often, a single Web application consists of many CGI or Active Server Page files. If you place all program files into a single Web site application node, such as asp-bin, the application contains many unrelated files. For example, suppose you create an ASP.NET application to process Clearwater Traders customer orders that consists of six different ASP.NET .aspx script files. You would place these six script files in the physical directory that you associate with the asp-bin application, which also contains all of the files for all of your other ASP.NET scripts. These multiple unrelated files become difficult to manage and maintain.

A better practice is to create a separate Web site application node for each individual Web application that contains one or more related script files. For the Clearwater Traders ordering system, you would create an application named ClearwaterOrders and then place the six .aspx files in the physical directory that you associate with this application.

Figure 5-18 shows a better Web site structure. On this Web site, the Images, Pages, and Documents physical directories are not within the home directory. Rather, the Web server administrator creates these physical directories outside of the home directory, and then creates virtual directories and associates them with these physical directories. The Pages directory contains all static Web pages that the Web site displays. The Images directory contains the files for the graphic images that appear in these static Web pages, and the Documents directory contains documents that these static Web pages reference.

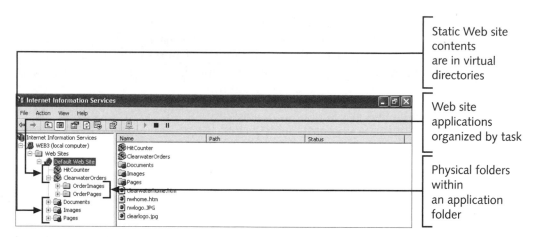

**Figure 5-18**   Preferred Web site structure

The Web server administrator creates a separate application that he or she associates with each separate Web application task. In this example, the administrator associates the HitCounter application with a physical directory that contains the files for the HitCounter program, and associates the ClearwaterOrders application with a physical directory that contains files for a program that enables Clearwater Traders customers to select items and then process an order. Note that the Clearwater Orders application contains physical directories named OrderPages and OrderImages that store the HTML files and graphic image files that the application references.

Now you will revise your Default Web Site so it has the structure shown in Figure 5-18. First, you will move your current Pages physical directory so it is outside the home directory. You will also delete the copies of the clearwaterhome.htm and nwhome.htm files that are in the Pages folder, because these files already exist in the home directory, and you do not want to have multiple copies of the same files on your Web server.

To move the Pages folder and delete the duplicate files:

1. In Windows Explorer, move the **Pages** folder from the Chapter5\Tutorials\wwwroot folder to the Chapter5\Tutorials folder on your Solution Disk, so that the folder is not in the home directory.

2. Delete the **clearwaterhome.htm** and **nwhome.htm** files from the Chapter5\Tutorials\Pages folder on your Solution Disk.

Next you will create folders named Documents and Images in the Chapter5\Tutorials folder on your Solution Disk. You will then create virtual directories associated with the Pages, Documents, and Images folders.

To create the folders and virtual directories:

1. In Windows Explorer, create folders named **Documents** and **Images** in the Chapter5\Tutorials folder on your Solution Disk. (Recall that your home directory is associated with the Chapter5\Tutorials\wwwroot folder, so these new folders are not physically within your home directory.)

2. Switch to the IIS console. To create the Pages virtual directory, select the **Default Web Site** node, right-click, point to **New**, and click **Virtual Directory** to start the Virtual Directory Creation Wizard. Click **Next**.

3. Type **Pages** in the *Alias* field and then click **Next**.

4. Click **Browse**, navigate to the Chapter5\Tutorials folder on your Solution Disk, select the **Pages** folder, click **OK**, and then click **Next**.

5. On the Access Permissions page, make sure that the *Read* check box is checked, and that all of the other check boxes are cleared. Click **Next** and then click **Finish** to create the virtual directory.

6. Repeat Steps 2 through 5 to create the Documents and Images virtual directories. Your IIS console display should contain the Documents, Images, and Pages virtual directories shown in Figure 5-18, as well as the HitCounter application. (Your Web site components may appear in a different order. Your console display does not yet show the ClearwaterOrders application, because you have not yet created it.)

Earlier in the chapter, you created a folder named Products in the Chapter5 folder on your Solution Disk. This folder contains the products.htm Web page HTML file and the files for the graphic images that this Web page references. Now you will move the products.htm Web page file to the Pages folder on your Solution Disk. Then, you will move the graphic image files that appear on the products.htm Web page into the Images folder on your Solution Disk. Finally, you will delete the Products folder.

To move the files and delete the Products folder:

1. Switch to Windows Explorer and move **products.htm** from the Chapter5\Products folder on your Solution Disk to the Chapter5\Tutorials\Pages folder on your Solution Disk.

2. Move the following files from the Chapter5\Products folder to the Chapter5\Tutorials\Images folder on your Solution Disk: **clearlogo.jpg**, **fleece.jpg**, **parka.jpg**, **sandals.jpg**, **shorts.jpg**, and **tents.jpg**.

3. Delete the **Products** folder on your Solution Disk.

To complete the Web server structure, you need to create the ClearwaterOrders application shown in Figure 5-18. The folder that you associate with this application contains folders (physical directories) named OrderPages and OrderImages. These physical directories contain the static Web pages and graphic image files that this application references. You must store these files in physical directories within the application. When an application creates dynamic Web pages that interact with static Web pages, you must place these static Web pages in physical directories that are subdirectories of the folder that you associate with the application. If you place these static Web pages in physical directories outside of the application in the IIS console tree, they are outside of the application's process space. If commands within the application attempt to navigate to these pages while the application is running, the commands cannot reference information from the application's process space, and the application will not run correctly.

Now you will create a folder named Cworders in the Chapter5\Tutorials folder on your Solution Disk. Within the Cworders folder, you will create folders named OrderPages and OrderImages. Then, you will copy the Clearwater Traders order application files into these folders. This application consists of three files: clearwater_orders.htm, clearlogo.jpg, and process_order.aspx. The clearwater_orders.htm file is a static Web page that contains a form that allows the user to select an item to order from Clearwater Traders. When the user submits the form to the Web server, the form calls the process_order.aspx ASP.NET script file. This script generates a dynamic Web page that summarizes the user's order.

To create the folders and copy the files:

1. In Windows Explorer, create a folder named **Cworders** in the Chapter5\Tutorials folder on your Solution Disk.

2. Create folders named **OrderPages** and **OrderImages** in the new Cworders folder.

3. Copy **process_order.aspx** from the Chapter5 folder on your Data Disk to the Chapter5\Cworders folder on your Solution Disk.

4. Copy **clearwater_orders.htm** from the Chapter5 folder on your Data Disk to the Chapter5\Cworders\OrderPages folder on your Solution Disk.

5. Copy **clearlogo.jpg** from the Chapter5 folder on your Data Disk to the Chapter5\Cworders\OrderImages folder on your Solution Disk.

Now you will create an application named ClearwaterOrders that you will associate with the Cworders folder in the Chapter5\Tutorials folder on your Solution Disk. You will specify that the application has *Read* and *Scripts only* access permissions. You will accept the default Medium (Pooled) memory model option for the application.

To create the ClearwaterOrders application:

1. Switch to the IIS console, select the **Default Web Site** node, right-click, point to **New**, and then click **Virtual Directory**. The Virtual Directory Creation Wizard opens. Click **Next**.

2. Type **ClearwaterOrders** in the *Alias* field, and then click **Next**.

3. On the Content Directory page, click **Browse**, navigate to the Chapter5\Tutorials folder on your Solution Disk, select the **Cworders** folder, click **OK**, and then click **Next**.

4. On the Access Permissions page, make sure that the *Read* and *Run scripts (such as ASP)* check boxes are checked, and that the other check boxes are cleared. Click **Next** and then click **Finish**. The ClearwaterOrders application appears under the Default Web Site node in the IIS console.

5. Click the **plus sign** beside the ClearwaterOrders node to view the physical directories within the application. Your IIS console display should look like Figure 5-18. (The order of your Web server components may be different.)

## REFERENCING FILES ON A WEB SERVER

Recall from Chapter 2 that the directory that contains the Web page that currently appears in the user's browser is called the browser's current working directory. When you reference objects such as graphic images in a Web page, you must either place the object file in the same directory as the Web page or specify an absolute or relative file path to the object file. (Recall that an absolute file path specifies the exact location of a file in the browser's file system, including the drive letter, path, and filename. A relative file path specifies a file location in relation to the current working directory.)

Similarly, when you reference an object on a Web page that is stored on a Web server, the referenced object must be in the same directory as the Web page that currently appears, or you must specify an absolute or relative path to the object on the Web server using absolute or relative URL addresses.

### Absolute URL Addresses

An **absolute URL address** specifies the Web server IP address or domain name, the complete path or virtual directory path to the Web page file, and the name of the Web page file. You can place an absolute URL address in a browser's *Address* field, in a hyperlink tag to specify the location of a Web page file, or as the src attribute value in an <img> tag. Figure 5-19 shows examples of a file URL, an absolute URL address that uses a virtual directory, and an absolute URL that uses a combination of a virtual directory and a physical directory.

The first example shows a file URL that uses an absolute path to show the actual physical location of the products.htm Web page file, which is stored in the Chapter5\Tutorials\Pages folder on your Solution Disk. The second URL shows the virtual directory path to the products.htm file, and assumes that the file is stored in the physical directory that you associate with the Pages virtual directory. The third URL shows how you can combine a virtual directory and a physical directory specification in an absolute URL to reference the location of the clearwater_orders.htm file. The file is stored in the OrderPages physical directory, which is in the physical directory that you associate with the ClearwaterOrders application.

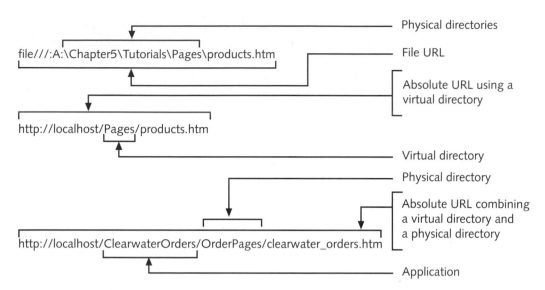

**Figure 5-19**    Absolute URL addresses

Now you will use the URLs in Figure 5-19 to display the products.htm and clearwater_orders.htm Web pages. Currently, these Web page files reference their graphic image files by assuming that the files are in the same directory as the Web page HTML files. Because you moved the graphic image files to the Images folder in the Chapter5\Tutorials folder on your Solution Disk, the images will not appear on the Web pages, because their paths are now incorrect.

To display the products.htm and clearwater_orders.htm Web page files using absolute URLs:

1. Switch to Internet Explorer, type **a:\chapter5\tutorials\pages\ products.htm** in the *Address* field, and press **Enter**. The Product Guide Web page appears, but none of the graphic images appear. This is because the src attribute values in the HTML document reference the graphic image files using relative paths, which assume that the files are in the same directory as the products.htm file.

2. To display the products.htm Web page using an absolute URL that specifies a virtual directory, type **http://localhost/pages/products.htm** in the *Address* box, and then press **Enter**. The Product Guide Web page appears again.

3. To display the clearwater_orders.htm Web page with an absolute URL that combines a virtual directory and a physical directory, type **http://localhost/ ClearwaterOrders/OrderPages/clearwater_orders.htm** and then press **Enter**. The Customer Orders Web page appears, as shown in Figure 5-20. The graphic image does not appear because the graphic image file is not in the same directory as the Web page's .htm file.

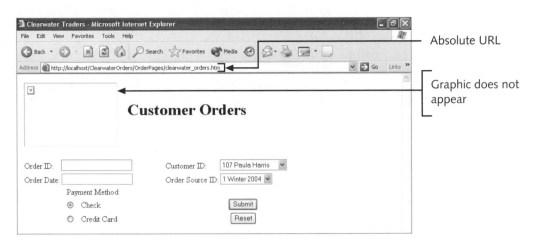

**Figure 5-20**     *Customer Orders Web page file*

Now you will modify the products.htm file so that the reference to the Clearwater Traders logo graphic image file uses an absolute URL. Earlier, you moved the file for the Clearwater Traders logo (clearlogo.jpg) to the Chapter5\Tutorials\Images folder on your Solution Disk. In addition, you created a virtual directory named Images that you associated with the Chapter5\Tutorials\Images folder. You will use the following absolute URL, which specifies the virtual directory, to reference the file location: *http://localhost/Images/clearlogo.jpg*.

To modify products.htm to use an absolute URL to specify the location of the graphic image file:

1. Start Visual Studio .NET, and open **products.htm** from the Chapter5\Tutorials\Pages folder on your Solution Disk.

2. Click the **HTML** tab to display the HTML source code. Change the <img> tag for the Clearwater Traders logo so the src attribute value is an absolute URL that specifies the Images virtual directory, as follows. (This tag should appear on approximately the 10th line of the HTML file.) Do not change any other attribute values of the img tag.

   ```
   <img height="102" src=↵
   "http://localhost/images/clearlogo.jpg" width="160">
   ```

3. Save the file.

4. Switch to Internet Explorer, click **File** on the menu bar, click **Open**, click **Browse**, navigate to the Chapter5\Tutorials\Pages folder on your Solution Disk, select **products.htm**, click **Open**, and then click **OK**. The products.htm Web page appears, and the Clearwater Traders logo image now appears. The other images on the page do not appear, because you have not modified the src attribute in their tags to reflect the new file locations outside of the current working directory.

 If the logo does not appear, make sure that the clearlogo.jpg file is located in the Chapter5\Tutorials\Images folder on your Solution Disk. Also make sure that you created a virtual directory named Images that is associated with the Chapter5\Tutorials\Images folder, and that you modified the image source reference as described in Step 2. You might also need to delete all of the cached files in your browser.

4. Switch back to Visual Studio .NET and close products.htm.

## Relative URL Addresses

A **relative URL address** specifies the location of a file relative to the current working directory. You can use relative URL addresses to specify files that you store in physical directories on the Web server. To reference a file that is in a physical directory within the current working directory, you type the physical directory name, a front slash (/), and then the filename, using the following syntax: *directory_name/filename*. Do not preface the *directory_name* with a slash. If you do, the path will start at the Web server's home directory rather than at the current working directory. To reference a file that is in the parent directory of the current working directory, you specify the parent directory using two periods (..) followed by a front slash (/), using the following syntax: *../filename*.

Currently, your Web server has the directory structure and files shown in Figure 5-21. The home directory contains the clearwaterhome.htm and nwhome.htm files and their associated graphic image files. There are three virtual directories: Documents, Pages, and Images. These virtual directories are directly below the home directory and contain the listed files. The HitCounter and ClearwaterOrders applications are also directly below the home directory and contain the listed files. (The HitCounter.txt file is a data file that the script creates the first time it runs and that keeps track of the current Page Hits value.) Recall that the physical directory that you associated with the ClearwaterOrders application contains physical directories named OrderPages and OrderImages, which contain the files shown in Figure 5-21.

You can use relative path addresses to specify file addresses that are below, above, and across a physical directory structure. Table 5-1 shows the relative URL path addresses that you would use to reference different files in the physical directory structure in the ClearwaterOrders application, depending on the current working directory.

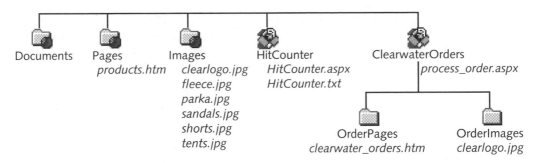

**Figure 5-21**    Current Web server directory structure

**Table 5-1**    Relative path addresses

| Browser Current Working Directory | Target File | Relative Path Address |
|---|---|---|
| ClearwaterOrders | clearwater_orders.htm | OrderPages/clearwater_orders.htm |
| OrderPages | process_order.aspx | ../process_order.aspx |
| OrderPages | clearlogo.jpg | ../OrderImages/clearlogo.jpg |

The first example in Table 5-1 shows how you can reference a file that is in a subdirectory of the current working directory by specifying the name of the directory and then the filename. The second example shows how you can reference a file that is in the parent directory of the current working directory by using the parent directory indicator (..) to move up the directory structure and then specifying the filename. The third example shows how to move across a directory structure by using the parent directory indicator (..) to move up to the ClearwaterOrders directory and then using a front slash plus the directory name to move down to the OrderImages directory.

You cannot use a relative URL to specify a file location in different virtual directories below the home directory. For example, you cannot use a relative URL to reference a file in the Images virtual directory if the current working directory is the Pages virtual directory.

Now you will open the clearwater_orders.htm Web page file in Visual Studio .NET and modify the file so it uses relative URL addresses. You will change the form's action attribute so it references the process_order.aspx file, which is in the parent directory of the current working directory. You will also change the src attribute value for the <img> tag for the Clearwater Traders logo so it references the file in the OrderImages physical directory, which is across the physical directory structure.

To modify the clearwater_orders.htm file to use relative URL addresses:

1. In Visual Studio .NET, open **clearwater_orders.htm** from the Chapter5\Tutorials\Cworders\OrderPages folder on your Solution Disk.

2. Click the **HTML** tab to view the page in HTML view. Modify the `<img>` tag as follows so the src attribute references the image file that is in the OrderImages folder, which is one directory up, and then in the OrderImages directory in the physical directory structure. (This tag is on approximately the eighth line of the file.) Do not modify any other properties of the `<img>` tag.

```
<img src="../OrderImages/clearlogo.jpg"
height="128" width="190">
```

3. Modify the action attribute of the `<form>` tag so it references the process_order.aspx file that is stored in the parent directory of the current working directory. (This tag is on approximately the 11th line of the file.)

```
<form name="frmCustOrders"
action="../process_order.aspx">
```

4. Save the file.

Next you will switch to Internet Explorer and open the Customer Orders Web page. You will confirm that the graphic image now appears, and confirm that when you click the Submit button, the process_order.aspx script file executes and creates a dynamic Web page that summarizes the order.

To open, view, and test the Customer Orders Web page:

1. Switch to Internet Explorer, type **http://localhost/ClearwaterOrders/ OrderPages/clearwater_orders.htm** in the *Address* field, and press **Enter**. The Web page appears as shown in Figure 5-20, except that now the image for the Clearwater Traders logo appears.

2. Type **1** in the *Order ID* field and type **2/10/2004** in the *Order Date* field. Accept all of the other default values, and then click **Submit** to submit the form to your Web server. (Normally, the application would automatically generate the Order ID value, but for testing purposes, you will manually insert it.) The dynamic Web page that the process_order.aspx script generates appears as shown in Figure 5-22, and summarizes the order information.

**Figure 5-22**    Dynamic Web page generated by script

3. Close Internet Explorer, Visual Studio .NET, the ITS console, and all other open applications.

## FACTORS IMPACTING WEB SITE PERFORMANCE

People who visit Web sites frequently experience delays while waiting for their browsers to display the pages they request. Some of the factors that affect the time it takes for a Web site to service a user request include:

- The speed of the Web server's network connection
- The amount of main memory that the Web server's administrator allocates to process Web page requests
- The Web server's processor speed
- The number of other visitors currently requesting pages or files from the Web site
- The size of Web page files and their embedded graphics objects
- The server resources required to execute Web-based programs and scripts in Web pages

Web server administrators can use a variety of tools to monitor Web site performance, and IIS offers many configuration options to tune the Web server and optimize performance. A discussion of these monitoring tools and configuration options is beyond the scope of this chapter. As a Web page developer, however, you need to be aware that an easy way to improve the performance of a Web site is to limit the size of your Web page files and the number of graphic objects on each page. Always assume that visitors will have fairly slow network connections that make Web page files take much longer to appear than they take to appear on your local workstation when you are testing the Web page. Each graphic image in an HTML file uses a separate Web server connection to transfer the file to the user's browser, which puts an additional load on your Web server. Try to use graphic images sparingly in your Web pages, and when you do use graphic images keep the graphic image files as small as possible.

## CHAPTER SUMMARY

- Internet Information Services (IIS) includes the IIS console for administering a Web server and the listener process for servicing user requests to a Web server.
- A Web server's home directory is the Web server directory that contains the Web server's default document. You can place the home directory anywhere in the Web server's file system, in a network share to which you have mapped a drive, or on a remote Web server identified by a URL.
- You use the Web Site Properties dialog box to configure general Web site properties, such as the home directory location, user access privileges to the home directory, and the default document filename.

❑ To connect to your local Web server, you use the *http://localhost* URL, which your workstation associates with the reserved IP address of 127.0.0.1 and which always refers to the IP address of the local computer.

❑ When a user connects to a Web server and does not specify an HTML document filename, IIS looks for the default document filename in the default document list in the home directory. If the Web server does not find a default document file, then a Web page appears stating that access is denied.

❑ When users access a Web server directory in which directory browsing is enabled, they see a listing of the files within the directory. Users can open, download, or print these files. It is useful to enable directory browsing for directories that you want to use to distribute files to users.

❑ A physical directory is a folder within the Web server's file system that is within the home directory, a virtual directory, or an application.

❑ A virtual directory is not necessarily physically within the home directory, but appears to client browsers as though it is. You associate a virtual directory with a physical directory in the Web server's file system or as a redirection to a URL. Every virtual directory has an alias, which is the name that client browsers use to access the directory. You create virtual directories to control access and security of the Web server file system, enable users to access Web pages and application files that are stored in locations outside of the home directory, and make it possible to change the physical location of Web page files on your Web server without changing the URLs that visitors use to access the files.

❑ Applications are virtual directories in which permissions exist to allow users to run scripts or executable files. Applications contain files for server-side executable programs or scripts. To create an application, you create a virtual directory that you associate with a physical directory containing the script files or executable files for the application, and specify that users can execute the scripts or executable files within the virtual directory.

❑ You can use the application Properties dialog box to specify whether an application runs using the Low, Medium, or High memory model. In the Low memory model, the application runs in the same process space as the Web server. In the Medium memory model, the application runs in a shared process space with other applications. In the High memory model, the application runs in its own isolated process space.

❑ To ensure Web server security and make the Web server easier to manage, you should place all static Web pages, and the images and documents they reference, in virtual directories whose physical directories are outside of the server's home directory. You should create a separate application for each Web application. In the application's folder, you should place all of the application's script or executable files, as well as the HTML document files and images that the application uses.

❑ When you reference an object on a Web page, the referenced object must be in the same physical or virtual directory as the Web page that currently appears, or you must specify an absolute or relative URL address to the object on the Web server. An absolute URL address specifies a location relative to the Web server home directory. A relative URL specifies a location relative to the current working directory. You can use relative URLs to navigate within physical directories that exist in applications or virtual directories.

❑ As a Web page developer, you should always assume that users have fairly slow network connections. To make Web pages appear faster, you should limit the size of your Web page files and minimize the number of graphic images.

**5**

---

# REVIEW QUESTIONS

1. Suppose that a Web server's home directory does not have a default document, and directory browsing is not enabled in the home directory. A user types a URL in the *Address* field in his or her Web browser that specifies the Web server's IP address, but does not specify a Web page file. What appears in the user's browser?

2. In the scenario described in Question 1, what will appear in the user's browser if directory browsing is enabled in the home directory?

3. True or false: When you delete a physical directory in the IIS console, you also delete the underlying folder and its contents.

4. Why do you usually disable script source access in Web site directories?

5. When you _____ a Web server, the Web server unloads the listener process from memory. When you _____ a Web server, the Web server listener is still active, but the Web server will not accept any new connections.

  a. Disable, enable

  b. Pause, start

  c. Pause, stop

  d. Stop, pause

6. When a computer has a _____ IP address, its IP address always stays the same. When a computer has a _____ IP address, its IP address changes whenever you reboot the computer.

  a. Local, remote

  b. Static, dynamic

  c. Dynamic, static

  d. Numerical, domain name

7. When should a computer have a static IP address?

8. When should a computer have a dynamic IP address?

9. A workstation associates the numerical IP address 127.0.0.1 with the _____ domain name.

10. What is the difference between a physical directory and a virtual directory, besides the type of icon that represents each node in the console tree?

11. How do you convert a virtual directory to an application?

12. List three ways to run a Web site application.

13. What is a process space?

14. The _____ memory model places all Web applications in the same process space as the Web server.

    a. Low

    b. Medium

    c. High

    d. Shared

15. For what types of applications should you use the High memory model? For what types of applications should you use the Low memory model?

16. True or false: A Web server can have only one default document file, and it must be in the home directory.

17. Why is it a poor practice to store Web site files in physical directories that are within the home directory?

18. The _____ access permission allows you to run CGI programs, Active Server Page files, and ASP.NET files in the same application.

    a. *Execute*

    b. *Scripts only*

    c. *Executables only*

    d. *Scripts and executables*

19. List three ways to speed up the time it takes a Web server to process user Web page requests.

20. Figure 5-23 shows the directory structure for a Web server. The Virtual Directory icon 🗂 designates virtual directories, the Physical Directory icon 📁 designates physical directories, and the Application icon 🌐 designates applications.

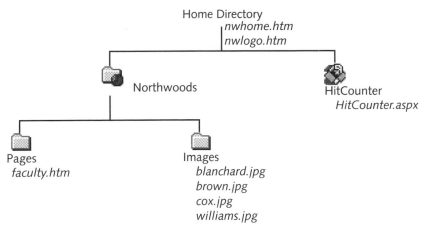

**Figure 5-23**

21. Specify the absolute URL addresses for the following files using localhost as the Web server domain name:

    a. nwhome.htm

    b. brown.jpg

    c. faculty.htm

    d. HitCounter.aspx

22. Using Figure 5-23 as the Web server directory structure, specify the relative URL addresses for the following target files, based on the specified current working directory:

| Target File | Current Working Directory |
| --- | --- |
| faculty.htm | Home Directory |
| nwhome.htm | Northwoods |
| nwhome.htm | Images |
| faculty.htm | Images |

# HANDS-ON PROJECTS

## Project 5-1 Configuring the Northwoods University Web Server

In this project, you will configure the Northwoods University Web server as shown in Figure 5-23.

1. Create a folder named 5Project1 in the Chapter5\Projects folder on your Solution Disk. Copy the nwhome.htm and nwlogo.htm files from the Chapter5 folder on your Data Disk into the new 5Project1 folder.

2. Create a folder named HitCounter in the Chapter5\Projects folder on your Solution Disk. Copy the hitcounter.aspx file from the Chapter5 folder on your Data Disk into the new HitCounter folder.

3. Create a folder named Northwoods in the Chapter5\Projects folder on your Solution Disk. Create folders named Pages and Images within the new Northwoods folder. Copy the faculty.htm file from the Chapter5 folder on your Solution Disk into the Pages folder, and copy the following files from the Chapter5 folder on your Data Disk into the Images folder: blanchard.jpg, brown.jpg, cox.jpg, and williams.jpg.

4. Delete all existing virtual directories and applications from your Default Web Site.

5. Modify your Default Web Site so its home directory is the 5Project1 folder on your Solution Disk, and disable directory browsing in the home directory. If necessary, add nwhome.htm to the default document list.

6. Create a virtual directory with the alias *Northwoods*. Associate the virtual directory with the Northwoods folder in the Chapter5\Projects folder on your Solution Disk. Specify that the virtual directory has the *Read* access privilege only, disable directory browsing, and disable the default document.

7. Create an application named HitCounter that you associate with the HitCounter folder in the Chapter5\Projects folder on your Solution Disk. Specify that the HitCounter application has *Read* and *Run scripts* access privileges.

8. Display the faculty.htm Web page file in your Web browser using an absolute URL address that specifies the Web page location using the localhost domain name and the Northwoods virtual directory. Specify the URL address you use. (Do not worry if the graphic images do not appear.)

9. Run the hitcounter.aspx script using an absolute URL address. Specify the URL address that you use.

To complete Project 5-2, you must have completed Project 5-1.

## Project 5-2 Using Absolute and Relative URL Addresses on the Northwoods University Web Site

In this project, you will modify the URL references in the HTML document files on the Northwoods University Web site so they work correctly within the Web server structure you created in Project 5-1.

1. Modify the nwhome.htm Web page file in the home directory so it uses an absolute URL address to reference the nwlogo.jpg graphic image file that is in the home directory.

2. Create a hyperlink in the nwhome.htm Web page file to link the Faculty unordered list item to the faculty.htm Web page file that is stored in the Northwoods\Pages physical directory. Use a relative URL address to create the link.

3. Modify the faculty.htm Web page file so the graphic images appear. Use an absolute URL address to reference the nwlogo.jpg file in the home directory, and use relative URL addresses to reference the other files, which are in the Images folder.

4. At the bottom of the faculty.htm Web page, create a hyperlink with the text "Count Hits." When the user clicks the hyperlink, the hitcounter.aspx script file should execute. Use an absolute URL address to reference the script file.

## Project 5-3 Configuring the Clearwater Traders Web Server

**5**

In this project, you will configure the Clearwater Traders Web server shown in Figure 5-24.

1. Create a folder named 5Project3 in the Projects folder on your Solution Disk. Copy the clearwaterhome.htm file from the Chapter5 folder on your Data Disk into the new 5Project3 folder.

2. Create a new folder named Clearwater in the Chapter5\Projects folder on your Solution Disk. Create folders named Pages and Images in the new Clearwater folder. Create folders named Products and Orders in the new Pages folder.

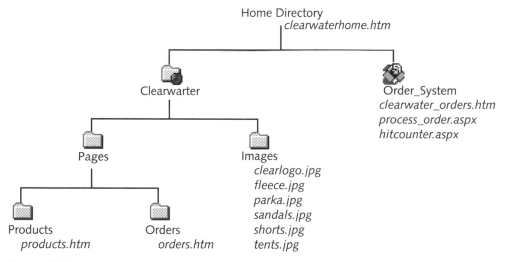

**Figure 5-24**

3. Create a new folder named Order_System in the Chapter5\Projects folder on your Solution Disk. Copy the files shown in the Order_System application in Figure 5-24 from the Chapter5 folder on your Data Disk into the new Order_System folder.

4. Copy the products.htm file from the Chapter5 folder on your Data Disk into the Products folder, and copy the orders.htm file from the Chapter5 folder on your Data Disk into the Orders folder. Copy the files shown in the Images physical directory in Figure 5-25 from the Chapter5 folder on your Data Disk into the new Images folder.

5. Delete all existing virtual directories and applications on your Default Web Site.

6. Modify your Default Web Site so its home directory is associated with the 5Project3 folder on your Solution Disk. Specify that clearwaterhome.htm is a default document. Disable directory browsing in the home directory.

7. Create a virtual directory with the alias "Clearwater" that corresponds with the Clearwater folder in the Chapter5\Projects folder on your Solution Disk. Specify that the virtual directory has the *Read* access privilege only, that directory browsing is disabled, and that the default document is not enabled.

8. Create a Web site application named Order_System. Associate the application with the Order_System folder in the Chapter5\Projects folder on your Solution Disk. Specify that the application has *Read* and *Run scripts* access permissions. Specify that the application uses the Medium memory model, and specify that clearwater_orders.htm is the application's default document.

To complete Project 5-4, you must have completed Project 5-3.

## Project 5-4 Using Absolute and Relative URL Addresses on the Clearwater Traders Web Site

In this project, you will modify the HTML files on the Clearwater Traders Web site in Figure 5-24 so they work correctly within the Web server structure you created in Project 5-3.

1. Modify the clearwaterhome.htm Web page file that is in the Chapter5\Projects\5Project3 folder on your Solution Disk so that the clearlogo.jpg graphic image appears, and so the How to Order text is a hyperlink anchor to the orders.htm Web page. Use absolute URL addresses.

2. Modify the orders.htm Web page file in the Chapter5\Clearwater\Pages\Orders folder on your Solution Disk so the graphic image appears. To accomplish this, specify a relative URL address to the tents.jpg file that is stored in the Images folder in the Clearwater virtual directory.

3. Create a hyperlink that associates the "Order Now" text with the Order_System application. The hyperlink should use an absolute URL path and specify the application name. Do not specify a filename, because the application has a default document.

4. Modify the clearwater_orders.htm Web page file that in the Order_System application so the graphic image for the Clearwater Traders logo appears correctly. To accomplish this, specify an absolute URL address to the clearlogo.jpg file that is in the Images folder in the Clearwater virtual directory.

5. Modify the products.htm Web page file in the \Pages\Products folder in the Clearwater virtual directory so the graphic images appear. Use relative URL addresses to reference the graphic images stored in the Images physical directory that is in the Clearwater virtual directory.

# CASE PROJECTS

## Case 5-1 Ashland Valley Soccer League

In this case, you will create a Web server structure similar to the one in Figure 5-21 for the Ashland Valley Soccer League Web site, which is described in Case 2-1 in Chapter 2. Create directories named Ashland, AshlandPages, and AshlandImages in the Chapter5\Cases folder on your Solution Disk. Copy the Ashland.htm file from the Chapter5\Cases\Ashland folder on your Data Disk to the Chapter5\Cases\Ashland folder on your Solution Disk. Copy the Fields.htm, Games.htm, and Teams.htm files from the Chapter5\Cases\Ashland folder on your Data Disk into the Chapter5\Cases\AshlandPages folder on your Solution Disk, and copy all of the .jpg files in the Chapter5\Cases\Ashland folder on your Data Disk to the Chapter5\AshlandImages folder on your Solution Disk.

Configure your Default Web Site so its home directory is associated with the Ashland folder on your Solution Disk. Create virtual directories named AshlandPages and AshlandImages, and associate these virtual directories with the new physical directories. Specify that Ashland.htm is the home directory's default document, and modify the image and hyperlink references in the Web pages so they use absolute URL addresses to reference the Web page documents and graphic image files. Create a new hyperlink on each page that uses an absolute URL to return to the home page. Test your Web pages using the *http://localhost* URL.

## Case 5-2 Al's Body Shop

In this case, you will create a Web server structure similar to the one in Figure 5-21 for the Al's Body Shop Web site, which is described in Case 2-2 in Chapter 2. Create directories named Als, AlsPages, and AlsImages in the Chapter5\Cases folder on your Solution Disk. Copy the Als.htm file from the Chapter5\Cases\Als folder on your Data Disk to the Chapter5\Cases\Als folder on your Solution Disk. Copy the Customers.htm, Services.htm, and Workorders.htm files from the Chapter5\Cases\Als folder on your Data Disk to the Chapter5\Cases\AlsPages folder on your Solution Disk, and copy the car.jpg file from the Chapter5\Cases\Als folder on your Data Disk to the Chapter5\Cases\AlsImages folder on your Solution Disk.

Configure your Default Web Site so the Chapter5\Cases\Als folder on your Solution Disk is the home directory, and specify that the Als.htm file is the default document. Create a virtual directory named AlsPages and associate it with the AlsPages folder, and create a virtual directory named AlsImages and associate it with the AlsImages physical directory. Modify the hyperlinks and image references in the Web pages so they use absolute or relative URLs to reference Web page documents and graphic image files. Create a new hyperlink on each page that uses an absolute URL to return to the home page. Test your Web pages using the *http://localhost* URL.

To complete Case 5-3, you must have completed Case 2-3 in Chapter 2.

## Case 5-3 Sun-Ray Videos

In this case, you will create a Web server structure similar to the one in Figure 5-21 for the Web pages you created in Case 2-3 for the Sun-Ray Videos Web site. Create a folder named Sunray in the Chapter5\Cases folder on your Solution Disk that will be the home directory, and store the home page in this folder. Store all Web pages other than the home page in a folder named SunrayPages in the Chapter5\Cases folder, and store all graphic image files in a folder named SunrayImages in the Chapter5\Cases folder. Create a virtual directory named SunrayPages and associate it with the SunrayPages folder, and create a virtual directory named SunrayImages and associate it with the SunrayImages folder. Specify that the home page HTML file is the default document in the home directory, and modify your Web pages so they use absolute or relative URLs to reference Web page documents and graphic image files. Create a hyperlink on each page that uses an absolute URL address to return to the home page. Test your Web pages using the *http://localhost* URL.

To complete Case 5-4, you must have completed Case 2-4 in Chapter 2.

## Case 5-4 Learning Technologies, Incorporated

In this case, you will create a Web server structure similar to the one in Figure 5-21 for the Web pages you created in Case 2-4 for the Learning Technologies, Incorporated (LTI), Web site. Create a folder named LTI in the Chapter5\Cases folder on your Solution Disk that will be the home directory, and store the home page in this folder. Store all Web pages other than the home page in a folder named LtiPages in the Chapter5\Cases folder on your Solution Disk. Store all graphic image files in a folder named LtiImages in the Chapter5\Cases folder on your Solution Disk. Create a virtual directory named LtiPages, and associate it with the LtiPages folder. Create a virtual directory named LtiImages and associate it with the LtiImages folder. Specify that the home page HTML file is the default document in the home directory, and modify your Web pages so they use absolute or relative URL addresses to reference Web page documents and graphic image files. Create a hyperlink on each page that uses an absolute URL to return to the home page. Test your Web pages using the *http://localhost* URL.

## CHAPTER 6

# INTRODUCTION TO ASP.NET

**In this chapter, you will:**

♦ Learn about the .NET framework, ASP.NET, and .NET server controls

♦ Become familiar with the .NET class libraries

♦ Learn how to create Web application projects

♦ Learn how to use the Visual Studio .NET integrated development environment to create and manage Web application projects

♦ Learn how to create and modify Web application project components

♦ Learn how to access and reference Web forms

♦ Learn how to move a Web application project's files to a different physical folder

In your quest to create database-driven Web sites, you have learned how to create HTML documents and client-side scripts that the Web browser processes on the client workstation. You have also learned how to configure a personal Web server and reference server-side programs that run on the Web server and create dynamic Web pages. Now you are ready to begin creating these server-side programs. Recall from Chapter 1 that you can create server-side programs that are compiled programs, scripts, or hybrid programs, which combine the advantages of compiled programs and scripts. This book focuses on creating server-side programs using ASP.NET. In this chapter, you will learn more about ASP.NET, and learn how to create Web application projects that contain server-side programs to create dynamic Web pages.

# THE .NET FRAMEWORK

Recall that a Web application consists of one or more files that developers create to solve a problem or provide a service through a Web site. A complex Web application may consist of multiple HTML document files, graphic image files, application files that contain code for server-side programs and scripts, and other related files. A Web application often integrates many different technologies.

As Web applications have become more complex over the years, a need has arisen for an Integrated Development Environment (IDE) that integrates all of these technologies. (Recall that an IDE is an environment for developing programs that displays multiple windows for performing different programming and debugging tasks.) Web developers need to be able to easily organize and manage all of the files in a Web application, and to easily debug Web pages that contain client-side script commands, server-side scripts, and compiled programs that create dynamic Web pages.

Microsoft developed the .NET framework in part to address these issues. The **.NET framework** is a set of code, objects, and standards for building computer applications. The .NET framework consists of three main parts: the Common Language Runtime, a hierarchical set of unified class libraries, and a new version of Active Server Pages called ASP.NET.

Currently you can create programs within the .NET framework using the Visual Basic programming language, which Microsoft now calls VB .NET. You can also create programs using the Visual C++, C# (C-Sharp), and Jscript programming languages. When you create a .NET program using any of these languages, you compile the code into a common intermediate language called the Microsoft Intermediate Language (MSIL). This MSIL program then runs using the **Common Language Runtime (CLR)** application. You can think of the CLR as the .NET framework's operating system: It executes the program commands and handles other operations that the operating system normally performs, such as memory management and input/output operations. Currently, the CLR runs on Windows-based computers, but work is under way to make the CLR available for other operating systems.

In the .NET framework, all elements are objects. The .NET framework defines these objects using a standard set of programs that are called **class libraries**. You will learn more about these class libraries later in this chapter.

You install the .NET framework when you install Visual Studio .NET on your computer. **ASP.NET** is the set of class libraries that contain code that defines objects that you use to create Web applications. When you create a new Web application using Visual Studio .NET, you can structure the application as a Web application project. A **Web application project** contains all of the related files in a Web application. A typical Web application project may consist of HTML documents, graphic files, XML files, and server-side programs and scripts. The Visual Studio .NET IDE provides a visual interface that enables you to access, configure, manage, and debug the different application components in a single integrated environment.

You have already used Visual Studio .NET to create HTML documents and add client-side scripts to these documents. You can also use .NET to create ASP.NET pages that contain server-side programs that generate Web pages. The following subsections describe ASP.NET in more detail, and introduce Web server controls, which provide important functionality in ASP.NET.

## Introduction to ASP.NET

Web developers first created dynamic Web pages using CGI and PERL server-side programs. As dynamic Web pages have become more sophisticated, developers have found that CGI programs process too slowly and PERL programs are difficult to write. To deal with these limitations, Microsoft developed Active Server Pages (ASPs), which were first supported in the 1996 NT Service Pack 4.0 upgrade to the Internet Information Services (IIS) Web server.

An ASP is a text file that has an .asp extension and contains ASP server-side script commands interleaved with HTML tags, Web page elements, and client-side script commands. When a browser submits an ASP to a Web server, the Web server processes the ASP server-side script commands. Some of these commands may involve processing HTML form inputs or retrieving data from a database. The server-side code then translates the outputs into HTML format and returns the outputs to the browser as a formatted Web page. ASPs can be difficult to maintain and debug because the ASP code interleaves the server-side script commands, client-side script commands, and HTML tags and Web page elements within the same .asp file. Another problem is that ASPs execute slower than compiled programs, because the Web server must interpret each ASP command and translate it to machine language each time a browser submits the ASP to the Web server.

To address the limitations of ASPs, Microsoft developed **ASP.NET pages**, which are also called ASPX pages or Web forms. From this point forward, we will refer to files with .aspx extensions as Web forms. A **Web form** is a text file with an .aspx file extension that contains Web page elements. These Web page elements contain links to programs that allow you to create dynamic Web pages using server-side processing. Although you could create a Web form using a text editor, you usually create Web forms in Visual Studio .NET because the IDE provides features such as IntelliSense lists, color coding, and debugging support that help you construct the programs. You can use Web forms to perform server-side Web processing tasks similar to those that ASPs perform, such as processing user inputs and executing database queries. You can also use Web forms to define the content and appearance of dynamic Web pages. Although ASPs and Web forms perform many of the same tasks, they are substantially different. The Web server stores a Web form as a compiled program rather than as a text file.

 A .NET Web application project can contain older-style ASPs along with newer-style Web forms.

Web programmers usually write programs associated with Web forms using the VB .NET programming language. They then compile and debug the programs, and place the finished, compiled program files on the Web server. Recall that VB .NET is the latest version of Visual Basic. VB .NET retains many of the strengths of earlier versions of Visual Basic, including its simplicity and excellent development and debugging environment. VB .NET also addresses some of the deficiencies in the older Visual Basic language. For example, VB .NET is a strongly typed language, which means that developers must always declare variables and specify the variable's data type before assigning a value to the variable. VB .NET also provides a more consistent way to write commands that call procedures, and it fully supports the object model. You will learn the basic structure and commands of VB .NET in Chapter 7.

## An Overview of ASP.NET Server Controls

Recall that one of the main problems with the older ASP technology is that the code interleaves the server-side script commands, client-side script commands, and the HTML tags and elements that define the Web page's content and appearance. This is a problem because often professionals called **HTML designers** are responsible for the HTML components of an application, whereas professionals called **Web programmers** are responsible for the program components, such as the client-side scripts and server-side programs. When an HTML designer modifies an application's HTML tags and Web page elements, he or she may accidentally delete or modify the script and program code in a way that causes the application's programs to fail. Similarly, Web programmers may accidentally change the formatting or appearance of the Web pages as they create or modify the application's programs.

To avoid these problems, Web forms can contain server controls. A **server control** is an element that an HTML designer creates in a Web form. A server control provides a more direct link between items on a Web page and programs running on the Web server. A server control can be similar to an HTML form element, such as a text input or selection list, or it can provide more sophisticated functions, such as a calendar. It can also serve to validate user inputs in other Web page controls. Server controls have associated events that the Web server associates with user actions. For example, you could create a server control that defines a command button on a Web page. This command button has an associated Click event that occurs, or is raised, when the user clicks the button.

 In JavaScript, when a user clicks a button, the event is called an onclick event. In VB .NET, the same event is called a Click event.

You would then create an associated **server-side event handler** that contains program commands that execute in response to events that the user raises on Web server controls, such as clicking a button or changing the text in a text input. Unlike a JavaScript event handler, which runs on the client, server-side event handlers execute on the Web server.

Server-side event handlers do not immediately execute when the user performs an event on a control. Rather, the Web form remembers the events that the user has raised in the form, and the event handlers execute when the user submits the form to the Web server. For example, a text input on a Web form might have a TextChanged event, which is raised when the user changes the text in the text input. If the user changes the text in the text input, the event handler does not execute immediately, but instead executes after the user submits the form to the server.

Server controls enable Web developers to create modular Web applications. An HTML designer can create a Web form that contains Web server controls along with the Web page's HTML tags and text. Web programmers can then write a separate VB .NET program that manipulates the server controls on the Web form. This enables the HTML designers and the Web programmers to save their work in separate files. The HTML tags, elements, and Web server definitions exist in the Web form's .aspx file. The commands that reference the Web server controls exist in a separate VB .NET program file. Figure 6-1 illustrates how a Web form that contains server controls interacts with a VB .NET program.

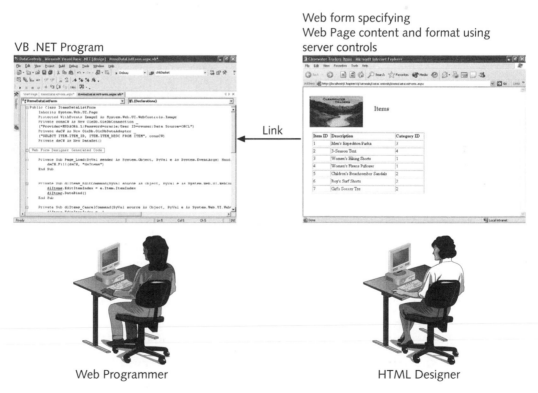

**Figure 6-1**    Using server controls to create modular Web applications

The main types of ASP.NET server controls are rich server controls, HTML server controls, and validation server controls. The following subsections describe these controls.

## Rich Server Controls

A **rich server control** can be similar to an HTML form element such as a text input or selection list. Rich server controls have a wide variety of properties, and Web programmers can reference these properties using VB .NET syntax. A rich server control can also provide more sophisticated functions in a Web page, such as a calendar that allows users to select past and future dates.

The .NET documentation refers to rich controls as Web server controls.

To create a rich server control, the HTML designer uses a **rich server control tag**, which has the following general syntax:

```
<asp:control_type ID="control_name" runat="server" />
```

In this syntax, *control_type* defines the type of the control, and *control_name* defines the control identifier. Common rich *control_type* values include Button, CheckBox, Image, and Label. The `runat="server"` attribute defines the control as a server-side control that server-side programs manipulate. Note that the rich server control follows the XHTML standard and uses the minimized tag syntax by including the closing front slash (/) at the end of the tag.

An example of a rich server control is a **Label**, which defines Web page text that the user cannot change. A Web page might display a Label rich server control that contains text that changes frequently, such as the current date or a value that a program retrieves from a database. An HTML designer would create a Label rich server control using the following rich server control tag:

```
<h1>Today's date is: <asp:Label ID="lblDate"
runat="server" /></h1>
```

Note that the HTML designer embeds the Web server control tag within other HTML tags and Web page elements, such as the text "Today's date is:." A Web programmer can then write a command in a VB .NET program that assigns the current date to the label. When processing the Web form, the Web server replaces the Web server control with the actual date value, which is the current date.

.NET provides several rich server controls to enhance Web page functionality. For example, the following rich server control tag creates the **calendar control** shown in Figure 6-2:

```
<asp:CalendarID="calDate" runat="server" />.
```

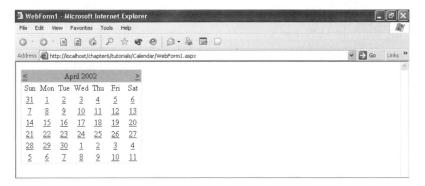

**Figure 6-2**   Calendar control

The user can select a date by clicking the date number on the calendar control. The user can scroll to future months by clicking the Next Month button ≥, and scroll to previous months by clicking the Previous Month button ≤. The selected date can appear in a Web page form and be sent to the Web server for processing. When an HTML designer adds a calendar control to a Web form, Visual Studio .NET automatically generates over 200 HTML tags, along with a JavaScript function that interacts with the tags to provide the calendar functionality.

Rich server controls automatically detect the browser type and version and then generate compatible HTML tags and JavaScript code. For example, if an older browser that doesn't support JavaScript requests the calendar control, the calendar control omits the JavaScript function. The processes that the JavaScript script formerly supported are now either omitted or supported by the Web server. This results in slower processing, but the calendar control will still work.

## HTML Server Controls

Although a Web server can receive input values from an HTML form, the Web server cannot directly respond to events that users raise in HTML form elements. As a consequence, in a typical HTML form, you cannot create a command button with an associated click event handler that executes on the Web server. However, you can use an HTML server control to sidestep this limitation. An **HTML server control** is almost identical to an HTML form element, except that its event handlers run on a Web server.

HTML server controls are similar to rich server controls, except that HTML server controls use the HTML DOM for referencing HTML document objects (see Chapter 3) and have event handlers that are similar to the event handlers you used with JavaScript. HTML server controls have the unique advantage that when a server-side event handler executes, the HTML form maintains its state, and the values that the user entered into the HTML server control still exist for which the Web server sends the Web page back to the browser. There are certain situations for which you should use rich server controls, and other situations for which you should use HTML server controls. Chapter 8 discusses the usage of these two control types in depth.

You can easily convert an HTML form element in a Web form to an HTML server control by adding the `runat="server"` attribute to its tag. For example, the following code creates an HTML server control command button named cmdUpdate that has the label "Update Values" and has an associated server-side event handler that runs on the Web server:

```
<input type="button" ID="cmdUpdate"/ value="Update Values"
runat="server" />
```

### Validation Server Controls

HTML designers and Web programmers can also create special Web server controls called **validation server controls** to validate user inputs. Recall from Chapter 4 that you can write JavaScript functions to validate form inputs by confirming that the user enters all necessary form input values and that all values are of the correct data type. Also recall that an ASP file contains a mix of server-side program commands, HTML tags, Web page content, and JavaScript code to validate form inputs and perform other client-side processing. When the Web server creates a dynamic Web page using an ASP, it processes the server-side command and then sends the resulting HTML tags, Web page content, and JavaScript commands directly to the browser. This resulting mix of HTML tags, Web page content, and client-side code can be confusing and difficult to maintain and debug. In contrast, a validation control automatically generates JavaScript code to validate HTML form input values. You will learn how to create and work with validation server controls in Chapter 8.

Validation server controls will not eliminate the need for JavaScript client-side form validation functions because they do not allow the programmer to validate inputs in controls such as check boxes. Also, programmers may want to create custom controls to provide the JavaScript commands that the controls generate to provide additional functionality, such as displaying alerts or selecting the input text that causes the error. When programmers create custom controls, they must write a custom JavaScript function that the custom control calls. Validation server controls are useful when the user's browser does not support JavaScript, because the validation server control automatically shifts validation processing to the Web server. Validation controls are also faster and easier to create than JavaScript form validation functions.

## THE .NET FRAMEWORK CLASS LIBRARIES

The .NET framework is built on the object-oriented model. Before you can begin creating Web forms and writing programs using VB .NET, you must be familiar with the .NET class library structure, and understand how to reference these libraries using dot syntax.

Recall from Chapter 3 that an object class defines the properties and actions of similar objects, and that you define a class by defining its properties, events, and methods. Object classes usually have a hierarchical structure that defines parent classes and child classes. A parent class has specific properties, events, and methods, and its child class may **inherit** these properties, events and methods. A child class may also have additional properties, events, and methods. For example, in the HTML DOM, an HTML document is a parent class, and an HTML form is a child class. The HTML form can also be a parent class, and a radio button group within the form is a child class. In addition, the radio button group is a parent class to a child class that defines the individual radio buttons. The individual radio buttons inherit the radio button group name attribute from the radio button group parent. Figure 6-3 shows these relationships.

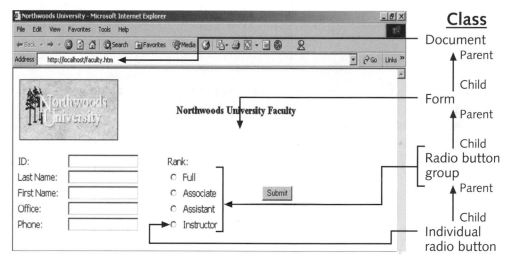

**Figure 6-3** Examples of parent and child classes

 A parent class is also called a base class, superclass, supertype, or generalization. A child class is also called a derived class, subclass, subtype, or specialization. This book will use the terms *parent class* and *child class*. Occasionally a parent class will be referred to as a *base class* because VB .NET uses the keyword myBase to reference parent class properties and methods from a child class.

In Chapter 3, you learned how to use dot syntax to reference elements in the HTML DOM. Recall that Visual Studio .NET represents child classes as properties of their parent class. Using Figure 6-3 as an example, assume you have an HTML document that contains a form named frmFaculty, and that the form has a radio button group named optRank. In Visual Studio .NET, when you type **document.** in this HTML document file, an IntelliSense list will display different properties and methods of the document class, as shown in Figure 6-4. The list will also display frmFaculty as a property value, although frmFaculty is actually a child class.

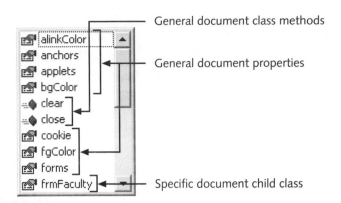

**Figure 6-4** Document class properties, methods, and child class

The document object inherits its general properties and methods from the document object class. The frmFaculty child class is specific to this particular document object. Similarly, the IntelliSense list in Figure 6-5 shows how the frmFaculty class obtains general properties, events, and methods from the Form class. The frmFaculty object also has the optRank child class, which appears in the list as a property.

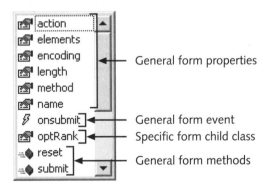

**Figure 6-5** Form class properties, events, methods, and child class

The .NET framework defines all of its elements using similar object classes, which are called **namespaces**. The .NET framework includes hundreds of predefined object classes that programmers can use to create objects quickly and easily within programs. It stores these predefined object classes in class libraries. When you create a new Web form, you can use the predefined ASP.NET namespaces to define items on the Web form. The .NET framework arranges its namespaces hierarchically using parent and child classes. Figure 6-6 illustrates the .NET framework namespaces you will use in this book.

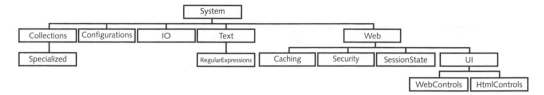

**Figure 6-6**   ASP.NET namespace hierarchy

The top-level ASP.NET namespace is *System*. Important child classes in the *System* namespace include *Collections*, *Configurations*, *IO*, *Text*, and *Web*. Figure 6-6 shows important child classes within these namespaces. You use the following general dot syntax to reference child classes within parent classes: ***parent_class.child_class***. In this syntax, a *child_class* can reference further *child_class* values by adding a dot (.) and then listing the next *child_class* name.

Table 6-1 shows the dot syntax for referencing the ASP.NET namespaces and describes each namespace.

**Table 6-1**   ASP.NET namespaces

| Namespace Dot Syntax Reference | Namespace Description |
|---|---|
| `System` | Defines fundamental data types. For example, `System.String` defines the string data type. Is the parent of nearly 100 additional namespaces that inherit the data types defined in System. |
| `System.Collections` | Contains definitions and classes for creating various collections, which are lists of similar objects. |
| `System.Collections.Specialized` | Contains specialized collections, which are collections with specific characteristics. |
| `System.Configuration` | Contains classes that you use to access .NET framework configuration settings programmatically and handle errors in configuration files. |
| `System.IO` | Contains definitions and classes that support file reading and writing operations. |
| `System.Text` | Contains definitions and classes representing ASCII, Unicode, UTF-7, and UTF-8 character encodings; classes for converting blocks of characters to and from blocks of bytes; and a class that manipulates and formats `System.String` objects. |

**Table 6-1**     ASP.NET namespaces (continued)

| Namespace Dot Syntax Reference | Namespace Description |
| --- | --- |
| `System.Text.RegularExpressions` | Contains definitions and classes providing functionality for regular expressions, which represent a concise and flexible notation for finding and replacing patterns of text. |
| `System.Web` | Contains classes and definitions that support browser/server communication. |
| `System.Web.Caching` | Contains classes for caching frequently used data on the server. |
| `System.Web.Security` | Contains classes for providing security for ASP.NET Web applications. |
| `System.Web.SessionState` | Contains classes and definitions that enable you to store data for a specific client session within a Web application on the server. |
| `System.Web.UI` | Contains the Control class, which provides server controls. It also includes the Page class, which automatically creates a Page object whenever a browser requests an .aspx file. |
| `System.Web.UI.WebControls` | Contains classes and definitions that allow you to create server controls. |
| `System.Web.UI.HtmlControls` | Contains classes and definitions that allow you to create HTML server controls on an ASP.NET Web page. |

## Creating a Web Application Project

One of the key advantages of using Visual Studio .NET to create Web applications is that it enables you to create and configure Web application projects that allow you to manage and control all of the application files. In this section, you will learn how to create an ASP.NET Web application project. The first project you will create contains a single Web form that displays information about a Clearwater Traders customer order, as shown in Figure 6-7. This Web form contains an Image rich server control that displays the Clearwater Traders logo, a Label rich server control that displays the text "Customer Orders," and a text input, which is called a TextBox control, that displays the current date.

In Chapter 5, you learned how to configure a Web server and how to create Web server applications and virtual directories. Recall that on a Web server, an application is a virtual directory that has the permissions that the Web server needs to run server-side executable programs and scripts. When you create a new Web application project in Visual Studio .NET, Visual Studio .NET automatically creates a **project folder** in a physical directory in which to store the project files. Visual Studio .NET also automatically creates a Web server application that it associates with the project folder. Before you can create a Web application project, you must configure your Web server in a certain way.

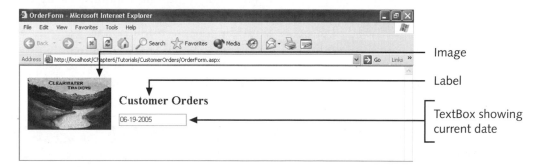

**Figure 6-7**   Customer Orders Web form

## Configuring the Web Server for Web Application Projects

Now you will start the IIS console and configure your local Web server. First you will confirm that your home directory is the C:\Inetpub\wwwroot folder on your work station.

To specify your home directory:

1. Start the IIS Console, click the **plus sign** beside the name of your local computer, click the **plus sign** beside the Web Sites folder, and open the **Default Web Site** node. If a dialog box opens stating the current path cannot be found, click **OK**. (If you are using Windows 2000, click the plus sign beside the name of your local computer, then open the default Web site node.)

2. Make sure that the Default Web Site node is selected, right-click, then click **Properties** to open the Web site Properties page.

3. Select the **Home Directory** tab. To specify that the home directory is the wwwroot folder on your Solution Disk, click **Browse**, navigate to the **C:\Inetpub\wwwroot** folder on your work station, then click **OK**. (This is the default IIS home directory.)

4. Make sure that the *Read*, *Log visits*, and *Index this resource* check boxes are checked, the other check boxes are cleared, and the *Execute Permissions* property is set to None. If the *Application name* field is enabled, click Remove. Then click **OK**.

Now you will create the **application root**, which is the Web server application whose associated folder contains the project folders for the Web application projects that you will create in this chapter. You will store your Web application project folders in the

Chapter6\Tutorials folder on your Solution Disk, so Chapter 6\Tutorials will be the application root. To configure the application root, you must create a Web server application and associate it with every folder in the folder path to the application root. It is very important to follow the Web server configuration instructions exactly, or your Web application project will not run correctly. Therefore, you need to make a Web server application that you will associate with the Chapter6 folder, and a second application that you will associate with the Tutorials subfolder. Now you will configure your Web server so it has the Web server application structure shown in Figure 6-8. (Your home directory may contain other physical folders, virtual directories, or applications.)

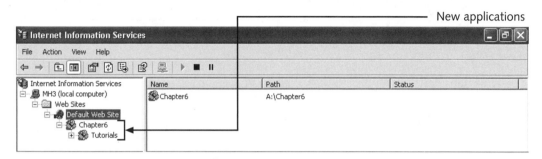

**Figure 6-8**    Web server application structure

Recall that when you create an application, you create a virtual directory and specify that the virtual directory has privileges to execute scripts, programs, or both. When you create a virtual directory or an application, you assign to it an alias that client browsers use to access the application. When you create an application that is on the URL path to a Web application project, its alias must have the same name as its associated physical folder. Otherwise, the Web application project may not run correctly. Therefore, you will give the new Web server applications the same alias names as their associated physical directories. Now you will create the Web server applications shown in Figure 6-8.

To create the Web server applications:

1. In the IIS console, select the **Default Web Site** node, right-click, point to **New**, and then click **Virtual Directory**. The Virtual Directory Wizard Welcome page opens. Click **Next**.

2. Type **Chapter6** in the *Alias* field, and then click **Next**.

3. On the Web Site Content Directory page, click **Browse**, navigate to the Chapter6 folder on your Solution Disk, select **Chapter6**, click **OK**, and then click **Next**.

4. Make sure that the *Read* check box and the *Run scripts (such as ASP)* check box are checked, check the **Browse** check box, click **Next**, and then click **Finish**. The new Chapter6 application appears in the console tree.

5. Right-click the new **Chapter6** application, point to **New**, click **Virtual Directory**, and then click **Next**.

6. Type **Tutorials** in the *Alias* field, then click **Next**.

7. Click **Browse**, navigate to the Chapter6\Tutorials folder on your Solution Disk, select **Tutorials**, click **OK**, and then click **Next**.

8. Make sure that the *Read* check box and the *Run scripts (such as ASP)* check box are checked, check the **Browse** check box, click **Next**, and then click **Finish**. The new Tutorials application appears in the console tree. Your finished Web server console tree should look like Figure 6-8. If your Home Directory or Chapter6 folder contains additional physical directories, these directories will also appear in the console tree.

If the Tutorials folder still appears as a physical directory within the Chapter6 virtual directory, click the Refresh button 🗊 on the IIS console toolbar. If it still appears, close the IIS console and then restart it.

## Creating Web Application Projects

The next step is to create the new Web application project in Visual Studio .NET. Recall from Chapter 2 that in Visual Studio .NET, a project consists of multiple files that comprise a Web application. A project solution consists of one or more projects. First you need to become familiar with the different files that comprise a Web application project, and you need to configure your Visual Studio .NET IDE to specify where it stores project files. Then you will create the project solution that contains the new project.

### Web Application Project Files

A Web application project consists of many interrelated files. When you create a new project, you specify the project name. Visual Studio .NET then automatically creates the project folder that stores the project files, and this folder has the same name as the project name. When you create a new Web application project, Visual Studio .NET also automatically creates a folder named \bin, which contains the compiled (binary) project files, and places it in the project folder. If the parent folder of a project folder does not contain any other Web application projects, Visual Studio .NET usually creates a folder named \VSMacros in the parent of the project folder. The \VSMacros folder contains support files for the project and the Visual Studio .NET IDE. Visual Studio .NET also automatically copies several files into a new project's project folder that the project requires to run correctly. Figure 6-9 shows the folder structure and file structure of a new Web application project, and Table 6-2 summarizes the project files.

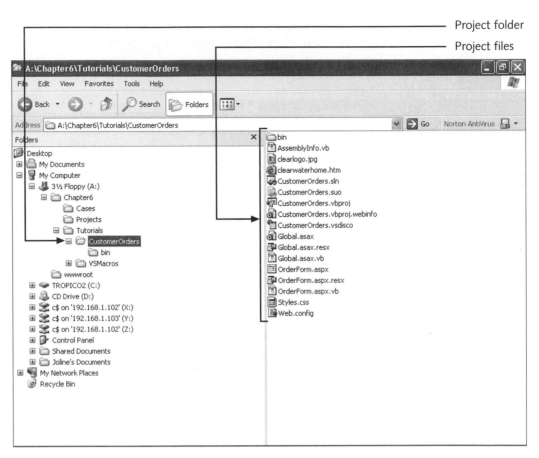

Project folder

Project files

**Figure 6-9**    Web application project folders and files

**Table 6-2**    Web application project files

| Filename | Function |
|----------|----------|
| AssemblyInfo.vb | Provides extra information about the compiled project output file, which is stored in the \bin folder and named *Project_name*.dll. |
| Global.asax | Contains event handler commands that are visible to all Web forms in the project. |
| Global.asax.resx | Edits and defines application resources, such as text strings, images, and objects. Storing data in a resource file allows you to change the resource data without recompiling the entire application. |
| Global.asax.vb | Contains ASP.NET code for responding to application-level events. This code is visible to all application Web forms. |
| *Project_name*.sln | Stores links to all project files. When the Web server is not your local computer, this is the only file that exists on your computer. |
| *Project_name*.suo | Contains information about the Visual Studio .NET IDE configuration for the project. |

**Table 6-2**    Web application project files (continued)

| Filename | Function |
|---|---|
| *Project_name*.vbproj | Contains the configuration and build settings and maintains a list of project files. |
| *Project_name*.vbproj.webinfo | Contains the URL path to the Web server on which the project runs. |
| *Project_name*.vsdisco | Enables non-browser-based client programs to search for Web services (Web services are Web-based programs that perform tasks that are common to many applications, that the project application offers.) |
| Styles.css | Defines Cascading Style Sheets (CSSs) within the project, which enable HTML designers to control the appearance of Web pages. |
| Web.config | Contains project application and folder configuration information. |
| *Web_form_name*.aspx | Contains project Web form ASPX files that define HTML and rich server controls to create the user interface. |
| *Web_form_name*.aspx.resx | Defines resources used in the corresponding Web form, such as strings, images, and objects. |
| *Web_form_name*.aspx.vb | Contains the code generated by the system or written by the developer for the associated Web form. |
| bin\\*Project_name*.dll | Contains the compiled project output file, which is called an assembly. |
| bin\\*Project_name*.pdb | Contains debugging information that the developer uses for debugging the project while it is running on the Web server. |

When you compile a project, Visual Studio .NET creates a compiled file called an assembly. Visual Studio .NET names the assembly file Project_name.dll, and stores it in the \bin folder within the project folder. Visual Studio .NET also creates a file named AssemblyInfo.vb, which is a text file that contains information about the assembly.

A project contains **global files**, which are visible to all project components. Projects contain one or more **resource files**, which contain data that supports the project, such as text data, images, or icons. Resource files have an .resx extension. The global resource file, which contains resources that are available to all project components, has the default filename Global.asax.resx. The global project code file which is named Global.asax.vb, contains code that is visible to all project components.

A project also contains several **project files**, which contain information about the project structure and contents. The *Project_name*.vbproj file is a text file that contains a listing of all of the project files. An important project file is the **project solution file**, which is a text file with an .sln extension. This file stores references to the files that make up the project. You open this file in Visual Studio .NET when you want to open an existing project. Another important project file is the **user option file**, which is a binary file with an .suo file extension. This file stores configuration settings for the solution. The *Project_name*.vbproj.webinfo file is a text file that contains configuration information about the project. The *Project_name*.vsdisco file, which supports non-browser searches, is optional for all projects. If you accidentally delete the *Project_name*.vbproj.webinfo or *Project_name*.suo file, Visual Studio .NET will automatically re-create these files the next time you open the project.

A project consists of one or more Web forms. The project stores each Web form in a separate file with an .aspx extension. When you create a new project, the project contains a default Web form named WebForm1 that the IDE stores in a file named WebForm1.aspx. Each Web form has an associated **code behind file**, which is a file with an .aspx.vb extension that contains the code that Web developers create to interact with the Web form's server controls. The default name for a Web form's code behind file is *Web_form_name*.aspx.vb.

A Web application project requires some of these files, and some of the files are optional. The required files include *Web_form_name*.aspx and bin\*project_name*.dll. The optional files include the .resx files, the .css file, and the .vsdisco file. The project requires the resource files if you explicitly create and store project resources in these files. Resource files are an advanced ASP.NET feature, and you will not use them in this book. You won't use cascading style sheets in your projects either, so for your purposes, the Styles.css file is also optional. If you delete any of the other project files or if the files become corrupt, errors will appear when you open or run the project. Therefore, it is a good practice to back up project files frequently. You should also avoid deleting any project files because it is easy to delete an essential file accidentally.

## Configuring Visual Studio .NET to Store Project Files in the Project Folder

By default, Visual Studio .NET places all new project folders in the **default Visual Studio Projects folder**, which has the following folder path on your workstation: *boot_drive*:\Documents and Settings\*user_name*\My Documents\Visual Studio Projects\. This folder path is on the drive from which your computer boots, which is usually the C drive, and *user_name* is the user name that you enter when you log on to your computer.

When you create a new project, you can specify to store the project folder in a different location than the default Visual Studio Projects folder. Regardless of where you specify to store the project folder, the Visual Studio .NET system always stores the project solution file and user option file in the default Visual Studio Projects folder. This makes it difficult for you to create projects and save them on floppy disks or on shared network drives. To resolve this problem, you will configure Visual Studio .NET so it stores solutions in the application root, which is the Chapter6\Tutorials folder on your Solution Disk. Configuring Visual Studio .NET this way automatically places the project solution file and user option file in the project folder.

To configure Visual Studio .NET to save the files in the project folder:

1. Start Visual Studio .NET, click **Tools** on the menu bar, and then click **Options**. The Options dialog box opens.

2. Make sure that the Environment folder is selected in the left window pane, and then select **Projects and Solutions**.

3. Type **a:\Chapter6\Tutorials** in the Visual Studio projects location field. (The drive letter or folder path to the Tutorials folder on your Solution Disk may be different.)

4. Make sure that both of the *Settings* check boxes are checked, make sure that the *Save changes to open documents* option button is selected, then click **OK**.

## Creating a New Web Application Project

A Web application project requires approximately 116 KB of free disk space for the files it creates. This does not count the disk space occupied by the .htm, .aspx, graphics, and other files within the Web application. If your Solution Disk is on a floppy disk, you will need to use multiple floppy disks to store your solution files. The directions in this book will instruct you when to insert a new disk to store your solution files.

Now you will create a new Web application project in Visual Studio .NET. When you create a new project, you specify the project location and the project name using the following general syntax: *http://URL_to_application_root/project_name*. In this syntax, *URL_to_application_root* represents the URL path to the application root, which is the Web server application whose associated folder contains the project folder. You will store the new Web application project in the Chapter6\Tutorials folder on your Solution Disk, and this folder is associated with the Web server application that has the URL *http://localhost/Chapter6/Tutorials/*. This application must already exist on your local Web server, as shown in Figure 6-8. The *project_name* represents the name you will assign to the project. You will name this project CustomerOrders. Therefore, you will specify the project location and project name as *http://localhost/Chapter6/Tutorials/CustomerOrders*.

To create the new Web application project:

1. In Visual Studio .NET, click **File** on the menu bar, point to **New**, and then click **Project**. The New Project dialog box opens.

You can also create a new project by clicking New Project on the Start Page.

2. In the left window pane, select the **Visual Basic Projects** folder if necessary, and then select the **ASP.NET Web Application** icon in the right window pane. Do not click OK yet.

If you accidentally click OK, click File on the menu bar, then click Close Solution. Switch to Windows Explorer, navigate to the Chapter6\Tutorials folder on your Solution Disk, and delete the WebApplication1 folder. Then repeat Steps 1 and 2.

3. Type **http://localhost/Chapter6/Tutorials/CustomerOrders** in the *Location* field. Your project specification should look like Figure 6-10.

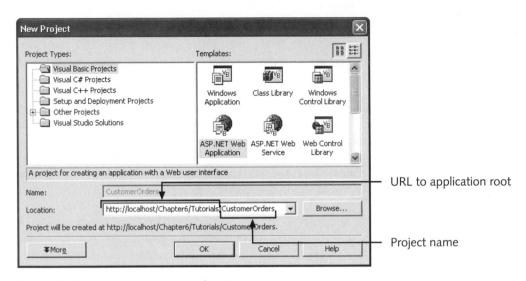

URL to application root

Project name

**Figure 6-10    New project specification**

4. Click OK to create the new project. The Create New Web alert appears briefly, and after a short while, Visual Studio .NET displays the project components. (You will learn more about the project components in Visual Studio .NET later in this chapter.)

When you create a new Web application project, Visual Studio .NET automatically creates the project folder and files shown in Figure 6-9. Visual Studio .NET also automatically creates a Web server application that it associates with the project solution folder. Now you will switch to Windows Explorer and view the project folder and files. Then you will open the IIS console and view the new Web application.

To view the project files and Web application on the IIS console:

1. Start Windows Explorer and navigate to the **CustomerOrders** folder in the Chapter6\Tutorials folder on your Solution Disk. The Chapter6\Tutorials folder on your Solution Disk should have the folder structure shown in Figure 6-9, and the CustomerOrders folder should contain the project files as shown. (Your Tutorials folder may contain a folder named \VSMacros, which Visual Studio .NET sometimes adds to the application root.)

2. Switch to the IIS console, and click the **Refresh** button 🔁 to refresh the console display. If necessary, click the plus sign beside the Tutorials application. A new Web server application named CustomerOrders appears as shown in Figure 6-11.

3. Select the **CustomerOrders** application to view the project files.

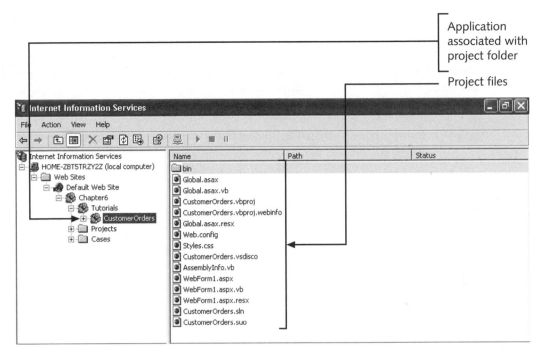

**Figure 6-11**   Web server application for the new project

Whenever you open an existing project on a different workstation than the one on which you created the project, you need to configure the local Web server so it contains the virtual directories that specify the path to the project, and you need to create a Web server application that you associate with the project folder. For example, if you close the CustomerOrders project you just created and then reopen it in Visual Studio .NET on an alternate workstation, you will need to open the IIS console on the alternate workstation and make sure that its configuration matches the one shown in Figure 6-11.

## Saving and Reopening Web Application Projects

You have seen that when you create a new Web application project, Visual Studio .NET automatically creates several files in the project folder. As you work with a project, you need to save the changes to your project explicitly. You can save changes to individual files, or you can save all of the changes to all of the project files. To save the changes to a specific file in a Web application project, you select the file node in the Solution Explorer and then click the Save button on the toolbar. For example, if you add server controls to a Web form, you need to save the changes to the Web form .aspx file. If you change the Web form's code behind file, you need to save the changes to the code behind file. You can save all of the project files in a Web application project by clicking the Save All button on the Visual Studio .NET toolbar.

You can close a Web application project in Visual Studio .NET, then reopen the project and work on it later. (Recall that if you reopen a project on a different workstation, you may need to reconfigure the local Web server so it contains the applications associated with the project.) Now you will save all of the project files. Then you will close the project in Visual Studio .NET and reopen the project.

To save, close, and reopen the project:

1. Switch back to Visual Studio .NET. To save all of the project files, click the **Save All** button 📁 on the toolbar.

2. To close the project, click **File** on the menu bar, and then click **Close Solution**. The Start Page appears in the Web Browser Window.

3. To reopen the project, click **File** on the menu bar, then click **Open Solution**. Navigate to the CustomerOrders folder in the Chapter6\Tutorials folder on your Solution Disk, select **CustomerOrders.sln**, and then click **Open**. The CustomerOrders project appears in Visual Studio .NET.

If you created the project on the same workstation you are currently using, you can also open the project by clicking the project link on the Start Page.

---

# THE VISUAL STUDIO .NET INTEGRATED DEVELOPMENT ENVIRONMENT

Recall that Visual Studio .NET has different windows that you use to develop applications. So far you have used Visual Studio .NET to create HTML documents and write and debug client-side scripts. You use different components of Visual Studio .NET depending on the type of application you are creating. Figure 6-12 shows the main IDE components that you use when working with Web application projects.

If your Visual Studio .NET IDE configuration looks very different from the one shown in Figure 6-12, click the My Profile link on the Start Page, open the Profile list, and select Visual Studio Developer. If your Visual Studio .NET IDE contains extra windows that are not shown in Figure 6-12, close these windows. If your IDE does not display the Toolbox tab, click View on the menu bar, and then click Toolbox. Right-click the Toolbox Window banner, click Auto Hide to display only the Toolbox tab, and then click anywhere in the Web Browser Window to hide the Toolbox. If your IDE does not display the Solution Explorer Window, click View on the menu bar, and then click Solution Explorer. If your IDE does not display the Properties Window, click View on the menu bar, and then click Properties Window.

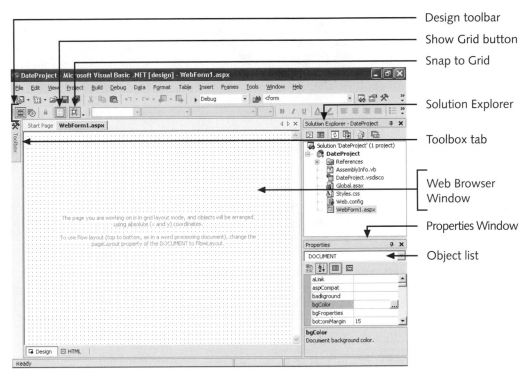

Design toolbar

Show Grid button

Snap to Grid

Solution Explorer

Toolbox tab

Web Browser Window

Properties Window

Object list

**Figure 6-12** Visual Studio .NET IDE configuration for working with Web application projects

The main Web application project IDE windows include:

- The *Solution Explorer* Window, which lists the Web application project components

- The *Web Browser* Window, which displays the design area and code window for the project's Web forms

- The *Toolbox*, which enables you to add elements to a Web form such as rich server controls, HTML server controls, and HTML elements

- The *Properties* Window, which lists the properties of the object that is currently active

The following subsections describe how you will use these IDE components as you work with Web application projects.

## The Solution Explorer

When you create or open a Web application project in Visual Studio .NET, the Solution Explorer displays the project and its components as a hierarchical tree. This tree contains a node to represent each open project, and nodes below the project to represent the project components. If a project component has multiple files, its node appears as a plus sign. For example, in Figure 6-12, the References node appears as a plus sign, which indicates that the project has multiple reference files. To view the individual components within a node, you click the plus sign to open the node. You can use the Solution Explorer to open individual project files, add and remove project items, and perform other project management tasks.

The Solution Explorer window has a toolbar with different buttons for performing different tasks. Table 6-3 illustrates the Solution Explorer toolbar buttons, shows when each button appears, and describes the button's function.

**Table 6-3**    Solution Explorer toolbar buttons

| Button | Appears | Function |
| --- | --- | --- |
| View Code button 📄 | When you select a project component that has code that you can edit | Enables you to view the selected component's code in the Browser Window's Code editor. |
| View Designer button 🗎 | When you select a Web form node in a project | Enables you to view the selected Web form's controls in the Browser Window in Visual view or HTML view. |
| Refresh button 🔁 | When you select a project or a project component | Makes the Solution Explorer window consistent with the underlying project files. If a project file has been deleted, renamed, or moved, the component node appears as the Item Not Found icon 🔘. |
| Copy Project button 📑 | When you select a project or a project component | Opens a dialog box that leads you through a series of steps to copy a project to a different Web server. |
| Show All Files button 📄 | Whenever a project is open in Visual Studio .NET | Shows all of the project files. Normally, the Solution Explorer does not display the files in the \bin folder and some of the other project files. |
| Properties button 📋 | Whenever the Solution Explorer window is open | Opens the Properties Window and displays the properties for the selected node. |

To open and modify an individual project file, you double-click the file node in the Solution Explorer. You can edit program files, text files, and Web form files in Visual Studio .NET, but you cannot edit files that are stored in machine language. When you double-click the node of a file that you cannot edit, the file does not open.

You use the Solution Explorer to add and remove project items. To add a new item to a project, you select the project node in the Solution Explorer, right-click, point to Add, and then select the item you wish to add. To remove a project item, you select the item, right-click, and then click Delete. Visual Studio .NET automatically creates a Web form named WebForm1 in every new project. Every Web application project contains at least one Web form on which you can place rich server controls, HTML server controls, and the HTML elements that specify the appearance of the Web form. A new project begins with one Web form, but you can add additional Web forms to the project as needed. By default, Visual Studio .NET gives all project Web forms the default names WebForm1, WebForm2, and so forth. To make the project easier to understand and manage, you should always assign descriptive names to project Web forms.

Now you will add a new Web form to the project. You will name the new Web form OrderForm, which is a more descriptive name than the existing Web form, which is named WebForm1. Then you will delete the default WebForm1 Web form.

Renaming existing Web forms becomes a little complicated. In this chapter, whenever you create a new Web application project, you will delete the default WebForm1 and then add a new form with a descriptive name. You will learn how to rename existing Web forms in Chapter 7.

To add and delete project items:

1. If necessary, click **View** on the Visual Studio .NET toolbar, and then click **Solution Explorer** to open the Solution Explorer.

2. To add a new Web form to the project, select the **CustomerOrders** node in the Solution Explorer, right-click, point to **Add**, and then click **Add Web Form**. The Add New Item - CustomerOrders dialog box opens with the Web form item template selected.

Another way to add a new Web form to a project is to select the project node in the Solution Explorer, click Project on the menu bar, and then click Add Web Form.

3. Change the *Name* field value to **OrderForm.aspx**, and then click **Open**. After a few moments, the new OrderForm.aspx Web form file appears in the Solution Explorer, and the new OrderForm.aspx tab appears in the Browser Window.

4. To delete the default WebForm1.aspx Web form, select the **WebForm1.aspx** node in the Solution Explorer, right-click, click **Delete**, and then click **OK** to confirm the deletion.

Another way to delete project items is to select the project item node in the Solution Explorer and then press Delete.

5. If necessary, select the **OrderForm.aspx** node in the Solution Explorer. If necessary, click the **Design** tab in the bottom-left corner of the Web Browser Window.

# The Web Browser Window

In earlier chapters, you used the Web Browser Window in the Visual Studio .NET IDE to create and view HTML documents and to write code for client-side scripts. Recall that the Web Browser Window displays Web forms in Design view and HTML view. The following sections describe how the different views in the Web Browser Window display Web forms.

## Web Form Visual View

In your .NET IDE, the Web Browser Window displays the OrderForm.aspx Web form in Design view, which shows the form and its components visually. If you click the View Code button ⊟ on the Solution Explorer toolbar, the Web Browser Window displays the Web form's code behind file. If you click the HTML button in the bottom-left corner of the Web Browser Window, the Web Browser Window displays the Web form's underlying HTML tags and elements.

In Figure 6-12, notice that a grid appears on the Web form display in the Web Browser Window. This grid enables you to align form objects. You can change the grid size, display or hide the grid, and specify to have form items automatically align to the gridlines. To create professional-quality Web forms, it is a good practice always to use the grid and configure the IDE to align form items to the gridlines automatically. Now you will configure the IDE to align form items to the gridlines automatically.

To configure the form grid:

1. In Visual Studio .NET, click **Tools** on the menu bar, click **Options**, select the **HTML Designer** folder in the left window pane, and then select **Display**. The HTML Designer Display Options window opens.

2. Make sure that the *Snap to grid* and *Show grid* check boxes are checked, and that the *Horizontal Spacing* and *Vertical spacing* settings for the gridlines is 8 pixels, as shown in Figure 6-13.

3. Confirm that the *Display Options* check boxes are configured as shown in Figure 6-13, then click **OK** to close the Options dialog box.

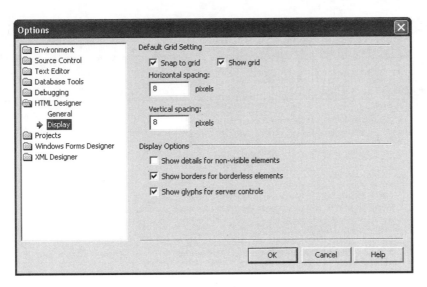

**Figure 6-13**    Design view grid specifications

 Another way to configure the IDE to show the gridlines is to click the Show Grid button ⊞ on the IDE Design toolbar, shown in Figure 6-12. Another way to configure the IDE to align controls to the grid automatically is to click the Snap to Grid button ⊞ on the .NET toolbar. (To display the IDE Design toolbar, click View on the menu bar, point to Toolbars, and then click Design. When a button is selected, it appears outlined in blue.)

 Sometimes Visual Studio .NET does not retain these setting when you close the IDE and then open it again. If this happens, you need to reconfigure the IDE using the preceding steps.

## Web Form HTML View

To display a Web form in HTML view, you click the HTML tab in the lower-left corner of the Web Browser Window. Now you will switch to HTML view and view the current form's HTML tags and text.

To switch to HTML view:

1. In the Web Browser Window, click the **HTML** tab to switch to HTML view.

2. Close the Solution Explorer and Properties Windows so you can view more of the HTML tags and text. (Close any other open windows if necessary.) Your screen display should look like Figure 6-14. (Your HTML code may contain extra blank lines.)

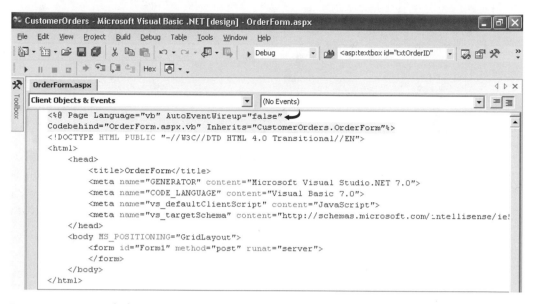

**Figure 6-14**    Web form in HTML view

The first command in the Web form HTML code is the @ Page directive. The **@ Page directive** specifies Web form configuration settings. The Visual Studio .NET IDE also uses the @ Page directive to reference the code behind file associated with the Web form. The @ Page directive contains the following attributes:

- **Language**, which specifies the language that you use to create commands in the Web form's HTML file. You can place server-side script commands directly in a Web form's HTML file, which is how developers created the older-style ASPs. In this book, however, you will not place code directly in .aspx files, so the language attribute isn't necessary.

- **AutoEventWireup**, which, when set to the value true, automatically associates page events to prenamed event handlers such as Page_Load, Page_Init, and so on. A disadvantage of setting AutoEventWireup to true is that it forces these page event handlers to have these specific names. If the AutoEventWireup attribute value is false, you can use different names for these event handlers. By default, the AutoEventWireup attribute value is set to false.

- **Codebehind**, which specifies the name of the code behind file associated with the Web form. This allows Visual Studio .NET to generate and place code in the code behind file automatically when HTML designers create server controls on the Web form. Note that in Figure 6-14, the code behind filename for the current Web form is OrderForm.aspx.vb.

The rest of the tags in HTML view specify the basic structure of an HTML document. Although you can use HTML view to define Web form elements manually using HTML tags, it is not a good practice, because the IDE does not generate the associated code and other links to the elements. For the most part, you do not use HTML view when you work with Web forms.

## The Toolbox

To add rich server controls, HTML server controls, and HTML elements to a Web form, you can select a tool in the Toolbox and draw the associated control on the Web form in Visual view. Earlier you configured the IDE so the Toolbox appears in minimized format as the Toolbox tab. This allows you to hide the Toolbox and then quickly display it when you need it. You display the Toolbox by placing the mouse pointer on the Toolbox tab. You hide the Toolbox by moving the mouse pointer to another location in the IDE.

Now you will reopen the Solution Explorer and Properties Windows in your IDE. Then you will open the Toolbox, disable the Auto Hide feature, and examine the Toolbox components.

To open the windows and examine the Toolbox:

1. Click the **Design** tab to redisplay the Web form in Design view.

2. Click **View** on the menu bar and then click **Solution Explorer** to open the Solution Explorer Window. Click **View** on the menu bar and then click **Properties Window** to open the Properties Window.

3. Move the mouse pointer onto the **Toolbox** tab. The Toolbox appears as shown in Figure 6-15.

**Figure 6-15**   Visual Studio .NET IDE Toolbox

4. To keep the Toolbox open, right-click **Toolbox**, then clear the check mark beside **Auto Hide**. (If there is not a check mark beside Auto Hide, do not check Auto Hide.) If necessary, click the Web Forms tab so your Toolbox looks like Figure 6-15.

The Toolbox contains tools that you use to create controls and other objects on Web forms. The Toolbox also contains multiple tabs. When you click a specific tab, a set of tools appears that supports a specific type of task. The default Toolbox tabs that appear when you are creating a Web application project are:

- **Data**, which contains tools for adding data components that support database operations. You will learn how to create and use Web form data components in Chapters 9 and 10.

- **Web Forms**, which contains tools for adding rich and validation server controls to a Web form.

- **Components**, which contains tools for adding special components to your project or form, such as an event log or a timer.

- **HTML**, which contains tools for adding HTML server controls and HTML form elements to a Web form.

- **Clipboard Ring**, which allows you to create a custom toolset of 12 items that you can copy from a Web form and store on the Clipboard Ring. For example, you could create a rich server control on a Web form, configure its size and property values, and then use the Clipboard Ring to easily create an exact copy of the control on the same Web form or on another Web form.

- **General**, which always appears by default when the Toolbox opens. The General tab contains only the default mouse pointer arrow.

You will learn how to use the Toolbox tools to create Web form server controls later in this chapter.

## The Properties Window

Recall that a Web form can contain items such as rich server controls, HTML server controls, or HTML form elements. Every item on a Web form is an object. Recall from Chapter 3 that an object has properties that specify its structure. For example, in Figure 6-7, the Image control has an ImageUrl property that specifies the name of the graphic image file that appears in the image, and the TextBox control has a MaxLength property that specifies the maximum number of characters that the user can enter into the TextBox control. You can set a control's property values at design time, which specifies the control's appearance and behavior when the Web form first opens. You can also use program commands to change the property values dynamically while the form is running, which is referred to as setting property values at run time.

The Properties Window lists the properties and their current design time values for the project component that is selected in the Solution Explorer or for the Web form item that is selected in the Web Browser Window in Visual view. The Object list appears at the top of the Properties Window and displays the name of the form object that is currently selected. If no object is selected, the Object list displays "DOCUMENT" and shows the Web form document's properties. For example, in Figure 6-12, the WebForm1.aspx Web form file is selected in the Solution Explorer, and the Properties Window displays the file's properties.

When you click the Categorized button 🔛 on the Properties Window toolbar, the property names appear under nodes that represent different property categories. For example, many rich server controls have a Font property node that contains properties, such as the font style and size, that allow you to specify how the font characters appear on the control. You can click the plus sign beside a property node to display its individual properties, and you can click the minus sign beside a property node to hide the individual properties. When you click the Alphabetic button 🔤 on the Properties Window, the properties appear in an alphabetized list. (In the alphabetized list, the Font properties still appear in a property node.)

When you click the Property Pages button 🖻 on the Properties Window toolbar, a dialog box opens that contains tab pages that allow you to set property values. You can optionally display or hide a description of the selected property in the bottom pane of the Properties Window. To toggle the description display on and off, right-click the Properties Window anywhere except in the window banner, and then click Description.

## WORKING WITH PROJECT COMPONENTS

HTML designers use Web form controls such as rich and HTML server controls and other Web page elements to create the visual elements that appear on a Web page. After an HTML designer creates a Web form control, he or she usually modifies the control's properties to specify how the control looks and behaves when the form first opens. Then, Web programmers write the code behind the controls to modify control properties at run time and perform the server-side processing. The following subsections describe how to create and configure Web form controls and how to write the code behind the controls.

### Creating Web Form Controls

Now you will create the visual items in the Web form in Figure 6-7. This Web form contains three rich server controls. The Clearwater Traders logo appears in an Image Control, the "The current date is:" text appears in a Label control, and the date value appears in a TextBox control. (Recall that a rich server control can be similar to an HTML form element, such as a text input or selection list, and can also provide more sophisticated functions in a Web page.) To create a rich server control on a Web form, you select the desired control in the Visual Studio .NET Toolbox, drag the control onto the form in Visual view, and then reposition and resize the control. Now you will add the rich server controls to the OrderForm Web form.

To create the Web form rich server controls:

1. Right-click the top bar of the Toolbox, and then check **Auto Hide**. Click the mouse pointer on the Web form to hide the Toolbox automatically.

2. Make sure that the OrderForm Web form appears in Visual view. Place the mouse pointer onto the **Toolbox** tab, and make sure that the Web Forms tab is selected.

3. Select the **Image** tool and drag it onto the Web form. The mouse pointer changes to the Precision Select pointer $+$ when you move the mouse pointer across the Web form.

4. Draw an image on the Web form that is approximately the same size as the Image control in Figure 6-16. Resize and reposition the Image control as necessary.

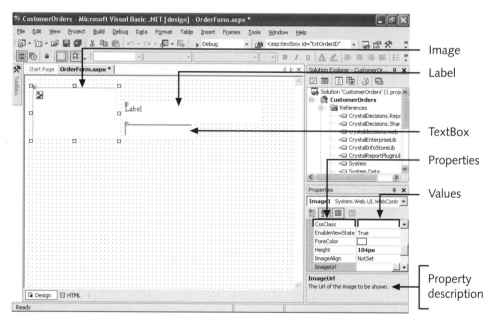

**Figure 6-16**    Creating the Web form rich server controls

Another way to create a control on a Web form is to double-click the control in the Toolbox. The new control automatically appears in the top-left corner of the current Web form. You can then select the control and drag it to the desired position and resize the control.

5. Move the mouse pointer onto the Toolbox tab again, select the **Label** tool, and draw the Label control template as shown in Figure 6-16.

6. Move the mouse pointer onto the Toolbox tab again, select the **TextBox** tool, and draw the TextBox control as shown in Figure 6-16.

7. Click the **Save** button on the toolbar to save the changes to the Web form.

Note that in Figure 6-16, a small green arrow appears on the top-left corner of each rich server control. This arrow indicates that the control is a server-side control and its event handler runs on the Web server. This green arrow appears on rich server controls, HTML server controls, and validation controls.

In a standard HTML document, all of the form elements appear in a **flow layout** style, which means that the elements appear in the same order as the underlying HTML tags. In Web forms, you usually use a **grid layout** style, which means that Visual Studio .NET specifies the element's location on the Web form using an absolute position. An **absolute position** specifies the element's location using values in the element's style tag that specify the number of pixels that the element appears from the top and left edges of the form. By using a grid layout style, you can easily reposition form elements by dragging and dropping the element in the desired position. This way, you do not need to use tables to display images beside text objects.

    When you display the grid in the Design Window in Visual view, you automatically specify that the Web form elements use a grid layout style.

When you create controls on a Web form, Visual Studio .NET automatically adds tags to the Web form to represent the controls. Now you will switch to HTML view to examine the tags that Visual Studio .NET created when you added the rich server controls to the Web form.

To examine the HTML tags for the controls:

1. Click the **HTML** tab to view the Web form in HTML view.

2. Scroll down until you see the tag for the Image control. The tag appears as follows:

```
<asp:Image id="Image1" style="style_specification">
</asp:Image>
```

Note that the *style_specification* contains the following style values: POSITION: absolute;LEFT: *n*px; TOP: *n*px. The values for *n* will be numbers. These style values specify that the control uses absolute positioning and show the number of pixels that that the control appears from the top and left edges of the form.

## Modifying Web Form Properties

Now you will modify the design time properties of the Web form's rich server controls. To change a control's design time property values, you select the control in the Browser Window, and then change the property values in the Properties Window. To apply the change, you select another property in the Properties Window.

Every control has an **ID property**, which specifies how the Web form internally references the control. The ID property is similar to the ID attribute of an HTML form element. Every Web form control must have a unique ID value. Normally, you accept the default ID values for static controls. A **static control** is a control whose properties are set at design time, and its properties do not change as a result of user actions or program commands. Web programmers do not reference static controls in program commands, so static controls do not need to have descriptive ID values. For example, the Image control that displays the Clearwater Traders logo and the Label control that displays the Web form title "Customer Orders" are static controls that do not change when the Web form executes.

Most Web forms contain **dynamic controls**, which are controls whose properties change while the form is running. For example, the TextBox control is a dynamic control that displays the order date and can be changed while the form is running. Because Web programmers reference dynamic controls in program commands, it is important to assign descriptive ID attribute values to them. You name Web form element ID values using prefixes that are similar to the ones you used in Chapter 2 for naming HTML form elements. Now you will change the ID property of the TextBox control to txtOrderDate.

To change the ID property value of the TextBox control:

1. Click the **Design** tab to switch to Design view, then select the **TextBox** control in the Browser Window. If necessary, open the Properties window. Note that the current ID property value, which is TextBox1, appears in the Object list at the top of the Properties Window.

2. If necessary, scroll in the Properties Window until you see the (ID) property. Because the ID property is one of the main control properties, it always appears at the top of the Properties Window.

 Another way to find the ID property is to click the Categorized button ▦ on the Properties Window and then open the Misc property node.

3. Select the **(ID)** property in the Properties Window, select the current ID value, which is TextBox1, delete it, and then type **txtOrderDate** as the new property value.

4. Select another property to save the new property value. The Properties Window with the modified ID value looks like Figure 6-17. Note that the new ID value now appears in the Object list at the top of the Properties Window.

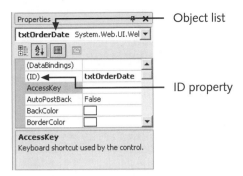

Object list

ID property

**Figure 6-17**    Changing the TextBox control's ID property value

Image rich server controls have an ImageUrl property that specifies the URL of the graphic image file that appears in the Image control. You can use either an absolute or relative URL to specify the ImageUrl property value. (Recall that an absolute URL specifies the absolute location of the file on the Web server, while a relative URL specifies the file location in relation to the current working directory.) Next you will copy the Clearwater Traders image file (clearlogo.jpg) to the project folder, and then change the Image control's ImageUrl property to a relative URL that specifies only the filename, because the file is in the current working directory.

To change the Image's ImageUrl property:

1. Switch to Windows Explorer and copy **clearlogo.jpg** from the Chapter6 folder on your Data Disk to the project folder, which is the Chapter6/Tutorials/ CustomerOrders folder on your Solution Disk.

2. Switch back to Visual Studio .NET and select the **Image** control in the Browser Window. If necessary, open the Properties Window and scroll down to the ImageUrl property.

3. Type **clearlogo.jpg** as the ImageUrl property value, and then select another property to apply the change. The logo image appears on the Web form.

Both Label and TextBox rich server controls have a **Text property** that specifies the text that the control displays when the form first opens. You can specify this value at design time, and you can write program commands to change the Text property value while the form is running. Because the text in the Label control does not change, you will specify its Text property as "*Customer Orders.*" You will also modify its font specification so the text appears in a large bold font style.

6

To modify the Label control's Text property:

1. Select the **Label** control in the Browser Window, scroll to the Text property, and change the Text property value to **Customer Orders**. Select another property value to apply the change.

2. Scroll down to the Font property, and then click the **plus sign** to open the property node.

3. Select the **Bold** property value to display the list that shows the legal property values. Open the list and select **True**.

4. Scroll down and select the **Size** property, open the list, and select **Large**. The Label control text now appears in a large bold font.

5. If necessary, adjust the size and position of the rich server controls so your Web form looks like Figure 6-7. The date value does not appear yet because you will use program code to set it at run time.

6. Click the **Save** button on the toolbar to save the Web form.

## Writing Server-Side Web Form Programs

In this chapter, you will learn the structure of a Web form code behind file. This will set the stage for learning the VB .NET language in Chapter 7. A code behind file contains some advanced programming features, and you do not need to understand all of its aspects fully.

The next step is to write the server-side program that provides the dynamic content for the Web page. In the OrderForm Web form, the program will retrieve the current date from the Web server and display the current date on the Web page. Recall that every Web form has an associated code behind file that contains the code that works with the Web form controls. You work with the code behind file in the Browser Window's Code editor.

The **Code editor** provides an environment in which you can enter, display, and edit program commands or text files. Figure 6-18 shows the OrderForm's code behind file in the Code editor.

You enter program commands in the **code pane**. The code pane organizes program commands into sections marked by nodes. You can open a node to view its underlying commands, and close a node to hide the commands. When you are programming in a Visual Studio .NET language, such as VB .NET and C#, the code pane provides IntelliSense lists to complete program commands automatically.

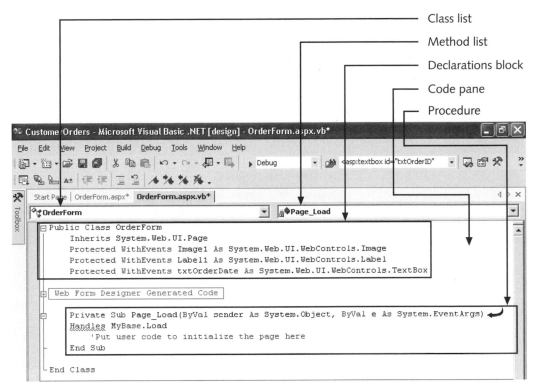

Class list
Method list
Declarations block
Code pane
Procedure

**Figure 6-18**    Code editor

To display a Web form's code behind file in the Code editor, you select the Web form node in the Solution Explorer Window and then click the View Code button [≣] on the Solution Explorer toolbar. Now you will open the code behind file for the OrderForm Web form. You will close the Toolbox, Solution Explorer, and Properties Windows to make more of the Code editor visible on the screen display.

To view the Web form's code behind file in the Code editor:

1. If necessary, select the **OrderForm.aspx** node in the Solution Explorer, and then click the **View Code** button [≣] on the Solution Explorer toolbar. The code for the OrderForm.aspx.vb file, which is the code behind file for the OrderForm Web form, appears in the Code editor.

Another way to view the code behind file for a Web form is to select the Web form in the Solution Explorer, click View on the menu bar, then click Code. Or, you can select the Web form in the Solution Explorer then press F7. Or, you can double-click anywhere on the Web form surface in Design view.

2. Close the Solution Explorer and Properties Windows so your screen display looks like Figure 6-18. Note that a new tab with the label "OrderForm.aspx.vb" appears in the Web Browser Window, which indicates that the Code editor is displaying the code for this Web form .aspx file.

A Web form's code behind file contains VB .NET commands that define and process Web form components. The first set of commands in the code behind file is called the Declarations block. The **Declarations block** contains the commands that define the Web form and its components. Next the code behind file contains **procedures**, which are self-contained code blocks written in one of the .NET programming languages. (In this book, you will write all Web form procedures in the VB .NET programming language.) Procedures can be functions and event handlers, which are similar to the JavaScript functions and event handlers that you learned about in Chapters 3 and 4. Recall that functions return a specific value, and event handlers execute in response to an object event. VB .NET procedures can also be **subroutines**, which are similar to functions and can receive and manipulate parameter values, but do not return a specific value.

The code for each procedure appears as a separate node in the Code editor. If you open the node, the procedure's individual commands appear. If you close the node, only the procedure header appears, which defines the procedure's name and parameter list. The following subsections describe the Declarations block and code behind file procedures.

## The Code Behind File Declarations Block

The .NET framework represents every Web form as an object class. When you create a new Web form, .NET creates a command as the first line in the code behind file's Declarations block that defines the Web form object class. This command has the following syntax:

```
Public Class Web_form_name
```

In this command, *Web_form_name* is the name of the Web form. Note that the first command in the OrderForm's code behind file in Figure 6-19 defines a class named OrderForm. The `Public` keyword specifies that any other .NET class can inherit the structure, properties, methods, and events of this class.

All Web forms have the same basic properties, methods, and events, which they inherit from the System.Web.UI.Page .NET reference library. (Recall that you learned about the .NET class libraries earlier in this chapter.) The second code line in the code behind file's Declarations block uses the following command to specify that the new Web form inherits its structures from this reference library: `Inherits System.Web.UI.Page`.

In VB. NET, a class can inherit elements from only one base (parent) class.

The Code editor contains a **class list** that displays the different object classes that exist in the Web form. The Web form class, which is OrderForm, appears as the first item in the class list. Other class list items include:

- *Overrides*, which allows you to create methods that **override**, or take precedence over, the methods that the Web form automatically inherits from the System.Web.UI.Page class.

- *Base Class Events*, which lists all of the events in the base class (System.Web.UI.Page). When you select this item in the class list, you can then open the method list and view a list of all of the base class's events. When you select one of these events, a code template appears for an event handler corresponding with the selected event. (A **code template** defines the basic structure of a procedure, and includes the procedure's declaration and parameter list specification. You add commands to the code template to define the procedure's specific parameters and commands.)

- *Form_objects*, which correspond to every form object, including rich, HTML, validation, and user server controls. The class list in Figure 6-18 contains items that represent the rich server controls that you created earlier.

The Code editor **method list** shows the associated methods for the current selection in the class list. Figure 6-19 shows the Code editor window in which the txtOrderDate TextBox control is selected in the class list, and the method list is opened and displaying the available methods for the selected control. If you select Declarations in the method list, the Code window insertion point moves to the Declarations block.

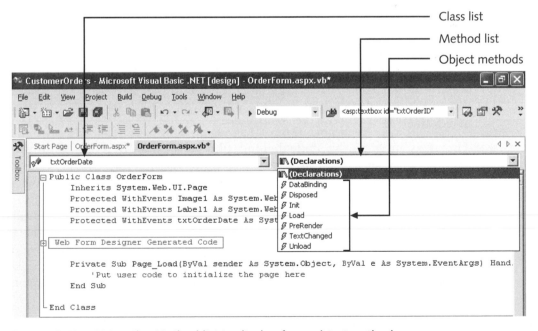

**Figure 6-19**    Using the Method list to display form object methods

Recall that when you create a Web server control in Design view, Visual Studio .NET automatically adds to the Declarations block commands that define the Web controls. In Figure 6-18, notice that the Declarations block contains commands that begin with the keyword Protected. These commands define the rich server controls you created earlier. Web server controls are objects that inherit from the base classes defined in the .NET class libraries. In Figure 6-18, notice that the Label control inherits from the System.WebControls.UI. Label class library, and the TextBox control inherits from the System.WebControls.UI. TextBox class library.

The `Protected` keyword in the control definitions specifies that the rich server controls are accessible only from within their own class. This means that you can write VB .NET commands within the OrderForm.aspx.vb code behind file that reference these controls, but you cannot reference these controls in another Web form's code behind file.

In the commands that define the rich server controls, the `WithEvents` keyword specifies that the rich controls can raise the events that their base classes define, and that the controls can have associated event handlers. For example, you can create a TextChanged event handler for the txtOrderDate TextBox rich server control that executes when the user changes the control's text.

## Code Behind File Procedures

You use procedures in the code behind file to manipulate the objects on a Web form. Code behind file procedures include server-side event handlers, subroutines, and functions that retrieve and manipulate database data based on user inputs. When you create a Web form, Visual Studio .NET automatically adds some standard procedures to support the form. In Figure 6-18, the first node under the Declarations block has the following syntax: `Web Form Designer Generated Code`. If you expand this node, the commands for these standard procedures appear. For now, do not worry about the commands within the Web Form Designer Generated Code node. When you add data objects to Web forms in Chapter 10, Visual Studio .NET adds a lot of code to this section to set up and manipulate database connections, so you will learn more about the standard commands then.

The next node in the code behind file declares a VB .NET subroutine named Page_Load. When you create a new Web form, Visual Studio .NET automatically creates a code template for the Page_Load event handler, which executes when the Web form loads. The `Private` keyword specifies that only other procedures that you define within the Web form code behind file and within the OrderForm class can call the Event handler. In most Web forms, you usually add VB .NET commands to the Page_Load subroutine. You will not work with or modify the parameter declarations in the Page_Load procedure, and you do not need to worry about what the declarations mean. Be careful not to change the syntax of the parameter list declaration accidentally, or the Web form will not run correctly.

In the OrderForm Web form, the txtOrderDate server control displays the current date when the Web page first appears. To implement this, you will add a command to the

Page_Load subroutine. This command will dynamically set the Text property of the txtOrderDate server control to the Web server's system date. To reference a property value of a Web form element in a VB .NET command, you use the following dot syntax: *element_ID.property_name*. In this syntax, *element_ID* is the ID property value of the element, and *property_name* is the name of the element property. For example, to reference the Text property of the txtOrderDate TextBox server control, you would use the following syntax: **txtOrderDate.Text**.

The DateString property represents the current Web server date. To set the Text property value of the server control to the current date, you will add the following command to the Page_Load subroutine:

```
txtOrderDate.Text = DateString
```

To add the command to the Page_Load subroutine:

1. In the Code editor, delete the text **'Put user code to initialize the page here** in the Page_Load event handler and replace it with the command shown in Figure 6-20.

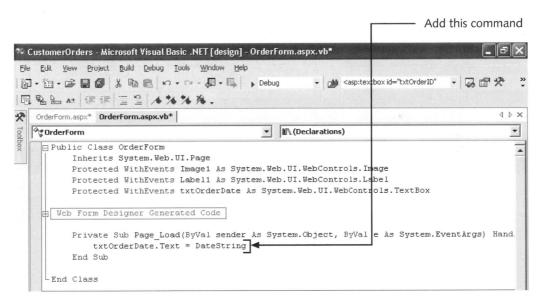

**Figure 6-20**    Adding the command to the Page_Load subroutine

2. Click the **Save** button on the toolbar to save the changes to the code behind file.

## Building and Testing the Project

After you create the Web server controls, modify their properties, and modify the code behind file, you must **build** the project. Building the project translates the project files into machine-readable code that your Web server can execute. Recall that Visual Studio .NET stores the compiled code of a Web application project in the project assembly file. Every time you make a change to your project, you must rebuild the project assembly file. One way to rebuild the project is to use the Build Solution or Rebuild Solution options on the Build menu. These options compile the files for all projects within a solution. You can also choose to build or rebuild the files for a specific project within a solution.

When you are developing a new project, another way to build or rebuild the project files is to run the project in the Visual Studio .NET IDE. Running the project automatically builds the project code, and then displays the project's Web form in Internet Explorer. You can then use the Visual Studio .NET Debugger, if necessary, to set breakpoints, step through commands, and view variable values during execution, just as you did with client-side scripts in Chapter 4. You will learn how to debug Web application projects in Chapter 8.

To run a project in the Visual Studio .NET Debugging environment, you select the project or one of its components in the Solution Explorer, and then click the Start button ▶ on the Visual Studio .NET Debug toolbar. (If you only have one project open, the project or one of its components is already selected.) Clicking the Start button ▶ causes Visual Studio .NET to automatically save the project files, build the project executable file, run the file on the Web server, and display the project in your Web browser.

Before you can run a project in Visual Studio .NET, you must specify the project **Start Page**, which is the Web form or HTML document that first appears in your Web browser when you run the project. A Web application project can contain many different Web forms. As you are developing these Web forms, you usually test each one independently. You can change the Start Page as you develop each separate form. Therefore, you must specify the project Start Page each time you create a new project and each time you reopen an existing project in Visual Studio .NET. After you build a project and place it on a production Web server, users can access any of the project's Web forms using a URL that specifies the Web form filename.

To specify the project Start Page, right-click the Web form or HTML document in the Solution Explorer that will be the project Start Page, and then click Set As Start Page. Now you will specify that OrderForm.aspx will be the project Start Page. Then you will run the project and view the Web form.

To specify the project Start Page and run the project:

1. Open the Solution Explorer, make sure that the **OrderForm.aspx** node is selected, right-click, and then click **Set As Start Page**.

 Each time you reopen an existing Web application project in Visual Studio .NET, you need to reset the Start Page.

2. If necessary, click **View** on the menu bar, point to **Toolbars**, and then click **Debug** to display the Debug toolbar.

3. Click the **Start** button ▶ on the Debug toolbar. The Output Window opens, which displays status messages about the project build process. After a few moments, the Web form appears in Internet Explorer as shown in Figure 6-7. (Your date will be different.)

Another way to run the project is to click Debug on the menu bar and then click Start.

An error message may appear stating "Error while trying to run project: Unable to start debugging on the Web server. The project is not configured to be debugged." If so, click No. Switch to the IIS console, and confirm that your Web server is configured as shown in Figure 6-11, that the project is saved in the Chapter6\Tutorials folder on your Solution Disk, and that the Chapter6 and Tutorials Web server applications are associated with the Chapter6 and Tutorials folders on your Solution Disk. Confirm that the project files appear in the application as shown in Figure 6-11. If the Web server configuration is not correct, correct the configuration. If the project is not saved in the correct location, proceed to the section titled "Moving Web Application Projects to Different Locations," and follow the instructions for modifying the project, then reopen the project in Visual Studio .NET and repeat Step 2.

4. Close Internet Explorer.

## ACCESSING AND REFERENCING WEB FORMS

So far you have created a Web application project, created a Web form, specified the Web form as the application's Start Page, and then run the application in the Visual Studio .NET debugging environment. After you successfully build and test a project, you can then make the project available to Web site users. One way a user can access a Web form is by entering the URL of the Web form in the *Address* field in their Web browser. Figure 6-7 shows the URL of the Customer Orders Web form in the CustomerOrders Web application project. Now you will start Internet Explorer and access the Web form using this URL.

To open a Web form in Internet Explorer:

1. Start Internet Explorer and type **http://localhost/Chapter6/Tutorials/CustomerOrders/OrderForm.aspx** in the Address field. (The URL path to a Web form is not case-sensitive.)

2. Press **Enter**. The Web form appears as shown in Figure 6-7.

You can also enable users to access Web forms through hyperlinks in static Web pages. You can add a static HTML document to a Web application project, and add any Web page elements to the document, including hyperlinks that reference Web forms. For example, Figure 6-21 shows a static Web page containing the text "Place an Order" that has an associated hyperlink. When the user clicks this hyperlink, the OrderForm Web form appears.

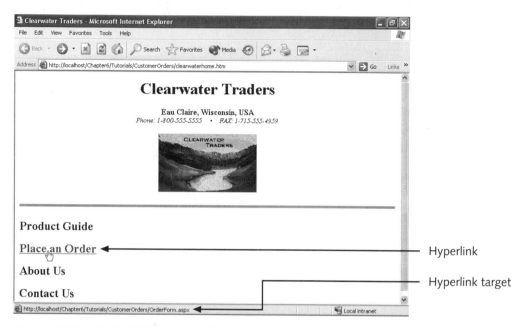

**Figure 6-21**    Static Web page with a hyperlink to Web form

Now you will add an existing HTML document to the CustomerOrders Web application project. Then you will add a hyperlink tag to link the text to the OrderForm.aspx Web form. To create a hyperlink that references a Web form, you specify the path to the Web form using either an absolute or relative URL folder path. The absolute URL to the OrderForm.aspx Web form is the URL path shown in Figure 6-7, so you will use this URL as the hyperlink tag's src attribute value. Then you will specify the static HTML document as the project's Start Page and run the project.

To add the static HTML document and create the hyperlink reference:

1. Switch to Windows Explorer, and copy **clearwaterhome.htm** from the Chapter6 folder on your Data Disk to the Chapter6\Tutorials\CustomerOrders folder on your Solution Disk.

2. Switch to Visual Studio .NET, select the **CustomerOrders** node in the Solution Explorer, right-click, point to **Add**, and then click **Add Existing Item**. The Add Existing Item - CustomerOrders dialog box opens.

3. Open the **Look in** list, if necessary navigate to the Chapter6\Tutorials\ CustomerOrders folder on your Solution Disk, open the **Files of type** list and select **All Files(\*.\*)**, select **clearwaterhome.htm**, and then click **Open**. The clearwaterhome.htm HTML document appears in the Solution Explorer.

When you add an existing item to a Web application project, you must specify the item's path from the file system rather than its URL path. If you select an existing item using its URL, the Web project will not run correctly.

4. Double-click the **clearwaterhome.htm** file, then click the **HTML** tab to view the HTML document in HTML view.

5. Add the following hyperlink tag to the Level 2 heading tag that contains the text "Place an Order." The completed tag should appear as follows:

```
<h2><a href="http://localhost/Chapter6/Tutorials/
CustomerOrders/OrderForm.aspx">Place an Order</a></h2>
```

6. Save the HTML document file.

7. Right-click the **clearwaterhome.htm** node in the Solution Explorer, and then click **Set As Start Page** to specify the static Web page as the project's Start Page.

8. Click the **Start** button ▶ on the Debug toolbar to run the project. The static Web page appears as shown in Figure 6-21.

9. Click the **Place an Order** hyperlink. The dynamic Web form appears as shown in Figure 6-7. Close Internet Explorer.

10. Switch back to Visual Studio .NET, if necessary, click **File** on the menu bar, then click **Close Solution** to close the CustomerOrders project solution. There should be no files currently open in Visual Studio .NET.

---

## MOVING WEB APPLICATION PROJECTS TO DIFFERENT LOCATIONS

Often you need to move Web application project files to new physical folder locations. The Web server's disk may become full or may fail. Or, you may want to reconfigure the structure of the Web server's file system. When you move a project to a new location, you must make some modifications both to the project and to the Web server structure. Otherwise, the project will not run correctly.

Recall that when you create a new Web application project, you specify the URL path to the application root, which is the project folder's parent folder. For example, when you created the CustomerOrders Web application project, you specified the URL path to the application root as *http://localhost/Chapter6/Tutorials* (see Figure 6-10). Visual Studio .NET then configured the project using this URL by writing this URL path into the project solution file. Now you will open the project solution file and view this path information. Recall that the project solution file is a text file. To view its contents, you open the file in Notepad or another text editor. You cannot open the file and view its contents in Visual Studio .NET, because Visual Studio .NET interprets the file as a project solution rather than as a text file.

To open the project solution file in Notepad:

1. Start Notepad, and if necessary, maximize the window.
2. Click **File** on the menu bar, click **Open**, and then navigate to the Chapter6\Tutorials\CustomerOrders folder on your Solution Disk. Open the **Files of type** list and select **All Files**, select **CustomerOrders.sln**, and then click **Open**. The text for the project solution file appears as shown in Figure 6-22.

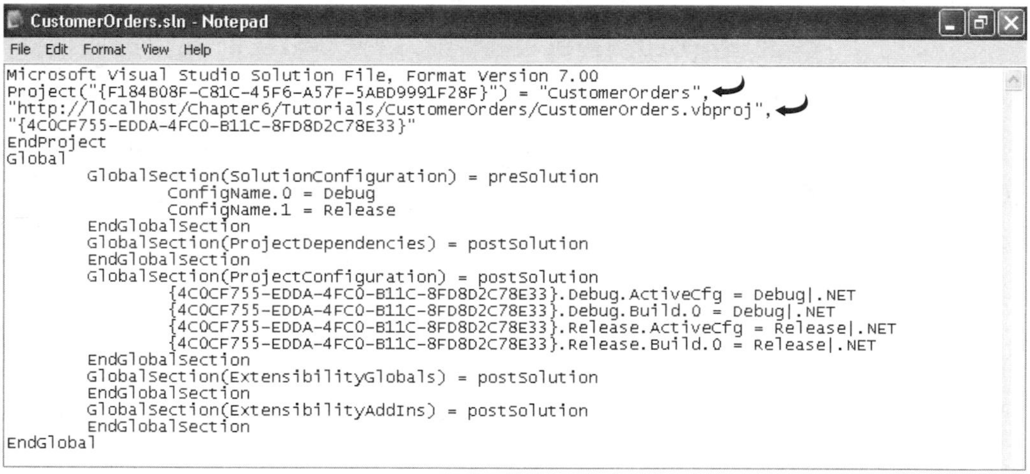


```
Microsoft Visual Studio Solution File, Format Version 7.00
Project("{F184B08F-C81C-45F6-A57F-5ABD9991F28F}") = "CustomerOrders",
"http://localhost/Chapter6/Tutorials/CustomerOrders/CustomerOrders.vbproj",
"{4C0CF755-EDDA-4FC0-B11C-8FD8D2C78E33}"
EndProject
Global
	GlobalSection(SolutionConfiguration) = preSolution
		ConfigName.0 = Debug
		ConfigName.1 = Release
	EndGlobalSection
	GlobalSection(ProjectDependencies) = postSolution
	EndGlobalSection
	GlobalSection(ProjectConfiguration) = postSolution
		{4C0CF755-EDDA-4FC0-B11C-8FD8D2C78E33}.Debug.ActiveCfg = Debug|.NET
		{4C0CF755-EDDA-4FC0-B11C-8FD8D2C78E33}.Debug.Build.0 = Debug|.NET
		{4C0CF755-EDDA-4FC0-B11C-8FD8D2C78E33}.Release.ActiveCfg = Release|.NET
		{4C0CF755-EDDA-4FC0-B11C-8FD8D2C78E33}.Release.Build.0 = Release|.NET
	EndGlobalSection
	GlobalSection(ExtensibilityGlobals) = postSolution
	EndGlobalSection
	GlobalSection(ExtensibilityAddIns) = postSolution
	EndGlobalSection
EndGlobal
```

**Figure 6-22** Project solution file

Note that the second command in the project solution file specifies the project name, which is CustomerOrders, and shows the URL to the project's .vbproj file. (Recall that the .vbproj file is an XML file that contains the configuration and build settings and lists the project's files.) You can copy the project folder to a new physical location, but Visual Studio .NET will continue to open the project files from the folder associated with the URL that the project solution file specifies.

To confirm that the project solution file opens the project files using this path, you will make a new folder named CustomerOrders_COPY in the Chapter6\Tutorials folder of your Solution Disk and copy all of the files in the CustomerOrders project folder to the new folder. Then you will open the project from the CustomerOrders_COPY folder and examine the project. You will see that even though you open the project using a different project solution file, Visual Studio .NET opens the project's component files from their original locations.

To copy the project and open the project copy:

1. Close Notepad, then switch to Windows Explorer and create a new folder named **CustomerOrders_COPY** in the Chapter6\Tutorials folder on your Solution Disk.

2. Copy all of the files and folders in the CustomerOrders folder to the CustomerOrders_COPY folder to make an exact copy of the project.

3. Switch to Visual Studio .NET, click **File** on the menu bar, point to **Open**, click **Project**, navigate to the CustomerOrders_COPY folder in the Chapter6\Tutorials folder on your Solution Disk, select **CustomerOrders.sln**, and then click **Open**. The copy of the CustomerOrders project opens in Visual Studio .NET.

4. Open the Solution Explorer if necessary, and then select **OrderForm.aspx**. Open the Properties Window if necessary, and view the File Name property value in a ScreenTip by placing the mouse pointer on the property value. Note that the File Name value for the Web form file specifies the Web form folder and file location of the original OrderForm.aspx file, as shown in Figure 6-23.

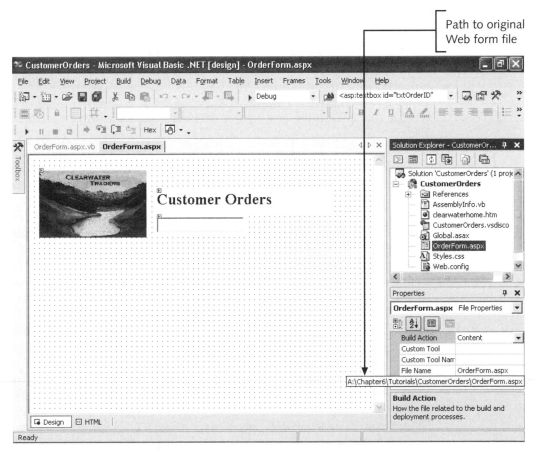

**Figure 6-23**   Path showing that the project copy references the Web form file from the original project

5. To confirm that the project still runs correctly, click the **Start** button ▶ on the Debug toolbar to run the project. The project's static Web page appears in Internet Explorer as shown in Figure 6-21.

6. Click **Place an Order**. The dynamic Web form showing the current date appears. Close Internet Explorer.

7. Close the CustomerOrders project solution in Visual Studio .NET.

Recall that when you create a Web application project, your Web server structure must contain applications that match the folder path to the project folder. In addition, the Web server must have a Web server application associated with the project folder, and the application must have the same name as the project folder. Even though you have not reconfigured your Web server so the Web server application specifies the new project folder location, the project still runs successfully. Why? The project still runs because it is referencing the original CustomerOrder project files in the Chapter6\Tutorials\CustomerOrders folder, rather than the copied files in the Chapter6\Tutorials\CustomerOrders_COPY folder. As long as the original project files are in their original location, the project will run correctly.

If you delete the original project files or move the original project files to a different location, however, the project will no longer run correctly. To confirm this, you will change the folder path of the original project. You will make the original project URL and folder paths invalid by renaming the CustomerOrders folder as CustomerOrders_TEMP. Then you will open the copy of the project and try to run the project.

To change the original project's folder path name and then try to run the project copy:

1. Switch to Windows Explorer and rename the CustomerOrders folder in the Chapter6\Tutorials folder on your Solution Disk as **CustomerOrders_TEMP**.

If an error message appears stating that you cannot rename CustomerOrders because another person or program is using it, click OK. This message appears because when you ran the project earlier, Visual Studio .NET cached the project code in main memory and is keeping the project files open. The ASP.NET process is a separate process from the Web server process and the Visual Studio .NET process, so closing Visual Studio .NET or the IIS console won't solve this problem. To stop the ASP.NET process, press Ctrl-Alt-Delete to open the Windows Task Manager. (Windows 2000 users will press Ctrl-Alt-Del, then click the Task Manager.) Select the Processes tab, select the Image Name column heading to organize the image list alphabetically, select aspnet_wp.exe, click End Process, and then click Yes. (Terminating aspnet_wp.exe is safe, but do not terminate other processes this way.) You will still see aspnet_wp.exe in the Task Manager's Processes window, because ASP.NET immediately restarts itself after being terminated, but you have released all cached programs from the ASP.NET process you terminated. Then close the Task Manager window and repeat Step 1.

If you still cannot rename the project folder, confirm that you closed the project solution file in Notepad, then repeat Step 1.

2. Switch to Visual Studio .NET, click **File** on the menu bar, point to **Open**, click **Project**, navigate to the CustomerOrders_COPY folder in the Chapter6\Tutorials folder on your Solution Disk, select **CustomerOrders.sln**, and then click **Open**. The Web Access Failed dialog box opens, indicating that the project folder path is no longer valid.

3. Make sure that the *Work offline* option button is selected, click **OK**, and then click **OK** again to confirm that you are not opening the project.

To move a project to a new location successfully, you must create a new Web server application and associate it with the new project folder. Then you must modify the project solution file to specify the URL to the new Web server application. To become familiar with this process, first you will reconfigure your Web server. You will create a new Web server application named CustomerOrders_COPY, and associate it with the CustomerOrders_COPY folder in the Chapter6\Tutorials folder on your Solution Disk.

To create the Web server application associated with the project copy:

1. Switch to the IIS console, select the **Tutorials** application in the console tree, right-click, point to **New**, and then click **Virtual Directory**. The Virtual Directory Creation Wizard Welcome page opens. Click **Next**.

2. Type **CustomerOrders_COPY** in the *Alias* field, and then click **Next**.

3. On the Web Site Content Directory page, click **Browse**, navigate to the Chapter6\Tutorials folder on your Solution Disk, select **CustomerOrders_COPY**, click **OK**, and then click **Next**.

4. On the Access Permissions page, make sure that the *Read* and *Run scripts (such as ASP)* check boxes are checked. Check the **Browse** check box, click **Next**, then click **Finish**. The new CustomerOrders_COPY Web server application appears under the Tutorials application node, as shown in Figure 6-24. (Your console tree may show different physical directories.)

 Another way to create a Web server application that you associate with the CustomerOrders_COPY folder is to right-click the CustomerOrders_COPY physical directory in the IIS console, click Properties, select the Directory properties page if necessary, and then click Create to create a Web server application based on the physical folder.

Application
associated with
project copy

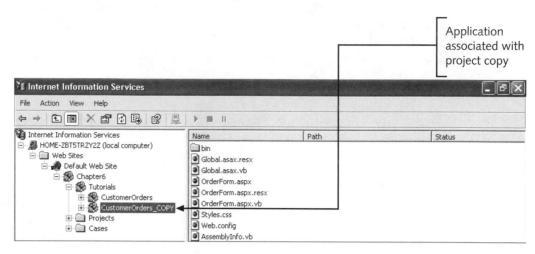

**Figure 6-24**   Creating the Web server application for the project copy

Next you will open the CustomerOrders.sln project solution file in the project copy in Notepad and change the project URL path so it specifies the URL to the new Web server application. This URL will specify the path to the CustomerOrders_COPY Web server application in Figure 6-24, which has the following URL: *http://localhost/Chapter6/ Tutorials/CustomerOrders_COPY*. You will also change the hyperlink in the static Web page to specify the new URL to the project's Web form.

To change the project URL path in the project solution file:

1. Start Notepad, and if necessary, maximize the window.

2. Click **File** on the menu bar, click **Open**, navigate to the Chapter6\Tutorials\CustomerOrders_COPY folder on your Solution Disk, open the **Files of type** list and select **All Files**, select **CustomerOrders.sln**, and then click **Open**. The text for the project solution file appears in Notepad.

3. In the second command in the file, change the URL to the .vbproj file so the project's Web server application name appears as follows:

   ```
   http://localhost/Chapter6/Tutorials ↵
   CustomerOrders_COPY/CustomerOrders.vbproj
   ```

4. Save the file and then exit Notepad.

5. Switch back to Visual Studio .NET. The File Modification Detected dialog box appears stating that the CustomerOrders solution has been modified outside of the Visual Studio .NET environment. Click **Reload**. The copy of the project appears in Visual Studio .NET.

If the File Modification Detected dialog box does not appear, open the CustomerOrders.sln file from the CustomerOrders_COPY folder in the Chapter6\Tutorials folder on your Solution Disk.

6. Open the Solution Explorer window if necessary, select the **OrderForm.aspx** node, and confirm that the File Name property value specifies that the project accesses the Web form from the CustomerOrders_COPY folder on your Solution Disk using the following folder path: Chapter6\Tutorials\CustomerOrders_COPY\OrderForm.aspx.

7. Double-click the **clearwaterhome.htm** node in the Solution Explorer, click the **HTML** tab to view the Web page in HTML view, and then change the hyperlink tag so it appears as follows. Then save the HTML document.

```
<a href="http://localhost/Chapter6/Tutorials/ ↵
CustomerOrders_COPY/OrderForm.asxp>
```

8. Right-click the **clearwaterhome.htm** node in the Solution Explorer, and then click **Set As Start Page** to specify the static Web page as the project's Start Page. (Recall that you must reset the Start Page every time you reopen an existing project in Visual Studio .NET.)

9. Click the **Start** button ▶ to run the project. After a few moments, the static Web page appears in Internet Explorer. Note that the URL in the *Address* field specifies the CustomerOrders_COPY Web server application.

10. Click **Place an Order**. The dynamic Web form showing the current date appears. Close Internet Explorer.

11. Switch back to Visual Studio .NET, if necessary, close the project solution, and close Visual Studio .NET and all other open applications.

Setting up a Web application project is a complicated process, and you need to follow the steps in the process carefully. Moving a Web application project is equally complicated, and you must take equal care when doing so. In summary, the steps for moving a Web application project to a new folder location are:

1. Move the project files to the new location

2. Create a new Web server application with the same name as the relocated project folder.

3. Use Notepad or another text editor to open the relocated project's project solution (.sln) file, and change the URL of the project's Web application to the new application path.

# CHAPTER SUMMARY

❑ The .NET framework is a set of code, objects, and standards for building computer applications. You can use ASP.NET to create a Web application project that contains all of the application's related files, such as HTML documents, graphic files, XML files, and server-side programs and scripts. The Visual Studio .NET IDE provides a visual interface that enables you to access, configure, manage, and debug the different application components in a single integrated environment.

❑ ASP.NET enables you to create Web forms that contain Web page elements with links to programs that interact with these elements and allow you to create dynamic Web pages using server-side processing.

❑ Web forms can contain server controls, which are elements that an HTML designer creates in a Web form. Server controls are similar to HTML form elements, except that they provide a more direct link between items on a Web page and programs running on the Web server. Web server controls can also provide more sophisticated functions, such as a calendar, and can be used to validate user inputs. Server controls have associated events that the Web server associates with user actions.

❑ Server controls enable Web developers to create modular Web applications in which HTML designers create Web forms that contain Web server controls, and Web programmers write separate programs that control and manipulate the server controls.

❑ Web server controls can be rich server controls, which are similar to HTML form elements except they have different properties and event handlers and can support more functionality; HTML server controls, which are almost identical to HTML form elements, except they have associated server-side event handlers; and validation server controls, which can validate user inputs.

❑ The .NET framework is built on the object-oriented model and contains an extensive class library with parent classes and associated child classes that inherit the properties, events, and methods of the parent classes. You use dot syntax to show the relationships between .NET class library parent classes and child classes.

❑ Before you can create a Web application project, you must configure your Web server so it contains the application root, which is a Web server application whose physical folder contains the project folder. If you open a Web application project on a different computer, that computer's IIS console must have the same Web server application structure as the computer on which you originally created the project.

❑ A Web application project consists of many interrelated files. When you create a new project, you specify the project name, and Visual Studio .NET then automatically creates the project folder that stores the project files. The project folder has the same name as the project name. The main files include the compiled project file, which is called an assembly; global files, which are visible to all project components; resource files, which contain data that supports the project, such as images or icons; the project solution file, which stores references to the files that comprise the project; and the user option file, which is a binary file with an .suo file extension that stores configuration settings for the solution.

❑ Visual Studio .NET stores every Web form in a file with an .aspx extension. Web forms have associated code behind files that contain the code that Web developers create to interact with the Web form's server controls.

❑ When you create a new Web application project, Visual Studio .NET automatically creates a new Web server application that it associates with the project folder.

❐ After you create a new Web application project, you use Visual Studio .NET to add or remove Web forms from the project, add new server controls to the Web forms, modify the properties of the server controls, and write code to create procedures and event handlers to manipulate the server controls.

❐ In Visual Studio .NET, you use the Solution Explorer to access and manage project components; you use the Web Browser Window to view Web forms in Visual and HTML view; you use the Toolbox to add server controls to Web forms; you use the Properties Window to view and modify item properties; and you use the Code editor to add and modify program code.

❐ Every Web form code behind file contains a Declarations block, which contains the commands that define the Web form and its components, and procedures, which are self-contained code blocks that other programs can call and to which they can pass parameters. Procedures can be functions, subroutines, or event handlers.

❐ After you create the Web server controls, modify their properties, and add procedures to the code behind file, you must build the project, which translates the project files into machine-readable code that your Web server can execute. You can explicitly build the project, or run the project in Visual Studio .NET to build it automatically. Before you can build a project, you must specify the project's Start Page, which is the Web form that appears when the project first opens.

❐ After you successfully build a Web application project, you can make the project's Web forms available to Web site users by having users enter the URL path to the project's Web form or by creating hyperlinks to the project's Web forms in HTML documents.

❐ When you create a new Web application project, Visual Studio .NET stores the URL path to the project application in the project's .vbproj file. If you move the project to a new location, the IDE accesses the project files from the original location if the files still exist. If the files have been moved or the path changes, the project will no longer run correctly.

❐ To move a Web application project to a new location, you must move the project files to the new location, create a new Web server application associated with the new project folder, and then modify the project's .vbproj file using a text editor.

## REVIEW QUESTIONS

1. _____ is a set of code, objects, and standards for building computer applications.

   a. VB .NET

   b. ASP.NET

   c. The .NET framework

   d. A Web application project

2. List three differences between older-style ASPs and Web forms that you create using ASP.NET.

3. What is the role of HTML designers in creating Web application projects, and what is the role of Web programmers in creating Web application projects?

4. List the three main types of Web server controls that ASP.NET provides.

5. Write the command to create a tag that specifies a rich server control with the ID property "lblHello" that contains the text "Hello World."

6. True or false: Server validation controls remove the need for JavaScript data validation functions.

7. Every Web form has an associated _____ file that contains the Web form's declarations and procedures.

   a. Code behind

   b. Resource

   c. Control

   d. Configuration

8. In a Web application project, _____ files are visible to all project components.

9. Match the Visual Studio .NET IDE component with the task for which you would use it.

| IDE Component | Task |
|---|---|
| 1. Solution Explorer | a. Create a new server control on a Web form |
| 2. Browser Window in HTML view | b. Write VB .NET commands to perform server-side processing |
| 3. Toolbox | c. Change the text that a rich server control label displays when a Web form first opens |
| 4. Properties Window | d. View the HTML tags and text for a Web form |
| 5. Code editor | e. Add a new Web form to a project |

10. When does a server-side event handler execute?

11. In the .NET framework, a child class inherits its properties, methods, and structure from its:

    a. Parent class

    b. Base class

    c. Collection

    d. Namespace

    e. Both a and b

12. When you create a new Web application project, Visual Studio .NET automatically creates a _____ on your Web server that it associates with the project's physical folder.

    a. Namespace

    b. Collection

    c. Base class

    d. Web server application

13. To reopen an existing Web application project, you open the _____ file in Visual Studio .NET, which has a(n) _____ extension.

14. What does the first command in a Web form's code behind file do?

15. True or false: In a code behind file, a subroutine always returns one or more values to the calling program.

16. Write the command to declare the object class for a Web form named myForm and to specify that the form inherits its structures from the UI.Page class library.

17. True or false: In Visual Studio .NET, a class can inherit its structures from only one parent class.

18. List two ways to build a new project assembly file.

19. What is the project Start Page? When do you need to specify the project Start Page?

20. When do you need to use a text editor to change the URL path in a project's .vbproj file?

## HANDS-ON PROJECTS

To solve these projects, you must first create a new Web server application that you associate with the Chapter6\Projects folder on your Solution Disk, and you must also modify the Visual Studio .NET IDE so it places all project solution files in the Chapter6\Projects folder on your Solution Disk.

### Project 6-1 Creating the Northwoods University Registration System Web Application Project

In this project, you will create a new Web application project named RegistrationProject that will store the Web forms for the Northwoods University Registration System. You will create a Web form for the project that contains rich server controls for the Northwoods University Log On Web page shown in Figure 6-25.

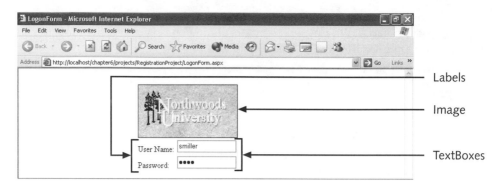

Labels

Image

TextBoxes

**Figure 6-25**

1. Create a new Web application project named RegistrationProject. The project's application root is the Projects application that you created based on the instructions in the Note before the first Hands-on project.

2. Delete the project's default Web form, and create a new Web form named LogonForm.

3. Create the Image control for the Northwoods University logo as shown in Figure 6-25. Copy the nwlogo.jpg file from the Chapter6 folder on your Data Disk to the Chapter6\Projects folder on your Solution Disk, then change the Image control's ImageUrl property value to specify the absolute URL path to the nwlogo.jpg file on your Web server.

4. Create the Label controls in Figure 6-25. Change the Text properties of the Label controls so the Web form appears as shown. Position the form controls so they appear centered on the Web page as shown.

5. Create the TextBox controls in Figure 6-25. Change the ID property value of the first TextBox control to txtUsername, and change the ID property value of the second TextBox control to txtPassword. Change the TextMode property of the txtPassword TextBox control to Password so the input text appears masked when the user enters a value.

6. Run the project to confirm that the Web form appears correctly in Internet Explorer and that the Password input value appears masked as shown.

## Project 6-2 Creating the Clearwater Traders Sales Order System Web Application Project

In this project, you will create a new Web application project named SalesProject that will store the Web forms for the Clearwater Traders Sales Order System. You will create a Web form for the project that contains rich server controls for the New Order Web page shown in Figure 6-26.

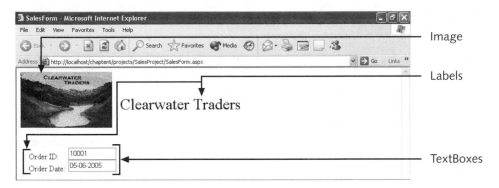

**Figure 6-26**

1. Create a new Web application project named SalesProject. The project's application root is the Projects application that you created based on the instructions in the Note before the first Hands-on Project.

2. Delete the project's default Web form, and then create a new Web form named SalesForm.aspx.

3. Create the Image control for the Clearwater Traders logo as shown in Figure 6-26. Copy the clearlogo.jpg file from the Chapter6 folder on your Data Disk to the Chapter6\Projects folder on your Solution Disk, then change the image's ImageUrl property value to specify the absolute URL path to the nwlogo.jpg file in the Projects folder on your Web server.

4. Create the "Clearwater Traders" Label control on the Web form. Change the Text property value to "Clearwater Traders." Change the Font property values so the text appears in 24-point Times Roman by changing the Font Name to Times New Roman, and the Font Size to 24.

5. Create the Label and TextBox controls for the Order ID and Order Date fields as shown. Assign descriptive ID property values to the TextBox controls using the appropriate ID prefixes.

6. Modify the Order ID TextBox control's Text property so the control displays the value "10001" when the form first opens.

7. Modify the Web form's code behind file so that when the form first opens, the Order Date TextBox control displays the current Web server system date.

8. Run the project to confirm that the Web form appears correctly in Internet Explorer.

## Project 6-3 Creating a Web Application Project with Hyperlinks to Web Forms

In this project, you will create a Web application project that contains the static Web page shown in Figure 6-27, which allows users to select different merchandise items on the Clearwater Traders Web site. When the user selects an item, a Web form opens, which describes the selected item.

Figure 6-27

1. Create a new Web application project named ItemsProject. The project's application root is the Projects application that you created based on the instructions in the Note before the first Hands-on Project.

2. Add a new HTML document named ItemsIndex.htm to the project, and create the Web form elements shown in Figure 6-27 in the HTML document.

3. Delete the project's default Web form, and then create a new Web form named ShortsForm.aspx as shown in Figure 6-28. Copy the shorts.jpg graphic image file from the Chapter6 folder on your Data Disk to the Chapter6\Projects folder on your Solution Disk, and then create an Image control. Set the Image control's ImageUrl property value to the URL of the shorts.jpg image on your local Web server using an absolute path. Create Label controls to display the item name ("Women's Hiking Shorts"), available sizes, colors, and price.

4. Create a new Web form named TentsForm.aspx as shown in Figure 6-29. Copy the tents.jpg graphic image file from the Chapter6 folder on your Data Disk to the Chapter6\Projects folder on your Solution Disk, and then create an Image control. Set the Image control's ImageUrl property value to the URL of the tents.jpg image on your local Web server. Create Label rich server controls to display the item name ("3-Season Tent"), available colors, and price.

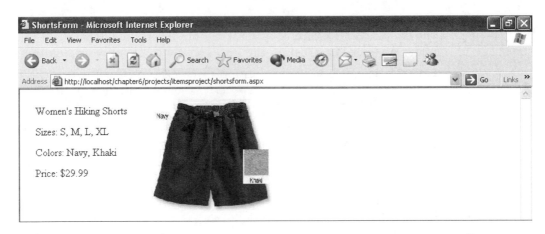

**Figure 6-28**

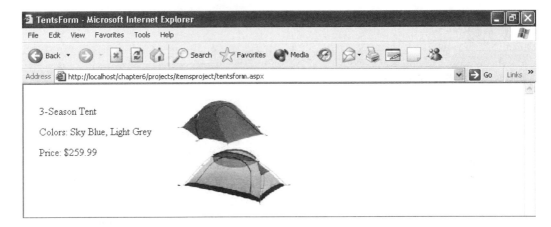

**Figure 6-29**

5. Create hyperlinks from the text items on the ItemsIndex.htm static Web page to the ShortsForm.aspx and TentsForm.aspx Web forms.

6. Specify the ItemsIndex.htm static Web page as the project's Start Page, and then run the project and confirm that it works correctly.

## Project 6-4 Copying a Project to a New Physical Folder Location

In this project, you will copy the files for a project named DateProject, which displays the current date on a Web form, to a new physical folder location. You will create a new folder for the project files, and copy the project files from your Data Disk to the new folder on your Solution Disk. Then you will create a new Web server application for the project, and modify the project's .vbproj file to reflect the new project URL.

1. Create a new folder named ProjectCopy in the Chapter6\Projects folder on your Solution Disk, and copy all of the files from the Chapter6\6Project4 folder on your Data Disk to the ProjectCopy folder on your Solution Disk.

2. Create a new Web server application named ProjectCopy within the Projects application on the IIS console. Associate the application with the ProjectCopy folder in the Chapter6\Projects folder on your Solution Disk.

3. Modify the URL path in the .vbproj file in the project solution file in the ProjectCopy project folder to reflect the new project URL.

4. Open the project copy in Visual Studio .NET, and modify the hyperlink on the StaticPage.htm Web page so it references the project's Web form using the modified project URL path.

5. Specify that StaticPage.htm is the project's Start Page, then run the project in Visual Studio .NET and confirm that it works correctly.

# CASE PROJECTS

If you are saving your Solution Disk files on a floppy disk, you will need to insert a new floppy disk in your disk drive to save your Case Project solutions because your current Solution Disk is almost full.

To solve the case projects in this chapter, you must first create a new Web server application that you associate with the Chapter6\Cases folder on your Solution Disk, and you must modify your Visual Studio .NET IDE so it places all project solution files in the Chapter6\Cases folder on your Solution Disk.

## Case Project 6-1 Ashland Valley Soccer League

In this Case Project, you will create a Web application project for the Ashland Valley Soccer League, which is described in Case 2-1 in Chapter 2. This project will contain a static Web page that is the Ashland Valley Soccer League's home page, and Web forms that contain information about the soccer league's fields, teams, and games. The Chapter6\Ashland folder on your Data Disk contains the HTML document that will be the home page and graphic image files you can display on these Web forms. Or, you can select your own images.

1. Create a new Web application project named AshlandProject that is in the Cases application on your Web server.

2. Copy the files from the Chapter6\Ashland folder on your Data Disk to the project folder. Then, add the AshlandHome.htm HTML document file to the project. This is a static Web page in which you will create links to the project's Web forms.

3. Create a Web form named FieldsForm.aspx that contains Label controls, which display the names and addresses of the league's soccer fields. (You can use any data values you want.)

4. Create a Web form named TeamsForm.aspx that contains Label rich server controls that display information about the names of the soccer league teams. (You can use any data values you want.)

5. Create a Web form named GamesForm.aspx that contains Label and TextBox controls that allow users to enter values for the game date, game time, home team name, visiting team name, and field name. Assign descriptive ID property values to all TextBox controls. Modify the Web form's code behind file so it automatically displays the current date in the Date TextBox control and the current time in the Time TextBox control when the form first opens. (*Hint*: Use the TimeString property to retrieve the current time on the Web server.)

6. On the AshlandHome.htm static Web page, create hyperlinks from the Games, Fields, and Teams bulleted items to the associated Web forms.

7. Set the home page as the project Start Page, then run the project in Visual Studio .NET to confirm that it runs correctly.

## Case Project 6-2 Al's Body Shop

In this Case Project, you will create a Web application project for Al's Body Shop, which is described in Case Project 2-2 in Chapter 2. This project will contain a static Web page that is Al's home page, and Web forms that contain information about the body shop's customers, services, and work orders. The Chapter6\Als folder on your Data Disk contains the HTML document file for the home page and a graphic image file that you can display on these Web forms. Or, you can select your own images.

1. Create a new Web application project named AlsProject that is in the Cases application on your Web server.

2. Copy the files from the Chapter6\Als folder on your Data Disk to the project folder. Then, add the AlsHome.htm HTML document file to the project. This is a static Web page in which you will create links to the project's Web forms.

3. Create a Web form named CustomerForm.aspx that contains Label rich server controls, which display the names, addresses, and telephone numbers of five different customers. (You can use any data values you want.)

4. Create a Web form named ServiceForm.aspx that contains Label rich server controls, which display the names and prices of five different services. (You can use any data values you want.)

5. Create a Web form named WorkOrderForm.aspx that contains Label and TextBox rich server controls that allow users to enter values for the Work Order ID, Date, Customer Name, and Service Name. Specify descriptive ID property values for the TextBox controls. (For now, include only one service per work order.) Modify the Web form's code behind file so it automatically displays the current date in the Date TextBox control when the form first opens.

6. On the AlsHome.htm static Web page, create hyperlinks from the Customers, Services, and Work Orders items to the associated Web forms.

7. Set the AlsHome.htm Web page as the project Start Page, then run the project in Visual Studio .NET to confirm that it runs correctly.

## Case Project 6-3 Sun-Ray Videos

In this Case Project, you will create a Web application project for Sun-Ray Videos, which is described in Case Project 2-3 in Chapter 2. This project will contain a static Web page that is the Sun-Ray home page, and Web forms that contain information about the video store's videos and rentals. The Chapter6\Sunray folder on your Data Disk contains the static Web page file and graphic image files that you can display on these Web forms. Or, you can select your own images.

1. Create a new Web application project named SunrayProject that is in the Cases application on your Web server.

2. Copy the files from the Chapter6\Sunray folder on your Data Disk to the project folder. Then, add the SunrayHome.htm HTML document file to the project. This is a static Web page in which you will create links to the project's Web forms.

3. Create a Web form named VideosForm.aspx that contains Label rich server controls, which display the titles of five different videos. (You can use any data values you want.)

4. Create a Web form named RentalsForm.aspx that contains Label and TextBox server controls that allow users to enter values for the Rental Date, Return Date, and Video Title. (For now, allow only one video title per rental.) Specify descriptive ID property values for the TextBox controls. Modify the Web form's code behind file so it automatically displays the current date in the Rental and Return Date TextBox controls when the form first opens.

5. On the SunrayHome.htm static Web page, create hyperlinks from the View Titles and Rent a Video text items to the associated Web forms.

6. Set the static Web page as the project Start Page, then run the project in .NET to confirm that it runs correctly.

## Case Project 6-4 Learning Technologies, Incorporated

In this Case Project, you will create a Web application project for Learning Technologies, Incorporated (LTI), which is described in Case Project 2-4 in Chapter 2. This project will contain a static Web page that is the LTI home page, and Web forms that contain information about LTI's authors, books, warehouses, and inventory. The Chapter6\LTI folder on your Data Disk contains the static Web page file and a graphic image file that you can display on these Web forms. Or, you can select your own images.

1. Create a new Web application project named LTIProject that is in the Cases application on your Web server.

2. Copy the files from the Chapter6\LTI folder on your Data Disk to the project folder. Then, add the LTIHome.htm HTML document file to the project. This is a static Web page in which you will create links to the project's Web forms.

3. Create a Web form named AuthorsForm.aspx that contains Label server controls that display the names, addresses, and telephone numbers of five different authors. (You can use any data values you want.)

4. Create a Web form named BooksForm.aspx that contains Label server controls that display the titles, publication dates, and prices of five different books. (You can use any data values you want.)

5. Create a Web form named WarehouseForm.aspx that contains Label server controls, which display the Warehouse ID, Address, and City of five different warehouses. (You can use any data values you want.)

6. Create a Web form named WarehouseQOHForm.aspx that contains Label and TextBox server controls, which allow users to enter values for a book title, warehouse ID, and quantity on hand of the specified book title. Specify descriptive ID property values for the TextBox server controls.

7. On the LTIHome.htm static Web page, create hyperlinks from the Authors, Books, Warehouses, and Update Warehouse QOH items to the associated Web forms.

8. Set the static Web page as the project Start Page, then run the project in Visual Studio .NET to confirm that it runs correctly.

6

# INTRODUCTION TO VB .NET

---

**In this chapter, you will:**

♦ Learn about the VB .NET programming language
♦ Learn how to declare variables and assign values to variables
♦ Use the VB .NET Debugger to monitor program execution
♦ Learn how to create user-defined procedures
♦ Work with complex numeric and string expressions in VB .NET
♦ Create decision and repetition (looping) structures
♦ Create and reference object classes
♦ Learn about the VB .NET collection class

---

In Chapter 6, you learned how to create Web application projects that enabled you to organize the components of a Web application. You learned how to create Web forms in Web application projects, and how to modify a Web form's code behind file to change the Web form's content dynamically. In Chapter 6, you also wrote simple VB .NET commands in Web form code behind files. To create database-driven Web sites, you must learn how to write more complex VB .NET programs in code behind files. This chapter presents the fundamentals of the VB .NET programming language.

# INTRODUCTION TO VB .NET

VB .NET is a full-featured object oriented programming language that you use to create executable programs. In this book, you will use VB .NET in Web form code behind files to perform server-side processing tasks that specify the content of dynamic Web pages. VB .NET is a strongly typed programming language, so you must always declare variables and specify their data types before you can assign values to variables. VB .NET has a rich set of built-in functions and procedures, and you can also write commands to create user-defined procedures. In addition, you can write commands to create new object classes in VB .NET. As with JavaScript commands, you use dot notation to reference program objects, properties, and methods. In contrast to JavaScript commands, VB .NET commands are not case-sensitive.

Recall that in JavaScript, a semicolon (;) marks the end of each program line. VB .NET program commands end when you press the Enter key to move to a new line in the Code editor. If you want to write a VB .NET command that continues to the next program line, you must use the **line continuation character**, which consists of a blank space followed by a single underline character ( _ ). You would use the following syntax to write a command that spans two lines in the  Code editor window:

```
lblMessage.Text = "Student Name: " & _
txtStudentName.Text
```

Recall that you use comment statements to document a program internally. The program interpreter or compiler does not verify the syntax of comment statements, and does not try to translate comment statements into machine language. To create a comment statement in a VB .NET program, you place a single quotation mark (') as the first character of the line. The following example shows a comment statement that spans two program lines:

```
'This is a block of comment
'statements in a VB .NET program
```

Sometimes in this chapter, you will be instructed to **comment out** one or more commands, which means that you will start the command with a single quotation mark ('). This causes the VB .NET compiler to skip the command when it compiles the program.

In this chapter, you will create a single Web application project named VBConcepts. Throughout the chapter, you will add new Web forms to this project and use these forms to write programs that illustrate different VB .NET programming concepts.

Recall that when you create a new Web application project, you must configure your Web server so it contains an application that corresponds to each folder in the path to the project folder. You will store the VBConcepts Web application project in the Chapter7\Tutorials folder on your Solution Disk. Therefore, you must create Web server applications that correspond to the Chapter7 folder and the Tutorials subfolder on your Solution Disk.

To start the IIS console and create the Web server applications:

1. Start the IIS console and open the node for the Default Web Site.

2. Create a new Web server application with the alias Chapter7 that you associate with the Chapter7 folder on your Solution Disk, and create a second Web server application within the Chapter 7 application with the alias Tutorials that you associate with the Tutorials folder in the Chapter7 folder on your Solution Disk. Your Web server configuration should look like Figure 7-1. On the Access Permissions page, make sure that the *Read* and *Run scripts (such as ASP)* check boxes are checked, and check the **Browse** check box.

 Don't worry if your Web server contains different physical directories than the ones shown in Figure 7-1.

**7**

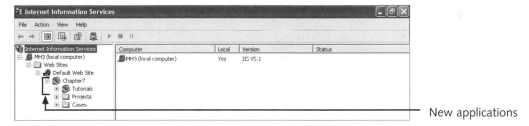
New applications

**Figure 7-1**    Web server configuration

Now you will start Visual Studio .NET and create a new Web application project named VBConcepts. Recall that when you create a new Web application project, you first need to configure the Visual Studio .NET IDE so it saves the project files in the application root, which is the Chapter7\Tutorials folder on your Solution Disk. Then you will create a new Web application project that has the URL *http://localhost/Chapter7/Tutorials/VBConcepts*.

To create the Web application project:

1. Start Visual Studio .NET, click **Tools** on the menu bar, click **Options**, make sure that the *Environment* folder is selected in the left pane, select **Projects and Solutions**, and change the *Visual Studio projects location* field to **a:\Chapter7\Tutorials**. (If your Solution Disk is on a different drive letter or has a different folder path, type that drive letter or folder path instead.) Click **OK**.

2. Click **File** on the menu bar, point to **New**, and then click **Project**. The New Project dialog box opens.

3. Make sure that the *Visual Basic Projects* folder is selected in the *Project Types* list, make sure that the *ASP.NET Web Application* template is selected in the

Templates pane, change the *Location* field value to **http://localhost/ Chapter7/Tutorials/VBConcepts**, and then click **OK**. After a few moments, the Visual Studio .NET IDE displays the project components.

4. If necessary, open the Browser Window, Solution Explorer, Properties Window, and Toolbox. Enable the Toolbox's Auto Hide feature so only the Toolbox tab appears. If any other windows are open in the IDE, close them.

5. Select the **Start Page** tab and then close the Start Page.

To learn about VB .NET, you will use the Clearwater Traders Order Summary Web form shown in Figure 7-2, which displays information about a customer order.

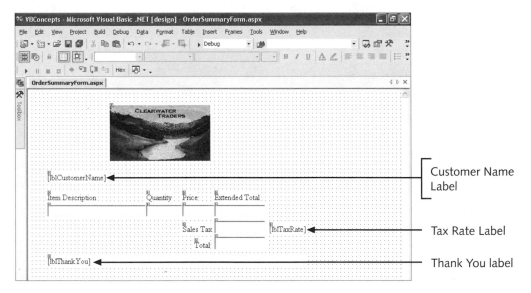

**Figure 7-2**   Clearwater Traders Order Summary Web form

 In this chapter, screenshots that focus on the contents of the Browser Window will not display the Solution Explorer or Properties Window, even though these windows are open and appear on your screen display.

This Web form contains several TextBox rich server controls. The Item Description TextBox describes the order item, the Quantity TextBox shows the order quantity, and the Price TextBox displays the item's unit price. The Extended Total TextBox displays the result of multiplying the order quantity times the unit price. The Sales Tax TextBox displays the sales tax amount, and the Total TextBox displays the sum of the Extended Total and Sales Tax. Label rich server controls describe the contents of each TextBox. The Web form also contains a Customer Label control that displays the customer's name, and a Tax Rate Label control on the right edge of the Sales Tax TextBox that displays the customer's state of residence and the associated tax rate. For example, if the customer lives in Wisconsin, this Label control will display the text "6% WI Sales Tax." The form also has a Thank You Label on its lower-left edge that displays a message thanking the customer for his or her order.

The files that define this Web form are in the Chapter7 folder on your Data Disk. Throughout the chapter, you will create copies of this form and then use these copies to practice using new VB .NET programming concepts. Now you will copy these files to the project folder, then add the files to your project.

To copy the form files and add the files to your project:

1. Switch to Windows Explorer and copy the following files from the Chapter7 folder on your Data Disk to the Chapter7\Tutorials\VBConcepts folder on your Solution Disk: **clearlogo.jpg**, **OrderSummaryForm.aspx**, **OrderSummaryForm.aspx.vb**.

2. Switch back to Visual Studio .NET, right-click the **VBConcepts** node in the Solution Explorer, point to **Add**, and then click **Add Existing Item**. The Add Existing Item – VBConcepts dialog box opens.

3. Open the **Look in** list, and navigate to the Chapter7\Tutorials\VBConcepts folder on your Solution Disk. Open the **Files of type** list and select **All Files (*.*)**.

4. Select the **OrderSummaryForm.aspx** file, press and hold the **Ctrl** key, and then select the **OrderSummaryForm.aspx.vb** file. Two files appear selected.

5. Click **Open**. The OrderSummaryForm.aspx file appears in the Solution Explorer.

 The code behind file with the .aspx.vb extension will appear in the Solution Explorer if you click the Show All Files button on the Solution Explorer toolbar, and then open the node for the form file.

6. Right-click the **WebForm1.aspx** node, click **Delete** to delete the default project form, then click **OK** to confirm the deletion.

Now you will make a copy of the OrderSummaryForm.aspx Web form, and name the copied form VariablesForm.aspx. (You will use the original form again later in the chapter.)

To create a copy of the Web form:

1. In Visual Studio .NET, select the **OrderSummaryForm.aspx** node in the Solution Explorer, right-click, and then click **Copy**.

2. Select the **VBConcepts project** node, right-click, and then click **Paste**. After a few moments, a new Web form named Copy of OrderSummaryForm.aspx appears in the project tree.

7

After you create a copy of the form, you must change its name. Changing the name of an existing Web form is a two-step process. First you change the form's File Name property to the new .aspx filename. Then you modify the command that defines the form's object class so it contains the new form name. First you will change the name of the copied Web form to VariablesForm.aspx.

To change the form name:

1. In Visual Studio .NET, select the **Copy of OrderSummaryForm.aspx** node in the Solution Explorer. In the Properties Window, change the Web form's *File Name* property value to **VariablesForm.aspx**.

2. Select another property value to save the change. The Web form node changes to VariablesForm.aspx in the Solution Explorer.

 Another way to change a Web form's File Name property is to select the Web form node in the Solution Explorer, click the Web form node again to open the form name for editing, and then change the Web form name.

 When you change a Web form's File Name property in the Properties Window or Solution Explorer, the Visual Studio .NET IDE automatically changes the filename of the Web form's .aspx file and the Web form's code behind file to the new Web form's filename.

3. Right-click the **VariablesForm.aspx** node in the Solution Explorer, and then click **Set As Start Page**.

Recall from Chapter 6 that when Visual Studio .NET creates a new Web form, commands within the form's code behind file create a class with the same name as the Web form. When you create the form copy, the original class declaration still appears in the copy of the form, which causes the project to have two form classes with the same name. This generates an error. When an error occurs in a command in the Code editor, the command text appears underlined in blue. When you place the mouse pointer on the underlined text, a ScreenTip appears that describes the error. Now you will open the copied Web form's code behind file, place the mouse pointer on the command that declares the form's class, and view the error message. Then you will change the class name to VariablesForm to correct the error.

To view the class name error and change the class name:

1. If necessary, select the *VariablesForm.aspx* node in the Solution Explorer, and then click the **View Code** button ⊞ to open the form's code behind file. Note that in the first line of the file, which is the form's class declaration, the text *OrderSummaryForm* is underlined in blue. This indicates that the command contains an error.

2. Place the mouse pointer on the underlined text. The error description states that there is a conflict in the VBConcepts namespace.

3. Change the first command that declares the form's object class so it appears as follows:

```
Public Class VariablesForm
```

4. Click on another command in the code behind file. Note that the blue underline no longer appears, which indicates that you corrected the error.

# VB .NET VARIABLES AND ASSIGNMENT STATEMENTS

Recall that programs use variables to store and reference values such as numbers, text strings, dates, and other types of data. When you declare a variable, the system sets aside space in main memory that contains information about the variable, such as its data type and maximum length, as well as the value that the variable stores. The following sections discuss VB .NET data types, variable names, the scope of variables, and how to declare variables and assign values to variables.

7

## VB .NET Data Types

In VB .NET, every variable has a data type that specifies the kind of data that the variable stores. Table 7-1 summarizes common VB .NET non-numeric data types and shows the amount of storage space the system allocates when you declare this type of variable, the value range for the data type, and the prefix you use for variable names of each data type. The table also shows the data type's **default initial value**, which is the value the system initially assigns to new variables of the specified data type.

**Table 7-1**    Common VB .NET non-numeric data types

| Data Type | Description | Memory Used | Value Range | Variable Name Prefix | Default Initial Value |
|-----------|-------------|-------------|-------------|----------------------|-----------------------|
| Boolean | Boolean (true or false) values | 2 bytes | True or False | bln | False |
| Date | Date and time values | 8 bytes | 0:00:00 on January 1, 0001 through 11:59:59 PM on December 31, 9999 | dtm | 12:00 AM if time is omitted; January 1, 0001 AD if date is omitted |
| Object | Pointer to an object in an application, such as a graphic image | 4 bytes | Any type can be stored in a variable of type Object | obj | No value |
| String (variable-length) | Text string | Depends on implementation platform | 0 to approximately 2 billion Unicode characters | str | Empty string ("") |

The four basic non–numeric data types are Boolean (True or False), Date, Object (for referencing objects such as images or sounds), and String. These data types are similar to data types you have worked with in other programming languages. Note that the Object data type can store any type of data, including numeric data.

Table 7-2 summarizes commonly used VB .NET numeric data types.

**Table 7-2**    Common VB .NET numeric data types

| Data Type | Description | Memory Used (Bytes) | Value Range | Variable Name Prefix |
|---|---|---|---|---|
| Byte | Unsigned integer number | 1 | 0 through 255 | byt |
| Decimal | Signed floating-point number | 16 | 0 through +/- 79,228,162,514,264,337,593,543,950,335 with no decimal point; 0 through +/−7.9228162514264337593543950335 with 28 places to the right of the decimal; smallest non-zero number is +/−0.0000000000000000000000000001 (+/−1E-28) | dec |
| Double (double-precision floating-point) | Signed floating-point number | 8 | −1.79769313486231570E+308 through −4.94065645841246544E−324 for negative values; 4.94065645841246544E−324 through 1.79769313486231570E+308 for positive values | dbl |
| Integer | Signed integer number | 4 | −2,147,483,648 through 2,147,483,647 | int |
| Long (long integer) | Signed integer number | 8 | −9,223,372,036,854,775,808 through 9,223,372,036,854,775,807 | lng |
| Short | Signed integer number | 2 | −32,768 through 32,767 | sho |
| Single | Signed floating-point number | 4 | −3.4028235E+38 through −1.401298E−45 for negative values; 1.401298E−45 through 3.4028235E+38 for positive values | sng |

The VB .NET numeric data types differ in the maximum number value they can store, whether they can store negative as well as positive values, and whether they can represent number values with decimal points. The Byte, Integer, Long, and Short data types store integer numbers without decimal values, and the Decimal, Double, and Single data types store numbers with decimal values. The Byte data type stores only positive number values. The default initial value for all numeric data types is 0.

When you declare a numeric variable, you should select the numeric data type that has an adequate value range and the ability to store decimal values and positive or negative values as necessary, but which occupies the least amount of memory space. For example, a variable that will store values for student ages does not need to store negative numbers, and the maximum age value would probably not be greater than 100. Therefore, the Byte data type would be adequate. You could use another data type, such as Decimal, but Decimal variables use more memory space to store each value (16 bytes instead of 1 byte), and student age values do not require the range of values, fractions, or negative values that Decimal variables support. If you are not certain of the range of values that a variable will store, you should select a data type that has an adequate range and features to store any values that your program could potentially ever assign to the variable.

## VB .NET Variable Names

When you declare a variable in a VB .NET program, you assign a name to the variable. VB .NET variable names can be a maximum of 255 characters long and can contain letters, numbers, or underscores (_). Variable names cannot begin with a number. It is a good practice to limit variables to no more than 25 or 30 characters because very long names become difficult to manage within program commands.

Usually VB .NET variable names begin with the three-letter prefixes shown in Tables 7-1 and 7-2, which identify the variable's data type. VB .NET variable names normally appear in mixed-case letters, with the first letter of each word beginning with an uppercase letter. For example, you might declare a variable that stores customer last names as strCustomerName or a variable that stores an item order quantity as bytQuantity.

Many programmers prefer to create a numeric variable named i for a loop counter. If several loops in the same code block require loop counters, programmers often name the additional loop counter variables j, k, and so forth.

## Assigning Values to Variables

You use an assignment statement to assign a value to a variable. In VB .NET, the basic syntax for an assignment statement is as follows:

```
variable_name assignment_operator expression
```

In this syntax, *variable_name* is the name of the variable to which you want to assign a value. The *assignment_operator* specifies the type of assignment. In this book, you will mainly use the simple = assignment operator to assign an expression to a variable.

VB .NET also supports complex assignment operators that allow you to perform arithmetic operations within assignment statements. These arithmetic/assignment operators are similar to the JavaScript arithmetic/assignment operators you used in Chapters 3 and 4. For example, the += operator adds a value to a variable and assigns the result to the variable.

7

The *expression* specifies the value that you assign to the variable. A **simple expression** is a literal value such as the number 2 or the text string "Paula Harris." A **complex expression** consists of multiple literal values, variables, built-in or user-defined functions, or object properties that you connect using arithmetic or concatenation operators. The following sections describe simple and complex expressions in VB .NET.

## Simple Expressions

You can create simple expressions using the VB .NET Boolean, numeric, string, and date data types. Table 7-3 shows how to create assignment statements using simple expressions with these data types.

**Table 7-3**　VB .NET assignment statements using literal values

| Data Type | Enclosing Character | Example Assignment Statements |
|---|---|---|
| Boolean | none | blnPmtStatus = True<br>blnEnrollmentStatus = False |
| Numeric data types (shown in Table 7-2) | none | intCounter = 5<br>bytQuantity += 3 |
| String | " | strCustomerName =<br>"Paula Harris" |
| Date | # | dtmOrderDate = # 6/14/2006 #<br>dtmStartTime = # 12:30 PM # |

In VB .NET, you express Boolean, numeric, and string literals using syntax that is similar to what you use in other programming languages. You express a Boolean literal using the mixed-case letters True or False. You express a numeric literal as a number with or without a decimal point or a sign, such as 42 or −3.14159. You express a string literal by enclosing the characters in double quotation marks, such as the value `"Paula Harris"`.

You use the following general syntax to express a date literal:

```
VariableName = # [date_value] [time_value] #
```

Notice that you must enclose a date literal within opening and closing pound signs (#). Recall that a date value has both a date and time component. If you omit the time component, the default time value is 12:00 AM. If you omit the date component, the default date value is January 1, 0001 AD. You can place one or more blank spaces between the opening #, the *date_value*, the *time_value*, and the closing #. The general format for specifying the *date_value* is as follows:

```
month_value date_separator ↵
day_value date_separator year_value
```

In this value, the *month_value*, *day_value*, and *year_value* are integers that represent the month number (1–12), day number (1–31), and year value as a four-digit year. The month and day number can optionally have leading zeroes. The *date_separator* can be a front slash (/), bar (|), or hyphen (–). Examples of legal date values include:

```
#  1/1/2001  #
#  07-14-1972  #
#  4|09|1955  #
```

The general format for the *time_value* is as follows:

```
hour_value [:minute_value] [:second_value] [AM|PM]
```

When you create a *time_value* expression in a date literal, you must include the *hour_value*, which is an integer from 1 to 24. The *minute_value* and *second_value* components are optional, and you express them as integers from 00 to 59 inclusive. You separate the *hour_value*, *minute_value*, and *second_value* components with colons (:). You can optionally use the characters AM or PM to express the meridian indicator. The following examples show legal time expressions:

```
#  1 PM  #
#  12:01 AM  #
#  18:24:32  #
```

To combine a date and time in a single expression, you separate the *date_value* and *time_value* with a blank space. The following example shows a combined date/time expression:

```
#  01/01/2001 12:00:00 AM  #
```

## Complex Expressions

You create a complex expression by joining literals, variables, function return values, or other values using arithmetic or concatenation operators. Table 7-4 summarizes the VB .NET arithmetic and concatenation operators, listed in order of evaluation precedence.

**Table 7-4**   VB .NET arithmetic and concatenation operators

| Operator | Symbol | Example Expression | Result |
|---|---|---|---|
| Exponentiation | ^ | 3^2 | 9 |
| Negation | – | –3 | –3 |
| Multiplication and division | *, / | 4*9/3 | 12.0 |
| Integer division | \ | 36\5 | 7 |
| Modulus | Mod | 36 Mod 5 | 1 |
| Addition and subtraction | +, – | 4+2–3 | 3 |
| String concatenation | & | "Paula" & " " & "Harris" | "Paula Harris" |

Most of the arithmetic operators in VB .NET are the same as those you used to write JavaScript client-side scripts. Two additional operators are the **integer division operator** (\), which divides two numbers, returns the integer portion of the result, and discards the remainder, and the **modulus operator (Mod)**, which divides two numbers and returns only the remainder. The following assignment statement shows how to use the arithmetic operator to increment the current value of a variable named bytQuantity by 1:

```
bytQuantity = bytQuantity + 1
```

An equivalent way to increment the bytQuantity variable by one is to use the increment assignment operator (+=), as follows: bytQuantity += 1.

VB .NET uses the ampersand operator (&) for string concatenation operations. You would use the following assignment statement to concatenate a string, an empty string literal (""), and another string, and assign the resulting value to a variable named strCustomerName:

```
strCustomerName = "Paula" & " " & "Harris"
```

VB .NET also supports using the plus sign (+) operator for concatenation operations, but this can become confusing because + is also used for addition operations. You should avoid using + for string concatenation operations.

Note that in the order of precedence, arithmetic operations evaluate before string concatenation operations. Later in the chapter, you will learn how to create complex expressions using the arithmetic and concatenation operators.

## VB .NET Variable Persistence and Scope

Recall that when you declare a variable, the system allocates space in the computer's memory for managing the variable and storing its value. When a program no longer needs the variable, the system reclaims the memory space and the variable is no longer available to program commands. In VB .NET programs in a Web form's code behind file, you can declare variables within the Declarations block or within different procedures. (Recall from Chapter 6 that the Declarations block contains the commands that define the Web form's class and its objects, and that procedures are self-contained code blocks such as functions or subroutines.) A variable's **persistence** specifies how long a variable is available to commands that need to reference the variable and modify its value. A variable's **scope** specifies the location of the commands that can reference and modify a variable. The location where you declare a variable and the command you use when you declare the variable determine the variable's persistence and scope.

In VB .NET, you control variable persistence and scope by defining variables as local or class variables. (VB .NET also supports global variables, but you will not use them in this book.) The following sections describe local and class variables and illustrate how to declare each variable type.

## Local Variables

A **local variable** is a variable that you declare within a procedure using the `Dim` declaration command. (`Dim` is short for *dimension*, and refers to allocating (dimensioning) a quantity of memory to maintain the variable.) The system creates the variable when the procedure executes, and destroys the variable when the procedure exits. The only program commands that can access and reference the local variable are the commands within the procedure that declares the local variable. You use local variables for storing values that you use in temporary calculations or operations that do not need to be visible outside of the scope of the current procedure. For example, a loop counter is usually a local variable.

You use the following general syntax to declare a local variable:

```
Dim variable_name As data_type
```

The *variable_name* specifies the name you assign to the variable, and the *data_type* specifies the variable's data type. You would use the following command to declare a local variable with the Byte data type named bytItemQuantity:

```
Dim bytItemQuantity As Byte
```

Sometimes it is useful to declare a variable and assign its initial value in a single command. To do this, you use the following syntax:

```
Dim variable_name As data_type = initial_value
```

For example, you would use the following command to initialize the local variable named bytItemQuantity as the value 3:

```
Dim bytItemQuantity As Byte = 3
```

Now you will add commands to the VariableForm.aspx form's Page_Load procedure to declare a Byte variable named bytItemQuantity and assign the value 3 to the variable. Then you will assign the variable value to the Quantity TextBox control's Text property so the variable's value appears when you run the form.

To declare and assign the local variable and run the form:

1. In the VariableForm.aspx Web form's code behind file, modify the Page_Load procedure so its commands appear as shown in Figure 7-3.

```
Private Sub Page_Load(ByVal sender As System.Object, ↵
ByVal e As System.EventArgs) Handles MyBase.Load
   Dim bytItemQuantity As Byte
   bytItemQuantity = 3
   txtQuantity.Text = bytItemQuantity
End Sub
```

**Figure 7-3**   Code to declare and assign a local variable

2. Save the Web form and then click the **Start** button ▶ on the Visual Studio .NET toolbar to run the project. The Web form appears in Internet Explorer and displays the local variable value 3 in the Quantity TextBox control.

 When you run a project in the Visual Studio .NET IDE, the system automatically saves the project files.

3. Close Internet Explorer. In Visual Studio .NET, close the Output window, which displays messages that describe the form's compilation and execution status. (From this point forward, always close the Output Window after you run a form.)

## Class Variables

A **class variable**, which is also called a **module-level variable**, is a variable that you declare within a code behind file's Declarations block using the `Private` declaration command. The `Private` keyword indicates that the variable is only available within the current module. Recall that when a Web form first opens, the first command in the code behind file creates the Web form's class. Further commands in the Declarations block create the class's objects, including class variables. The system destroys class variables when the form exits. A class variable is visible to all procedures within the code behind file, but is not visible to procedures within other classes in the Web application project.

You use class variables to store values that different procedures within a Web form need to share. For example, you might create a form that allows users to log on to a system by entering a user name and a password, but allows only three attempts before terminating the application. To implement this, you would create a class variable that stores the number of times the user has tried to log on. This variable would be visible to all of the file's procedures, including the procedure that validates the user name and password information.

You use the following general syntax to declare a class variable:

```
Private variable_name As data_type
```

In this syntax, `Private` signifies that the variable is accessible only to commands in procedures within the current form's code behind file. You would use the following command to declare a class variable named strItemDescription that has the String data type:

```
Private strItemDescription As String
```

Now you will add a single command to the VariablesForm.aspx Web form's code behind file to declare a class variable named strItemDescription and assign to it the value "Women's Hiking Shorts." Then you will assign the variable value to the Item Description TextBox control's Text property so the value appears on the form when you run the project.

To add the class variable to the Web form and run the form:

1. In the VariablesForm.aspx Web form's code behind file, add the command shown in Figure 7-4 to declare the class variable in the Declarations block.

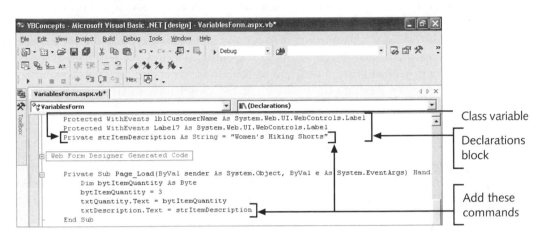

**Figure 7-4**  Declaring and assigning a class variable

2. Add the command shown in Figure 7-4 to the Page_Load procedure to display the class variable value in the TextBox control.

3. Click the **Start** button ▶ on the Visual Studio .NET toolbar to run the form. The Web form appears in Internet Explorer, and the Item Description TextBox control now displays the value of the class variable.

4. Close Internet Explorer.

How do you decide when to use a local variable and when to use a class variable? Use a local variable whenever possible because it has the narrowest scope and least persistence, and therefore consumes the fewest system resources. **Narrowest scope** means that a variable is visible to the fewest number of procedures or commands. **Least persistence** means the variable lasts in memory for the shortest amount of time. You could successfully create a class variable named bytCounter to serve as a loop counter in a procedure, but you would be consuming system resources unnecessarily, because the loop counter needs to persist only while the procedure within the loop executes.

# USING THE VB .NET DEBUGGER

As you create VB .NET programs in Web form code behind files, you can use the VB .NET Debugger to help find and correct errors. The VB .NET Debugger is similar to the Script Debugger that you used in Chapter 4 to debug JavaScript client-side scripts. The VB .NET Debugger allows you to step through programs one command at a time to view how execution proceeds and examine variable values and other object values during execution. Like the Script Debugger, the VB .NET Debugger allows you to set breakpoints to pause execution on specific program lines.

Recall that when a program executes in the Script Debugger, the execution arrow appears in the gray area on the left edge of the Code editor window and points to the statement that will execute next. The command that will execute next also appears shaded in yellow. Also recall that to set a breakpoint, you click the mouse pointer in the gray area on the left edge of the Code editor window. As with most debugging environments, you can create breakpoints only on executable program commands. You cannot create breakpoints on non-executable commands such as commands that declare variables or comment lines.

To control program execution in the VB .NET Debugger, you use buttons on the Debug toolbar that are similar to the ones you used in the Script Debugger, although some of the buttons have slightly different names. You use the Start button ▶ to start execution, the Continue button ▶ to resume execution after a break, and the Stop Debugging button ■ to halt program execution and stop debugging. Now you will create a breakpoint on the command that declares the Page_Load procedure.

To create a breakpoint and run the form in the Debugger:

1. If the Debug toolbar is not currently visible in the Visual Studio .NET IDE, click **View** on the menu bar, point to **Toolbars**, and then click **Debug**. The Debug toolbar appears as shown in Figure 7-5.

**Figure 7-5**    Setting a breakpoint in the Code editor

2. To create a breakpoint, move the mouse pointer onto the gray area to the left of the Page_Load procedure declaration, and then click the mouse pointer. The Breakpoint icon ● marks the breakpoint as shown in Figure 7-5.

3. Click the **Start** button ▶ on the Debug toolbar. After a few moments, the execution arrow appears on the command with the breakpoint.

As with the Script Debugger, the VB .NET Debugger provides multiple ways to view variable values during program execution. If you place the mouse pointer on the variable in the Code editor, the variable's value appears in a ScreenTip. You can also create a watch to monitor the variable value during execution. Now you will use both of these approaches to view variable values during program execution.

To view variable values during program execution:

1. With the execution arrow on the Page_Load procedure declaration, place the mouse pointer on the second command in the Page_Load procedure, which is the command that assigns the value to the bytItemQuantity variable. A ScreenTip appears with the text "bytItemQuantity = 0," which indicates that the variable currently stores its default value, which is 0.

2. To set a watch on the local variable, right-click any instance of **bytItemQuantity** in the Code editor, and then click **Add Watch**. The Watch 1 window opens, and displays the variable name and its associated value, which is currently 0.

3. Click the **Step Into** button ⊊. The execution arrow moves to the second command in the procedure, which is the command that assigns the value to the local variable. Note that the execution arrow skips the command that declares the local variable because this is not an executable command.

4. Click the **Step Into** button ⊊ again. Note that the value of the local variable changes to 3 in the Watch 1 window, and the value appears in red. The red highlighting indicates that the value just changed.

Sometimes while you are debugging, you may want to examine some commands and skip other commands that you know are working correctly. To do this, you can set a breakpoint on the next command on which you want execution to pause. Then when you click the Continue button ▶, execution continues and then pauses on the next breakpoint. Now you will set a breakpoint on the last command in the Page_Load subroutine, and then click the Continue button ▶ to resume execution to this breakpoint.

To set another breakpoint and then resume execution:

1. Set a breakpoint on the End Sub command in the Page_Load procedure.

2. Click the **Continue** button ▶. Execution resumes and then pauses on the new breakpoint.

3. Click the **Continue** button ▶ again. The Web form appears in Internet Explorer.

4. Close Internet Explorer.

When you are finished debugging, there are two ways to close the Debugger environment. You can close the Internet Explorer window, which automatically stops the Debugger, or you can click the Stop Debugging button ■ on the Debug toolbar.

After you create breakpoints in a form, the breakpoints still exist even after you close the form in the Visual Studio .NET IDE. And when you create a watch on a form variable, the watch still exists even after you close the form. When you are finished debugging a form, it is a good idea to remove all breakpoints and watches before you close the form. To remove an individual breakpoint, you click the Breakpoint icon ● in the Code editor window. To clear all form breakpoints, you click Debug on the menu bar, and then click Clear All Breakpoints.

You can remove a watch only while you are debugging. To remove a watch, you select the watch in the Watch window while you are debugging, right-click, and then click Delete Watch. Now you will run the form again and delete the watch. Then you will remove the breakpoints and close the form.

To remove the watch, stop debugging, and remove the breakpoints:

1. Click the **Start** button ▶ to start debugging. The execution arrow appears on the breakpoint in the Page_Load procedure declaration, and the Watch 1 window appears.

2. Right-click the **bytItemQuantity** variable in the Watch 1 window, and then click **Delete Watch**.

 If the Watch 1 window is not open, click Debug on the menu bar, point to Windows, point to Watch, and then click Watch 1.

3. Click the **Stop Debugging** button ■ to stop debugging.

4. Click **Debug** on the menu bar, and then click **Clear All Breakpoints** to remove the breakpoints.

5. You are now finished working with the VariablesForm.aspx Web form, so close all open windows within the Browser Window. Only the Solution Explorer, Properties window, and Toolbox tab should be open in the Visual Studio .NET IDE.

## CREATING VB .NET PROCEDURES

Recall from Chapter 6 that in a Web form's code behind file, VB .NET procedures are self-contained code blocks that commands in other programs can call and pass parameters to. You create procedures to make your code more modular and easier to maintain and debug. In VB .NET, procedures can be subroutines or functions. The following subsections describe how to create and use these two types of procedures.

To learn about procedures, you will use a Web form named ProceduresForm.aspx that is a copy of the OrderSummaryForm.aspx Web form in Figure 7-2. Now you will create a copy of the OrderSummaryForm.aspx Web form in your project and change the Web form's name to ProceduresForm.aspx.

To make a copy of the Web form and change its name:

1. In Visual Studio .NET, select the **OrderSummaryForm.aspx** node in the Solution Explorer, right-click, and then click **Copy**.

2. Select the **VBConcepts** node, right-click, and then click **Paste**. After a few moments, a new Web form named Copy of OrderSummaryForm.aspx appears in the project tree.

3. Select the **Copy of OrderSummaryForm.aspx** node in the Solution Explorer, change the Web form's *File Name* property value to **ProceduresForm.aspx**, and then select another property value to save the change. The Web form node changes to ProceduresForm.aspx in the Solution Explorer.

4. Make sure that the *ProceduresForm.aspx* node is selected in the Solution Explorer, and then click the **View Code** button 📝 on the Solution Explorer toolbar to open the form's code behind file. Change the command that declares the form class so it appears as follows:

```
Public Class ProceduresForm
```

5. Right-click the **ProceduresForm.aspx** node in the Solution Explorer and then click **Set As Start Page**.

## Subroutines

Recall that in VB .NET, a subroutine is a procedure that manipulates variable values but does not return a specific value to the calling program. Figure 7-6 shows the general syntax for a subroutine.

```
Sub subroutine_name ([ByVal|ByRef parameter1 As data_type, ↵
                      ByVal|ByRef parameter2 As data_type, ...])
   subroutine_commands
End Sub
```

**Figure 7-6**    General syntax for a VB .NET subroutine

A subroutine begins with a declaration statement that contains the keyword **Sub**, which identifies the code block as a subroutine, followed by the *subroutine_name* and the subroutine parameter list. The *subroutine_name* identifies the subroutine and follows the same naming rules as VB .NET variables. You enclose the subroutine parameter list in parentheses. Each list item represents the declaration for each individual parameter. You can include any number of parameters in the subroutine parameter list, or you can specify that there are no parameters in the parameter list. (The square brackets in the general syntax indicate that the parameter declarations are optional.) If a procedure does not require parameters, you declare the parameter list as an empty list, `( )`.

You declare each parameter using the syntax `ByVal|ByRef parameter_name As data_type`. (The bar (|) in the syntax definition indicates you use either `ByVal` or `ByRef`. You will learn how to use these keywords a little later in the chapter.) Each *parameter_name* value follows the naming rules for VB .NET variables, and *data_type* can be any legal VB. NET data type. You separate each parameter declaration with a comma (,). The subroutine body follows the subroutine declaration, and can contain any legal VB .NET commands. The `End Sub` command marks the end of the subroutine.

To call a subroutine, you use the following command syntax:

```
subroutine_name(parameter1_value, parameter2_value, ...)
```

In this syntax, *subroutine_name* is the name of the subroutine, followed by the list of parameter values that you wish to pass to the subroutine. You must include a parameter value for each parameter that appears in the subroutine declaration. The parameter values must be in the same order as the parameters appear in the subroutine declaration, and the values must be of the correct data types. (You will learn more about passing parameters later in this chapter.) If the subroutine does not have any parameters, you must include an empty list, `( )`, in the subroutine call.

Now you will create a subroutine in the ProceduresForm.aspx Web form. You will name the subroutine SetCustomerName and specify that it has an empty parameter list. The subroutine body will contain a command to set the Text property of the form's Customer Name Label control to the text string "Paula Harris." You will place the command to call the subroutine in the Web form's Page_Load procedure. Then you will run the project.

To create and run the subroutine:

1. In Visual Studio .NET, create and call the subroutine by adding the commands shown in Figure 7-7 to the ProceduresForm.aspx.vb code behind file.

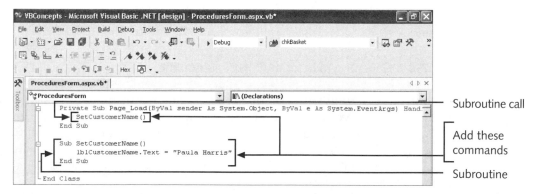

**Figure 7-7**    Creating and calling a subroutine

2. Click the **Start** button ▶ on the Debug toolbar to run the project. The Web form appears in Internet Explorer, and the text "Paula Harris" appears in the Customer Name Label control.

3. Close Internet Explorer.

# Functions

Recall that in VB .NET, a function is a procedure that manipulates variable values and returns a specific value to the calling program. Figure 7-8 shows the general syntax for creating a function.

```
Function function_name ([ByVal|ByRef parameter1 As data_type, ↵
                         ByVal|ByRef parameter2 As data_type, ... ]) ↵
As data_type
   function_commands
   function_name = return_value
End Function
```

**Figure 7-8**   General syntax for a VB .NET function

A function begins with a declaration statement that contains the keyword **Function**, which identifies the code block as a function, followed by the *function_name* and parameter list declaration. After the parameter list declaration, the function declaration contains the command **As *data_type***, which specifies the data type of the value that the function returns. For example, you would use the following command to declare a function named myFunction that has an empty parameter list and returns a String value:

```
Function myFunction() As String
```

The function body contains the function's program commands. The final command in the function body is ***function_name = return_value***, which specifies the value the function returns to the calling program. Sometimes the function body contains only a single command that assigns a value to the *return_value*. The *return_value* can be any legal VB .NET expression, such as a string or numeric literal, a variable value, or a combination of variable values in an arithmetic calculation or string concatenation expression. The *return_value* must have the same data type that you specify in the **As *data_type*** clause in the function declaration. The **End Function** command marks the end of the function.

To call a function, you use the following command syntax:

```
object = function_name(parameter1_value, ↵
parameter2_value, ...)
```

In this syntax, *object* is the name of the program object to which you assign the function's return value. The *object* can be a variable or a control property, such as the Text property of a Label or TextBox control. The *function_name* is the name of the function you wish to call, followed by its parameter list.

Now you will create a function in the ProceduresForm.aspx Web form. You will name the function DescriptionValue, and specify that it has an empty parameter list. The function will return a value that has the String data type. The function body will set the function's return value to the text string "Women's Hiking Shorts." You will place the command to call the function in the Web form's Page_Load procedure, and specify that the function returns its value to the Item Description TextBox control's Text property.

To create and test the function:

    1. In Visual Studio .NET, create and call the function by adding the commands shown in Figure 7-9 to the ProceduresForm.aspx.vb code behind file.

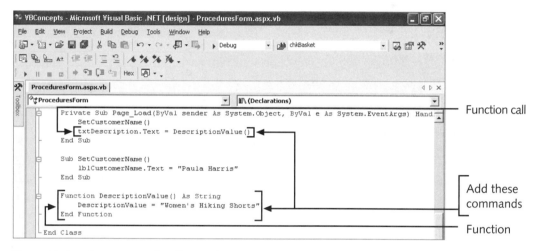

**Figure 7-9**　Creating and calling a function

    2. Click the **Start** button ▶ to run the project. The Web form appears in Internet Explorer, and the text "Women's Hiking Shorts" appears in the Item Description TextBox control.

    3. Close Internet Explorer.

## Scope of Procedures

As with variables, VB .NET procedures have scopes that limit the location of commands that can call the procedures. A procedure's scope can be **public**, which specifies that commands in other code modules can call the procedure and that commands in custom classes can call the procedure. (You will learn to create custom classes later in this chapter.) Or a procedure's scope can be **private**, which specifies that only commands within the code behind file in which you declare the procedure can call the procedure.

To create a public or private procedure, you place the keyword `Public` or `Private` before the `Sub` or `Function` keyword in the procedure declaration. For example, you would use the following commands to declare a public subroutine and a private function:

```
Public Sub mySubroutine
Private Function myFunction
```

In the subroutine and function you created earlier, you omitted the scope declaration. When you omit the scope declaration, the procedure has the default scope, which is private. For now, all of the procedures you create will be in the same code behind file, so you will omit the scope declaration and always create private procedures.

## Scope of Variables in Procedures

Earlier you learned about VB .NET's local and class variables. Now you will learn how to reference local and class variables within form procedures.

### Referencing Local Variables in Procedures

Recall that a local variable is visible only within the procedure that declares it. Commands within other procedures cannot reference a procedure's local variables. For example, if you declare a local variable in the PageLoad procedure in the ProceduresForm.aspx Web form, you cannot reference this local variable in the SetCustomerName subroutine. To learn about referencing variables in subroutines, you will create a subroutine named ScopeSubroutine. This subroutine will not perform any real function in the ProceduresForm.aspx Web form, but you will use it to learn how VB .NET handles the scope of variables. First, in the Page_Load procedure, you will declare a local variable named bytQuantity and assign its value as the number 3. Then you will create the ScopeSubroutine, and add a command that attempts to set the value of the Quantity TextBox control's Text property to the bytQuantity variable. Because the variable is not visible outside of its scope, which is the Page_Load procedure, the command will fail.

To create a local variable and attempt to reference it outside of its scope:

1. After the last command in the Page_Load procedure, which is the command that calls the DescriptionValue function, add the following commands to declare the bytQuantity local variable, assign its value, and call the ScopeSubroutine. (You will create the ScopeSubroutine in the next step.)

```
Dim bytQuantity As Byte = 3
ScopeSubroutine()
```

2. In the ProceduresForm.aspx.vb code behind file, place the insertion point after the **End Sub** command in the Page_Load procedure, press **Enter** two times, then add the following commands to create the ScopeSubroutine:

```
Sub ScopeSubroutine()
   txtQuantity.Text = bytQuantity
End Sub
```

3. Note that a blue line appears under the bytQuantity variable in the subroutine. Place the mouse pointer on the underlined text, and note the ScreenTip that appears stating "Name 'bytQuantity' is not declared." This error appears because you are referencing the variable outside of its scope.

4. Click the **Start** button ▶. A Microsoft Development Environment message box appears stating that there were build (compile) errors and asking whether you want to continue. The build error message appears because your command in the subroutine attempted to reference a local variable outside of its scope.

5. Click **No** to close the error message dialog box. The Task List window opens, which lists the error, the line that causes the error, and a description of the error. Close the Task List window.

## Referencing Class Variables in Procedures

Recall that when you declare a class variable in a Web form's Declarations block, the class variable is visible to all procedures in the Web form's code behind file. Now you will declare a class variable and then reference the variable in the form's procedures. Because class variables are visible to all form procedures, the class variable will be visible within the Page_Load procedure and within the ScopeSubroutine. You will assign the variable's value in the Page_Load procedure and then reference the variable's value in the ScopeSubroutine.

To create a class variable and reference it within form procedures:

1. To declare the bytQuantity class variable, add the following command as the last command in the Declarations block:

   ```
   Private bytQuantity As Byte
   ```

2. Modify the third command in the Page_Load procedure so it assigns the value 3 to the class variable, rather than declaring a local variable, using the following command:

   ```
   bytQuantity = 3
   ```

To confirm that the class variable is visible in both the Page_Load procedure and the ScopeSubroutine subroutine, you will create a breakpoint on the third command in the Page_Load procedure and step through the program commands in the Debugger.

To create a breakpoint and run the form in the Debugger:

1. Create a breakpoint on the third command in the Page_Load procedure, which is the command that assigns the value to the class variable, and then click the **Start** button ▶. After a few moments, execution pauses on the breakpoint.

2. Move the mouse pointer onto the text **bytQuantity** in the shaded command. A ScreenTip appears with the text "bytQuantity = 0." This indicates that the class variable has not yet been assigned a value, and 0 is its default value.

3. Click the **Step Into** button ⤓≣. The execution arrow and yellow shading move to the next command, which calls the subroutine.

4. Move the mouse pointer onto the text **bytQuantity** in the previous command to examine the variable's value again. A ScreenTip with the text "bytQuantity = 3" appears, indicating that the previous command assigned the class variable to the value.

5. Click the **Step Into** button ⤓≣ again. The execution arrow moves to the subroutine declaration. Click the **Step Into** button ⤓≣ again. The execution arrow moves to the first command in the subroutine, which assigns the Label's Text property to the class variable's value.

6. Click the **Step Into** button ⤓≣ again. The execution arrow moves to the `End Sub` command in the subroutine.

7. Highlight the text **txtQuantity.Text** in the previous command and then place the mouse pointer on the highlighted text. A ScreenTip appears with the text "txtQuantity.Text = "3,"" which shows the value of the Label control's Text property.

8. Click the **Continue** button ▶ to resume execution. The form appears in Internet Explorer and displays the value "3" in the Quantity TextBox control. Close Internet Explorer to end the debugging session, and then clear the breakpoint.

## Referencing Local and Class Variables with the Same Names in Procedures

You can create two or more Web form variables that have the same name as long as the scope of the variables is different. For example, you can create a variable named bytCounter in two different procedures in the same Web form to serve as loop counters. Because each variable persists only within its procedure, no conflict occurs.

VB .NET also allows you to create a class variable and a local variable with the same name, but this can be confusing. Recall that a class variable persists as long as the form is running, and a local variable persists only while its procedure is running. If you create a class variable and a local variable with the same name, the system creates two separate memory areas for the variables. The system uses the local variable value within the local variable's scope, and the class variable value outside of the local variable's scope. (Recall that the local variable's scope is the procedure in which you create it.)

When you create a variable, you should define the variable so it has the narrowest scope that is sufficient to do the required task. This avoids confusion among variables that have the same names but have different scopes. When a code behind file contains both class and local variables, always give the class and local variables different names.

## Persistence of Variables in Procedures

Recall that a variable's persistence specifies the time between when you declare a variable and when the system destroys the variable. The following subsections explore the persistence of local and class variables.

### Persistence of Local Variables

A local variable persists from the time you declare the variable to the time that the procedure in which you declare the variable ends. To test the persistence of a local variable, you will create a subroutine named PersistenceSubroutine. In the subroutine, you will declare a local variable named sngPrice and initialize its value as 29.99. You will add a command to add the value 1 to this variable, and then add a second command to display the variable value in the form's Price TextBox control. You will also add commands to the form's Page_Load procedure to call the subroutine two separate times. Because the sngPrice variable persists only in the subroutine, the system creates a new variable each time it calls the subroutine, and destroys the variable each time the subroutine exits.

To test the persistence of a local variable:

1. In the ProceduresForm.aspx.vb code behind file, place the insertion point after the **End Sub** command in the Page_Load procedure, press **Enter** two times, then add the following commands to create the PersistenceSubroutine:

```
Sub PersistenceSubroutine()
    Dim sngPrice As Single = 29.99
    sngPrice +=  1
    txtPrice.Text = sngPrice
End Sub
```

Recall that you use the += assignment operator to add a value to a variable and then assign the result back to the variable.

2. Add the following commands to the Page_Load procedure immediately after the command that calls the ScopeSubroutine. (These commands call the new PersistenceSubroutine subroutine two times.)

```
PersistenceSubroutine()
PersistenceSubroutine()
```

3. Create a breakpoint on the fifth command in the Page_Load procedure, which is the first call to the PersistenceSubroutine, and then click the **Start** button ▶ to run the project. The execution arrow appears on the breakpoint.

4. Right-click **sngPrice** in the first command in the PersistenceSubroutine, then click **Add Watch**. Highlight the text **txtPrice.Text** in the third command in the PersistenceSubroutine, right-click, then click **Add Watch**. The watches

currently show that the sngPrice variable is not yet declared, and the TextBox's Text property is an empty string (" "), which is its default initial value.

5. Click the **Step Into** button ⧨. The execution arrow moves to the subroutine declaration. The watch shows that the value of sngPrice is 0.0, which is its default initial value.

6. Click the **Step Into** button ⧨ two times. The execution arrow moves to the command that adds 1 to the variable's current value. The sngPrice variable value appears as 29.99 in the watch.

7. Click the **Step Into** button ⧨ again. The sngPrice variable value appears as 30.99 in the watch.

8. Click the **Step Into** button ⧨ again. The execution arrow moves to the End Sub command, and the TextBox's Text property appears as "30.99" in the watch.

9. Click the **Step Into** button ⧨ again. The execution arrow moves back to the first subroutine call in the Page_Load procedure. The sngPrice variable appears as undeclared in the watch.

Recall that a local variable persists as long as the procedure in which you declare it executes. Because execution is no longer in the subroutine, the system has destroyed the sngPrice variable, and its value appears as undeclared in the watch. However, note that the value of the txtPrice.Text property still appears as "30.99." Control property values are similar to class variables, and persist as long as the form is running. Now you will continue to step through the form commands and view how the system creates the local variable again.

To view how the system creates the local variable again:

1. Click the **Step Into** button ⧨ again. The execution arrow moves to the second subroutine call in the Page_Load procedure.

2. Click the **Step Into** button ⧨ again. The execution arrow moves to the subroutine declaration. Note that the value of the sngPrice variable has been reinitialized to 0.0, indicating that the system has created a new variable. Also note that the TextBox's Text property is still 30.99. Recall that control properties are similar to class variables and persist across different form procedures.

3. Click the **Step Into** button ⧨ two times. Note that the value of the sngPrice variable has been set to 29.99 again.

4. Click the **Continue** button ⧨ to resume execution. The form appears in Internet Explorer, and the value 30.99 appears in the Price TextBox on the Web form.

5. Close Internet Explorer.

7

## Persistence of Class Variables

A class variable persists as long as the form in which you declare it is running. To test the persistence of a class variable, you will declare the sngPrice variable as a class variable instead of as a local variable. Then, you will use the Debugger to step through the commands and view how the class variable value persists each time the Page_Load procedure calls the subroutine.

To declare the variable as a class variable and see how the class variable value persists:

1. Add the following command as the last command in the Web form's Declarations block to declare sngPrice as a class variable:

   **Private sngPrice As Single**

2. Change the first command in the PersistenceSubroutine so it assigns the value to the sngPrice variable rather than declaring it as a local variable:

   **sngPrice = 29.99**

3. Make sure that the breakpoint is still set on the fifth command in the Page_Load procedure and then click the **Start** button ▶ to run the project. The execution arrow appears on the breakpoint. Make sure that a watch is still set on the sngPrice variable and the txtPrice.Text property. The watches show that the current value of the variable is 0.0 and the TextBox control's Text property value is an empty string.

4. Click the **Step Into** button 모. The execution arrow appears on the subroutine declaration.

5. Click the **Step Into** button 모 two times. The execution arrow moves to the command that adds 1 to the variable's value. The watch shows the value of sngPrice as 29.99.

6. Click the **Step Into** button 모 again. The watch shows that the current value of sngPrice is now 30.99.

7. Click the **Step Into** button 모 again. The watch shows that the current value of the TextBox control's Text property is now 30.99.

Now you will continue executing the program, and see how the class variable value persists across multiple calls to the subroutine.

To continue executing the program:

1. Click the **Step Into** button 모 three times. The execution arrow moves to the subroutine declaration for the second time. Note that the value of sngPrice is still 30.99, indicating that the class variable value persists from the last command that assigned its value in the subroutine. Also note that the TextBox's Text property is still 30.99.

2. Click the **Step Into** button 모 two times. The watch shows that the variable value is reset to 29.99.

3. Delete the two watches.

4. Click the **Stop Debugging** button ■ to stop debugging, and then clear the breakpoint.

5. You are finished working with the ProceduresForm.aspx, so close all open windows within the Visual Studio .NET Browser Window.

# Passing Parameters to Procedures

Recall that when you create a procedure, you can specify a parameter list in the procedure declaration. A parameter list enables the command that calls the procedure to pass data values to the procedure. Parameters can be literal values, such as the number 10 or the string "Paula Harris." Parameters can also be variables. When you call the procedure, you pass the parameters to the procedure by listing the parameter values in the same order in which the parameters appear in the procedure declaration. When you call a procedure that has a parameter list, you must include a parameter value for each parameter that appears in the procedure declaration. The parameter values must be in the same order as they appear in the procedure declaration, and each parameter value must have the same data type as its associated parameter in the procedure declaration.

Figure 7-10 shows an example of a subroutine declaration that has a parameter list containing three parameters. The figure also shows a command that calls the subroutine and passes parameter values to the subroutine.

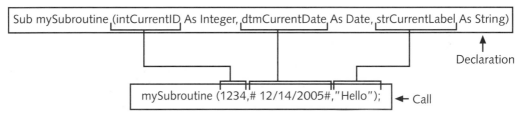

**Figure 7-10**   Parameters in a subroutine declaration and subroutine call

In the parameter list, the first parameter has the Integer data type, the second parameter has the Date data type, and the third parameter has the String data type. Note that in the command that calls the subroutine, the parameter values appear in the same order as the parameter declarations, and the parameter values are of the same data types as the associated parameter in the subroutine declaration.

To gain experience working with parameters, you will make a copy of the OrderSummaryForm.aspx Web form, and rename the copied form as ParametersForm.aspx.

To create the ParametersForm.aspx Web form:

1. In Visual Studio .NET, make a copy of the OrderSummaryForm.aspx Web form, select the **Copy of OrderSummaryForm.aspx** node in the Solution

Explorer and change the Web form's *File Name* property value to **ParametersForm.aspx**.

2. Open the new form's code behind file and change the class declaration so it appears as `Public Class ParametersForm`.

3. Right-click the **ParametersForm.aspx** node in the Solution Explorer and then click **Set As Start Page**.

When you create a procedure that has a non-empty parameter list, you must specify whether the calling program passes each parameter value either by value or by reference in the parameter list declaration. The following subsections describe these two methods.

## Passing Parameters by Value

Passing a parameter **by value** means that when you call the procedure and pass the parameter value, the system creates a memory space for each parameter and copies the parameter value into this memory space. To declare a parameter by value, you use the following general syntax:

```
(ByVal parameter1 As data_type, …)
```

By default, VB .NET passes parameters by value. When you create the declaration of a subroutine or function that has a non-empty parameter list, Visual Studio .NET automatically inserts the `ByVal` keyword in the Code editor if you omit it when you type the parameter list declaration.

You would use the following command to declare a subroutine named CalcExtendedTotal that has a parameter named bytQuantity and a second parameter named sngPrice that you pass by value:

```
Sub CalcExtendedTotal(ByVal bytQuantity As Byte, ↵
ByVal sngPrice As Single)
```

You would use the following command to call the subroutine and pass the values 3 and 29.99 as the parameter values:

```
CalcExtendedTotal(3, 29.99)
```

When this command executes, the system creates two new local variables in the subroutine that have the same names as the parameter names and then copies the passed values to these variables. When the subroutine exits, the system destroys these variables.

Now you will create a subroutine named CalcExtendedTotal that receives two parameters, which represent the item quantity and item price, multiplies these values to calculate the extended total, and then displays the result in the form's Extended Total TextBox control. You will also create a command in the Page_Load procedure that calls the subroutine and passes the values 3 and 29.99 to the subroutine. Then you will step through the commands and view how the system passes the values to the subroutine.

To create and call the subroutine:

1. To create the subroutine, add the commands in Figure 7-11.

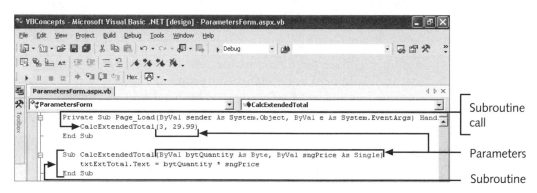

**Figure 7-11**    Creating and calling a subroutine with parameters

2. To call the subroutine, add the command in the Page_Load procedure in Figure 7-11.

3. Create a breakpoint on the command in the Page_Load procedure that calls the subroutine, and then click the **Start** button ▶ to run the project. The execution arrow appears on the breakpoint.

4. Create watches on the **bytQuantity** and **sngPrice** parameters. Currently, the parameter values appear as not yet declared.

5. Click the **Step Into** button ⊊≡. The execution arrow moves to the subroutine declaration. Note that the value for bytQuantity is now 3, and the value for sngPrice is now 29.99, because execution is within the subroutine's scope.

6. Click the **Step Into** button ⊊≡ again. The execution arrow moves to the command that multiplies the two parameter values and assigns the product to the Text property of the form's txtExtTotal TextBox control.

7. Delete the watches you created, and then click the **Continue** button ▶ to resume execution. The Web form appears in Internet Explorer, and displays the value 89.97 in the Extended Total TextBox control.

8. Close Internet Explorer, and then clear the breakpoint.

Recall that when you call a procedure that has a parameter list, you must pass a value for each parameter, and the values must be of the correct data type. If you violate either of these rules, an error will occur. Now you will intentionally create parameter passing errors by not passing enough parameter values and passing values of the wrong data type.

To create parameter passing errors:

1. Modify the command in the Page_Load procedure so it passes only one parameter to the CalcExtendedTotal subroutine, as follows:

```
CalcExtendedTotal(3)
```

2. Click the mouse pointer on another command. A blue line appears under the command. Place the mouse pointer on the command. A ScreenTip appears stating "Argument not specified for parameter 'sngPrice.'" This error appears because you did not pass a value for both subroutine parameters.

3. In the Page_Load procedure, change the command that calls the subroutine so it passes a value with the String data type for the second parameter value as follows. Notice that the second parameter does not use the correct data type.

```
CalcExtendedTotal(3, "29.99")
```

4. Click the mouse pointer on another command. Note that no error appears on the procedure call. This is because VB .NET automatically converts string values that are numbers to numeric values when required.

5. Modify the command in the Page_Load procedure as follows so it passes a string parameter value that is not a number:

```
CalcExtendedTotal(3, "Hello")
```

6. Click the **Start** button ▶ to run the project. An error appears in Internet Explorer with the message "Input string was not in a correct format." This error occurs because VB .NET cannot convert the text string "Hello" to a number. Close Internet Explorer.

7. Change the subroutine call back to the following:

```
CalcExtendedTotal (3,29.99).
```

So far you have passed parameters by value using literal values. You can also pass parameters as variables. Recall that when you pass a parameter by value, the system creates a new memory space and copies into the new memory space the value that you place in the procedure call. If you pass a parameter as a variable, the system copies the variable's value into the parameter's memory space. If you change the parameter's value in the procedure, the value changes in the parameter's memory space, but the value of the original variable remains the same.

When you pass a parameter as a variable, the name of the variable in the parameter list in the calling command does not need to be the same as the name of the parameter in the procedure declaration. For example, suppose you use the following commands to create a subroutine named AddQuantity that receives a parameter value and increments it by one:

```
Sub AddQuantity(bytQuantity As Byte)
    bytQuantity += 1
End Sub
```

You could use the following commands to declare a variable named bytCurrentQuantity, call the AddQuantity subroutine, and pass the variable value as a parameter:

```
Dim bytCurrentQuantity As Byte = 3
AddQuantity(bytCurrentQuantity)
```

Note that the parameter name in the subroutine declaration is bytQuantity, but the variable name in the command that calls the subroutine is bytCurrentQuantity. This code executes successfully because the system associates the variable value with the parameter based on its position in the parameter list rather than based on matching the variable name to the parameter name.

Now you will create a subroutine named AddQuantity that receives a parameter value, increments it by 1, and then displays the result in the form's txtQuantity TextBox control. You will declare a local variable in the Page_Load subroutine named bytCurrentQuantity to which you will assign an initial value of 3. You will then pass the bytCurrentQuantity variable as a parameter to the AddQuantity subroutine.

To pass a variable as a parameter:

1. Add the following commands to the ParametersForm.aspx.vb code behind file's Page_Load procedure immediately after the procedure declaration, so they appear as the first two commands in the procedure:

```
Dim bytCurrentQuantity As Byte = 3
AddQuantity(bytCurrentQuantity)
```

2. To create the AddQuantity subroutine, add the following commands to the ParametersForm.aspx.vb code behind file, after the CalcExtendedTotal subroutine:

```
Sub AddQuantity(ByVal bytQuantity As Byte)
    bytQuantity += 1
    txtQuantity.Text = bytQuantity
End Sub
```

3. Create a breakpoint on the first command in the Page_Load subroutine, which is the command that declares the bytCurrentQuantity variable and assigns the value 3 to the variable, and then click the **Start** button ▶ to run the project. The execution arrow appears on the line with the breakpoint.

Now you will create watches on the bytCurrentQuantity variable and on the bytQuantity parameter in the procedure. Then you will step through the program commands and see how the variable value changes in relation to the parameter value.

To create watches on the variable and parameter values and step through the commands:

1. Create a watch on the **bytCurrentQuantity** variable, and create a second watch on the **bytQuantity** parameter in the AddQuantity subroutine. The bytCurrentQuantity variable value appears as 0, which is its initial value. The bytQuantity parameter value appears as the text "Name 'bytQuantity' is not declared," because the command that declares the parameter has not executed yet.

7

2. Click the **Step Into** button ⬘≡ to execute the next command. The watch shows that the value for bytCurrentQuantity is now 3.

3. Click the **Step Into** button ⬘≡ again. The execution arrow moves to the command that declares the subroutine.

The watch now shows that bytCurrentQuantity is not declared, because execution is outside its scope. The Watch 1 window also shows that the bytQuantity parameter value is 3, which is the value that the calling command passed to the subroutine. Now you will continue to step through the commands and see how the watch values change.

To continue to step through the commands and monitor the watch values:

1. Click the **Step Into** button ⬘≡ again. The execution arrow moves to the command that increments the parameter value by 1. The watch values do not change.

2. Click the **Step Into** button ⬘≡ again. The execution arrow moves to the command that displays the parameter value in the form's Quantity TextBox control. Note that the parameter value now appears as 4 in the Watch 1 window.

3. Click the **Step Into** button ⬘≡ two times so the execution arrow appears on the original subroutine call in the Page_Load procedure. Note that in the Watch 1 window, the bytCurrentQuantity variable value appears as 3 again, which confirms that the subroutine commands did not change the original variable's value. The bytQuantity parameter now appears as undeclared, because the parameter's scope is only within its subroutine.

4. Click the **Continue** button ▶ to resume execution. The Web form appears in Internet Explorer, and the Quantity TextBox control displays the value 4, which is the value that the subroutine command assigned to its Text property.

5. Close Internet Explorer.

## Passing Parameters by Reference

When you pass a parameter **by reference**, you pass the parameter as a variable rather than as a literal value. When you call the procedure and pass the parameter value by reference, you pass the memory location of the variable to the procedure. In the procedure commands, the system references the variable's underlying memory location instead of creating a new memory location. When you pass a parameter by reference, if the called procedure changes the parameter's value, the value in the variable's memory location changes, and the change persists outside of the scope of the procedure. The system does not retain the variable's original value as it did when you passed the parameter by value.

In the previous exercise, you passed a parameter by value to a subroutine that incremented the parameter's value by 1. The change was visible only inside the subroutine because the change was written in the parameter's memory space rather than in the original variable's memory space. If you had passed the parameter by reference, the parameter's memory space and the variable's memory space would be one and the same, and the change would be visible outside of the subroutine.

To declare a parameter by reference, you use the following general syntax:

```
(ByRef parameter1 As data_type, ...)
```

You would use the following code to declare a subroutine named AddQuantity that has a parameter named bytQuantity that you pass by reference:

```
Sub AddQuantity(ByRef bytQuantity As Byte)
```

When you pass a parameter by reference, the command to call the subroutine is the same as it is when you pass a parameter by value; the only difference is in how you declare the parameter in the procedure declaration. Now you will modify the AddQuantity subroutine to declare the bytQuantity parameter so the calling command passes the parameter value by reference. Then you will run the form and see that the incremented parameter value is now visible outside of the subroutine.

To pass a parameter by reference:

1. Modify the AddQuantity subroutine declaration so it appears as follows:

```
Sub AddQuantity(ByRef bytQuantity As Byte)
```

2. Make sure that the breakpoint is still set on the first command in the Page_Load subroutine, and then click the **Start** button ▶ to run the project. The execution arrow appears on the command with the breakpoint.

3. Make sure that the watches are still set on the bytCurrentQuantity variable and the bytQuantity parameter. Note that the variable value is currently 0 and the parameter value is undeclared.

4. Click the **Step Into** button ⬇≣. The variable value appears as 3.

5. Click the **Step Into** button ⬇≣ again. Now the variable value is undeclared, because execution is outside its scope. The parameter value is now 3.

6. Click the **Step Into** button ⬇≣ two times. The subroutine increments the parameter value, which now is 4.

7. Click the **Step Into** button ⬇≣ two times. The execution arrow appears on the original subroutine call in the Page_Load procedure again. Note that the variable value now appears as 4, which confirms that the system preserves the modified variable value because the variable was passed by reference.

8. Delete the watches.

9. Click the **Continue** button ▶ to execute the rest of the procedure's commands without pausing. The value 4 appears in the Quantity TextBox control in Internet Explorer. Close Internet Explorer.

10. Clear the breakpoint. You are finished working with the ParametersForm.aspx Web form, so close all open windows within the Visual Studio .NET Browser Window.

Usually local variables are visible only within the procedure in which you declare them. If you pass a local variable to a procedure by reference, however, you extend the variable's scope to the procedure to which you pass it. This is useful when you want to change a variable value in a procedure. For example, you might want to create a procedure that tracks the number of times that a user tries to log on to a system. You would create a procedure that verifies each log on attempt, and then pass the variable that counts the number of log on attempts as a parameter. However, recall that you should always keep the scope of variables as narrow as possible to avoid inadvertently changing variable values when you do not want to. For this reason, you should use ByRef parameters with care.

## WORKING WITH COMPLEX EXPRESSIONS IN VB .NET

Recall that a simple expression is a literal value such as the number 3, a variable, or a value returned by a function. A complex expression combines multiple simple expressions using arithmetic or concatenation operators. When you create a complex expression that combines simple expressions that have different data types, you must be aware of how VB .NET handles the different data types. To learn about complex expressions, you will create and work with a copy of the Clearwater Traders Order Summary Form named ExpressionsForm.aspx.

To create the ExpressionsForm.aspx Web form:

1. In Visual Studio .NET, make a copy of the OrderSummaryForm.aspx Web form, and change the new form's name to **ExpressionsForm.aspx**.

2. Open the new form's code behind file and change the class declaration so it appears as `Public Class ExpressionsForm`.

3. Right-click the **ExpressionsForm.aspx** node in the Solution Explorer and then click **Set As Start Page**.

The following subsections illustrate complex numeric expressions and complex string expressions and describe the VB .NET data type conversion functions.

### Creating Complex Numeric Expressions

You can create complex numeric expressions in VB .NET using the arithmetic operators summarized in Table 7-4. You can combine multiple operations in a single command, and you can nest operations. For example, the following complex expression divides one number by a second number, and then adds the result to the first number:

```
bytNumber1/bytNumber2 + bytNumber1
```

The following subsections explore complex numeric expressions in more detail. Specifically, they address mixing numeric data types in expressions, converting numeric expressions to currency formats, and handling overflow errors.

## Mixing Numeric Data Types in Expressions

Suppose you create a complex expression that uses arithmetic operators to combine numeric data types that represent whole numbers, such as Short and Integer, with numeric data types that contain decimal fractions, such as Single and Decimal. If you assign the result to a variable with a data type that represents fractional values, the result will retain its fractional value. If you assign the result to a variable with a data type that represents only whole numbers, VB .NET rounds the result to the nearest whole number.

Now you will create a subroutine named CalcComplexTotal that declares variables to represent the Quantity, Price, and Extended Total on the Order Summary form. These variables will have the following names and associated data types:

| Variable Name | Data Type |
|---------------|-----------|
| bytQuantity   | Byte      |
| sngPrice      | Single    |
| bytExtTotal   | Byte      |

The subroutine will contain a complex expression that calculates the Extended Total as the product of the Quantity times the Price, and assigns the result to the bytExtTotal variable. Because this variable has the Byte data type, which does not represent decimal fractions, VB .NET will round the value to the nearest whole number. The subroutine will also contain commands that display the variable values in the associated TextBox controls on the form.

To create a complex numeric expression:

1. To create the CalcComplexTotal subroutine, add the commands shown in Figure 7-12 to the end of the ExpressionsForm.aspx.vb code behind file, just before the **End Class** command.

```
Sub CalcComplexTotal()
   Dim bytQuantity As Byte = 3
   Dim sngPrice As Single = 29.99
   Dim bytExtTotal As Byte
   bytExtTotal = bytQuantity * sngPrice
   'display values in TextBox controls
   txtQuantity.Text = bytQuantity
   txtPrice.Text = sngPrice
   txtExtTotal.Text = bytExtTotal
End Sub
```

**Figure 7-12**　Creating a complex numeric expression using variables with different numeric data types

2. Add the following command to the Page_Load procedure to call the subroutine:

```
CalcComplexTotal()
```

3. Click the **Start** button ▶ to run the project. The values "3" and "29.99" appear in the Quantity and Price TextBox controls, and the value "90" appears in the Extended Total TextBox control.

4. Close Internet Explorer.

The actual product of 3 times 29.99 is 89.97. However, because you assigned the product to a variable with the Byte data type, which represents only whole values, VB .NET rounds the result to the nearest whole number, which is 90. To retain the fractional part of the result, you will modify the commands in the CalcComplexTotal subroutine so the variable that represents the extended total uses the Single data type, which represents decimal fractions. Then you will run the project again and view the results.

To modify the variable's data type to retain the fraction portion of the product:

1. In Visual Studio .NET, change the commands in the CalcComplexTotal subroutine that declare the bytExtTotal variable and assign the product to the variable so the commands appear as follows:

```
Dim sngExtTotal As Single
sngExtTotal = bytQuantity * sngPrice
```

2. In the subroutine, change the final command that assigns the variable to the Extended Total TextBox control so it appears as follows:

```
txtExtTotal.Text = sngExtTotal
```

3. Click the **Start** button ▶ to run the project. The extended total now appears as 89.97, because the variable with the Single data type retains the fractional portion of the product.

4. Close Internet Explorer.

## Formatting Numeric Values as Currency

Often Web applications display currency data values. VB .NET provides a built-in function named **FormatCurrency** that automatically formats numbers as currency values based on your system preferences. For example, United States currency values truncate to two decimal places, display a comma between every three digits, and use the dollar sign ($) currency marker.

 To change your system's currency preference, click *Start* on the taskbar, click *Control panel*, click the *Date, Time, Language and Regional Options* link, click *Change the format of numbers, dates, and times,* and then select the desired format from the top list on the dialog box. If you are using Windows 2000, click *Start*, point to settings, click *Control Panel*, double-click *Regional and Language Options*, then select the desired format from the top list.

The general format of the FormatCurrency function is as follows:

```
FormatCurrency(expression)
```

In this syntax, *expression* represents the expression that you want to format as currency. The expression can be a literal value, a variable, a control property, or a value returned by a function. For example, the following function formats as currency the value represented by a variable named dblNumber3:

```
FormatCurrency(dblNumber3)
```

Now you will modify the ExpressionsForm.aspx Web form so the code formats as currency the numbers that appear in the form's Price and Extended Total TextBox controls.

To format the control values as currency:

1. In Visual Studio .NET, change the last two commands in the CalcComplexTotal subroutine so they appear as follows:

```
txtPrice.Text = FormatCurrency(sngPrice)
txtExtTotal.Text = FormatCurrency(sngExtTotal)
```

2. Click the **Start** button ▶ to run the project. After a few moments, the values appear as "$29.99" and "$89.97" in Internet Explorer, which is the appropriate currency format.

3. Close Internet Explorer.

## Handling Overflow Errors

Recall that VB .NET numeric data types differ according to the maximum values they can store. For example, the Byte data type can store integer numbers to a maximum value of 255, whereas the Short data type can store integer numbers to a maximum value of 32,767. If you attempt to assign a numeric value to a variable but the value is too large for the variable's data type, an **overflow error** occurs.

If you assign a literal value to a variable but the literal value is too large for the variable's data type, Visual Studio .NET will detect the overflow error at design time. To illustrate this, you will assign the value 300 to the bytQuantity variable in the CalcComplexTotal subroutine. Because the maximum value that a Byte variable can store is 255, an overflow error occurs.

To create an overflow error at design time:

1. In Visual Studio .NET, modify the command that declares the bytQuantity variable and assigns its initial value so that the command appears as follows:

```
Dim bytQuantity As Byte = 300
```

2. Click the mouse pointer on another code line. Note that 300, which is the value that is causing the overflow error, appears underlined in blue.

7

3. Move the mouse pointer over the underlined text. The error message "Constant expression not representable in type 'Byte'" appears, advising you that the data value is not legal for the variable's data type.

Overflow errors occur at run time when you assign one variable to another variable but the source variable's value is too large for the target variable to store. Overflow errors also occur when you create a complex expression that calculates and then assigns a value to a variable that is too large for the variable to store. To create a runtime overflow error, you will modify the commands in the CalcComplexTotal subroutine and assign an initial value of 200 to the bytQuantity variable, which is a legal value. Then you will add a command that adds 100 to the variable's value, which causes an overflow error. Then you will run the project and view the overflow error message.

To create a runtime overflow error:

1. Change the first command in the CalcComplexTotal subroutine so it appears as follows:

```
Dim bytQuantity As Byte = 200
```

2. Add the following command so it appears as the second command in the CalcComplexTotal subroutine. Although this command will cause an overflow error, it does not appear underlined in blue because it causes a runtime overflow error.

```
bytQuantity += 100
```

3. Click the **Start** button ▶ to run the project. The error message "Arithmetic operation resulted in an overflow" appears in the Internet Explorer window. Close Internet Explorer.

4. To remove the errors in the form, change the first two commands in the CalcComplexTotal subroutine so they appear as follows:

```
Dim bytQuantity As Byte = 3
'bytQuantity += 100
```

How do you avoid overflow errors? You always need to select data types that will handle the largest possible value that the program will assign to a variable. You also need to include in your Web pages client-side error handlers that evaluate user inputs and advise the user if an input value is out of range.

## Creating Complex String Expressions

The following subsections describe how to concatenate strings, how to use common VB .NET built-in string methods and functions, and why you should avoid using the plus sign (+) to perform string concatenation operations.

## Concatenating Strings

Recall that you use the ampersand (&) concatenation operator to create a single string value by joining two or more string expressions. For example, the following code joins three separate string expressions into a single string value:

```
Dim strFirstName As String = "Paula"
Dim strLastName As String = "Harris"
Dim strFullName As String = strFirstName & " " ↵
& strLastName
```

When this code executes, the last command concatenates a string literal that contains a blank space (" ") with the two string variables to create the blank space between the first and last name. The resulting value of strFullName is "Paula Harris."

When you create a complex string expression using the ampersand (&) concatenation operator, VB .NET expects the simple expressions on either side of the concatenation operator to be of the String data type. If either expression is not of the String data type, VB .NET automatically converts the expression to a string and then performs the concatenation operation.

Now you will create a subroutine named ShowTaxRate that displays the customer's sales tax rate in the Tax Rate Label on the left side of the Sales Tax TextBox control. For example, for a customer who lives in Wisconsin, the label displays the value "6% WI State Tax." The ShowTaxRate subroutine receives a numeric parameter value that specifies the customer's sales tax rate as a decimal value, such as .06, and a string parameter that specifies the customer's state of residence, such as "WI." The subroutine contains a complex expression that converts the decimal value to a percentage by multiplying it by 100, and then concatenates the percentage value with the string literal "%," the string that specifies the customer's state of residence, and the string literal " State Tax Rate." You will also add a command to the Page_Load procedure that calls the ShowTaxRate subroutine and passes the values .06 and "WI" to the subroutine as parameters.

To create and test the ShowTaxRate subroutine:

1. To create the ShowTaxRate subroutine, add the commands shown in Figure 7-13 to the end of the ExpressionsForm.aspx.vb code behind file, just before the **End Class** command.

```
Sub ShowTaxRate(ByVal sngTaxRate As Single, ByVal strCustState As String)
  lblTaxRate.Text = (sngTaxRate * 100) & ↵
  "% " & strCustState &  " State Tax Rate"
End Sub
```

**Figure 7-13**    Code to create a complex string expression

2. To call the ShowTaxRate subroutine, add the following command so it appears as the second command in the Page_Load procedure, after the first command that calls the CalcComplexTotal subroutine.

```
ShowTaxRate(.06, "WI")
```

3. Click the **Start** button ▶ to run the project. Internet Explorer opens and the Tax Rate Label control displays the text "6% WI State Tax Rate." Close Internet Explorer.

Note that the preceding concatenation operation involves a numeric expression that calculates the product of the sngTaxRate variable times 100. VB .NET automatically converts the numeric value to a string value and then performs the concatenation operations.

## Using Built-In String Methods and Functions

VB .NET supports several built-in string functions and methods to support string operations. One string operation that you sometimes need to perform is converting a string to all uppercase characters or to all lowercase characters. To do this, you use the ToUpper and ToLower methods. For example, suppose you have a string variable named strExample that currently has the string value "Hello." You would use the following code to convert this value to all uppercase characters ("HELLO") and all lowercase characters ("hello"):

```
strExample.ToUpper
strExample.ToLower
```

Sometimes you need to **parse** a string, which means to extract one or more characters from the string and represent the extracted characters as separate string variables. For example, suppose you have a variable named strCustomerName that stores a customer's name as "Paula Harris." You might want to parse this string into two separate string variables that represent the individual first and last name components. Parsing the string requires that you use several operations.

The first important parsing operation is finding the number of characters in a string. To do this, you use the VB .NET **Length property**, which returns an integer value that represents the number of characters in the string. The Length function has the following general syntax:

```
string.Length
```

In this syntax, *string* represents the string for which you want to determine the length. You would use the following command to determine the length of the string stored by the variable strCustomerName:

```
strCustomerName.Length
```

If the variable currently stores the value "Paula Harris," this function returns the value 12, which represents the number of characters in the string.

Another important parsing operation is finding the starting position of a specific character within a string. To do this, you use the VB .NET **IndexOf method** to search the string and find the position of the search character. The IndexOf method has the following general syntax:

```
string.IndexOf("char")
```

In this syntax, *string* represents the string being searched, and *char* represents the search character. For example, you would use the following command to find the position of the blank space (" ") in the strCustomerName string variable that stores the value "Paula Harris":

```
strCustomerName.IndexOf(" ")
```

This method returns the integer value 6, which represents the position of the blank space within the text string "Paula Harris." If the strCustomerName text string contains multiple blank spaces, the IndexOf method returns the position of the first blank space.

The final important string parsing operation you need to perform is done by the VB .NET **Substring method**, which extracts a substring from an existing string based on the starting position and the length of the substring. The Substring function has the following general syntax:

```
String.Substring(start, length)
```

In this syntax, *String* is the string from which you are extracting the substring. The *start* parameter represents the starting position of the string. The first character in the string is at position 0, the second character is at position 1, and so forth. The *length* parameter specifies the number of characters to extract. For example, suppose you want to extract the substring "Paula" from the variable named strCustomerName, which contains the text string "Paula Harris." The starting position of the substring is the first string character, which is at position 0. The length of the string that you want to extract is five characters, which is the number of characters in "Paula." You would use the following command to call the substring method and return the extracted string value to a string variable named strFirstName:

```
Dim strFirstName As String = strCustomerName.Substring(0, 5)
```

To parse all of the characters in a string that appear before a delimiting character, you use the IndexOf and Substring methods. (A delimiting character is a character that divides a string into different parts, such as a blank space or a comma.) You use the IndexOf method to find the position of the delimiting character, then use the Substring method to return all of the string characters from the beginning of the string to the position just before the delimiting character. For example, you use the following commands to parse the characters that appear before the blank space ("Paula") in the text string "Paula Harris":

```
Dim bytPosition As Byte = strFullName.IndexOf(" ")
strFirstName = strFullName.Substring(0, bytPosition)
```

In this code, the bytPosition variable is assigned the value 5. (The first character in the string "Paula Harris" is at position 0, so the blank space is at position 5.) The Substring method returns the first five characters of strFullName, which are *Paula*.

To parse the characters in a string that follow a delimiting character, you first use the Length property to find the total string length, and then use the IndexOf method to find the position of the delimiting character. You then find the length of the substring by subtracting the total string length from the position of the delimiting character, minus 1, to account for the delimiting character. You then use the results in the Substring method to return all of the string characters from the position just after the delimiting character to the final string character. For example, you use the following commands to parse the characters that appear after the blank space in the text string "Paula Harris":

```
Dim bytStrLength As Byte = strFullName.Length
Dim bytPosition As Byte = strFullName.IndexOf(" ")
Dim bytSubStrLength As Byte = ↵
bytStrLength — bytPosition - 1
strLastName = ↵
strFullName.Substring(bytPosition + 1, bytSubStrLength)
```

In this code, bytStrLength evaluates as 12, which is the number of characters in "Paula Harris." The value of bytPosition is 5, which is the position of the blank space. (Recall that the first string character is at position 0.) The value of bytSubStrLength is six, which is the difference of the string length (12) minus the delimiter position (5) minus 1. The Substring method then extracts the final six characters in the strFullName variable, which are *Harris*.

## Avoiding Using the Plus Sign (+) as a Concatenation Operator

Recall that VB .NET supports using the plus sign (+) in addition to the ampersand (&) as a string concatenation operator. Also recall that you should not use the plus sign for concatenation operations because it can cause errors or unpredictable results when you concatenate string values that contain numeric expressions. When you concatenate string values that contain numeric expressions, VB .NET tries to use the plus sign (+) as an addition operator and add the string value to the numeric expression. Unless the string value contains numeric characters, an error occurs.

To illustrate this error, you will change the concatenation operators from & to + in the complex string expression you created earlier to display the Tax Rate Label control value. Then you will run the project and analyze the error.

To use the plus sign concatenation operator and generate an error:

1. In Visual Studio .NET, change the command in the ShowTaxRate subroutine by replacing the & concatenation operators with + so the command appears as follows:

```
lblTaxRate.Text = (sngTaxRate * 100) + ↵
"% " + strCustState + " State Tax Rate"
```

2. Click the **Start** button ▶ to run the project. After a few moments, an error with the message "Input string was not in a correct format" appears in the Internet Explorer window.

3. Close Internet Explorer.

What happened? Recall from Table 7-4 that in the operator order of precedence, string concatenation is always the final operation. When you use the plus sign (+) as a concatenation operator to create a complex expression using a string expression and a number expression, VB .NET tries to perform an addition operation instead of a concatenation operation. To perform the addition operation, VB .NET tries to convert the string variable to a number. If the string variable does not contain numeric characters, an error occurs. In this case, VB .NET tries to convert the text literal "%" to a numeric value, which generates the error.

You can write complex expressions that combine arithmetic and string concatenation operations if you always use the ampersand (&) concatenation operator. Now you will correct the error in the ShowTaxRate subroutine by replacing the plus sign (+) operator with the ampersand (&) concatenation operator between the numeric and string expressions.

To correct the error:

1. In Visual Studio .NET, modify the command in the ShowTaxRate subroutine so it appears as follows:

```
lblTaxRate.Text = (sngTaxRate * 100) & ↵
"% " + strCustState + " State Tax Rate"
```

2. Click the **Start** button ▶ to run the project. The Tax Rate Label appears correctly in Internet Explorer.

3. Close Internet Explorer.

Note that VB .NET correctly interpreted the plus sign (+) as a concatenation operator between the command's string expressions. To avoid errors, however, it is a good practice to avoid using the plus sign as a concatenation operator.

## Converting Data Types in VB .NET

So far you have seen that in many numeric and string expressions, VB .NET automatically performs data type conversions so that the expressions evaluate correctly. In some situations, however, VB .NET does not automatically perform data type conversions, or does not perform the data type conversions that you expect. For example, in the previous section you saw how VB .NET incorrectly tried to convert the text string "%" to a number in order to perform a numeric operation in an expression.

You cannot always predict when VB .NET will perform an automatic data type conversion. Therefore, it is a good practice always to convert a value to the correct data type

7

explicitly before you use it in an expression that involves a numeric or string operation. You can convert the data types of VB .NET variables and object properties (such as the Text property of a Label or TextBox control) using the VB. NET data conversion functions and the ToString string conversion method. The following subsections describe these data type conversion approaches.

## Using the VB .NET Data Conversion Functions

VB .NET has several built-in functions that perform data conversion operations. Table 7–5 summarizes the VB .NET data conversion functions.

**Table 7-5**     VB .NET data conversion functions

| Function | Description | Return Value Data Type |
| --- | --- | --- |
| CBool | Converts an expression to a Boolean data type | Boolean |
| CByte | Converts an expression to a Byte data type | Byte |
| CDate | Converts an expression to a Date data type | Date |
| CDbl | Converts an expression to a Double data type | Double |
| CDec | Converts an expression to a Decimal data type | Decimal |
| CInt | Converts an expression to an Integer data type | Integer |
| CLng | Converts an expression to a Long data type | Long |
| CObj | Converts an expression to an Object data type | Object |
| CShort | Converts an expression to a Short data type | Short |
| CSng | Converts an expression to a Single data type | Single |
| CStr | Converts an expression to a String data type | String |
| Val | Converts a numeric text string to an appropriate numeric data type | Appropriate numeric data type |

All of these functions except the Val function begin with the letter *C*, which stands for *convert*, followed by an abbreviation of the resulting data type (such as Bool or Str). You use the following general syntax to call a data conversion function:

```
new_value = Function(expression)
```

In this syntax, *new_value* represents a variable or object with the new data type. *Function* represents the function name, and *expression* represents either a simple or complex expression. For example, you would use the following command to convert the date #12/14/2006# to a string and assign its value to a variable named strTodaysDate:

```
strTodaysDate = CStr(#12/14/2006#)
```

You can use data conversion functions directly within expressions. For example, you could use the following command to create an expression that converts a date value to a string and concatenates the value with a string literal:

```
strTodaysDate = "Today is " & CStr(#12/14/2006#)
```

To gain experience using the VB .NET data conversion functions, you will create a subroutine named CalcTax that receives the customer's tax rate as a parameter, then calculates the order's sales tax as the product of the tax rate times the Extended Total value, and displays the result in the Sales Tax TextBox control. Because the Extended Total TextBox's Text property stores the extended total as a string value, you will use the CSng data conversion function to convert the string value to a Single data type prior to the calculation. You will also include a command that uses the FormatCurrency function to apply a currency format to the sales tax value.

To use the data conversion function:

1. To create the CalcTax subroutine, add the following commands to the end of the ExpressionsForm.aspx.vb code behind file, just before the **End Class** command:

```
Sub CalcTax(sngTaxRate As Single)
    txtTax.Text = CSng(txtExtTotal.Text) * sngTaxRate
    txtTax.Text = FormatCurrency(txtTax.Text)
End Sub
```

2. To call the new subroutine, add the following command as the last command in the Page_Load procedure:

```
CalcTax(.06)
```

3. Click the **Start** button ▶ to run the project. The form appears in Internet Explorer and shows the Sales Tax value as $5.40. Close Internet Explorer.

In this case, you do not absolutely have to use the CSng function to convert the string value in the TextBox control to a number. VB .NET will see that you are performing the multiplication operation on the numeric string, and will automatically perform the conversion. However, VB .NET does not automatically perform this conversion when you perform an addition arithmetic operation on two strings. Instead, VB .NET assumes you are performing a concatenation operation. To illustrate this problem, you will create a subroutine named CalcTotal that adds the value in the Extended Total TextBox control to the value in the SalesTax TextBox control and displays the sum in the Total TextBox control. First you will attempt to perform the addition operation without converting the strings to numeric data values.

To perform an addition operation on two strings:

1. To create the CalcTotal subroutine, add the following command to the end of the ExpressionsForm.aspx.vb code behind file, just before the **End Class** command:

```
Sub CalcTotal()
    txtTotal.Text = txtExtTotal.Text + txtTax.Text
End Sub
```

2. To call the new subroutine, add the following command as the last command in the Page_Load procedure:

```
CalcTotal()
```

3. Click the **Start** button ▶ to run the project. The form appears in Internet Explorer and shows the Total value as $89.97$5.40. Close Internet Explorer.

As you can see, VB .NET concatenated the two text strings rather than adding their numeric values as you intended. Now you will modify the CalcTotal subroutine so it uses the CSng data conversion function to convert the string values in the Extended Total and Sales Tax TextBox controls to numeric values prior to adding them.

To convert the strings to numbers before adding them:

1. Modify the command in the CalcTotal subroutine, which calculates the sum of the Extended Total and Sales Tax values, so it appears as follows:

```
txtTotal.Text = CSng(txtExtTotal.Text) + ↵
CSng(txtTax.Text)
```

2. Click the **Start** button ▶ to run the project. The form appears in Internet Explorer and shows the Total value as $95.37, which is the sum of the Extended Total and Sales Tax values.

3. Close Internet Explorer. Because you are finished working with the ExpressionsForm.aspx Web form, close all open windows within the Visual Studio .NET Browser Window.

### Using the VB .NET ToString Method

You can use the **ToString method** instead of the CStr function to convert non-string values to the String data type. The general syntax of the ToString method is as follows:

```
value.ToString
```

In this syntax, *value* can be a variable, a reference to a server control Text property, or a complex expression such as the sum of two numbers. If *value* is a complex expression, you must enclose it in parentheses. For example, the following code calculates the product of two numbers and then converts the result to a string:

```
(intNumber1 * intNumber2).ToString
```

Is there a corresponding ToNumber or ToInteger method to convert a string to a number? The answer is no. You must use one of the VB .NET data conversion functions to convert a string to a number.

## VB .NET Decision Control and Repetition (Looping) Structures

Recall that a decision control structure enables a program to execute alternate statements based on a condition that is either true or false, and a repetition (looping) structure processes multiple values the same way until an exit condition is true. The following subsections explore VB .NET decision control and looping structures in more detail. To gain practice with these structures, you will create and work with a copy of the OrderSummaryForm.aspx Web form named StructuresForm.aspx.

To create the StructuresForm.aspx Web form:

1. In Visual Studio .NET, make a copy of the OrderSummaryForm.aspx Web form, and change the new form's name to **StructuresForm.aspx**.

2. Open the new form's code behind file and change the class declaration so it appears as `Public Class StructuresForm.`

3. Right-click the **StructuresForm.aspx** node in the Solution Explorer and then click **Set As Start Page**.

# Decision Control Structures

In this section, you will learn how to use the `If` and `Select Case` decision control structures. You will also learn how to use the AND, OR, and NOT logical operators within decision control conditions.

## The `If` Control Structure

The general syntax of the VB .NET `If` control structure is as follows:

```
If condition Then
    program_statements
End If
```

In this syntax, `If` marks the beginning of the `If` control structure.

 VB .NET commands are not case-sensitive, so if you type the command as `IF` or `if`, VB .NET will automatically reformat the command using mixed-case letters so that the result is `If`.

If the *condition* is true, the *program_statements* will execute. If the *condition* is false, execution will skip the *program_statements*. Notice that unlike JavaScript, VB .NET doesn't use curly braces to delimit the code within an `If` control structure. The beginning of the code belonging to the *condition* starts after the `Then` keyword, and ends at the `End If` keyword.

Recall that the general syntax of a *condition* is *expression1 comparison_operator expression2*. The *comparison_operator* is the symbol that defines the type comparison being made between *expression1* and *expression2*. Table 7-6 summarizes the VB .NET comparison operators.

**Table 7-6** VB .NET comparison operators

| Operator | Description | Example | Result |
|---|---|---|---|
| = | Compares two expressions to determine whether they are equal | `intCounter = 10` | Returns True if intCounter is equal to 10 |
| <> | Compares two expressions to determine whether they are not equal | `intCounter <>10` | Returns True if intCounter is not equal to 10 |
| ><br><<br>>=<br><= | Greater than<br>Less than<br>Greater than or equal to<br>Less than or equal to | `intCounter > 10`<br>`intCounter < 10`<br>`intCounter >= 10`<br>`intCounter <= 10` | Returns True if the condition is true, or False if the condition is False |

Recall that sometimes in a decision control structure, the program needs to execute one set of commands if the condition is true and an alternate set of commands if the condition is false. To create this kind of a decision control structure, you use the `If/Else` form of the `If` decision control structure. The general syntax for an `If/Else` decision control structure in VB .NET is:

```
If condition Then
    program_statements
Else
    alternate_program_statements
End If
```

Finally, sometimes you need to create an `If` decision control structure that evaluates multiple different conditions and executes different commands for each condition. To do this, you use the `If/ElseIf` form of the `If` decision control structure. The `If/ElseIf` structure has the following general syntax:

```
If condition1 Then
    program_statements1
ElseIf condition2 Then
    program_statements2
ElseIf condition3 Then
    program_statements3
...
Else
    alternate_program_statements
End If
```

Note that in the VB .NET syntax, ElseIf within the command is a single word.

In this syntax, the program first evaluates *condition1*. If *condition1* is true, the program executes *program_statements1* and then exits the control structure. If *condition1* is false, the program evaluates *condition2*. If *condition2* is true, the program executes *program_statements2* and then exits the control structure. The program continues to evaluate each condition, one after another, until it finds a true condition. If the program does not find a true condition, it executes the *alternate_program_statements* following the **Else** command.

To gain experience using decision control structures, you will create a subroutine in the StructuresForm.aspx Web form named CalcTax, which receives a string parameter that specifies the customer's state of residence. For example, if a customer lives in Wisconsin, the subroutine will receive the string parameter "WI." The subroutine will use a decision control structure to determine the customer's tax rate based on his or her state of residence. For example, if the customer is a Wisconsin resident, the tax rate is 6 percent, and if the customer is an Alaska resident, the tax rate is 3 percent. You will also add commands to the Page_Load procedure to declare a variable to represent the customer's state of residence, assign initial values to the Item Description, Quantity, Price, and Extended Total TextBox controls, and call the CalcTax subroutine.

To include an **If/ElseIf** decision control structure in the Web form:

1. Add the commands shown in Figure 7-14 to the StructuresForm.aspx.vb code behind file to initialize the form values in the Page_Load procedure and create the CalcTax subroutine. (The CalcTax subroutine would theoretically contain tax rates for all 50 states, but this example contains rates for only a few states so you get the idea of how it works.)

Note that when you type If to create a decision control structure, the Visual Studio .NET IDE automatically adds End If in the Code editor.

2. Click the **Start** button ▶ to run the project. The form appears in Internet Explorer, and displays $5.40 for the Sales Tax value, which is the correct amount for Wisconsin residents.

3. Close Internet Explorer.

```
Private Sub Page_Load(ByVal sender As System.Object, ↵
ByVal e As System.EventArgs) Handles MyBase.Load
   Dim strCurrCustState As String = "WI"
   txtDescription.Text = "Women's Hiking Shorts"
   txtQuantity.Text = "3"
   txtPrice.Text = FormatCurrency("29.99")
   txtExtTotal.Text = CSng(txtQuantity.Text) * CSng(txtPrice.Text)
   txtExtTotal.Text = FormatCurrency(txtExtTotal.Text)
   CalcTax(strCurrCustState)
End Sub

Sub CalcTax(ByVal strCustState As String)
   strCustState = strCustState.ToUpper
   If strCustState = "AK" Then
      txtTax.Text = 0.03 * CSng(txtExtTotal.Text)
   ElseIf strCustState = "MN" Then
      txtTax.Text = 0.08 * CSng(txtExtTotal.Text)
   ElseIf strCustState = "WI" Then
      txtTax.Text = 0.06 * CSng(txtExtTotal.Text)
   ElseIf strCustState = "WY" Then
      txtTax.Text = 0.05 * CSng(txtExtTotal.Text)
   Else
      txtTax.Text = "0"
   End If
   txtTax.Text = FormatCurrency(txtTax.Text)
End Sub
```

**Figure 7-14**    Commands to create an `If/ElseIf` decision control structure

## The `Select Case` Control Structure

Sometimes a decision control structure tests multiple conditions that compare the same variable value. Recall that in Chapter 3, you used the `switch` control structure to do this in JavaScript. In VB .NET, you use the `Select Case` control structure to test multiple conditions that compare the same variable value and then perform associated programming commands. The general syntax for the VB .NET `Select Case` control structure is:

```
Select Case controlling_expression
    Case expression1
        program_statements1
    Case expression2
        program_statements2
    ...
    Case Else
        alternate_program_statements
End Select
```

In this syntax, the *controlling_expression* specifies the expression that the structure compares to each of the individual expressions (*expression1*, *expression2*, and so forth.) For example, in the preceding StructuresForm.aspx Web form, the *controlling_expression* would be the variable that represents the customer's state of residence, which you would represent as strCustState. *Expression1* would be the literal value "AK," *expression2* would be the literal value "MN," and so forth.

Now you will modify the StructuresForm.aspx Web form by adding a new subroutine named AltCalcTax that uses a `Select Case` structure rather than an `If/ElseIf` structure to evaluate the customer's state of residence and then display the appropriate sales tax value.

To add a `Select Case` structure to the Web form:

1. Create the AltCalcTax subroutine that contains the `Select Case` structure commands by adding the code shown in Figure 7-15 just before the `End Class` command in the StructuresForm.aspx.vb code behind file.

```
Sub AltCalcTax(ByVal strCustState As String)
   strCustState = strCustState.ToUpper
   Select Case strCustState
      Case "AK"
         txtTax.Text = 0.03 * CSng(txtExtTotal.Text)
      Case "MN"
         txtTax.Text = 0.08 * CSng(txtExtTotal.Text)
      Case "WI"
         txtTax.Text = 0.06 * CSng(txtExtTotal.Text)
      Case "WY"
         txtTax.Text = 0.05 * CSng(txtExtTotal.Text)
      Case Else
         txtTax.Text = "0"
   End Select
   txtTax.Text = FormatCurrency(txtTax.Text)
End Sub
```

**Figure 7-15**   Commands to create a `Select Case` decision control structure

2. In the Page_Load procedure, comment out the command that calls the CalcTax subroutine, then add the following command to call the AltCalcTax subroutine:

   **AltCalcTax(strCurrCustState)**

3. Click the **Start** button ▶ to run the project. After a few moments, the Web form appears in Internet Explorer and shows the Sales Tax value as $5.40.

4. Close Internet Explorer.

## Using the AND, OR, and NOT Logical Operators within Conditions

Recall that you can use the AND and OR logical operators to test multiple conditions in a single condition comparison. If you join two separate condition statements with the

AND operator, both conditions must be true for the overall condition to be true. If you join two separate condition statements with the OR operator, if either condition is true, the overall condition is true. VB .NET condition statements that use these logical operators have the following general syntax:

```
((condition1) And (condition2))
((condition1) Or (condition2))
```

Note that you enclose each separate condition in parentheses and enclose the overall condition in parentheses. The following examples illustrate condition comparisons using the VB .NET logical operators:

```
((3 < 4) And (5 > 6))
((3 < 4) Or (5 > 6))
```

In these examples, the first condition comparison would evaluate as false. Recall that with an AND operator, both condition statements must be true for the overall condition comparison to be true. Because one of the condition statements (5 > 6) is not true, the overall condition comparison is not true. The second condition comparison would evaluate as true, because with an OR operator, if either condition is true, the overall condition comparison is true. Because the first condition statement (3 < 4) is true, the overall condition comparison is true.

Now you will add a condition comparison containing an OR operator to the StructuresForm.aspx Web form. Suppose that residents of Iowa pay the same sales tax as Minnesota residents. You will modify the condition in the **If** control structure that tests whether the customer is a Minnesota resident so that it uses an OR logical operator to test also whether the customer is an Iowa resident. If the customer is a resident of either state, the command executes and shows the correct sales tax amount. You will also change the command in the Page_Load procedure so that the form calls the CalcTax subroutine, which contains the **If/ElseIf** decision structure, and specify that the customer is an Iowa resident.

To add an OR logical operator to the Web form:

1. In the StructuresForm.aspx Web form code behind file, modify the first **ElseIf** command within the **If/ElseIf** control structure so it appears as follows:

```
ElseIf ((strCustState = "MN") Or ↵
(strCustState = "IA")) Then
```

2. Modify the first command in the Page_Load procedure as follows to specify that the customer is an Iowa resident:

```
Dim strCurrCustState As String = "IA"
```

3. Comment out the command that calls the AltCalcTax subroutine, and remove the comment character from the command that calls the CalcTax subroutine

so that the form now calls the CalcTax subroutine. The final two commands in the Page_Load subroutine should appear as follows:

```
CalcTax(strCurrCustState)
'AltCalcTax(strCurrCustState)
```

4. Click the **Start** button ▶ to run the project. After a few moments, the Web form appears in Internet Explorer and displays the Sales Tax value as $7.20, which is the correct amount for both Iowa and Minnesota residents.

5. Close Internet Explorer.

You use the NOT logical operator to execute commands if a condition is not true. In VB .NET, the NOT logical operator has the following general syntax in an `If` decision structure: `If Not (condition)`. For example, you would use the following structure to execute commands if a customer's state of residence is not Wisconsin:

```
If Not (strCustState = "WI) Then
```

## Creating Looping Structures

Recall that you use a loop to process multiple values the same way. The loop systematically executes a series of program statements and periodically evaluates an exit condition that determines whether the loop repeats or exits. A pretest loop evaluates the exit condition before any program commands execute, and a posttest loop executes one or more program commands before evaluating the exit condition the first time. VB .NET supports many types of loops. In this book, you will learn to use three loops that should support most situations: `Do` loops, `Do While` loops, and `For/Next` loops.

### Do Loops

In a `Do` loop, you need to declare a variable that serves as the loop counter. The loop's exit condition evaluates the value of the loop counter and determines how many times the loop executes. You need to explicitly increment the loop counter so the exit condition eventually becomes true and the loop terminates. The general syntax for a `Do` loop is:

```
Do
        [pretest_program_statements]
        If condition Then
              Exit Do
        End If
        [posttest_program_statements]
Loop
```

In a `Do` loop, you declare and initialize the loop counter variable in a command before the loop. The `Do` keyword marks the beginning of the loop structure. You can optionally place program commands as well as the command to increment the loop counter in the *pretest_program_statements*. Next, you write the code to explicitly test for a *condition* that determines whether the loop exits using an `If` decision control structure. You can optionally include additional program statements as the *posttest_program_statements*. This allows you to structure the loop as a pretest loop, a posttest loop, or a combination of both. If the loop contains commands before the `If` structure, the loop is a posttest loop. If the loop contains no commands before the `If` structure, the loop is a pretest loop. This capacity to create either a pretest or a posttest loop makes the `Do` loop one of the most flexible loops in VB .NET.

Now you will create a subroutine named DoLoop that contains a `Do` loop that displays the text "Thank You" multiple times in the form's Thank You Label control. You will declare a local variable within the subroutine named intCounter that will be the loop's counter and set its initial value as 1. You will then add the commands for the `Do` loop, and structure it as a posttest loop. The loop first contains a command that appends the text literal " **Thank You** " to the current value of the Thank You Label's Text property. You will then write a command that increments the counter by one. You will specify the `If` control structure so that the loop exits when the counter is greater than 5.

To create the subroutine that contains the `Do` loop:

1. To create the DoLoop procedure, add the commands shown in Figure 7-16 to the StructuresForm.aspx.vb code behind file just before the `End Class` command.

```
Sub DoLoop()
    Dim intCounter As Integer = 1
    Do
        lblThankYou.Text = lblThankYou.Text & " **Thank You** "
        intCounter = intCounter + 1
        If intCounter > 5 Then
            Exit Do
        End If
    Loop
End Sub
```

**Figure 7-16**   Commands to create a `Do` loop

2. To call the DoLoop procedure, add the following code as the last command in the Page_Load procedure:

   **DoLoop()**

3. Click the **Start** button ▶ to run the project. The Web form appears in Internet Explorer and displays the Thank You Label, which displays the text "**Thank You **" five times. This confirms that the loop executed successfully.

4. Close Internet Explorer.

## Do While Loops

A **Do While** loop is a pretest loop that you often use to process records that a program retrieves from a database. Because you usually do not know exactly how many records the program will retrieve, you structure the loop's exit condition so the loop exits after it processes all of the records.

The general syntax for a **Do While** loop is:

```
Do While condition
  program_statements
Loop
```

During program execution, the system first evaluates the *condition*. If the *condition* is true, the system executes the *program_statements*, and then reevaluates the *condition*. The loop continues to execute the *program_statements* until the *condition* becomes false. The *program_statements* must contain a command that changes the *condition* so the loop eventually terminates.

Now you will modify the StructuresForm.aspx Web form by adding a subroutine named DoWhileLoop() that contains a **Do While** loop to initialize the text in the Thank You Label. In the subroutine, you will declare a local variable named intCounter as the loop counter and initialize its value as 1. You will then add the commands for the **Do While** loop. The condition will specify that the loop appends the text "** Thank you for your order **" to the Thank You Label's Text property as long as the loop counter is less than 3.

To create the subroutine that contains the **Do While** loop:

1. To create the DoWhileLoop procedure, add the commands in Figure 7-17 to the StructuresForm.aspx.vb code behind file just before the **End Class** command.

```
Sub DoWhileLoop()
   Dim intCounter As Integer = 1
   Do While (intCounter < 3)
      lblThankYou.Text = lblThankYou.Text ⤶
      & " **Thank you for your order** "
      intCounter = intCounter + 1
   Loop
End Sub
```

**Figure 7-17**   Commands to create a Do While loop

2. In the Page_Load procedure, comment out the command that calls the DoLoop procedure and add the following command to call the DoWhileLoop procedure:

```
DoWhileLoop()
```

3. Click the **Start** button ▶ to run the project. The Web form appears in Internet Explorer and displays " **\*\*Thank you for your order\*\*** " two times, which confirms that the loop executed successfully.

4. Close Internet Explorer.

## For/Next Loops

A VB .NET **For/Next** loop is similar to the JavaScript **for** loop because you use the loop structure to declare and increment the loop counter. You use a **For/Next** loop when you know at design time exactly how many times the loop will execute. A **For/Next** loop is useful for processing database records because you can easily step through a set of retrieved records sequentially or move to a specific record number.

The general structure of a **For/Next** loop is:

```
For counter = start To end [Step interval]
    program_statements
Next counter
```

In this syntax, *counter* is any legal VB .NET variable name, and represents the loop counter. You must declare the counter variable before you use it in the **For/Next** loop declaration.

 Programmers often use a variable named i for loop counters in For/Next loops.

The *start* and *end* markers represent integer numbers that specify the loop counter's start value and end value. By default, the loop automatically increments the loop counter's start value by 1 until the loop counter reaches the end value. The optional **Step** keyword and *interval* value allow you to increment the start by an alternate amount. The *interval* value can be a positive or negative integer.

Now you will add to the StructuresForm.aspx Web form a subroutine named ForNextLoop that contains a **For/Next** loop. You will structure the loop so the start value is 5 and the end value is 1. You will decrement the loop counter so that the program statement displays the numbers 1 through 5 in reverse order in the form's Thank You Label control. The command uses the ToString method to convert the integer loop counter to a string when it appends the loop counter value to the string.

To create the subroutine that contains the **For/Next** loop:

1. To create the ForNextLoop subroutine, add the commands in Figure 7-18 to the StructuresForm.aspx.vb code behind file just before the **End Class** command.

```
Sub ForNextLoop()
   Dim i As Integer
   For i = 5 To 1 Step -1
      lblThankYou.Text = lblThankYou.Text & " " & i.ToString
   Next
End Sub
```

**Figure 7-18**    Commands to create a `For/Next` loop

2. In the Page_Load procedure, comment out the command that calls the DoWhileLoop subroutine and add the following command to call the ForNextLoop subroutine:

**ForNextLoop()**

3. Click the **Start** button ▶ to run the project. The Web form appears in Internet Explorer, and the Thank You Label displays the text "5 4 3 2 1," which confirms that the loop executed successfully.

4. Close Internet Explorer.

5. Because you are finished working with the StructuresForm.aspx Web form, close all open windows within the Visual Studio .NET Browser Window.

## CREATING CUSTOM CLASSES IN VB .NET

Recall that an object is an abstract representation of something in the real world, and that an object class defines the properties and actions of similar objects. For example, a Web form is an abstract representation of a paper form that people use to enter data values. In Visual Studio .NET, when you create a new Web form, the form's code behind file creates a form object. An object has properties and methods that specify its behavior. A Web form inherits its properties and methods from the System.Web.UI.Page base class. So far, all of the objects you have used in Visual Studio .NET have been instances of predefined object classes.

VB .NET is a full-featured object-oriented programming language that allows programmers to define **custom classes**, which are classes for which programmers define specific properties and methods. Once you have created a custom class, you can use it in a variety of different Web forms and different Web application projects to perform common processing tasks.

You can create a custom class in a Web application project, and then use VB .NET commands to define class properties and create class methods. You create a custom class when you need to create an object within a Web application project that many forms within the project might use, or that forms within many different projects might use. For example, many pages in a Web-based order form would use a shopping cart, so you would create a class object to implement the shopping cart application. The shopping cart has a definite structure that defines the items and associated quantities it contains. The shopping cart object would have methods for adding items, removing items, and checking out when the user finishes shopping.

To use a custom class in a Web application project, you first define the class in the project. Next, you create an instance of the class in a Web form. You can then use the object instance to perform operations within the form, such as calling a class method. For example, you might define an object class to represent a shopping cart, create an instance of a shopping cart in a specific form, and then create methods to add and remove shopping cart items.

To become familiar with custom classes, you will create a custom class in the VBConcepts project that has a method that calculates sales tax based on the customer's state of residence. This is an appropriate object application because you might want to use this object in multiple project forms. You might also want to export the class to different Web application projects. The following subsections describe how to create a new custom class, write a method in the custom class, and then use the custom class within a Web form.

## Creating a Custom Class

When you create a custom class in a Web application project, ASP.NET stores information about the custom class in a **class definition file** with a .vb file extension. All of the project's Web forms can then use the custom class's methods.

Visual Studio .NET allows you to create class libraries that are available to multiple projects, but developing class libraries is beyond the scope of this book. For now, when you use classes, they will always be in the same project as the forms that use them.

Now you will create a new custom class named SalesTaxClass in the VBConcepts project.

To create a custom class:

1. Select the **VBConcepts** project node in the Solution Explorer, right-click, point to **Add**, and then click **Add Class**. The Add New Item – VBConcepts dialog box opens.

Another way to create a custom class is to click Project on the menu bar and then click Add Class.

2. Make sure that the *Class* template is selected, change the *Name* field to **SalesTaxClass.vb**, and then click **Open**. After a few moments, a new class node named SalesTaxClass.vb appears in the Solution Explorer.

The Visual Studio .NET IDE has created a class definition file named SalesTaxClass.vb that contains the command that defines the class. You can now add commands to the class definition file to define class properties and methods.

## Defining Class Properties and Methods

In the class definition file, you can declare variables that specify the class's properties. You can also create procedures that specify the class's methods. Now you will create a method in the SalesTaxClass class. This method will be a function named StateTaxRate that receives a string parameter that is the two-character abbreviation for the customer's state of residence (such as "WI"). The method will then return the sales tax rate for the state. The method will use a `Select Case` decision control structure to evaluate the state value and then return the associated sales tax rate.

To add the code to define the StateTaxRate method:

1. To create the StateTaxRate class method, add the commands shown in Figure 7-19 to the SalesTaxClass.vb class definition file.

```
Public Function StateTaxRate(ByVal strState As String) As Single
    Dim strSt As String = strState.ToUpper
    Select Case strSt
        Case "AK"
            StateTaxRate = 0.03
        Case "MN"
            StateTaxRate = 0.08
        Case "WI"
            StateTaxRate = 0.06
        Case "WY"
            StateTaxRate = 0.05
        'assume values are entered for other states
        Case Else
            StateTaxRate = 0
    End Select
End Function
```

**Figure 7-19**    Code to create the custom class method

2. Click the **Save** button on the toolbar to save the class.

## Creating Class Instances and Calling Class Methods

The next steps in using a custom class are to create a new object instance of the class in a Web form and use the object to call the class methods. First you will create a copy of the OrderSummaryForm.aspx Web form named ClassesForm.aspx.

To create the ClassesForm.aspx Web form:

1. In Visual Studio .NET, make a copy of the OrderSummaryForm.aspx Web form, and change the new form's name to **ClassesForm.aspx**.

2. Open the new form's code behind file and change the class declaration so it appears as `Public Class ClassesForm`.

3. Right-click the **ClassesForm.aspx** node in the Solution Explorer and then click **Set As Start Page**.

The following subsections describe how to create a new object in a Web form and how to use the object to call the class methods.

## Creating a New Object Instance

Before a Web form can interact with a class, the form must first contain an object that is a member of the class. Creating an object that is a member of a class is called **instantiating** the class. In the ClassesForm.aspx Web form, you need to create an object that is a member of the SalesTaxClass object class in order to instantiate the class. When you write the command to instantiate a class, you must decide whether the new class object will have local or module-level scope. A **local object** is visible only within the procedure that creates it. A **module-level object** is visible to all procedures within the Web form that creates it.

You use the following general syntax to create local and module-level objects, respectively:

```
Dim object_name As New project_name.class_name
Private object_name As New project_name.class_name
```

In this syntax, the *object_name* can be any legal VB .NET variable name. Usually, object names have an `obj` prefix to signal that they are objects. Notice that the command to instantiate an object from a class looks a lot like the command for declaring a variable. The only differences are that you include the `New` keyword and specify the *project_name.class_name* instead of a data type. Note that you must specify the project name along with the class name using dot syntax. You must specify the name of the project in which the class exists in case you place the class in a class library outside of the current project.

You would use the following command to create a new local object named objTaxRate in the SalesTaxClass class in the VBConcepts project:

```
Dim objTaxRate As New VBConcepts.SalesTaxClass
```

Now you will add commands to the ClassesForm.aspx Web form's Page_Load procedure to instantiate the SalesTaxClass class using a local object.

To add the command to instantiate the SalesTaxClass class using a local object:

1. In the ClassesForm.aspx.vb code behind file, add the following command to the Page_Load procedure:

```
Dim objTaxRate As New VBConcepts.SalesTaxClass()
```

2. Save the form.

## Calling Class Methods

To use a custom class object instance in a Web form, you add commands that call the object class's methods. To call a class method from a Web form, you use the following general syntax:

```
object_name.method_name(parameter1, parameter2, ...)
```

You would use the following command to declare a variable named sngTaxRate and then call the StateTaxRate method and pass to it the parameter "WI":

```
Dim sngTaxRate As Single= objTaxRate.StateTaxRate("WI")
```

Note that after you instantiate a class, you do not need to preface the *method_name* with its class name. The *object_name* links the class to the method.

Now you will also declare a variable named strCustomerState that stores the two-letter abbreviation for the customer's state of residence. Then you will create a command to declare a variable named sngTaxRate and then call the StateTaxRate method and pass to it the strCustomerState variable that represents the customer's state of residence. You will also add a command to display the retrieved tax rate percentage in the Tax Rate Label control on the Web form. Recall that because the SalesTaxRate method returns the tax rate as a decimal value, this command will multiply the decimal tax rate by 100 to convert it to a percentage. It will then concatenate the returned value in a string that displays the tax percentage, the text literal "%," the customer's state of residence, and the text literal "Tax Rate." For example, for a Wisconsin customer, the label will appear as "6% WI Tax Rate."

To instantiate the class, call the method, and assign the label value:

1. In the ClassesForm.aspx.vb code behind file, add the shaded commands to the Page_Load procedure as shown in Figure 7-20.

```
Private Sub Page_Load(ByVal sender As System.Object, ↵
ByVal e As System.EventArgs) Handles MyBase.Load
    Dim objTaxRate As New VBConcepts.SalesTaxClass()
    Dim strCustomerState As String = "WI"
    Dim sngTaxRate As Single = objTaxRate.StateTaxRate(strCustomerState)
    lblTaxRate.Text = (sngTaxRate * 100).ToString & ↵
    "% " & strCustomerState & " Tax Rate"
End Sub
```

**Figure 7-20**   Code to call the class method

2. Click the **Start** button ▶ to run the Web form. The Web form appears in Internet Explorer, and the Tax Rate Label appears as "6% WI Tax Rate." Close Internet Explorer.

3. In the ClassesForm.aspx.vb code behind file, change the command that specifies the customer's state of residence as follows:

```
Dim strCustomerState = "AK"
```

4. Click the **Start** button ▶ to run the Web form again. The Web form appears in Internet Explorer, and the Tax Rate Label appears as "3% AK Tax Rate." Close Internet Explorer.

## Class Inheritance

Recall that in object-oriented programming, a class can inherit properties and methods from a base, or parent, class. In VB .NET, you can create a custom class that inherits properties and methods from a base class. For example, you could create a class named ShoppingCartClass that contains properties and methods to process a customer's purchases. However, suppose that you create a new Web application project that uses the properties and methods in this class, but also requires additional properties and methods that are not in the base ShoppingCartClass. To solve this problem, you could create a new custom class named SpecialShoppingCart, and you could specify that the SpecialShoppingCart class inherits from the base ShoppingCartClass. You would use the following syntax to define the SpecialShoppingCart class and specify that it inherits from the ShoppingCartClass class:

```
Public Class SpecialShoppingCart
Inherits ShoppingCartClass
```

By specifying that the SpecialShoppingCart class inherits ShoppingCartClass's properties and methods, you can include commands within methods of the SpecialShoppingCart class that call methods in the parent ShoppingCartClass. To reference a property or method in a parent class, you preface the property or method with the `MyBase` keyword, using the following dot syntax: `MyBase.`*`name`*. In this syntax, *name* represents the property or method in the parent class. For example, you would use the following command to call a method named StateTaxRate in the parent ShoppingCartClass from a method in the child SpecialShoppingCart class:

```
sngTaxRate = MyBase.StateTaxRate("WI")
```

In VB .NET, a child class can inherit from only one base class. Therefore, when you create custom classes, you must plan the class structure so the base classes contain the basic properties and methods that your child classes need to inherit.

## THE VB .NET COLLECTION CLASS

In VB .NET, a **collection class** is an object class that has methods that enable you to manipulate class objects in VB .NET programs. You can instantiate a collection and then add objects to the new collection. Each individual object within a collection is called a **collection element**. A collection is similar to a JavaScript array. (Recall that an array is similar to a spreadsheet, where the row number is the index of each array element, and the columns contain data values that you associate with each index.) In VB .NET, you could use a collection to track all of the controls on a Web form. Programmers who create data-based Web pages often use collections to store and process retrieved database data values.

You use the following general syntax to instantiate a collection:

```
Private collection_name As New Collection()
```

The *collection_name* is any legal VB .NET variable name. A collection has standard methods that you use to manipulate the collection objects. The Add method adds an object to a collection using the following general syntax:

```
collection_name.Add(object)
```

For example, you would use the following syntax to create a **Private** collection named CustomerCollection and add two string objects containing the text "Paula Harris" and "Mitch Edwards" to the collection:

```
Private CustomerCollection As New Collection()
CustomerCollection.Add("Paula Harris")
CustomerCollection.Add("Mitch Edwards")
```

Although this collection contains only string objects, a collection can contain objects of any data type. A collection can have any number of objects, and it automatically expands as you add new objects.

To access the individual objects within a collection, you use a **For Each/Next** loop. A **For Each/Next** loop sequentially steps through the objects in a collection and allows you to manipulate them. The general syntax for a **For Each/Next** loop is:

```
Dim object_name As Object
For Each object_name In collection_name
    program_statements
Next
```

To use a **For Each/Next** loop, you must first declare a variable with the data type Object that you use to reference the individual objects in the collection. The loop then sequentially accesses each object in the collection, and you can use the *program_statements* to manipulate each individual object. For example, you would use the following code to access each object in the CustomerCollection and display the name in a Label control named lblCustomerName on a Web form:

```
Dim objCustomer As Object
For Each objCustomer In CustomerCollection
    lblCustomerName.Text = objCustomer
Next
```

In this example, the loop will execute two times, and the label will display "Paula Harris" the first time and "Mitch Edwards" the second time.

Now you will create a collection named CustomerCollection in the ClassesForm.aspx Web form. This collection will store the names of Clearwater Traders customers. You will declare the collection in the form's Declarations block, and declare a class variable named objCustomer. You will create a subroutine named AddCustomers to add the customer names to the collection. You will then add commands to the Page_Load procedure to call the subroutine and create a `For Each/Next` loop that appends each customer's name to the Text property of the lblCustomerName Label control on the form. (Normally, you would not display two customer names on the same Order Summary Form, but this example illustrates how the `For Each/Next` loop works.)

To create and access the collection:

1. In the ClassesForm.aspx.vb code behind file, add the following commands to the Declarations block, just under the declarations of the form controls:

```
Public CustomerCollection As New Collection()
Private objCustomer As Object
```

2. To create the subroutine to add the customer names to the collection, add the following commands at the end of the code behind file, just before the `End Class` command:

```
Sub AddCustomers()
    CustomerCollection.Add("Paula Harris")
    CustomerCollection.Add("Mitch Edwards")
End Sub
```

3. Add the shaded commands shown in Figure 7-21 to the ClassesForm.aspx.vb Page_Load procedure. These commands step through the collection elements and append each element's value to the Text property of the form's Customer Name Label control.

```
Private Sub Page_Load(ByVal sender As System.Object, ↵
ByVal e As System.EventArgs) Handles MyBase.Load
    Dim objTaxRate As New VBConcepts.SalesTaxClass()
    Dim strCustomerState As String = "AK"
    AddCustomers()
    For Each objCustomer In CustomerCollection
        lblCustomerName.Text = lblCustomerName.Text & " " & objCustomer
    Next
    Dim sngTaxRate As Single = objTaxRate.StateTaxRate(strCustomerState)
    lblTaxRate.Text = (sngTaxRate * 100).ToString & ↵
    "% " & strCustomerState & " Tax Rate"
End Sub
```

**Figure 7-21** Code to step through the collection using a `For Each/Next` loop

4. Click the **Start** button ▶ to run the project. After a few moments, the Web form appears in Internet Explorer and displays the two customers' names in the Customer Name Label control, which confirms that the `For Each/Next` loop correctly retrieved the collection elements.

5. Close Internet Explorer and then close Visual Studio .NET.

The VB .NET programming language is a powerful tool for writing programs that create visual applications. You will put these commands to use in later chapters when you learn to create Web forms that retrieve and manipulate database data.

## CHAPTER SUMMARY

❑ VB .NET is a full-featured object-oriented programming language that you use in Web form code behind files to specify the content of dynamic Web pages.

❑ When you declare a variable in VB .NET, you must specify the variable name and the data type of the data that the variable will store. VB .NET supports several numeric and non-numeric data types. When you declare a numeric variable, you should select the numeric data type that has an adequate value range and the ability to store decimal values and positive/negative values that you need, but occupies the least amount of memory space.

❑ A VB .NET variable name can have from 1 to 255 characters, and can contain letters, numbers, and underscores (_). Variable names usually begin with a three-character prefix that identifies the variable's data type.

❑ You can use assignment statements to assign to variables the values of simple or complex expressions. A simple expression is a single value such as a literal value, a control property value, or the value that a function returns. A complex expression combines multiple simple expressions using arithmetic or concatenation operators.

❑ A variable's persistence specifies how long the variable remains in memory and determines when commands can reference the variable and modify its value. A variable's scope specifies the location of the commands that can reference and modify the variable. You control variable persistence and scope in VB .NET by defining variables as local variables or as class variables. You should always use a variable with the narrowest scope and least persistence that will perform the required task.

❑ You can use the VB .NET Debugger to create breakpoints that pause execution on a command. You can then step through program commands and examine variable values during execution using ScreenTips or watches. When you are finished debugging, you should clear all program breakpoints and delete any watches you set.

❑ In VB .NET, a subroutine is a procedure that manipulates variable values, but does not return a specific value to the calling program. A function is a procedure that manipulates variable values and returns a specific value to the calling program. A procedure's scope can be public, which specifies that commands in other Web form code behind files can call the procedure and that commands in custom classes can call the procedure. A procedure's scope can also be private, which specifies that only commands within the code behind file in which you declare the procedure can call the procedure.

❑ When you create a procedure, you can declare a parameter list that enables the command that calls the procedure to pass data values, called parameters, to the procedure. Parameters can be literal values or variables. When you call the procedure, you pass the parameters to the procedure by listing the parameter values in the same order in which the parameters appear in the procedure declaration.

❑ You can pass procedure parameters by value, which means that when you call the procedure and pass the parameter value, the system creates a memory space for each parameter and copies the parameter value into this memory space. You can also pass parameters by reference, in which case you pass the parameter as a local or class variable. When you pass a variable parameter by reference, the system passes the variable's underlying memory location instead of creating a new memory location. The procedure can then change the parameter value, and the change persists outside of the scope of the procedure.

❑ When you create a complex expression that uses arithmetic operators to combine numeric data types that represent whole numbers with numeric data types that contain decimal fractions, if you assign the result to a variable with a data type that represents fractional values, the result will retain its fractional value. If you assign the result to a variable with a data type that does not represent fractional values, VB .NET rounds the result to the nearest whole number.

❑ If you attempt to assign to a variable a numeric value that is too large for the variable's data type, an overflow error occurs. To avoid overflow errors, select data types that will handle the largest possible value that the program will assign to a variable, and create client-side error handlers that evaluate user inputs and advise the user if an input value is out of range.

❑ When you perform concatenation operations using the ampersand (&) concatenation operator, VB .NET automatically converts both expressions to the String data type. When you perform concatenation operations using the plus sign (+), both expressions must already be of the String data type. If either expression is of a numeric data type, VB .NET assumes you want to perform an addition operation. To avoid errors, avoid using + as a concatenation operator.

❑ VB .NET provides several built-in functions for converting expressions to specific data types. VB .NET also provides the ToString method to convert expressions to the String data type.

❑ You can create decision control structures in VB .NET using the If, If/ElseIf, and Select Case decision structures. You can create looping structures using Do loops, Do While loops, and For/Next loops.

❏ VB .NET allows programmers to create custom object classes, add object instances to these classes, and create associated object methods. When you create a custom class in a Web application project, ASP.NET stores the custom class's properties and methods in a class definition file with a .vb file extension. To call a class method from a form procedure, you must instantiate the class by creating a class object within the form. A custom class can inherit properties and methods from only one base class.

❏ A collection class is an object class that has methods that enable you to manipulate class objects in VB .NET programs. You can instantiate a collection and then add objects to the collection. You use the `For Each/Next` loop to step through the collection and access each individual element.

---

## REVIEW QUESTIONS

7

1. Specify the location where you declare each of the following variable types, and indicate the keyword you use to declare the variable type:

| Variable Type | Location Where You Declare It | Declaration Keyword |
|---|---|---|
| Local variable | | |
| Class variable | | |

2. Write a command to declare a class variable that stores student ID values that will have a range from 0 to 999,999,999. Specify a descriptive name for the variable.

3. Write a command to declare a local variable that stores student grade point average (GPA) values that will have a range from 0 to 4.0 and contain floating-point decimal values. Make up a descriptive name for the variable.

4. Describe the difference between a simple expression and a complex expression.

5. Write commands to declare local variables that store the following data. Select the appropriate data type, create a descriptive name for the variable, and assign each variable the associated initial value.

| Variable Data | Data Description | Initial Value |
|---|---|---|
| Inventory ID values | Integers from 1 to 50,000 | 1 |
| Inventory color values | String | Red |
| Inventory prices | Decimal values from 0.00 to 999.99 | 1.00 |
| Date the last inventory shipment was received | Date | 02/02/2006 |

6. A variable's _____ specifies the location of the commands that can reference and modify the variable.

   a. Scope

   b. Persistence

   c. Data type

   d. Base class

7. True or false: A local variable is less persistent than a class variable.

8. Describe the difference between a function and a subroutine.

9. When you pass a parameter by _____, the system creates a memory space for the parameter and makes a copy of the parameter value in this memory space. When you pass a parameter by _____, the system references the parameter using the same memory space as the variable.

10. Write commands to create a subroutine named DisplayNumbers that receives two number values as parameters that you declare using the Byte data type. In the subroutine, use a single command to convert the parameter values to the String data type, concatenate them to form a single string, and then display the string in a form TextBox control named txtDisplay.

11. Write commands to create a function named AddValues that receives two string values as parameters. In the function, use a single command to convert the values to numbers of the Decimal data type, add them, and return the sum as the function's return value. Also write a command to call the function, pass to it the values "5" and "7," and assign the value returned by the function to a Decimal variable named decResult.

12. When should you pass a parameter by reference?

13. If you attempt to assign a numeric value to a variable, and the value is too large for the variable's data type, a(n) _____ error occurs.

    a. Data type

    b. Data conversion

    c. Assignment

    d. Overflow

14. If you use the plus sign (+) operator to concatenate two expressions, and one of the expressions has a numeric data type, a(n) _____ error occurs.

    a. Data type

    b. Data conversion

    c. Assignment

    d. Overflow

16. True or false: VB .NET detects overflow errors only at run time.

17. A Web form contains a Label server control whose ID property value is lblResult.

    a. The code behind file that VB .NET associates with this form contains the commands shown in Figure 7-22. (The Page_Load procedure will automatically run when you run the Web form.) When you run the Web form, what appears in the lblResult Label control?

```
Private Sub Page_Load(ByVal sender As System.Object, ↵
ByVal e As System.EventArgs) Handles MyBase.Load
    Dim strChoice As String
    strChoice = "one"
    mySub(strChoice)
    lblResult.Text = strChoice
End Sub

Private Sub mySub(ByRef strTemp As String)
    strTemp = "Give it up . . . Bwah ha ha"
End Sub
```

**Figure 7-22**

    b. The code behind file that VB .NET associates with this form contains the commands shown in Figure 7-23. (The Page_Load procedure will automatically run when you run the Web form.) When you run the Web form, what appears in the lblResult Label control?

```
Private strMessage As String = "Hello"

Private Sub Page_Load(ByVal sender As System.Object,
ByVal e As System.EventArgs) Handles MyBase.Load
Dim strMessage As String = "Goodbye"
lblResult.Text = myFunction(strMessage)
End Sub

Private Function myFunction(ByVal strMsg As String) As String
    strMessage = "Give it up . . . Bwah ha ha"
    strMsg = "Help, I've fallen and I can't get up"
    myFunction = strMessage
End Function
```

**Figure 7-23**

    c. The code behind file that VB .NET associates with this form contains the code shown in Figure 7-24. (The Page_Load procedure will automatically run when you run the Web form.) When you run the Web form, what appears in the lblResult Label control?

```
Private Sub Page_Load(ByVal sender As System.Object, ↵
ByVal e As System.EventArgs) Handles MyBase.Load
   Dim strResult As String = "two"
   Dim strChoice As String = "one"
   mySub(strResult, strChoice)
   lblResult.Text = strChoice & strResult
End Sub

Private Sub mySub(ByVal strTwo As String, ByRef strOne As String)
    strTwo = "Give it up . . . Bwah ha ha"
    strOne = "Help, I've fallen and I can't get up"
End Sub
```

**Figure 7-24**

18. Write a function named CompareNumbers that receives two parameters that you declare using the Byte data type. Specify to pass the parameters by value. In the function, write commands that compare the two numbers and return the string value "Numbers are equal" if the values are equal, the string value "Number 1 is greater than Number 2" if the first number is greater than the second number, or "Number 2 is greater than Number 1" if the second number is greater than the first number. If for any reason none of the comparisons are true, the function should return the string "Comparison error."

19. Create a subroutine named SumIntegers that uses a `Do loop` to sum the integers from 1 to 10 and displays the result in a form Label control named lblSum.

20. Create a subroutine named SumIntegers that uses a `For/Next` loop to sum the integers from 1 to 10 and displays the result in a form Label control named lblSum.

21. Write a command to create a new object named objMyObject that instantiates a custom class named MyCustomClass that is defined in the MyProject Web application project.

22. In VB .NET, you use a _____ loop to access the elements in a collection class.

    a. `Do`

    b. `Do While`

    c. `For/Next`

    d. `For Each/Next`

23. Write a command to create a collection named CourseCollection. Create a subroutine named AddCourses that adds the course names "MIS 101," "MIS 341," and "MIS 441" to the collection. Declare a class object named objCourse, then create a subroutine named AppendCourses that steps through the collection, concatenates the text string " is a great course" to the name of each collection element, and displays the concatenated string in a form Label control named lblResult.

# HANDS-ON PROJECTS

To complete the Chapter 7 Hands-on Projects, you will first need to create a Web server application named Projects that you associate with the Projects folder in the Chapter7 folder on your Solution Disk. You will also need to create a Web application project named VBProjects whose application root is the Projects folder in the Chapter7 folder on your Solution Disk. Then you will add the solution for each Hands-on project as an individual Web form to this Web application project. Be sure to configure the Visual Studio .NET IDE so it places the project solution file in the Chapter7\Projects folder on your Solution Disk. Copy the nwlogo.jpg and clearlogo.jpg files to the VBProjects folder that Visual Studio creates when it creates the Web application project.

7

## Project 7-1 Creating the Northwoods University Estimated Costs Form

In this project, you will create the Web form shown in Figure 7-25. This form displays estimated costs for students who are considering attending Northwoods University.

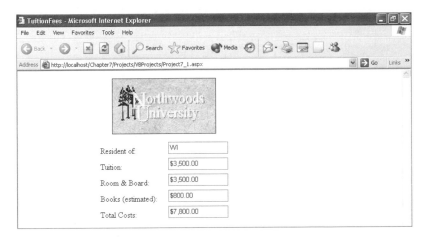

**Figure 7-25**

1. Add to the VBProjects Web application project a new Web form named Project7_1.aspx.

2. Create the Image, Label, and TextBox rich server controls shown in Figure 7-25. Change the ID property values of the TextBox controls to descriptive names.

3. Add a command to create a class variable named strStudentState that represents the student's state of residence, and assign the variable an initial value of "MN."

4. Create a subroutine named ShowTuition that receives the strStudentState variable as a parameter and uses an **If** selection structure to display the student's

tuition amount in the Tuition TextBox control. Northwoods University bases tuition costs on the student's state of residence. Students who are Wisconsin ("WI") residents pay $3,500 for tuition. Students who are Minnesota ("MN") or Illinois ("IL") residents pay $3,700 for tuition, and students who are residents of other locations pay $12,000 for tuition.

5. Add a command to the Page_Load procedure to display the value of the strStudentState variable in the Resident of TextBox control. Also add commands to display the room and board costs ($3,500) and estimated book costs ($800) in the form TextBox controls. (Room and board and book costs are the same for all students regardless of residency.)

6. Add to the Page_Load procedure a command to add the tuition, room and board, and book costs and display the total in the Total Costs TextBox control.

## Project 7-2 Creating the Northwoods University Registration System Logon Form

In this project, you will create the Web form shown in Figure 7-26. This form enables Northwoods University students to log on to the university's registration system.

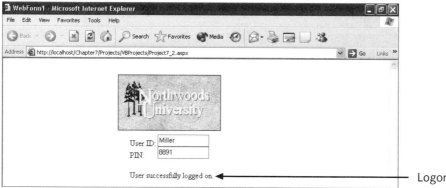

**Figure 7-26**

1. Add to the VBProjects Web application project a new Web form named Project7_2.aspx.

2. Create the Image, Label, and TextBox controls shown in Figure 7-26. Change the ID property values of the TextBox controls to descriptive names.

3. Add the Logon OK Label control that appears below the TextBox control. Delete the Label's Text property value, and change the Label's ID property value to lblLogonOK.

4. Add commands to the Page_Load procedure to initialize the value of the User ID TextBox control to "Miller" and the value of the PIN TextBox control to "8891."

5. Create a subroutine named ProcessLogon that evaluates the values in the User ID and PIN TextBox controls and uses an `If` selection structure to determine whether they are valid. If the User ID/PIN combination is valid, the form's Logon OK Label control displays the text "User successfully logged on." If the combination is not valid, the lblLogonOK Label displays the text "Invalid User ID or PIN." The following values represent valid User ID/PIN combinations:

| User ID | PIN |
|---------|------|
| Miller | 8891 |
| Umato | 1230 |
| Black | 1613 |

6. Add a command in the Page_Load procedure to call the ProcessLogon subroutine.

## Project 7-3 Finishing the Clearwater Traders Order Summary Form

7

In this project, you will complete the Clearwater Traders Order Summary Web form so it looks like Figure 7-27. You will use the SalesTaxClass.vb custom class to calculate the order sales tax and create a custom class that calculates shipping and handling charges. Be sure to display all currency values using a currency format.

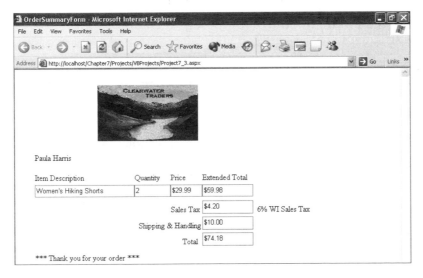

**Figure 7-27**

1. Copy the OrderSummaryForm.aspx and OrderSummaryForm.aspx.vb files from the Chapter7 folder on your Data Disk to the Chapter7\Projects\VBProjects folder on your Solution Disk, then add these files to the VBProjects Web application project. Change the form name to Project7_3.aspx and the form class name to Project7_3.

2. Reposition the existing form controls as necessary, then create the new Label and TextBox control for the Shipping & Handling amount as shown in Figure 7-27. Change the ID property value of the TextBox control to txtSH.

3. Add commands to the Page_Load procedure to initialize the value of the Customer Name, Thank You, and Tax Rate Labels and the Item Description, Quantity, and Price TextBox controls to the values shown in Figure 7-27. Also add a command to calculate and display the value in the Extended Total TextBox control as the product of the price and quantity values.

4. Copy the SalesTaxClass.vb class definition file that you created in the tutorial from the Chapter7\Tutorials\VBConcepts folder on your Solution Disk to the Chapter7\Projects\VBProjects folder on your Solution Disk. Then add the class definition file to the VBProjects Web application project. (If you did not create the class definition file in the tutorial, you can find a completed copy of the SalesTaxClass.vb file in the Chapter7 folder on your Data Disk.) Then use the SalesTaxClass.vb custom class to retrieve the sales tax rate and calculate the sales tax amount. Assume the customer's state of residence is "WI."

5. Create a new custom class called ShippingHandlingClass that has a method named CalcSH. This method receives the order extended total as a parameter and returns the shipping and handling value based on the extended total amount, as follows:

| Extended Total Amount | Shipping & Handling Fee |
| --- | --- |
| Less than $50 | $5.00 |
| $50 – $100 | $10.00 |
| Over $100 | $15.00 |

6. Add a command to the Page_Load procedure that uses the ShippingHandlingClass class to retrieve the shipping and handling fee and then display the value in the Shipping & Handling TextBox control. Also add a command that calculates and displays the order total as the sum of the Extended Total, Sales Tax, and Shipping & Handling values.

## Project 7-4 Creating the Northwoods University Grade Report Form

In this project, you will create the Web form shown in Figure 7-28. This form displays a Northwoods University student's grade report.

1. Add to the VBProjects Web application project a new Web form named Project7_4.aspx.

2. Create the Image, Label, and TextBox controls shown in Figure 7-28. The grade report will always show grades for only three courses. Change the ID property values of the first row of TextBox controls to txtCourse1, txtCredits1, and txtGrade1; the second row of TextBox controls to txtCourse2, txtCredits2, and txtGrade2; and the third row of TextBox controls to txtCourse3, txtCredits3, and txtGrade3. Change the Text property values of the Label and TextBox controls so the controls have the initial values shown in Figure 7-28.

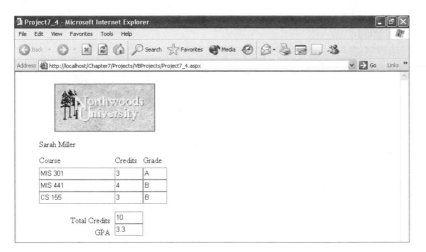

**Figure 7-28**

3. Change the (ID) property value of the Total Credits TextBox control to txtTotalCredits and the (ID) property value of the GPA TextBox control to txtGPA.

4. Add to the Page_Load procedure a command that sums the total credits and displays the sum in the Total Credits TextBox control.

5. To calculate the student's GPA, create a custom class named StudentGPAClass. Include in the class a method named CalcGPA that receives an input parameter that is a collection object. Each collection element represents the number of credits in a course and the associated course grade as a concatenated string. For the grade report in Figure 7-28, this collection will contain the elements "3A," "4B," and "3B." Add commands to the Page_Load procedure to create the collection by concatenating the values in the form TextBox controls.

6. In the StudentGPAClass class, add commands to the CalcGPA method to parse each collection element to determine the credit and grade value for each course. Then calculate the GPA using the following formula:

SUM(Individual Course Credits * Individual Course Grade Points)

SUM(Course Credits)

To determine student grade point averages, Northwoods University awards course grade points as follows:

| Grade | Grade Points |
| --- | --- |
| A | 4 |
| B | 3 |
| C | 2 |
| D | 1 |
| F | 0 |

7

## Project 7-5 Creating a Collection of Perfect Numbers

A perfect number is a number that equals the sum of all numbers that divide equally into it. For example, 6 is perfect because 1, 2, and 3 divide equally into it and their sum is 6. (Mathematicians do not consider a number to be a divisor of itself when evaluating perfect numbers.) In this project, you will create the Web form in Figure 7-29. This Web form creates a collection that contains all of the perfect numbers between 1 and 1,000. The Web form then displays the collection in a form Label as shown, with two blank spaces between each number.

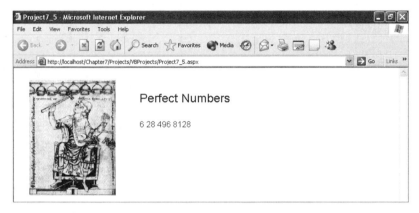

**Figure 7-29**

1. Add to the VBProjects Web application project a new Web form named Project7_5.aspx.

2. Copy the Pythagoras.jpg file from the Chapter7 folder on your Data Disk to the Chapter7\Projects\VBProjects folder on your Solution Disk.

3. Create the Image and Label controls shown in Figure 7-29. Change the ImageUrl property value of the Image control to Pythagoras.jpg, and change the ID property value of the Label control that displays the Perfect Number collection to lblPerfectNumbers.

4. In the form's code behind file, create a collection named PerfectCollection.

5. Create a subroutine named AddPerfect that receives two integer parameters named intStart and intStop. The subroutine adds all of the perfect numbers between intStart and intStop, inclusive, to PerfectCollection. For example, if intStart is 1 and intStop is 100, the AddPerfect subroutine adds to PerfectCollection all perfect numbers between 1 and 100, inclusive. (*Hint*: Use the Mod arithmetic operator.)

6. Create a subroutine named DisplayPerfect that uses a **For Each/Next** loop to step through the PerfectCollection collection and display all the perfect numbers in the form Label control as shown.

7. Add commands to the Page_Load procedure to call the CreatePerfect subroutine, and pass to the subroutine a start value of 1 and a stop value of 1,000. Also add a command to call the DisplayPerfect subroutine. When you run the form, it should look like Figure 7-29.

## CASE PROJECTS

To solve the case projects in this chapter, you must first create a new Web server application that you associate with the Cases folder in the Chapter7 folder on your Solution Disk, and you must modify your Visual Studio .NET IDE so it places all project solution files in the Chapter7\Cases folder on your Solution Disk.

### Case Project 7-1   Ashland Valley Soccer League

Create a Web application project named AshlandProject in the Chapter7\Cases folder on your Solution Disk. Copy all of the files from the Chapter7\Cases\Ashland folder on your Data Disk to the Chapter7\Cases\AshlandProject folder on your Solution Disk. (Visual Studio .NET creates the AshlandProject folder when you create the Web application project.) Then add to the project the AshlandHome.htm static HTML document and the GamesForm.aspx Web form file and its associated code behind file. Modify the Page_Load procedure in the GamesForm.aspx Web form so it contains commands that declare local variables to represent the values in all of the form controls and assigns the initial values to the form controls using VB .NET commands. Assign the game date as the current system date, and assign initial values to the other form controls using literal expressions.

### Case Project 7-2   Al's Body Shop

Create a Web application project named AlsProject in the Chapter7\Cases folder on your Solution Disk. Copy all of the files from the Chapter7\Cases\Als folder on your Data Disk to the Chapter7\Cases\AlsProject folder on your Solution Disk. (Visual Studio .NET creates the AlsProject folder when you create the Web application project.) Then add to the project the AlsHome.htm static HTML document and the WorkOrderForm.aspx Web form file and its associated code behind file. Modify the Page_Load procedure in the WorkOrderForm.aspx Web form so it contains commands that automatically display literal values of your choice for the work order ID, customer name, service description, and price. Also add commands to calculate and display the sales tax amount as 6 percent of the work order service price and the work order total amount as the price plus the sales tax amount. Display all currency values using a currency format.

## Case Project 7-3  Sun-Ray Videos

To complete Case Project 7-3, you must have completed Case Project 6-3 in Chapter 6.

Create a Web application project named SunrayProject in the Chapter7\Cases folder on your Solution Disk. Add to the project the SunrayHome.htm HTML document, and the VideosForm.aspx and RentalsForm.aspx Web forms that you created in Case 6-3. (You first will need to create the Web application project, then copy the files from the Chapter6\Cases\SunrayProject to the Chapter7\Cases\SunrayProject folder that Visual Studio .NET creates, and then add the individual files to the project.)  If necessary, modify all URL references so the files run correctly in the new project location. Then modify the Page_Load procedure in the RentalsForm.aspx Web form so it contains commands that declare local variables to represent the values in all of the form controls, and assigns literal values of your choice as initial values to the form controls using VB .NET commands. Assign the rental date and return date as the current system date. Add a TextBox control to display the rental price, and display the price value using a currency format.

## Case Project 7-4  Learning Technologies, Incorporated

To complete Case Project 7-4, you must have completed Case Project 6-4 in Chapter 6.

Create a Web application project named LtiProject in the Chapter7\Cases folder on your Solution Disk. Add to the project the LTIHome.htm HTML document, and the AuthorsForm.aspx, BooksForm.aspx, WarehouseForm.aspx, and WarehouseQOHForm.aspx Web forms that you created in Case 6-3. (You first will need to create the Web application project, then copy the files from the Chapter6\Cases\LtiProject to the Chapter7\Cases\LtiProject folder that Visual Studio .NET creates, and then add the individual files to the project.) If necessary, modify all URL references so the files run correctly in the new project location. Then modify the Page_Load procedure in the WarehouseQOHForm.aspx Web form so it contains commands that declare local variables to represent the values in all of the form controls and assigns literal values of your choice as initial values to the form controls using VB .NET commands.

# 8

# PROCESSING ASP.NET WEB FORMS AND WORKING WITH SERVER CONTROLS

## In this chapter, you will:

♦ Learn how Web servers use server-side processing to create dynamic Web pages

♦ Learn how to create event handlers for ASP.NET server controls

♦ Understand the differences between HTML server controls and rich server controls

♦ Create HTML elements in Web forms

♦ Create HTML server controls

♦ Create list, radio button, check box, and calendar rich server controls

♦ Learn how to create validation controls

Database-driven Web sites create dynamic Web pages based on user inputs and data retrievals from databases. In this chapter, you will learn how Web forms process user inputs and create dynamic Web pages based on these user inputs. To do this, you will learn how Web forms interact with the Web server. You will also learn more about HTML and rich server controls, how to create controls such as command buttons, radio buttons, and selection lists, and how to create and use validation server controls to validate user inputs.

Before you start your exploration of Web form processing, you will configure your Web server so it contains the application structure you need to create and run Web application projects that you store in the Chapter8\Tutorials folder on your Solution Disk.

To configure your Web server:

1. Start IIS, open the node for the Default Web Site, and make sure that the home directory is associated with the C:\Inetpub\wwwroot folder on your workstation.

2. In IIS, create an application that you associate with the Chapter8 folder on your Solution Disk, and create a second application that is a child application of the Chapter8 application, and that you associate with the Chapter8\Tutorials folder on your Solution Disk. Your Default Web Site configuration should look like Figure 8-1. (Your Default Web Site may display additional applications, virtual directories, and physical directories.)

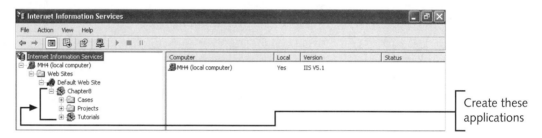

**Figure 8-1**    Default Web site configuration

Now you will start Visual Studio .NET and change its configuration so it saves your Web application project solution files in the Chapter8\Tutorials folder on your Solution Disk. Then you will create a new Web application project named ServerControls. You will delete the project's default WebForm1.aspx Web form, and you will add new Web forms to this project as you learn about server controls throughout the chapter.

To create the new Web application project:

1. Start Visual Studio .NET, click **Tools** on the menu bar, click **Options**, make sure the *Environment* folder is selected in the left pane, select **Projects and Solutions**, click **Browse**, navigate to the Chapter8\Tutorials folder on your Solution Disk, click **Open**, and then click **OK.**

2. Click **File** on the menu bar, point to **New**, click **Project**, make sure the *ASP.NET Web Application* template is selected, and then type **http://localhost/Chapter8/Tutorials/ServerControls** in the *Location* field to specify the new project name. Click **OK** to create the project. After a few moments, the new project appears in the Solution Explorer.

3. Select the **WebForm1.aspx** node in the Solution Explorer, right-click, click **Delete**, and then click **OK** to confirm the deletion.

# CREATING DYNAMIC WEB PAGES USING SERVER-SIDE PROCESSING

Recall that when a user runs a dynamic Web page that uses server-side processing, the Web server receives a request from a user's browser, processes the commands to create the dynamic Web page, and sends the finished Web page back to the user's browser. The following subsections describe server-side processing using HTML forms and Web forms.

## Server-Side Processing Using HTML Forms

Recall that an HTML form contains elements, such as text inputs, radio buttons, and selection lists, that allow the user to enter or select values and then submit these values to the Web server for processing. Figure 8-2 illustrates how the client browser interacts with the Web server to process a standard HTML form.

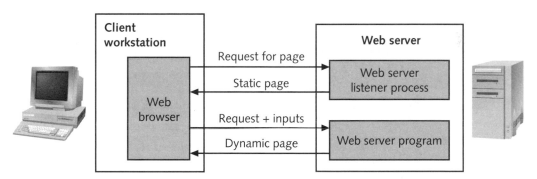

**Figure 8-2**   Standard HTML form processing

The client browser first requests a static Web page from the Web server. The Web server returns the static Web page, which contains an HTML form. The user enters data values in the HTML form and clicks the form's Submit button. This causes the browser to run the Web server servicing program that the HTML form's action attribute specifies. The browser also submits the form input values to the Web server. The servicing program processes the form inputs and creates a dynamic Web page, which the Web server then returns to the client browser.

To work with standard HTML form processing, you will copy a static Web page to the Chapter8\Tutorials folder on your Solution Disk. This Web page contains the Clearwater Traders Customer Order form shown in Figure 8-3.

This HTML form allows Clearwater Traders customers to specify order information, such as the date and form of payment. Now you will copy the file, open it, and examine the page's HTML **<form>** tag.

**Figure 8-3** Clearwater Traders Customer Orders HTML form

To copy and open the static Web page and examine its **<form>** tag:

1. Switch to Windows Explorer, and copy **clearwater_orders.htm**, **process_order.aspx**, and **clearlogo.jpg** from the Chapter8 folder on your Data Disk to the Chapter8\Tutorials folder on your Solution Disk.

2. Switch to Visual Studio .NET, click **File** on the menu bar, point to **Open**, click **File**, navigate to the Chapter8\Tutorials folder on your Solution Disk, select **clearwater_orders.htm**, and then click **Open**. The HTML document appears in the Browser Window.

3. Click the **HTML** tab to view the document in HTML view, and scroll down to approximately line 15 to examine the document's **<form>** tag. The tag defines the form name and action attributes as follows:

```
<form name="frmCustOrders" ↵
action="process_order.aspx">
```

4. Close clearwater_orders.htm in Visual Studio .NET.

The **<form>** tag's action attribute specifies that when the user submits the Customer Order form to the Web server, the browser requests a processing program named process_order.aspx. Now you will start Internet Explorer and observe the HTML form processing steps shown in Figure 8-2.

To observe the HTML form processing steps:

1. Start Internet Explorer, type **http://localhost/Chapter8/Tutorials/ clearwater_orders.htm** in the browser's *Address* field, then press **Enter** to request the static Web page from the Web server. The Web page appears in Internet Explorer and displays the HTML form.

2. Type **12345** in the *Order ID* text input and **7/14/2006** in the *Order Date* text input, and then click **Submit** to submit the HTML form to the Web server. The Web server returns the dynamic Web page, which summarizes the order inputs, to Internet Explorer, as shown in Figure 8-4.

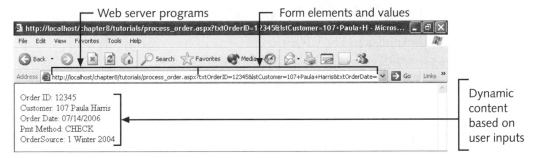

**Figure 8-4**   Dynamic Web page created by processing an HTML form

3. On the dynamic Web page, click the insertion point in the *Address* field, and press **Home** to move to the beginning of the *Address* field text. Note that the URL displays the name of the Web server program, which is the same as the form's action attribute. The URL also displays the form's elements and values, as shown in Figure 8-4.

4. Close Internet Explorer.

You can see that the client browser requests the name of the Web server program, which is process_order.aspx, in the URL address that it submits to the Web server. Following the program name, the URL address displays a question mark (?), followed by a parameter list that shows the names of the HTML form inputs and their associated values. In Figure 8-4, the first form input name is txtOrderID, and its value is "12345." The parameter list separates each form input name and value pair with an ampersand (&), and separates the form input name from the value with an equals sign (=). When the Web server receives this parameter list, it runs the process_order.aspx program using the input parameters and returns the dynamic Web page to the client browser.

HTML form processing proceeds in a linear fashion: When the client browser requests a processing program, the commands in the processing program execute sequentially to create the dynamic Web page. The same commands execute in the same order every time the user requests the processing program. The only way the user interacts with the Web server is by submitting the form. Other user actions, such as entering values in a form input or clicking buttons other than the Submit button, are client-side actions that do not communicate with the Web server.

You use standard HTML form processing to create Web applications that display a series of Web pages that do not require a high level of interaction between the user and the Web server. In contrast, to create dynamic Web pages with richer interfaces that allow the user to interact with the Web server in ways other than just by submitting an HTML form, you use Web forms. Web forms support an event-driven style of processing, in which different event handlers execute in response to specific user events.

## Server-Side Processing Using Web Forms

Recall that a Web form is similar to an HTML form: A Web form can contain HTML tags, text, and form elements. However, a Web form can also contain server controls, which are similar to HTML form elements except that they provide a more direct link between items on a Web page and programs running on the Web server. The following sections explain how a client browser interacts with a Web server during Web form processing and describe the HTML document that ASP.NET generates based on a Web form. The final section describes the Web form processing life cycle.

### Web Form Client/Server Interactions during Form Processing

Figure 8-5 illustrates how a client browser interacts with a Web server when it processes a Web form. The client browser initially requests the Web form using the Web form's URL. The Web server returns to the client browser an HTML document that represents the Web form. The user interacts with the form by performing actions or initiating events, such as entering data values into the form controls or clicking commands buttons on the form. The browser keeps track of all of the events that the user initiates, or raises, on the form.

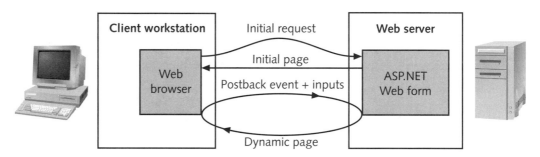

**Figure 8-5**    Web form processing

Certain user events cause the browser to send, or **post**, the Web form back to the server. When the browser posts the Web form back to the server, the server runs the event handlers associated with the events that the user raises on the form. (Recall that an event handler is a series of program commands that execute in response to an event such as clicking a button.) After the Web server runs the event handlers, ASP.NET generates, or **renders**, an HTML document that contains standard HTML tags and elements that represent the Web form's server controls and other Web page elements. This HTML document is called the Web form's **HTML source code**. The Web server returns the Web form's HTML source code to the client browser, which displays the source code as a Web page. The user can then interact with the form and raise form events again. Each time that the browser sends the form to the server and then receives back its HTML source code is called a **round trip**. This process of repeatedly raising events on the client, executing event handlers on the Web server, and then returning the form's HTML source code to the client is called **postback processing**.

Recall that with an HTML form, processing proceeds in a linear fashion: When the client browser requests a processing program, the commands in the processing program execute sequentially to create a dynamic Web page, and then do not execute again until the user submits a form that requests that processing program again. In contrast, in Web form processing, the client browser interacts with the same Web form over the course of many round trips between the client and server. Processing is **event driven**, which means that different commands execute in response to different user actions.

However, Web form processing is not event driven in the same way that programs written in other languages, such as Visual Basic, are event driven. In a Visual Basic program, each time the user raises an event in a program, such as clicking a button, selecting an option button, or changing the text in a text box, the event handler associated with the event immediately executes. If a Web form behaved this way, the form would constantly make round trips between the client and server, and processing would be very slow. In a Web form, the user raises the events in the browser, but the event handler associated with each event does not execute until the browser posts the Web form back to the Web server.

To post the Web form back to the server, the user must perform an action that raises the **postback event**. What actions raise the postback event? Typically button controls that have **click events**, which are events that the user raises when he or she clicks the button, automatically raise the postback event. For a Web form that has only one TextBox control, pressing the Enter key raises the postback event.

To work with postback processing in a Web form, you will use the CustomerOrders.aspx Web form shown in Figure 8-6.

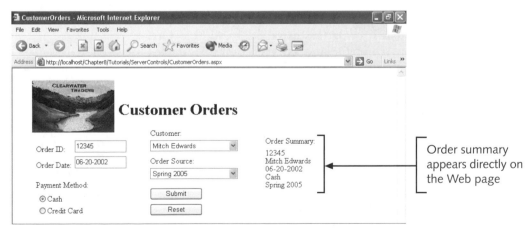

**Figure 8-6**   CustomerOrders.aspx Web form

This Web form looks similar to the HTML form in Figure 8-3, but it is a Web form and not an HTML form. When the form first appears, it automatically displays values for the *Order ID* and *Order Date*. The user can change these values, if necessary, and select the *Payment Method (Cash or Credit Card)*, *Customer*, and *Order Source*. When the user clicks the Submit button, the form raises a postback event that posts the Web form to the Web server. The Web server executes the Submit button event handler, which displays the Order Summary information. The Order Summary information, which summarizes the form's input values in Label controls, appears directly on the Web form. The Web server then posts the Web form back to the user's browser.

When the user clicks the Reset button, the form raises the postback event and the Web server executes the Reset button event handler. The Reset button event handler clears the Order Summary information and option button selection. The Web server then posts the Web form back to the browser. The user can then change the form inputs and click either the Submit or Reset button again. Each time the user clicks a button, the browser posts the form to the Web server, and the Web server processes the button's event handler and posts the form back to the browser. Now you will add this Web form to the ServerControls Web application project that you created earlier.

To add the Web form to your project:

1. Switch to Windows Explorer and copy the following three files from the Chapter8 folder on your Data Disk to the Chapter8\Tutorials\ServerControls folder on your Solution Disk: **clearlogo.jpg**, **CustomerOrders.aspx**, and **CustomerOrders.aspx.vb**.

2. Switch back to Visual Studio .NET, select the **ServerControls** project node in the Solution Explorer, right-click, point to **Add**, and then click **Add Existing Item**. The Add Existing Item – ServerControls dialog box opens.

3. Navigate to the Chapter8\Tutorials\ServerControls folder on your Solution Disk, open the **Files of type** list, and select **All Files (\*.\*)**. Select **CustomerOrders.aspx**, press and hold **Ctrl**, select **CustomerOrders.aspx.vb**, and then click **Open**. The CustomerOrders.aspx Web form appears in the project tree.

If an error message stating "Unable to get file" appears, make sure that you navigate to the Chapter8\Tutorials\ServerControls folder on your Solution Disk rather than the Chapter8/Tutorials/ServerControls URL on your Web server.

4. Right-click the **CustomerOrders.aspx** node in the Solution Explorer, and then click **Set As Start Page**.

Recall that when you created HTML forms in Chapter 2, you created opening and closing `<form>` tags to enclose the tags that defined the form elements. When you view a Web form in HTML view, it also has `<form>` tags, but Web form tags have slightly different attribute values than HTML form tags. Now you will view the Web form's `<form>` tags.

To view the Web form's `<form>` tags:

1. In the Visual Studio .NET IDE, make sure that the *CustomerOrder.aspx* node is selected in the Solution Explorer, and then click the **View Designer** button ▤ on the Solution Explorer toolbar. The form appears in Design view.

2. Click the **HTML** tab at the bottom of the window to display the Web form's underlying HTML tags and elements.

Note that the opening `<form>` tag appears within the HTML document's `<body>` tags and has the following syntax:

```
<form id="Form1" method="post" runat="server">
```

In this syntax, Form1 is the form's default ID attribute value. The **method attribute** specifies how the browser passes the values of the form inputs to the Web server and can have one of two possible values: "get" or "post." If the method attribute value is "get," which is the default value, then the browser sends the form input values to the Web server as a parameter list, and the form input values appear in the URL as shown in Figure 8-4. If the method attribute value is "post," the browser submits the form input values directly to the Web server as though the user enters them from the keyboard.

The **runat attribute** specifies where the system processes the Web form's code. The runat attribute can have the values "client," which is the default value, or "server." If you omit the runat attribute, the default value is "client," the form tag looks like a standard HTML form tag, and the Web browser processes the Web form just as it processes an ordinary HTML form. When the runat attribute value is "server," the Web browser processes the Web form using postback processing.

Note that the tags that define the Web form's rich server controls appear within the `<form>` tags. For example, the following tag defines the Label control that displays the customer name in the order summary:

```
<asp:Label id="lblCustomer" style="style_definition" ↵
runat=" server"></asp:Label>
```

HTML server controls and rich server controls normally appear within Web forms, but you can also create tags that define server controls anywhere within an HTML document. For example, you could programmatically insert the text that defines the `<asp:Label>` tag anywhere in an HTML document. You could not reference such a tag in commands in a Web form code behind file or perform dynamic operations such as changing the Label control's Text property, but the Label server control would still appear in the HTML document. You cannot reference the element in the code behind file because the element is not defined in the Web form's Declarations block.

To become familiar with postback processing, you will run the Web form, enter input values, and raise events.

To perform postback processing:

1. In Visual Studio .NET, click the **Start** button ▶ to run the Web form. The Web form appears in Internet Explorer. If necessary, maximize the Internet Explorer window. Note that the value "12345" appears as the Order ID value, and the current date appears for the Order Date value. Also note that the Order Summary information does not yet appear.

2. Select the **Cash** option button, select **Mitch Edwards** for the Customer ID, select **Winter 2004** for the Order Source ID, and then click **Submit** to raise the postback event and post the Web form to the server. The Web server executes the Submit button event handler, then posts the Web form back to your browser, which displays the Order Summary information. The Order Summary information appears similar to the information shown in Figure 8-6.

3. Click the **Reset** button to raise the postback event and post the Web form to the server. The Web server executes the Reset button event handler, which clears the Order Summary information and the option button selection, and then posts the Web form back to your browser.

4. Select the **Credit Card** option button and then click **Submit** again. The Web server executes the Submit button event handler again and displays the modified Order Summary information, which now shows the payment method value as "Credit Card."

## Viewing a Web Form's Underlying HTML Document

Recall that when a client browser requests a Web form from a Web server, ASP.NET renders the Web form's HTML source code. The HTML source code contains standard HTML form element tags rather than the server control tags that appear in HTML view in the Visual Studio .NET Browser Window. For example, suppose a Web developer creates a Web form that defines an Image server control. In HTML view, the tag for this control appears as follows:

```
<asp:Image id="Image1" style="style_specification" ↵
ImageUrl="clearlogo.jpg"></asp:Image>
```

The *style_specification* refers to the control's style attributes. HTML style attributes are described in Chapter 2.

When ASP.NET renders the Web form's source code, it translates this definition into the following <img> tag that defines a standard HTML graphic image:

```
<img id="Image1" src="clearlogo.jpg" border="0" ↵
style="style_specification" />
```

Web developers can create **Button** rich server controls on Web forms, and ASP.NET translates these controls into standard HTML button elements. Recall that every Button control on a Web form raises the postback event that posts the Web form to the Web server. Therefore, when ASP.NET renders the Web form's HTML source code, it renders every Button server control as a Submit button, which causes the browser to submit the form to the Web server.

Now you will view the HTML source code for the Customer Order Web form that currently appears in Internet Explorer and see how ASP.NET translates the Web form control specifications to standard HTML element tags. To view the underlying HTML source code for any Web page, you click View on the browser menu bar, and then click Source.

To view the Web form's HTML source code:

1. Make sure that the Customer Orders form still appears in Internet Explorer, click **View** on the menu bar, and then click **Source**. The CustomerOrders[1] – Notepad window opens, which shows the HTML tags and text that define the Customer Orders Web page.

2. Scroll down to the opening `<form>` tag, which appears as follows:

```
<form name="Form1" method="post" ↵
action="CustomerOrders.aspx" id="Form1">
```

Note that this tag specifies that the browser calls the CustomerOrders.aspx Web form when the user submits the form to the server.

3. Scroll down to the tag that defines the Submit button on the Web form, which appears as follows:

```
<input type="submit" name="cmdSubmit" value="Submit" ↵
id="cmdSubmit" style="style_specification" />
```

Note that this tag specifies the Submit button as a standard Submit button form element.

Standard HTML forms are **stateless**, which means that the HTML form does not store or retain form input values after the browser submits the form to the Web server. However, when you processed the Customer Orders Web form, the form retained the values that you selected for the *Payment Method*, *Customer ID*, and *Order Source ID*. ASP.NET saves Web form and control property values, or **view states**, between round trips. ASP.NET also retains information that specifies whether the Web form is appearing to the user for the first time or whether the form is being posted back to the user.

To save a Web form's view state and form status information, ASP.NET uses a hidden form input called the **ViewState input**. (Recall from Chapter 2 that a hidden form input is a form input that contains data values that are not visible to the user.) The Web server automatically adds to the HTML source code the ViewState input that the server renders for the Web form. Now you will view the ViewState input in the Web form's HTML source code.

To view the ViewState input:

1. In Notepad, scroll up to the ViewState input definition, which appears just below the opening `<form>` tag. This definition appears as follows:

```
<input type="hidden" name="__VIEWSTATE" ↵
value="value_specification" />
```

2. Close Notepad, and then close Internet Explorer.

3. In Visual Studio .NET, close the Output window. (When you run a form in Visual Studio .NET, compile and debugging messages appear in the Output window. You will need to close the Output window each time after you run a form.)

In this tag, the *value_specification* is an encoded string of letters and numbers that store information about the Web form, such as the current property values of server controls at the time the page is generated, and whether the form is appearing to the user for the first time or is being posted back. The ViewState input retains all of the property values of server controls, including the control's ID, value, size, font, and so forth.

## The Web Form Processing Life Cycle

So far you have learned that during Web form processing, the Web server receives a request for a Web form from a client browser. If the Web server receives the request for the first time, the Web server renders the Web form's HTML source code and posts it to the client. If the Web server receives the request a second or subsequent time as a result of the postback event, the Web server processes the form inputs, executes the event handlers associated with events that the user performed on the form, and then renders the Web form's HTML source code and posts it back to the client.

To develop Web forms, you must understand exactly how ASP.NET implements these processes. Table 8-1 summarizes the Web form processing stages.

**Table 8-1** Web form processing stages

| Stage | Description | Actions |
|-------|-------------|---------|
| ASP.NET Page Framework Initialization | Creates the form objects and raises the form's Page_Init event | 1. Initializes the class and object definitions in the form's code behind file<br>2. For postback request, loads ViewState data into form<br>3. Executes the Page_Init procedure |
| User Code Initialization | Raises the form's Page_Load event | 1. Loads form objects<br>2. Executes the Page_Load procedure |
| Validation | Invokes the Validate method of any server controls | 1. Validates control values |

**Table 8-1**   Web form processing stages (continued)

| Stage | Description | Actions |
| --- | --- | --- |
| Event Handling | Executes the form's event handlers raised by user events | 1. For postback requests, executes event handlers<br>2. For postback requests, executes the event handler associated with the control that raised the postback event<br>3. Saves current control property values in the ViewState hidden input<br>4. Renders the form's HTML source code and forwards it to the client browser |
| Cleanup | Raises a Dispose event | 1. Closes files and database connections<br>2. Destroys objects used to render HTML source code |

The actions that the system performs during each stage depend on whether the user's request is a first-time request or a postback request. In the *ASP.NET Framework Initialization* stage, for both first time and postback requests, ASP.NET initializes the form object class and form objects. Next, for postback requests only, ASP.NET reads the values in the ViewState hidden input, and updates the values of the form's server controls if any of the values were changed based on user inputs.

In the next initialization stage step, ASP.NET executes the Page_Init procedure. When a Web developer creates a new Web form, ASP.NET automatically creates a template for the Page_Init procedure. (The code for this procedure appears in the **Web Form Designer Generated Code** section in the Web form's code behind file.) This template does not contain any commands, and so far, you have not added any commands to this procedure. When you create Web pages that interact with databases, you will add commands to the Page_Init procedure that create database connections.

In the *User Code Initialization* stage, ASP.NET loads the form objects into the Web server's memory and then executes the Page_Load procedure. Recall that in Chapters 6 and 7, you added commands to the Page_Load procedure to initialize form control property values and call procedures.

In the *Validation* stage, the Web server runs the code that the developer associates with validation controls. (Recall that validation controls are server controls that validate Web form user inputs. You will learn how to create validation server controls later in this chapter.) The Validation stage executes during postback processing only after the user has entered form inputs.

8

In the *Event Handling* stage, the Web server executes the event handlers that are associated with events that the user raised on the form. For example, if the user changes the text in a text input and the developer has written an event handler associated with the event of changing the text in this input, this event handler executes. Recall that some events, such as clicking a button, raise the postback event that posts the Web form to the Web server. The event handler that the system associates with the control that raises the postback event always executes last. For example, suppose you change the text in a form input, and then click a button on the form. Clicking the button raises the postback event and posts the form to the Web server. When the form event handlers execute, the event handler associated with changing the input text executes first, and the event handler associated with clicking the button executes last.

If a user raises multiple events on a form, the event handlers execute in the order in which they appear in the form's HTML code. For example, if the user changes the text in two different text inputs on the form, the event handlers for these events execute in the order in which the text input tags appear in the HTML source code.

After all of the event handlers execute, ASP.NET renders the form's HTML source code, which contains the HTML tags and text to represent the Web form. Then it forwards the rendered HTML document to the client browser. After ASP.NET renders the form's HTML source code, the system no longer needs the form objects. It then performs the final *Cleanup* stage, which closes files and database connections associated with the form. During this stage, ASP.NET also destroys all of the form objects and makes their memory space available for other processing tasks.

To work with the Web form processing life cycle, you will modify the CustomerOrders.aspx Web form by adding a command to the Page_Init procedure. Currently, the Page_Load procedure contains commands that initialize the value of the *Order ID* TextBox control to "12345" and the value of the *Order Date* TextBox control to the current date. You will move the command that initializes the Order ID value to the Page_Init procedure.

To move the command to the Page_Init procedure:

1. If necessary, select the *CustomerOrders.aspx* node in the Solution Explorer, and then click the **View Code** button ▤ to display the Web form's code behind file.

2. Scroll down in the Code editor and click the **plus sign** beside the node titled *Web Form Designer Generated Code*. A code block titled `#Region "Web Form Designer Generated Code "` appears in the Code editor. This code block contains procedure definitions and commands that ASP.NET uses to initialize Web forms. It also contains the template for the Page_Init procedure.

3. To move the command from the Page_Load procedure to the Page_Init procedure, scroll down in the Code editor until you see the Page_Load procedure code and select the command `txtOrderID.Text = 12345`. (This command is within an `If` decision control structure. Don't worry about how this code works for now.)

4. Click **Edit** on the menu bar, click **Cut**, place the insertion point after the `Initialize_Component()` command in the Page_Init procedure, and press **Enter** to create a new blank line.

5. Click **Edit** on the menu bar, and then click **Paste**. The command to initialize the value in the TextBox control that displays the Order ID value now appears in the Page_Init procedure.

Now you will set breakpoints on the first commands in the Page_Init and Page_Load procedures, and on the first commands in the Submit and Reset button event handlers in the code behind file. (For now, do not worry about how the event handlers work; you will learn how to create event handlers a little later in the chapter.) Then you will run the form and observe how the Web form moves through the processing stages the first time the browser requests the Web form.

To set breakpoints, run the form, and observe how it moves through the processing stages:

1. In the Code editor, create breakpoints on the following commands:

| Procedure | Command |
|---|---|
| Page_Init | `txtOrderID.Text = 12345` |
| Page_Load | `If IsPostBack = False Then` |
| cmdSubmit_Click | `lblSummaryLabel.Visible = True` |
| cmdReset_Click | `txtOrderDate.Text = DateString` |

2. Click the **Start** button ▶ to run the form. The Web form process begins with the ASP.NET Framework Initialization stage, which runs the Page_Init procedure, so the execution arrow pauses on the breakpoint in the Page_Init procedure.

3. Click the **Continue** button ▶ to resume execution. The Web form process moves to the User Code Initialization stage, which executes the Page_Load procedure, so the execution arrow pauses on the breakpoint on the first command in the Page_Load procedure.

4. Click the **Continue** button ▶ to resume execution. Because this is the first time the client browser requests the Web form, none of the event handlers execute, and the Web form appears in Internet Explorer.

5. Select the **Cash** option button, accept the default values for the Customer and Order Source, and then click **Submit** to post the Web form back to the Web server. The execution arrow appears on the first command in the Page_Init procedure.

Because the Submit button raises the postback event and posts the Web form back to the Web server, a new Web form processing cycle begins, and the execution arrow appears on the first command in the Page_Init procedure. Now you will continue to execute the form and observe how the Web form moves through the processing stages during a postback request. Because you clicked the Submit button, the commands in the Submit button's event handler will execute. The commands in this event handler initialize and display the values that appear in the Order Summary text on the Web page.

To observe the processing stages during a postback request:

1. Currently the execution arrow is on the first command in the Page_Init procedure. Click the **Continue** button ▶ to resume execution. The execution arrow moves to the first command in the Page_Load procedure again.

2. Click the **Continue** button ▶ again to resume execution. The execution arrow moves to the first command in the cmdSubmit_Click procedure. Because this is a postback request and you clicked the Submit button on the Web form, the commands for the Submit button's event handler execute. These commands display the Order Summary information on the Web page.

3. Click the **Continue** button ▶ again to resume execution. The Web form appears in Internet Explorer and displays the Order Summary information on the Web page.

4. Click the **Reset** button. This raises the postback event again, so the execution arrow again appears on the breakpoint on the command in the Page_Init procedure.

5. Click the **Continue** button ▶ to resume execution. The execution arrow moves to the breakpoint on the first command in the Page_Load procedure again.

6. Click the **Continue** button ▶ again to resume execution. The execution arrow moves to the breakpoint on the first command in the cmdReset_Click procedure. Because this is a postback request and you clicked the Reset button on the Web form, the commands for the Reset button's event handler execute. These commands clear the Order Summary items.

7. Click the **Continue** button ▶ again to resume execution. The Web form appears in Internet Explorer, and the Order Summary information no longer appears on the Web page.

8. Close Internet Explorer, and clear all breakpoints in Visual Studio .NET.

## Determining Web Form Processing Status

Sometimes during Web form processing, you need to determine whether execution is occurring as a result of a first-time request or as a result of a postback request. For example, in the CustomerOrders.aspx Web form, the command in the Page_Load procedure that displays the *Order Date* as the current system date executes only for first-time requests. To determine whether execution is a result of a first-time request or a postback request, you use the IsPostBack property. The **IsPostBack property** is a Boolean property that has the value True if page processing is a result of a postback request and has the value False if page processing is a result of a first-time request. To use the IsPostBack property to determine the Web form's processing status, you create an `If` decision control structure using the following syntax:

```
If IsPostBack = False Then
     commands_to_execute_for_first_time_requests
Else
     commands_to_execute_for_postback_requests
End If
```

You will gain experience using the IsPostBack property in the next section, which describes how to create Web form event handlers.

## CREATING EVENT HANDLERS IN WEB FORMS

When you create a Web form, you usually first create a design sketch of how the Web form will look. Then you open the Web form in the Design window in Design view, and create and position the Web form controls. Finally, you add event handlers to the form controls to control the form processing. Recall that event handlers are procedures that execute in response to user events such as clicking a button or changing the text in a TextBox control. You first learned how to create event handlers in JavaScript client-side scripts. An event handler has an associated control, such as a button, and an associated event, such as the user clicking the button.

To create an event handler in a Web form, you open the Web form in the Design window in Design view and then double-click the control to which you want to add an event handler. This displays a template for the control's event handler in the form's code behind file in the Code editor. In a Web form, a server control usually has only one event for which you can create an event handler. This event is the most common event that users perform on the control, such as clicking a Button control or changing the text in a TextBox control. Then, you add the event handler's VB .NET commands to the template.

To see the event for each control on a Web form, you open the Web form's code behind file in the Code editor, open the *Class* list and select the control, and then open the *Method* list, which displays the control's event in boldface type. (Recall that the *Class* list appears on the top border of the Code editor window on the left side, and the *Method* list appears on the top border of the Code editor window on the right side.)

Another way to create an event handler is to select the control in the *Class* list, and then select the control's event in the *Method* list.

An event handler has the following general syntax:

```
Private Sub controlID_Event(parameter_list) ↵
Handles controlID.Event
     event_handler_commands
End Sub
```

In this syntax, *controlID* is the value of the control's ID property that you specify in the Properties Window when you create the control. *Event* is the name of the event that you associate with the event handler. The *parameter_list* must include the parameters that ASP.NET expects for the event handler. The `Handles` keyword links the control and event to the procedure. The *event_handler_commands* are any legal VB .NET commands that the Web developer adds to the event handler.

 You can manually type the code for an event handler, including the parameter list and `Handles` keyword, in the Code editor. However, it is easier and more accurate to let Visual Studio .NET create the event handler template. To have Visual Studio .NET generate the template, double-click the form control in Design view.

Now you will add event handler templates to the Customer Orders form for events that the user raises when he or she changes the text in the Order ID and Order Date TextBox controls. These event handlers will display the text string "(changed)" after the Order ID and Order Date values in the Order Summary. First you will create the event handler template for the Order ID and Order Date TextBox controls.

To add the event handler templates to the Web form:

1. In Visual Studio .NET, click the **CustomerOrders.aspx** tab to display the Web form. If necessary, click the Design tab to display the form in Design view.

2. To create the event handler template for the *Order ID* TextBox control, double-click the **txtOrderID** TextBox control that appears just to the right of the *Order ID* Label control. The Code editor opens and displays the event handler template for the TextBox control's default event.

3. To create the event handler template for the *Order Date* TextBox control, open the Class list at the top-left side of the Code editor window (see Figure 8-7) and select **txtOrderDate**. Then open the *Method* list that at the top-right side of the Code editor window (see Figure 8-7), and select **TextChanged**. The event handler template appears in the Code editor.

4. Save the Web form.

Now you will add the VB .NET commands for the event handlers. If the user changes the value of the Order ID or Order Date, you want the TextBox control event handlers to append the text string "(changed)" to the end of these values in the Order Summary. To do this, you will create class variables to represent the text that the Order Summary Labels display. (Recall that you use class variables for variable values that must be visible to multiple procedures within a form.) You will add commands to the Page_Load procedure that assign to these variables the values that appear in the *Order ID* and *Order Date* TextBox controls. If the user changes the *Order ID* or *Order Date* values, the event handlers for the TextChanged events for these controls modify these class variables so that the variables store the TextBox control values plus the text string "(changed)." Then you will modify the commands in the Submit button event handler so the Order Summary Label controls display the class variable values.

To add the commands for the event handlers:

1. In the CustomerOrders.aspx.vb code behind file in the Code editor, add the following commands to the end of the Declarations block. These commands declare the class variables that will display the *Order ID* and *Order Date* Order Summary information.

```
Private strOrderIDValue As String
Private strOrderDateValue As String
```

2. Scroll down in the Code editor to the Page_Load procedure, and add the following commands as the last two commands of the procedure, just before the `End Sub` command:

```
strOrderIDValue = txtOrderID.Text
strOrderDateValue = txtOrderDate.Text
```

3. Scroll down in the Code editor to the new event handler templates and add the commands shown in Figure 8-7 to the event handler templates.

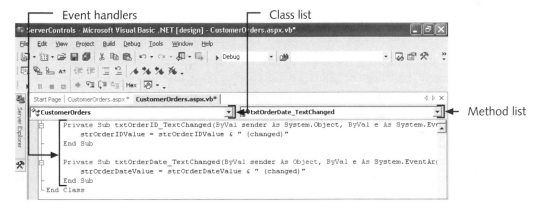

**Figure 8-7**    Event handler commands

4. Scroll up in the Code editor to the Submit button event handler (`Private Sub cmdSubmit_Click`), and modify the commands that display the Label controls in the Order Summary so they appear as follows:

```
lblOrderID.Text = strOrderIDValue
lblOrderDate.Text = strOrderDateValue
```

Now you will add breakpoints to your code behind file and then run the project. (Recall that when you run a project in Visual Studio .NET, the IDE automatically saves your file.) You will change the values in the *Order ID* and *Order Date* text inputs, and examine how the event handlers execute.

To examine how the event handlers execute:

1. Create a breakpoint on the following command in the cmdSubmit_Click procedure: `lblOrderID.Text = strOrderIDValue`.

2. Create breakpoints on the first commands in the txtOrderID_TextChanged and txtOrderDate_TextChanged event handlers.

3. Click the **Start** button ▶ to run the project. The Customer Orders form appears in Internet Explorer. If necessary, maximize the window.

4. Change the Order ID value to **12346**, change the *Order Date* value so the year is one year in the future from today, select the **Cash** option button, and accept the default values for the *Customer* and *Order Source*.

5. Click **Submit** to post the Web form back to the Web server. The execution arrow appears on the breakpoint in the txtOrderID_TextChanged event handler.

6. Click the **Continue** button ▶ to resume execution. The execution arrow appears on the breakpoint in the txtOrderDate_TextChanged event handler.

7. Click the **Continue** button ▶ to resume execution. The execution arrow appears on the breakpoint in the cmdSubmit_Click event handler.

8. Click the **Continue** button ▶ to resume execution. The Web form appears in Internet Explorer, and the Order Summary displays the text string "(changed)" after the modified *Order ID* and *Order Date* values. Close Internet Explorer. Do not clear the breakpoints.

Note that the event handler for the txtOrderID_TextChanged event executes first and the event handler for the textOrderDate_TextChanged event executes second. Recall that if a user raises multiple events on a form, the event handlers execute in the order in which the tags for their associated controls appear in the form in the Design window in HTML view. Now you will open the Web form in HTML view, and note the order that the controls appear in HTML view. Sometimes it is difficult to find HTML tags for server controls, because Visual Studio .NET does not place the tag for each control on a separate line in the HTML editor. To make it easier to find the tags, you will use the Visual Studio .NET Find and Replace feature.

To view the order of the control tags:

1. In Visual Studio .NET, select the **CustomerOrders.aspx** tab, and then click the **HTML** tab to view the Web form in HTML view.

2. Click **Edit** on the menu bar, point to **Find and Replace**, and then click **Find**. To find the tag for the *Order ID* TextBox control, type **<asp:textbox id="txtOrderID"** in the *Find what* field, and then click **Find Next**. The search text appears highlighted in the HTML editor.

Sometimes Visual Studio .NET removes quotation marks that enclose attribute values. If the search does not find the tag, remove the quotation marks around "txtOrderID" in the Find what field, then click Find Next.

3. To find the tag for the *Order Date* TextBox control, type **<asp:textbox id="txtOrderDate"** in the *Find what* field, and then click **Find Next**. The search text appears highlighted in the HTML editor.

If the search does not find the tag, remove the quotation marks around "txtOrderDate" in the Find what field, then click Find Next.

4. Click **Close** to close the Find dialog box.

Note that in the HTML editor, the tag for the *Order ID* TextBox control appears before the tag for the *Order Date* TextBox control. This specifies the order in which the controls' event handlers execute. Now you will change the order of the tags so the *Order Date* TextBox tag appears before the *Order ID* TextBox tag. (Changing the order that the control tags appear in HTML view will not change the appearance of the form. Each control's style attribute specifies the control's position on the Web page.)

To change the order of the TextBox tags:

1. To move the tag for the *Order Date* TextBox control, select all of the text in the tag that begins **<asp:Textbox id="txtOrderDate"** through the tag's closing **</ asp:Textbox>** tag, click **Edit** on the menu bar, and then click **Cut**.

2. Place the insertion point just before the opening angle bracket for the **<asp:Textbox id="txtOrderID"** tag, and press **Enter** two times to create a new blank line just above the tag.

3. Place the insertion point on the new blank line. Click **Edit** on the menu bar, and then click **Paste** to paste the tag for the *Order Date* TextBox control so it appears before the tag for the *Order ID* TextBox control.

Now you will run the form again and confirm that changing the order of the HTML tags changes the order in which the event handlers execute. Now the txtOrderDate_TextChanged event handler should execute first, and the txtOrderID_TextChanged event handler should execute second. As before, the event handler for the Submit button executes last, because this event raised the postback event.

To run the form and view the revised order that the event handlers execute:

1. Click the **Start** button ▶ to run the project. The Customer Orders form appears in Internet Explorer. If necessary, maximize the window.

2. Change the *Order ID* value to **12346**, change the *Order Date* value so the year is one year in the future from today, select the **Cash** option button, and accept the default values for *Customer* and *Order Source*.

3. Click **Submit** to post the Web form back to the Web server. The execution arrow now appears on the breakpoint in the txtOrderDate_TextChanged event handler. Because you placed the tag for the *Order Date* TextBox control so it appears first, its event handler now executes first.

4. Click the **Continue** button ▶ to resume execution. The execution arrow appears on the breakpoint in the txtOrderID_TextChanged event handler, again confirming that the order of the HTML tags specifies the order that the control event handlers execute.

5. Click the **Continue** button ▶ to resume execution. The execution arrow appears on the breakpoint in the cmdSubmit_Click event handler.

6. Click the **Continue** button ▶ to resume execution. The Web form appears in Internet Explorer, and the Order Summary displays the text string "(changed)" after the modified *Order ID* and *Order Date* values.

7. Close Internet Explorer.

8. Clear all of the breakpoints in CustomerOrders.aspx. Because you are finished working with the CustomerOrders.aspx Web form, close all open windows in the Browser Window.

## CREATING HTML ELEMENTS AND SERVER CONTROLS IN WEB FORMS

Web forms can contain standard HTML elements, such as text and tags that represent images, text inputs, hyperlinks, and so forth. Web forms can also contain HTML server controls. HTML server controls are almost identical to HTML form elements, except they have associated event handlers that run on the server. Web forms can also contain rich server controls, which are similar to HTML server controls, except that they have a wider array of properties and richer functionality. (Recall that rich server controls are also sometimes called Web server controls.) When you create a Web form, how do you decide when to use standard HTML elements, HTML server controls, or rich server controls?

A disadvantage of rich server controls is that they require more processing than HTML form elements or HTML server controls. Rich server controls require more processing because ASP.NET must render the associated HTML source code to represent the control. To minimize Web server processing and optimize the performance of your Web applications, you should use standard HTML elements to create items that program commands do not reference or modify, such as static labels and images.

HTML elements do not support server-side processing, and you cannot dynamically change the appearance of an HTML element. In contrast, HTML server controls and rich server controls have associated server-side event handlers, and you can dynamically change HTML server control and rich server control values during postback processing. Therefore, use HTML server controls or rich server controls for items for which you want to create event handlers or whose properties you want to change during form processing.

HTML server controls use the HTML DOM that you learned about in Chapter 3, so their properties are very similar to HTML form element properties. In contrast, rich server controls are VB .NET objects and have different properties. In general, VB .NET objects have a more extensive set of properties than HTML DOM objects, and VB .NET programmers find it easier to configure and reference rich server controls than HTML DOM objects using VB .NET commands. Therefore, you should usually use rich server controls rather than HTML server controls to create items that program commands reference or modify, such as user input values or dynamic labels that display messages to the user. Use HTML server controls when there is no comparable rich server control. For example, there is no rich server control that allows the user to upload files to a specified location. If you want to allow users to upload files easily, you must create this control as an HTML server control.

The following sections describe how to create standard HTML elements, HTML server controls, and rich server controls in Web forms. To learn how to work with these elements and controls, you will use a Web form named CustomerOrdersControls.aspx that will contain many of the same elements as the Customer Orders Web form in Figure 8-6. Now you will create this Web form.

To create the CustomerOrdersControls.aspx Web form:

1. In Visual Studio .NET, right-click the **ServerControls** node in the Solution Explorer, point to **Add**, and then click **Add Web Form**.

2. Make sure that the *Web Form* template is selected, change the *Name* field value to **CustomerOrdersControls.aspx**, and then click **Open**. After a few moments, the new CustomerOrdersControls.aspx Web form appears in the Solution Explorer project tree and in the Browser Window.

3. Right-click the **CustomerOrdersControls.aspx** node in the Solution Explorer, and then click **Set As Start Page**.

## CREATING HTML ELEMENTS IN WEB FORMS

In Visual Studio .NET, you can easily create HTML elements on a Web form by selecting the desired element on the Toolbox HTML tab and then drawing the element on the form's Design view display. Figure 8-8 shows the elements in the HTML Toolbox that you can add to Web forms.

The Toolbox contains tools to create HTML elements that you learned about in Chapter 2, such as buttons, text fields (which Chapter 2 calls text inputs), text areas, and radio buttons. When you select one of the Toolbox tools and draw its associated element on the form, Visual Studio .NET creates the corresponding HTML tag. When you modify the element's attributes using the Properties Window, Visual Studio .NET modifies the HTML tag attributes and style tag attributes to reflect the modified attribute values.

The HTML Toolbox also contains two elements that are not standard HTML elements: Label and File Field. An HTML **Label element** represents a distinct text element that appears on the Web form. When you create a Label element on a Web form, Visual Studio .NET creates a **<div> tag**, which creates a division in the Web page that encloses the Label element's text. An HTML **File Field element** consists of a text input and a Browse button. When the user clicks Browse, the system allows the user to select a file from his or her local workstation and upload the file to a location on the Web server. When you create a File Field element, Visual Studio .NET creates an **<input>** tag of type "file," which you will learn about later in the chapter.

8

**Figure 8-8** HTML form elements that you can add to Web forms

The HTML Toolbox tab also contains Flow Layout Panel and Grid Layout Panel selections. Recall that in a standard HTML document, all of the form elements appear in a flow layout style, which means that the elements appear in the same order as the underlying HTML tags. In Web forms, you usually use a grid layout style, which means that Visual Studio .NET specifies the element's location on the Web form using an absolute position. An absolute position specifies the element's location using values in the element's style tag that specify the number of pixels that the element appears from the top and left edges of the form.

When you display the grid in the Design window in Design view, you automatically specify that the Web form elements use a grid layout style.

When you create a **Flow Layout Panel** on a Web form, Visual Studio .NET creates a distinct area on the Web form in which the elements appear within a flow layout. Similarly, when you create a **Grid Layout Panel** on a Web form, Visual Studio .NET creates a distinct area in which the elements appear within a grid layout. To specify these panels, Visual Studio .NET creates a `<div>` tag, then adds the elements that appear in the panel, and formats the elements using either a flow or grid layout. You would create a Flow Layout or Grid Layout panel to specify an area on the Web form in which the elements appear in specific positions relative to one another, but which allows the entire panel to move to different locations on the Web form. For example, you would use a panel to create a toolbar. The toolbar contains buttons that remain in the same positions relative to each other, but the user can move the toolbar to a different position on the Web form.

To gain experience creating HTML elements in a Web form, you will create and configure elements to represent the Clearwater Traders logo image, form title, and form input labels shown in Figure 8-9. The logo image will be an Image element, and the form input labels will be Label elements.

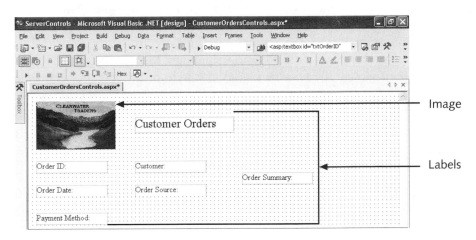

**Figure 8-9**    Web form HTML elements

To create the Web form HTML elements:

1. In Visual Studio .NET, make sure that the CustomerOrdersControls.aspx Web form appears in the Browser Window in Design view, then move the mouse pointer onto the **Toolbox** tab on the left side of the screen display to open the Toolbox.

2. Click the **HTML** tab on the Toolbox to display the HTML elements, and then select the **Image** tool. (You may need to scroll down in the Toolbox list to display the Image tool.) Draw the image on the form, and then resize and reposition the image so it appears in the position shown in Figure 8-9. (You will configure the Image element's properties later.)

 If the HTML tab does not appear on the Toolbox, click Tools on the menu bar, click Customize Toolbox, and then click Reset to reset the Toolbox to its default configuration.

3. Open the Toolbox again, select the **Label** tool, and draw a Label in the position of the Customer Orders Label in Figure 8-9.

4. Repeat Step 3 for the *Order ID*, *Order Date*, *Payment Method*, *Customer*, *Order Source*, and *Order Summary* Label elements in Figure 8-9. (You will modify the Label properties later.)

To create several Label elements quickly on a Web form, draw the first Label element, then copy and paste it several times to create the other Label elements.

5. Save the Web form.

Recall that you can modify the attributes of HTML elements using the Visual Studio .NET Properties Window. The element property names correspond to the HTML attribute names you learned for the elements in Chapter 2. To specify the file that an Image element displays, you modify the element's src attribute. To specify the text that appears in a Label element, you select the Label in Design view so an insertion point appears in the Label, and then change the text. To modify the style of the text in a Label element, you open the Style Builder and change the font style properties. Now you will change the text and attributes of the HTML elements. Because the properties of these elements will not change while the form runs, you will not change their default ID values.

To change the HTML element text and attributes:

1. If necessary, open the Properties Window. Select the **Image** element on the Web form, change its src property value to **clearlogo.jpg** in the Properties Window, and select another property to apply the change. The Image element now displays the Clearwater Traders logo.

2. Click the **Label** element on the right side of the Image element, and then click the element again so the insertion point appears in the Label text. Delete the existing text, and then type **Customer Orders** to change the Label text. Click anywhere on the Web form outside the Label to apply the change.

3. Repeat Step 2 to change the text in the other Label elements so they appear as shown in Figure 8-9.

4. To change the font style of the *Customer Orders* Label, select the **Customer Orders** Label, select the **style** property value, and then click the **More** button [...] to open the Style Builder dialog box. Make sure that the Font tab is selected, then select the **Absolute** option button in the *Size* option button group.

5. Open the **Absolute** list, select **Large**, and then click **OK** to apply the change.

6. Click the **HTML** tab to view the Web form in HTML view. Note that Visual Studio .NET has created the HTML tags for the elements, placed the Label text between the opening and closing `<div>` tags, and specified the element attribute values.

7. Click the **Design view** tab to redisplay the Web form in Design view, and then save the form.

# CREATING HTML SERVER CONTROLS IN WEB FORMS

An HTML server control is a standard HTML element whose tag contains the `runat="server"` attribute specification. To convert an HTML element to an HTML server control in Visual Studio .NET, you create the HTML element in Design view, right-click the element, and then check *Run As Server Control* so a check mark appears before this selection. This action automatically adds the `runat="server"` attribute to the element's tag. To change an HTML server control back to an HTML element, right-click the control and clear the check mark beside *Run As Server Control*. You can distinguish a server control from an HTML element because a server control displays a small green arrow on its top-left corner, as shown in the HTML server controls in Figure 8-10.

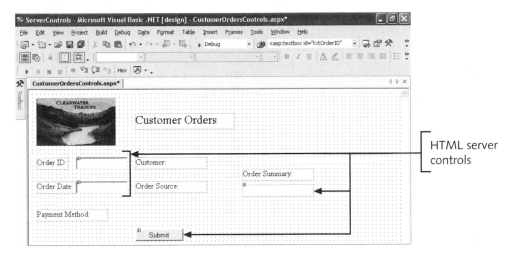

**Figure 8-10**   Web form HTML server controls

To learn about HTML server controls, you will create the HTML server controls shown in Figure 8-10 to represent the *Order ID* and *Order Date* text inputs, the Submit button, and the Label control that displays the *Order ID* value in the Order Summary. (In practice, you would probably create these elements as rich server controls, but you will create them as HTML server controls here to practice making HTML server controls.) The following subsections describe how to create HTML server controls and how to create HTML server control event handlers.

## Creating New HTML Server Controls

To create a new HTML server control, you open the Web form in the Browser Window in Design view, create the server control as an HTML element, convert the element to a server control, and then modify the control's ID attribute value in the Properties Window. This process creates the server control's object declaration in the Declarations block of the Web form's code behind file. If you manually type the HTML tag for the server control in HTML view, or if you manually change the server control's ID attribute value in HTML view, the server control's object declaration will be missing or incorrect, and the server control will not work correctly.

Now you will add the Text Field, Submit button, and Label server controls by creating the corresponding HTML elements and then converting them to server controls. Then you will use the Properties Window to change the ID attribute values to descriptive names.

To create the HTML server controls:

1. In Visual Studio .NET, make sure that the CustomerOrdersControls.aspx Web form appears in the Design Window in Design view, then move the mouse pointer onto the **Toolbox** tab.

2. Make sure that the *HTML* tab is selected in the Toolbox, then select the **Text Field** tool and draw a new Text Field element on the form. Resize and reposition the Text Field element so it appears on the right edge of the *Order ID* Label element, as shown in Figure 8-10. (If necessary, resize the *Order ID* Label element so the Text Field element and Label element do not overlap.)

3. Select the **Order ID** Text Field, right-click, and then click **Run As Server Control**. A small green arrow appears on the top-left corner of the element to indicate that the element is now a server control.

4. Repeat Steps 2 and 3 to create the *Order Date* Text Field.

5. Open the Toolbox, select the **Submit Button** tool, and draw the Submit Button control on the form as shown in Figure 8-10. Right-click the new **Submit** button and then click **Run As Server Control**.

6. Open the Toolbox, select the **Label** tool, and draw the Label element that is under the *Order Summary* Label, as shown in Figure 8-10. Delete the Label's text so it appears as a blank Label, right-click the new **Label**, and then click **Run As Server Control**.

7. Select the **Order ID** Text Field, open the Properties Window if necessary, and change the Text Field's (id) property value to **txtOrderID**.

8. Repeat Step 7 to change the *Order Date* Text Field's (id) property value to **txtOrderDate** and the Submit button's (id) property value to **cmdSubmit.**

9. Change the (id) property value of the HTML Label server control, which is under the *Order Summary* Label, to **lblOrderID**.

10. Save the form.

## Creating HTML Server Control Event Handlers

Earlier you learned that rich server controls have events that users raise in forms, and that Web programmers can create associated event handlers that execute when users raise the control's event. Some HTML server controls also have associated events and event handlers. Table 8-2 lists the HTML server controls that have events and the name of the associated event handler.

**Table 8-2**    HTML server control events and event handlers

| HTML Server Control | Event | Event Handler Name |
| --- | --- | --- |
| Button, Reset Button, Submit Button | Click | *ElementID*_ServerClick |
| Text Field, Text Area, Password Field, Checkbox, Radio Button, Hidden, Listbox, Dropdown | Change | *ElementID*_ServerChange |

You create event handlers for HTML server controls the same way you create event handlers for rich server controls: You double-click the control on the Web form in Design view, and Visual Studio .NET creates a template for the event handler in the Web form's code behind file. Event handlers for HTML server controls execute in the same order as rich server control event handlers: The event handlers execute in the order in which their associated HTML tags appear in HTML view in the Web form. The event handler associated with the control that raises the postback event executes last.

Recall that HTML server controls use the HTML DOM, so they have different properties than rich server controls. Because an HTML server control is an HTML element, its Properties Window displays HTML attributes and style tag attributes. These attributes are different from the rich server control property names you used in Chapter 7 to reference control properties. Therefore, you use different VB .NET commands to reference HTML server control properties. The main properties that you reference in HTML server controls are the properties that represent the value that the user enters or that the system displays in the control.

To reference the value that appears in an HTML Text Field server control, you use the Text Field's Value property. For example, you would use the following command to reference the current value that appears in the txtOrderID HTML Text Field server control: `txtOrderID.value`. To reference the current value that appears between an HTML Label server control's `<div>` tags, you use the Label's InnerText property. For example, you would use the following command to reference the text that appears in the lblOrderID HTML Label server control: `lblOrderID.InnerText`.

 To view a complete listing of an HTML server control's properties and methods, type the name of the server control in the Code editor, followed by a dot (.). An IntelliSense list appears to show you the properties and methods. When you select a property or method, a ScreenTip appears that describes the selection.

Now you will add code to the CustomerOrdersControls.aspx Web form so the Web form automatically displays the *Order ID* value "12345" and displays the current date in the Order Date text input when the user first requests the form. You will add event handlers for the Submit button click event and for the txtOrderID Server_Change event.

The Submit button's event handlers will display the Order Summary, and the txtOrderID's event handler will note in the Order Summary whether the *Order ID* value has changed.

To add the code and event handlers:

1. Click the **View Code** button 🗐 on the Solution Explorer to open the Web form's code behind file. Add the following command to the Declarations block to declare the class variable to represent the *Order ID* value:

```
Private strOrderID As String
```

2. Delete the current comments in the Page_Load procedure, then add the following commands to the Page_Load procedure to initialize the Text Field values for first-time requests and to display the class variable value in the lblOrderID server control for postback requests:

```
If IsPostBack = False Then
        txtOrderID.Value = "12345"
        txtOrderDate.Value = DateString
Else
        strOrderID = "Order ID: " & txtOrderID.Value
End If
```

3. To create the event handler template for the Submit button, click the **CustomerOrdersControls.aspx** tab to display the Web form in Design view, and then double-click the **Submit** button. The Code editor opens again, and the event handler template appears. Add the following command to display the *Order ID* value in the *Order Summary* Label:

```
lblOrderID.InnerText = strOrderID
```

4. To create the event handler for the txtOrderID Text Field server control, open the **Class** list and select **txtOrderID**, then open the **Method** list and select **ServerChange**. The event handler template appears in the Code editor. Add the following command to the event handler to display the text string " (changed)" after the new Order ID value:

```
strOrderID = strOrderID & " (changed)"
```

5. Click the **Start** button ▶ to run the form. The Web form appears in Internet Explorer, and the initial values appear in the Text Field controls.

6. Click **Submit**. The text "Order ID: 12345" appears in the Order Summary.

7. Change the Order ID value to **12346** and then click **Submit**. The value "Order ID: 12346 (changed)" appears in the *Order Summary* Label.

 If your *Order Summary* Label wraps to two lines, close Internet Explorer, switch back to Visual Studio .NET, and make the Label wider on the Web form in Design view.

8. Close Internet Explorer.

## Creating a File Field HTML Server Control

Recall that Web programmers use File Field HTML server controls to allow users to upload files to the Web server. A File Field HTML server control consists of a text input field, a Browse button, and an associated Submit button. When the user clicks Browse, a Choose file dialog box opens, which allows the user to select a file from the file system on his or her workstation. The selected filename appears in the File Field text input. When the user clicks the Submit button that is associated with the File Field, the browser posts the Web form back to the server, and an event handler executes that uploads the selected file to a location in the Web server's file system. Figure 8-11 shows an HTML File Field server control on the Customer Orders Web form. In this example, the Submit button displays the text "Send File." This example also has a Message HTML Label server control that displays a message about the status of the upload operation.

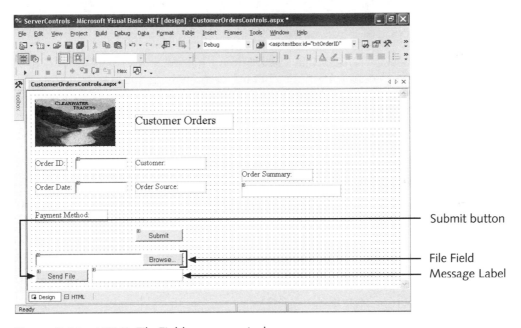

**Figure 8-11**   HTML File Field server control

   To use a File Field server control, users must have Internet Explorer Version 3.02 or later.

Now you will add the File Field HTML server control and Send File button shown in Figure 8-11. The (id) property value of a File Field element usually has the prefix `file` to identify the element as a File Field. You will also add an HTML Label server control that displays a message either stating that the file was successfully sent or prompting the user to select a file.

To add the elements and modify their properties:

1. In Visual Studio .NET, click the CustomerOrdersControls.aspx tab on the Web Browser Window if necessary to display the Web form in Design view. Move the mouse pointer onto the Toolbox, make sure that the HTML tab is selected, and then select the **File Field** tool. Draw the File Field element on the Web form, and then resize and reposition the File Field so it appears as shown in Figure 8-11.

2. Create a Submit button HTML element on the Web form, and then resize and reposition it so it appears as the Send File button in Figure 8-11. (You will modify the button's properties a little later. For now, the button displays the text "Submit.")

3. Create a Label HTML element on the Web form for the Message Label. Position the Label element so it appears on the right edge of the Send File button as shown in Figure 8-11. (You will modify the Label's properties a little later. For now, the Label's text appears as "Label.")

4. Convert the new File Field, Submit button, and Label elements to HTML server controls by right-clicking each element and then clicking **Run As Server Control**.

5. If necessary, open the Properties Window, and then change the (id) property values of the new server controls to the following values:

   | Server Control | (id) Property Value |
   | --- | --- |
   | File Field | **fileUpload** |
   | Submit button | **cmdUpload** |
   | Label | **lblMessage** |

6. Delete the text in the Message Label control so the Label appears blank.

7. Change the Submit button's value property to **Send File**.

8. Save the Web form.

When you create a File Field element in a Web form, Visual Studio .NET creates an `<input>` tag in which the type attribute value is *file*. To use the File Field server control in a Web form, you must add the encType attribute to the Web form's `<form>` tag. HTML forms use the **encType attribute** to specify the format of data that the form passes to the Web server. For a File Field server control, the encType attribute value is multipart/form-data, which is the data format that Web servers require for receiving file data. Visual Studio .NET does not add this attribute automatically, so you must manually enter this attribute in HTML view. You will do this next.

To modify the `<form>` tag:

1. In Visual Studio .NET, and click the **HTML** tab to display the CustomerOrdersControls.aspx Web form in HTML view.

2. Add the following attribute to the `<form>` tag so it appears as follows:

```
<form id="Form1" method="post"
encType="multipart/form-data" runat="server">
```

To make the File Field server control operational, you create an event handler for the Send File button that uploads the selected file to the Web server. You use the File Field control's **PostedFile.FileName property**, which references the filename that appears in the text input of the File Field HTML server control, and the control's **PostedFile.SaveAs method**, which uploads the specified file to the Web server. This event handler uses an `If` decision control structure that determines whether a filename appears in the File Field text input. If a filename appears, the event handler calls the PostedFile.SaveAs method. If a filename does not appear, the event handler displays an error message in the Message Label.

You will first create a folder named Uploads in the Chapter8\Tutorials folder on your Solution Disk. The event handler will specify to save the uploaded file as a file named *temp* in the Uploads folder on your Solution Disk. The file does not have a file extension, because you do not know the file type that the user will upload. The uploaded file could be a text file, word processor file, spreadsheet file, or another type of file.

To create the folder and event handler:

1. Switch to Windows Explorer, and create a folder named **Uploads** in the Chapter8\Tutorials folder on your Solution Disk.

2. Switch back to Visual Studio .NET, click the **Design** tab to switch to Design view, and then double-click the **Send File** button to create an event handler. The event handler template appears in the Code editor.

3. Add to the event handler template the shaded code shown in Figure 8-12. (If your Solution Disk is on a different drive or has a different path, enter that drive letter or path instead.)

4. Add the following command as the last command in the Web form's Page_Load procedure to reset the text that appears in the Message Label to an empty string:

```
lblMessage.InnerText = ""
```

```
Private Sub cmdUpload_ServerClick (ByBVal sender As ↵
System.Object, ByVal e As System.EventArgs) Handles ↵
cmdUpload.ServerClick
    If fileUpload.PostedFile.FileName <> "" Then
        fileUpload.PostedFile.SaveAs ↵
        ("a: \chapter8\tutorials\uploads\temp")
        lblMessage.InnerText = "File successfully sent"
    Else
        lblMessage.InnerText = "Please select a file to send"
    End If
End Sub
```

**Figure 8-12**　Event handler for File Field server control

Now you will run the project and test the File Field server control. You will select a file named letterfile.txt that is in the Chapter8 folder on your Data Disk, and upload this file to the Chapter8\Tutorials\Uploads folder on the Web server.

To test the File Field server control:

1. Click the **Start** button ▶ to run the project. The Customer Orders Web page appears in Internet Explorer.

2. Click **Browse**, navigate to the Chapter8 folder on your Data Disk, select **letterfile.txt**, and then click **Open**. The drive letter, path, and filename appear in the File Field server control's text input.

3. Click **Send File**. After a few moments, "File successfully sent" appears in the Message Label.

4. Switch to Windows Explorer, navigate to the Chapter8\Tutorials\Uploads folder on your Solution Disk, and confirm that you successfully uploaded the temp file.

5. Switch to Internet Explorer, click **Browse** again, do not select a file, and then click **Cancel**. Click **Send File**. The "Please select a file to send" message appears in the Message Label.

6. Close Internet Explorer.

Currently, the Send File button's event handler always saves the uploaded file as a file named temp in the Uploads folder. If you upload multiple files, the last file is overwritten. You can upload files to the Web server using the file's original name, but to do this, you must add code to parse the file's original filename from the string in the PostedFile.FileName property that references the file's drive letter and folder. For example, if your Data Disk is on drive A, the PostedFile.FileName property stores the text string "a:\Chapter8\letterfile.txt." Extracting the filename requires using VB .NET string functions to find the position of the last back slash, and then extracting the remaining characters, which are *letterfile.txt*.

# CREATING RICH SERVER CONTROLS IN WEB FORMS

Table 8-3 summarizes commonly used rich server controls and shows the name of each control's associated event handler. (Recall that most rich server controls have an event for which Web form developers can create an associated event handler.)

**Table 8-3**    Commonly used rich server controls

| Rich Server Control | Description | Event |
|---|---|---|
| Button | Creates a button that posts the Web form back to the Web server | OnClick |
| Calendar | Creates a calendar that displays one month at a time, and allows the user to move to future and previous months and select dates | OnSelectionChanged |
| CheckBox | Creates a check box that allows the user to select between two options, such as Yes and No or True and False | OnCheckedChanged |
| CheckBoxList | Creates a series of related check boxes whose text labels you can dynamically generate using a data source such as a database or data file | OnCheckedChanged |
| DropDownList | Creates a drop-down list that allows the user to select a single item from a list | OnSelectedIndexChanged |
| Label | Displays formatted text whose values users cannot change | None |
| ListBox | Creates a list that allows the user to select a single item or multiple items | OnSelectedIndexChanged |
| Panel | Creates a container for other rich server controls | None |
| RadioButton | Creates a single radio button that you can add to a radio button group | OnCheckedChanged |
| RadioButtonList | Creates a radio button group whose text labels you can dynamically generate using a data source such as a database or data file | OnSelectedIndexChanged |
| TextBox | Creates a single- or multiline text input in which users can enter and modify data values | OnTextChanged |

**8**

You have already created Image, Label, and TextBox rich server controls. Earlier in the chapter, you worked with a Button control when you learned about the Web form processing stages. The following subsections describe how to use rich server controls to create lists, radio buttons, check boxes, and calendars on Web forms.

## Using Rich Server Controls to Create Lists

You can use rich server controls to create lists that are similar to the selection lists you created in Chapter 2 using HTML form element tags. A **ListBox** rich server control is similar to a selection list and displays multiple items on the screen from which the user can make a selection. A **DropDownList** rich server control is similar to a selection list in which the size attribute value is 1: The list displays only the selected item, and the user must open the list to view the list items. The differences between a ListBox control and a DropDownList control is that the ListBox control allows the person designing the Web form to display multiple selections on the Web form. The ListBox control also allows the user to make multiple selections at one time. The DropDownList control allows the user to make only a single selection.

To create a ListBox or DropDownList rich server control, you select the associated tool in the Toolbox, and then draw the control on the Web form. You change the (ID) property value of a list to a descriptive name, and preface the (ID) property with `lst` to denote the control as a list. Now you will add to the Customer Orders Web form the lists that display the *Customer* and *Order Source* values. You will create both of these lists as DropDownList rich server controls.

To create the DropDownList rich server controls:

1. In Visual Studio .NET, select the **CustomerOrdersControls.aspx** tab, open the Toolbox, make sure that the Web Forms tab is selected, select the **DropDownList** tool, and draw the list control below the *Customer* Label as shown in Figure 8-13. Draw a second list control below the *Order Source* Label as shown.

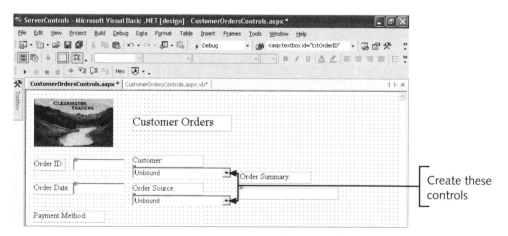

**Figure 8-13**　Creating the DropDownList rich server controls

2. Change the (ID) property value of the first list to **lstCustomer** and the (ID) property value of the second list to **lstOrderSource**. (Note that the prefix of the (ID) property begins with a lowercase letter *L*, not the number 1.)

Note that "Unbound" appears in the list controls. This is because the lists do not yet contain any items. You can specify list items at design time either by directly specifying the items using literal values or by specifying a data source, such as a database, for the lists. In this chapter, you will specify list items using literal values. In Chapter 10, you will learn how to create lists that display database data.

Each item in a ListBox or DropDownList rich server control is a member of a collection class named Items. (Recall from Chapter 7 that a collection class is a predefined class that has methods that enable you to manipulate multiple similar objects, and is similar to a JavaScript array.) To reference a list item, you specify the list item's position in the list's Items collection using an index value that corresponds to the item's list position. (Recall that you used an index to denote the position, or row number, of each item in an array or collection.) For example, suppose you create a ListBox rich server control and specify that the server control's (ID) property value is lstNames. You would reference the first list item as `lstNames.Items(0)`, the second list item as `lstNames.Items(1)`, and so forth.

To specify list items using literal values, you add the items using the ListItem Collection Editor. To open the ListItem Collection Editor, you click the More button ⌷ beside the list's Items collection in the Properties Window. Figure 8-14 shows the ListItem Collection Editor window.

**8**

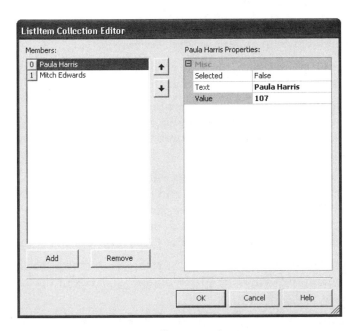

**Figure 8-14**   ListItem Collection Editor

In the ListItem Collection Editor, you create objects in the list's Items collection and specify their properties. To create a new object, you click Add. To remove an existing object, you select the object in the Members list and click Remove. You can specify three properties for each object: Selected, Text, and Value. The Selected property indicates whether the object is selected when the Web form first opens, and can have a value of True or False. Only one item in a DropDownList rich server control can have a Selected value of True.

The Text property specifies the value that appears in the list, such as the customer name "Paula Harris." The Value property specifies an additional property that corresponds to the list selection. Often databases use numeric identifiers to identify data items uniquely. (You will learn more about these numeric identifiers, which are called primary keys, in Chapter 9.) For example, a database might contain a *Customer ID* value such as "107" to identify customer "Paula Harris." This numeric value does not appear in the *Customer* list, but the underlying program code uses the value to process the customer order.

Now you will open the ListItem Collection Editor for the DropDownList rich server controls, and add the list items.

To add the list items:

1. If necessary, open the Properties Window. Select the **lstCustomer** DropDownList rich server control, and then select the **Items** property in the Properties Window. Note that the Items property value is *(Collection)*, which indicates that the property value is a collection.

2. Click the **More** button ⌊...⌋. The ListItem Collection Editor dialog box opens.

3. Click **Add**. A new list item appears in the *Members* list.

4. Click the insertion point beside the Text property in the ListItem Properties list, and type **Paula Harris** for the first list item's Text property.

5. Click the insertion point beside the Value property, delete the default value, which is the same as the Text property value, type **107** for the item's Value property, and then press **Enter**. "Paula Harris" appears as the first list item beside index value 0.

6. Click **Add** to add the next list item. Type **Mitch Edwards** for the Text property and **232** for the Value property, and then press **Enter**. Mitch Edwards appears as the second list item beside index value 1. Your completed ListItem Collection Editor window should look like Figure 8-14. Click **OK** to save your changes and close the ListItem Collection Editor.

7. Select the **lstOrderSource** DropDownList rich server control, select the **Items** property, and then click the **More** button ⌊...⌋ to open the ListItem Collection Editor.

8. Add the following items to the list, and then click **OK** to save your changes and close the ListItem Collection Editor.

| Item Text | Item Value |
| --- | --- |
| **Winter 2004** | 1 |
| **Spring 2005** | 2 |

To reference a property of a list item, you reference the list item followed by the property name, using the following syntax: *listID(index).PropertyName*. For example, to reference the Text property of the second item in the lstCustomer DropDownList rich server control, you would use the following syntax: `lstCustomer(1).Text`. This reference returns the value "Mitch Edwards," because this is the Text property of the second list item.

To reference the index value of the item that the user selects in a list, you use the SelectedItem property. For example, if the user selects the second item in the lstCustomer DropDownList control, the SelectedItem property value is 1. To reference the Text property of the selected item, you use the following syntax: *listID.SelectedItem.Text*. For example, to reference the Text property of the current selection in the lstCustomer list, you use the following syntax: `lstCustomer.SelectedItem.Text`. To reference the Value property of the selected item, you use the following syntax: *listID.SelectedItem.Value*. For example, to reference the Value property of the current selection in the lstCustomer list, you use the following syntax: `lstCustomer.SelectedItem.Value`.

Recall from Table 8-3 that the primary event for the ListBox and DropDownList rich server controls is SelectedIndexChanged. The user raises this event when he or she selects a list item. Now you will add two Label rich server controls to the Web form that appear under the txtOrderID HTML Label server control in the Order Summary. These controls will display the *Customer* and *Order Source* selections. You will add event handlers to the Web form so that when the user selects list items, the list event handlers assign the Text property values of the list selections to the new Label controls.

To add the Label controls and event handlers to display the list selections:

1. In Visual Studio .NET, create the Label server controls shown in Figure 8-15. Change the (ID) property value of the first Label to **lblCustomer**, and the (ID) property value of the second Label to **lblOrderSource**. Delete the Text property value of both Labels.

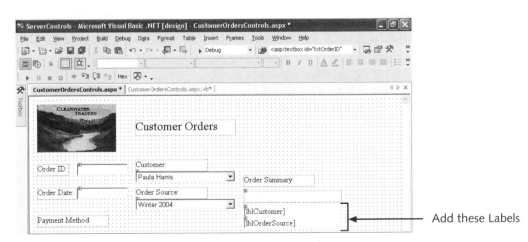

**Figure 8-15**   Creating Label controls to display the list selections

2. In the Browser Window in Design view, double-click the **lstCustomer** DropDownList control. The Code editor opens, and displays the template for the lst_Customer_SelectedIndexChanged event handler. Add the following command to the event handler template to display the list selection in the lblCustomer Label control:

```
lblCustomer.Text = lstCustomer.SelectedItem.Text
```

3. Open the **Class** list at the top of the Code editor window and select **lstOrderSource**, then open the **Method** list and select **SelectedIndexChanged**. An event handler template for the control appears in the Code editor. Add the following command to the event handler template to display the list selection in the lblOrderSource Label control:

```
lblOrderSource.Text = lstOrderSource.SelectedItem.Text
```

Now you will run the Web form and select items from the *Customer* and *Order Source* lists. Then you will submit the form to the Web server and view the list selections in the Order Summary.

To run the Web form and view the list selections:

1. Click the **Start** button ▶ on the Debug toolbar to run the form. The Web form appears in Internet Explorer.

2. Select **Mitch Edwards** from the *Customer* list, **Spring 2005** from the *Order Source* list, accept all of the other form values, and then click **Submit**. The list selections "Mitch Edwards" and "Spring 2005" appear in the *Order Summary* Label controls.

3. Close Internet Explorer.

## Using Rich Server Controls to Create Radio Buttons

Recall that you use radio buttons to allow the user to select a single value from a group of related values, and that you define related radio buttons as a radio button group to allow the user to select only one button in the group at one time. One way to represent radio buttons on a Web form is to create a RadioButtonList. A RadioButtonList rich server control is a special kind of a list that displays its list items as radio buttons. You can use the ListItem Collection Editor to add the radio button labels and associated values at design time, or you can use a data source to retrieve the radio button labels and values at run time. You use *listID(index).PropertyName* to reference a specific radio button, *listID*.SelectedItem.Text to reference the selected radio button's Text property, and *listID*.SelectedItem.Value to reference the selected radio button's Value property. Now you will create a RadioButtonList rich server control on the Customer Orders Web form to represent the payment method, which can be either "Cash" or "Credit Card." You will create the RadioButtonList rich server control on the form, and then change its (ID) property value to optPaymentMethod. You will also add a Label rich server control that will display the selected radio button's value.

To create the RadioButtonList and Label rich server controls:

1. Make sure that the CustomerOrdersControls.aspx Web form appears in Design view, then place the mouse pointer on the *Toolbox* tab, and make sure that the Web Forms tab is selected. Select the **RadioButtonList** tool.

2. Draw the RadioButtonList rich server control shown in Figure 8-16. Resize and reposition the control as shown. Currently, the control only has one radio button.

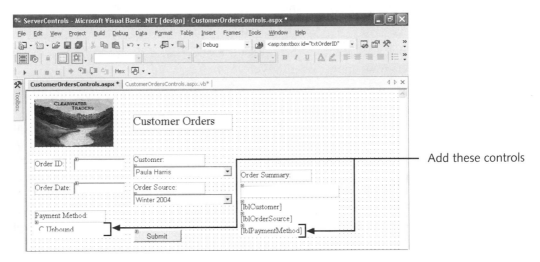

**Figure 8-16**    Creating a RadioButtonList rich server control

3. Create a new Label rich server control as shown in Figure 8-16 to display the selected radio button's value.

4. Select the new **RadioButtonList** rich server control, open the Properties Window if necessary, and change the control's (ID) property value to **optPaymentMethod**.

5. Select the new Label rich server control, change its (ID) property value to **lblPaymentMethod**, and delete its current Text property value.

You use the ListItem Collection Editor to add the individual radio buttons to a RadioButtonList rich server control. Recall that in the ListItem Collection Editor, each item has a Text property and a Value property. For a RadioButtonList, the Text property specifies the text that appears beside the radio button. The Value property represents the button's associated data value, which may or may not be the same as the button's Text property. Now you will open the new RadioButtonList control's Items collection, and add the individual radio buttons.

To add the individual radio buttons to the RadioButtonList:

1. Select the **optPaymentMethod** RadioButtonList control on the Web form, select the **Items** property in the Properties Window, and then click the **More** button ⬚. The ListItem Collection Editor window opens.

2. Add the following items to the RadioButtonList rich server control:

| Item Index | Text | Value |
|---|---|---|
| 0 | **Cash** | **C** |
| 1 | **Credit Card** | **CC** |

3. Click **OK** to close the ListItem Collection Editor. The individual radio buttons now appear on the Web form.

As with other rich server controls lists, the primary event for a RadioButtonList rich server control is SelectedIndexChanged. The user raises this event when he or she selects a radio button. To reference an individual radio button within a RadioButtonList, you use the button's index value. For example, to reference the first radio button in the optPaymentMethod RadioButtonList, you use the following syntax: `optPaymentMethod(0)`. To reference the Text property of the first radio button, you use the following syntax: `optPaymentMethod(0).Text`. To reference the selected radio button, you use the SelectedItem property. For example, to reference the Value property of the selected radio button in the optPaymentMethod RadioButtonList, you use the following syntax: `optPaymentMethod.SelectedItem.Value`.

Now you will add an event handler to the RadioButtonList rich server control form so that when the user selects one of the radio buttons, the RadioButtonList event handler assigns to the new Label control the Text property value of the selected radio button. Then you will run the form and view the selection in the *Order Summary* Label control.

To add the event handler to the RadioButtonList rich server control:

1. In Visual Studio .NET in Design view, double-click the **optPaymentMethod** RadioButtonList rich server control. The Code editor opens and displays an event handler template for the optPaymentMethod_SelectedIndexChanged.

2. Add the following command to the event handler:

```
lblPaymentMethod.Text = "Payment Method: " & ↵
optPaymentMethod.SelectedItem.Text
```

3. Click the **Start** button ▶ to run the Web form. The Web form appears in Internet Explorer.

4. Select the **Cash** option button, select **Mitch Edwards** in the *Customer* list, select **Spring 2005** in the *Order Source* list, accept all of the other values, and then click **Submit**. The Order Summary now displays the text "Payment Method: Cash" in the lblPaymentMethod Label control. (If the message wraps to two lines, close Internet Explorer, make the lblPaymentMethod Label wider in Design view, then run the form again.)

5. Close Internet Explorer.

Another way to add radio buttons to a Web form is to use the RadioButton rich server control. The RadioButton rich server control is very similar to the radio button HTML form element: You create the individual radio buttons, and then change the GroupName attribute value of each individual radio button to the name of the radio group. Each radio button has a Text property that specifies the text value that appears next to the radio button and a Checked property that can have a value of either True or False that specifies whether or not the button is selected. The RadioButtonList rich server control is easier to work with and more flexible, so in almost all cases, you should create a RadioButtonList when you add radio buttons to a Web form.

# Using Rich Server Controls to Create Check Boxes

Recall from Chapter 2 that you use a check box to define an element that can have one of two distinct values, such as on or off, or true or false. In a Web form, you can use two different rich server controls to create check boxes. You use the CheckBox rich server control to create a single check box, such as a check box that appears on an order form and indicates whether or not the order will use overnight delivery. You use the CheckBoxList control to create a series of check boxes. For example, you might create a CheckBoxList on a Web form that lists all merchandise items that are available for sale and includes a check box that the customer can check to indicate whether he or she wants to purchase the item. The following subsections describe how to create CheckBox and CheckBoxList server controls.

## Creating a CheckBox Rich Server Control

The CheckBox rich server control is very similar to the HTML check box form element: It has a Value property that specifies the text that appears beside the check box, and it has a Checked property to indicate whether or not it is checked. If the Checked property has the value True, the CheckBox is checked, and if the Checked property has the value False, the CheckBox is cleared. To learn how to create a CheckBox rich server control, you will add a CheckBox rich server control that specifies whether or not the current order uses overnight delivery. When you create a new CheckBox rich server control, you preface its ID property value with the prefix chk. You will also add the *Shipment Status* Label control to the Order Summary.

To create the CheckBox rich server control and Label control:

1. Select the **CustomerOrdersControls.aspx** tab in the Web Browser Window, open the Toolbox, and make sure that the Web Forms tab is selected. Select the **CheckBox** tool, and draw a CheckBox rich server control on the Web form. Resize and reposition the CheckBox so it looks like the one in Figure 8-17.

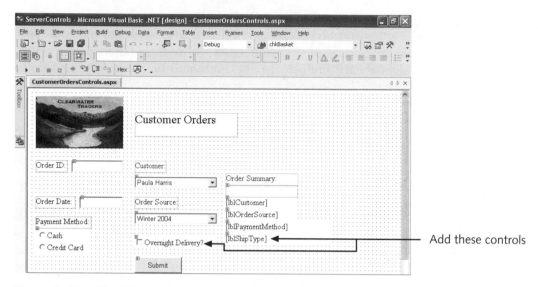

**Figure 8-17**   CheckBox rich server control

2. Make sure that the new CheckBox is selected, and open the Properties Window if necessary. Change the (ID) property value to **chkShipType** and the Text property value to **Overnight Delivery?**

3. Select the **Label** tool from the Toolbox, and draw the *Shipment Status* Label shown in Figure 8-17. Change the ID property value to **lblShipType**, and delete the Text property value.

Next you will create an event handler for the CheckBox rich server control that corresponds to the CheckBox's CheckedChanged event. The user raises this event when he or she either checks or clears the CheckBox. Initially, the CheckBox is cleared. If the user checks the CheckBox, the CheckBox control's Checked property is set to True, and the lblShipType Label will report that the order uses overnight delivery.

To create the CheckBox event handler:

1. Double-click the **CheckBox** rich server control. The Code editor opens and displays the template for the chkShipType_CheckedChanged event handler.

2. Add the following commands to the event handler:

```
If chkShipType.Checked = True Then
        lblShipType.Text = "Order uses overnight delivery"
Else
        lblShipType.Text = "Order uses regular delivery"
End If
```

3. Click the **Start** button ▶ to run the form. Select the **Cash** option button, select **Mitch Edwards** from the *Customer* list and **Spring 2005** from the *Order Source* list, check the **Overnight Delivery?** check box, and then click **Submit**. The

message "Order uses overnight delivery" appears in the lblShipType Label. (If the message wraps to two lines, close Internet Explorer, make the shipping message Label wider in Design view, then run the form again.)

4. Close Internet Explorer. Because you are finished working with the CustomerOrdersControls.aspx Web form, close all open windows within the Browser Window.

## Creating a CheckBoxList Rich Server Control

Recall that you use the CheckBoxList rich server control to display multiple check boxes on a Web form. The check boxes can be checked or cleared independently. The CheckBoxList rich server control is very similar to the RadioButtonList rich server control: You can use the ListItem Collection Editor to specify the check box text labels and values at design time, or you can retrieve the text labels and values from a data source at run time. You reference an individual check box within the CheckBoxList using the Items collection with the check box's index value. To gain experience creating a CheckBoxList rich server control, you will use the Order Items Web form shown in Figure 8-18.

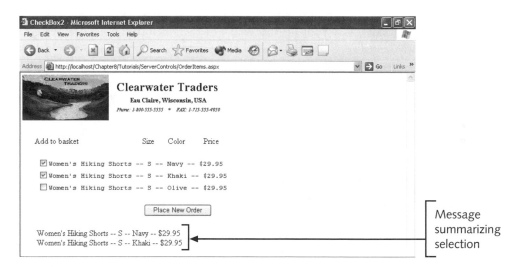

**Figure 8-18**   Order Items Web form

On this Web form, the user can select one or more order items by checking the check box beside the item description, and then clicking Place Order Now. A message then appears on the Web form that summarizes the order.

A partially completed Order Items Web form is in the Chapter8 folder on your Data Disk. This Web form contains the static HTML form elements, including the image logo and the heading information. Now you will copy the files for this Web form to your Solution Disk and add the Web form to the ServerControls project.

To copy the files and add the form to the project:

1. Switch to Windows Explorer, and copy **OrderItems.aspx** and **OrderItems.aspx.vb** from the Chapter8 folder on your Data Disk to the Chapter8\Tutorials\ServerControls folder on your Solution Disk.

2. Switch to Visual Studio .NET, right-click the **ServerControls** project node in the Solution Explorer, point to **Add**, and then click **Add Existing Item**.

3. Navigate to the Chapter8\Tutorials\ServerControls folder on your Solution Disk, open the **Files of type** list and select **All Files (*.*)**, select **OrderItems.aspx**, press and hold **Ctrl**, then select **OrderItems.aspx.vb**.

4. Click **Open** to add the files to the project.

5. Right-click the **OrderItems.aspx** node in the Solution Explorer, and then select **Set As Start Page**.

Next you will add the CheckBoxList, Place New Order, and Message Label rich server controls to the Web form, and modify the properties of these new controls.

To add the rich server controls to the form:

1. Open the OrderItems.aspx form in Design view, open the Toolbox, select the **CheckBoxList** tool on the Web Forms tab, and draw the CheckBoxList shown in Figure 8-19. Change the CheckBoxList (ID) property value to **chkBasket**, Font Name to **Courier New**, and Font Size to **X-Small**.

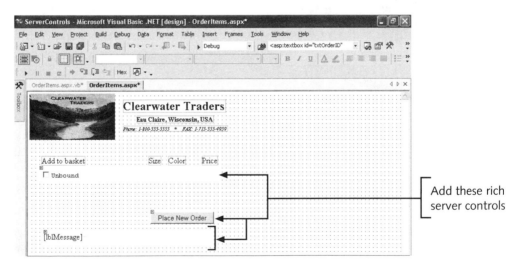

**Figure 8-19**    Creating the form's rich server controls

2. Create the Button rich server control shown in Figure 8-19. Change the Button's (ID) property value to **btnOrder** and Text property value to **Place New Order**.

3. Create the Message Label rich server control shown in Figure 8-19. Change the Label's (ID) property value to **lblMessage**, and delete the Text property value.

Next you will add the check box list items to the CheckBoxList. You will use the ListItems Collection Editor to add a text description for each merchandise item for the Text property and an Item ID value for the Value property.

To add the items to the CheckBoxList:

1. Select the **chkBasket** CheckBoxList, select the **Items** property in the Properties Window, and then click the **More** button [...] to open the ListItem Collection Editor.

2. Add the following items to the collection:

| Index | Text | Value |
| --- | --- | --- |
| 0 | **Women's Hiking Shorts -- S -- Navy -- $29.95** | 17778 |
| 1 | **Women's Hiking Shorts -- S -- Khaki -- $29.95** | 17779 |
| 2 | **Women's Hiking Shorts -- S -- Olive -- $29.95** | 17780 |

3. Click **OK** to save your changes. The CheckBoxList items appear on the Web form. If necessary, resize and reposition the rich server controls so your Web form looks like the Order Items Web form in Figure 8-18.

The final step is to add the event handler for the Place New Order button. This event handler will call a function named RetrievedItems that evaluates the Selected property value for each CheckBoxList item, adds each selected item's Text property to a local variable named strItemDescriptions, and returns the variable value as the function result. Each item description ends with a line break tag (`<br />`) so each item description appears on a separate line.

To create the event handler for the Place New Order button:

1. Select the **OrderItems.aspx** node in the Solution Explorer, click the **View Code** button [≡] to open the Code editor, and then add the code shown in Figure 8-20 to create the RetrievedItems function at the end of the file, just before the **End Class** command.

2. Open the **Class** list and select **btnOrder**, and then open the **Method** list and select **Click**. The event handler template for the Button rich server control appears in the Code editor.

8

```
Private Function RetrievedItems() As String
   Dim strItemDescriptions As String
   If chkBasket.Items(0).Selected Then
      strItemDescriptions = chkBasket.Items (0).Text & "<br />"
   End If
   If chkBasket.Items(1).Selected Then
      strItemDescriptions = strItemDescriptions & ↵
      chkBasket.Items(1).Text & "<br />"
   End If
   If chkBasket.Items(2).Selected Then
      strItemDescriptions = strItemDescriptions & ↵
      chkBasket.Items(2).Text & "<br />"
   End If
   RetrievedItems = strItemDescriptions
End Function
```

**Figure 8-20**    Code to evaluate CheckBoxList items

3. Add the following command to call the RetrievedItems function and assign the result to the Message Label:

   **lblMessage.Text = RetrievedItems()**

4. Click the **Start** button ▶ to run the project. The Web form appears in Internet Explorer.

5. Check the **Women's Hiking Shorts -- S -- Navy** and **Women's Hiking Shorts -- S -- Khaki** check boxes, and then click **Place New Order**. The Message Label summarizing the order appears as shown in Figure 8-18.

6. Close Internet Explorer. Because you are finished working with the OrderItems.aspx Web form, close all open windows within the Browser Window.

## Creating a Calendar Rich Server Control

The Calendar rich server control displays a calendar that shows the days in the current month. The user can move to future and previous months, and select a date that then appears in a text input on the form. To learn about the Calendar control, you will use the Receive Shipment Web form shown in Figure 8-21, which allows employees at Clearwater Traders to enter information about incoming merchandise shipments.

This Web form allows the employee to select a *Shipment ID* from a list of incoming shipments, and then select an *Inventory ID* from a list of inventory ID values for the selected shipment. The employee then clicks the Show Calendar button 🖽▾, which displays the Calendar rich server control. The employee can select a date on the Calendar control. The selected date then appears in the *Date Received* text input, and the Calendar control closes. Now you will copy the project files to the project folder and add the Web form files to the project.

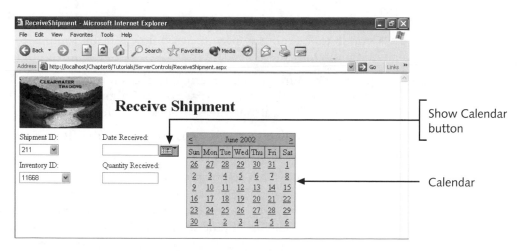

**Figure 8-21**   Receive shipment Web form

To add the Receive Shipment form to your project:

1. Switch to Windows Explorer, and copy the following files from the Chapter8 folder on your Data Disk to the Chapter8\Tutorials\ServerControls folder on your Solution Disk: **calendar1.gif**, **ReceiveShipment.aspx.vb**, and **ReceiveShipment.aspx**.

2. Switch to Visual Studio .NET, right-click the **ServerControls** project node in the Solution Explorer, point to **Add**, click **Add Existing Item**, navigate to the Chapter8\Tutorials\ServerControls folder on your Solution Disk, open the **Files of type** list and select **All Files (*.*)**, select **ReceiveShipment.aspx**, press and hold **Ctrl**, then select **ReceiveShipment.aspx.vb** and click **Open** to add the files to the project.

3. Right-click the **ReceiveShipment.aspx** node in the Solution Explorer, and then click **Set As Start Page**.

First you will add the Calendar rich server control and the Show Calendar button to the form. The Show Calendar button is an Image Button rich server control, which is similar to a standard Button rich server control, except that it displays a graphic image rather than a text label.

To add the rich server controls:

1. If necessary, double-click the **ReceiveShipment.aspx** node in the Solution Explorer to display the form in the Browser Window in Design view.

2. Open the Toolbox, make sure that the Web Forms tab is selected, then select the **ImageButton** tool and draw the Show Calendar button on the right edge of the Date Received text input, as shown in Figure 8-21. Resize and reposition the Image Button as necessary.

3. Open the Toolbox, make sure that the Web Forms tab is selected, then select the **Calendar** tool. (You may need to scroll down in the Toolbox to locate the Calendar tool.) Draw the Calendar on the Web form as shown in Figure 8-21.

4. Select the **Image Button** rich server control, open the Properties Window if necessary, and change the (ID) property to **btnCalendar** and the ImageUrl to **calendar1.gif**. The Calendar image appears on the Button.

5. Select the **Calendar** rich server control, and change the (ID) property to **calDateReceived**.

The Calendar rich server control has approximately 200 properties that Web programmers can use to specify the control's appearance and behavior. Fortunately, you can accept most of the default property values. Now you will modify the Calendar rich server control properties to modify its outline style and background colors. You will also change the Calendar's Visible property to False, so the Calendar does not appear when the form first opens.

To modify the Calendar properties:

1. If necessary, select the Calendar rich server control in the Browser Window.

2. Select the **BackColor** property, which specifies the Calendar's background color. Open the list, make sure that the Custom tab is selected, then select a **light gray** square.

3. Select the **BorderColor** property, which specifies the color of the Calendar's border, open the list, make sure that the Custom tab is selected, then select a **dark gray** square.

4. Select the **BorderStyle** property and select **Outset** to make the calendar appear three-dimensional on the Web form.

5. Type **1** in the BorderWidth property value to specify the width of the Calendar's border.

6. Select the **DayHeaderStyle** property node to specify the following properties of the header bar that shows the days of the week:

| Property | Value |
| --- | --- |
| BackColor | Select a **light red** square |
| BorderColor | Select a **dark red** square |
| BorderStyle | **Inset** |
| BorderWidth | **1** |

7. Change the Visible property value to **False**.

Users can use the Calendar to select a single day, week, or month. You use the SelectDate property to reference a single selection, and the SelectedDates collection to reference multiple selections. You use the Calendar's SelectionMode property to specify how many selections a user can make. When the SelectionMode value is Day, the user can select a single date. When SelectionMode is DayWeek, the user can select either a single day or an entire week. When SelectionMode is DayWeekMonth, the user can select a single day, an entire week, or an entire month. If the user selects an entire week or an entire month, you use the SelectedDates collection to reference the selections. You can use the SelectedDates.Count property to determine the number of dates that the user selects.

 The SelectedDate property always references the first user selection, so SelectedDate and SelectedDates[0] have the same value.

Now you will create the event handlers to open the Calendar when the user clicks the Open Calendar button, display the selected date in the *Date Received* text input, and close the Calendar after the user makes a selection. Because the Receive Shipment form allows the user to select only a single date, you will first confirm that the SelectionMode property value is Day.

To create the event handlers:

1. Make sure that the Calendar control is selected, open the Properties Window if necessary, and confirm that the SelectionMode property value is Day.

2. Double-click the **Show Calendar** button. The btnCalendar_Click event handler template appears in the Code editor. Add the following command to display the Calendar rich server control:

   ```
   calDateReceived.Visible = True
   ```

3. Select the **ReceiveShipment.aspx** tab at the top of the Browser Window to redisplay the Web form in Design view, then double-click the **Calendar** control. The calDateReceived_SelectionChanged event handler template appears in the Code editor. Add the following commands to the event handler:

   ```
   txtDateReceived.Text = calDateReceived.SelectedDate
   calDateReceived.Visible = False
   ```

4. Click the **Start** button ▶ to run the form. The Web form opens, but the Calendar does not yet appear.

5. Click the **Show Calendar** button ▦▾. The calendar appears and displays the current month.

6. Click the **Move Next** button ▷. The Calendar displays the next month.

7. Click the **Move Previous** button ◁. The calendar displays the current month.

8. Select the **current date** on the calendar. The date appears in the *Date Received* text input, and the Calendar rich server control no longer appears.

9. Close Internet Explorer.

How does the Web server process a Calendar control? Each time the user selects a date, the control raises the postback event. Similarly, each time the user clicks the Move Next ⟩ or Move Previous ⟨ button to scroll through months, the control raises the postback event. This generates a lot of network traffic, so you should use Calendar controls sparingly in Web forms.

## Setting the Tab Order of Web Form Controls

In Web applications, users should be able to press the Tab key to move to form controls in a top-down, left-to-right order. You may have noticed that when you run the ReceiveShipment.aspx Web form, the insertion point moves somewhat randomly through the form controls when you press Tab. To control the order that the insertion point moves through Web form HTML server and rich server controls, you use the TabIndex property. You set the TabIndex property value for the first form control to 1. When the user presses Tab, the insertion point moves to the control whose TabIndex property is 2. When the user presses Tab again, the insertion point moves to the control whose TabIndex property is 3, and so on. Now you will modify the TabIndex property values of the form controls so the insertion point moves in a top-down, left-to-right order.

To modify the TabIndex property values of the form controls:

1. If necessary, click the ReceiveShipment.aspx tab at the top of the Browser Window to display the Web form in Design view.

2. Select the **Shipment ID** list, open the Properties Window if necessary, change the TabIndex property value to **1,** then select another property to apply the change.

3. Select the **Inventory ID** list, and change the TabIndex property value to **2**.

4. Select the **DateReceived** TextBox control, and change the TabIndex property to **3**.

5. Select the Show Calendar button ▦▾, and change the TabIndex property to **4**.

6. Select the **Quantity Received** TextBox control, and change the TabIndex property to **5**.

7. Click the **Start** button ▸ to run the project. Press **Tab**. The URL for the form is selected, which is always the first TabIndex selection.

8. Press **Tab**. The *Shipment ID* list appears selected. Press **Tab** again. The *Inventory ID* list appears selected. Continue to press **Tab** and observe how the insertion point or form focus moves through the form controls based on the TabIndex values.

Sometimes when the insertion point is in the first text input on a Web form and you press Tab, Internet Explorer raises the postback event and submits the Web form to the server.

9. Close Internet Explorer. Because you are finished working with the ReceiveShipment.aspx Web form, close all open windows within the Visual Studio .NET Browser Window.

## CREATING VALIDATION CONTROLS IN WEB FORMS

In Chapter 4, you learned how to create client-side form validation functions to validate user inputs in commonly used Web form input elements such as text inputs, radio buttons, and selection lists. These functions evaluate user inputs to ensure that the user enters the required field values and that the values are within allowable ranges or are in the correct formats. You may have noticed that the code in these validation controls is very similar: You confirmed that users entered values for required fields, and entered values within allowable ranges. For values that require a certain format, such as dates and telephone numbers, the values must follow this format. To expedite creating form validation functions, Microsoft has created a series of JavaScript libraries that contain standard functions that perform these validation tasks. You can access these JavaScript libraries using Web form server-side validation controls.

Server-side validation controls, or simply validation controls, automatically generate client-side JavaScript commands that perform the same tasks as the form validation functions you manually created using JavaScript. When the Web server renders the Web form's HTML source code, it places commands in the HTML source code that call standard JavaScript validation functions from a JavaScript code library named WebUIValidation.js that is in a subdirectory within the Web server's home directory.

Because validation controls automatically generate client-side form validation function commands, they save development time and effort. In addition, if a user's browser doesn't support JavaScript, the validation controls automatically perform the validation tasks using validation functions that the Web server processes during the Validation Web form processing stage. Table 8-4 summarizes the different types of validation controls.

**Table 8-4**    Server-side validation controls

| Validation Control Name | Description |
| --- | --- |
| RequiredFieldValidator | Validates a user input by determining whether or not the user enters a required value |
| RangeValidator | Validates a user input by determining whether or not the value is within specified upper and/or lower bounds |
| CompareValidator | Validates a user input based on allowable values or properties |
| RegularExpressionValidator | Validates a user input by determining whether the value matches a regular expression, which requires an explicit pattern of characters and/or numbers |
| ValidationSummary | Summarizes error messages from all validation controls in a single control |
| CustomValidator | Validates a user input using a custom function you write in either JavaScript or VB .NET |

8

The RequiredFieldValidator, RangeValidator, CompareValidator, and RegularExpression-Validator validation controls are the standard validation controls that use JavaScript library functions to evaluate inputs in text input, radio button, and selection list Web form elements. The ValidationSummary validation control summarizes the error messages that the other validation controls generate. You use the CustomValidator validation control to associate your own custom JavaScript validation functions with Web form controls. CustomValidator validation controls are useful for evaluating inputs in Web form elements that the standard validation controls do not support, such as check boxes and Calendar control inputs.

The following subsections describe how to create these validation controls. You will work with the Validation.aspx form in Figure 8-22 to demonstrate validation controls.

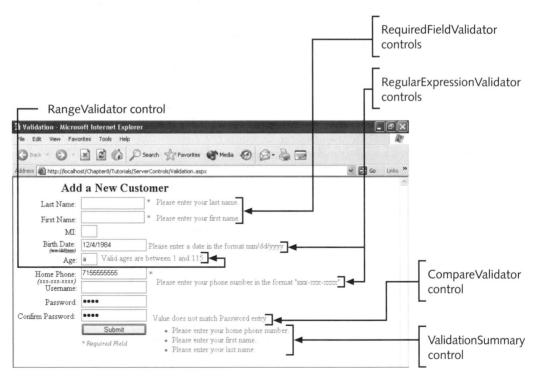

**Figure 8-22**    Validation.aspx Web form

This Web form contains TextBox rich server controls that allow the user to enter personal information. The red asterisks (*) denote required fields. When the Web form first opens, the error messages in Figure 8-22 do not appear. If the user places the insertion point in a TextBox that has an associated validation control but does not enter a required value or enters a value that is not legal or is not formatted correctly, and then presses Enter or Tab, clicks Submit, or moves the insertion point to a different TextBox control, the error message for the field with the missing or incorrect value appears. Now you will add this Web form to your project.

To add the Validation.aspx form to your project:

1. Switch to Windows Explorer and copy **Validation.aspx** and **Validation.aspx.vb** from the Chapter8 folder on your Data Disk to the Chapter8\Tutorials\ServerControls folder on your Solution Disk.

2. Switch to Visual Studio .NET, right-click the **ServerControls** project node in the Solution Explorer, point to **Add**, click **Add Existing Item**, navigate to the Chapter8\Tutorials\ServerControls folder on your Solution Disk, open the **Files of type** list and select **All Files (\*.\*)**, select **Validation.aspx**, press and hold **Ctrl**, then select **Validation.aspx.vb** and click **Open** to add the files to the project.

3. Right-click the **Validation.aspx** node in the Solution Explorer, and then select **Set As Start Page**.

## Creating RequiredFieldValidator Validation Controls

One of the most common data entry validation tasks is to ensure that the user enters values in TextBox controls that contain required input values. You use a **RequiredFieldValidator validation control** to confirm that the user enters a value in a specific TextBox control. You must create a separate RequiredFieldValidator for each TextBox control that represents a required value. When you run the form, ASP.NET generates JavaScript procedures that call commands in JavaScript library files that validate whether or not the input's value has changed. The Web server downloads these JavaScript library files to the client browser when the client requests the Web form. Now you will add a RequiredFieldValidator for each required field on the Validation.aspx Web form.

To create the RequiredFieldValidator controls:

1. Make sure that the **Validation.aspx** node in the Solution Explorer is selected, then click the **View Designer** button ▣ on the Solution Explorer toolbar to open the Web form in Design view. The Web form appears. The red asterisks (\*) indicate that the *Last Name*, *First Name*, and *Home Phone* number TextBox inputs are required.

2. Open the Toolbox, make sure that the Web Forms tab is selected, then select the **RequiredFieldValidator** tool. (You may need to scroll down in the Toolbox.)

3. Draw a RequiredFieldValidator control to the right of the first asterisk beside the *Last Name* TextBox control, as shown in Figure 8-23.

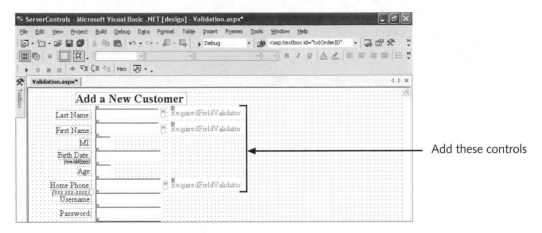

Add these controls

**Figure 8-23**    Creating the RequiredFieldValidator controls

4. Add the RequiredFieldValidator controls for the *First Name* and *Home Phone* TextBox controls, as shown in Figure 8-23. Resize and reposition the new controls as necessary.

When you create a RequiredFieldValidator validation control, you must specify two properties: the ControlToValidate property, which determines the TextBox control that the validation control validates, and the ErrorMessage property, which specifies the error message text that appears on the Web form when the validation control fails. You usually do not modify the (ID) property of a validation control, because you do not directly reference the control in VB .NET commands. Now you will modify the properties of the RequiredFieldValidator validation controls to specify which TextBox controls these controls validate and to specify the validation control error messages.

To modify the validation control properties:

1. Select the first validation control beside the *Last Name* TextBox control, open the Properties Window if necessary, select the **ControlToValidate** property, open the selection list, and select **txtLast**.

2. Change the ErrorMessage property value to **Please enter your last name**. If necessary, resize the validation control so the text appears on one line.

3. Select the second validation control beside the *First Name* TextBox control, and change the ControlToValidate property to **txtFirst** and the Error Message to **Please enter your first name**. If necessary, resize the validation control so the text appears on one line.

4. Select the third validation control beside the *Home Phone* TextBox control, and change the ControlToValidate property to **txtHPhone** and the Error Message to **Please enter your home phone number**. If necessary, resize the validation control so the text appears on one line.

Now you will run the project and test the validation controls.

To test the validation controls:

1. Click the **Start** button ▶ to run the project. The Web form appears in Internet Explorer.

2. Click **Submit**. The RequiredFieldValidator control error messages appear on the form.

3. Type **Harris** in the *Last Name* TextBox, and then press **Tab**. Note that the validation control ErrorMessage for this TextBox no longer appears.

4. Type **Paula** in the *First Name* TextBox and then press **Tab**. Note that the validation control ErrorMessage for this TextBox no longer appears.

5. Do not enter a value in the *Home Phone* TextBox, then click **Submit**. The error message beside the *Home Phone* TextBox still appears. When a Web form contains validation controls, all validation occurs on the client workstation. The Submit button does not raise the postback event and post the Web form back to the Web server until all validation controls evaluate as true.

6. Type **715-555-5555** in the *Home Phone* TextBox control and then click **Submit**. The message "Paula Harris has been submitted" appears in the Message Label, indicating the validation controls all evaluate as true and the Web form has been submitted to the Web server.

7. Close Internet Explorer.

The RequiredFieldValidator validation control evaluates whether or not the user enters a value in a TextBox control, but it does not confirm that the value is legal or reasonable. You use the RangeValidator, CompareValidator, and RegularExpressionValidator controls to evaluate input values.

## Creating RangeValidator Validation Controls

The **RangeValidator validation control** evaluates input values to confirm that the values are of a specific data type that fall within a specific range. This range can be a numeric range, such as 1 through 10; an alphabetic range, such as the letters *A* through *M*; or a date range, such as any date during the past year. A RangeValidator validation control works the same way as a RequiredFieldValidator validation control: You create a separate RangeValidator control for each TextBox in which the value must fall within a specific range, and specify the associated TextBox control's (ID) value and the validation control's ErrorMessage.

A RangeValidator validation control has three additional properties: MaximumValue specifies the maximum range value; MinimumValue specifies the minimum value; and Type specifies the data type. The MinimumValue must always be less than the MaximumValue, or an error occurs. The Type property value can have a value of String, Integer, Double, Date, or Currency. If you select one of the numeric data types (Integer, Double, Date, or Currency), the MaximumValue and MinimumValue properties must be numbers.

If you select the String data type, the MaximumValue and MinimumValue property values can be letters or numbers. Recall that the MaximumValue must always be larger than

8

the MinimumValue. Sometimes evaluating relationships among String data values is not straightforward: For example, is the number 0 less than or greater than the letter *a*?

RangeValidator validation controls evaluate string values using ASCII (American Standard Code for Information Interchange) character codes. Recall that computers translate all data values, including characters, to binary numbers. When users enter letters and decimal numbers as Web form inputs, the computer must translate these inputs to binary numbers. Because binary numbers are difficult for most people to understand and interpret, the ASCII character codes represent data values such as numbers, letters, and symbols (such as # or &) using decimal numbers. For example, the ASCII code for the number 0 is 48, and the ASCII code for the lowercase letter *a* is 97. (Since the ASCII character code 48 is less than the ASCII character code 97, the number 0 is in fact less than the letter *a*.)

When you set the Type property of a RangeValidator validation control to String, you can set the MaximumValue and MinimumValue properties to any printable ASCII character value. Table 8-5 shows the printable ASCII character codes and their associated values. (The non-printable ASCII character codes, which are not shown, represent keyboard instructions that a printer cannot display, such as Esc or Shift.)

**Table 8-5**   Printable ASCII character codes

| Code | Value | Code | Value | Code | Value | Code | Value | Code | Value |
|------|-------|------|-------|------|-------|------|-------|------|-------|
| 33 | ! | 53 | 5 | 73 | I | 93 | ] | 113 | q |
| 34 | " | 54 | 6 | 74 | J | 94 | ^ | 114 | r |
| 35 | # | 55 | 7 | 75 | K | 95 | _ | 115 | s |
| 36 | $ | 56 | 8 | 76 | L | 96 | ` | 116 | t |
| 37 | % | 57 | 9 | 77 | M | 97 | a | 117 | u |
| 38 | & | 58 | : | 78 | N | 98 | b | 118 | v |
| 39 | ' | 59 | ; | 79 | O | 99 | c | 119 | w |
| 40 | ( | 60 | < | 80 | P | 100 | d | 120 | x |
| 41 | ) | 61 | = | 81 | Q | 101 | e | 121 | y |
| 42 | * | 62 | > | 82 | R | 102 | f | 122 | z |
| 43 | + | 63 | ? | 83 | S | 103 | g | 123 | { |
| 44 | , | 64 | @ | 84 | T | 104 | h | 124 | \| |
| 45 | - | 65 | A | 85 | U | 105 | i | 125 | } |
| 46 | . | 66 | B | 86 | V | 106 | j | 126 | ~ |
| 47 | / | 67 | C | 87 | W | 107 | k | | |
| 48 | 0 | 68 | D | 88 | X | 108 | l | | |
| 49 | 1 | 69 | E | 89 | Y | 109 | m | | |
| 50 | 2 | 70 | F | 90 | Z | 110 | n | | |
| 51 | 3 | 71 | G | 91 | [ | 111 | o | | |
| 52 | 4 | 72 | H | 92 | \ | 112 | p | | |

To specify a String value range, you enter the minimum value in the RangeValidator's MinimumValue property, and you enter the maximum value in the RangeValidator's MaximumValue property. For example, to specify that a TextBox control must contain a lowercase letter between *a* and *z*, you type *a* in the Minimum property and *z* in the MaximumValue property. This specifies that the user can only enter character values whose ASCII codes are between the ASCII codes for *a*, which is 97, and *z*, which is 122. If the user enters a value that is outside this range, such as an uppercase *A*, which has the ASCII code value 65, an error occurs.

To gain experience using the RangeValidator validation control, you will add a RangeValidator validation control to the Validation.aspx Web form and use it to confirm that the value that the user enters in the Age TextBox is a number between 1 and 115.

To create a RangeValidaton validation control:

1. If necessary, select the Validation.aspx tab in the Browser Window to display the Validation.aspx Web form in Design view.

2. Open the Toolbox, make sure the Web Forms tab is selected, then select the **RangeValidator** tool. (You may need to scroll down in the Toolbox.) Add a RangeValidator control beside the *Age* TextBox control, as shown in Figure 8-22.

3. If necessary, select the new RangeValidator control. Open the Properties Window if necessary, then set the RangeValidator control's ControlToValidate property to **txtAge**, ErrorMessage to **Valid ages are between 1 and 115**, MaximumValue to **115**, MinimumValue to **1**, and Type to **Integer**. (If necessary, resize the RangeValidator control so the error message text appears on a single line.)

4. Click the **Start** button ▶ to run the project. Type **a** in the *Age* TextBox, and then press **Tab**. The RangeValidator's ErrorMessage appears because the input is not of the correct data type.

5. Change the *Age* value to **25** and press **Tab**. The error message no longer appears.

6. Close Internet Explorer.

## Creating CompareValidator Validation Controls

You use the CompareValidator control to compare an input value with another input value or to compare an input value with a predefined literal value. For example, you would use a CompareValidator control to compare a *Password* field with the value in a second field that you use to validate the password value. You can also use a CompareValidator validation control to validate that an input value is of a specific data type by specifying the required data type in the control's Type property.

As with the other validation controls, you use the ControlToValidate property to specify the TextBox that you associate with the validation control, and you use the ErrorMessage property to define the error message that appears on the Web form. To use the validation control to compare the input value to the value of another TextBox rich server control on the Web form, you specify the other TextBox's (ID) value in the validator control's ControlToCompare property. To use the validation control to compare the input value to a literal value, you specify the literal value in the validation control's ValueToCompare property. If you assign values to both the ControlToCompare and ValueToCompare properties, an error occurs.

Now you will create a CompareValidator validation control that you will associate with the *Confirm Password* TextBox control. You will use the validation control to confirm that the *Confirm Password* input value contains the same value as the *Password* TextBox.

To add a CompareValidator control to the validation Web page:

1. If necessary, click the Validation.aspx tab to open the Validation.aspx Web form in Design view, then open the Toolbox and select the **CompareValidator** tool.

2. Draw the **CompareValidator** validation control on the right edge of the *Confirm Password* Textbox, as shown in Figure 8-22.

3. If necessary, select the new CompareValidator validation control, open the Properties Window if necessary, set the ControlToValidate property to **txtConfirmpassword**, ControlToCompare to **txtPassword** and the ErrorMessage to **Value does not match Password entry**. Make sure that the Type property value is String.

4. Click the **Start** button ▶ to run the project.

5. Type **asdf** in the *Password* TextBox, type **jklm** in the *Confirm Password* TextBox, then press **Tab**. The validation control message beside the *Confirm Password* TextBox appears. (The error messages beside the required fields may also appear.)

6. Change the *Confirm Password* TextBox value to **asdf**, then press **Tab**. The error message beside the *Confirm Password* TextBox no longer appears.

7. Close Internet Explorer.

## Creating RegularExpressionValidator Validation Controls

Another important data validation task is to ensure that users enter input values such as dates and telephone numbers in the correct formats. For example, the *Birth Date* TextBox requires users to enter date values using the format *mm/dd/yyyy*. An example of a date in this format is 12/04/1984. If a user enters the date in a different format, such as 04-DEC-1984, an error will occur when the program on the Web server tries to process the value.

The RegularExpressionValidator confirms that an input value is in a specific format based on a regular expression. A **regular expression** is a concise and specific syntax that programmers use to specify a pattern of letters, numbers, and formatting characters. As with the other validation controls, you create a RegularExpressionValidator validation control for each TextBox that you wish to validate. You assign the TextBox (ID) value to the validation control's ControlToValidate property, and the desired error message to the ErrorMessage property. You specify the required format as a regular expression in the validation control's ValidationExpression property.

You can use the Regular Expression Editor dialog box shown in Figure 8-24 to select or specify the ValidationExpression property value. The Regular Expression Editor dialog box displays choices for Standard Expressions such as telephone numbers, e-mail addresses, URLs, postal codes, and social security numbers.

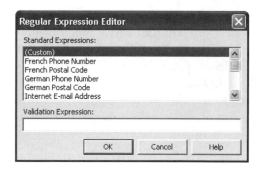

**Figure 8-24**    Regular Expression Editor dialog box

Now you will create a RegularExpressionValidator validation control that evaluates whether the user enters the *Home Phone* value using the format *xxx-xxx-xxxx*, such as the value 715-555-5555. Notice that you can assign multiple validation controls to the same TextBox control. Recall that the *Home Phone* TextBox already has a RequiredFieldValidator validation control to validate that the user enters a value. You will place the new validation control directly below the existing validation control.

To create RegularExpressionValidator validation control:

1. If necessary, click the Validation.aspx tab to display the form in Design view. Open the Toolbox, select the **RegularExpressionValidator** tool, and draw a **RegularExpressionValidator** validation control directly below the RequiredFieldValidator validation control for the *Home Phone* TextBox, as shown in Figure 8-22.

2. If necessary, select the new RegularExpressionValidator validation control, open the Properties Window if necessary, and change the ControlToValidate value to **txtHPhone** and ErrorMessage to **Please enter your phone number in the format "xxx-xxx-xxxx"**.

3. Select the **ValidationExpression** property, and then click the **More** button [...]. The Regular Expression Editor dialog box opens.

4. Scroll down the Standard Expressions list and select **U.S. Phone Number**. The regular expression syntax for the format *xxx-xxx-xxxx* appears in the *Validation Expression* field. You will learn about this syntax later. Click **OK** to accept the selection and close the Regular Expression Editor dialog box.

5. Click the **Start** button ▶ to run the project.

6. Type **7155555555** in the *Home Phone* TextBox and then press **Tab**. Because this value is not in the correct format, a message appears prompting you to enter the value in the correct format.

7. Change the *Phone Number* value to **715–555–5555**, which is the correct format, and then press **Tab**. The error message no longer appears.

8. Close Internet Explorer.

Unfortunately, the *Standard Expressions* list in the Regular Expressions Editor dialog box does not provide standard date format selections. You can verify that an input value has the Date data type by creating CompareValidator or RangeValidator validation controls, but this does not ensure that a date value has a specific format. For example, 01/01/06, 1/1/2006, and 01-January-2006 are all valid Date data type values, but they use very different formats. To ensure that a date value is in a specific format, you must create a RegularExpressionValidator validation control and specify the date format as a regular expression.

When you specify a regular expression, you specify characters that must appear in the expression. For example, the regular expression that specifies the *xxx-xxx-xxxx* telephone number format contains hyphens (-) as formatting characters. A regular expression also contains special characters, called **metacharacters**, which specify items such as numbers or repeating characters within the expression.

The back slash (\) signals the beginning of a metacharacter sequence. An important metacharacter sequence is \d, which specifies that the expression must contain a digit with a value between 0 and 9. The \d metacharacter sequence usually appears with a set of curly braces ({}) that enclose a number. This number specifies that the expression contains a specific number of digits. For example, the regular expression \d{2} specifies that the data value must contain exactly two digits, such as 01 or 12. The following regular expression specifies a date in the format *mm/dd/yyyy*, which consists of two digits, a front slash, two more digits, another front slash, and then four digits: \d{2}/ \d{2}/\d{4}. Figure 8-25 illustrates a date value in this format and shows the corresponding regular expression specification.

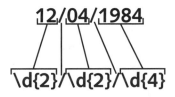

**Figure 8-25**    Date value and its associated regular expression specification

Now you will create a RegularExpressionValidator validation control for the *Birth Date* TextBox. You will specify the regular expression manually using the syntax in Figure 8-25.

To create a RegularExpressionValidator validation control by specifying the regular expression manually:

1. In the Validation.aspx Web form in Design view, create a RegularExpressionValidator validation control beside the *Birth Date* TextBox.

2. Make sure that the new *RegularExpressionValidator* is selected, open the Properties Window if necessary, then set the ControlToValidate value to **txtBirthDate** and the ErrorMessage value to **Please enter a date in the format mm/dd/yyyy**.

3. Select the **ValidationExpression** property, click the **More** button $\boxed{...}$ to open the Regular Expression Editor dialog box, then type **\d{2}/\d{2}/ \d{4}** in the *Validation Expression* field to specify the regular expression.

4. Click **OK** to save your expression and close the Regular Expression Editor dialog box.

5. Click the **Start** button ▶ to run the project. Type **12-4-84** in the *Birth Date* TextBox, then press **Tab**. The error message prompting you to enter the date in the correct format appears.

6. Change the *Birth Date* value to **12/4/84**, then press **Tab** again. Because the date is still not in the correct format, the error message still appears.

7. Change the *Birth Date* value to **12/04/1984**, which is the correct format, then press **Tab** again. The error message no longer appears.

8. Close Internet Explorer.

Many more options exist for creating regular expressions that allow the user to enter data values in different formats. For example, in the regular expression you created, the user must enter the date exactly as 12/04/1984, rather than as 12/4/1984.

## Creating ValidationSummary Validation Controls

Every validation control you have created so far displays its error message as a separate text message on the Web form. A **ValidationSummary validation control** displays all form validation error messages in a single error message. You can configure a ValidationSummary validation control to display the error summary in a JavaScript alert or to display the summary as text directly on the Web form, as shown in Figure 8-26.

To display the alert, you set a ValidationSummary validation control's ShowMessageBox property value to True. To display the text summary, you set the control's ShowSummary property value to True. If you set both of these properties to True, the validation control displays both the alert and the text message, as shown in Figure 8-26.

8

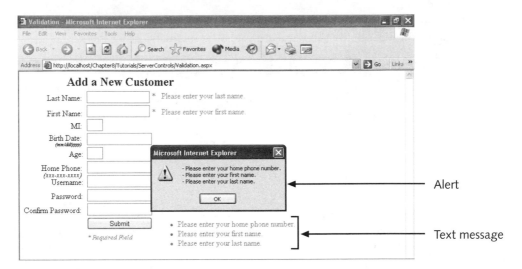

**Figure 8-26**   ValidationSummary alert and text message

When do you need to create a ValidationSummary validation control? Sometimes you create a Web form that contains many controls. If all of the controls are not visible on the user's screen display at the same time, the user must scroll up or down the screen display to view different form controls. Suppose a validation error occurs within a TextBox control that is at the top of the form, and the top of the form doesn't currently appear on the user's screen display. When the user tries to submit the form to the Web server, the error message appears, but the user cannot see it. As a result, the user will not understand why he or she cannot successfully submit the form to the Web server. Now you will add a ValidationSummary validation control to the Validation.aspx Web form.

To add a ValidationSummary validation control to the Web form:

1. If necessary, click the Validation.aspx tab to open the Web form in Design view, then open the Toolbox, select the **ValidationSummary** tool, and draw a ValidationSummary validation control in the position of the text message in Figure 8-26.

2. If necessary, select the new ValidationSummary validation control, open the Properties Window if necessary, and change the ShowMessageBox property to **True**. Make sure that the ShowSummary property value is True.

3. Click the **Start** button ▶ to run the project. Do not enter any inputs in the form TextBox controls, and then click **Submit**. The ValidationSummary alert and text message appear as shown in Figure 8-26. Note that the form first displays the RequiredFieldValidator validation controls.

4. Click **OK** to close the alert, then close Internet Explorer.

Recall that you can display the ValidationSummary validation control information either in the alert, the text summary, or both. It is probably best to display only the alert, because the alert always appears on the user's screen display regardless of which part of the Web form is currently visible.

## Creating CustomValidator Validation Controls

In the standard validation controls you have created so far, if the user input does not match the control specifications, an error message specified by the control's ErrorMessage property appears in the validation control. Sometimes you want to create custom validation controls that work differently. For example, you may want to display an alert that contains a specific message for a specific validation control. Or, you may want to place the insertion point in the TextBox control where the error occurs and select the current text. To create custom validation controls, you use a **CustomValidator validation control**, which calls a custom client-side JavaScript function or a server-side VB .NET procedure that a Web programmer creates to validate the input values. These custom functions or procedures can validate input values for one or more Web form controls.

To create a CustomValidator validation control, you create the validation control on the Web form and then specify its ControlToValidate property as one of the form controls. When the user changes the value in this control, the client-side function associated with the CustomValidator control executes.

 To use JavaScript commands to validate the values of other form control values besides the selected one, do not specify a value in the ControlToValidate property.

You change the CustomValidator validation control's ClientValidationFunction property to the name of the JavaScript function that the validation control calls. Then, you add the code for the JavaScript client-side form validation function to the Web form in HTML view. This custom validation function uses syntax similar to what you learned in Chapter 4 for creating client-side form validation functions.

Now you will add a CustomValidator validation control to the Validation.aspx Web form, and associate it with the *Username* TextBox control. You will use this validation control to ensure that the Username value that the user enters is at least eight characters long. You will specify that the validation control will call a client-side JavaScript function named ValidateInputs.

To add a CustomValidator validation control to the Web form:

1. If necessary, select the Validation.aspx tab in the Browser window to display the Web form in Design view.

2. Open the Toolbox, make sure that the Web Forms tab is selected, select the **CustomValidator** tool, and draw a new validation control to the right of the *Username* TextBox control.

3. Make sure that the new CustomValidator control is selected, open the Properties Window if necessary, and change the ClientValidationFunction property to **ValidateEntries**, the ControlToValidate property to **txtUsername**, and the ErrorMessage property to **Please enter a Username that has at least 8 characters**.

Next you will open the Validation.aspx Web form in HTML view and add the code for the JavaScript function. The function declaration must contain two separate parameters: the first parameter is named val, and the second parameter is named args. (You can use different names for these parameters; the position of the parameter specifies its purpose.) The system uses the val parameter to process the validation function, and it uses the args parameter to represent the value that the function returns. The args parameter has an IsValid property that you set within the function as either true or false. If `args.IsValid` is true, the form validation function succeeds, the form raises the post-back event, and the browser posts the form back to the Web Server. If `args.IsValid` is false, the form validation function fails, the postback event is not raised, and the browser continues to process the form until the validation function succeeds.

Now you will add the JavaScript commands to create the client-side validation function and then run the form. The JavaScript function will create a new String object to represent the text that the user enters in the *Username* TextBox. It will use the JavaScript length property to evaluate whether the String object is at least eight characters long. If the *Username* value is not at least eight characters long, the form validation function returns the value false and selects the current *Username* value. The CustomValidator control displays the error message on the form, and the ValidationSummary control displays the error message in an alert.

When you run the form, you must press Enter or click Submit to execute the CustomValidator validation function. Pressing the Tab key or clicking the insertion point in a different form control does not execute the CustomValidator validation function.

To add the custom JavaScript client-side validation function to the Web form:

1. In the Browser Window in Design view, click the **HTML** tab to display the Web form in HTML view.

2. Place the insertion point after the closing angle bracket (>) in the opening **<body>** tag, press **Enter** to create a new blank line, then add the commands in Figure 8-27 to create the JavaScript function.

3. Click the **Start** button ▶ to run the project. Type the required field values of **Harris** in the *Last Name* TextBox control, **Paula** in the *First Name* TextBox control, and **715–555–5555** in the *Home Phone* TextBox control.

```
<script language="javascript">
<!--
    function ValidateEntries (val, args) {
        args.IsValid = false;
        var currentUsername = new String();
        currentUsername.value = document.Form1.txtUsername.value;
        if (currentUsername.value.length < 8) {
            document.Form1.txtUsername.select();
        } else {
            args.IsValid = true;
        }
    }
//-->
</script>
```

**Figure 8-27**    Client-side JavaScript validation function

4. Type **asdf** in the *Username* TextBox control, and then click **Submit**. Because this is not a valid *Username* value, a ValidationSummary alert appears prompting you to enter a user name that has at least eight characters. Click **OK** to close the alert. The error message also appears in the CustomValidator validation control on the form.

5. Type **asdfjklm** in the *Username* TextBox control, and then click **Submit**. Because this is a valid *Username* value, the validation function succeeds, the Web form is posted back to the server, and the message "Paula Harris has been submitted" appears in the form's Message Label.

6. Close Internet Explorer.

To minimize network traffic, Web forms process validation functions on the client workstation. However, because some users' browsers do not support JavaScript functions, you should always create alternate server-side validation procedures for CustomValidator validation controls. To create a server-side validation procedure, you double-click the CustomValidator validation control in the Browser Window in Design view, and Visual Studio .NET creates an event handler template for the validation procedure. Now you will reopen the Web form in Design view, and create the server-side validation event handler template.

To create the server-side validation event handler template:

1. In Visual Studio .NET, click the **Design** tab to display the Web form in Design view.

2. Double-click the **CustomValidator** validation control to create the event handler template. The Code editor window opens and displays the event handler template, which is named CustomValidator1_ServerValidate.

The event template appears as follows in the Code editor:

```
Private Sub CustomValidator1_ServerValidate ↵
(ByVal source As System.Object, ByVal args As ↵
System.Web.UI.WebControls.ServerValidateEventArgs) ↵
Handles CustomValidator1.ServerValidate
End Sub
```

The event handler procedure's declaration contains a parameter named source and a parameter named args. The source parameter references the CustomerValidator control, and the args parameter specifies whether the validation procedure succeeds or fails. In the event handler, you set the **args.IsValid** property to True if the procedure succeeds, and you set the value to False if the procedure fails.

To make the server-side event handler operational, you must also add a decision control structure to the Submit button's Click event handler. This decision control structure evaluates whether the Web form's IsValid property value is True or False. If the value is True, the event handler processes the Click event commands. If the value is False, the event handler does not execute the Click event commands. In the Click event handler, you reference the IsValid property value using the syntax **Me.IsValid**. The keyword **Me** references the current Web page.

Now you will modify the code in the Submit button's Click event handler by adding the VB .NET commands to process or skip the Click event actions based on the outcome of the validation. You will also add the commands to the validation control's event handler template to determine whether the *Username* value has at least eight characters. In addition, you will disable the client-side validation function by setting the CustomValidator validation control's EnableClientScript property to False. Then you will run the form and test the server-side validation procedure.

To create and test the server-side validation procedure:

1. In the Code editor, add the shaded the commands to the btnSubmit_Click event handler as shown in Figure 8-28.

2. Add the shaded commands to the server-side validation event handler to evaluate the *Username* length as shown in Figure 8-28. (Note that these commands perform processing tasks similar to the client-side JavaScript validation function in Figure 8-27, except that you cannot select the text that appears in a Web form using postback processing.)

3. Click the **Validation.aspx** tab on the Browser window, select the **CustomValidator** validation control, make sure the Properties Window is open, and then change the EnableClientScript property to **False**.

4. Click the **Start** button ▶ to run the project. Type the required field values of **Harris** in the *Last Name* TextBox control, **Paula** in the *First Name* TextBox control, and **715-555-5555** in the *Home Phone* TextBox control.

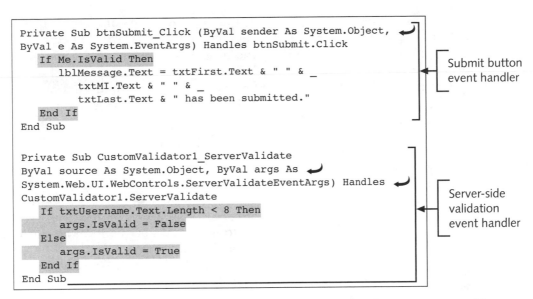

```
Private Sub btnSubmit_Click (ByVal sender As System.Object,
ByVal e As System.EventArgs) Handles btnSubmit.Click
    If Me.IsValid Then
        lblMessage.Text = txtFirst.Text & " " & _
        txtMI.Text & " " & _
        txtLast.Text & " has been submitted."
    End If
End Sub


Private Sub CustomValidator1_ServerValidate
ByVal source As System.Object, ByVal args As
System.Web.UI.WebControls.ServerValidateEventArgs) Handles
CustomValidator1.ServerValidate
    If txtUsername.Text.Length < 8 Then
        args.IsValid = False
    Else
        args.IsValid = True
    End If
End Sub
```

Submit button event handler

Server-side validation event handler

**Figure 8-28**    Code to modify Submit button event handler and create a server-side validation event handler

5.  Type **asdf** in the *Username* TextBox control, and then click **Submit**. Because this is not a valid value, a ValidationSummary alert appears prompting you to enter a user name that has at least eight characters. Click **OK** to close the alert. The error message appears in the CustomValidator validation control and in the ValidationSummary control on the form.

6.  Type **asdfjklm** in the *Username* TextBox control, and then click **Submit**. Because this is a valid *Username* value, the validation function succeeds, the Web form is posted back to the server, and the message "Paula Harris has been submitted" appears in the form's Message Label.

7.  Close Internet Explorer, then close all open windows in the Browser window and close Visual Studio .NET.

For the most part, the non-custom Web form validation controls provide a convenient way to validate user inputs in TextBox controls. When you need to create more complex validation functions, you can easily do so using the CustomValidator control and creating an associated client-side JavaScript validation function.

There are a few disadvantages to using server-side validation controls to validate Web form inputs. First, the only way to show the user which Web form control generates a validation error is by displaying the error message beside the control. To flag an error by placing the insertion point in the control or selecting the incorrect text, you must create a CustomValidator validation control using a client-side JavaScript validation function, which requires more effort on the part of the Web programmer. Second, when you create a CustomValidator validation control, you cannot create separate client-side form validation functions and call them using the HTML form's onsubmit attribute. When a Web form contains server-side validation controls, the HTML source code that Visual Studio .NET renders automatically specifies a different function name in the HTML form's onsubmit attribute. Finally, you cannot create validation controls to validate the Calendar, CheckBoxList, and CheckBox rich server controls. To validate inputs in these controls, you must write CustomValidator validation functions using client-side JavaScript functions.

## CHAPTER SUMMARY

❑ During HTML form processing, the only way the user interacts with the Web server is through submitting the form. ASP.NET Web form processing is much more interactive, and allows the user to raise events on the form by performing actions such as changing text inputs or clicking buttons. The Web server executes event handlers associated with these events when the user performs an action that posts the Web form back to the server.

❑ Web form processing consists of the following stages: Initialization, in which ASP.NET initializes the form object class and objects and executes the Page_Init procedure; User Code Initialization, in which the system loads the form objects into memory and executes the Page_Load procedure; Validation, in which the Web server runs the code for server-side validation controls; Event Handling, in which the Web server executes event handlers associated with user events, then renders the HTML source code for the form's Web page that is returned to the user; and Cleanup, in which the system closes all open files and connections, and destroys objects used to render the source code.

❑ When a user raises multiple events on a Web form, the event handlers execute in the order in which the event's associated controls appear in the Web form's HTML code.

❑ Web developers should use HTML form elements to create static form items whose values do not change and are not referenced in program commands. They should use HTML server controls to create controls for which there is no comparable rich server control, and rich server controls to create form items that program commands reference.

❑ VB .NET commands in Web forms reference HTML form element and HTML server control properties and methods using HTML DOM referencing syntax, and they reference rich server controls using VB .NET referencing syntax.

❑ The RadioButtonList rich server control creates a radio button group in which you reference the individual radio buttons as list items. The CheckBoxList rich server control creates a series of related check boxes that you reference as list items.

❑ Validation controls are Web form controls that validate user inputs. These validation controls generate client-side JavaScript form validation functions. If a user's browser does not support JavaScript, the validation functions evaluate user inputs on the Web server during the Validation stage of Web form processing.

❏ The RequiredFieldValidator validation control evaluates whether a user enters a value in a required field. The CompareValidator compares a user input to another value. The CustomValidator associates a user input with a client-side JavaScript function or a server-side VB. NET procedure. The RangeValidator determines whether a user input is within an allowable range of values. The RegularExpressionValidator determines whether a user input matches an explicit input pattern or format. The ValidationSummary displays all error messages in a text summary or JavaScript alert.

## REVIEW QUESTIONS

1. In standard HTML form processing, the client browser passes form input values to the Web server:

    a. As a parameter list that appears on the Web page URL

    b. As `Private` class variables

    c. In the ViewState hidden form input

    d. As a result of a postback event

2. Describe the difference between the "get" and "post" form method attributes.

3. Write the HTML `<form>` tag for a Web form with the ID value "myForm" that has the "post" method attribute value.

4. True or false: During Web form processing, the client browser executes the Web form's .aspx file.

5. _____ processing involves repeatedly raising events on the client computer, executing event handlers on the Web server, and then returning the Web form's HTML source code to the client.

    a. HTML form

    b. Postback

    c. Event-driven

    d. Validation

6. List two Web form events that raise the postback event.

7. Write the HTML tags for a TextBox rich server control with the (ID) value "txtTextBox1," and for a second TextBox rich server control with the (ID) value "txtTextBox2." Omit the style specifications. Write the tags so that the event handler for "txtTextBox2" executes first during Web form processing.

8. When does the Web server create the ViewState input, and what does the ViewState input represent?

9. The Web server executes the Page_Init procedure during the _____ processing stage, and executes the Page_Load procedure during the _____ processing stage.

   a. User Code Initialization, Page Framework Initialization

   b. Page Framework Initialization, Event Handling

   c. User Code Initialization, Event Handling

   d. Page Framework Initialization, User Code Initialization

10. True or false: The Validation stage executes only during Web form processing for postback requests.

11. The Web server renders the Web form's HTML source code during the _____ stage of Web form processing.

12. You use the _____ property to determine whether a Web form is processing a first-time request or a postback request.

13. During Web form processing, which event handler always executes last?

14. How do you change the order in which event handlers execute during Web form processing?

15. Why should you create static Web form controls as standard HTML form elements rather than as HTML server controls or rich server controls?

16. A File Field is a(n) _____ that allows users to upload files to the Web server.

   a. Rich server control

   b. HTML server control

   c. HTML form element

   d. Validation control

17. In Visual Studio .NET, a small green arrow on the top-left corner of a control indicates that the control is a(n):

   a. HTML form element

   b. rich server control

   c. HTML server control

   d. Either b or c

18. Write the VB .NET command to reference the Text property of the third item in a ListBox rich server control that has the (ID) property "MyList."

19. Describe the differences between the CheckBox and the CheckBoxList rich server controls.

20. Why should you create Calendar rich server controls sparingly in Web forms?

21. Write a regular expression to specify the following formats:

    a. United States social security numbers formatted as 111-11-1111

    b. United States nine-digit postal codes formatted as 54701-1234

    c. Telephone numbers formatted as (715)555-5555

    d. Dates formatted as 12-04-1984

22. List the user actions that execute the client-side script commands for the non-custom validation controls.

23. What is a ValidationSummary validation control, and when should a form contain one?

---

## HANDS-ON PROJECTS

To complete the Chapter 8 Hands-on Projects, you will first need to create a Web server application named Projects that you associate with the Chapter8\Projects folder on your Solution Disk. You will also need to create a Web application project named VBProjects whose application root is the Chapter8\Projects application on your Web server. Then you will add the files for each Hands-on project to this Web application project as individual Web forms. Copy the clearlogo.jpg, nwlogo.jpg, and calendar1.gif files from the Chapter8 folder on your Data Disk to the Chapter8\Projects\VBProjects folder on your Solution Disk so the graphic images appear correctly on the Web forms. (Visual Studio .NET creates the VBProjects folder when you create the new VBProjects Web application project.)

### Project 8-1 Creating the Northwoods University Student Information Web Form

In this project, you will create the Web form shown in Figure 8-29. This form allows Northwoods University students to enter student information.

1. Create a new Web form named StudentInfo.aspx in the VBProjects Web application project that you created based on the instructions in the Note at the beginning of the Hands-on projects.

2. Create HTML form elements to represent the logo image and static form labels.

3. Create TextBox rich server controls to represent the text inputs. Assign descriptive values to the (ID) properties of the TextBox controls.

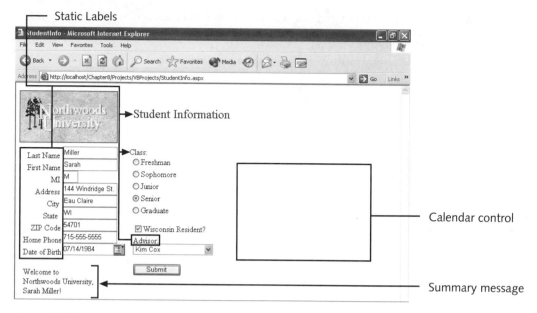

**Figure 8-29**

4. Create a RadioButtonList rich server control to represent the student's class. Change the ID property value of the RadioButtonList to optClass. Assign the following values to the list items:

| Index | Text | Value |
|-------|------|-------|
| 0 | Freshman | FR |
| 1 | Sophomore | SO |
| 2 | Junior | JR |
| 3 | Senior | SR |
| 4 | Graduate | GR |

5. Create a CheckBox rich server control to specify whether the student is a Wisconsin resident, as shown in Figure 8-29. Change the CheckBox's (ID) property to chkResident.

6. Create a DropDownList rich server control to list the names of the student advisors. Specify the list's (ID) property value as lstAdvisor, and specify the list items as follows:

| Index | Text | Value |
|-------|------|-------|
| 0 | Kim Cox | 1 |
| 1 | John Blanchard | 2 |
| 2 | Jerry Williams | 3 |

7. Create a Calendar rich server control with the (ID) property value calDOB that appears on the right side of the form, as shown in the outline in Figure 8-29. Configure the Calendar so that it does not appear when the form first opens. Also create an Image Button rich server control with the (ID) property value btnCalendar. The control should appear on the right edge of the *Date of Birth* TextBox, as shown in Figure 8-29. Display the calendar1.gif image on the Image Button. Create event handlers so that when the user clicks the Image Button, the Calendar appears. When the user selects a date in the calendar, the date appears in the *Date of Birth* TextBox and the Calendar no longer appears.

8. Create a Button rich server control that has the label "Submit," and create a Label rich server control on the left side of the button, as shown in Figure 8-29. The Label should not display any text when the form first opens. When the user clicks the Submit button, display a message showing the student's first and last name formatted as shown in Figure 8-29.

9. Adjust the TabIndex properties of the Web form controls so the insertion point or form focus moves through the items in a top-down, left-to-right order.

## Project 8-2 Creating the Northwoods University Faculty Information Web Form

In this project, you will create the Web form shown in Figure 8-30. This form allows Northwoods University faculty members to enter information.

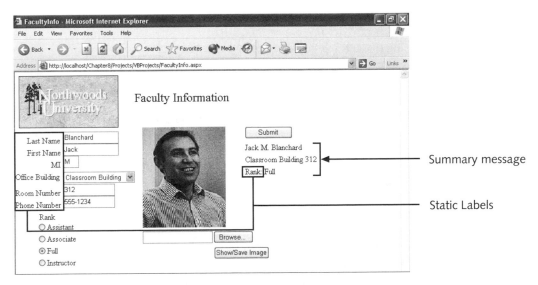

**Figure 8-30**

1. Copy the blanchard.jpg file from the Chapter8 folder on your Data Disk to the Chapter8\Projects\VBProjects folder on your Solution Disk.

2. Create a new Web form named FacultyInfo.aspx in the VBProjects Web application project that you created based on the instructions in the Note at the beginning of the Hands-on projects.

3. Create HTML form elements to represent the logo image and static form labels.

4. Create TextBox rich server controls to represent the text inputs. Assign descriptive values to the TextBox control (ID) properties.

5. Create a DropDownList rich server control to list the names of Northwoods University building locations. Specify the list's (ID) property value as lstBldgCode, and specify the list items as follows:

| Index | Text | Value |
|-------|------|-------|
| 0 | Classroom Building | CR |
| 1 | Business Building | BUS |
| 2 | Library | LIB |

6. Create a RadioButtonList rich server control to represent the faculty member's rank. Change the property value of the RadioButtonList to optRank. Assign the following values to the list items:

| Index | Text | Value |
|-------|------|-------|
| 0 | Assistant | ASST |
| 1 | Associate | ASSO |
| 2 | Full | FULL |
| 3 | Instructor | INST |

7. Create an Image rich server control to display the faculty member's photograph. Change the (ID) property value of the Image to imgPhoto.

8. Create a File Field HTML server control and a Button rich server control with the Label "Show/Save Image." The user clicks Browse and then selects the image file. (You will select the blanchard.jpg file from the Chapter8\Projects\VBProjects folder on your Solution Disk.) Then the user clicks Show/Save Image, which causes the image file to appear in the imgPhoto rich server control and causes the system to upload the image file to the Web server. Create a folder named Uploads in the Chapter8\Projects folder on your Solution Disk, then save the uploaded file in the Uploads folder and specify that the filename is the faculty member's last name as it appears in the *Last Name* text input. Do not specify a file extension on the uploaded filename. (Hint: To display the image in the Image control dynamically, set the Image control's ImageUrl to the name of the selected file in the File Field HTML server control.)

9. Create three separate Label rich server controls to summarize the faculty member's full name, office location and room number, and rank, as shown in Figure 8-30. Also create a Button rich server control with the label "Submit." Create an event handler for the Submit button that displays the summary Label controls after the user clicks Submit.

10. Configure the TabIndex properties of the server controls so the insertion point moves through the form in a top-down, left-to-right order.

## Project 8-3 Creating the Northwoods University Enrollment Web Form

In this project, you will create the Web form shown in Figure 8-31. This form allows Northwoods University students to enroll in courses.

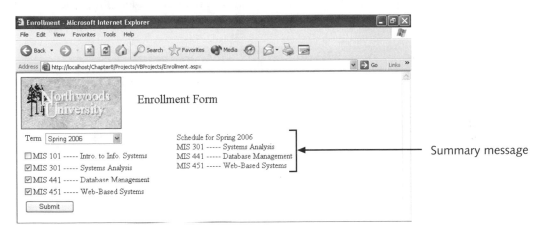

**Figure 8-31**

1. Create a new Web form named Enrollment.aspx in the VBProjects Web application project that you created based on the instructions in the Note at the beginning of the Hands-on projects.

2. Create HTML form elements to represent the logo image and static form labels.

3. Create a DropDownList rich server control to list the term descriptions. Specify the list's (ID) property value as lstTerms, and specify the list items as follows:

| Index | Text | Value |
|-------|-------------|-------|
| 0 | Fall 2005 | 1 |
| 1 | Spring 2006 | 2 |
| 2 | Summer 2006 | 3 |

4. Create a CheckBoxList rich server control that displays course call ID and name information as shown in Figure 8-31. Specify the (ID) property of the CheckBoxList as chkCourses. Specify the Text properties of the list items as shown in Figure 8-31, and specify that the Value property is the same as the Text property for each item.

5. Create a Button rich server control with the (ID) property value btnSubmit and the Text property "Submit." Also create a Label rich server control that summarizes the course selections as shown in Figure 8-31.

## Project 8-4 Validating the Clearwater Traders Receive Shipment Web Form

In this project, you will add validation controls to the Receive Shipment Web form shown in Figure 8-32. This form allows Clearwater Traders employees to enter information about incoming merchandise shipments.

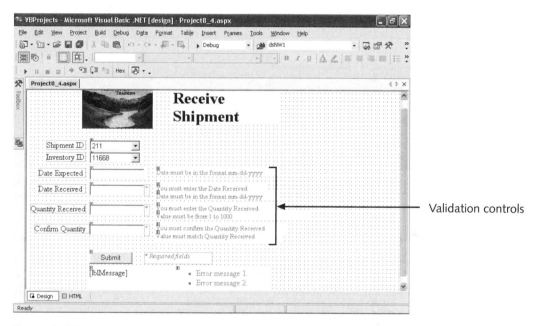

**Figure 8-32**

1. Copy the Project8_4.aspx and Project8_4.aspx.vb files from the Chapter8 folder on your Data Disk to the Chapter8\Projects\VBProjects folder on your Solution Disk, then add the files to your VBProjects Web application project that you created based on the instructions in the Note at the beginning of the Hands-on Projects.

2. Create RequiredFieldValidator validation controls for the TextBox controls that are marked as required fields. Configure the validation controls so their error messages appear as shown in Figure 8-32.

3. Create a RangeValidator validation control to confirm that the Quantity Received input value is an integer that is greater than or equal to 1 and less than or equal to 1,000. Display the validation control's error message directly below the TextBox control's RequiredFieldValidator validation control message.

4. Create a CompareValidator validation control that confirms that the *Quantity Received* and *Confirm Quantity* values are the same. If the values are not the same, display the error message beside the *Confirm Quantity* TextBox.

5. Create RegularExpressionValidator validation controls to confirm that the *Date Expected* and *Date Received* input values are in the date format *mm-dd-yyyy*. A valid date value would be 07-15-2006. Display the error messages beside the associated TextBox controls and just below any existing error messages.

6. Create a ValidationSummary validation control that displays all of the validation error messages in an alert only.

## Project 8-5 Validating the Clearwater Traders Receive Shipments Web Form Using a CustomValidator

In this project, you will create a CustomValidator validation control to validate the user inputs in the Clearwater Traders Receive Shipments Web form in Figure 8-32.

1. Copy the Project8_5.aspx and Project8_5.aspx.vb files to the Chapter8\Projects\ VBProjects folder on your Solution Disk, and add the files to the VBProjects Web application project that you created based on the instructions in the Note at the beginning of the Hands-on Projects.

2. Add a CustomValidator validation control to the Project8_5.aspx Web form. Specify its client-side JavaScript function as ValidateItems and its error message text as "Invalid input values," and place the error message on the left side of the Submit button.

3. Write an associated JavaScript form validation function to validate the form inputs. Confirm that the user enters values in the required fields, that the Quantity Received value is greater than or equal to 1 and less than or equal to 1,000, and that the Quantity Received and Confirm Quantity input values are the same. (Refer to Chapter 4 if necessary to review the JavaScript syntax for form validation functions.) Display a custom alert for each validation test to advise the user of the nature of the error, and then add a command to select the form control that causes the error. For example, if the user does not enter a value in the *Date Received* input, display an alert with the message "Please enter a value for Date Received," and place the insertion point in the *Date Received* input.

8

## CASE PROJECTS

To solve the case projects in this chapter, you must first create a new Web server application that you associate with the Chapter8\Cases folder on your Solution Disk, and you must modify your Visual Studio .NET IDE so it places all project solution files in the Chapter8\Cases folder on your Solution Disk.

### Case Project 8-1 Ashland Valley Soccer League

Create a Web application project named AshlandProject whose application root is the Chapter8/Cases application on your Web server. Copy all of the files from the Chapter8\Cases\Ashland folder on your Data Disk to the Chapter8\Cases\AshlandProject folder on your Solution Disk. (You will need to create the Web application project first, then copy the files into the project folder that Visual Studio .NET creates.)

Add the AshlandHome.htm static Web page and the FieldsForm.aspx, GamesForm.aspx, and TeamsForm.aspx Web forms and their associated code behind files to the project. Then modify the GamesForm.aspx Web form to allow the user to select the Home Team, Visiting Team, and Field values using DropDownList rich server controls. Specify the list values using the data on the TeamsForm.aspx and FieldsForm.aspx Web forms. Add a CheckBox rich server control to specify whether or not the game has been played. Add a Button rich server control with the Text "Submit" to the Web form, and a Label rich server control that displays a summary of the game information when the user submits the form. Add validation controls to confirm that the user enters values in the Date and *Time* TextBox controls, that the *Date* value has the format *mm/dd/yyyy*, and that the *Time* value has the format *hh:mi*, where *hh* represents the hours and *mi* represents the minutes. Also confirm that the *Home Team* and *Visiting Team* values are not the same.

### Case Project 8-2 Al's Body Shop

Create a Web application project named AlsProject whose application root is the Chapter8/Cases application on your Web server. Copy all of the files from the Chapter8\Cases\Als folder on your Data Disk to the Chapter8\Cases\AlsProject folder on your Solution Disk. (You will need to create the Web application project first, then copy the files into the project folder that Visual Studio .NET creates.)

Add to the project the AlsHome.htm static Web page and the CustomerForm.aspx, ServiceForm.aspx, and WorkOrderForm.aspx Web forms and their associated code behind files. Then modify the WorkOrderForm.aspx Web form to allow the user to select the *work order date* using a Calendar control and the *customer* using a DropDownList rich server control. Specify the list values using the data on the CustomerForm.aspx Web form. Add a CheckBoxList rich server control to list the available services. Add a Button rich server control with the Text "Submit" to the Web form, and add a Label rich server control that displays a summary of the service order information when the user submits the form.

To complete Case 8-3, you must have completed Case 7-3 in Chapter 7.

## Case Project 8-3 Sun-Ray Videos

Create a Web application project named SunrayProject in the Chapter8\Cases application on your Web server. Copy the SunrayHome.htm static Web page file and the RentalsForm.aspx and VideosForm.aspx Web forms files and their associated code behind files that you created in Case 7-3 to the Chapter8\Cases\SunrayProject folder that Visual Studio .NET creates. Then add the individual files to the project.

Modify the RentalsForm.aspx Web form by deleting the current commands in the Page_Load() procedure, then adding Calendar controls to allow the user to select the *Rental Date* and the *Return Date*. (You will need to create a separate Calendar for each date.) Add a DropDownList rich server control to allow the user to select the video title based on the titles that the VideosForm displays. Add a Button rich server control with the Text "Submit" to the Web form, and add a Label rich server control that displays a summary of the rental information when the user submits the form.

To complete Case 8-4, you must have completed Case 7-4 in Chapter 7.

## Case Project 8-4 Learning Technologies, Incorporated

Create a Web application project named LtiProject in the Chapter8\Cases folder on your Solution Disk. Copy the LtiHome.htm HTML document and the AuthorsForm.aspx, BooksForm.aspx, WarehouseForm.aspx, and WarehouseQOHForm.aspx Web form files that you created in Case 7-4. Then add the individual files to the project.

Delete the commands in the Page_Load procedure in the WarehouseQOHForm.aspx Web form, then modify the form so it displays DropDownList rich server controls that allow the user to select the *Warehouse ID* and *Book* values based on the data values that appear on the WarehouseForm.aspx and BooksForm.aspx Web forms. Add a validation control to confirm that the user enters a *QOH* value. Add a Button rich server control with the Text "Submit" to the Web form, and add a Label rich server control that displays a summary of the rental information when the user submits the form.

## CHAPTER 9

# INTRODUCTION TO DATABASE CONCEPTS

## In this chapter, you will:

♦ Learn what a relational database is, become familiar with the structure of a relational database, and understand relational database concepts and terms

♦ Understand the differences between personal and client/server databases, and become familiar with the Oracle9*i* client/server database

♦ Explore the structure of the Clearwater Traders and Northwoods University relational databases

♦ Understand how Web forms communicate with databases and learn how to create a data connection in Visual Studio .NET

♦ Write SQL queries to retrieve records from a single database table, and learn how to sort and filter retrieved values

♦ Write SQL queries that join multiple database tables

♦ Write SQL queries to perform operations on groups of data values

♦ Write SQL queries to insert, update, and delete data records

To create Web pages that interact with data that is stored in a relational database, you must first have a basic understanding of relational databases. This chapter will familiarize you with relational database concepts. Because this book provides instructions for creating data-based Web pages using Oracle9*i*, which is a client/server database, and using Access, which is a personal database, you will also learn about the differences between client/server and personal databases.

Recall that data-based Web pages allow users to enter new data values, update and delete existing data values, and retrieve data values from a database. These Web pages call programs that use SQL commands to process user inputs that manipulate database data. This chapter describes how to create a connection to a database in Visual Studio .NET and how to create SQL commands in the Visual Studio .NET IDE to view, insert, update, and delete data.

All of the tutorials, projects, and cases in this book provide instructions using both the Oracle9*i* client/server database and the Access personal database.

---

## OVERVIEW OF RELATIONAL DATABASES

When organizations first began converting from manual to computerized data processing systems, each individual application had its own set of data files that were used only for that application. Figure 9-1 shows an example of a data file that contains information about students. This file contains individual data items, or **fields**, that describe characteristics about Northwoods University students, such as each student's last name, first name, middle initial, address, city, state, ZIP code, telephone number, class, date of birth, identification number, and the student's advisor's last and first name. Fields are also called **columns**. Each field value is separated by a comma. A collection of related fields that contain information about a single student is called a **record**. Each student record appears on a separate line in the file.

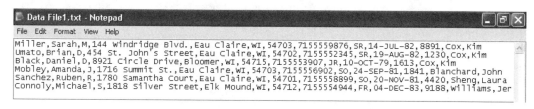

**Figure 9-1**    Example student data file

As applications became more complex, organizations encountered problems with managing data stored in data files. One problem was the proliferation of data management programs. Because each data file contained different data fields, programmers had to write and maintain a separate program to insert, update, delete, and retrieve data that is stored in each different data file. For a large organization with many data files, this involved a lot of programs that all performed essentially the same tasks.

Another problem with data files was the presence of redundant data. Figure 9-2 shows an example of a data file that contains information about the courses in which each student is enrolled.

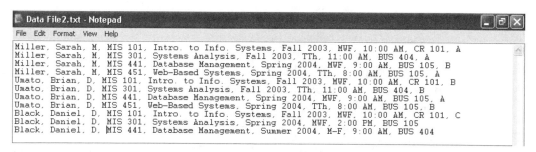

**Figure 9-2**    Enrollment data file containing redundant data

This file contains fields representing the student's last name, first name, and middle initial. The file also contains enrollment information for the student, including the associated course call number (such as MIS 101), course name, term, course section day, time, and location, and the student's course grade, if assigned. Note that the student names repeat for each course in which each student enrolls. Because each student will probably take many courses during his or her academic career, the file will store the student's last name, first name, and middle initial many times, which takes up valuable file space. Also, note that the information for each course section repeats for each student who enrolls in the course. If data about a course needs to be updated, such as the day, time, or location, it must be updated for each student/enrollment record, which makes the application for updating enrollment records more complex.

Yet another problem with data files is that they might contain inconsistent data. If a student changes his or her name, the name data must be updated in both the student file shown in Figure 9-1 and the enrollment file shown in Figure 9-2. If different files contain different data values for the same student, the system is inconsistent and errors occur.

To address these problems with data files, programmers developed databases to store and manage application data. A **database** stores data in a central location. A database strives to eliminate redundant data in order to reduce the possibility of inconsistent data. In a database system, a single application called the **database management system (DBMS)** performs all routine data handling operations. The DBMS provides a central set of common functions for managing a database, which include inserting, updating, retrieving, and deleting data values. The person who is responsible for installing, administering, and maintaining the database is called the **database administrator**, or **DBA**.

Most modern databases are **relational databases**, which store data in a tabular format. A relational database organizes data in **tables**, or matrixes with columns and rows. Columns represent different data fields, and rows contain individual records. Figure 9-3 shows an example of two relational database tables.

 In this book, database table and field names appear in all capital letters, such as STUDENT and S_LAST_NAME. Individual words are separated by underscores, such as S_ID and S_ADDRESS.

In database terminology, an **entity** is an object about which you want to store data. In a relational database, different tables store data about different entities. For example, one table stores data about students, a second table stores data about faculty members, and a third table stores data about courses. This minimizes storing redundant data. To connect information about different entities, you must create **relationships**, which are links that show how different records are related. For example, when you create a student enrollment record, you must create a relationship between the enrollment record and the student record, and between the enrollment record and the course record. Relationships among records in different tables are established through **key fields**. There are five main types of key fields in a relational database: primary keys, candidate keys, surrogate keys, foreign keys, and composite keys. The following sections describe these types of key fields in more detail.

Fields

Records

STUDENT

| S_ID | S_LAST_NAME | S_FIRST_NAME | S_MI | S_ADDRESS | S_STATE | S_ZIP |
|------|-------------|--------------|------|-----------|---------|-------|
| 100 | Miller | Sarah | M | 144 Windridge Blvd. | WI | 54703 |
| 101 | Umato | Brian | D | 454 St. John's Place | WI | 54702 |
| 102 | Black | Daniel | | 8921 Circle Drive | WI | 54715 |
| 103 | Mobley | Amanda | J | 1716 Summit St. | WI | 54703 |
| 104 | Sanchez | Ruben | R | 1780 Samantha Court | WI | 54701 |
| 105 | Connoly | Michael | S | 1818 Silver Street | WI | 54712 |

FACULTY

| F_ID | F_LAST_NAME | F_FIRST_NAME | F_MI | F_PHONE | F_RANK |
|------|-------------|--------------|------|---------|--------|
| 1 | Cox | Kim | J | 7155551234 | ASSO |
| 2 | Blanchard | John | R | 7155559087 | FULL |
| 3 | Williams | Jerry | F | 7155555412 | ASST |
| 4 | Sheng | Laura | M | 7155556409 | INST |
| 5 | Brown | Phillip | E | 7155556082 | ASSO |

**Figure 9-3**   Examples of relational database tables

## Primary Keys

A **primary key** is a field in a relational database table whose value must be unique for each record, and which serves to identify the record. Every record must have a primary key, and the primary key cannot be NULL. **NULL** means that a value is indeterminate or undefined. In the STUDENT table in Figure 9-3, the S_ID field is a good choice for the primary key because a unique value can be assigned for each student. The S_ADDRESS (student address) field might be another choice for the primary key, but there are two problems with using this field. First, two different students might have the same address. Second, the field contains text data that is prone to data entry errors, such as spelling errors and variations in capitalization. Being prone to data entry errors is a problem because database developers use primary key values to create relationships with other database tables, and the values must *exactly* match in the different tables. The best choice for a primary key field is a field that contains numerical data.

## Candidate Keys

When you are designing a relational database table, many fields might be possible choices for the table's primary key. A **candidate key** is a field that could be used as the primary key. A candidate key should be a numeric field that is unique for each record and does not change. Good candidate key choices include identification numbers such as product stock-keeping units (SKUs), book ISBN numbers, and student identification numbers.

Telephone numbers are not good candidate keys, because different people might share the same telephone number, and telephone numbers can change when a person moves to a new location. Social security numbers are not good candidate keys, because for security reasons many people are reluctant to provide their social security numbers for non-governmental purposes.

## Surrogate Keys

What do you do when a table does not contain any suitable candidate keys? Figure 9-4 shows a CUSTOMER table with this problem.

CUSTOMER table

| LAST_NAME | FIRST_NAME | ADDRESS | PHONE |
|-----------|-----------|---------|-------|
| Brown | John | 101 Main Street | 7155554321 |
| Brown | John | 3567 State Street | 7155558901 |
| Carlson | Mike | 233 Water Street | 7155557890 |
| Carlson | Martha | 233 Water Street | 7155557890 |
| Davis | Carol | 1414 South Street | 7155555566 |
| | | | |

**Figure 9-4**    Table lacking suitable candidate keys

The LAST_NAME or FIRST_NAME field, or even the combination of the two fields, is not a suitable candidate key because many people have the same name. Multiple people can share the same address and telephone number, and telephone numbers are not good candidate keys because people often change their telephone numbers. To address this problem, a good database development practice is to create a surrogate key. A **surrogate key** is a field that the database designer creates to be the record's primary key identifier. A surrogate key has no real relationship to the record to which it is assigned, other than to identify the record uniquely. Usually, developers configure the database to generate surrogate key values automatically.

In an Oracle9*i* database, you can automatically generate surrogate key values using a sequence. **Sequences** are sequential lists of numbers that the database generates automatically and that guarantee that each primary key value will be unique. In an Access database, you can automatically generate surrogate key values using the AutoNumber data type, which automatically inserts the next numerical value every time you create a new record.

For the CUSTOMER table in Figure 9-4, you would probably create a new surrogate key field named CUSTOMER_ID, and you might start the CUSTOMER_ID values at 1 or 100. The CUSTOMER_ID numbers will not change, and every customer gets a unique number. In Figure 9-3, S_ID and F_ID are additional examples of surrogate keys. Surrogate keys are always numerical fields, because the database usually generates values automatically by incrementing the previous value by one.

## Foreign Keys

How do you use key fields to create relationships among records? One way to represent this relationship is to combine the FACULTY and STUDENT fields into a single table, and store the data for each student's faculty advisor directly in each student record. Figure 9-5 shows how the combined fields might look. Some of the fields in the table shown in Figure 9-5 have been omitted to allow the figure to fit on the page.

STUDENT

| S_ID | S_LAST_NAME | S_FIRST_NAME | F_ID | F_LAST_NAME | F_FIRST_NAME | |
|------|-------------|--------------|------|-------------|--------------|---|
| 100 | Miller | Sarah | 1 | Cox | Kim | Data values repeat for each student |
| 101 | Umato | Brian | 1 | Cox | Kim | |
| 102 | Black | Daniel | 1 | Cox | Kim | |
| 103 | Mobley | Amanda | 2 | Blanchard | John | |
| 104 | Sanchez | Ruben | 4 | Sheng | Laura | |
| 105 | Connoly | Michael | 3 | Williams | Jerry | |

**Figure 9-5** Creating relationships by repeating data

The problem with this approach is that it causes you to store redundant data. Note that the data for faculty member Kim Cox repeats three times, once for each student she advises. If Kim advises 50 or 100 students, her data repeats 50 or 100 times. Recall that storing redundant data is undesirable because it occupies valuable storage space. And, when the same data is stored in multiple places, it can become inconsistent.

Relational databases provide a better way to create relationships by using foreign keys. A **foreign key** is a field in a table that is a primary key in another table. The foreign key creates a relationship between the two tables. Rather than storing all of the faculty member's data in each associated student's record, you can simply store the F_ID, which is the primary key of the FACULTY table, in each student record. Figure 9-6 shows the STUDENT table, now containing the F_ID field for each student's advisor as a foreign key in each student record. This creates a relationship between the STUDENT table and the FACULTY table.

By using foreign keys to create relationships, you repeat only the foreign key values. If the data values for a faculty member change, you update the values only in the FACULTY table. The primary key of the FACULTY table, which is the F_ID value, will not change, so the STUDENT table will not need to be updated if the faculty data changes.

A foreign key value must exist in the table where it is a primary key. For example, suppose you have a new record for S_ID 106 that specifies that the student's F_ID (advisor ID) value is 6. Currently, there is no record for F_ID 6 in the FACULTY table, so the student record is invalid. Foreign key values must match the value in the primary key table *exactly*. That is why it is best to use number values for primary keys rather than text values, which are prone to typographical, punctuation, spelling, and case variation errors.

Foreign keys ———

STUDENT

| S_ID | S_LAST_NAME | S_FIRST_NAME | S_MI | S_ADDRESS | S_STATE | S_ZIP | F ID |
|------|-------------|--------------|------|-----------|---------|-------|------|
| 100 | Miller | Sarah | M | 144 Windridge Blvd. | WI | 54703 | 1 |
| 101 | Umato | Brian | D | 454 St. John's Place | WI | 54702 | 1 |
| 102 | Black | Daniel | | 8921 Circle Drive | WI | 54715 | 1 |
| 103 | Mobley | Amanda | J | 1716 Summit St. | WI | 54703 | 2 |
| 104 | Sanchez | Ruben | R | 1780 Samantha Court | WI | 54701 | 4 |
| 105 | Connoly | Michael | S | 1818 Silver Street | WI | 54712 | 3 |

——— Primary keys

FACULTY

| F_ID | F_LAST_NAME | F FIRST_NAME | F_MI | F_PHONE | F_RANK |
|------|-------------|--------------|------|---------|--------|
| 1 | Cox | Kim | J | 7155551234 | ASSO |
| 2 | Blanchard | John | R | 7155559087 | FULL |
| 3 | Williams | Jerry | F | 7155555412 | ASST |
| 4 | Sheng | Laura | M | 7155556409 | INST |
| 5 | Brown | Phillip | E | 7155556082 | ASSO |

**Figure 9-6**   Creating relationships using foreign keys

9

## Composite Keys

Sometimes you have to combine multiple fields to create a unique primary key. The ENROLLMENT table in Figure 9-7 shows an example of this situation. In this table, the S_ID field is not a candidate key, because one student may enroll in many courses. Similarly, the COURSE_ID field is not a candidate key, because one course may enroll many students. The GRADE field is not a candidate key, because many students receive the same grade in courses. Because each student enrolls in each course only once, however, the combination of the S_ID field and the COURSE_ID field represents a unique identifier for each record. The combination of fields to create a unique primary key is called a **composite key**. The S_ID field in the ENROLLMENT table is part of the table's primary key, and is also a foreign key that references an S_ID value in the STUDENT table. Similarly, the COURSE_ID field in the ENROLLMENT table is part of the primary key, and is also a foreign key that references a COURSE_ID value in the COURSE table.

Foreign key references

Composite key

STUDENT

| S_ID | S_LAST_NAME | S_FIRST_NAME | S_MI | S_ADDRESS | S_STATE | S_ZIP |
|------|-------------|--------------|------|-----------|---------|-------|
| 100 | Miller | Sarah | M | 144 Windridge Blvd. | WI | 54703 |
| 101 | Umato | Brian | D | 454 St. John's Place | WI | 54702 |
| 102 | Black | Daniel | | 8921 Circle Drive | WI | 54715 |
| 103 | Mobley | Amanda | J | 1716 Summit St. | WI | 54703 |
| 104 | Sanchez | Ruben | R | 1780 Samantha Court | WI | 54701 |
| 105 | Connoly | Michael | S | 1818 Silver Street | WI | 54712 |

COURSE

| COURSE_ID | CALL_ID | COURSE_NAME | CREDITS |
|-----------|---------|-------------|---------|
| 1 | MIS 101 | Intro. to Info. Systems | 3 |
| 2 | MIS 301 | Systems Analysis | 3 |
| 3 | MIS 441 | Database Management | 3 |
| 4 | CS 155 | Programming in C++ | 3 |
| 5 | MIS 451 | Web-Based Systems | 3 |

ENROLLMENT

| S_ID | COURSE_ID | GRADE |
|------|-----------|-------|
| 100 | 1 | A |
| 100 | 2 | A |
| 100 | 3 | B |
| 101 | 5 | B |
| 101 | 1 | C |
| 101 | 2 | B |
| 101 | 3 | A |
| 101 | 5 | B |

**Figure 9-7**   Example of a composite key

# DATABASE MANAGEMENT SYSTEMS

Recall that a database management system (DBMS) provides the common functions for managing a database. A DBMS consists of a **database engine**, which manages the physical storage and data retrieval. A DBMS also provides software for creating **database applications**, which provide the interface that allows users to interact with the database. When organizations first started using databases, the database engine and the database applications were housed on large centralized mainframe computers that users accessed using terminals. **Terminals** are devices that do not perform any processing, but only send keyboard input and display video output from a central computer. As distributed computing and microcomputers became popular during the 1980s, two new kinds of database management systems emerged: personal databases and client/server databases.

## Personal Database Management Systems

A **personal database** is a database management system that is primarily for creating single-user database applications, which are applications that only one person uses at one time. For example, you might use a personal database to create an address book or track information about your personal finances. With a personal database, the database engine and the database applications run on the same workstation, and appear to the user as a single integrated application.

 Microsoft Access is the dominant personal database in the marketplace today, so the discussion of personal databases focuses on Microsoft Access. Although Microsoft Access and Personal Oracle9i are both considered personal databases, they differ extensively in their approach to managing data. Personal Oracle9i derives its features from full Oracle9i's client/server database, which the next section describes. Conversely, Access has no client/server features. Oracle Corporation has imposed limits on the Personal Oracle9i database to prevent people from using it for large multi-user database applications.

Organizations sometimes use personal databases to create simple multi-user database applications that multiple people use at the same time. For example, a computer laboratory manager might use a personal database to create a multi-user database application to track laboratory equipment or employee schedules that multiple employees use at the same time. Personal databases such as Microsoft Access support small multi-user database applications by storing the database application files on a file server instead of a single user's workstation and then transmitting the files or the parts of files containing the desired data to various users across a network, as shown in Figure 9-8.

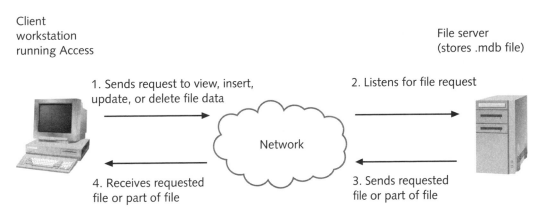

**Figure 9-8**   Using a personal database for a multi-user application

The Microsoft Access personal database stores all data for a database in a single file with an .mdb extension. To run a multi-user personal database application, the database administrator stores the .mdb file on a central file server. Each client workstation loads the entire DBMS into main memory, along with the database applications to view, insert, update, or print data. As an individual user interacts with the database, his or her workstation sends requests to the file server for all or part of the database .mdb file. A request for a small amount of data sometimes requires the file server to transmit the entire file, which may contain hundreds of megabytes of data, to the client's workstation. The client workstation then filters out the requested data. As a result, Microsoft Access and other similar personal database management systems sometimes impose a heavy load on client workstations and on the network. The network must be fast enough to handle the traffic generated when transferring database files to the client workstation and sending them back to the server for database additions and updates.

As a general rule, you should use a personal database only for non–mission-critical applications. In a personal database system, when a client workstation requests a data file, parts of the data file are locked and unavailable to other users. If a client workstation fails due to a software malfunction or power failure during a database operation, the locked parts of the data file are unavailable to other users and may become damaged. The central database file might be reparable, but all users must log off during the repair process, which can take several hours. Updates, deletions, and insertions taking place at the time of the failure usually cannot be reconstructed. If repair is not possible, the DBA can restore the database to its state at the time of the last regular backup, but transactions that occurred since the backup are lost.

Another problem with using personal databases involves how they support transaction processing. **Transaction processing** refers to grouping related database changes into units of work that must either all succeed or all fail. For example, assume a customer writes a check to deposit money from a checking account into a money market account. The bank must ensure that the checking account is debited for the amount and the money market account is credited for the same amount. If any part of the transaction fails, then neither account balance should change. When you perform a transaction using a Microsoft Access personal database, the personal database records the related changes in the client workstation's main memory in a record called a **transaction log**. If the user decides to abort the transaction, or if some part of the transaction does not succeed, the DBMS can use the transaction log to reverse, or **roll back**, the changes. However, recall that the transaction log is in the client workstation's main memory. If the client workstation fails in the middle of the transaction, the transaction log is lost, so the changes cannot be rolled back. Depending on the order of the transactions, a failed client could result in a depleted checking account and unchanged money market account, or an enlarged money market account and unchanged checking account.

Although personal databases such as Microsoft Access are not really suitable for creating large, mission-critical database systems, they are excellent for creating smaller systems. They provide all of the required database functionality for learning to create data-based Web pages.

## Client/Server Database Management Systems

Today's organizations often need databases that support tens of thousands of simultaneous users and support mission-critical tasks. To accomplish this, they use client/server databases, which take advantage of distributed processing and networked computers by distributing processing across multiple computers. The following subsections describe client/server database concepts and the Oracle9*i* client/server DBMS.

## Client/Server Database Concepts

In a **client/server database**, the DBMS server process runs on one workstation, and the database applications run on separate client workstations across the network. Figure 9-9 illustrates the client/server database architecture.

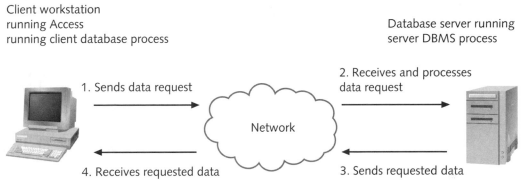

Client workstation running Access running client database process

Database server running server DBMS process

1. Sends data request
2. Receives and processes data request

Network

4. Receives requested data
3. Sends requested data

**Figure 9-9**   Client/server database architecture

The **client process** sends data requests across the network. The server DBMS process runs on the database server and listens for requests from clients. When the **server DBMS process** receives a data request, it retrieves the data from the database, performs the requested functions on the data (retrieving, inserting, updating, sorting, and so on), and sends *only* the requested data, rather than the entire database, back to the client. As a result, client/server databases generate less network traffic than personal databases and are less likely to get bogged down due to an overloaded network.

Another important difference between client/server and personal databases is how they handle hardware and software malfunctions. Most client/server DBMS servers have extra features to minimize the chance of failure, and when they do fail, they have powerful recovery mechanisms that often operate automatically. Client/server systems also differ from personal database systems in how they handle transaction processing. Client/server systems maintain a file-based transaction log on the database server. If a client workstation fails before finishing a transaction, the database server automatically rolls back all of the transaction changes.

Web-based database applications usually support multiple users and require a high level of fault tolerance and transaction processing capabilities. As a result, client/server databases are appropriate for Web-based database systems on production Web sites. Client/server databases are harder to install and configure than personal databases. However, from a Web developer's viewpoint, once the client/server database is up and running, it works almost identically as a personal database such as Access.

### The Oracle9*i* Client/Server DBMS

Oracle9*i* is the latest release of Oracle Corporation's relational DBMS. Oracle9*i* is a client/server database, so you must consider its environment in terms of server-side programs and client-side programs. On the server side, the DBA installs and configures the Oracle9*i* database. After the DBA installs and configures the database, a process on the database server listens for incoming user requests and commands.

You will not perform database administration tasks in the tutorials or end-of-chapter projects in this book. Instead, you will be learning to use the Oracle9*i* database as a Web application developer. Therefore, you will be using client-side applications that connect to server-side products that your instructor or technical support person installs and configures.

If you are using the Oracle9*i* Personal database on your computer, you will install and configure the database yourself, and run both the server-side and client-side programs on the same workstation.

On the client side, Oracle9*i* provides utilities for executing SQL commands and designing and creating custom applications, as well as specific applications for supporting tasks such as accounting, finance, production, and sales. All Oracle9*i* server- and client-side programs use SQL*Net, which is a utility that enables the network communication between the client and the server. Whenever you start an Oracle9*i* client-side program, a SQL*Net process automatically starts on the client workstation. The client SQL*Net process communicates with a SQL*Net process running on the database server. The process running on the server forwards user requests to the Oracle9*i* DBMS.

Usually, people interact with an Oracle9*i* database using application programs that run on their client workstations. For example, students might enroll in courses using a program that displays a list of courses that are available during a specific term, select desired courses, and then view a copy of their completed schedule on their workstation screen.

## THE CASE STUDY DATABASES

You have created Web pages for Clearwater Traders and Northwoods University in previous chapters. The remaining chapters contain tutorial and end-of-chapter cases that illustrate data-based Web page development using databases for Clearwater Traders and Northwoods University. Each database has data examples to illustrate the concepts that this book addresses.

Because the focus of this book is on data-based Web page development rather than on database design, the rationale behind the design of the case study database tables is not a focus of this discussion. Nevertheless, it is important that you understand a few general database design principles. You should follow these principles when creating database tables:

- To avoid creating tables that contain redundant data, group related items that describe a single entity together in a common table. For example, a CUSTOMER table groups all data fields describing customers, a STUDENT table groups all data fields about students, and a COURSE table groups all data fields describing courses. If a table seems to describe more than one entity, then it probably needs to be split into two tables, and one table needs to contain a foreign key that references records in the other table.

- Do not create tables that duplicate values many times in different rows. For example, if a specific customer places several customer orders, you should place the order information in a separate table named CUSTOMER_ORDERS. Then link the CUSTOMER_ORDERS table to the CUSTOMER table by placing the primary keys from the CUSTOMER table in the relevant rows of the CUSTOMER_ORDERS table. When you place the CUSTOMER and CUSTOMER_ORDERS data values in separate tables, the database will contain duplicates of the CUSTOMER_ID primary key field for some customers as a foreign key in the CUSTOMER_ORDERS table. However, this is preferable to duplicating additional customer information, such as the customer name or address, which customers are likely to enter with occasional spelling errors.

- When a database programmer creates a database and inserts data values, he or she must specify the data type for each column. Different database management systems have specific names for their data types, but in general, data values are numbers, text strings, or date/time values. Recall that primary key fields should use a number data type to avoid typographical, punctuation, and case variation errors. In general, you should use a number data type only for columns that store values that involve numbers that are involved in calculations. For example, you would store inventory quantity-on-hand values in number columns, but you would not store telephone numbers in number columns. You store data values that contain numeric characters that are not used in calculations, such as telephone numbers and postal codes, as text strings.

## The Clearwater Traders Sales Order Database

Recall that Clearwater Traders markets a line of clothing and sporting goods via mail-order catalogs and wants to add a Web site to its operations. Processes running on the Web site must allow customers to view the available merchandise using the company's Web site. When a customer selects an item, these processes must determine whether the ordered item is in stock. If the item is in stock, the processes must update the available quantity on hand to reflect that the item has been sold. If the item is not in stock, a Web page must advise the customer when the item will be available. The Web site must process customer payments and display an order summary to provide customers with the details of their order. These processes require the following data items:

- Customer name, address, and daytime and evening telephone numbers.

- Order date, payment method (check or credit card), order source (catalog description or Web site), and associated item numbers, sizes, colors, and quantities ordered.

- Item descriptions and photo images, as well as item categories (women's clothing, outdoor gear, and so on), prices, and quantities on hand. Many clothing items are available in multiple sizes and colors. Sometimes the same item has different prices depending on the item size.

Figure 9-10 shows sample data for Clearwater Traders. Each database table displays the table name, column names, and the type of data (Number, String, or Date/Time) the column stores. The CUSTOMER table displays six customer records. Customer 1 is Paula Harris, who lives at 1156 Water Street, Apt. #3, Osseo, WI, and her ZIP code is 54705. Her daytime telephone number is 715-555-8943, and her evening telephone number is 715-555-9035. C_ID has been designated as the table's primary key.

CUSTOMER

| C_ID | C_LAST | C_FIRST | C_MI | C_BIRTHDATE | C_ADDRESS | C_CITY |
|---|---|---|---|---|---|---|
| Number | String | String | String | Date/Time | String | String |
| 1 | Harris | Paula | E | 04/09/1953 | 1156 Water Street, Apt. #3 | Osseo |
| 2 | Garcia | Maria | H | 07/14/1958 | 2211 Pine Drive | Radisson |
| 3 | Miller | Lee | | 01/05/1936 | 699 Pluto St. NW | Silver Lake |
| 4 | Chang | Alissa | R | 10/01/1976 | 987 Durham Rd. | Apple Valley |
| 5 | Edwards | Mitch | M | 11/20/1986 | 4204 Garner Street | Washburn |
| 6 | Nelson | Kyle | E | 12/04/1984 | 232 Echo Rd. | Minnetonka |

CUSTOMER (continued)

| C_STATE | C_ZIP | C_DPHONE | C_EPHONE | C_USER_ID | C_PASSWORD |
|---|---|---|---|---|---|
| String | String | String | String | String | String |
| WI | 54705 | 7155558943 | 7155559035 | harrispe | asdfjk |
| WI | 54867 | 7155558332 | 7155558332 | garciamm | 12345 |
| WI | 53821 | 7155554978 | 7155559002 | miller1 | zxcvb |
| MN | 55712 | 7155557651 | 7155550087 | changar | qwerui |
| WI | 54891 | 7155558243 | 7155556975 | edwardsmm | qwerty |
| MN | 55438 | 7151113333 | 7155552222 | nelsonke | clever |

**Figure 9-10**    Clearwater Traders database

ORDER_SOURCE

| OS_ID | OS_DESC |
|--------|---------|
| Number | String |
| 1 | Winter 2005 |
| 2 | Spring 2006 |
| 3 | Summer 2006 |
| 4 | Outdoor 2006 |
| 5 | Children's 2006 |
| 6 | Web Site |

ORDERS

| O_ID | O_DATE | O_METHPMT | C_ID | OS_ID |
|------|--------|-----------|------|-------|
| Number | Date/Time | String | Number | Number |
| 1 | 5/29/2006 | CC | 1 | 2 |
| 2 | 5/29/2006 | CC | 5 | 6 |
| 3 | 5/31/2006 | CHECK | 2 | 2 |
| 4 | 5/31/2006 | CC | 3 | 3 |
| 5 | 6/01/2006 | CC | 4 | 6 |
| 6 | 6/01/2006 | CC | 4 | 3 |

CATEGORY

| CAT_ID | CAT_DESC |
|--------|----------|
| Number | String |
| 1 | Women's Clothing |
| 2 | Children's Clothing |
| 3 | Men's Clothing |
| 4 | Outdoor Gear |

ITEM

| ITEM_ID | ITEM_DESC | CAT_ID | ITEM_IMAGE |
|---------|-----------|--------|------------|
| String | Number | Number | String |
| 1 | Men's Expedition Parka | 3 | parka.jpg |
| 2 | 3-Season Tent | 4 | tents.jpg |
| 3 | Women's Hiking Shorts | 1 | shorts.jpg |
| 4 | Women's Fleece Pullover | 1 | fleece.jpg |
| 5 | Children's Beachcomber Sandals | 2 | sandals.jpg |
| 6 | Boy's Surf Shorts | 2 | surfshorts.jpg |
| 7 | Girls' Soccer Tee | 2 | girlstee.jpg |

**Figure 9-10**   Clearwater Traders database (continued)

INVENTORY

| INV_ID | ITEM_ID | COLOR | INV_SIZE | INV_PRICE | INV_QOH |
|--------|---------|-------|----------|-----------|---------|
| Number | Number | String | String | Number | Number |
| 1 | 2 | Sky Blue | | 259.99 | 16 |
| 2 | 2 | Light Grey | | 259.99 | 12 |
| 3 | 3 | Khaki | S | 29.95 | 150 |
| 4 | 3 | Khaki | M | 29.95 | 147 |
| 5 | 3 | Khaki | L | 29.95 | 0 |
| 6 | 3 | Navy | S | 29.95 | 139 |
| 7 | 3 | Navy | M | 29.95 | 137 |
| 8 | 3 | Navy | L | 29.95 | 115 |
| 9 | 4 | Eggplant | S | 59.95 | 135 |
| 10 | 4 | Eggplant | M | 59.95 | 168 |
| 11 | 4 | Eggplant | L | 59.95 | 187 |
| 12 | 4 | Royal | S | 59.95 | 0 |
| 13 | 4 | Royal | M | 59.95 | 124 |
| 14 | 4 | Royal | L | 59.95 | 112 |
| 15 | 5 | Turquoise | 10 | 15.99 | 121 |
| 16 | 5 | Turquoise | 11 | 15.99 | 111 |
| 17 | 5 | Turquoise | 12 | 15.99 | 113 |
| 18 | 5 | Turquoise | 1 | 15.99 | 121 |
| 19 | 5 | Bright Pink | 10 | 15.99 | 148 |
| 20 | 5 | Bright Pink | 11 | 15.99 | 137 |
| 21 | 5 | Bright Pink | 12 | 15.99 | 134 |
| 22 | 5 | Bright Pink | 1 | 15.99 | 123 |
| 23 | 1 | Spruce | S | 199.95 | 114 |
| 24 | 1 | Spruce | M | 199.95 | 17 |
| 25 | 1 | Spruce | L | 209.95 | 0 |
| 26 | 1 | Spruce | XL | 209.95 | 12 |
| 27 | 6 | Blue | S | 15.95 | 50 |
| 28 | 6 | Blue | M | 15.95 | 100 |
| 29 | 6 | Blue | L | 15.95 | 100 |
| 30 | 7 | White | S | 19.99 | 100 |
| 31 | 7 | White | M | 19.99 | 100 |
| 32 | 7 | White | L | 19.99 | 100 |

**Figure 9-10**    Clearwater Traders database (continued)

COLOR

| COLOR |
| --- |
| *String* |
| Sky Blue |
| Light Grey |
| Khaki |
| Navy |
| Royal |
| Eggplant |
| Blue |
| Red |
| Spruce |
| Turquoise |
| Bright Pink |
| White |

**9**

ORDER_LINE

| O_ID | INV_ID | OL_QUANTITY |
| --- | --- | --- |
| *Number* | *Number* | *Number* |
| 1 | 1 | 1 |
| 1 | 14 | 2 |
| 2 | 19 | 1 |
| 3 | 24 | 1 |
| 3 | 26 | 1 |
| 4 | 12 | 2 |
| 5 | 8 | 1 |
| 5 | 13 | 1 |
| 6 | 2 | 1 |
| 6 | 7 | 3 |

SHIPMENT

| SHIP_ID | SHIP_DATE_EXPECTED |
| --- | --- |
| *Number* | *Date/Time* |
| 1 | 09/15/2006 |
| 2 | 11/15/2006 |
| 3 | 06/25/2006 |
| 4 | 06/25/2006 |
| 5 | 08/15/2006 |

**Figure 9-10**    Clearwater Traders database (continued)

SHIPMENT_LINE

| SHIP_ID | INV_ID | SL_QUANTITY | SL_DATE_RECEIVED |
|---------|--------|-------------|------------------|
| Number | Number | Number | Date/Time |
| 1 | 1 | 25 | 09/10/2006 |
| 1 | 2 | 25 | 09/10/2006 |
| 2 | 2 | 25 | |
| 3 | 5 | 200 | |
| 3 | 6 | 200 | |
| 3 | 7 | 200 | |
| 4 | 12 | 100 | 08/15/2006 |
| 4 | 13 | 100 | 08/25/2006 |
| 5 | 23 | 50 | 08/15/2006 |
| 5 | 24 | 100 | 08/15/2006 |
| 5 | 25 | 100 | 08/15/2006 |

STATE

| S_ABBREVIATION | S_NAME |
|----------------|--------|
| String | String |
| AK | Alaska |
| AL | Alabama |
| AR | Arkansas |
| (all rows not shown) | |
| WV | West Virginia |
| WY | Wyoming |

**Figure 9-10**    Clearwater Traders database (continued)

The ORDER_SOURCE table has OS_ID as the primary key and contains a field named OS_ DESC, which describes the order source as a specific catalog or the company Web site. The ORDERS table shows six customer orders. The table fields include O_ID, which is a surrogate key that is the table's primary key. The O_DATE field shows the date the customer places the order. The O_METHPMT field indicates the payment method: CC (credit card) or CHECK. C_ID is a foreign key that creates a relationship to the CUSTOMER table. OS_ID is a foreign key that creates a relationship to the ORDER_SOURCE table. The first record shows information for O_ID 1, dated 5/29/2006, method of payment CC (credit card), and ordered by customer 1, Paula Harris. The OS_ID foreign key indicates that the Spring 2006 catalog was the source for the order.

The CATEGORY table displays different product categories: Women's Clothing, Children's Clothing, Men's Clothing, and Outdoor Gear. The CAT_ID field is this table's primary key. The ITEM table contains seven different items. ITEM_ID is the table's primary key. The CAT_ID field is a foreign key that creates a relationship with the CATEGORY table. Item 1, Men's Expedition Parka, is in the Men's Clothing category. The ITEM_IMAGE field contains a text string that represents the name of the JPEG image file that stores an image of each item.

The INVENTORY table contains specific inventory numbers for specific merchandise item sizes and colors. It also shows the price and quantity on hand (QOH) for each item. Items that are not available in different sizes contain NULL, or undefined, values in their INV_SIZE columns. Notice that some items have different prices for different sizes. For example, for ITEM_ID 1 (Men's Expedition Parka), the small (S) and medium (M) inventory items are priced at $199.95, while the large (L) and extra large (XL) items are priced at $209.95. INV_ID is the primary key of this table, and ITEM_ID is a foreign key that creates a relationship with the ITEM table.

The ORDER_LINE table represents the individual inventory items in a customer order. The first line of O_ID 1 specifies one sky blue 3-Season Tent, and the second line of this order specifies two large royal-colored Women's Fleece Pullovers. This information is used to create the printed customer order invoice and to calculate sales revenues. Note that the primary key of this table is not O_ID, because more than one record might have the same O_ID. The primary key is a composite key comprised of the combination of O_ID and INV_ID. An order might have several different inventory items, but it will never have the same inventory item listed more than once. Along with being part of the primary key, O_ID and INV_ID are also foreign keys because they create relationships to the ORDERS and INVENTORY tables.

The COLOR table is a lookup table. A **lookup table** is also sometimes called a pick list. It contains a list of legal values for a field in another table. Notice the variety of colors shown in the INVENTORY table (Sky Blue, Light Grey, Khaki, Navy, Royal, and so on). If users have to type these colors each time they add an inventory item to the table, data entry errors might occur. For example, a query looking for sales of items with the Light Grey color will not find instances if Light Grey is spelled as *Light Gray*, or is specified with a different combination of upper- and lowercase letters, such as *Light grey* or *LIGHT GREY*. Typically, when a Clearwater Traders employee user enters a new inventory item, he or she will select a color from a pick list that displays values from the COLOR table. Thus the user need not type the color directly, which reduces errors. Small lists that are unlikely to change over time might be coded directly into an application, but lists to which many items might be added over time are usually stored in a separate lookup table.

The STATE table is a second lookup table that provides values for the C_STATE field in the CUSTOMER table. The S_ABBREVIATION field shows the two-letter abbreviations for all states and territories within the United States, and the S_NAME shows the corresponding state or territory name. S_ABBREVIATION is the table's primary key.

Figure 9-11 shows a visual representation of the Clearwater Traders database tables. In this representation, the primary key for each table appears in boldface, and relationships between tables are represented by join lines. For example, note that in Figure 9-11, a join line

9

connects the C_ID field in the CUSTOMER table to the C_ID field in the ORDERS table. The relationship beside the CUSTOMER table has the digit 1 beside it, and the relationship beside the ORDERS table displays the infinity symbol (∞). This symbol indicates a **one-to-many relationship**, in which each C_ID value in the CUSTOMER table can have many associated C_ID values in the ORDERS table, so one customer can have many orders. Conversely, for each C_ID value in the ORDERS table, there is only one associated C_ID value in the CUSTOMER table, so each customer order is placed by one and only one customer.

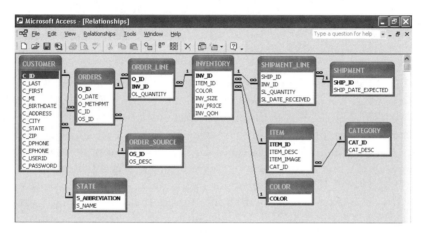

**Figure 9-11**    Visual representation of the Clearwater Traders database

# The Northwoods University Student Registration Database

Recall that the Northwoods University Web-based registration system will allow students to retrieve information about courses, such as course names, call IDs (such as MIS 101), section numbers, days, times, locations, and the availability of open seats in the course. Students will be able to register for courses, as well as view information about the courses they have taken, and print transcript reports showing past course grades and grade point averages. Faculty members will be able to retrieve student course lists, add students to and drop students from courses, and record course grades using their Web browsers.

The data items for the Northwoods database are:

- Student name, address, telephone number, class (freshman, sophomore, junior, or senior), date of birth, personal identification number (PIN), and advisor ID

In a production system, PIN or password values are usually stored as encrypted values.

- Course call number, name, credits, location, maximum enrollment, instructor, and term offered

- Instructor name, office location, telephone number, rank, and PIN
- Student enrollment and grade information

Figure 9-12 shows sample data for the Northwoods database. The LOCATION table identifies building codes, room numbers, and room capacities. LOC_ID is the primary key. The FACULTY table describes five faculty members. The first record shows faculty member Kim Cox, whose office is located at BUS 424, and her telephone number is 715-555-1234. She has the rank of ASSO (associate professor), and her PIN is 1181. This F_PIN (faculty PIN) will be used as a password to determine whether a faculty member can update specific student or course records. F_ID is the primary key, and LOC_ID is a foreign key that references the LOCATION table. The F_IMAGE field specifies a text string that represents the name of a JPEG image file that contains an image of each faculty member.

LOCATION

| LOC_ID | BLDG_CODE | ROOM | CAPACITY |
|--------|-----------|------|----------|
| Number | String | String | Number |
| 1 | CR | 101 | 150 |
| 2 | CR | 202 | 40 |
| 3 | CR | 103 | 35 |
| 4 | CR | 105 | 35 |
| 5 | BUS | 105 | 42 |
| 6 | BUS | 404 | 35 |
| 7 | BUS | 421 | 35 |
| 8 | BUS | 211 | 55 |
| 9 | BUS | 424 | 1 |
| 10 | BUS | 402 | 1 |
| 11 | BUS | 433 | 1 |
| 12 | LIB | 217 | 2 |
| 13 | LIB | 222 | 1 |

FACULTY

| F_ID | F_LAST | F_FIRST | F_MI | LOC_ID | F_PHONE | F_RANK | F_PIN | F_IMAGE |
|------|--------|---------|------|--------|---------|--------|-------|---------|
| Number | String | String | String | Number | String | String | String | String |
| 1 | Cox | Kim | J | 9 | 7155551234 | ASSO | 1181 | cox.jpg |
| 2 | Blanchard | John | R | 10 | 7155559087 | FULL | 1075 | blanchard.jpg |
| 3 | Williams | Jerry | F | 12 | 7155555412 | ASST | 8531 | williams.jpg |
| 4 | Sheng | Laura | M | 11 | 7155556409 | INST | 1690 | sheng.jpg |
| 5 | Brown | Phillip | E | 13 | 7155556082 | ASSO | 9899 | brown.jpg |

Figure 9-12    Northwoods University database

STUDENT

| S_ID | S_LAST | S_FIRST | S_MI | S_ADDRESS | S_CITY | S_STATE |
|--------|--------|---------|--------|---------------------|------------|---------|
| Number | String | String | String | String | String | String |
| 1 | Miller | Sarah | M | 144 Windridge Blvd. | Eau Claire | WI |
| 2 | Umato | Brian | D | 454 St. John's Place | Eau Claire | WI |
| 3 | Black | Daniel | | 8921 Circle Drive | Bloomer | WI |
| 4 | Mobley | Amanda | J | 1716 Summit St. | Eau Claire | WI |
| 5 | Sanchez | Ruben | R | 1780 Samantha Court | Eau Claire | WI |
| 6 | Connoly | Michael | S | 1818 Silver Street | Elk Mound | WI |

STUDENT (continued)

| S_ZIP | S_PHONE | S_CLASS | S_DOB | S_PIN | F_ID |
|--------|------------|---------|-----------|--------|--------|
| String | String | String | Date/Time | String | Number |
| 54703 | 7155559876 | SR | 07/14/85 | 8891 | 1 |
| 54702 | 7155552345 | SR | 08/19/85 | 1230 | 1 |
| 54715 | 7155553907 | JR | 10/10/82 | 1613 | 1 |
| 54703 | 7155556902 | SO | 9/24/86 | 1841 | 2 |
| 54701 | 7155558899 | SO | 11/20/86 | 4420 | 4 |
| 54712 | 7155554944 | FR | 12/4/87 | 9188 | 3 |

STATE

| S_ABBREVIATION | S_NAME |
|-----------------------|---------------|
| String | String |
| AK | Alaska |
| AL | Alabama |
| AR | Arkansas |
| (all rows not shown) | |
| WV | West Virginia |
| WY | Wyoming |

**Figure 9-12** Northwoods University database (continued)

TERM

| TERM_ID | TERM_DESC | STATUS |
|---------|-----------|--------|
| Number | String | String |
| 1 | Fall 2005 | CLOSED |
| 2 | Spring 2006 | CLOSED |
| 3 | Summer 2006 | CLOSED |
| 4 | Fall 2006 | CLOSED |
| 5 | Spring 2007 | CLOSED |
| 6 | Summer 2007 | OPEN |

COURSE

| COURSE_ID | CALL_ID | COURSE_NAME | CREDITS |
|-----------|---------|-------------|---------|
| Number | String | String | Number |
| 1 | MIS 101 | Intro. to Info. Systems | 3 |
| 2 | MIS 301 | Systems Analysis | 3 |
| 3 | MIS 441 | Database Management | 3 |
| 4 | CS 155 | Programming in C++ | 3 |
| 5 | MIS 451 | Web-Based Systems | 3 |

COURSE_SECTION

| C_SEC_ID | COURSE_ID | TERM_ID | SEC_NUM | F_ID | C_SEC_DAY | C_SEC_TIME | LOC_ID | MAX_ENRL |
|----------|-----------|---------|---------|------|-----------|------------|--------|----------|
| Number | Number | Number | Number | Number | String | Date/Time | Number | Number |
| 1 | 1 | 4 | 1 | 2 | MWF | 10:00 AM | 1 | 140 |
| 2 | 1 | 4 | 2 | 3 | TR | 9:30 AM | 7 | 35 |
| 3 | 1 | 4 | 3 | 3 | MWF | 8:00 AM | 2 | 35 |
| 4 | 2 | 4 | 1 | 4 | TR | 11:00 AM | 6 | 35 |
| 5 | 2 | 5 | 2 | 4 | TR | 2:00 PM | 6 | 35 |
| 6 | 3 | 5 | 1 | 1 | MWF | 9:00 AM | 5 | 30 |
| 7 | 3 | 5 | 2 | 1 | MWF | 10:00 AM | 5 | 30 |
| 8 | 4 | 5 | 1 | 5 | TR | 8:00 AM | 3 | 35 |
| 9 | 5 | 5 | 1 | 2 | MWF | 2:00 PM | 5 | 35 |
| 10 | 5 | 5 | 2 | 2 | MWF | 3:00 PM | 5 | 35 |
| 11 | 1 | 6 | 1 | 1 | MTWRF | 8:00 AM | 1 | 50 |
| 12 | 2 | 6 | 1 | 2 | MTWRF | 8:00 AM | 6 | 35 |
| 13 | 3 | 6 | 1 | 3 | MTWRF | 9:00 AM | 5 | 35 |

9

**Figure 9-12**    Northwoods University database (continued)

ENROLLMENT

| S_ID | C_SEC_ID | GRADE |
|------|----------|-------|
| Number | Number | String |
| 1 | 1 | A |
| 1 | 4 | A |
| 1 | 6 | B |
| 1 | 9 | B |
| 2 | 1 | C |
| 2 | 5 | B |
| 2 | 6 | A |
| 2 | 9 | B |
| 3 | 1 | C |
| 3 | 12 | |
| 3 | 13 | |
| 4 | 11 | |
| 4 | 12 | |
| 5 | 1 | B |
| 5 | 5 | C |
| 5 | 9 | C |
| 5 | 11 | |
| 5 | 13 | |
| 6 | 11 | |
| 6 | 12 | |

**Figure 9-12**    Northwoods University database (continued)

The STUDENT table displays six student records. Its primary key field is S_ID. The first record displays data for student Sarah Miller, who lives at 144 Windridge Blvd. in Eau Claire, Wisconsin. Her telephone number is 715-555-9876, she is a senior, her date of birth is 7/14/85, and her faculty advisor is Kim Cox. Note that the S_PIN (student PIN) field stores her student personal identification number to control data access. F_ID (faculty ID) is a foreign key that refers to the F_ID field in the FACULTY table.

The STATE table is a lookup table that provides values for the S_STATE field in the STUDENT table. The S_ABBREVIATION field shows the two-letter abbreviations for all states and territories within the United States, and the S_NAME shows the corresponding state or territory name. S_ABBREVIATION is the table's primary key.

The TERM table has an ID number that links terms to different course offerings. TERM_ID is the primary key. The table contains a text description of each term and a STATUS field that shows whether enrollment is open or closed. The first record shows a TERM_ID of 1 for the Fall 2005 term, with enrollment status as CLOSED.

The COURSE table shows records for five courses. The first course record, COURSE_ID 1, has the CALL_ID MIS 101 and is named "Intro. to Info. Systems." It provides three credits. COURSE_ID is the primary key, and the table contains no foreign keys.

The COURSE_SECTION table shows the course offerings for specific terms and includes fields that display the course ID, section number, ID of the instructor teaching the section, and course day, time, location, and maximum allowable enrollment. C_SEC_ID is the primary key, and COURSE_ID, TERM_ID, F_ID, and LOC_ID are all foreign key fields. The first record shows that C_SEC_ID 1 is section 1 of MIS 101. It is offered in the Fall 2006 term and is taught by John Blanchard. The section meets on Mondays, Wednesdays, and Fridays at 10:00 A.M. in room CR 101. It has a maximum enrollment of 140 students.

Day and time are reserved words in Access that should not be used as field names. This is why the field names c_sec_day and c_sec_time are not shortened to day and time.

The ENROLLMENT table shows students who currently are enrolled in each course section and their associated grade if one has been assigned. The primary key for this table is a composite key comprised of S_ID and C_SEC_ID.

Figure 9-13 shows a visual representation of the tables in the Northwoods University database. As with the visual representation of the Clearwater Traders database in Figure 9-11, primary key fields appear in boldface, and foreign key relationships appear as join lines.

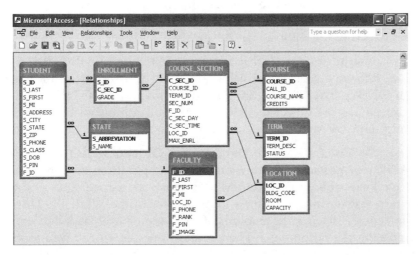

**Figure 9-13**   Visual representation of the Northwoods University database

# RETRIEVING DATABASE DATA USING VISUAL STUDIO .NET

In this book, you are using Visual Studio .NET to create Web application projects that contain Web forms that retrieve and manipulate data in Oracle9*i* or Access databases. To retrieve and manipulate data in a database, you must create a **data connection**, which is a communication path between a Web application and a data source, such as a database. To create a data connection, you must first understand how Web forms and data sources communicate. Then you will create a data connection using Visual Studio .NET.

## How Web Forms Communicate with Data Sources

Programs supplied by different vendors need to work together. For example, many companies use an Oracle9*i* database to store and manage data for a Microsoft e-mail server process. To enable programs to work together successfully, vendors have developed standard **application program interfaces (APIs)** that establish rules for how programs interact and share data.

When programmers write applications that interact with another vendor's database, the programmers must use a special software program called an Open Database Connectivity (ODBC) driver. **ODBC (Open Database Connectivity)** is an API that specifies how program commands connect to databases and communicate with databases. An **ODBC driver** translates database application program commands to a format that the database understands. A **driver** is a program that translates commands between different programs. Database vendors such as Oracle Corporation write ODBC drivers for their databases and make them available to programmers. When you develop data-based Web pages, you use the ODBC driver for the specific database with which your Web pages interact. If you use an Oracle9*i* database, you must use an Oracle9*i* ODBC driver; if you use an Access database, you must use an Access ODBC driver.

Programmers can write commands that interact directly with ODBC drivers, but these commands are difficult to write and debug. To make it easier to write programs that interact with ODBC drivers, Visual Studio .NET provides **ADO.NET**, which is a set of built-in procedures and object models that translate commands between application programs and ODBC drivers.

Previous versions of Visual Basic used **Data Access Objects (DAO)** and **Active Data Objects (ADO)** to provide procedures to enable applications to communicate with databases. A weakness of both DAO and ADO is that both technologies establish a database connection that remains open for a long period of time. While the DAO or ADO database connection is open, large amounts of data automatically pass between the database server and the client computer. This situation bogs down the Web server and the database server, clogs the network with unnecessary traffic, and hurts the performance of Web applications. Microsoft designed ADO.NET specifically to work with Web applications. ADO.NET creates a connection between the database and the Web application to retrieve and update data, but as soon as data has been retrieved, the connection terminates.

Figure 9-14 shows how Web forms use ADO.NET and ODBC to interact with databases. A series of processes run on the Web server that allow Web forms to interact with databases, such as Oracle9*i* and Access, or with other types of server processes that provide data to Web forms, such as e-mail servers or file servers. The Web form communicates with the ADO.NET processes, and the ADO.NET processes communicate with OLE DB drivers. An **OLE DB (Object Linking and Embedding Database) driver** is an intermediary layer of procedures and objects that translate ADO.NET commands into the commands that specific ODBC drivers expect. Different OLE DB drivers are needed to communicate with different ODBC drivers. OLE DB is necessary because it allows ADO.NET to communicate with other data sources besides databases. Figure 9-14 shows that OLE DB can interact with Oracle9*i* and Access ODBC drivers as well as with other types of drivers.

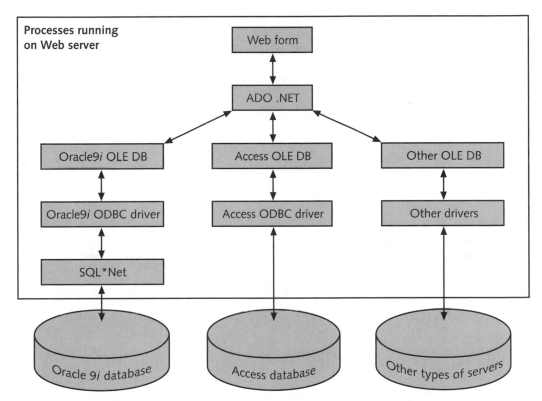

**Figure 9-14**    How Web forms interact with databases using ADO.NET and ODBC

Recall from earlier in Chapter 9 that all Oracle9*i* server- and client-side programs use SQL*Net to enable network communication between the client and the server. Figure 9-14 shows that the Web server must also run SQL*Net to enable the communication between the Oracle9*i* ODBC driver and the Oracle9*i* database.

## Creating a Data Connection in Visual Studio .NET

 If you are using an Oracle9*i* client/server database, the client browser and the Web server processes run on your workstation and retrieve data from a remote database server. If you are using a Personal Oracle9*i* database or an Access database, the client browser, the Web server, and the database all run on your workstation.

The first step in creating a Web form that displays database data is to make a data connection. When you create a new data connection, the connection exists in the Visual Studio .NET IDE, and is available to any Web application project that you open. Before you begin learning how to create a new data connection, you need to configure your Web server so it contains the application structure for Web application projects that you store in the Chapter9\Tutorials folder on your Solution Disk. Then you will create a new Web application project named DBConcepts that you will use in the chapter tutorials.

To configure your Web server and create the Web application project:

1. Start IIS, then create a Web server application named **Chapter9** that you associate with the Chapter9 folder on your Solution Disk. Create a second application named **Tutorials** within the Chapter9 application that you associate with the Chapter9\Tutorials folder on your Solution Disk. Configure the applications so users have *Read*, *Run scripts*, and *Browse* privileges. Your Default Web Site configuration should look like Figure 9-15. (Your Default Web site may display additional applications, virtual directories, and physical directories.)

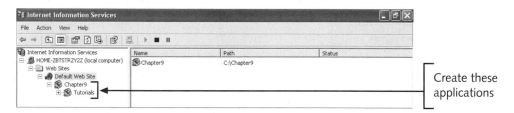

**Figure 9-15**    Default Web site configuration

2. Start Visual Studio .NET, click **Tools** on the menu bar, click **Options**, make sure the *Environment* folder is selected in the left pane, select **Projects and Solutions**, click **Browse**, navigate to the Chapter9\Tutorials folder on your Solution Disk, click **Open**, and then click **OK**.

3. In Visual Studio .NET, click **File** on the menu bar, point to **New**, click **Project**, select **Visual Basic Projects** for the Project Type, make sure the *ASP.NET Web Application* template is selected, and then type **http://localhost/Chapter9/Tutorials/DBConcepts** in the *Location* field to specify the new project name. Click **OK** to create the proj-ect. After a few moments, the new project appears in the Solution Explorer.

4. Open the Solution Explorer if necessary, and select the **WebForm1.aspx** node. Open the Properties window if necessary, change the *File Name* value to **DBForm.aspx**, then select another property to apply the change.

5. Make sure that the *DBForm.aspx* node is selected in the Solution Explorer, click the **View Code** button 📝 on the Solution Explorer toolbar, then change the first command in the code behind file so it appears as follows:

```
Public Class DBForm
```

Next you will initialize your Clearwater Traders database. If you are using an Oracle9*i* database, you will start SQL*Plus, which is an Oracle9*i* client-side utility that allows you to send commands to the database. You will run a **SQL script**, which is a text file that contains commands that create database tables and perform other database operations. (You will not learn how to create database tables in this book, but instead you will run SQL scripts that are on your Data Disk; these scripts will automatically create your database tables. Unless you are a DBA, you develop applications using existing databases rather than designing and developing your own databases.) This SQL script will create the tables in the Clearwater Traders database in Figure 9-10 and insert all of the data records. If you are using an Access database, you will copy the Clearwater.mdb database file to your Solution Disk.

If you are using an Access database, skip these steps and proceed to the next set of steps.

To initialize your database if you are using an Oracle9*i* database:

1. Click **Start** on the taskbar, point to **All Programs**, point to **Oracle – OraHome92**, point to **Application Development**, and then click **SQL Plus**. The Log On dialog box opens. (Windows 2000 users will click Start, point to Programs, point to Oracle – OraHome92, point to Application Development, and then click SQL Plus.)

2. Type **cwuser** in the *User Name* field, **oracle** in the *Password* field, leave the *Host String* field blank, and then click **OK**. The Oracle SQL*Plus window opens, and the SQL prompt appears.

If you are using a client-server database, your instructor or technical support person will tell you the connection information you need to use. If you are using a Personal Oracle9*i* database, you needed to create this user account based on the steps in the installation instructions that are provided with the software.

3. Type **start a:\Chapter9\Clearwater.sql** at the SQL prompt, and then press **Enter**. (If your Data Disk is stored on a different drive or has a different folder path, type that drive or path instead.) The SQL*Plus window displays series of messages that confirm that the database tables are created and the

records are inserted. When the "Commit complete" message appears, close the Oracle SQL*Plus window.

Don't worry if the SQL*Plus window displays the message "ORA-00942: table or view does not exist." This message indicates that the script is trying to drop a table that does not exist. The script attempts to drop all existing Clearwater Traders database tables before creating the new tables, because if a script tries to create a table that already exists, SQL*Plus generates an error and does not re-create the table.

To initialize your database if you are using an Access database:

1. Start Windows Explorer.

2. Copy **Clearwater.mdb** from the Chapter9 folder on your Data Disk to the Chapter9\Tutorials folder on your Solution Disk.

To create and manage data connections in your Visual Studio .NET IDE, you will use the **Server Explorer**, which is a server management console. (Recall from Chapter 5 that a console is an environment for administering remote computers.) You can use the Server Explorer to log on to different servers and interact with their resources. Now you will open the Server Explorer. As with the Toolbox, you can display the Server Explorer in a minimized format in the Visual Studio .NET IDE by right-clicking the Server Explorer title bar and then checking Auto Hide. When you do this, the Toolbox tab appears as the Toolbox icon 🔨, and the Server Explorer appears as a tab under the Toolbox icon. Now you will open the Server Explorer and change its configuration so it appears minimized in the Visual Studio .NET IDE.

To open and configure the Server Explorer:

1. In Visual Studio .NET, click **View** on the menu bar, and then click **Server Explorer**. The Server Explorer opens.

2. If necessary, click the *plus sign* beside the Servers node, then click the *plus sign* beside the node that represents your local computer. Your Server Explorer should look similar to the Server Explorer shown in Figure 9-16. Your local computer name will be different, and your local computer may display different components.

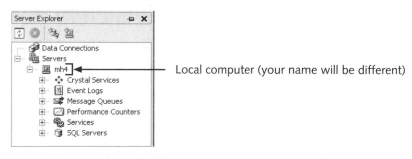

**Figure 9-16**    Server Explorer window

3. Right-click the Server Explorer window title bar, and then check **Auto Hide**. (If Auto Hide is already checked, do not clear it.)

4. Click the mouse pointer anywhere off of the Server Explorer window, and note that the Server Explorer appears as a tab on the left edge of the Browser Window and the Toolbox tab appears as the Toolbox icon ⚒.

When you select the Toolbox icon ⚒, the Toolbox opens, and the Server Explorer appears as the Server Explorer icon 🖳.

In the Server Explorer, the Data Connections node displays the data connections within your Visual Studio .NET IDE. Your Data Connections node will be empty if you have not yet created any data connections. The nodes under your local computer represent different hardware and software components on your workstation that you can configure and manage.

To create a data connection, you must know the type of database to which you are connecting, such as Oracle9*i*, Access, or SQL Server, and you must select a compatible OLE DB driver. The OLE DB driver then communicates with the correct ODBC driver to connect to the database. Many database vendors provide multiple OLE DB drivers, so you must know which OLE DB driver to use. Different drivers have different features, and vendors implement different drivers to work with different database versions. How do you know which drivers to select? The driver names are descriptive, so you select a likely candidate, and then test it to confirm that it works correctly with your applications.

To create a data connection, you also need to know vendor-specific and database-specific connection information. For an Oracle9*i* database, you need to know the *Server Name* or *Data Source* name, which identifies the database server to which you are connecting. For an Access database, you need to know the folder path and filename of the Access database file.

The *Server Name* or *Data Source* name both refer to an entry in an Oracle9*i* database configuration file named tnsnames.ora. The Oracle9*i* tnsnames.ora configuration file associates a name with the IP address and Oracle9*i* database system identifier (SID).

Now you will create a new data connection. You will use the **Data Link Properties dialog box**, which you open through the Data Connections node. The Data Link Properties dialog box has the following pages:

- *Provider*, which allows you to select an OLE DB driver
- *Connection*, which allows you to specify connection information for the database to which you are connecting
- *Advanced*, which allows you to specify network connection information
- *All*, which summarizes the information about the connection

9

To create a new data connection:

1. Move the mouse pointer onto the Server Explorer tab to open the Server Explorer, right-click the **Data Connections** node, and then click **Add Connection**. The Data Link Properties dialog box opens. Click the **Provider** tab to select the database OLE DB driver.

2. *If you are using an Oracle9i database*, select **Microsoft OLE DB Provider for Oracle**, then click **Next**.

   *If you are using an Access database*, select **Microsoft Jet 4.0 OLE DB Provider**, then click **Next**.

3. The Connection page appears.

   *If you are using an Oracle9i database*, type **ORCL** in the *Enter a server name* field, **cwuser** in the *User name* field, **oracle** in the *Password* field, and check the **Allow saving password** check box. (When you check the *Allow saving password* check box, the system saves your password and does not prompt you to enter your password every time you interact with the database.)

 These values will work only if you are connecting to a Personal Oracle9i database and you exactly followed the installation and configuration instructions in the Personal Oracle9i software kit that comes with this textbook. If you are connecting to an Oracle9i client/server database, your instructor or technical support person will tell you the values that you should type on the Connection page.

   *If you are using an Access database*, click the **More** button ⌊…⌋, navigate to the Chapter9\Tutorials folder on your Solution Disk, select **Clearwater.mdb**, and then click **Open**.

4. Click **Test Connection**. The Microsoft Data Link message box displays the message "Test connection succeeded." Click **OK**.

5. Click **OK** to close the Data Link Properties dialog box.

   *If you are using an Oracle9i database*, a message appears stating that your password will not be encrypted before it is saved. This message appears because you instructed Visual Studio .NET to save your password. Users who open the Web application project files in Visual Studio .NET can view your Oracle9i password. Therefore, you should make sure that your Visual Studio .NET project files are in a secure location. Click **OK**.

The new data connection appears in the Server Explorer as a node below the Data Connections node. You can use this node to access database tables and other items in your database. Now you will open the new data connection and examine its contents.

To open the new data connection:

1. *If you are using an Oracle9i database*, click the **plus sign** beside the ORCL.CWUSER node. (If you specified a different database or user name when you created the connection, the node will have these values.)

   *If you are using an Access database*, click the **plus sign** beside the ACCESS.A:\Chapter9\Tutorials\clearwater.mdb.Admin node. (The path you will see may be different, depending on where your Access database file is located.)

2. Nodes representing Tables, Views, and Stored Procedures appear.

In a database, a **view** is similar to a table, except that it shows a different aspect of the table, such as a subset of the table fields or a combination of fields from multiple tables. A **stored procedure** is a program that you store in the database and which other users can execute. You can use a stored procedure to retrieve data values and manipulate them using program commands.

Now you will open the Tables node and view your database tables. Then you will open the CUSTOMER table to view the table fields.

 If you are using an Oracle9i database, you will see other tables besides the ones in Figure 9-10. This is because an Oracle9i database contains special tables called system tables that the DBMS uses to manage data. When you connect to an Oracle9i database, your user account has privileges to use these system tables, so you will see many system tables along with the Clearwater Traders database tables.

To view your database tables:

1. Click the **plus sign** beside the Tables node. An alphabetic listing of all of your database tables appears.

2. *If you are using an Oracle9i database*, type **c** to move the window focus to the name of the first table that begins with the letter *c*. Scroll down the list to find the CUSTOMER table.

3. Click the **plus sign** beside the CUSTOMER node. A listing of the CUSTOMER table fields appears.

You can view, insert, update, and delete data records using Visual Studio .NET. To open a database table, you right-click the table name in the Server Explorer Table node, then click Retrieve Data from Table. The table appears in a worksheet format in the Browser Window. Now you will open the CUSTOMER table.

To open the CUSTOMER table:

1. Right-click the **CUSTOMER** node, then click **Retrieve Data from Table**.

2. *If you are using an Oracle9i database*, a tab named CWUSER.CUSTOMER: Table(ORCL) appears in the Browser Window. (Some of the tab label text may not appear in the Browser Window.)

*If you are using an Access database*, a tab named CUSTOMER: Table (...\clearwater.mdb) appears in the Browser Window. (Some of the tab label text may not appear in the Browser Window.)

To insert a new record, you type the data values in the blank row that appears after the existing records. To change a data value, you replace an existing value with a new value. To delete a record, you click the left edge of the record so the record appears selected, right-click, then click Delete. Now you will update customer Paula Harris's middle initial value.

To update a record:

1. Place the insertion point in the C_MI field for the first record, which is the record for customer Paula Harris, and change Paula's C_MI value to **F**.

2. Click the insertion point in another column to apply the change, then close the CUSTOMER table window to save the change and close the table.

To delete a data connection, you select the connection in the Server Explorer, right-click, and then click Delete. Delete data connections with care. Recall that data connections are associated with the Visual Studio .NET IDE, and may be used by multiple projects. Even if you may no longer need a data connection in your current project, you may have used the connection in another project, and this project will not run correctly if its connection has been deleted.

---

# WRITING SQL QUERIES TO RETRIEVE DATA FROM A SINGLE DATABASE TABLE

To create Web pages that allow users to manipulate database data, you must write program commands that can interact with relational databases. These program commands often use **query languages** to retrieve existing database data and insert, update, and delete data values. Query languages use English words such as SELECT, CREATE, ALTER, INSERT, and UPDATE. The primary query language for relational databases is **Structured Query Language (SQL)**. The basic SQL language consists of about 30 commands that enable users to create database structures and manipulate and view data. In this section, you will become familiar with the syntax of SQL commands that you use to retrieve database data from a single database table. SQL commands that retrieve database data are called **queries**, because they often answer a question. SQL commands that insert, update, or delete database data are called action queries, because they perform an action that changes the data values in the database.

To create database queries in Visual Studio .NET, you create a Web form component called an OleDbDataAdapter. To help you write SQL queries that retrieve data from a single database table, Visual Studio .NET provides **Query Builder**, which is a graphical environment that allows you to visually select the database tables and table fields from which you want to retrieve values. Visual Studio .NET then automatically generates the SQL syntax for the associated query and puts it in the Web form's code behind file.

It is important for you to understand the syntax of the SQL query, however, in case you need to modify or debug the query syntax. The following subsections describe how to create a data adapter, and how to use Query Builder to create SQL queries that retrieve data from a single database table.

## Creating a Data Adapter

To retrieve database data in a Web form, you create a Web form component called a data adapter. A **Web form component** is similar to a control and provides functionality to the Web form. However, a Web form component does not actually display on the Web form, and users cannot interact with it directly. A **data adapter** is a Web form component that retrieves specific data values from a data source such as a database, and places the values in a data set. A data set is a structure that is similar to an array or a collection, except that it stores data that you retrieve from a database. In this chapter, you will not actually create and manipulate data sets, but you will learn how to configure data adapters so they can retrieve data into data sets. You will learn how to create and manipulate data sets in Chapter 10.

Now you will use the Data Adapter Configuration Wizard to create a new data adapter in the DBForm.aspx Web form.

To create the data adapter:

1. Select the **DBForm.aspx** tab to open the Web form in Design view, then click the **Toolbox** icon 🛠 on the left edge of the screen display to open the Toolbox.

2. Click the **Data** tab, and then double-click the **OleDbDataAdapter** tool. The Data Adapter Configuration Wizard Welcome page appears.

The Data Adapter Configuration Wizard has the following pages:

- *The Welcome page*, which introduces the Wizard.

- *The Data Connection page*, which allows you to select the data connection for the data adapter. You can select an existing connection or create a new connection.

- *The Query Type page*, which allows you to specify whether the data adapter uses a SQL statement or a stored procedure to access the data.

- *The SQL statement page*, which you use either to specify the SQL query syntax directly or to access the Query Builder. Within the Query Builder, you can visually create the SQL query syntax.

- *The Results page*, which summarizes the tasks that the Wizard performs.

9

Now you will use the Data Adapter Configuration Wizard to create the new data adapter. You will configure the data adapter so it uses the data connection you created earlier.

To create the data adapter:

1. On the Data Adapter Configuration Wizard Welcome page, click **Next**. The Data Connection page appears.

2. *If you are using an Oracle9i database*, make sure that *ORCL.CWUSER* is selected in the *Which data connection should the data adapter use* list.

   *If you are using an Access database*, make sure that *ACCESS.A:\Chapter9\ clearwater.mdb.Admin* is selected in the *Which data connection should the data adapter use* list. (The connection displays *Admin* because you are using the Admin user account in the Access database.)

3. Click **Next**. On the Query Type page, make sure that the *Use SQL statements* option button is selected, and then click **Next**. The SQL statements page appears.

On the SQL statements page, you can directly enter the SQL query in the *What data should the data adapter load into the dataset* field. Or, you can click the Query Builder button to start Query Builder and create the query syntax visually. The following section describes how to use Query Builder to create SQL queries that retrieve data from a single database table.

## Using Query Builder to Create SQL Queries That Retrieve Data from a Single Database Table

 At publication time, a documented bug in the Query Builder prevents it from retrieving data from three or more database tables in the Access database environment. You will use Query Builder only when you retrieve data from a single database table.

To use Query Builder to create queries that retrieve data from a single database table, you select the database table from which you want to retrieve data, specify the table columns that the query retrieves, specify a sort order for the retrieved data values, and specify search conditions to filter the retrieved values. Figure 9-17 shows the Query Builder window.

When you first open Query Builder, a dialog box appears that lists all of the database tables that are available through the data connection. After you select the database tables you want to use, the Diagram pane displays a visual representation of each table and its associated columns. To select the table columns that the query will retrieve, you check the column name in the Diagram pane display. The selected columns then appear in the Grid pane, and the SQL command syntax appears in the SQL pane. To run the query, right-click anywhere in the Query Builder window, except on one of the tables in the Diagram pane, and then click Run. The retrieved data values appear in the Results pane.

Within the Grid pane, the Column field displays the names of the columns that the query retrieves. The Alias field allows you to specify an alternate column heading in the Results pane. The Table field shows the name of the database table from which the column data is retrieved. The Output field allows you to specify whether the column's values appear in the Results pane. The Sort Type and Sort Order fields allow you to specify how the output is sorted. The Criteria field allows you to specify a search condition to filter the query results, and the Or columns allow you to specify alternate search conditions.

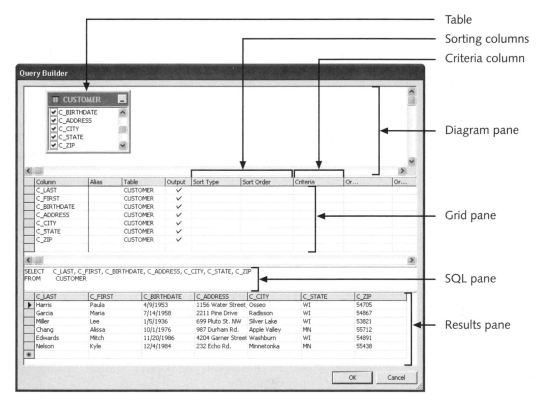

**Figure 9-17**   Query Builder window

Now you will use Query Builder to create a query that retrieves the C_LAST, C_FIRST, C_ADDRESS, C_CITY, C_STATE, C_ZIP, and C_BIRTHDATE columns from the CUSTOMER database table. Then you will examine the SQL query syntax.

To create the query visually:

1. On the SQL statements page, click **Query Builder**. The Add Table dialog box opens.

2. *If you are using an Oracle9i database*, type **c** to move to the tables that begin with the letter *c*, scroll down to CUSTOMER, select **CUSTOMER**, click **Add**, and then click **Close**.

*If you are using an Access database*, select **CUSTOMER**, click **Add**, and then click **Close**.

3. A visual representation of the CUSTOMER table appears in the Diagram pane in the Query Builder window, as shown in Figure 9-17. To select the table columns, check **C_LAST**, **C_FIRST**, **C_BIRTHDATE**, **C_ADDRESS**, **C_CITY**, **C_STATE**, and **C_ZIP**. You must select the columns in the order listed so the column names will appear in the correct order in the *Column* field in the Grid pane and so the results will appear in the correct order in the Results pane.

If you are using Access, the column names will appear in a different order in the Diagram pane.

4. Right-click anywhere in the Query Builder window, and then click **Run**. The retrieved data values appear in the Results pane as shown in Figure 9-17. (You may need to resize your Query Builder window or adjust the sizes of the individual window panes to display all of the values in the Results pane.)

Note the SQL query that appears in the SQL pane. The basic syntax for a SQL query that retrieves data from a single database table is:

```
SELECT column1, column2, ...
FROM table
```

In this syntax, the SELECT clause lists the names of the columns whose values you want to retrieve. The FROM clause specifies the name of the database table. In the SQL pane in Figure 9-17, the selected CUSTOMER column names appear in the SELECT clause, and CUSTOMER appears as the *table* name.

You can modify the column selections by checking new columns or clearing checked columns in the Diagram pane. To update the Results pane after changing the query selections, right-click, then click Run.

## Using Query Builder to Sort Data Values

Currently, the data records do not appear in a particular order. (Actually they appear in order of their associated C_ID values, but this will not necessarily be the case as you add new records to the CUSTOMER table.) To retrieve records so they appear in a specific order, you specify a sort key. A **sort key** is a column on which you want to sort the data values. To select the sort key, you click the Sort Type cell for the sort key column. (Recall that the *Sort Type* field is the fifth column in the Grid pane in Figure 9-17.) A list opens that allows you to select the sort type, which can be *Ascending* or *Descending*. If you select *Ascending*, the query sorts numerical records in ascending order from lowest to highest. If the sort key is a text string, the query sorts the records in alphabetical ascending order (from *A* to *Z*). If the sort key is a date, the query sorts the dates from oldest to most recent. If you select *Descending*, SQL sorts the records in the opposite order.

You can sort retrieved data values using multiple sort keys. For example, you could specify first to sort the values in Figure 9-17 by state, and then to sort the values by customer last names. When you specify multiple sort keys, the sort key's *Sort Order* cell specifies whether the associated sort key is the first sort key, the second sort key, and so on. (Recall that the *Sort Order* field is the sixth column in the Grid pane in Figure 9-17.) Now you will modify the query so it displays the data sorted first by state, then by customer last names.

To sort the data values by state and by last name:

1. Click the insertion point in the **C_STATE Sort Type** cell, open the list, and then select **Ascending** to sort the retrieved data values by state, in alphabetical order. (If you select *Descending*, the results will appear in reverse alphabetical order.) Note that the value "1" appears in the *Sort Order* field, which indicates that C_STATE is the first sort key. Also note that the Sort Ascending glyph ⇩ appears beside the C_STATE field in the Diagram pane.

2. Click the insertion point in the **C_LAST Sort Type** cell, open the list, then select **Ascending** to sort the retrieved data values by customer last name. Note that the value "2" appears in the *Sort Order* cell, which indicates that C_LAST is the second sort key.

3. Right-click anywhere in the Query Builder window, and then click **Run**. The retrieved values in the Results pane now appear sorted by state and then by customer last name within states.

Notice that in the SQL pane, the ORDER BY clause appears after the FROM clause, and specifies the query sort order. The general syntax for the ORDER BY clause is ORDER BY *column1, column2, ...*. The column names specify the sort keys, and appear in the order in which the query performs the sorting operations.

## Using Query Builder to Filter Retrieved Data

Currently, your query retrieves all of the customer records. Sometimes, however, you need to create a query that retrieves only certain records based on criteria such as the state in which the customer lives or the first letter in the customer's last name. You can specify an **exact search condition**, for which a field value must exactly match a search condition. An example of an exact search condition is retrieving all records for which the C_STATE value is equal to "MN." You can also specify an **inexact search condition**, for which a field value falls within a range of values. An example of an inexact search condition is retrieving all records for which C_LAST is greater than the letter *M*. This query would retrieve all records for which C_LAST begins with a letter from *N* through *Z*.

To filter data in a SQL query, you use the WHERE clause to specify a search condition. The general syntax for the WHERE clause is:

WHERE *column comparison_operator search_expression*

In this syntax, *column* is the name of the column that must match the search condition, such as C_LAST. The *search_expression* specifies the value to which the column is compared, and may be a literal value, such as "MN," or a variable value. The *comparison_operator* compares the *column* value to the *search_expression* value. Table 9-1 lists common SQL comparison operators.

**Table 9-1**    Common search condition comparison operators

| Operator | Description | Example Oracle9*i* Syntax | Example Access Syntax |
|---|---|---|---|
| = | Equal to | C_STATE = 'MN' | C_STATE = 'MN' |
| > | Greater than | INV_QUANTITY > 50 | INV_QUANTITY > 50 |
| < | Less than | INV_QOH < 100 | INV_QOH < 100 |
| >= | Greater than or equal to | C_BIRTHDATE >= TO_DATE ('01-JAN-1980', 'DD-MON-YYYY') | C_BIRTHDATE >= #01-JAN-1980# |
| <= | Less than or equal to | INV_QOH <= 30 | INV_QOH <= 30 |
| < > | Not equal to | O_METHPMT <> 'CHECK' | O_METHPMT <> 'CHECK' |
| IS NULL | Values that are NULL | C_MI IS NULL | C_MI IS NULL |
| IS NOT NULL | Values that are not NULL | C_MI IS NOT NULL | C_MI IS NOT NULL |

Search expressions for text values are case-sensitive, and you must enclose text search expressions in quotation marks. Note that in Oracle9*i*, you use single quotation marks, as in the search condition C_STATE = 'MN'. In Access, you can use either double or single quotation marks. Query Builder automatically converts double quotation marks to single quotation marks. Values within quotation marks are case-sensitive. If you type C_STATE = 'mn', you will not retrieve rows in which the C_STATE value is MN. To specify a search condition that contains an embedded single quotation mark, such as the quotation mark in the text string "Mike's," you insert the embedded single quotation mark twice. For example, you would specify a search condition for the value "Women's Hiking Shorts" in the ITEM_DESC column in the ITEM table in the Clearwater Traders database as follows: ITEM_DESC = 'Women''s Hiking Shorts'.

When you are searching for a date or time data value, Oracle9*i* users must use the TO_DATE function in the search expression. TO_DATE is a data conversion function that converts a text string to a date value. The general syntax for the Oracle9*i* TO_DATE function is:

TO_DATE('*date_text_string*', '*date_format_mask*')

The *date_text_string* represents the date as a text string, such as "January 1, 1980." The *date_format_mask* indicates the date text string's format using a format mask. A **format mask** is an expression that specifies a data value's format when you enter the value into the database or display it to users. A format mask represents data using specific formatting characters, and is similar to the regular expressions that you learned about in Chapter 8. Table 9-2 shows common Oracle9*i* date format masks.

Table 9-2    Common date format masks

| Format Mask | Description | Displayed Value |
|---|---|---|
| YYYY | Displays all four digits of the year. | 2004 |
| MM | Displays the month as digits (01–12). | 01 |
| MONTH | Displays the name of the month, spelled out, in uppercase. For months with fewer than nine characters in their name, the DBMS adds trailing blank spaces to pad the name to nine characters. | FEBRUARY |
| Month | Displays the name of the month, spelled out, in mixed case. The DBMS adds trailing blank spaces to pad the name to nine characters. | February |
| DD | Displays the day of the month (01–31). | 15 |
| DAY | Displays the day of the week, spelled out, in uppercase. | SUNDAY |
| Day | Displays the day of the week, spelled out, in mixed case. | Sunday |
| AM, PM, A.M., P.M. | Displays the meridian indicator (without or with periods). | PM |
| HH | Displays the hour of the day using the 12-hour clock. | 05 |
| HH24 | Displays the hour of the day using the 24-hour clock. | 17 |
| MI | Displays minutes (0–59). | 45 |
| SS | Displays seconds (0–59). | 35 |

9

You can specify to include front slashes (/), hyphens (-), and colons (:) as embedded characters between different date format mask elements. For example, the format mask MM/DD/YYYY would appear as 02/15/2006, and the format mask HH:MI:SS would appear as 05:45:35. You can also specify to include additional characters, such as commas, periods, and blank spaces. For example, the format mask DAY, MONTH DD, YYYY would appear as SUNDAY, FEBRUARY 15, 2006.

To search for dates that are before a given date, you use the less than operator (<). To search for dates that are after a given date, you use the greater than operator (>). To search for dates that exactly match a given date, you use the equal to operator (=). An example of an Oracle9*i* search condition that searches for all dates after January 1, 1980, is as follows:

```
WHERE C_BIRTHDATE > TO_DATE('01/01/1980', 'MM/DD/YYYY')
```

An example of an Oracle9*i* search condition that searches for all times after 3:00 P.M. is as follows:

```
WHERE C_SEC_TIME > TO_DATE('03:00 PM', 'HH:MI PM')
```

As with VB .NET, you must enclose Access date values in pound signs (#). The equivalent search conditions for an Access database are as follows:

```
WHERE C_BIRTHDATE > #01/01/1980#
WHERE C_SEC_TIME > #3:00 PM#
```

Note that to search for values that are NULL (undefined), you use the search condition IS NULL. Similarly, to search for values that are not NULL, you use the search condition IS NOT NULL. For example, you would use the following search conditions to retrieve all records from the CUSTOMER table in which the C_MI (middle initial) column value is NULL and not NULL respectively:

```
WHERE C_MI IS NULL
WHERE C_MI IS NOT NULL
```

Now you will add an exact search condition to the query so it retrieves customer records only for customers whose C_STATE value is equal to "WI." To do this, you type the search condition in the *Criteria* column, which is the seventh column in the Grid pane in Figure 9-17.

To add a search condition to the query:

1. Click the insertion point in the **Criteria** cell for the C_STATE row, then type **='WI'**, then click another cell to apply the change.

 When you type a double quotation mark ("), Query Builder automatically converts it to a single quotation mark ('), regardless of which database you use.

2. In the Diagram pane, scroll down in the CUSTOMER table, if necessary, to display the C_STATE column. Notice that the Funnel glyph ▽ appears beside the C_STATE column, which indicates the column has a search condition.

3. Right-click anywhere in the Query Builder window, and then click **Run**. The Results pane now displays values only for customers whose C_STATE value is "WI."

Note that the search condition now appears in the SQL pane after the FROM clause. Query Builder places parentheses around each search condition, so the search condition appears as WHERE (C_STATE = 'WI').

You can combine multiple search conditions using the AND and OR operators. When you use the AND operator to connect two search conditions, both conditions must be true for the row to satisfy the search conditions. If no rows exist that match *both* conditions, the search finds no matching records. When you use the OR operator to connect two search conditions, only one of the conditions must be true for the row to satisfy the search conditions.

When you add a new search condition to a query that already contains a search condition, Query Builder uses the AND operator if the new search condition specifies a different column than the existing search condition. Query Builder uses the OR operator if the new search condition specifies the same column as the existing search condition. In addition, Query Builder appends the search conditions to the SQL query in the same order you specify the search conditions in the graphical window. To add an additional search expression to a column that already contains a search condition, you type the additional expression in the column's *Or* cell.

Now you will add another search condition to your query. You will specify to retrieve the records for all customers whose birth date is after January 1, 1980.

To add an additional search condition to the query:

1. Click the insertion point in the C_BIRTHDATE's **Criteria** cell.

2. *If you are using an Oracle9i database*, type **> TO_DATE('01/01/1980', 'MM/DD/YYYY')**.

   *If you are using an Access database*, type **> #01/01/1980#**.

3. Click another cell to apply the change, and then run the query. Figure 9-18 shows how the query syntax appears in the SQL pane for an Oracle database user. Notice that Query Builder joined the search conditions for the different columns using the AND operator. The Results pane displays the record for the only Wisconsin customer whose date of birth is after January 1, 1980, which is customer Mitch Edwards.

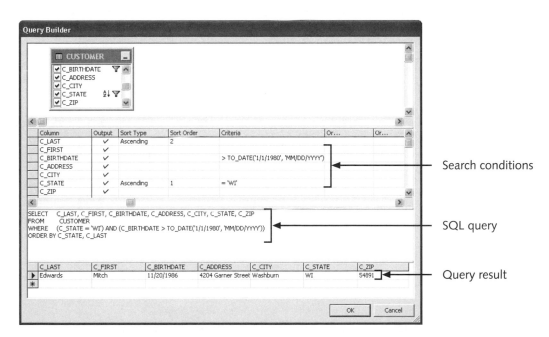

**Figure 9-18**   Query combining search conditions using the AND operator

You can combine multiple AND and OR operators in a single query. This operation is quite powerful, but can be tricky to use. The query retrieves the records based on search conditions joined by an AND operator first, and then evaluates the result of the records retrieved using the AND search condition against the records that the OR search condition retrieves. To illustrate this, you will add another search condition to your query.

You will specify that the search condition for the C_STATE column can include values where C_STATE equals either "WI" or "MN." Recall that when you specify an additional search expression for a column, Query Builder automatically adds the expression using the OR operator and appends the new search condition to the end of the query. Now you will add the additional search expression and view the query results.

To add the additional search expression:

1. To add an additional search expression to the C_STATE column, click the insertion point in the C_STATE column's first **Or** cell. (You may need to make your Query Builder window wider to display the *Or* column, or scroll to the right edge of the Grid pane to display the first *Or* column.)

2. Type **= 'MN'**, then click any other cell to apply the change. The WHERE clause in the SQL pane appears for an Oracle user as shown in Figure 9-19. Recall that when you add additional search conditions to a query, Query Builder appends the search condition to the end of the existing search condition. Note that Query Builder joins the new search expression for the C_STATE column using the OR operator, because the C_STATE column already has a search condition.

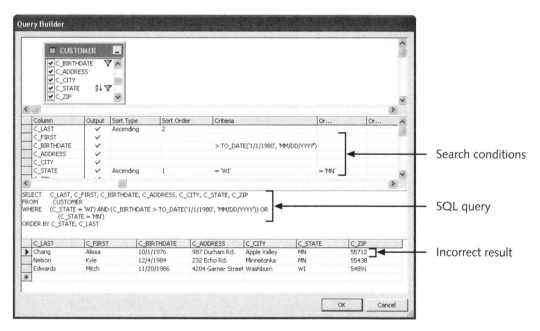

**Figure 9-19**   Query combining search conditions using the AND and OR operators

3. Run the query. The Results pane displays the records shown in Figure 9-19. The results are not correct, because they show the record for Alissa Chang, who was born in 1976.

What happened? The query was supposed to retrieve records only for customers whose birth date was after January 1, 1980. Why is Alissa Chang in the results? Recall that the query first retrieves the records specified by search conditions joined by the AND operator. This retrieves the records shown in the Results pane in Figure 9-18, which displays the Wisconsin customer whose date of birth is after January 1, 1980 (Mitch Edwards). The query then retrieves the records specified by the OR search condition, which is `C_STATE = 'MN'`. This search condition retrieves the records for all Minnesota customers (Alissa Chang and Kyle Nelson). The query then combines the results of the first search condition with the results of the second search condition, and retrieves the records shown in Figure 9-19, which displays Wisconsin customers whose date of birth is after January 1, 1980, plus *all* Minnesota customers.

To overcome this problem, you must manually edit the query and place the operation that should be performed first in parentheses. The query always evaluates search conditions joined by AND and OR operators that are enclosed in parentheses first. You will manually edit the query and modify the WHERE clause by placing the search conditions that the OR operator joins in parentheses, so the query retrieves the customers from both states. Then you will place the search condition that evaluates the C_BIRTHDATE column last, so the query then retrieves only customers whose date of birth is after January 1, 1980. When you manually edit a query, the query text is not case-sensitive, and the SQL interpreter ignores extra blank spaces and hard returns.

To edit the query manually:

1. *If you are using an Oracle9i database*, edit the WHERE clause in the SQL pane so it appears as follows (do not modify any other parts of the query:)

   ```
   WHERE ((C_STATE = 'WI') OR (C_STATE = 'MN'))
   AND (C_BIRTHDATE > TO_DATE('01/01/1980', 'MM/DD/YYYY'))
   ```

   *If you are using an Access database*, edit the WHERE clause in the SQL pane so it appears as follows (do not modify any other parts of the query:)

   ```
   WHERE ((C_STATE = 'WI') OR (C_STATE = 'MN'))
   AND (C_BIRTHDATE > #01/01/1980#)
   ```

2. Run the query. The Results pane now displays only the records for customers Nelson and Edwards, which is correct.

 When you run the query, Query Builder removes the inner parentheses around the individual search conditions, but retains the outer parentheses, so the query runs correctly. If you do not type both sets of parentheses, Query Builder will remove all parentheses and the query will not run correctly.

## Finishing the Data Adapter

Now you will finish creating the data adapter. When you create a new data adapter using the Data Adapter Configuration Wizard, the Wizard automatically creates action queries based on the data adapter's SQL query. (Recall that action queries are commands that insert, update, and delete database records.) Because you are not interested in creating action queries using this data adapter, you need to configure the data adapter so the Wizard does not try to generate these action queries. (You will learn to create action queries later in this chapter.) To configure the data adapter so it does not create action queries, you open the Advanced SQL Generation Options dialog box and clear the *Generate Insert, Update and Delete statements* check box. Now you will instruct the Wizard not to generate the action queries, and finish creating the data adapter.

To finish creating the data adapter:

1. Click **OK** to close Query Builder. The SQL statement page appears again, and displays the completed SQL query.

2. Click **Advanced Options** to open the Advanced SQL Generation Options dialog box.

3. Clear the **Generate Insert, Update and Delete statements** check box, and then click **OK** to close the Advanced SQL Generation Options dialog box.

4. Click **Next**. The Results page appears.

5. Click **Finish**. Icons representing the new data connection and data adapter appear in the component tray in the Browser Window in Design view, as shown in Figure 9-20.

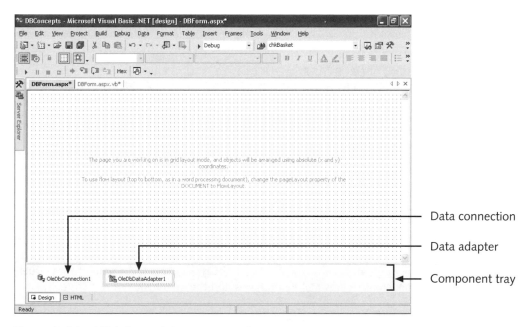

**Figure 9-20**    Web form data components

The Designer Window **component tray** displays application components that do not appear directly on a Web form, but which you create and configure to make the form functional. You can select existing Web form data components from the component tray and modify their properties using the Properties Window. Now you will change the names of the data connection and data adapter to descriptive names. In this book, you will preface data connections names with the text string "conn" and data adapter names with the text string "da."

To modify the data component names:

1. If necessary, open the Properties Window.

2. Select **OleDbConnection1** in the component tray. The Properties Window displays the data connection properties. Change the (Name) property value to **connDBForm**, then select another property to apply the change. The new name appears in the component tray.

3. Select **OleDbDataAdapter1** in the component tray, change the *(Name)* property value to **daQuery1**, then select another property to apply the change. The new name appears in the component tray.

4. Click the **Save All** button [image] on the toolbar to save your changes. Because you are finished working with the DBForm.aspx Web form, close all open windows in the Browser Window.

You can also modify the properties of the data adapter using the Data Adapter Configuration Wizard. For example, you can change the data adapter's SQL query or other property values. To reopen the data adapter in the Wizard, right-click the data adapter in the component tray, then click Configure Data Adapter. The Data Adapter Configuration page opens, and you can click Next to move to different Wizard pages and change the adapter configuration.

## CREATING SQL QUERIES THAT RETRIEVE DATA FROM MULTIPLE TABLES

One of the strengths of SQL is its ability to **join**, or combine, data from multiple database tables using foreign key references. For example, suppose you want to create a query that retrieves the item description, inventory ID, color, size, and quantity on hand for every product in the INVENTORY table in the Clearwater Traders database in Figure 9-10. Your query must retrieve data values from the ITEM table, which displays the item descriptions in the ITEM_DESC column, and the remaining fields from the INVENTORY table. The ITEM table and INVENTORY table are linked through the ITEM_ID field, which is a foreign key in the INVENTORY table and the primary key in the ITEM table.

The general syntax of a SELECT query that joins two tables is:

```
SELECT table.column1, table.column2, ...
FROM table1, table2
WHERE table1.joincolumn = table2.joincolumn
[AND search_condition(s)]
```

SQL supports multiple types of join queries. In this book, you will use only the simplest type of join, which you create by joining two or more tables when values in one table are equal to values in another table.

In this book, you will use the SQL syntax for joining multiple tables that Oracle9i databases use, because this syntax is also compatible with Access databases. Access supports alternative syntax for joining multiple tables that is not compatible with Oracle9i databases.

The SELECT clause lists the names of the columns that appear in the query output. Because the query now involves more than one table, you should preface each column name with the name of its associated database table, followed by a period. For example, to display the ITEM_DESC column in the ITEM table, you will specify that its column name appears as `ITEM.ITEM_DESC` in the SELECT clause. This is called **qualifying** the column name.

The FROM clause lists the names of all of the tables involved in the query. The FROM clause must include all tables whose fields appear in the SELECT clause, as well as tables whose fields are used in search conditions.

The WHERE clause contains the **join condition**, which specifies the table and column names on which to join the tables. The join condition contains the foreign key reference in one table and the primary key reference in the other table. The WHERE clause can contain additional search conditions that you specify using the AND and OR operators. In the search conditions, you must qualify the column names by prefacing the column name with its associated table name. For example, the following SQL query retrieves the item description, inventory ID, color, size, and quantity on hand for every product in the INVENTORY table in the Clearwater Traders database in Figure 9-10:

```
SELECT ITEM.ITEM_DESC, INVENTORY.INV_ID, INVENTORY.COLOR,
INVENTORY.INV_SIZE, INVENTORY.INV_QOH
FROM ITEM, INVENTORY
WHERE ITEM.ITEM_ID = INVENTORY.ITEM_ID
```

To practice creating queries that join multiple tables, you will use the Query form shown in Figure 9-21.

For the rest of the chapter, you will use the Query form to test database queries. Although you can use Query Builder to create single-table database queries, you will not use it to create and test queries that join multiple database tables, because at publication time it does not work with three or more tables in the Access database environment.

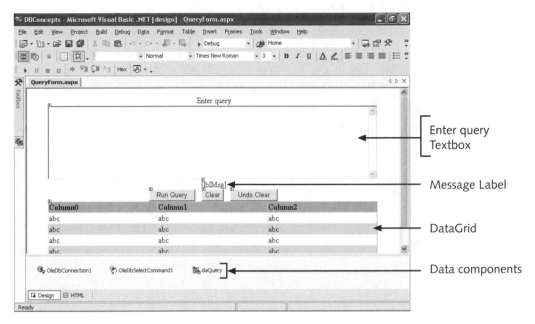

**Figure 9-21**    Query Form

The Query form contains an *Enter query* TextBox rich server control in which you can type a SQL query. When you click *Run Query,* the Web form submits the query to the database and displays the retrieved records on the form in the DataGrid. (A DataGrid is a rich server control that you use to display retrieved data. You will learn how to create DataGrid rich server controls in Chapter 10.) When you click *Clear*, the *Enter query* TextBox is cleared. When you click *Undo Clear* after clicking *Clear*, the previous text in the *Enter query* TextBox appears again. If an error occurs, an error message appears in the Message Label. Now you will add the Query form to your project.

To add the Query form to your project:

1. Start Windows Explorer if necessary, and copy **QueryForm.aspx** and **QueryForm.aspx.vb** from the Chapter9 folder on your Data Disk to the Chapter9\Tutorials\DBConcepts folder on your Solution Disk.

2. Switch to Visual Studio .NET, open the Solution Explorer if necessary, right-click the **DBConcepts** project node, point to **Add**, and then click **Add Existing Item**. Navigate to the Chapter9\Tutorials\DBConcepts folder on your Solution Disk, open the **Files of type** list, select **All Files (\*.\*)**, select **QueryForm.aspx** and **QueryForm.aspx.vb**, and click **Open**. The QueryForm.aspx node appears in the project tree.

3. Right-click the **QueryForm.aspx** node, then click **Set As Start Page**.

4. Make sure that the *QueryForm.aspx* node is selected, and then click the **View Designer** button 🔲. The Web form appears in Design view, as shown in Figure 9-21.

The Query form contains three data components in the component tray: a data connection named OleDbConnection1, a data adapter named daQuery, and an OleDbCommand component named OleDbSelectCommand1 that the form uses to store and process the queries that you type in the *Enter query* TextBox control. (An OleDbCommand component stores information about a data query.)

Before you can run the Query form, you must change the data connection's ConnectionString property. A data connection's **ConnectionString property** specifies information that the data connection passes to the OLE DB and ODBC drivers about the target database, as well as user information, such as the user name and password. You need to change the ConnectionString so it specifies the correct information to connect to the database you are using. The ConnectionString value contains many parameters, and it is easy to make errors when you type its syntax, so it is a good idea to use the ConnectionString property value from an existing connection rather than typing the value manually.

Earlier in the chapter, you used the Data Link Properties dialog box to create a data connection, and Visual Studio .NET automatically configured the ConnectionString property value. When you open the Properties Window for any data connection in your Visual Studio .NET IDE, a list appears that shows the names of your existing data connections. Now you will change the ConnectionString property of the OleDbConnection1 data connection to the connection string of your existing data connection.

To change the OleDbConnection1 data connection's ConnectionString property:

1. Open the Properties Window if necessary, then select the **OleDbConnection1** data connection in the component tray. The Properties Window displays the data connection's properties.

2. Select the **ConnectionString** property and open the list.

3. *If you are using an Oracle9i database*, select **ORCL.CWUSER**. (If your database name or user account is different, select that connection instead.)

   *If you are using an Access database*, select **ACCESS.A:\Chapter9\Tutorials\ clearwater.mdb**. (Your drive letter or folder path may be different.)

Now you will run the Query form and type in the *Enter query* TextBox the SQL query that joins the ITEM and INVENTORY tables. You will add a search condition to the query so it retrieves only records where the ITEM_DESC field value is "Women's Hiking Shorts."

To run the Query form and type the SQL query:

1. Click the **Start** button ▶ to run the project. The Query form appears in Internet Explorer.

2. Type the query shown in Figure 9-22 to retrieve the data values, then click **Run Query**. The retrieved data values appear in the DataGrid as shown.

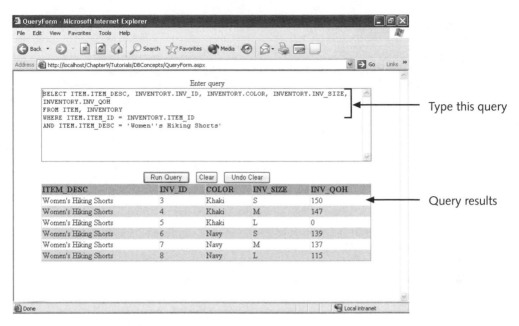

Figure 9-22    Query that joins two database tables

If you are using an Oracle9*i* database, an error message may appear that states "Oracle client and networking components were not found." This error message appears when the access permissions are not configured properly on the folders that contain your Oracle9*i* software. Close Internet Explorer, then close Visual Studio .NET. Switch to Windows Explorer, navigate to the C:\oracle\ora92 folder, right-click the ora92 folder, then click Properties. If the Security Tab appears, select the Security tab, click *Add*, click *Advanced* on the Select Users or Groups dialog box, click *Find Now* on the Select Users or Groups Dialog box, scroll down in the list, and select IUSR_*computer_name*. (In this item, *computer_name* is the name of your computer.) Click *OK*, and then click *OK* again to close the Select Users or Groups dialog box. In the ora92 Properties dialog box, make sure that *Internet Guest Account* is selected in the *Group or user names* list, check the *Allow* check box beside *Full Control*, then click *OK*. This will give Internet users the permissions they need to access the Oracle9*i* software. It may take several minutes to reset all of the permissions in the Oracle9*i* folder. Then restart Visual Studio .NET, reopen the project, and run the project again. (If the Security tab did not appear and you are using Windows XP, in Windows Explorer, select Tools from the menu, and then select Folder Options. In the Folder Options dialog box select the View tab. Scroll to the bottom of the Advanced Settings list box and clear the option Use Simple File Sharing (Recommended). After doing this, repeat the preceding steps.) (If the Security tab did not appear and you are using Windows 2000, right-click the ora92 folder, click Properties, then click the Sharing tab. On the Sharing tab, click the *Share this folder* option button, click Permissions, click Add, then select IUSR_*computer_name* from the list, click Add, and click OK.)

If you are using an Access database, an error message may appear that states, "The Microsoft Jet database engine cannot open the file 'A:\Chapter9\Tutorials\ clearwater.mdb." This error message appears when the access permissions are not configured properly on the folder that contains your Access database .mdb file. Close Internet Explorer, then close Visual Studio .NET. Switch to Windows Explorer, navigate to the Chapter9\Tutorials folder on your Solution Disk, right-click the Tutorials folder, and then click *Properties*. If the Security tab appears, select the Security tab, click *Add*, and then type *Everyone* in the *Enter the object names to select* field. Click *OK* to close the Select Users or Groups dialog box. In the Tutorials Properties dialog box, make sure that *Everyone* is selected in the *Group or user names* list, check the *Allow* check box beside *Full Control*, then click *OK*. This will give Internet users the permissions they need to access the Access database file. Then restart Visual Studio .NET, reopen the project, and run the project again. You will need to reset the folder properties this way whenever you create a data connection that references an Access database in a different folder. (If the Security tab did not appear and you are using Windows XP, in Windows Explorer, select Tools from the menu, and then select Folder Options. In the Folder Options dialog box select the View tab. Scroll to the bottom of the Advanced Settings list box and clear the option Use Simple File Sharing (Recommended). After doing this, repeat the preceding steps.) (If the Security tab did not appear and you are using Windows 2000, right-click the Tutorials folder, and then click Properties. Click the Sharing tab, select the *Share this folder* option button, then click the Permissions button. In the Permissions dialog box, select Everyone from the Name pane, and check the Full Control check box in the Permission pane. Click OK, and click OK again.)

You can join any number of tables in a SELECT command. To structure the query, you must include in the SELECT clause the names of all of the fields you wish to display. In addition, you must include in the FROM clause the names of all of the tables that contain display fields or fields used in the search condition. And, you must include a join condition in the WHERE clause to specify each foreign key/primary key link between tables.

Suppose you want to create a query that displays the item description, size, color, price, and order quantity of every item that customer Alissa Chang has ever ordered. This query involves the following tables:

- ITEM, to display the item description
- INVENTORY, to display the item size, color, and price
- ORDER_LINE, to display the order quantity
- CUSTOMER, to specify the search conditions "Alissa" and "Chang"
- ORDERS, to link the CUSTOMER table to the ORDER_LINE table

When you identify the tables in a query, sometimes you must include tables that do not necessarily contribute fields that appear in the SELECT clause. For example, in this query, you must include the CUSTOMER table because it provides the fields in the search condition. You must also include the ORDERS table, because it provides the link between the CUSTOMER and ORDER_LINE tables, even though the query doesn't display any fields from the ORDERS table. To make it easier to identify the tables in a multiple-table query, it is helpful to create a query design diagram such as the one shown in Figure 9-23.

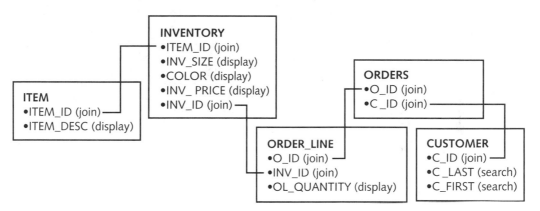

**Figure 9-23** Query design diagram

To create a query design diagram, you first identify all of the tables in the query. You draw the tables that contribute display and search fields, and label the fields to indicate whether they are display or search fields. Then you draw the primary key/foreign key links between each table, and identify the corresponding primary and foreign key fields as join fields. By creating a query design diagram, you can easily identify when you need to include a table such as the ORDERS table, which does not contribute any display or search fields, but is required because it contributes join fields.

Table 9-3 describes the process for deriving the SQL query based on the query design diagram in Figure 9-23.

Note that in Figure 9-23, there are five tables and four links between the tables. Because there are four links, there must be four join conditions. You must always have one fewer join condition than the total number of tables that the query joins. In this query, you are joining five tables, so you have four join conditions.

**Table 9-3**    Deriving a SQL query from a query design diagram

| Step | Process | SQL Query Syntax |
|---|---|---|
| 1 | Create the SELECT clause by listing the display fields | `SELECT ITEM.ITEM_DESC, INVENTORY.INV_SIZE, ORDER_LINE.OL_QUANTITY, INVENTORY.INV_COLOR,INVENTORY.INV_PRICE` |
| 2 | Create the FROM clause by listing the table names | `FROM ITEM, INVENTORY, ORDER_LINE, ORDERS, CUSTOMER` |
| 3 | Create a join condition for every link between the tables | `WHERE ITEM.ITEM_ID = INVENTORY.ITEM_ID AND INVENTORY.INV_ID = ORDER_LINE.INV_ID AND ORDER_LINE.O_ID = ORDERS.O_ID AND ORDERS.C_ID = CUSTOMER.C_ID` |
| 4 | Add search conditions for search fields | `AND C_LAST = 'Chang' AND C_FIRST = 'Alissa'` |

Now you will type and run the SQL query in the *Enter query* TextBox control in the Query form, and run the query.

To enter and run the query that joins five tables:

1. Click **Clear** to delete the current query text in the *Enter query* TextBox, then type the SQL query shown in Figure 9-24.

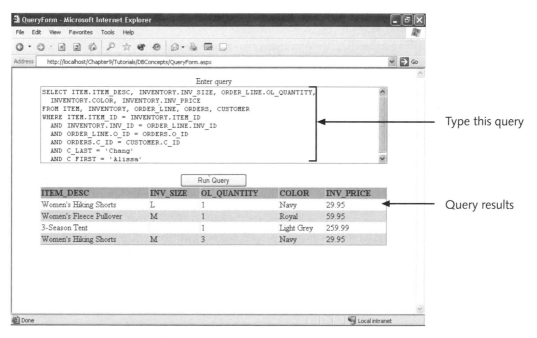

**Figure 9-24**    Query that joins five tables

2. Click **Run Query**. The query results should appear as shown in Figure 9-24.

If you are an Oracle9*i* user and an error message appears stating "invalid identifier," confirm that you entered all of the table and field names exactly as they appear in the Clearwater Traders database tables in Figure 9-10.

If you are an Access user and an error message appears stating "No value given for one or more required parameters," confirm that you entered all of the table and field names exactly as they appear in the Clearwater Traders database tables in Figure 9-10.

If you create a multiple table query that retrieves many more records than you expect, you probably forgot a join clause. Remember that you must always include one less join clause than the total number of tables that the query joins.

## PERFORMING QUERY OPERATIONS ON GROUPS OF RECORDS

So far, you have learned how to retrieve data from a single table and from multiple tables that have been joined. SQL also has commands that allow you to retrieve information about groups of similar records. For example, Clearwater Traders managers might want to retrieve the sum of all revenues generated by orders placed using the Web site as the order source, or they might want to know the total inventory quantity on hand for all sizes and colors of an item such as "Girl's Soccer Tee." The following subsections describe how to use SQL group functions and how to group related records in query outputs.

### SQL Group Functions

A SQL **group function** performs an operation on a group of retrieved records and returns a single result, such as a column sum. Table 9-4 describes and gives examples of commonly used SQL group functions.

**Table 9-4**    SQL group functions

| Function | Description | Example Query | Result |
|---|---|---|---|
| AVG (*fieldname*) | Returns the average value of a numeric column's returned values | SELECT AVG(INVENTORY.INV_QOH) FROM INVENTORY | 98.21875 |
| COUNT (*fieldname*) COUNT(*) | Returns an integer representing a count of the number of returned rows. COUNT (*fieldname*) counts only rows where the specified field is not NULL, whereas COUNT(*) counts all rows. | SELECT COUNT (INVENTORY.INV_SIZE) FROM INVENTORY<br><br>SELECT COUNT(*) FROM INVENTORY | Rows for which an INV_SIZE value exists = 30;<br><br>all rows = 32 |
| MAX (*fieldname*) | Returns the maximum value of a numeric column's returned values. | SELECT MAX (INVENTORY.INV_PRICE) FROM INVENTORY | 259.99 |
| MIN (*fieldname*) | Returns the minimum value of a numeric column's returned values. | SELECT MIN INVENTORY (INV_PRICE) FROM INVENTORY | 15.95 |
| SUM (*fieldname*) | Sums a numeric column's returned values. | SELECT SUM(INVENTORY.INV_QOH) FROM INVENTORY | 3143 |

To use a group function in a SQL query, you list the function name, followed by the column name on which to perform the calculation in parentheses. Now you will write a SQL query that retrieves the maximum, minimum, and average quantity on hand values for the INVENTORY table.

To write a query that uses group functions:

1. Click **Clear** to delete the current query in the *Enter query* TextBox, then type the following query:

```
SELECT MAX(INVENTORY.INV_QOH),
MIN(INVENTORY.INV_QOH), AVG(INVENTORY.INV_QOH)
FROM INVENTORY
```

2. Click **Run Query**. The maximum value is 187, the minimum value is 0, and the average value is 98.21875.

In an Oracle9*i* database, the group function expressions serve as the column headings. For example, the first column heading is "MAX(INVENTORY.INV_QOH)." In an Access database, the column headings appear as undefined expressions, such as "Expr1000." To correct this problem, when you retrieve data in a query, you can display alternate column headings by creating a column alias. A **column alias** is a descriptive text string that you can assign to any column in the SELECT clause. The alias replaces the column name in the retrieved data value display. The general syntax for creating a column alias is *fieldname* AS *alias_name*. For example, you would use the following query to retrieve the sum of all of the INV_QOH values in the INVENTORY table and display the result using the column heading "TOTAL_INVENTORY":

```
SELECT SUM(INVENTORY.INV_QOH) AS TOTAL_INVENTORY
FROM INVENTORY
```

Now you will modify the query so it includes column aliases for the group function columns.

To create column aliases for the group function columns:

1. Modify the SELECT clause of the query so it appears as follows:

```
SELECT MAX(INVENTORY.INV_QOH) AS MAX_INVENTORY,
MIN(INVENTORY.INV_QOH) AS MIN_INVENTORY,
AVG(INVENTORY.INV_QOH) AS AVG_INVENTORY
```

2. Click **Run Query**. The group function values appear with the modified column headings.

## Using the GROUP BY Clause to Group Related Records

If a query retrieves multiple records, and one of the columns has duplicate values, you can group the output by the column with duplicate values and apply group functions to the grouped data. For example, you might want to list the descriptions of the different Clearwater Traders merchandise items and list the sum of the quantity on hand for all colors and sizes of each item. To do this, you use the GROUP BY clause, which has the following syntax: GROUP BY *fieldname*. The *fieldname* parameter is the name of the column on which you want to group the values. In this example, the GROUP BY clause would be GROUP BY ITEM_DESC. Now you will create a query that uses a group function with the GROUP BY clause.

To use the GROUP BY clause to group rows:

1. Click **Clear** to delete the current query in the *Enter query* TextBox, then type the query in Figure 9-25 to list the item description and the quantity on hand for each item.

2. Click **Run Query**. The query results appear as shown in Figure 9-25.

**9**

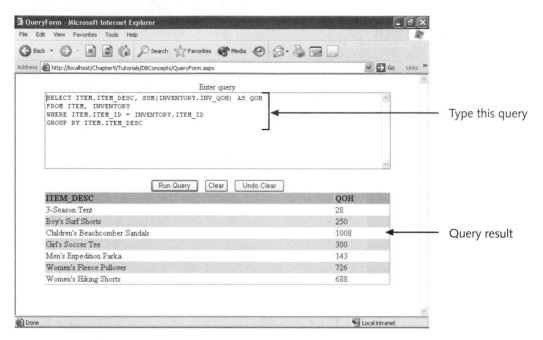

**Figure 9-25**   Query using the GROUP BY clause

If you create a query in which one or more columns in the SELECT clause are in a group function and one or more columns are not in a group function, then you must always place the columns that are *not* in a group function in the GROUP BY clause. For example, notice in Figure 9-25 that there are two columns in the SELECT clause: ITEM_ID and INV_QOH. The ITEM_ID column is not in the group function, while the INV_QOH column is in the SUM group function. Therefore, the ITEM_DESC column must appear in the GROUP BY clause. If you do not place the non-grouped columns in a GROUP BY clause, an error occurs.

## INSERTING, UPDATING, AND DELETING DATABASE DATA

As users interact with data-based Web pages, they enter input values and make selections that may generate action queries. Recall that action queries involve operations that change the database by inserting, updating, or deleting data values. The following sub-sections describe the SQL commands for inserting, updating, and deleting data.

### Inserting Database Data

You use the SQL **INSERT** action query to add new data records to database tables. The basic syntax of an INSERT action query for inserting a value for each table field is:

```
INSERT INTO table (column1_name, column2_name, ...)
VALUES (column1_value, column2_value, ...)
```

In this command, the INSERT INTO keywords are followed by *table*, which is the name of the table in which you want to insert data values.

 You can insert values into only one table at a time using a single SQL INSERT statement. If you want to insert values into multiple tables, you must use multiple SQL INSERT statements.

After the INSERT INTO clause, the command lists the name of each table column for which you wish to insert a value. You can list the column names in any order. Although you do not need to insert a value into every column, you must always insert a value for the record's primary key column, and the primary key value cannot be the same as any primary key values that already exist in the table. For example, if you insert a new record in the CUSTOMER table, you cannot insert the value 1 for the C_ID field, because C_ID is the table's primary key, and the value 1 already exists for another record. If the table has a composite primary key, you must insert values for all columns that comprise the primary key, and the combination of the columns that comprise the primary key must be unique.

The next component in the command is the **VALUES** keyword, which is followed by a list that specifies the data value for each column name that appears in the list in the INSERT INTO clause. The values in the VALUES list must appear in the same order as the column names in the INSERT INTO list. For example, you would use the following command to insert all of the values into the first record in the ITEM table:

```
INSERT INTO ITEM (ITEM_ID, ITEM_DESC,
CAT_ID, ITEM_IMAGE)
VALUES (1, 'Men''s Expedition Parka',
3, 'parka.jpg')
```

Note that the list that specifies the column names contains four items, and the list that specifies the column values also contains four items.

When you insert data values into fields that contain numbers, you simply type the number. To insert text string values, you must enclose the values in single quotation marks, and the text within the single quotation marks is case-sensitive. Note that if you want to enter a text string that includes a single quotation mark, you type the single quotation mark two times, as in `'Men''s Expedition Parka'`.

To insert date and time values, Oracle9*i* users must use the TO_DATE function to convert the date text string to a date value. Recall that the general syntax of the TO_DATE function is as follows:

```
TO_DATE('date_text_string', 'date_format_mask')
```

Oracle9*i* users would use the following INSERT statement to insert the C_ID and C_BIRTHDATE fields for the first record in the CUSTOMER table in the Clearwater Traders database:

```
INSERT INTO CUSTOMER (C_ID, C_BIRTHDATE)
VALUES (1, TO_DATE('04/09/1953', 'MM/DD/YYYY'))
```

If you are using an Access database, you enclose date values in pound signs. Access users would use the following INSERT statement to insert the C_ID and C_BIRTHDATE fields for the first customer record:

```
INSERT INTO CUSTOMER (C_ID, C_BIRTHDATE)
VALUES (1, #04/09/1953#)
```

Before you can insert a new record, you must ensure that the database contains all of the foreign key records that the new record references. For example, suppose you want to insert the first record into the INVENTORY table. The INVENTORY table contains a foreign key reference to the ITEM table, and the first record references ITEM_ID 2. The record for ITEM_ID 2 must already exist in the ITEM table before you can insert the value for ITEM_ID 2 as a foreign key in the INVENTORY table.

Now you will insert a new record into the ITEM table. You will specify the ITEM_ID value as 8, which is the next unique primary key value. You will specify the ITEM_DESC value as 'Children's Denim Overalls,' the CAT_ID as 2, and the ITEM_IMAGE value as 'overalls.jpg.' Recall that the CAT_ID field is a foreign key in the ITEM table. The CAT_ID value of 2 already exists in the CATEGORY table, so the foreign key reference exists.

To insert a new record into the ITEM table:

1. In the Query form in Internet Explorer, click **Clear** to delete the current query text in the *Enter query* TextBox, then type the following action query:

```
INSERT INTO ITEM (ITEM_ID, ITEM_DESC,
CAT_ID, ITEM_IMAGE)
VALUES (8, 'Children''s Denim Overalls',
2, 'overalls.jpg')
```

2. Click **Run Query**. The message "Query succeeded, 1 record(s) affected" appears in the Message Label.

To confirm that the action query successfully inserted the record, you will run a query that displays all of the column values in all of the records in the ITEM table. Rather than typing all of the column names in the SELECT clause, you will substitute the * wildcard character.

To confirm that the record was inserted:

1. Click **Clear** to delete the current query text in the *Enter query* TextBox, and then type the following query to display all of the columns in all of the records:

```
SELECT * FROM ITEM
```

2. Click **Run Query**. The new record for ITEM_ID 8 appears in the DataGrid, which confirms that the record was successfully inserted.

When you insert new database records, you often use surrogate keys as primary keys. Recall that a surrogate key is artificially created to be the record's primary key identifier, and has no intrinsic relation to the record to which it is assigned, other than to identify the record uniquely. Usually, developers configure the database to generate surrogate key values automatically. The following subsections describe how to generate surrogate key values automatically in Oracle9*i* and Access databases.

## Generating Surrogate Key Values in an Oracle9*i* Database

 If you are using an Access database, you can skip this section and proceed to the section titled "Generating Surrogate Key Values in an Access Database."

In an Oracle9*i* database, you retrieve surrogate key values using a sequence. (Recall that sequences are sequential lists of numbers that the Oracle9*i* DBMS automatically generates.) The DBMS guarantees that each primary key value will be unique. You create and manipulate sequences using SQL commands.

**Creating New Sequences**    The following command creates a new sequence:

```
CREATE SEQUENCE sequence_name
START WITH start_value;
```

Every sequence in your user account must have a unique name. The name must be from 1 to 30 characters, must begin with a letter, and can contain the special characters _, #, and $. The CREATE SEQUENCE command is the only command required to create a sequence. The START WITH clause is optional, and when you omit it, the sequence automatically starts with the value 1.

Now you will create a sequence named ITEM_ID_SEQUENCE that will generate values for the ITEM_ID field in the ITEM table. You will specify that the sequence will start with 10, to ensure that the new ITEM_ID values differ from any existing values.

1. Click **Clear** to delete the current query in the *Enter query* TextBox, then type the following SQL command to create the new sequence:

```
CREATE SEQUENCE ITEM_ID_SEQUENCE
START WITH 10
```

2. Click **Run Query**. The message "Query succeeded, 0 record(s) affected" appears, indicating that you successfully created the sequence.

**Viewing Sequence Information**    Sometimes you need to review the names of the sequences you have created. To review the names of your sequences, you can open your data connection in the Visual Studio .NET Server Explorer and view the names of your sequences in a system table named USER_SEQUENCES. (Recall that a system table is a table that the DBMS uses to manage the database.) Now you will query the USER_SEQUENCES system table and view your sequences to confirm that you have successfully created the ITEM_ID_SEQUENCE sequence. You can do this while the Query form is running by multitasking between Internet Explorer and Visual Studio .NET.

To view your sequences:

1. Switch to Visual Studio .NET. (The Server Explorer tab is not currently visible because you are running a project.) Click **View** on the menu bar, and then click **Server Explorer**. The Server Explorer opens.

2. Click the plus sign beside the *Data Connections* node if necessary, click the plus sign beside the *ORCL.CWUSER* node if necessary, and click the plus sign beside the *Tables* node if necessary.

3. Type **u** to move to the first table that begins with the letter *U*. Scroll down the window until the USER_SEQUENCES table appears, right-click **USER_SEQUENCES**, then click **Retrieve Data from Table**. The USER_SEQUENCES: Table(ORCL) page appears in the Browser Window and displays ITEM_ID_SEQUENCE in the SEQUENCE_NAME column. (If you have created other sequences, the table displays these sequences also. You may need to adjust the column widths to view the entire sequence name.)

If you are using an Oracle9*i* Enterprise Edition database, the USER_SEQUENCES table will not be visible under the Tables node.

4. Close the User Sequences table in the Browser Window, then close the Server Explorer.

**Using Sequences in INSERT Action Queries** To use sequences in INSERT queries, you must first understand pseudocolumns. A **pseudocolumn** is an Oracle9*i* construct that acts like a column, but is actually a command that returns a specific value. You can use the NEXTVAL sequence pseudocolumn within SQL commands to retrieve the next value of a sequence. You use the following general syntax to access the next sequence value using the NEXTVAL pseudocolumn and insert the sequence value into a new record:

```
INSERT INTO tablename (column1_name, column2_name)
VALUES(sequence_name.NEXTVAL, column2_value)
```

This syntax assumes that the primary key associated with the sequence is the first table field.

Now you will insert another record into the ITEM table, but this time you will use the ITEM_ID_SEQUENCE and the NEXTVAL pseudocolumn to generate the ITEM_ID value. You will retrieve all of the table columns and records to confirm that the record was successfully inserted.

To insert a new ITEM record using the ITEM_ID_SEQUENCE sequence:

1. Switch back to Internet Explorer, click **Clear**, then type the following query:

```
INSERT INTO ITEM (ITEM_ID, ITEM_DESC,
CAT_ID, ITEM_IMAGE)
VALUES (ITEM_ID_SEQUENCE.NEXTVAL,
'Children''s Snow Boots', 2, 'boots.jpg')
```

2. Click **Run Query**. The Message Label displays the message "Query succeeded. 1 record(s) affected."

3. Click **Clear**, then type the following query to display all of the columns in all of the records:

```
SELECT * FROM ITEM
```

4. Click **Run Query**. The new record appears in the DataGrid, which confirms that the record was successfully inserted. Note that the ITEM_ID value for the new record is 10, which is the value you specified as the sequence's start value.

## Generating Surrogate Key Values in an Access Database

9

 If you are using an Oracle9*i* database, you can skip this section.

In an Access database, when you create a database table that contains a column that will store surrogate key values, you assign the column a numeric data type named AutoNumber. The AutoNumber data type generates a unique sequential number whenever a user inserts a new record into the table. In an Access database table, only one column can have the AutoNumber data type. Table 9-5 summarizes the primary key columns in the Clearwater Traders and Northwoods University databases that have the AutoNumber data type.

**Table 9-5**   Primary key columns with the AutoNumber data type in the Clearwater Traders and Northwoods University databases

| Clearwater Traders Database Table | Primary Key Column with AutoNumber Data Type | Northwoods University Database Table | Primary Key Column with AutoNumber Data Type |
|---|---|---|---|
| CUSTOMER | C_ID | LOCATION | LOC_ID |
| ORDER_SOURCE | OS_ID | FACULTY | F_ID |
| ORDERS | O_ID | STUDENT | S_ID |
| CATEGORY | C_ID | TERM | TERM_ID |
| ITEM | ITEM_ID | COURSE | COURSE_ID |
| INVENTORY | INV_ID | COURSE_SECTION | C_SEC_ID |
| SHIPMENT | SHIP_ID | | |

The tables that have composite primary keys do not have an AutoNumber column. This is because the composite primary keys include foreign key references to other tables. For example, the ORDER_LINE table has a composite primary key comprised of the O_ID (order ID) and INV_ID (inventory ID) columns. Before you can insert the first record in the ORDER_LINE table (O_ID = 1 and INV_ID = 1), you must insert the O_ID value of 1 in the ORDERS table and the INV_ID value of 1 in the INVENTORY table.

To retrieve the next value in an AutoNumber field, you create a SQL action query that inserts a record, but you omit from the INSERT INTO clause the name of the column that contains the AutoNumber data type. The Access database automatically inserts the next AutoNumber value into the column. For example, note from Table 9-5 that the ITEM_ID column in the ITEM table has the AutoNumber data type. You would use the following command to insert a new record into the ITEM table:

```
INSERT INTO ITEM (ITEM_DESC, CAT_ID, ITEM_IMAGE)
VALUES ('Children''s Snow Boots, 2, 'boots.jpg')
```

Note that the column name list does not include the ITEM_ID column. This causes the Access DBMS to retrieve and insert the next AutoNumber value into the record automatically. If you try to insert a number value in the ITEM_ID column, an error will occur.

Now you will insert a new record in the ITEM table. You will omit the ITEM_ID column in the column list so the Access database will retrieve the next AutoNumber value.

To insert a new record in the ITEM table using the AutoNumber value:

1. In Internet Explorer, click **Clear** to delete the current query text in the *Enter query* TextBox, then type the following query:

```
INSERT INTO ITEM (ITEM_DESC, CAT_ID, ITEM_IMAGE)
VALUES ('Children''s Snow Boots', 2, 'boots.jpg')
```

2. Click **Run Query**. The Message Label displays the message "Query succeeded. 1 record(s) affected."

3. Click **Clear**, then type the following query to display all of the columns in all of the records:

```
SELECT * FROM ITEM
```

4. Click **Run Query**. The new record appears in the DataGrid, which confirms that the record was successfully inserted. Note that the ITEM_ID value for the new record is 9, which is the next value in the AutoNumber sequence.

## Updating Database Records

Updating existing data values is an important data maintenance operation. Customer addresses change, product prices and specifications change, and customers change their minds about which items they want to order. To update an existing database record, you use an **UPDATE** action query. In an UPDATE action query, you specify the name of the table to update, and list the name of the column (or columns) to update along with the new data value (or values). You also specify a search condition to identify the row to update. The general syntax of an UPDATE action query is:

```
UPDATE tablename
SET column1 = new_value1, column2 = new_value2, ...
WHERE search_condition
```

Although you can update multiple columns in multiple records using a single UPDATE action query, you can update records in only one table at a time. You use the WHERE clause to specify a search condition to make the command update specific records. Recall that the general syntax for a search condition is WHERE `column_name comparison_ operator search_expression`. An example of a search condition is WHERE CUSTOMER.C_ID = 1. The following UPDATE action query updates customer Paula Harris's ZIP code value to "54702." (Figure 9-10 shows that Paula's C_ID value is 1.)

```
UPDATE CUSTOMER
SET C_ZIP = '54702'
WHERE CUSTOMER.C_ID = 1
```

You can update multiple records in a table using a single UPDATE command that has an inexact search condition that matches multiple records. You can also combine multiple search conditions using the AND and OR operators. If you omit the search condition in the UPDATE action query, then the command updates all table rows. For example, the following action query updates the value of C_STATE to "WI" for all records in the CUSTOMER table:

```
UPDATE CUSTOMER
SET C_STATE = 'WI'
```

Now you will update customer Paula Harris's birth date value from April 9, 1953, to April 9, 1954. Oracle9*i* database users will use the TO_DATE function to specify the new date, and Access database users will enclose the date value in pound signs (#). Recall from Figure 9-10 that Paula's C_ID value is 1, so you will use this value as the search condition. Then you will display the CUSTOMER records to confirm that the update was successful.

To update the birth date value:

1. In Internet Explorer, click **Clear**.

2. *If you are using an Oracle9i database*, type the following query:

```
UPDATE CUSTOMER
SET CUSTOMER.C_BIRTHDATE =
TO_DATE('04/09/1954', 'MM/DD/YYYY')
WHERE CUSTOMER.C_ID = 1
```

*If you are using an Access database*, type the following query:

```
UPDATE CUSTOMER
SET CUSTOMER.C_BIRTHDATE = #04/09/1954#
WHERE CUSTOMER.C_ID = 1
```

3. Click **Run Query**. The "Query succeeded. 1 record(s) affected" message appears in the Message Label.

4. Click **Clear**, then type the following query to display the C_ID and C_BIRTHDATE columns in all of the records in the CUSTOMER table:

```
SELECT CUSTOMER.C_ID, CUSTOMER.C_BIRTHDATE
FROM CUSTOMER
```

5. Click **Run Query**. The C_BIRTHDATE value for C_ID 1 appears as 4/9/1954, which confirms that the record was successfully updated. (The Query form DataGrid displays the date value using a slightly different date format than the format you used when you updated the value.)

## Deleting Existing Database Records

As you are developing new database applications, you often insert new records to test your applications, and you eventually need to delete these records. Occasionally you need to delete database records in business systems; for example, a customer may cancel an order, or a product may be discontinued. You use the **DELETE** action query to remove records from database tables. The general syntax for the DELETE action query is:

```
DELETE FROM tablename
WHERE search_condition
```

You can delete records from only one table at a time using a single DELETE action query. (If you want to delete records from multiple tables, you must use multiple DELETE action queries.) The *search_condition* can be an exact search condition that matches and therefore deletes a single record. The *search_condition* can also be an inexact search condition that matches and therefore deletes multiple records. Be very careful when you use the DELETE action query, because it is very difficult to restore records that you delete in error. You should always include a WHERE clause when deleting a record from a table to ensure that you delete the correct record(s). If you omit the WHERE clause, you will delete every record in the table! Now, you will delete the record that you inserted in the ITEM table that had the ITEM_DESC value "Children's Snow Boots."

To delete the record from the ITEM table:

1. In Internet Explorer, click **Clear**, then type the following query:

```
DELETE FROM ITEM
WHERE ITEM.ITEM_DESC = 'Children''s Snow Boots'
```

2. Click **Run Query**. The "Query succeeded. 1 record(s) affected" message appears in the Message Label.

3. Click **Clear**, then type the following query to display all of the columns in all of the records in the ITEM table to confirm the deletion:

```
SELECT * FROM ITEM
```

4. Click **Run Query**. The record for "Children's Snow Boots" no longer appears, which confirms that the record was deleted.

You cannot delete a record if it contains a value that another record references as a foreign key. For example, you cannot delete the record for C_ID (customer ID) 1 (Paula Harris) unless you first delete the records in which the foreign key value exists. (C_ID 1 is a foreign key in the first record in the ORDERS table.) Now you will attempt to delete a record that contains a field that is a foreign key reference to display the error message.

To try to delete a record that contains a value that another record references as a foreign key:

1. In Internet Explorer, click **Clear**, then type the following query:

```
DELETE FROM CUSTOMER
WHERE CUSTOMER.C_ID = 1
```

2. Click **Run Query**. An error message appears in the Message Label as a result of the foreign key violation.

3. Close Internet Explorer, then close Visual Studio .NET.

This message indicates that the record that you tried to delete is referenced as a foreign key in the ORDERS table. To delete the record for C_ID 1, you must first delete the record for O_ID 1, which is the record that references the value as a foreign key. However, the record for O_ID 1 is referenced as a foreign key in the first two records in the ORDER_LINE table. You would need to delete the first two records in the ORDER_LINE table first, then delete the record for O_ID 1 in the ORDERS table second, then finally delete the record for C_ID 1.

You now have a basic understanding of how to create data connections and data adapters in Visual Studio .NET, and how to write SQL queries to retrieve, insert, update, and delete data records. In Chapter 10, you will learn how to make Web forms that interact with databases.

## CHAPTER SUMMARY

- When organizations first began converting from manual to computerized data processing systems, each individual application had its own set of data files that was used only for that application. As applications became more complex, data files became difficult to manage because each data file required a separate program to maintain its contents and because data files for related applications contained redundant data. Redundant data takes up valuable file space, and can become inconsistent. To address these problems, organizations began using databases to store and manage application data.

- Most modern databases are relational databases, which store data in a tabular format. Columns represent different data fields, and rows contain individual data records. Relational databases store data about different entities in separate tables. You use key fields to create relationships that link related data.

- A primary key is a field that uniquely identifies a specific record in a database table. Primary key values must be unique within a table and cannot be NULL. Primary key fields should contain numeric data rather than text data, because text data is more prone to data entry errors. A candidate key is a field that could be used as the primary key.

- When a database table does not contain any suitable candidate keys, you should create a surrogate key, which is a numeric field that has no intrinsic relation to the record and is used for the sole purpose of identifying the record. Usually, the DBMS automatically generates surrogate key values.

- A foreign key is a field in a table that is a primary key in another table and that creates a relationship between the two tables. A foreign key field in a table must exist as a primary key in another table.

- A composite key is a primary key composed of the combination of two or more fields. The combination of the two field values must be unique for every record.

- Personal database systems are best suited for single-user database applications, which usually are stored on a single user's desktop computer. When organizations use personal databases for a multi-user application, the personal database downloads to the user's client workstation some or all of the data that a user needs. This process can be slow and cause network congestion.

- Client/server databases divide the database into a server process that runs on a network server and user application processes that run on individual client workstations. Client/server databases send data requests to the server and return the results of data requests to the client workstation. This process minimizes network traffic and congestion. Client/server databases have better failure recovery mechanisms than personal databases, and automatically handle competing user transactions.

- In an Oracle9i client/server database, Oracle9i provides client-side utilities for executing SQL commands and designing and creating custom applications, and a server-side DBMS. All Oracle9i server- and client-side programs use SQL*Net, which is a utility that enables the network communication between the client and the server.

- Programmers use ODBC drivers to translate program commands into formats that databases understand. Every database has a specific ODBC driver. Visual Studio .NET provides a set of built-in procedures and models called ADO.NET, which translates commands between Web application projects and ODBC drivers. ADO.NET uses an OLE DB driver to translate its commands to the commands that ODBC drivers understand.

- To create a Web application project that retrieves and manipulates database data, you must create a data connection, which is a communication path between a Web application and a database. To create a data connection, you must specify the connection's OLE DB driver and information about the data source. After you create a data connection, the data connection is available to all forms and projects within your Visual Studio .NET IDE.

❒ You can access your data connections using the Server Explorer. You can view, insert, update, and delete data records using the data connection's Tables node.

❒ Web forms that interact with databases contain SQL commands to retrieve, insert, update, and delete data. SQL is the primary language for interacting with relational databases. SQL commands that retrieve database data are called queries, and SQL commands that insert, update, or delete database data are called action queries.

❒ To create database queries in Visual Studio .NET, you create a Web form component called a data adapter, which retrieves specific data records from a data source and places them in a container called a data set. You can use Query Builder to create SQL queries that retrieve data from a single database table, to sort retrieved data values, and to filter data values using search conditions.

❒ You can create SQL queries that combine, or join, fields in multiple tables that are related by primary key/foreign key relationships. In a join query, the FROM clause must specify the name of every table that displays data, is used in a search condition, or is used to join other tables. The WHERE clause must contain a join condition that specifies every primary key/foreign key link.

❒ A SQL group function returns the sum, minimum, maximum, or average value of a group of numerical records that a query retrieves. The SQL COUNT group function returns the number of records that a query retrieves. You can create a column alias to specify an alternate column heading for the values that a group function retrieves.

❒ You can use the GROUP BY clause to perform operations on repeating values in a query result. If you create a query in which one or more columns in the SELECT clause are in a group function and one or more columns are not in a group function, then you must always place the columns that are *not* in a group function in the GROUP BY clause.

❒ You use the SQL INSERT action query to add new data records to database tables. When you insert a new record into a table, you do not need to insert a value into every column, but you must always insert a value for the record's primary key column, and the primary key value cannot be the same as any primary key values that already exist in the table. Before you can insert a new record, you must ensure that the database contains all of the foreign key records that the new record references.

❒ In an Oracle9*i* database, you use sequences to generate surrogate key values automatically. In an Access database, you use an AutoNumber data type for the surrogate key column.

❒ To update an existing database record, you use an UPDATE action query in which you specify the name of the table to update, and list the name of the column (or columns) to update, along with the new data value (or values). You specify a search condition to identify the row or rows to update.

❒ You use the DELETE action query to remove records from database tables. You can delete records from only one table at a time, and you should delete records with care because it is very difficult to restore records that you delete by mistake.

9

## REVIEW QUESTIONS

1. List two problems that can occur when you store application data in data files.
2. What is a database management system (DBMS)?
3. A _____ key uniquely identifies a record in a relational database table.
   a. Primary key
   b. Foreign key
   c. Candidate key
   d. Both a and c
4. What is a foreign key?
5. What is a surrogate key?
6. What is a composite key?
7. When a data value is _____, it is unknown or undefined.
8. Why should primary key values be numerical rather than text?
9. Describe the differences in the way client/server and personal databases handle and process data in a multi-user environment.
10. What is an ODBC driver?
11. _____ provides a set of procedures and objects that allow Web forms to communicate with ODBC drivers.
    a. SQL*Net
    b. ADO.NET
    c. ASP.NET
    d. DAO.NET
12. Write a search condition for the following Clearwater Traders database queries:
    a. INV_QOH values in the INVENTORY table that are greater than or equal to 50
    b. CAT_DESC values in the CATEGORY value equal to "Children's Clothing"
    c. O_DATE values in the ORDERS table that were placed after June 1, 2006 (specify the syntax for both Oracle9*i* and Access)
    d. O_METHPMT values in the ORDERS table in which the method of payment is not "CC"
13. Write a single SQL action query to delete every record in the Clearwater Traders INVENTORY table.
14. To generate surrogate key values automatically, you use a(n) _____ in an Access database, and a(n) _____ in an Oracle9*i* database.
15. Write a query to retrieve all rows and all columns from the Clearwater Traders ORDER_LINE table. Structure the query so that you do not need to specify the name of each field in the SELECT clause.

16. How many join conditions must you include in a query that joins six tables?

17. In a SQL query, you use the _____ clause to change the order in which SQL displays retrieved records.

a. WHERE

b. SORT BY

c. ORDER BY

d. NEXTVAL

18. When is it necessary to use the GROUP BY clause in a SELECT query that contains a group function?

19. Write SQL queries that retrieve the following values from the Clearwater Traders database. Use the table and column names in Figure 9-10.

a. The order date, payment method, and order source description for every order placed after June 1, 2006 (write the query using both Access and Oracle9i syntax).

b. The date expected, item ID, size, color, and shipment line quantity for every incoming shipment item. Sort the retrieved values by ascending shipment line quantity.

c. The last name of each customer and the total number of items each customer has ordered.

d. The total number of orders in which the payment method is "CC."

20. Write SQL queries that retrieve the following values from the Northwoods University database. Use the table and column names in Figure 9-12.

a. The first and last name of every faculty member, and the building code and room number of the faculty member's office. Sort the retrieved values by faculty member last names.

b. The term description, course name, day, and time for all courses that meet after 2 P.M. (write the query using both Access and Oracle9i syntax).

c. The building code and the total number of rooms listed for every separate building code.

d. The average maximum enrollment for every course ever taught by faculty member John Blanchard. Use "John" and "Blanchard" for the search conditions.

21. Write the following SQL action queries for the Clearwater Traders database:

a. Insert a new record in the CUSTOMER table. Use the data values for C_ID 6 (Kyle Nelson), as shown in Figure 9-10. (If you are using an Oracle9i database, write the query using an Oracle9i sequence named C_ID_SEQUENCE. If you are using an Access database, write the query assuming the C_ID column has the AutoNumber data type.)

b. Update the record for ITEM_ID 2 in the ITEM table so the ITEM_DESC value is "4-Season Tent."

c. Delete every record in the INVENTORY table in which the price is less than $20.

22. Write the following SQL action queries for the Northwoods University database:

    a. Insert a new record in the STUDENT table. Use the data values for S_ID 1 (Sarah Miller), as shown in Figure 9-12. (If you are using an Oracle9*i* database, write the query using an Oracle9*i* sequence named S_ID_SEQUENCE. If you are using an Access database, write the query assuming the S_ID column has the AutoNumber data type.)

    b. Update the record for student Brian Umato so his address is "454 St. John's Street."

    c. Delete every record in the TERM table in which the term status value is "CLOSED."

## HANDS-ON PROJECTS

To complete the Chapter 9 Hands-on Projects, you will first need to create a Web server application named Projects that you associate with the Chapter9\ Projects folder on your Solution Disk. Then create a Web application project named DBProjects whose application root is the Chapter9\Projects folder on your Solution Disk. Delete the default WebForm1.aspx form from the project. Copy QueryForm.aspx and QueryForm.aspx.vb from the Chapter9 folder on your Data Disk to the Chapter9\Projects\DBProjects folder on your Solution Disk, and add the Query form files to the project.

*If you are using an Oracle9i database*, start SQL*Plus, log on by entering cwuser in the User Name field and Oracle in the Password field, and run the Northwoods.sql script in the Chapter9 folder on your Data Disk to initialize the Northwoods University database.

*If you are using an Access database*, copy the Clearwater.mdb and Northwoods.mdb database files from the Chapter9 folder on your Data Disk to the Chapter9\Projects folder on your Solution Disk.

### Project 9-1 Creating Clearwater Traders Database Single-Table Queries

In this project, you will create a data connection for the Clearwater Traders database. Then you will create two separate data adapters and use the Query Builder to specify the data that the data adapters retrieve.

1. Create a new Web form named ClearwaterDBForm.aspx in the DBProjects Web application project that you created based on the instructions in the Note at the beginning of the Hands-on Projects.

2. Create a new data connection named connClearwater.

    *If you are using an Oracle9i database*, do not create this connection if you already created the connection in your Visual Studio .NET IDE in the tutorial exercises. If you did not create the connection before, specify that the data connection uses the *ORCL* data source and the *cwuser* Oracle user account, which is identified by the password *oracle*. (Your connection information may be different if you are using a client/server database.)

*If you are using an Access database*, specify that the data connection uses the Clearwater.mdb file in the Chapter9\Projects folder on your Solution Disk.

3. Create a new data adapter named daInventory that uses the connClearwater data connection. Use the Query Builder to specify that the data adapter's query retrieves the INV_ID, INV_SIZE, COLOR, and INV_QOH columns for inventory items in which the QOH is greater than 0. Sort the records by ascending INV_QOH and then by color.

4. Create a new data adapter named daShipment that uses the connClearwater data connection. Use the Query Builder to specify that the data adapter's query displays all fields in the SHIPMENT_LINE table for records that were received after September 1, 2006. Do not display records in which the date received value is NULL. Sort the records so the shipments that were received most recently appear first. (Hint: You will need to modify the search condition manually.)

## Project 9-2 Creating Northwoods University Database Single-Table Queries

In this project, you will create a data connection for the Northwoods University database. Then you will create two separate data adapters, and use the Query Builder to specify the data that the data adapters retrieve.

1. Create a new Web form named NorthwoodsDBForm.aspx in the DBProjects Web application project that you created based on the instructions in the Note at the beginning of the Hands-on Projects.

2. Create a new data connection named connNorthwoods.

*If you are using an Oracle9i database*, specify that the data connection uses the *ORCL* data source and the *cwuser* Oracle user account, which is identified by the password *oracle*. (Your connection information may be different if you are using a client/server database. Be sure that you initialized the Northwoods database based on the instructions in the Note at the beginning of the Hands-on Projects.)

*If you are using an Access database*, specify that the data connection uses the Northwoods.mdb file in the Chapter9\Projects folder on your Solution Disk.

3. Create a new data adapter named daStudents that uses the connNorthwoods data connection. Use the Query Builder to specify that the data adapter's query retrieves the S_LAST, S_FIRST, S_CLASS, and S_DOB columns for students who were born after January 1, 1984, and who are not seniors (S_CLASS = 'SR'). Sort the records by ascending last names.

4. Create a new data adapter named daFaculty that uses the connNorthwoods data connection. Use the Query Builder to specify that the data adapter's query displays the F_LAST, F_FIRST, and F_RANK fields in the FACULTY table. Display the records for all faculty members except those who have the rank of instructor (F_RANK = "INST"). Sort the records so they appear sorted by faculty rank, then by faculty last names.

## Project 9-3 Creating Clearwater Traders Database Queries

In this project, you will create a series of queries that join multiple tables or use group functions in the Clearwater Traders database. You will save the query text in a text file named 9Project3.sql, and you will test the queries using the Query form that you used in the chapter tutorials.

1. In the DBProjects Web application project that you created based on the instructions in the Note at the beginning of the Hands-on Projects, change the ConnectionString property of the Query form's OleDB Connection1 data adapter so it connects to the Clearwater Traders database. (If you are using an Access database, make sure that the data adapter uses a data connection that connects to the Clearwater.mdb database file in the Chapter9\Projects folder on your Solution Disk. You may have already created this data connection in Project 9-1.)

2. Create a new text file named 9Project3.sql in the Chapter9\Projects folder on your Solution Disk. Write the syntax for the following SQL queries in the 9Project3.sql file, and test the queries in the project's Query form:

   ❑ List the first and last names of every customer who placed orders using the Web site as an order source. Display the records in alphabetical order by customer last name.

   ❑ List the item description and total inventory quantity on hand for every item. For example, you will show the total number of "Women's Hiking Shorts" on hand. Include all sizes and colors in the total. Create an alias named "QOH" for the sum of the quantities on hand, and sort the output by the sum of the quantities on hand.

   ❑ List the total number of orders that have been placed since June 1, 2006. (Include orders placed on June 1, 2006.) Display the result using a column alias named TOTAL_ORDERS.

   ❑ List the item description, color, and quantity on hand for every item in the INVENTORY table for which no size value is specified.

   ❑ Display the item description, size, color, shipment quantity, and date expected for all shipments that have not been received (DATE_RECEIVED in the SHIPMENT_LINE table is NULL) of every item where the quantity on hand is 0 in the INVENTORY table.

## Project 9-4 Creating Northwoods University Database Queries

In this project, you will create a series of queries that join multiple tables or use group functions on tables in the Northwoods University database. You will save the query text in a text file named 9Project4.sql, and you will test the queries using the Query form that you used in the chapter tutorials.

1. In the DBProjects Web application project that you created based on the instructions in the Note at the beginning of the Hands-on Projects, change the ConnectionString property of the OleDbConnection1 data adapter in the Query form so it connects to the Northwoods University database. You may need to create a new data connection. (Make sure that you initialized this database using the instructions in the Note at the beginning of the Hands-on Projects. If you are using an Access database, make sure that the connection uses the Northwoods.mdb database file in the Chapter9\Projects folder on your Solution Disk.)

2. Create a new text file named 9Project4.sql in the Chapter9\Projects folder on your Solution Disk. Then create the following SQL queries in the 9Project4.sql file, and test the queries in the Query form in the project:

   ❐ List the first and last names of every student that faculty member Kim Cox advises. Use "Kim" and "Cox" as the search conditions, and sort the output by student last names.

   ❐ Display the call ID, course name, section number, and day for every course offered during the Spring 2007 term. Use "Spring 2007" as the search condition.

   ❐ Calculate the total credits earned to date by student Brian Umato. Display the result using a column alias named TOTAL_CREDITS. Use "Brian" and "Umato" as the search conditions.

   ❐ Display a listing of the call ID, course section number, and day that all courses meet in BUS 105 during the Spring 2007 term. Use "BUS," "105," and "Spring 2007" as the search conditions.

## Project 9-5 Creating Clearwater Traders Database Action Queries

In this project, you will create a series of action queries that insert, modify, or delete records in the Clearwater Traders database. You will save the query text in a text file named 9Project5.sql, and you will test the queries using the Query form that you used in the chapter tutorials.

1. Change the ConnectionString property of the OleDbConnection1 data adapter in the Query form so it connects to the Clearwater Traders database. (If you are using an Access database, make sure that you are using a connection that connects to the Clearwater.mdb database file in the Chapter9\Projects folder on your Solution Disk. You may have already created this data connection in a previous project.)

2. Create a new text file named 9Project5.sql in the Chapter9\Projects folder on your Solution Disk. Then create the following SQL queries in the 9Project5.sql file, and test the queries in the Query form in the project:

   ❐ Insert a new record in the CUSTOMER table. Create your own data values for the data fields.

(*If you are using an Oracle9i database*, if necessary create a new sequence named C_ID_SEQUENCE that starts with 10, then use the sequence to generate the C_ID value. If you are using an Access database, recall that the C_ID column in the CUSTOMER table has the AutoNumber data type.)

❐ Update customer Paula Harris's address to "321 Marvin's Place." Use C_ID 1 as the search condition in the UPDATE action query.

❐ Delete the color "Red" from the COLOR table.

## Project 9-6 Creating Northwoods University Database Action Queries

In this project, you will create a series of action queries for tables in the Northwoods University database. You will save the query text in a text file named 9Project6.sql, and you will test the queries using the Query form that you used in the chapter tutorials.

1. Change the ConnectionString property of the OleDbConnection1 data adapter in the Query form so it connects to the Northwoods University database. (Make sure that you initialized this database using the instructions in the Note at the beginning of the Hands-on Projects. If you are using an Access database, make sure that the connection uses the Northwoods.mdb database file in the Chapter9\ Projects folder on your Solution Disk. You may have already created this data connection in a previous project.)

2. Create a new text file named 9Project6.sql in the Chapter9\Projects folder on your Solution Disk. Then create the following SQL action queries in the 9Project6.sql file, and test the queries in the Query form in the project:

❐ Insert a new record in the STUDENT table. Create your own data values for the data fields.

(*If you are using an Oracle9i database*, create a new sequence named S_ID_ SEQUENCE that starts with 10, then use the sequence to generate the S_ID value. *If you are using an Access database*, recall that the S_ID column in the STUDENT table has the AutoNumber data type.)

❐ Update faculty member Kim Cox's office location to LIB 222. Use F_ID 1 as the search condition in the UPDATE action query.

❐ Delete the ENROLLMENT record for student Michael Connoly in C_SEC_ID 11.

# CASE PROJECTS

To solve the case projects in this chapter, first create a new Web server application that you associate with the Cases folder in the Chapter9 folder on your Solution Disk, and modify your Visual Studio .NET IDE so it places all project solution files in the Chapter9\Cases folder on your Solution Disk.

## Case 9-1 Ashland Valley Soccer League

Figure 9-26 shows the tables in the Ashland Valley Soccer League database, and Figure 9-27 shows a visual representation of the database tables.

ASHLAND_FIELD

| FIELD_ID | FIELD_NAME | FIELD_ADDRESS |
|----------|------------|---------------|
| Number | String | String |

ASHLAND_TEAM

| TEAM_ID | TEAM_NAME |
|---------|-----------|
| Number | String |

ASHLAND_GAME

| GAME_ID | GAME_DATE | HOME_TEAM_ID | VISITING_TEAM_ID |
|---------|-----------|--------------|------------------|
| Number | Date/Time | Number | Number |

ASHLAND_GAME (continued)

| FIELD_ID | STATUS |
|----------|--------|
| Number | String |

**Figure 9-26**

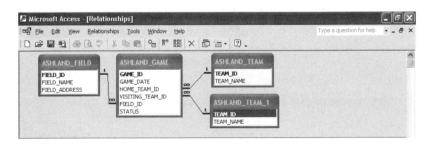

**Figure 9-27**

The ASHLAND_FIELD table displays information about the league's soccer fields, and the ASHLAND_TEAM table displays information about league teams. The FIELD_ID column is the primary key in the ASHLAND_FIELD table, and TEAM_ID is the primary key in the ASHLAND_TEAM table. In the ASHLAND_GAME table, GAME_ID is the primary key, and the HOME_TEAM_ID and VISITING_TEAM_ID columns are foreign keys that reference TEAM_ID values in the ASHLAND_TEAM table. (In Figure 9-27, ASHLAND_TEAM and ASHLAND_TEAM_1 both represent the ASHLAND_TEAM table, but ASHLAND_TEAM_1 is a copy of the ASHLAND_TEAM table that explicitly shows the foreign key relationship with the VISITING_TEAM_ID column.) The FIELD_ID column in the ASHLAND_GAME table is a foreign key that references the FIELD_ID column in the ASHLAND_FIELD table and shows the field on which the game is played.

In this case, you will initialize the Ashland Valley Soccer League database on your workstation, create a new Web application project, and then use the Query form in Figure 9-21 to insert records into the database and perform a variety of SQL queries. You will save the queries in a file named AshlandQueries.sql in the Chapter9\Cases folder on your Solution Disk.

1. To initialize the database:

   *If you are using an Oracle9i database*, start SQL*Plus, log on by entering *cwuser* in the *User Name* field and *oracle* in the *Password* field. Create the database tables by running the Ashland.sql script that is in the Chapter9\Cases folder on your Data Disk.

   *If you are using an Access database*, copy the Ashland.mdb file from the Chapter9\Cases folder on your Data Disk to the Chapter9\Cases folder on your Solution Disk.

2. Create a Web application project named AshlandProject in the Chapter9/Cases application on your Web server. Copy the QueryForm.aspx and QueryForm.aspx.vb files from the Chapter9 folder on your Data Disk to the Chapter9\Cases\AshlandProject folder on your Solution Disk. (You will need to create the Web application project in Visual Studio .NET first, then copy the files into the project folder that Visual Studio .NET creates.) Then add the Query form to the project. Create a new data connection to the Ashland database, and configure the Query form so it uses the new data connection.

3. Create a text file named AshlandQueries.sql in the Chapter9\Cases folder on your Solution Disk, then write action queries to insert at least two records into each database table. (If you are using an Oracle9i database, create a sequence to generate the primary key values automatically for all tables. If you are using an Access database, all of the table's primary key columns have the AutoNumber data type.)

4. Write a query that displays the name of every team.

5. Write a query that retrieves the start date and time and playing field name for every game in which a specific team is the home team. Search for the team by team name.

6. Write a query to list each team name and display the total number of visiting games that each team will play. List the teams by team name.

## Case 9-2 Al's Body Shop

Figure 9-28 shows the tables in the Al's Body Shop database, and Figure 9-29 shows a visual representation of the database tables.

The ALS_CUSTOMER table displays information about Al's customers, and the ALS_CAR table displays information about customer cars. The CUST_ID column is the primary key in the ALS_CUSTOMER table, and the VIN (vehicle identification number) column is the primary key in the ALS_CAR table. The ALS_CUSTOMER_CAR table is a linking table that links customers and cars, and its composite primary key comprises the CUST_ID and VIN columns. The ALS_WORKORDER table describes customer work orders, and the VIN column is a foreign key that links the car to the work order. The ALS_SERVICE table describes the services that Al's offers, and the ALS_WORKORDER_SERVICE table is a linking table that shows the services that are performed on each work order. The ALS_WORKORDER_SERVICE table has a composite primary key that comprises the WORKORDER_ID and SERVICE_ID columns.

ALS_CUSTOMER

| CUST_ID | CUST_NAME | CUST_ADDRESS | CUST_PHONE |
|---------|-----------|--------------|------------|
| Number  | String    | String       | String     |

ALS_CAR

| VIN    | CAR_MAKE | CAR_MODEL | CAR_YEAR |
|--------|----------|-----------|----------|
| String | String   | String    | String   |

ALS_CUSTOMER_CAR

| CUST_ID | VIN    |
|---------|--------|
| Number  | String |

ALS_WORKORDER

| WORKORDER_ID | WORKORDER_DATE | VIN    |
|--------------|----------------|--------|
| Number       | Date/Time      | String |

ALS_SERVICE

| SERVICE_ID | SERVICE_DESC | SERVICE_CHARGE |
|------------|--------------|----------------|
| Number     | String       | Number         |

ALS_WORKORDER_SERVICE

| WORKORDER_ID | SERVICE_ID |
|--------------|------------|
| Number       | Number     |

**Figure 9-28**

9

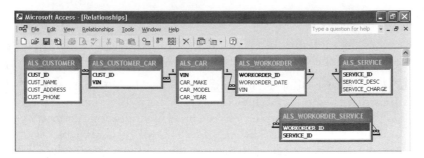

**Figure 9-29**

In this case, you will initialize the database on your workstation, create a new Web application project, and then use the Query form in Figure 9-21 to insert records into the database and perform a variety of SQL queries. You will save the queries in a file named AlsQueries.sql in the Chapter9\Cases folder on your Solution Disk.

1. To initialize the database:

   *If you are using an Oracle9i database*, start SQL*Plus, log on by entering *cwuser* in the *User Name* field and *oracle* in the *Password* field. Create the database tables by running the Als.sql script that is in the Chapter9\Cases folder on your Data Disk.

   *If you are using an Access database*, copy the Als.mdb file from the Chapter9\Cases folder on your Data Disk to the Chapter9\Cases folder on your Solution Disk.

2. Create a Web application project named AlsProject in the Chapter9/Cases application on your Web server. Copy the QueryForm.aspx and QueryForm.aspx.vb files from the Chapter9 folder on your Data Disk to the Chapter9\Cases\ AlsProject folder on your Solution Disk. (You will need to create the Web application project in Visual Studio .NET first, then copy the files into the project folder that Visual Studio .NET creates.) Then add the Query form to the project. Create a new data connection to the Al's Body Shop database, and configure the Query form so it uses the new data connection.

3. Create a text file named AlsQueries.sql in the Chapter9\Cases folder on your Solution Disk, then write action queries to insert at least two records into each database table. (If you are using an Oracle9i database, create a sequence to generate the primary key values in the CUSTOMER, WORKORDER, and SERVICE tables automatically. If you are using an Access database, the CUST_ID, WORKORDER_ID, and SERVICE_ID primary key columns in the CUSTOMER, WORKORDER, and SERVICE tables have the AutoNumber data type.)

4. Write a query that lists the make, model, year, and owner name for each car in the database.

5. Write a query that retrieves the work order date and the descriptions of all work order services for all work orders associated with a specific customer.

6. Write a query that retrieves the work order ID, work order date, and the total charges for all services on all work orders performed on a specific date. Group the

output by work order ID values, and change the total charges column heading to "TOTAL_CHARGES."

## Case 9-3 Sun-Ray Videos

Figure 9-30 shows the tables in the Sun-Ray Videos database, and Figure 9-31 shows a visual representation of the database tables.

SUNRAY_CUSTOMER

| CUSTOMER_ID | LAST_NAME | FIRST_NAME | CUST_ADDRESS | CITY | STATE | ZIP |
|---|---|---|---|---|---|---|
| Number | String | String | String | String | String | String |

SUNRAY_CUSTOMER (continued)

| USER_NAME | USER_PASSWORD |
|---|---|
| String | String |

SUNRAY_CATEGORY

| CATEGORY_ID | CATEGORY_DESC |
|---|---|
| Number | String |

SUNRAY_VIDEO

| VIDEO_ID | TITLE | CATEGORY_ID |
|---|---|---|
| Number | String | Number |

SUNRAY_FORMAT

| FORMAT_ID | FORMAT_DESC |
|---|---|
| Number | Number |

SUNRAY_VIDEO_FORMAT

| VIDEO_FORMAT_ID | VIDEO_ID | FORMAT_ID | COST |
|---|---|---|---|
| Number | Number | Number | Number |

SUNRAY_RENTAL

| RENTAL_ID | DATE_OUT | DATE_DUE | DATE_IN | DELIVERY_STATUS | COST |
|---|---|---|---|---|---|
| Number | Date/Time | Date/Time | Date/Time | String | Number |

SUNRAY_RENTAL (continued)

| LATE_FEE | CUSTOMER_ID | VIDEO_FORMAT_ID |
|---|---|---|
| Number | Number | Number |

**Figure 9-30**

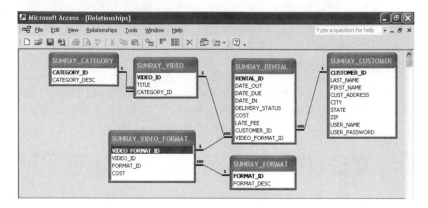

**Figure 9-31**

The SUNRAY_CUSTOMER table displays information about Sun-Ray customers. The SUNRAY_CATEGORY table displays different video categories, such as "Action" or "Children's." The SUNRAY_VIDEO table lists all video titles, and contains the CATEGORY_ID column as a foreign key to indicate each video's category. The SUNRAY_FORMAT table lists the different video formats that are available, such as DVD or VHS. The SUNRAY_VIDEO_FORMAT table is a linking table that indicates the different formats that are available for different video titles and the cost of renting each title in each available format. Its primary key is VIDEO_FORMAT_ID, which uniquely identifies each video title/format combination. The SUNRAY_RENTAL table contains information about customer rentals, and includes the CUSTOMER_ID and VIDEO_FORMAT_ID as foreign key fields.

In this case, you will initialize the database on your workstation, create a new Web application project, then use the Query form in Figure 9-21 to insert records into the database and perform a variety of SQL queries. You will save the queries in a file named SunrayQueries.sql in the Chapter9\Cases folder on your Solution Disk.

1.  To initialize the database:

    *If you are using an Oracle9i database*, start SQL*Plus, log on by entering *cwuser* in the *User Name* field and *oracle* in the *Password* field. Run the Sunray.sql script that is in the Chapter9\Cases folder on your Data Disk to create the database tables.

    *If you are using an Access database*, copy the Sunray.mdb file from the Chapter9\Cases folder on your Data Disk to the Chapter9\Cases folder on your Solution Disk.

2.  Create a Web application project named SunrayProject in the Chapter9/Cases application on your Web server. Copy the QueryForm.aspx and QueryForm.aspx.vb files from the Chapter9 folder on your Data Disk to the Chapter9\Cases\SunrayProject folder on your Solution Disk. (You will need to create the Web application project in Visual Studio .NET first, then copy the files into the project folder that Visual Studio .NET creates.) Then add the Query form to the project. Create a new data connection to the Sun-Ray Videos database, and configure the Query form so it uses the new data connection.

3. Create a text file named SunrayQueries.sql in the Chapter9\Cases folder on your Solution Disk, then write action queries to insert at least two records into each database table. (If you are using an Oracle9i database, create a sequence to generate the primary key values automatically for the primary keys in the SUNRAY_ CUSTOMER, SUNRAY_CATEGORY, SUNRAY_VIDEO, SUNRAY_ FORMAT, SUNRAY_VIDEO_FORMAT, and SUNRAY_RENTAL tables. If you are using an Access database, these primary key columns have the AutoNumber data type.)

4. Write a query that lists the title of each video, its category description, the description of each format in which the video is available, and the associated cost for each title/format combination.

5. Write a query that lists each video category and counts the number of video titles in each separate category. Display the heading for the column that shows the number of titles in each category as "TITLES_IN_CATEGORY."

6. Write a query that retrieves the total cost of all rentals for a specific customer.

7. List the customer first and last name, date due, and title for each unreturned video (DATE_IN is NULL).

## Case 9-4 Learning Technologies, Incorporated (LTI)

Figure 9-32 shows the tables in the LTI database, and Figure 9-33 shows a visual representation of the database tables.

LTI_AUTHOR

| AUTHOR_ID | AUTHOR_LAST_NAME | AUTHOR_FIRST_NAME | AUTHOR_ADDRESS |
|-----------|------------------|-------------------|----------------|
| Number | String | String | String |

LTI_AUTHOR (continued)

| AUTHOR_CITY | AUTHOR_STATE | AUTHOR_ZIP | AUTHOR_PHONE |
|-------------|--------------|------------|--------------|
| String | String | String | String |

LTI_BOOK

| ISBN | TITLE | PUBLISH_DATE | PRICE |
|------|-------|--------------|-------|
| String | String | Date/Time | Number |

LTI_BOOK_AUTHOR

| ISBN | AUTHOR_ID |
|------|-----------|
| String | Number |

**Figure 9-32**

LTI_WAREHOUSE

| WAREHOUSE_ID | WAREHOUSE_ADDRESS | WAREHOUSE_CITY | WAREHOUSE_STATE |
|---|---|---|---|
| Number | String | String | String |

LTI_WAREHOUSE_BOOK

| WAREHOUSE_ID | ISBN | QOH |
|---|---|---|
| Number | Number | Number |

**Figure 9-32** (continued)

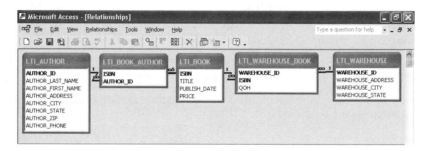

**Figure 9-33**

The LTI_AUTHOR table displays information about LTI authors, and the LTI_BOOK table displays information about LTI books. The AUTHOR_ID column is the primary key of the LTI_AUTHOR table, and the ISBN column is the primary key of the LTI_BOOK table. The LTI_BOOK_AUTHOR table is a linking table that shows which author or authors wrote different books, and its primary key is a composite key comprised of the AUTHOR_ID and ISBN columns. The LTI_WAREHOUSE table shows information about different book warehouses, and its primary key is WAREHOUSE_ID. The LTI_WAREHOUSE_BOOK table is a linking table that shows the quantity on hand of different books at different warehouses. The primary key of the WAREHOUSE_BOOK table is a composite key comprised of WAREHOUSE_ID and ISBN.

In this case, you will initialize the database on your workstation, create a new Web application project, and then use the Query form in Figure 9-21 to insert records into the database and perform a variety of SQL queries. You will save the queries in a file named LtiQueries.sql in the Chapter9\Cases folder on your Solution Disk.

1. To initialize the database:

   *If you are using an Oracle9i database*, start SQL*Plus, log on by entering *cwuser* in the *User Name* field and *oracle* in the *Password* field. Create the database tables by running the Lti.sql script that is in the Chapter9\Cases folder on your Data Disk.

   *If you are using an Access database*, copy the Lti.mdb file from the Chapter9\Cases folder on your Data Disk to the Chapter9\Cases folder on your Solution Disk.

2. Create a Web application project named LtiProject in the Chapter9/Cases application on your Web server. Copy the QueryForm.aspx and QueryForm.aspx.vb files from the Chapter9 folder on your Data Disk to the Chapter9\Cases\LtiProject folder on your Solution Disk. (You will need to create the Web application project in Visual Studio .NET first, then copy the files into the project folder that Visual Studio .NET creates.) Then add the Query form to the project. Create a new data connection to the LTI database, and configure the Query form so it uses the new data connection.

3. Create a text file named LtiQueries.sql in the Chapter9\Cases folder on your Solution Disk, then write action queries to insert at least two records into each database table. (If you are using an Oracle9*i* database, create a sequence to generate the primary key values automatically for the AUTHOR_ID and WAREHOUSE_ID primary keys in the LTI_AUTHOR and LTI_WAREHOUSE tables respectively. If you are using an Access database, these columns have the AutoNumber data type.)

4. Write a query that lists the first and last names of each author, and the titles of all books the author has written.

5. Write a query that lists the city and state of each warehouse and the total number of books at that warehouse. Sort the output by the city in which the warehouse is located, and label the column that displays the book total as "TOTAL_QOH."

6. Write a query that retrieves book titles and the last name of the author(s) for books that were published after a specific date.

7. Write a query that lists the warehouse city, state, and quantity on hand for a specific book title.

**9**

# RETRIEVING AND DISPLAYING DATABASE DATA IN WEB FORMS

**In this chapter, you will:**

♦ Write VB .NET commands to create data components and retrieve and display database data on Web forms

♦ Create DataList and DataGrid rich server controls that allow users to display, update, and delete database data

♦ Learn how to validate user inputs in DataList and DataGrid controls

♦ Create a Web form that allows users to insert data into a database

♦ Create a Web form that displays data that has master-detail relationships

In a database-driven Web site, the Web server presents the user with a Web form in which the user can make selections or enter inputs. The user then posts the Web form back to the Web server, and the Web server executes program commands that send queries to a database based on the user's inputs. These programs create dynamic Web pages that display query results in the user's browser. So far in this book, you have learned how to create Web forms that process user inputs, and you have learned how to write SQL queries that retrieve, insert, update, and delete database data. In this chapter, you will integrate this knowledge. You will learn how to create Web forms that display database data and allow the user to insert and modify data records. First you will learn how to write program commands to create a data connection and a data adapter. Then you will learn how to use Web form data components to display database data.

Before you begin, you will configure your Web server so it contains the application structure you need to create and run Web application projects that you store in the Chapter10\Tutorials folder on your Solution Disk. Then you will create a new Web application project named DataControls that you will use in the chapter tutorials.

To configure your Web server and create the Web application project:

1. Start IIS, and create an application named **Chapter10** that you associate with the Chapter10 folder on your Solution Disk. Create a second application named **Tutorials** within the Chapter10 application that you associate with the Chapter10\Tutorials folder on your Solution Disk. Configure the applications so users have *Read*, *Run scripts*, and *Browse* privileges.

2. Start Visual Studio .NET, click **Tools** on the menu bar, click **Options**, make sure the *Environment* folder is selected in the left pane, select **Projects and Solutions**, click **Browse**, navigate to the Chapter10\Tutorials folder on your Solution Disk, click **Open**, and then click **OK**.

3. Click **File** on the menu bar, point to **New**, click **Project**, make sure the *ASP.NET Web Application* template is selected, and then type **http://localhost/Chapter10/Tutorials/DataControls** in the *Location* field to specify the new project name. Click **OK** to create the project. After a few moments, the new project appears in the Solution Explorer.

4. In the Solution Explorer, select the **WebForm1.aspx** node, right-click, click **Delete**, then click **OK** to confirm the deletion.

Next you will initialize your Clearwater Traders database. If you are using an Oracle9i database, you will start SQL*Plus, which is the Oracle9i client-side utility that allows you to send commands to the database, and run the Clearwater.sql SQL script in the Chapter10 folder on your Data Disk. This script creates the database tables. (The SQL script commands will create the tables in the Clearwater Traders database in Figure 9-10 in Chapter 9, and insert all of the data records.)

 If you are using an Access database, skip these steps and proceed to the next set of steps.

To initialize your database if you are using an Oracle9i database:

1. Click **Start** on the taskbar, point to **All Programs**, point to **Oracle − OraHome92**, point to **Application Development**, and then click **SQL Plus**. The Log On dialog box opens. (Windows 2000 users will click *Start*, point to *Programs*, point to Oracle − *OraHome92*, point to *Application Development*, and then click *SQL Plus*.)

2. Type **cwuser** in the *User Name* field, and **oracle** in the *Password* field. Leave the *Host String* field blank. Then click **OK**. The Oracle SQL*Plus window opens, and the SQL prompt appears.

3. To run the script, type **start a:\Chapter10\Clearwater.sql** at the SQL prompt, and then press **Enter**. (If your Data Disk is stored on a different drive or has a different folder path, type that drive letter or path instead.) The SQL *Plus window displays a series of messages that confirm that the database tables are created and the records are inserted. When the "Commit complete" message appears, close the Oracle SQL*Plus window.

 Don't worry if the SQL*Plus window displays the message "ORA-00942: table or view does not exist." This message indicates that the script is trying to delete a table that does not exist. The script attempts to delete all existing Clearwater Traders database tables before creating the new tables, because if a script tries to create a table that already exists, SQL*Plus generates an error and does not re-create the table.

To initialize your database if you are using an Access database:

1. Start Windows Explorer.

2. Copy **Clearwater.mdb** from the Chapter10 folder on your Data Disk to the Chapter10\Tutorials\DataControls folder on your Solution Disk.

**10**

# CREATING AND CONFIGURING DATA COMPONENTS USING PROGRAM COMMANDS

In Chapter 9, you learned how to create data components using visual configuration tools: You used the Data Link Properties dialog box to create a data connection, and you used the Data Adapter Configuration Wizard to create a data adapter. In this chapter, you will learn how to create and modify data connections and data adapters using VB .NET program commands. You will also learn how to display the retrieved data using Web form controls.

Why do you need to learn to create data components using program commands rather than visual configuration tools? One reason is that it is more efficient to configure the properties of the data components using program commands. When you create data connections and data adapters using visual configuration tools (Wizards), you must configure and modify the properties and settings on different Wizard or dialog box pages, which can be a slow process.

Another reason to configure data components using program commands is that when you create a data connection to an Access database, the Data Link Properties dialog box places the absolute path to the Access .mdb file in the data connection's ConnectString property. For example, if your Access database file is named Clearwater.mdb and is stored in the A:\Chapter10\Tutorials folder on your workstation, the Data Link Properties dialog box stores this path, including the drive letter, in the ConnectString property. If you move the .mdb file to another location, you must update the data connection to reflect the new file location; otherwise, your Web form will not be able to query the database successfully. In contrast, when you create an Access data connection using program commands, you can specify a relative path location for the database .mdb file, which makes your application easier to maintain.

Furthermore, as you learn how to create different kinds of data components to store and manipulate database data, you must use program commands for tasks such as updating and deleting data, and for creating data components that display data values from multiple tables. By creating and configuring all data components using program commands, you can view all of the commands in a single location, which makes it easier to ensure that the components work together correctly.

To retrieve data from a database and display the retrieved values on a Web form, you perform the following steps:

1. Create the data connection.

2. Create a data adapter that uses this data connection and specifies the SQL query that retrieves the data that will appear on the Web form.

3. Create a new data set, which stores the retrieved data, and then fill the data set with the retrieved values.

4. Display the data set values on the Web form.

The following subsections describe how to write program commands to accomplish these four steps. As you work with these program commands, you will use the Clearwater Traders Items Web form shown in Figure 10-1. This Web form, which is saved in a file named ItemsForm.aspx, displays data from the ITEMS table in the Clearwater Traders database (see Figure 9-10). Now you will add this Web form to your Web application project.

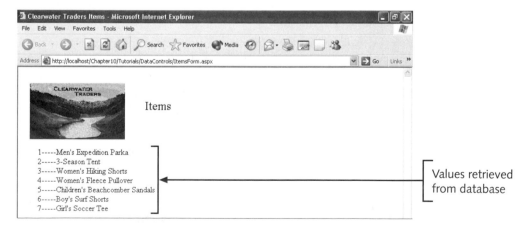

**Figure 10-1**    Clearwater Traders Items Web form

To add the Web form to your Web application project:

1. If necessary, start Windows Explorer, then copy **clearlogo.jpg**, **ItemsForm.aspx**, and **ItemsForm.aspx.vb** from the Chapter10 folder on your Data Disk to the Chapter10\Tutorials\DataControls folder on your Solution Disk.

2. In Visual Studio .NET, open the Solution Explorer if necessary, right-click the **DataControls** project node, point to **Add**, then click **Add Existing Item**. Open the **Files of type** list and select **All Files (*.*)**. Navigate to the Chapter10\Tutorials\DataControls folder on your Solution Disk, select **ItemsForm.aspx**, press and hold **Ctrl**, then select **ItemsForm.aspx.vb** and click **Open** to add the files to the project.

3. Right-click the **ItemsForm.aspx** node in the Solution Explorer, then click **Set As Start Page** to set the Web form as the project's Start Page.

## Using Program Commands to Create a Data Connection

Recall that the first step in creating a Web form that displays database data is to make a data connection, which provides the communication path from your Web form to the database. To create a data connection, you must specify the connection's OLE DB driver, which allows the Web form to communicate with the database. You must also specify database-specific information. For an Oracle9i database, you must specify the user account, password, and host name. For an Access database, you must specify the location of the database .mdb file.

When you created a new data connection in Chapter 9 using the Data Link Properties dialog box, the new connection was visible in your Visual Studio .NET IDE, and you could use the connection in any Web form and in any Web application project. However, when you create a new data connection using a program command, you create the data connection in a specific Web form as either a local or module-level object. (Recall from Chapter 7 that a local object is visible only within the procedure that creates it, and a module-level object is an object that is visible to all procedures within the Web form that creates it.)

If you create the connection as a module-level object, commands anywhere in the form's code behind file can reference the data connection. If you create the connection as a local object, only commands in the procedure that creates the data connection can reference the data connection.

Recall from Chapter 6 that the .NET framework has a set of class libraries that provide common functions to .NET programs. To create a new data connection, you create an object instance of the OleDb.OleDbConnection class library. (OleDb is the parent class, and OleDbConnection is a child class.) To create a new module-level object instance of the OleDb.OleDbConnection class library, you use the following general syntax:

```
Private object_name As New OleDb.OleDbConnection ↵
("connection_string")
```

To create a new local object instance of the OleDb.OleDbConnection class library, you use the following general syntax:

```
Dim object_name As New OleDb.OleDbConnection ↵
("connection_string")
```

Recall that to create a module-level object, you use the **Private** keyword and declare the object in the Declarations block. To create a local object, you use the **Dim** keyword and declare the object in a procedure. The **New** keyword signifies that you are creating a new object, and **OleDb.OleDbConnection** specifies the new object's class. The *connection_string* parameter specifies information about the connection object, including the OLE DB adapter and the database-specific connection information. Figure 10-2 shows the code to create new data connection objects named connCW for both an Oracle9*i* or Access database.

```
' code to create an Oracle database connection
Dim connCW As New OleDb.OleDbConnection ("Provider=MSDAORA.1; ↵
    Password=oracle; User ID=cwuser; Data Source=ORCL;")

'code to create an Access database connection
'using an absolute path
    Dim connCW As New OleDb.OleDbConnection = ↵
    ("Provider=Microsoft.Jet.OLEDB.4.0; ↵
     Data Source=a:\chapter10\tutorials\clearwater.mdb;")

'code to create an Access database connection
'using a relative path
Dim connCW As New OleDb.OleDbConnection = ↵
    ("Provider=Microsoft.Jet.OLEDB.4.0; Data Source= " & ↵
     AppDomain.CurrentDomain.BaseDirectory & "clearwater.mdb;")
```

**Figure 10-2**    Code to create new data connection objects

In Figure 10-2, the "Provider" parameter in the *connection_string* specifies the OLE DB adapter. The other connection string parameters specify information about the data connection, such as the user account, password, and connect string for an Oracle9*i* database, and the location of the .mdb file for an Access database.

Notice that Figure 10-2 shows connection strings for an Access database file using both absolute and relative paths. The absolute path example specifies the drive letter and folder path where the Access .mdb file is located. The relative path example structures the connection string so the data connection looks for the database file in the current working directory, which is the project folder. To do this, the relative path connection string uses the following syntax:

```
"Data Source=" & AppDomain.CurrentDomain.BaseDirectory
& "clearwater.mdb"
```

To specify the *Data Source* parameter, the command concatenates a string that first references the AppDomain class, which specifies the environment where applications execute. It then references the AppDomain class's CurrentDomain property, which specifies the memory space for the current application. The command next references the BaseDirectory property, which specifies the path to the Web form's project folder. Finally, the command concatenates the .mdb filename to the project folder path to complete the Data Source specification. If you use this syntax to create your Access data connection, you can move your project files to a different drive location or folder without having to change the path in your Access data connection.

You can use the AppDomain.CurrentDomain.BaseDirectory property only in data connections you create using program commands. If you try to use this value in the ConnectString property when you create a data connection using the Data Link Properties dialog box, an error will occur.

Now you will add a command to the ItemsForm.aspx.vb code behind file to create a new data connection. You will create the data connection as a local object in the Page_Load procedure.

To create a data connection using a program command:

1. In Visual Studio .NET, select the *ItemsForm.aspx* node in the Solution Explorer if necessary, then click the **View Code** button 📄 on the Solution Explorer toolbar to open the Web form's code behind file.

2. Type the following as the start of the first command in the Page_Load procedure:

```
Dim connCW As New OleDb.OleDbConnection("
```

The next step is to specify the connection string. As Figure 10-2 shows, the connection string has many parameters, so it is easy to make typing errors. Recall from Chapter 9 that when you created a data connection using the Data Link Properties dialog box, the resulting data connection had a ConnectString property. This property has the same parameters as the connection string in the program command that creates a new data connection. To avoid errors, it is a good practice to first create a data connection using the Data Link Properties dialog box, and then copy the resulting ConnectString property value to your program command that creates the database connection. This way, your Web form creates the data connection object, but always has the correct connection string syntax.

Data connections become invalid if the database that the connection references is no longer available. This may occur with an Oracle9*i* database if the user name or password values are no longer valid, or if the database is shut down. This may occur with an Access database if the path to the database .mdb file is no longer valid because the folder path has been changed or the file has been moved.

10

Now you will specify the data connection's connection string. You will use the ConnectString property value from the data connection that you created in Chapter 9 as the data connection object's connection string value.

To specify the data connection's connection string:

1. In the Visual Studio .NET IDE, open the Server Explorer.

 If the Server Explorer tab is not visible in the Visual Studio .NET IDE, click *View* on the menu bar, then click *Server Explorer*. Right-click the *Server Explorer* window title bar, and check *Auto Hide*.

2. If necessary, open the *Data Connections* node.

   *If you are using an Oracle9i database*, right-click the **ORCL.CWUSER** node, then click **Properties** to open the Properties window, which displays the data connection's properties.

 If the ORCL.CWUSER node does not appear, make a new data connection using the instructions in Chapter 9 in the section titled "Creating a Data Connection in Visual Studio .NET." If the connection node appears but the Properties window appears empty, the data connection probably is no longer valid because the database has been shut down or the user name and password are no longer valid. To make sure that your Oracle9i database is started, start SQL*Plus and log on as user name *cwuser* and password *oracle*. If the Properties window is still empty, make a new data connection.

   *If you are using an Access database*, right-click the **Data Connections** node, then click **Add Connection**. Click the **Provider** tab, select **Microsoft Jet 4.0 OLE DB Provider** from the list, click **Next**, click the **More** button [...], navigate to the Chapter10\Tutorials\DataControls folder on your Solution Disk, select **Clearwater.mdb**, click **Open**, then click **OK** to create a new data connection. Right-click the new data connection, then click **Properties** to open the Properties Window, which displays the data connection's properties.

3. To copy the ConnectString property value, double-click the mouse pointer on the **ConnectString** property value to select the value, then press **Ctrl-C**.

4. Close the Properties Window.

5. In the ItemsForm.aspx.vb code behind file, if necessary place the insertion point at the end of the command in the Page_Load procedure that creates the connCW object. Click **Edit** on the menu bar, then click **Paste**. The copied ConnectString property value appears in the Code editor.

6. Type **" )** at the end of the copied connection string.

If you are using an Oracle9*i* database, the copied connection string appears exactly as shown in Figure 10-2. If you are using an Access database, the copied connection string has additional parameters that do not appear in Figure 10-2, and the pairs of double quotation marks indicating empty strings, for example `password=""`, will cause concatenation errors if they are not replaced with two single quotation marks, as in (`password='`). (Because the only required connection string parameter values for an Access data connection are Provider and Data Source, we avoid the double quotation marks problem by simplifying the connection string to these two parameters.) Also, the copied connection string does not specify a relative path to the Access database file. If you are using an Access database, you will now edit your connection string so it uses the relative path specification shown in Figure 10-2.

If you are using an Oracle9*i* database, you can skip these steps.

To edit your Access connection string:

1. In the Code editor, edit the Access connection string value so it appears as follows:

```
("Provider=Microsoft.Jet.OLEDB.4.0; Data Source= " & ⤸
AppDomain.CurrentDomain.BaseDirectory & "clearwater.mdb")
```

You can make your connection string appear on multiple Code editor lines by using the line continuation character, which is a blank space followed by an underscore (_). However, you cannot use the line continuation character in the middle of a string enclosed in quotation marks.

2. Save the file.

## Using Program Commands to Create a Data Adapter

The next step in writing program commands to retrieve database data in a Web form is to create a data adapter. Recall from Chapter 9 that a data adapter retrieves specific data values from a database. A data adapter is an object instance of the OleDb.OleDbDataAdapter class library. (OleDb is the parent class, and OleDbDataAdapter is a child class.) To create a new module-level object instance of the OleDb.OleDbDataAdapter class library, you use the following general syntax:

```
Private object_name As New OleDb.OleDbDataAdapter ⤸
("SQL_query", data_connection)
```

To create a new local object instance of the OleDb.OleDbDataAdapter class library, you use the following general syntax:

```
Dim object_name As New OleDb.OleDbDataAdapter ⤸
("SQL_query", data_connection)
```

In this syntax, the New keyword signifies that you are creating a new object, and OleDb.OleDbDataAdapter specifies the new object's class. The *SQL_query* parameter specifies the values that the data adapter retrieves, and can be any SQL query. The *data_connection* parameter specifies the (ID) value of the data connection object that the data adapter uses to connect to the database. The *data_connection* must be within the scope of the command that creates the data adapter. If you create the data adapter as a local object, the *data_connection* can be either a local object in the same procedure or a class object. If you create the data adapter as a class object, the *data_connection* must also be a class object.

Now you will create a new data adapter named daCW that is a local object in the Page_Load procedure. This data adapter will retrieve the ITEM_ID and ITEM_DESC columns from the ITEM table in the Clearwater Traders database, and will use the connCW data connection object that you created earlier in the Page_Load procedure.

To create the data adapter:

1. In the Code editor, add the following command to the Page_Load procedure below the command that creates the connCW data connection object:

```
Dim daCW As New OleDb.OleDbDataAdapter ↵
("SELECT ITEM.ITEM_ID, ITEM.ITEM_DESC FROM ITEM", connCW)
```

2. Save the file.

As you are developing Web forms that retrieve database data, you will write many SQL queries. Inevitably, some of these queries will contain errors. Therefore, it is a good practice always to test your SQL queries before you try to run the Web form and retrieve the data. This way, if your form contains an error, you'll know that the SQL query is not causing the error. In Chapter 9, you used a Web form named QueryForm.aspx to test SQL queries. Now you will test the SQL query in the connCW data connection object by adding the QueryForm.aspx Web form to your project, then pasting the query into the Query form's *Enter query* TextBox and running the query.

To add the Query form to the project and test the query:

1. Switch to Windows Explorer, and copy **QueryForm.aspx** and **QueryForm.aspx.vb** from the Chapter10 folder on your Data Disk to the Chapter10\Tutorials\DataControls folder on your Solution Disk.

2. Switch back to Visual Studio .NET, add the **QueryForm.aspx** and **QueryForm.aspx.vb** files to the DataControls project, and then set the QueryForm.aspx node as the project's Start Page.

3. Make sure that the *QueryForm.aspx* node is selected, then click the **View Designer** button ▣ on the Solution Explorer toolbar to open the Query form in Design view. Right-click **OleDbConnection1** in the component tray, then click **Properties**.

4. Select the ConnectString property value, then open the list.

*If you are using an Oracle9i database*, select the **ORCL.CWUSER** connection string.

*If you are using an Access database*, select the connection string associated with the Clearwater.mdb file in the Chapter10\Tutorials\DataControls folder on your Solution Disk.

5. Select the **ItemsForm.aspx.vb** tab in the Browser Window, select the query text for the SQL query in the command that creates the data adapter, click **Edit** on the menu bar, and then click **Copy**. (Do not copy the quotation marks that enclose the query.)

6. Click the **Start** button ▶ to run the project. The Query form appears in Internet Explorer.

7. Make sure that the insertion point is in the *Enter query* TextBox, click **Edit** on the menu bar, and then click **Paste**. The query text appears in the *Enter query* TextBox.

8. Click **Run Query**. The ITEM_ID and ITEM_DESC values from the Clearwater Traders ITEM table appear in the DataGrid.

If you are using an Access database, the following message may appear: "The Microsoft Jet database engine cannot open the file 'A:\Chapter10\Tutorials\ DataControls\Clearwater.mdb'. It is already opened exclusively by another user, or you need permission to view its data." If so, you need to change the security permissions on your project folder using the instructions in Chapter 9 in the section titled "Creating SQL Queries That Retrieve Data from Multiple Tables."

9. Close Internet Explorer.

10. In Visual Studio .NET, right-click the **ItemsForm.aspx** node in the Solution Explorer, then click **Set As Start Page**.

You have now confirmed that your data adapter's SQL query is correct. Whenever you create a data adapter, you should repeat this process of running the Query form, testing the SQL query text, then debugging the query if necessary.

## Using Program Commands to Create and Fill a Data Set

A **data set** is a memory structure that stores the data that a data adapter retrieves from a database. A data set stores data in one or more **data tables**, which are memory structures that contain rows and columns that store related data. You retrieve and process data in a data set using a loop that sequentially accesses each record in a specific table.

The next step in displaying database data on a Web form is to create a data set and fill the data set with the values that the data adapter retrieves. To create a new data set object, you create an instance of the .NET DataSet object class. You use the following general syntax to create a new module-level .NET DataSet object:

```
Private object_name As New DataSet()
```

You use the following general syntax to create a new local .NET DataSet object:

```
Dim object_name As New DataSet()
```

For example, you would use the following command to create a new local data set named dsCW:

```
Dim dsCW As New DataSet()
```

After you create the data set, you use the data adapter **Fill method** to fill the data set with the data that the data adapter retrieves. You use the following command to call the Fill method:

```
data_adapter_object.Fill(data_set_object, "table_name")
```

In this command, the *data_adapter_object* is the name of the data adapter that retrieves the data that you wish to place in the data set. The *data_set_object* is the name of the target data set. The *table_name* parameter specifies the data table within the data set where the Fill method places the retrieved data. By specifying a different value for the *table_name* parameter for each Fill operation, you can store the results of multiple Fill operations in the same data set. (In the next section, you will learn how to use the *table_name* parameter to reference the retrieved data.)

You would use the following command to fill a data set named dsCW with the data that the daCW data adapter retrieves and place the results in a data table named dsItems:

```
daCW.Fill(dsCW, "dsItems")
```

Now you will add program commands to the ItemsForm.aspx Web form to create a new data set, open the database connection, fill the data set with the values that the data adapter retrieves, and then close the connection.

To add the commands to create and fill the data set:

1. In the Code editor, add the following program commands to the end of the Page_Load procedure, just before the **End Sub** command:

```
Dim dsCW As New DataSet()
daCW.Fill(dsCW, "dsItems")
```

2. Save the file.

## Displaying Data Set Values on a Web Form

At this point, you have created a data connection and a data adapter, and you have created and filled a data set. You are probably more than ready to display retrieved data values on the ItemsForm.aspx Web form. There are many ways you can display data on a

Web form, and you will learn different approaches throughout this chapter. The simplest way to display data on a Web form is to display the data in a Label control, which you will do next.

Recall that a data set contains one or more data tables, and a data table contains multiple rows. Each data table within a data set is an object, and each row within a data set table is also an object. To display data set values in a Web form, you use a `For Each/Next` loop to access each record in a data set's data table. (Recall from Chapter 7 that you use a `For Each/Next` loop to access individual objects within an object collection.)

To use a `For Each/Next` loop to access the data set contents, you must first create a **data row**, which is an object that references a row within a data set's data table. To create a new data row object, you create an instance of the .NET DataRow object class. You use the following general syntax to create a new local DataRow object:

> `Dim object_name As DataRow`

You use the following general syntax to create a new module-level DataRow variable:

> `Private object_name As DataRow`

Note that you do not use the `New` keyword when you declare the data row variable. This is because you are not creating a new data row object. Instead, the data row creates a variable that references an existing memory location.

 Note that an empty parameter list, ( ), does not follow the DataRow class name when you create a new data row. If you add an empty parameter list, Visual Studio .NET will generate a compile error.

For example, you would use the following command to create a new local data row named rowItems:

> `Dim rowItems As DataRow`

To use a data row to process each row in a data set, you structure the `For Each/Next` loop as follows:

```
For Each data_row In data_set.Tables("table_name").Rows
    commands_to_process_row
Next
```

In this command, you use the data set's Tables property to reference the *table_name* of the data set table that you wish to process. You use the Rows property to move the contents of each row into the data row object. The *commands_to_process_row* can be any VB .NET commands, and usually specify how to display the retrieved data on the Web form. You would use the following `For Each/Next` loop to process each row in the dsCW data set:

```
For Each rowItems In data_set.Tables("dsItems").Rows
    commands_to_process_row
Next
```

When you fill a data set using a data adapter, each data set table column has the same name as the associated database column. For example, in the dsCW data set, the first column is named ITEM_ID, and the second column is named ITEM_DESC. To reference the value of an individual column in a data row that contains retrieved database data, you use the following syntax:

```
data_row_name("column_name")
```

For example, to reference the first column in the rowItems data row, you would use the following syntax:

```
rowItems("ITEM_ID")
```

Now you will add the commands to the ItemsForm.aspx Web form to display the data set values and then run the project. You will create a data row object named rowItems and use a **For Each/Next** loop to process each row in the dsCW data set. You will specify to display each ITEM_ID and ITEM_DESC value in the Label control on the Web form. You will separate the ITEM_ID and ITEM_DESC values with a text string that contains five hyphens ("-----"), and you will add a line break tag (**<br />**) after each ITEM_DESC value so each record appears on a separate line.

To add the commands to display the data set values and then run the project:

1. Add the shaded commands shown in Figure 10-3 to create the data row and the **For Each/Next** loop. Figure 10-3 shows the complete code for the Page_Load procedure.

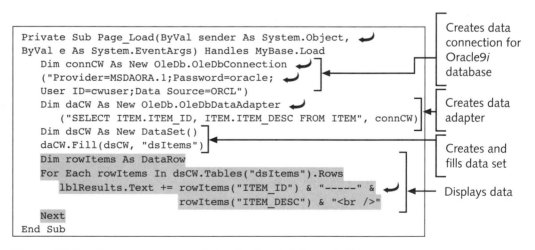

```
Private Sub Page_Load(ByVal sender As System.Object, ↵
ByVal e As System.EventArgs) Handles MyBase.Load
   Dim connCW As New OleDb.OleDbConnection ↵
   ("Provider=MSDAORA.1;Password=oracle; ↵
   User ID=cwuser;Data Source=ORCL")
   Dim daCW As New OleDb.OleDbDataAdapter ↵
      ("SELECT ITEM.ITEM_ID, ITEM.ITEM_DESC FROM ITEM", connCW)
   Dim dsCW As New DataSet()
   daCW.Fill(dsCW, "dsItems")
   Dim rowItems As DataRow
   For Each rowItems In dsCW.Tables("dsItems").Rows
      lblResults.Text += rowItems("ITEM_ID") & "-----" & ↵
                         rowItems("ITEM_DESC") & "<br />"
   Next
End Sub
```

Creates data connection for Oracle9*i* database

Creates data adapter

Creates and fills data set

Displays data

**Figure 10-3**   Program commands to display database data

In Figure 10-3, the connection string in the command that creates the data connection connects to an Oracle9*i* database. The code for Access users will be the same except for the connection string value in the command that creates the data connection.

2. Click the **Start** button ▶ to run the project. The Clearwater Traders Items form appears as shown in Figure 10-1.

If an error appears, make sure that your connection string looks exactly like the correct connection string for your database in Figure 10-2. Also make sure that you have tested and debugged your SQL query using the Query form.

3. Close Internet Explorer.

## Changing Retrieved Data Values at Runtime

The Web developer specifies the SQL query that retrieves the data that appears on the Items Web form at design time. To make interactive Web pages that respond to user inputs, Web developers must use a program command that specifies the data records that the data adapter retrieves while the Web form is running. For example, the user should be able to select an item ID value on the Items form in Figure 10-1 and run a query that retrieves the selected item's associated size, color, and price inventory information. To do this, you will add the *Item ID* TextBox and *Show Details* Button controls shown in Figure 10-4.

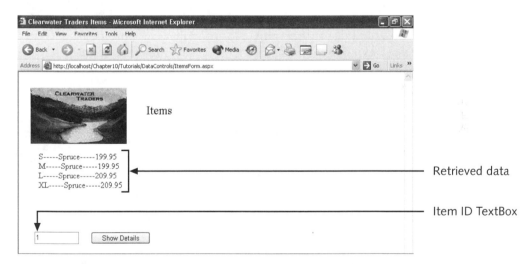

**Figure 10-4**    Items form that uses a dynamic query

When the user enters a value in the Item ID TextBox and then clicks Show Details, the available item sizes, colors, and prices appear in the form Label control that shows the retrieved data in Figure 10-4. First you will add the TextBox and Label rich server controls to the form.

To add the TextBox and Label controls:

1. Select the **ItemsForm.aspx** node in the Solution Explorer if necessary, then click the **View Designer** button 🔳 to display the form in Design view.

2. Open the Toolbox, select the Web Forms tab if necessary, select the **TextBox** tool, and create the *Item ID* TextBox control shown in Figure 10-4.

3. Open the Toolbox, select the **Button** tool, and create the *Show Details* button shown in Figure 10-4.

4. Select the new **TextBox** control, right-click, then click **Properties** to open the Properties Window. Change the *(ID)* property of the TextBox to **txtItemID**.

5. Select the new Button control, change the *(ID)* property of the Button to **btnShowDetails**, the *Text* property to **Show Details**, then select another property to apply the change.

6. Save the Web form.

In this form, the event handler for the *Show Details* button will use the same data connection, data adapter, and data set that you used earlier to retrieve the item values. Originally, you created these components as local objects in the Page_Load procedure. Because these objects must also be visible to the Show Details event handler, you will modify the form and declare the objects as module-level objects. To declare the objects as module-level objects, you will move the commands that create the objects to the Declarations block and change them so they use the `Private` keyword.

To change the data connection, data adapter, and data set to module-level objects:

1. Select the **ItemsForm.aspx.vb** tab at the top of the Browser window to open the Web form's code behind file.

2. Select the first three commands in the Page_Load procedure, click **Edit** on the menu bar, and then click **Cut**.

3. Place the insertion point at the end of the last command in the Declarations block and press **Enter** to create a new blank line.

4. Click **Edit** on the menu bar, then click **Paste** to paste the object definitions.

5. Modify the pasted commands by replacing the `Dim` keyword with `Private` so the commands appear as follows:

```
Private connCW As New ↵
OleDb.OleDbConnection("connection_string")
Private daCW As New OleDb.OleDbDataAdapter ↵
("SELECT ITEM.ITEM_ID, ITEM.ITEM_DESC FROM ITEM", connCW)
Private dsCW As New DataSet()
```

In your code, *connection_string* will be the actual value of your connection string.

6. Save the file.

Now you will add an event handler for the *Show Details* button that dynamically changes the daCW data adapter's SQL query. To change a data adapter's SQL query dynamically, you modify the data adapter's SelectCommand.CommandText property, using the following syntax:

```
data_adapter.SelectCommand.CommandText = "SQL_query"
```

In this syntax, *data_adapter* is the name of the data adapter, and *SQL_query* is the text of the new SQL query. Now you will create and test the event handler for the *Show Details* button. The first command in the event handler will reset the Label control's Text property to an empty string literal. The next command will modify the data adapter's SQL query so the query retrieves the INV_SIZE, COLOR, and INV_PRICE values from the INVENTORY table in the Clearwater Traders database for the value the user specifies in the *Item ID* TextBox control. Finally, the event handler commands will refresh the data set by calling the Fill method, then use a **For Each/Next** loop to display the new data values on the Web form.

To create and test the event handler for the *Show Details* button:

1. Select the **ItemsForm.aspx** tab to display the Web form in Design view, then double-click the **Show Details** button. The event handler template appears in the Code editor.

2. Add to the event handler template the shaded commands in Figure 10-5.

```
Private Sub btnShowDetails_Click(ByVal sender As System.Object ↵
ByVal e As System.EventArgs) Handles btnShowDetails.Click
    lblResults.Text = ""
    daCW.SelectCommand.CommandText = _
    ("SELECT INVENTORY.INV_SIZE, INVENTORY.COLOR, INVENTORY.INV_PRICE ↵
     FROM INVENTORY WHERE INVENTORY.ITEM_ID =" & txtItemID.Text)
    daCW.Fill(dsCW, "dsInventory")
    Dim rowInventory As DataRow
    For Each rowInventory In dsCW.Tables("dsInventory").Rows
        lblResults.Text += rowInventory("INV_SIZE") & "-----" & _
                           rowInventory("COLOR") & "-----" & _
                           rowInventory("INV_PRICE") & "<br />"
    Next
End Sub
```

**Figure 10-5** Commands to change the retrieved data at runtime

3. Click the **Start** button ▶ to run the form. The Items form appears in Internet Explorer.

If the *Item ID* TextBox or *Show Details* Button control overlap onto the retrieved data display area, close Internet Explorer. In Visual Studio .NET Design view, move the TextBox and Button so they are lower on the form, then run the form again.

4. Type **1** in the *Item ID* TextBox, then click **Show Details**. The data values based on the user input appear on the Web form as shown in Figure 10-4.

If an error occurs, close Internet Explorer, make the Query form the project Start Page, copy the SQL_query text from the command that sets the value of the SelectCommand.CommandText property in the code behind file, run the project, then paste the SQL_query text into the Query form, run the query, and debug the query if necessary.

5. Change the *Item ID* TextBox value to **3**, then click **Show Details**. The data values for Item ID 3 (Women's Hiking Shorts) appear on the Web form. (On a production Web server, the Web form would probably redisplay the items in Figure 10-1 before entering another *Item ID* value, but this form illustrates the concept of changing the query results based on user inputs.)

6. Close Internet Explorer. Close the ItemsForm.aspx Web form in the Web Browser window. Leave the ItemsForm.aspx.vb code behind file open, because you will copy the data connection's connection string into other Web forms.

You now know the basic steps for retrieving and displaying database data on a Web form. The rest of the chapter describes how to use these commands and techniques to create professional-quality interfaces that display database data and allow users to display and manipulate database data.

## DISPLAYING DATA USING RICH SERVER CONTROLS

In Web forms, you can use **data binding** to link rich server controls to a data source such as a database. The system queries the data source at runtime to retrieve the current data values, and then configures the control dynamically and displays the most current data values. For example, you can use data binding to link the ImageUrl property of an Image rich server control to a database field that specifies an image filename. When the form runs, the system retrieves the image filename and loads the correct graphic image. Similarly, you can link a TextBox control to a specific database field and display the retrieved value in the TextBox when the form runs.

The two main rich server controls that use data binding to display multiple columns and rows of retrieved data are the DataList and DataGrid controls. A DataList and a DataGrid both display data values on a Web page in a tabular format. Web developers configure DataList controls using commands embedded within HTML tags, so DataLists display data in a very flexible way on Web pages. Visual Studio .NET provides visual configuration tools for creating and configuring DataGrid displays, so it is easier to create a DataGrid, but the data display is not as configurable as the data display that a DataList control provides.

To use DataList and DataGrid controls, you create a data connection and data adapter, and then fill a data set with retrieved values. You then bind the data set to the control, and the control displays the data set's contents on the Web page. Using these controls enables you to display the contents of a data set in a professional format without using loops and labels. The following sections describe how to create DataList and DataGrid rich server controls.

You can also use a Repeater rich server control to display multiple data items, but this control does not allow you to specify an absolute position for the retrieved items on the Web form. This forces you to format your Web form using older-style tables to control the placement of items, and does not give the designer as much control over the Web form's appearance.

**10**

## Using a DataList Control to Display and Edit Database Data

A **DataList rich server control** displays the contents of a data set in a matrix of rows and columns. Figure 10-6 shows an example of a DataList control that displays values retrieved from the ITEMS table in the Clearwater Traders database. You can configure the DataList control to display data as read-only values, as shown in Figure 10-6. You can also configure the DataList control so users can edit and delete data items, which you will learn how to do later.

Creating a DataList control involves two steps: First, you create and configure the DataList control on the Web form. Then you create Web server control templates to specify how the DataList control displays the data values on the form. To learn about DataList controls, you will use the ItemsDataListForm.aspx Web form, which is similar to the Items form you completed in the last section. The ItemsDataListForm.aspx.vb file contains the code to create a module-level data connection and data adapter. The data adapter retrieves the ITEM_ID, ITEM_DESC, and CAT_ID fields from the Clearwater Traders ITEMS table. The form's Page_Load procedure contains commands to create and fill a data set named dsCW. Now you will add the ItemsDataListForm.aspx Web form and its associated code behind file to your project and configure the data connection's connection string so it is compatible with your database.

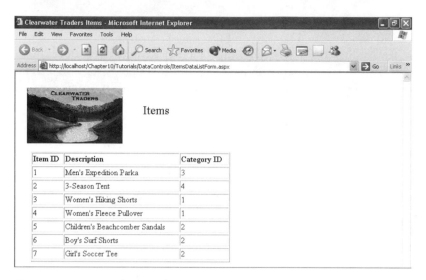

**Figure 10-6**     Displaying data using a DataList control

To add the Web form to the project and configure the connection string:

1. Switch to Windows Explorer and copy **ItemsDataListForm.aspx** and **ItemsDataListForm.aspx.vb** from the Chapter10 folder on your Data Disk to the Chapter10\Tutorials\DataControls folder on your Solution Disk.

2. In Visual Studio .NET, add the **ItemsDataListForm.aspx** and **ItemsDataListForm.aspx.vb** files to the DataControls project, and set **ItemsDataListForm.aspx** as the project's Start Page.

3. Make sure that the *ItemsDataListForm.aspx* node is selected in the Solution Explorer, then click the **View Code** button 🗐 on the Solution Explorer toolbar to open the Web form's code behind file. Figure 10-7 shows that the file contains commands to create the data connection and data adapter, and to create and fill the data set.

4. To modify the data connection so it works with your database, copy the connection string from the ItemsForm.aspx.vb file by selecting the ItemsForm.aspx.vb tab to open the file in the Code editor, then selecting the text that defines the connection string. Do not select the quotation marks.

   *If you are using an Oracle9i database*, this is the text that begins with "Provider=MSDAORA.1" and ends with "Data Source=ORCL."

   *If you are using an Access database*, this is the text that begins with "Provider=Microsoft.Jet.OLEDB.4.0," and ends with "clearwater.mdb;."

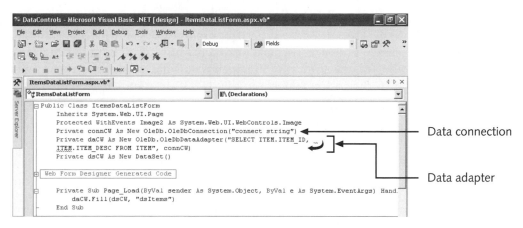

**Figure 10-7**  Commands to create the data connection and data adapter and to create and fill the data set

5. Click **Edit** on the menu bar, then click **Copy** to copy the connection string. Because you will no longer be using the ItemsForm.aspx.vb file, close the ItemsForm.aspx.vb window in the Browser Window.

6. Make sure that the ItemsDataListForm.aspx.vb code behind file appears in the Browser Window, then delete the **connect_string** text in the command that defines the data connection. Do not delete the quotation marks.

7. Place the insertion point inside the empty quotation marks, click **Edit** on the menu bar, and then click **Paste**. The pasted connection string appears in the file. Make sure that the connection string looks like the connection string in Figure 10-2. (If you are using an Access database, your connection string should use the relative path specification shown in Figure 10-2.)

8. Save the file.

## Creating and Configuring a DataList Control

You create a DataList control by drawing it on the Web form using the DataList tool on the Web Forms Toolbox tab. Then, you configure the DataList control by changing its (ID) property value and adding program commands that specify the data set that you will bind to the control. These program commands assign values to the DataList control's DataSource and DataMember properties. The DataSource property specifies the name of the data set to which you bind the DataList, and the DataMember property specifies the name of the data set's data table to which you bind the DataList. Finally, you will add a command to call the DataBind method, which binds the DataList to the data set. You perform these tasks using the following general program commands:

```
data_list_object.DataSource = data_set_object
data_list_object.DataMember = "table_name"
data_list_object.DataBind()
```

In these commands, *data_list_object* references the (ID) property value of the DataList control. *Data_set_object* references the (ID) property of the data set, and *table_name* references the name of the data set table to which you want to bind the control. For example, you would use the following commands to bind a DataList object with the (ID) value dlItems to the "dsItems" table in the dsCW data set:

```
dlItems.DataSource = dsCW
dlItems.DataMember = "dsItems"
dlItems.DataBind()
```

Now you will create a new DataList control on the ItemsDataListForm.aspx Web form. Then you will add the commands to the form's code behind file to configure and bind the control to the data set.

To create and bind the DataList control:

1. In Visual Studio .NET, make sure that the ItemsDataListForm.aspx node is selected in the Solution Explorer, then click the **View Designer** button to open the form in Design view.

2. Open the Toolbox, make sure that the Web Forms tab is selected, then select the **DataList** tool. Create a new DataList control, and resize and reposition the new control so your Web form looks like Figure 10-8.

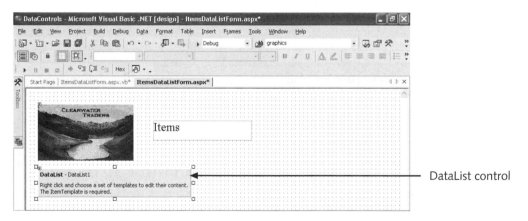

**Figure 10-8**    Creating a DataList control

3. Right-click the **DataList** control, then click **Properties** to open the Properties Window. Change the control's (ID) property value to **dlItems**, select another property to apply the change, then close the Properties Window.

4. Select the **ItemsDataListForm.aspx.vb** tab in the Browser Window to open the Web form's code behind file. To bind the DataList control to the

"dsItems" table in the dsCW data set, add the following commands just before the **End Sub** command in the Page_Load procedure:

```
dlItems.DataSource = dsCW
dlItems.DataMember = "dsItems"
dlItems.DataBind()
```

## Creating a Web Server Control Template to Display DataList Values

A **Web server control template** consists of HTML elements, server controls, and other commands that specify how a Web server control, such as a DataList control, displays data on a Web form. You place the template within the Web server control tags in HTML view. Table 10-1 summarizes some of the different Web server control template types and shows their associated tags.

**Table 10-1**    Web server control template types

| Template Type | Description | Tag |
|---|---|---|
| Header template | Specifies the text and HTML elements that appear at the top of the control | `<HeaderTemplate>` |
| Item template | Specifies the text and HTML elements to render for each data source row | `<ItemTemplate>` |
| Footer template | Specifies the text and HTML elements that appear after the data items | `<FooterTemplate>` |
| Alternating item template | Similar to an item template, but specifies template alternate formatting that appears for every other data source row | `<AlternatingItemTemplate>` |
| Selected item template | Specifies the formatting for a selected item in an item template | `<SelectedItemTemplate>` |
| Edit item template | Specifies the formatting when an item is opened for editing | `<EditItemTemplate>` |
| Separator template | Specifies the elements to render between each item in an item template, such as a horizontal rule `<hr>` | `<SeparatorTemplate>` |

**10**

You can create a **header template**, which specifies the HTML elements that appear before the control values; an **item template**, which specifies the appearance of the control item values; and a **footer template**, which specifies HTML elements that appear after the control values. Within the different template types, you can use any HTML elements or server controls to format the control's appearance on the Web page.

For example, for the DataList control in Figure 10-6, the header template defines the HTML table in which the data values appear and displays the table headings. The item template formats the individual data items in each table row. The footer template contains the closing `</table>` tag.

Figure 10-9 shows the basic structure of a Web server control template for a DataList control. Note that the template tags are within the `<asp:DataList>` tags that define the DataList control. The `<HeaderTemplate>`, `<ItemTemplate>`, and `<FooterTemplate>` tags enclose the tags that define the elements within the respective templates. These tags can contain any HTML elements, including text, images, or table definitions.

```
<asp:DataList id="DataList1" style="style_specification">
  <HeaderTemplate>
    header_template_tags_and_text
  </HeaderTemplate>
  <ItemTemplate>
    item_template_tags_and_text
  </ItemTemplate>
  <FooterTemplate>
    footer_template_tags_and_text
  </FooterTemplate>
</asp:DataList>
```

**Figure 10-9**   Basic Web server control template structure for a DataList control

Within the `<ItemTemplate>` tags, you use the following syntax to display the data set values that are bound to the DataList control:

```
<%# DataBinder.Eval(Container.DataItem, ↵
"column_name") %>
```

You enclose this command in **script delimiter tags** (`<% %>`), which instruct the system to process the enclosed elements as server-side script commands rather than pass them to the client browser as HTML elements. Script delimiter tags appear shaded in yellow in the HTML editor to highlight that they enclose script commands. When a # follows the opening script delimiter tag, this tells ASP.NET that a data binding expression will be included. The DataBinder.Eval method inserts the current value of the specified *column_name* into the tag. Because this method is within the `<ItemTemplate>` tags, the system displays all of the data set records.

Consider the following `<ItemTemplate>` tag:

```
<ItemTemplate>
<%# DataBinder.Eval ↵
(Container.DataItem, "ITEM_DESC") %><br />
</ItemTemplate>
```

If the data set that is bound to the DataList control contains the first two ITEM_DESC values in the ITEMS table in the Clearwater Traders database, the template tag displays the following data on the Web form:

Men's Expedition Parka

3-Season Tent

Note that the data items appear on different lines, because the line break tag (**<br />**) appears within the item template. Now you will add a Web server header, item, and footer template to the ItemsDataListForm.aspx Web form to display the DataList control data values using an HTML table as shown in Figure 10-6. Then you will test the form.

To create and test Web server control templates:

1. Select the **ItemsDataListForm.aspx** tab in the Browser window, then click the **HTML** tab to display the Web form in HTML view.

2. In the HTML editor, find the opening **<asp:DataList>** tag, scroll to the right edge of the window, then place the insertion point before the opening angle bracket in the closing **</asp:DataList>** tag. Press **Enter** two times to create a new blank line between the DataList control's opening and closing tags.

3. Add the shaded code in Figure 10-10 on the blank line after the opening DataList tag to create the Web server template.

**10**

```
<asp:DataList id="dlItems" style="style_specification">
    <HeaderTemplate>
        <table width="400px" border cellspacing="1">
            <tr><th align="left">Item ID</th>
                <th align="left">Description</th>
                <th align="left">Category ID</th></tr>
    </HeaderTemplate>
    <ItemTemplate>
        <tr>
            <td><%# DataBinder.Eval(Container.DataItem, "ITEM_ID") %></td>
            <td><%# DataBinder.Eval(Container.DataItem, "ITEM_DESC") %></td>
            <td><%# DataBinder.Eval(Container.DataItem, "CAT_ID") %></td>
        </tr>
    </ItemTemplate>
    <FooterTemplate>
        </table>
    </FooterTemplate>
</asp:DataList>
```

**Figure 10-10**   Creating Web server control templates to display data values in an HTML table

4. Click the **Start** button ▶ to run the project. The DataList control items appear as shown in Figure 10-6.

5. Close Internet Explorer.

You can use an **alternating item template** along with an item template to specify that every other DataList item appears in a different format. You specify the format of the first set of items, which are the odd-numbered items, in the item template, and the format of the alternating set of items, which are the even-numbered items, in the alternating item template. For example, you might specify that the odd-numbered list items appear on a white background and the even-numbered list items appear on a gray background. Now you will modify the DataList control template so it uses an alternating item template that displays the even-numbered list items on a light gray background.

To add an alternating item template to the DataList control display:

1. Make sure that the ItemsDataListForm.aspx Web form appears in HTML view, then add the shaded alternating item template tags and elements just below the closing `</ItemTemplate>` tag, as shown in Figure 10-11.

```
<asp:DataList id="dlItems" style="style_specification">
   <HeaderTemplate>
      <table width="400px" border cellspacing="1">
         <tr><th align="left">Item ID</th>
            <th align="left">Description</th>
            <th align="left">Category ID</th></tr>
   </HeaderTemplate>
   <ItemTemplate>
      <tr>
         <td><%# DataBinder.Eval(Container.DataItem, "ITEM_ID") %></td>
         <td><%# DataBinder.Eval(Container.DataItem, "ITEM_DESC") %></td>
         <td><%# DataBinder.Eval(Container.DataItem, "CAT_ID") %></td>
      </tr>
   </ItemTemplate>
   <AlternatingItemTemplate>
      <tr style="background-color: gainsboro">
         <td><%# DataBinder.Eval(Container.DataItem, "ITEM_ID") %></td>
         <td><%# DataBinder.Eval(Container.DataItem, "ITEM_DESC") %></td>
         <td><%# DataBinder.Eval(Container.DataItem, "CAT_ID") %></td>
      </tr>
   </AlternatingItemTemplate>
   <FooterTemplate>
      </table>
   </FooterTemplate>
</asp:DataList>
```

**Figure 10-11** Adding alternating item template tags to the Web server control templates

2. Click the **Start** button ▶ to run the project. The DataList control items appear with alternating background shading.

3. Close Internet Explorer.

You have learned how to create templates for read-only DataList controls. Now you will learn how to use the edit item template to create templates that enable users to edit list items.

## Editing Data in a DataList Control

You can configure a DataList control to allow users to edit individual list items. For example, on a Web page that shows a shopping cart of merchandise that a user selects for purchase, the customer would directly edit the selected items and item quantities. On a Web page that displays the merchandise that Clearwater Traders offers for sale, Clearwater Traders employees would need to be able to edit merchandise item descriptions and prices.

To enable users to edit database values using a DataList control, you place an *Edit* button beside each list item, which the user can click to open the item for editing. Figure 10-12 shows the Items form DataList control in which each list item has an associated *Edit* button. Clearwater Traders employees would use this Web form to edit merchandise descriptions and category ID values.

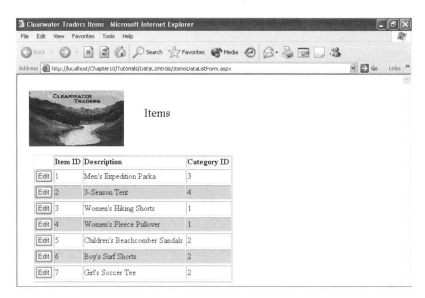

**Figure 10-12**    Buttons to allow users to edit DataList items

When you configure a DataList to allow users to edit items, you need to specify the appearance of the list item when the user clicks *Edit* and opens the item for editing. For example, when the user clicks *Edit* beside "Men's Expedition Parka" in Figure 10-12, the Web page shown in Figure 10-13 appears, with the "Men's Expedition Parka" and Category ID "3" selections opened for editing. The user can edit the item description text and Category ID value in the associated TextBox controls, then click *Update* to update the values in the database or click *Cancel* to close the item for editing and redisplay the Web page as shown in Figure 10-12.

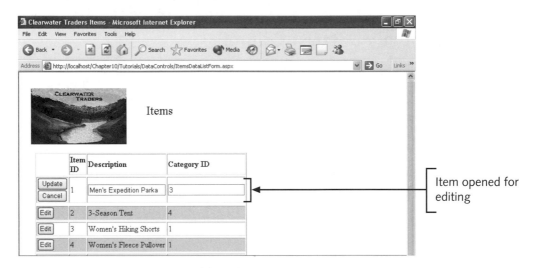

**Figure 10-13** List item opened for editing

To add this functionality to the DataList control, you first add the tags to create the *Edit* buttons in the item template and the alternating item template. Then, you create the **edit item template**, which specifies the appearance of the list item when the user opens the item for editing and creates *Update* and *Cancel* buttons. Finally, you add event handlers for the *Edit*, *Cancel*, and *Update* buttons. The following subsections outline how to perform these tasks.

## Adding *Edit* Buttons to the Item Template

To display the *Edit* buttons beside the DataList control items as shown in Figure 10-12, you add a Button rich server control to the item and alternating item templates. You cannot add this button visually in Design view. You must manually type the tag in HTML view. The *Edit* button will raise the EditCommand event for the DataList control. To associate the button with the EditCommand event, you add the following attribute in the button tag: `CommandName="Edit"`.

Now you will add the *Edit* Button rich server control to the ItemsDataListForm.aspx Web form. You will create a new column in the HTML table, and then add the Button control tag to the item and alternating item templates.

To add the *Edit* Button control to the form:

1. Make sure that the ItemsDataListForm.aspx Web form is open in HTML view.

2. Add the shaded tags as shown in Figure 10-14 to create a new blank table data element in the header template, and to create new table data elements and *Edit* buttons in the item template and alternating item template.

```
<HeaderTemplate>
   <table width="400px" border cellspacing="1">
   <tr><th></th><th align="left">Item ID</th>
   <th align="left">Description</th>
   <th align="left">Category ID</th></tr>
</HeaderTemplate>
<ItemTemplate>
   <tr><td><asp:Button ID="btnEdit" Text="Edit" CommandName="Edit"
   Runat="server"></asp:Button></td>
   <td><%# DataBinder.Eval(Container.DataItem, "ITEM_ID") %></td>
   <td><%# DataBinder.Eval(Container.DataItem, "ITEM_DESC") %></td>
   <td><%# DataBinder.Eval(Container.DataItem, "CAT_ID") %></td>
   </tr>
</ItemTemplate>
<AlternatingItemTemplate>
   <tr style="background-color: gainsboro">
   <td><asp:Button ID="btnAltEdit" Text="Edit" CommandName="Edit"
   Runat="server"></asp:Button></td>
   <td><%# DataBinder.Eval(Container.DataItem, "ITEM_ID") %></td>
   <td><%# DataBinder.Eval(Container.DataItem, "ITEM_DESC") %></td>
   <td><%# DataBinder.Eval(Container.DataItem, "CAT_ID") %></td>
   </tr>
</AlternatingItemTemplate>
```

**Figure 10-14**     Adding the *Edit* buttons to the DataList control display

10

3. Click the **Start** button ▶ to run the project. The *Edit* buttons appear on the Web form as shown in Figure 10-12.

4. Close Internet Explorer.

## Creating the Edit Item Template

When the user opens an item for editing, the Web page displays the item using edit item template elements rather than the normal item or alternating item template elements. As with the other Web server control templates, you can specify the edit item template elements using HTML elements, server control elements, or other commands.

Now you will create the edit item template to display the item that the user opens for editing, as shown in Figure 10-13. The template will display *Update* and *Cancel* Button rich server controls. Because ITEM_ID is the primary key in the ITEM table, the template will display the ITEM_ID value as a read-only value that the user cannot edit. The template will display the ITEM_DESC and CAT_ID values in TextBox controls so the user can edit these values. To display these values in TextBox controls, you set the TextBox control's Text property using the DataBinder.Eval method, and you place the commands in single quotation marks so the value returned by the DataBinder.Eval method is placed in the TextBox. Otherwise, the command that calls the method would appear in the TextBox.

To create the edit item template:

1. Make sure that the ItemsDataListForm.aspx Web form is open in HTML view, place the insertion point after the closing `</AlternatingItemTemplate>` tag, then press **Enter** to create to a new line in the HTML editor.

2. Add the code in Figure 10-15 to create the edit item template.

```
<EditItemTemplate>
   <tr>
      <td><asp:Button ID="btnUpdate" Text="Update"
      CommandName="Update" Runat="server"></asp:Button>
      <asp:Button ID="btnCancel" Text="Cancel" CommandName="Cancel"
      Runat="server"></asp:Button></td>
      <td><%# DataBinder.Eval(Container.DataItem, "ITEM_ID") %></td>
      <td><asp:TextBox ID="txtDescription"
      Text= '<%# DataBinder.Eval(Container.DataItem, "ITEM_DESC") %>'
      Runat="server" /></td>
      <td><asp:TextBox ID="txtCatID"
      Text= '<%# DataBinder.Eval(Container.DataItem, "CAT_ID") %>'
      Runat="server" /></td>
   </tr>
</EditItemTemplate>
```

**Figure 10-15**  Code to create the edit item template

3. Save the file.

## Creating the *Edit* Button Event Handler

When the user clicks an *Edit* button associated with a list item on the Web page in Figure 10-12, the selected item opens for editing, as shown in Figure 10-13. When you created the *Edit* buttons in the templates, you included the attribute `CommandName="Edit"` in the Button tags, which associates the *Edit* button with the DataList control's EditCommand event. The EditCommand event handler has the following general syntax:

```
Protected Sub data_list_object_Edit(ByVal sender As Object, ↵
ByVal e As DataListCommandEventArgs) Handles ↵
data_list_object.EditCommand
    data_list_object.EditItemIndex = e.Item.ItemIndex
    data_list_object.DataBind()
End Sub
```

The Visual Studio .NET IDE configures the event handler header, so you should not edit the event handler name or parameters. The system returns data for the event in the DataListCommandEventArgs object, e. For example, if the user selects the first item, the e.Item.ItemIndex value is 0, if the user selects the second item, it is 1, and so on.

The first command in the event handler assigns the selected index value to the DataList object's EditItemIndex property. The event handler then calls the DataList control's DataBind method, which binds the values for the selected index value into the edit item template. Now you will create the EditCommand event handler.

To create the EditCommand event handler:

1. Select the **ItemsDataListForm.aspx.vb** tab in the Browser Window to view the form's code behind file in the Code editor.

2. To create the event handler template, open the **Class** list in the top-left corner of the Code editor, and select **dlItems**.

3. Open the **Method** list in the top-right corner of the Code editor and select **EditCommand**. The event handler template appears in the Code editor.

4. Add the following commands to the EditCommand event handler:

```
dlItems.EditItemIndex = e.Item.ItemIndex
dlItems.DataBind()
```

5. Save the file.

Before you can test the *Edit* button and confirm that it displays the selected item using the edit item template, you must modify the Page_Load procedure in the code behind file. Recall that whenever you click a button on a Web form, the client browser posts the form back to the Web server. During postback processing, the Web server performs a series of steps, which include executing the Page_Load procedure. Then, the Web server executes the event handlers for the events the user raises, such as the EditCommand event handler. When the Web server executes the DataBind method in the Page_Load procedure the first time the user requests the Web form, the DataBind method configures the DataList control so no list item is open for editing. If the Web server executes the Page_Load() procedure during postback processing, the call to the DataBind method resets the Web form, so once again the selected item is not open for editing.

To overcome this problem and allow editing, you must modify the Page_Load procedure so the Web server executes the DataBind method only for first-time requests. To do this, you use the **If Not IsPostBack** decision structure that you learned about in Chapter 8. (Recall that this decision structure tests to see whether the Web page request is a first-time request or a postback request.) After you modify the Page_Load procedure, you will run the form and open an item for editing.

To modify the Page_Load procedure and run the form:

1. Make sure that the ItemsDataListForm.aspx.vb code behind file is open in the Code editor, then modify the Page_Load procedure so its commands appear as follows:

```
daCW.Fill(dsCW, "dsItems")
dlItems.DataSource = dsCW
dlItems.DataMember = "dsItems"
```

10

```
If Not IsPostBack Then
    dlItems.DataBind()
End If
```

2. Click the **Start** button ▶ to run the project. The Items form appears as shown in Figure 10-12.

3. Click **Edit** beside "Men's Expedition Parka." The Web form appears as shown in Figure 10-13, with the Description and Category ID columns available for editing. (You can edit the items, but if you click *Update*, the item is not updated because you have not yet written the *Update* button event handler.)

4. Close Internet Explorer.

## Creating the *Cancel* Button Event Handler

When an item is open for editing and the user clicks the *Cancel* button, the system restores the DataList control to its initial state, as shown in Figure 10-12. When you created the *Cancel* button in the edit item template, you included the attribute `CommandName="Cancel"` in the Button tag, which associates the *Cancel* button with the DataList control's CancelCommand event. To implement the *Cancel* button, you create a CancelCommand event handler, which has the following general syntax:

```
Private Sub data_list_object _CancelCommand(↵
ByVal sender As Object, ↵
ByVal e As DataListCommandEventArgs) ↵
Handles data_list_object.CancelCommand
    data_list_object.EditItemIndex = -1
    data_list_object.DataBind()
End Sub
```

The first event handler command resets the list index to the value–1, which specifies that no list item is selected. The second command calls the DataBind method, which refreshes the list display. Now you will create the CancelCommand event handler in the Web form and then run the form to test the event handler.

To create and test the event handler:

1. Make sure that the ItemsDataListForm.aspx.vb file appears in the Code editor. To create the event handler template, open the **Class** list in the top-left corner of the Code editor and select **dlItems**.

2. Open the **Method** list in the top-right corner of the Code editor and select **CancelCommand**. The event handler template appears in the Code editor.

3. Add the following commands to the CancelCommand event handler:

```
dlItems.EditItemIndex = -1
dlItems.DataBind()
```

4. Click the **Start** button ▶ to run the project. The Items form appears as shown in Figure 10-12.

5. Click **Edit** beside "Men's Expedition Parka." The Items form appears as shown in Figure 10-13.

6. Click **Cancel**. The Items form appears as shown in Figure 10-12 again.

7. Close Internet Explorer.

## Creating the *Update* Button Event Handler

When the user clicks the *Update* button for a selected list item, the browser posts the Web form back to the Web server, and the Web server sends an action query to the database to update the selected list item's values. To implement the *Update* button, you create an event handler associated with the UpdateCommand event. The UpdateCommand event handler contains commands that create an OleDbCommand object that the Web server uses to process the update, specify the object's SQL command, execute the SQL command, then refresh the list display. The following subsections describe these commands.

**Creating an OleDbCommand Object**  An **OleDbCommand object** is a child object within the OleDb class that represents a SQL statement that the Web server sends to the database. You use the following syntax to create a new local OleDbCommand object:

```
Dim object_name As New OleDb.OleDbCommand
```

You use the following syntax to create a new module-level OleDbCommand object:

```
Private object_name As New OleDb.OleDbCommand
```

After you create a new OleDbCommand object, you must assign a value to its Connection property to specify the data connection that the object uses to retrieve data. You would use the following commands to create a new local OleDbCommand object named sqlCommand and set its Connection property to the connCW connection:

```
Dim sqlCommand As New OleDb.OleDbCommand
sqlCommand.Connection = connCW
```

Now you will create a new UpdateCommand event handler in the Web form, and add commands to create an OleDbCommand object and specify the object's connection.

To create the OleDbCommand object:

1. Make sure that the ItemsDataListForm.aspx.vb tab is selected in the Browser Window, then open the **Class** list and select **dlItems**.

2. Open the **Method** list and select **UpdateCommand**. The template for the UpdateCommand event handler appears in the Code editor.

3. Add the following commands to create a new OleDbCommand object named sqlCommand and set its Connection property to the connCW data connection:

```
Dim sqlCommand As New OleDb.OleDbCommand()
sqlCommand.Connection = connCW
```

4. Save the file.

**Specifying the OleDbCommand Object's SQL Query**  After you create a new OleDbCommand object, you must set the object's CommandText property, which specifies the text of the SQL command that the object represents. (You used the CommandText property earlier in this chapter when you specified the SQL query for a data adapter.) You specify the command text of an OleDbCommand object using the following syntax:

```
command_object_name.CommandText = "SQL_query_text"
```

In this command, *command_object_name* is the name of the OleDbCommand object, and "*SQL_query_text*" is a string that represents the SQL query that the database processes. When you create SQL queries at runtime, parameters such as search conditions often reference variable or property values in Web form controls. For example, you might create a SQL query that retrieves all of the INVENTORY records for the ITEM_ID value that the user selects in a DataList control. Or, you might want to update the ITEM_DESC field to the value that currently appears in a TextBox control named txtDescription.

Recall from Chapter 9 that the general format for an UPDATE action query is as follows:

```
UPDATE tablename
SET column1 = new_value1, column2 = new_value2, …
WHERE search_condition
```

When you create the *SQL_query_text* for an OleDbCommand object, the values for *new_value1*, *new_value2*, and so forth will be represented by variables or property values. Note that each *new_value* marker is separated from the next column name by a comma. Therefore when you create the *SQL_query_text*, you must concatenate a comma immediately after the variable or property name in the command.

Furthermore, in a SQL command, string values must appear in single quotation marks. When you write a SQL command that contains text values that are represented by variables or control properties, you must embed the single quotation marks within the query text. Figure 10-16 shows how a VB .NET command that defines a SQL query concatenates commas and single quotation marks to enclose a text value represented by a variable.

In Figure 10-16, the VB .NET command contains an UPDATE action query that updates the ITEM_DESC and CAT_ID columns to values that are in TextBox controls named txtDescription and txtCatID. The resulting SQL query text assumes that the txtDescription.Text property value is "3-Season Tent," and that the txtCatID.Text property value is 2. Notice that in the first command, the text `"SET ITEM_DESC = '"` ends with a single quotation mark followed by a double quotation mark. The single quotation mark specifies the opening single quotation mark in `'3-Season Tent'`.

In the VB .NET command, the string `"', CAT_ID = "` begins with the single quotation mark that ends the text string specifying the ITEM_DESC value. The single quotation mark is followed by the comma that separates the ITEM_DESC value from the name of the CAT_ID column. Note that the value for the CAT_ID column is not enclosed in single quotation marks, because CAT_ID is a number, not a text string. Finally, the string " WHERE ITEM.ITEM_ID = 1" specifies the search condition.

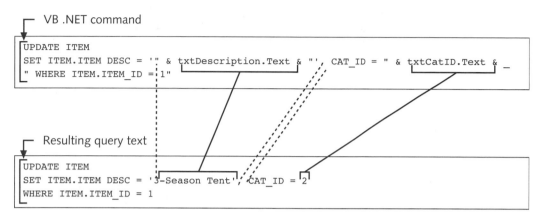

**Figure 10-16**    Embedding commas and single quotation marks within commands that create SQL queries

You must remember to include blank spaces in the query string so the SQL command is formatted correctly. For example, in the string " WHERE ITEM.ITEM_ID = 1", a blank space appears before the WHERE command because there must be a blank space between the CAT_ID value (2) and the WHERE keyword.

When you write program commands that create SQL queries using variables, you must also correctly represent the text strings that contain embedded single quotation marks. Recall that in a SQL command, you must replace a single quotation mark with two single quotation marks. For example, you specify the text string "Children's Clothing" as "Children''s Clothing." Whenever a VB .NET command creates a SQL query that references a text string as a variable or property value, the command should replace each single quotation mark (') with two single quotation marks (''). The most convenient way to do this is to use the VB .NET Replace function, which has the following syntax:

```
return_value = Replace(input_string, "str1", "str2")
```

In this syntax, *input_string* represents the string value within which you want to search and replace values. "*str1*" is the search string, and "*str2*" is the replacement string. You would use the following command to replace every single quotation mark with two single quotation marks in the Text property of a Control named txtDescription, and return the result to a variable named strReplacedText:

```
Dim strReplacedText As String = ↵
Replace(txtDescription.Text, "'", "''")
```

When you type program commands that create SQL queries, the commands can become very long. It is a good practice to use ampersands and the underscore line continuation character (_) to break up long lines of code so they appear on multiple lines and do not scroll off the right edge of the screen display. This makes the commands easier to read and debug. However, it also introduces the possibility of creating concatenation errors.

Now you will add the commands to the UpdateCommand event handler to create the SQL query. This query references the ITEM_ID, ITEM_DESC, and CAT_ID values of the selected list items, using the following general syntax:

```
UPDATE ITEM
SET ITEM_DESC = item_desc_value,
CAT_ID = category_id_value
WHERE ITEM_ID = item_id_value
```

The system must configure this query at runtime by placing the updated value that the user enters in the TextBox controls in Figure 10-13 as the *item_desc_value* and *category_id_value*, and specifying the ITEM_ID of the selected item as the *item_id_value*. To reference the TextBox controls, you create new TextBox objects in the event handler that have the same structure as the TextBox controls in which the user edits the item description and category ID values. You use the following syntax to create these TextBox objects:

```
Dim object_name As New TextBox = e.Item.FindControl
("control_ID")
```

In this syntax, the system calls the **e.Item.FindControl** method, which references the current selection in the DataList control and finds the control with the specified *control_ID*. Recall from Figure 10-15 that the ID of the TextBox control in which the user edits the item description is txtDescription. You would use the following command to create a new TextBox object named txtItemDesc that references the txtDescription TextBox in the Web form.

```
Dim txtItemDesc As New TextBox = ⮠
  e.Item.FindControl("txtDescription")
```

 You cannot directly reference the txtDescription TextBox control in code behind file commands because this TextBox is not defined in the form class declarations in the Declarations block. You cannot define template items in the form class declarations.

Because the ITEM_ID column is the primary key of the ITEM table, the best way to reference the ITEM_ID value is to set the DataList control's DataKeyField property to the name of the primary key column in the Properties Window. Now you will add the commands to the event handler to specify the OleDbCommand object's SQL query.

To add the commands to specify the OleDbCommand object's SQL query:

1. Select the **ItemsDataListForm.aspx** tab in the Browser Window, then click the **Design** tab to open the form in Design view.

2. Select the **DataList** control, right-click, and then click **Properties** to open the Properties Window. Change the DataKeyField property value to

**ITEM_ID**, select another property to apply the change, and then close the Properties Window.

3. Select the **ItemsDataListForm.aspx.vb** tab to open the code behind file, then add the shaded commands in Figure 10-17 to create the variables that reference the DataList values and to create the SQL command text.

```
Private Sub dlItems_UpdateCommand(ByVal source As Object, ↵
ByVal e As System.Web.UI.WebControls.DataListCommandEventArgs ↵
Handles dlItems.UpdateCommand
    Dim sqlCommand As New OleDb.OleDbCommand()
    sqlCommand.Connection = connCW
    Dim txtItemDesc As TextBox = e.Item.FindControl("txtDescription")
    Dim txtItemCatID As TextBox = e.Item.FindControl("txtCatID")
    'replace single quotes with double quotes
    Dim strReplacedDescText As String = ↵
        Replace(txtItemDesc.Text, "'", "''")
    Dim intItemID As Integer = dlItems.DataKeys.Item(e.Item.ItemIndex)
    sqlCommand.CommandText = "UPDATE ITEM SET ITEM.ITEM_DESC = '" & _
            strReplacedDescText & "', CAT_ID = " & txtItemCatID.Text & _
            " WHERE ITEM.ITEM_ID = " & intItemID
```

**Figure 10-17**   Code to create the SQL action query

10

4. Save the file.

**Executing the Query**   The next step is to execute the query represented by the OleDbCommand object. When you execute a query using an OleDbCommand object, you must first explicitly open the data connection. To open a data connection, you use the Open method, which has the following syntax: *data_connection*.Open(). After the query executes, there is no need to leave the data connection open, because the connection uses client and server memory resources. Therefore, you close the data connection using the Close method, which has the following syntax: `data_connection.Close()`.

To execute the SQL query, you call the OleDbCommand object's ExecuteNonQuery method using the following general syntax:

> *command_object_name*.ExecuteNonQuery()

The ExecuteNonQuery method executes the query specified by the object's CommandText property using the object's connection. Unfortunately, queries that you compose using program commands and user inputs can fail for a wide variety of reasons. Validating user entries with validation controls helps to alleviate this problem, but there is always the possibility that a user will enter a value that a validation control or function does not catch, and the query will fail. To avoid query errors, you call the ExecuteNonQuery method using a `Try/Catch/End Try` code block, which VB .NET provides for executing commands that may cause runtime errors. This code block has the following general structure:

```
Try
    test_command
    commands_that_execute_if_test_command_succeeds
Catch
    commands_that_execute_if_test_command_fails
End Try
```

In this structure, the system attempts to execute the *test_command* in the Try section. If the *test_command* succeeds, the system executes the remaining commands in the Try section. If the *test_command* fails, the system executes the commands in the Catch section. To use a `Try/Catch/End Try` code block to execute a query, you use the command that calls the ExecuteNonQuery method as the *test_command*. You display a message confirming the query was successful as the next command in the Try section, and you display a message stating that the query failed in the Catch section.

In the error message, you can use the Err.Description property to display the error message that the system returns. The Err object is a system object that contains information about runtime errors. The Description message is usually quite technical and is aimed toward programmers rather than users. As a general rule, you should use this message as a debugging aid and remove the message when you move the program to a production Web server and make it available to users.

Now you will add a Label rich server control to the Web form to display a message that describes the query's status. Then you will add the commands to open the data connection, execute the query and display the messages, and then close the data connection.

To add the Label control and the commands to execute the query:

1. Select the **ItemsDataListForm.aspx** tab to display the Web form in Design view, open the Toolbox, select the **Web Forms** tab, select the **Label** tool, and then draw a new Label control on the right edge of the DataList server control. Align the top edge of the Label with the top edge of the DataList control.

2. Right-click the new **Label** control, then click **Properties** to open the Properties Window. Change the Label's (ID) property value to **lblMessage**, delete the Label's Text property value, select another property to apply the change, and then close the Properties Window.

3. Select the **ItemsDataListForm.aspx.vb** tab to open the code behind file, then add the following commands as the last commands in the UpdateCommand event handler, just before the `End Sub` command:

```
sqlCommand.Connection.Open()
Try
        sqlCommand.ExecuteNonQuery()
        lblMessage.Text = "Record successfully updated"
```

```
Catch
    lblMessage.Text = "Query error: " & Err.Description
End Try
sqlCommand.Connection.Close()
```

    4. Save the file.

**Refreshing the List Display**   To finish the UpdateCommand event handler, you need to add commands to close the opened list item, then refresh the list display so it shows the updated value. To close the opened list item, you reset the list index to the value–1, which specifies that no list item is selected. Then, you add a command to update the data set by removing the data table that contains the updated item. To remove a data table from a data set, you call the Remove method using the following syntax:

    *data_set_object*.Tables.Remove("*table_name*")

The next command calls the Fill method to refill the data set, and the final command calls the DataBind method, which refreshes the list display. Now you will finish the UpdateCommand event handler. Then you will run the project and test the event handler.

To finish and test the UpdateCommand event handler:

    1. Make sure that the ItemsDataListForm.aspx.vb code behind file is open in the Code editor, then add the shaded commands in Figure 10-18. Figure 10-18 shows the completed UpdateCommand event handler.

    2. Click the **Start** button ▶ to run the project. The Items form opens in Internet Explorer. Click **Edit** beside Item ID 1 (Men's Expedition Parka). The item opens for editing.

    3. Change the item description value to **Men's Tundra Parka**, then click **Update**. The Message Label displays the message "Record successfully updated," the selected item is closed for editing, and the updated value appears in the DataList control.

 If an error message appears, double-check your commands to make sure they appear exactly as shown in Figure 10-18. If you cannot locate your error, set a breakpoint on the first command in the UpdateCommand event handler, then step through the commands in the Debugger to determine which command is causing the error. If the command that assigns the sqlCommand.CommandText value is causing the error, create a watch on sqlCommand.CommandText, and view the SQL query string that the event handler submits to the database to see whether you made a concatenation error. Copying the query text and pasting it into the Query form to see whether the query runs outside of the UpdateCommand event handler may help you discover the error.

    4. Click **Edit** beside Item ID 2 ("3-Season Tent"). The item opens for editing.

```
Private Sub dlItems_UpdateCommand(ByVal source As Object, ByVal e As
System.Web.UI.WebControls.DataListCommandEventArgs) Handles dlItems.Update
Command
    Dim sqlCommand As New OleDb.OleDbCommand()
    sqlCommand.Connection = connCW
    Dim txtItemDesc As TextBox = e.Item.FindControl("txtDescription")
    Dim txtItemCatID As TextBox = e.Item.FindControl("txtCatID")
    'replace single quotes with double quotes
    Dim strReplacedDescText As String = Replace(txtItemDesc.Text, "'", "''")
    Dim intItemID As Integer = dlItems.DataKeys.Item(e.Item.ItemIndex)
    sqlCommand.CommandText = "UPDATE ITEM SET ITEM.ITEM_DESC = '" & _
        strReplacedDescText & "', CAT_ID = " & txtItemCatID.Text & _
        " WHERE ITEM.ITEM_ID = " & intItemID
    sqlCommand.Connection.Open()
    Try
        sqlCommand.ExecuteNonQuery()
        lblMessage.Text = "Record successfully updated"
    Catch
        lblMessage.Text = "Query error: " & Err.Description
    End Try
    sqlCommand.Connection.Close()
    dlItems.EditItemIndex = -1
    dsCW.Tables.Remove("dsItems")
    daCW.Fill(dsCW, "dsItems")
    dlItems.DataBind()
End Sub
```

**Figure 10-18**    Code for the completed DataList UpdateCommand event handler

5. Change the Category ID value to **10**, then click **Update**. An error message appears because the CAT_ID column is a foreign key in the ITEM table, and you cannot insert a foreign key value unless the value is a primary key in the related table.

6. Close Internet Explorer.

7. Because you are finished working with the ItemsDataListForm.aspx Web form, close all open windows in the Web Browser Window.

You can also use a DataList control to delete data values. To do this, you add a Delete Button rich server control to the item template and place the attribute value `CommandName="Delete"` in the Button's tag. Then, you create a DeleteCommand event handler that contains the command for a DELETE action query. This event handler has the same syntax as the UpdateCommand event handler, except the *SQL_query* specifies a DELETE action query.

## Formatting DataList Control Data Values

Sometimes you need to format data values that appear in a DataList control. For example, you might want to format price values as currency or date values using a specific date format. To do this, you add an optional third parameter to the DataBinder.Eval method that contains a formatting expression. Table 10-2 shows format string expressions for numeric data values.

**Table 10-2** DataBinder.Eval numeric formatting expressions

| Format String | Description | Example | Data Value | Result |
|---|---|---|---|---|
| {0:C} or {0:c} | Displays numeric values in currency format | "{0:C}" | 259.99 | $259.99 |
| {0:E} or {0:e} | Displays numeric values in scientific (exponential) format | "{0:E}" | 259.99 | 2.599900E+002 |
| {0:Fn} or {0:fn} | Displays numeric values rounded to n decimal places | "{0:F1}" | 259.99 | 260.0 |
| {0:Pn} or {0:pn} | Displays numeric values in percent format, rounded to n decimal places | "{0:P1}" | .06 | 6.0% |

For example, in a call to the DataBinder.Eval method, you would use the following command to format the INV_PRICE field as currency:

```
<%# DataBinder.Eval(Container.DataItem, "INV_PRICE", ↵
"{0:C}")
```

Table 10-3 shows the DataBinder.Eval method formatting expressions for date/time data values using an example date/time value of Friday, October 1, 2006, 12:00 AM.

**Table 10-3** DataBinder.Eval date/time formatting expressions

| Format String | Description | Result |
|---|---|---|
| {0:d} | Short date pattern | 10/1/2006 |
| {0:D} | Long date pattern | Friday, October 01, 2006 |
| {0:t} | Short time pattern | 12:00 AM |
| {0:T} | Long time pattern | 12:00:00 AM |
| {0:g} | Short date/short time pattern | 10/1/2006 12:00 AM |
| {0:G} | Short date/long time pattern | 10/1/1976 12:00:00 AM |
| {0:f} | Long date/short time pattern | Friday, October 01, 2006 12:00 AM |
| {0:F} | Long date/long time pattern | Friday, October 01, 2006 12:00:00 AM |
| {0:M} or {0:m} | Month/date pattern | October 01 |

For example, you would use the following command to format the C_BIRTHDATE date values from the CUSTOMER table in the Clearwater Traders database using the short date pattern:

```
<%# DataBinder.Eval(Container.DataItem, ↵
"C_BIRTHDATE", "{0:d}") %>
```

10

In this example, customer Paula Harris's birth date would appear as 4/9/1953.

The DataList control provides a powerful and highly configurable way to display and edit database data. You can use HTML tags and elements to configure the Web server control templates so they display the data values in almost any way you can display data on a Web page.

A disadvantage of the DataList control is that it takes a lot of time to create and configure because it requires the Web developer to write a lot of code. The Web developer must write the HTML commands to configure the templates, and write the VB .NET commands to create the event handlers that perform the action queries. To overcome these deficiencies, you can use a DataGrid control, which provides much of the same functionality as the DataList control, but is easier to configure.

## USING A DATAGRID CONTROL TO DISPLAY AND EDIT DATA

A DataGrid rich server control is very similar to a DataList control: A **DataGrid rich server control** displays retrieved data values, and Web developers can configure a DataGrid control to allow users to update and delete data values. The main difference between a DataList and a DataGrid involves how you create them. Recall that with a DataList, you create an item template to specify the appearance of the data display and an edit item template to specify the appearance of the editing display. With a DataGrid control, the Visual Studio .NET IDE provides visual configuration tools that allow you to easily specify the data and editing display. You can also create Web server control templates to configure the DataGrid's appearance, but in many situations you can create an attractive, professional-looking interface entirely with the visual configuration tools. As a result, using a DataGrid usually requires less custom programming.

The Visual Studio .NET IDE provides visual configuration tools to assist in creating DataList controls, but the tools have limited functionality and do not work as well as the DataGrid visual configuration tools.

With a DataGrid control, as with a DataList control, the Web developer still writes the event handlers for opening an item for editing, updating or deleting an item, or canceling an editing operation. The commands in these event handlers are almost identical to the commands you wrote in the EditCommand, UpdateCommand, and CancelCommand event handlers for the DataList control. (You will learn how to create a DeleteCommand event handler to delete an item later in this section.)

To learn about the DataGrid control, you will use a Web form named InventoryDataGrid Form.aspx that is in the Chapter10 folder on your Data Disk. This Web form displays data from the INVENTORY database table in the Clearwater Traders database. Now you will add this form to your DataControls project.

To add the InventoryDataGridForm.aspx Web form to the project:

1. Switch to Windows Explorer and copy **InventoryDataGridForm.aspx** and **InventoryDataGridForm.aspx.vb** from the Chapter10 folder on your Data Disk to the Chapter10\Tutorials\DataControls folder on your Solution Disk.

2. In Visual Studio .NET, add the **InventoryDataGridForm.aspx** and **InventoryDataGridForm.aspx.vb** files to the DataControls project, and set **InventoryDataGridForm.aspx** as the project's Start Page.

A DataGrid control uses a data connection and a data adapter to retrieve data. To use the visual configuration tools to configure the DataGrid control that you will make in this form, you cannot create the data connection and data adapter using program commands. If you create these data components using program commands, the components will not appear in the visual tool selection lists. Therefore, you will use the data connection that you created earlier in your Visual Studio .NET IDE, and create a data adapter using the Data Adapter Configuration Wizard. (You used this Wizard in Chapter 9 to create a data adapter.) Now you will create the data adapter.

To create the data adapter:

1. In Visual Studio .NET, select the **InventoryDataGridForm.aspx** node in the Solution Explorer if necessary, then click the **View Designer** button ⊞ to open the form in Design view.

2. Open the Toolbox, click the **Data** tab, and then double-click the **OleDbDataAdapter** tool. The Data Adapter Configuration Wizard Welcome page appears. Click **Next**.

3. The Data Connection page appears.

   *If you are using an Oracle9i database,* make sure that *ORCL.CWUSER* is selected in the *Which data connection should the data adapter use* list, and then click **Next**.

   *If you are using an Access database,* make sure that *ACCESS.A:\Chapter10\ Tutorials\DataControls\Clearwater.mdb.Admin* is selected in the *Which data connection should the data adapter use* list, and then click **Next**.

4. On the Query Type page, make sure that the *Use SQL statements* option button is selected, and then click **Next**. The SQL statements page appears.

5. Type **SELECT * FROM INVENTORY** in the *What data should the data adapter load into the dataset* field.

6. Click **Advanced Options**, clear the **Generate Insert, Update, and Delete statements** check box, click **OK**, click **Next**, then click **Finish**. The Web form appears in Design view, and the data connection and data adapter appear in the component tray.

**10**

If you are using an Access database, do not use the wildcard character (*) in a query that joins multiple tables. Access assigns alternate names to the join columns, and you cannot reference these columns in your DataGrid. You can use the wildcard character (*) in this query, because it retrieves values from only one table.

Recall that to use the data that a data adapter retrieves, you must create and fill a data set. When you create a new data set, the data set object appears in the component tray, and the data set's XML schema definition file appears in the project tree in the Solution Explorer. The data set's **XML schema definition file** defines the data set's tables and the fields within each table.

To create and fill the data set, you right-click the data adapter in the component tray, then click *Generate Dataset*. This opens the Generate Dataset dialog box, which allows you to specify the new data set's name, define its tables, and fill the data set with the data adapter's data values. Now you will generate a new data set using the Generate Dataset dialog box.

To generate a new data set:

1. Right-click **OleDbDataAdapter1** in the component tray, then click **Generate Dataset**. The Generate Dataset dialog box opens, as shown in Figure 10-19.

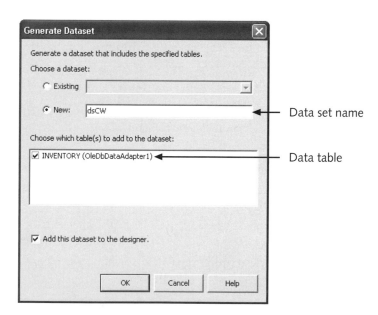

**Figure 10-19**    Generate Dataset dialog box

2. Make sure that the *New* option button is selected, then change the value in the *New* field to **dsCW**. The *Choose which table(s) to add to the dataset* field

specifies that the data adapter fills the data set and places the values in a data table named INVENTORY, and the *Add this dataset to the designer* check box specifies that the data set appears in the component tray.

3. Click **OK** to close the Generate Dataset dialog box and save your changes. The new DsCW1 data set appears in the component tray, and a new object named dsCW.xsd appears in the project tree to represent the data set's schema definition file, as shown in Figure 10-20.

 When you generate a data set using the General Dataset dialog box, the configuration tool always appends a number to the data set name.

The following subsections describe how to create and configure a DataGrid control, how to allow users to edit data items in a DataGrid control, and how to format data values that appear in a DataGrid.

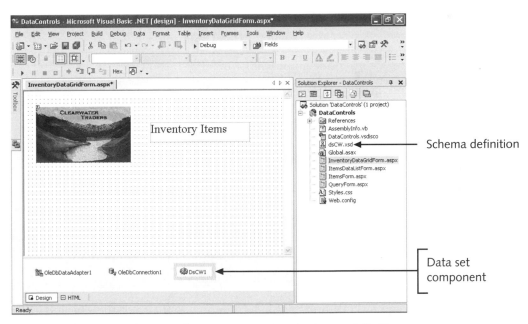

**Figure 10-20**   New data set data component and schema definition

# Creating and Configuring a DataGrid Control

You use the DataGrid tool on the Web Forms tab in the Toolbox to create a new DataGrid control. Then, you use the Property Builder visual configuration tool to configure the DataGrid's properties. Now you will create a new DataGrid control on the Web form. You will specify the DataGrid's (ID) property value. You will also specify the DataGrid's Height property, which determines the height of each row in the grid. (If you do not explicitly set the Height value, the Web form automatically adjusts the height depending on how many data values it retrieves, and the results are unpredictable.) Then you will open the Property Builder dialog box to specify other DataGrid property values.

To create the DataGrid control:

1. Make sure that the InventoryDataGridForm.aspx Web form is open in Design view, open the Toolbox, select the **Web Forms** tab, select the **DataGrid** tool, and then draw a new DataGrid control on the Web form, as shown in Figure 10-21.

2. Select the **DataGrid** control, right-click, click **Properties** to open the Properties Window, change the *(ID)* property value to **dgInventory** and the *Height* property value to **55px**, then select another property to apply the change.

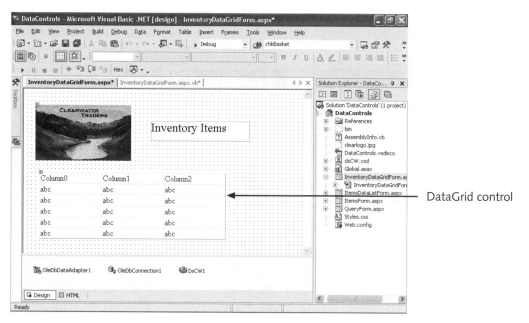

**Figure 10-21** Creating a new DataGrid control

3. To open the Property Builder window, right-click the **DataGrid** control, then click **Property Builder**. The Property Builder window opens and displays the General page, as shown in Figure 10-22.

The DataGrid Property Builder window has tabs that allow you to view the following pages:

- *General*, which allows you to specify properties about the DataGrid data, such as the data set and data table within the data set, and select the key field within the table

- *Columns*, which allows you to specify the columns that appear in the DataGrid and configure the column properties

- *Paging*, which allows you to specify whether the DataGrid displays values in sets that the user can page through

- *Format*, which allows you to specify formatting properties such as font styles and background colors

- *Borders*, which allows you to specify the properties of the DataGrid borders

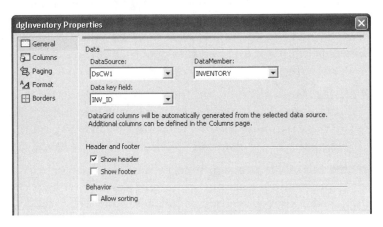

**Figure 10-22**   Property Builder General page

The following subsections describe how to configure the DataGrid using the General, Columns, Format, and Borders pages. Paging is an advanced topic that this book will not address.

## Property Builder General Page

The Property Builder General page (see Figure 10-22) allows you to bind the DataGrid control to a data set, specify the data table within the data set that the DataGrid displays, and select one of the table columns as a key field. (You will use the key field later in action query search conditions.) You can use the *Show header* and *Show footer* check boxes to specify whether to display a header or footer on the DataGrid. You usually display a header which shows the column names. (You will learn how to specify the header text and properties later on the Column page.) You check the *Allow sorting* check box to enable sorting within the DataGrid. The DataGrid does not sort the records, but checking this box enables the SortCommand event handler, which contains program commands to sort the data values. Now you will configure the DataGrid's General properties by specifying the data set, data set table, and key field.

To configure the DataGrid's General properties:

1. On the dgInventory Properties General page, open the **DataSource** list, and select **DsCW1** to bind the DataGrid to the data set.

2. Open the **DataMember** list, and select **INVENTORY** to select the data table within the data set from which the DataGrid retrieves its values.

3. Open the **Data key field** list, and select **INV_ID** to specify the DataGrid's key field.

4. Make sure that the *Show header* check box is checked and that the other check boxes are cleared, then click **OK** to close the Property Builder dialog box.

The DataGrid appears in Design view and shows a template for the selected data set. The template shows the column heading names and displays numerical template values (0, .1, .2, and so forth) in the table columns that contain number values (INV_ID, ITEM_ID, INV_PRICE, and INV_QOH), and text template values ("abc") in the table columns that contain text data (COLOR and INV_SIZE). However, the template does not yet actually show data values.

To dynamically fill the DataGrid control with data values from the data set so the control displays retrieved data values, you write program commands to call the data adapter Fill() method to update the data values that the data adapter retrieves, and then call the DataGrid control's Bind method to dynamically bind the DataGrid to the new values.

You cannot fill and bind the values at design time, because the database data values may change, so you want to perform these actions at the time the user requests the form. To fill and bind the values at runtime, you will add commands to the Web form's code behind file to create a procedure called FillAndBind that calls the Fill method to refresh the data adapter, then calls the Bind method to bind the DataGrid to the data values. (The Web form code will perform these two actions many times, so it makes sense to expedite them using a procedure.) Then you will add commands to the Page_Load procedure to call the FillAndBind procedure. This command will use an **If** decision control structure, and call the procedure only for first-time requests. Then you will run the form.

To create the FillAndBind procedure, call it from the Page_Load procedure, and then run the form:

1. Right-click anywhere on the InventoryDataGridForm.aspx Web form in Design view, then click **View Code** to open the Web form's code behind file.

2. Add the following commands just before the **End Class** command at the end of the code behind file to create the FillAndBind procedure:

```
Sub FillAndBind()
     OleDbDataAdapter1.Fill(DsCW1, "INVENTORY")
     dgInventory.DataBind()
End Sub
```

3. Add the following command to the Page_Load procedure to call the FillAndBind procedure:

```
If Not IsPostBack Then
     FillAndBind()
End If
```

4. Click the **Start** button ▶ to run the form. The Web form appears in Internet Explorer, and the DataGrid control displays the INVENTORY data values, as shown in Figure 10-23. (The order of your columns may be different. You will learn how to specify the column order in the next section.)

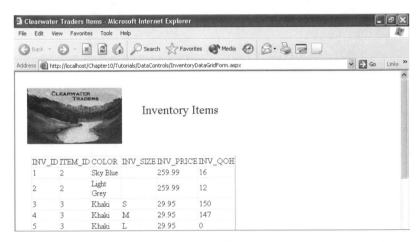

**Figure 10-23**    DataGrid control displaying INVENTORY data values

5. Close Internet Explorer.

The next step is to enhance the appearance of the output using the other Property Builder pages. Next, you will use the Property Builder Column page to specify the properties of individual columns.

## Property Builder Columns Page

Figure 10-24 shows the Property Builder Columns page. You can use the Columns page to specify which columns appear on the DataGrid output display and to modify the column properties. When the *Create columns automatically at run time* check box is checked, the DataGrid automatically displays all of the columns in the data set. If you want to configure the properties of individual columns, you must clear this check box, then select the columns to display in the *Available columns* list and move the selected column to the *Selected columns* list.

The *Available columns* list has the following nodes: *Data Fields*, which represents each column in the data set; *Button Column*, which allows you to create a new column that contains buttons that allow users to perform actions on individual list items, such as editing or updating the item; *HyperLink Column*, which allows you to create a column that contains a hyperlink associated with each list item; and *Template Column*, which allows you to create a Web server template to specify the column's contents. Now you will open the Property Builder Columns page and modify the DataGrid so it displays all columns except the ITEM_ID column.

To modify the DataGrid to display all columns except ITEM_ID:

1. Select the **InventoryDataGridForm.aspx** tab on the Browser Window, right-click the **DataGrid** control, then click **Property Builder** to open the dgInventory Properties dialog box.

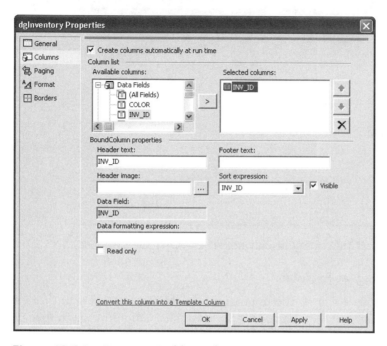

**Figure 10-24**    Property Builder Columns page

2. Click the **Columns** tab to display the Columns page.

3. Clear the **Create columns automatically at run time** check box.

4. Select **INV_ID** under the Data Fields node in the *Available columns* list, then click the **Add** button to move INV_ID to the *Selected columns* list.

5. Repeat Step 4 to move the **COLOR**, **INV_SIZE**, **INV_PRICE**, and **INV_QOH** columns to the *Selected columns* list.

6. Select **COLOR** in the *Selected columns* list, then click the **Down arrow** beside the *Selected columns* list to move COLOR so it appears just after INV_SIZE in the list.

7. Click **Apply** to save your changes, but leave the dgInventory Properties dialog box open.

When you select a column in the *Selected columns* list, you can configure that column's properties in the BoundColumn properties frame on the Columns page. The *Header text* field specifies the column heading, and can include text as well as HTML tags. The

*Footer text* field specifies the text that appears at the end of the column. The *Header image* field can specify the URL of an image file that can appear as the column heading. If you specify a value for both the *Header text* and *Header image* fields, the image value overrides the text value. The *Sort expression* list specifies the column name that is passed to the optional SortCommand event handler if you want to enable sorting in the DataGrid. The *Visible* check box specifies whether the column appears in the control. The *Data Field* field is read-only, and shows the data set table field to which the column is bound. The *Data formatting expression* field allows you to specify a formatting expression, such as the ones in Tables 10-2 and 10-3, for the selected column. When you check the *Read only* check box, users cannot edit the column value when they open the item for editing.

Now you will modify the column properties. You will specify descriptive column headings for each column, specify that the INV_ID column cannot be edited, and format the INV_PRICE column using a currency format. Then you will run the project and view your changes.

To modify the column properties and view the changes:

1. Select **INV_ID** in the *Selected columns* list, change the *Header text* field value to **Inventory ID**, and check the **Read only** check box.

2. Select **INV_SIZE** in the *Selected columns* list, then change the *Header text* field value to **Size**.

3. Repeat Step 2 to change the column headings for the COLOR, INV_PRICE, and INV_QOH columns to **Color**, **Price**, and **Quantity on Hand** respectively.

4. Select **Price** in the *Selected columns* list, then type **{0:c}** (the number zero) in the *Data formatting expression* field to specify the column format as currency. (Tables 10-2 and 10-3 summarize the data formatting expressions.)

5. Click **OK** to save your changes and close the Property Builder dialog box.

6. Click the **Start** button ▶ to run the project. The formatted columns appear as shown in Figure 10-25. Note that the columns have different headings, and the Price column values appear with a currency format.

7. Close Internet Explorer.

## Property Builder Format Page

The Property Builder Format page allows you to specify the foreground and background colors of different sections of the DataGrid and to specify the font properties of these sections. Figure 10-26 shows the Property Builder Format page.

The *Objects* list shows the DataGrid elements for which you can specify formatting properties. You can select *DataGrid* to specify properties for the overall control, or select *Header, Footer,* or *Pager* to specify properties for individual sections within the control.

(The *Pager* selection applies only when you enable paging in the DataGrid, which is an advanced topic that this book does not address.) When you specify a property for an individual section, it overrides the property selection for the overall control.

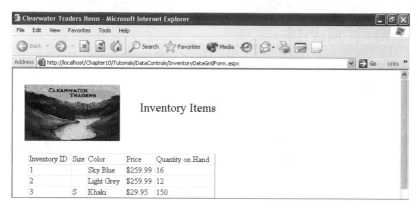

**Figure 10-25**    DataGrid with formatted columns

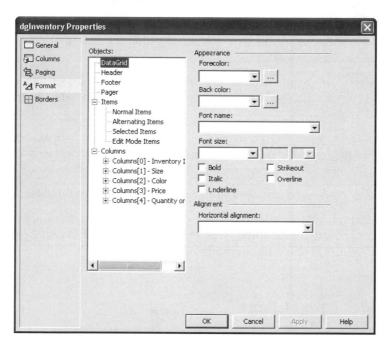

**Figure 10-26**    Property Builder Format page

The *Items* node allows you to specify properties for specific items. Item choices include *Normal Items* and *Alternating Items*, which allows you to specify properties for alternating items as you did with the DataList alternating item template. Other Items choices include *Selected Items*, which specifies properties for an item that the user selects, and *Edit*

*Mode Items*, which specifies properties for an item that a user opens for editing. The *Columns* node displays all of the columns in the DataGrid and allows you to modify the formats of individual columns.

Now you will modify the DataGrid formats. First you will change the background color of the column headings and display the column headings in a bold font. Then you will display the DataGrid items using alternating background colors, in which the odd-numbered items appear on a white background and the even-numbered items appear on a light gray background.

To format the DataGrid control:

1. Select the **DataGrid** control in Design view, right-click, click **Property Builder** to open the dgInventory Properties dialog box, then click the **Format** tab to open the Format page.

2. Select **Header** in the *Objects* list, click the **More** button [...] beside the *Back color* list to open the **Color Picker**, select the **Named Colors** tab, select **Seashell** (which is in the sixth row in the 15th column), and then click **OK**. The color name appears in the *Back color* list.

3. Check the **Bold** check box to display the *Header* text in a bold font.

4. Open the **Items** node in the *Objects* list, select the **Normal Items** node, open the **Back color** list, and select **White**.

5. Select the **Alternating Items** node in the *Objects* list, click the **More** button [...] beside the *Back color* list, select the **Named Colors** tab, select **Gainsboro** (which is in the fourth row in the last column), and then click **OK**. The color name appears in the *Back color* list.

6. Click **OK** to apply the changes and close the dgInventory Properties dialog box. The formatted DataGrid control appears in Design view. If necessary, adjust the color properties until you find shades that coordinate.

## Property Builder Borders Page

The Property Builder Borders page allows you to specify the cell margins, which determine how much space appears between the cell borders and the cell contents and between adjacent cells. This page also allows you to specify the properties of the gridlines between the cells. Figure 10-27 shows the Property Builder Borders page.

On the Borders page, the *Cell padding* field specifies the number of pixels between the cell contents and the gridlines, and the *Cell spacing* field specifies the number of pixels between adjacent cells. By default, the *Cell spacing* value is 0, so DataGrid cells appear directly adjacent to each other. The *Grid lines* list allows you to display horizontal gridlines, vertical gridlines, both, or no gridlines. By default, both horizontal and vertical gridlines appear. The *Border color* and *Border width* lists allow you to configure the border color and width. Now you will modify the DataGrid borders so the gridlines are 2 pixels thick and appear in a dark gray color.

10

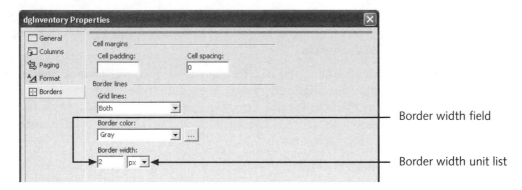

**Figure 10-27** Property Builder Borders page

To modify the DataGrid borders:

1. Select the **DataGrid** control in Design view, right-click, click **Property Builder** to open the dgInventory Properties dialog box, then click the **Borders** tab to open the Borders page.

2. Open the **Border color** list and select **Gray**. (If Gray does not appear in your list, select an alternate color.)

3. Type **2** in the *Border width* field. Note that *px* appears in the *Border width unit* list, which specifies the border width measurement unit.

4. Click **OK** to close the dgInventory Properties dialog box, then click the **Start** button ▶ to run the project. The formatted DataGrid control appears as shown in Figure 10-28.

**Figure 10-28** Formatted DataGrid control

5. Close Internet Explorer.

## Allowing Users to Edit DataGrid Values

You can create button columns that display buttons that allow users to perform actions on DataGrid items. Then, as with the DataList control buttons, you write associated event handlers for the buttons. The following subsections describe these tasks.

### Adding Button Columns to the DataGrid

In a DataGrid, a **button column** displays one or more buttons that allow users to select an item and perform different actions on the item. You can create buttons that allow the user to select an item, open an item for editing, or delete an item. To create a button column, you open the Property Builder Columns page and add a new button column to the *Selected columns* list. Then you specify the button properties. Now you will open the Property Builder Columns page, and create one button column that displays *Edit*, *Update*, and *Cancel* buttons, and a second button column that displays *Delete* buttons. The *Edit* and *Delete* buttons appear when the form initially opens. As with the DataList control, when the user clicks *Edit* beside an item, the item opens for editing, and the *Update* and *Cancel* buttons appear. After the user clicks *Update* or *Cancel*, the item is closed for editing, and the *Edit* and *Delete* buttons appear again.

To add button columns to the DataGrid control:

1. Right-click the **DataGrid** control in Design view, click **Property Builder**, then click the **Columns** tab to open the Columns page.

2. Scroll down the *Available columns* list, open the **Button Column** node, select **Edit**, **Update**, **Cancel**, and then click the **Add** button ⟩ to add the button column to the *Selected columns* list.

3. Make sure that *Edit, Update, Cancel* is selected in the *Selected columns* list, then click the **Up arrow** until *Edit, Update, Cancel* appears as the first list item.

4. Accept the default *Edit* text, *Cancel* text, and *Update* text values for the button labels, then open the **Button type** list and select **PushButton** so the buttons appear as command buttons rather than as hyperlinks.

5. In the *Available columns* list, select **Delete** under the Button Column node, and then click the **Add** button ⟩ to move *Delete* to the *Selected columns* list.

6. Make sure that *Delete* is selected in the *Selected columns* list, then click the **Up arrow** until *Delete* appears as the second list item.

7. Accept the default *Text* and *Command name* field values, then open the **Button type** list and select **PushButton** so the *Delete* button appears as a command button rather than as a hyperlink.

8. Click **OK**. The button columns appear in the DataGrid, as shown in Figure 10-29. Resize the DataGrid control so the column headings all appear on one line.

**10**

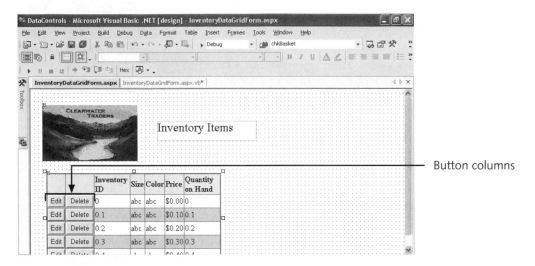

**Figure 10-29** DataGrid control with button columns

9. Save the file.

## Creating the *Edit* and *Cancel* Button Event Handlers

The commands for the *Edit* and *Cancel* button event handlers are almost identical to the commands you used earlier for these event handlers in the DataList control. Recall that in the DataList Control's *Edit* button event handler, the first command sets the control's EditItemIndex property to the value of the selected control item, and the second command calls the control's DataBind method and binds the data set items to the control. In the *Cancel* button event handler, the first command sets the control's EditItemIndex property to–1 to indicate that no item is selected, then calls the DataBind method.

Because the DataGrid control uses a data adapter that you configured in Visual Studio .NET, you must call the data adapter's Fill method to refresh the data adapter before binding the data values to the control. To do this, you will call the FillAndBind procedure that you created earlier. Now you will create the event handlers for the *Edit* and *Cancel* buttons, then run the form and test the event handlers.

To create and test the *Edit* and *Cancel* button event handlers:

1. Select the **InventoryDataGridForm.aspx.vb** tab in the Browser Window to display the form's code behind file.

2. Open the **Class** list, select **dgInventory**, then open the **Method** list and select **EditCommand**. The event handler template appears in the Code editor.

3. Add the following commands to the EditCommand event handler:

```
dgInventory.EditItemIndex = e.Item.ItemIndex
FillAndBind()
```

4. Open the **Class** list, select **dgInventory**, then open the **Method** list and select **CancelCommand**. The event handler template appears in the Code editor.

5. Add the following commands to the CancelCommand event handler:

```
dgInventory.EditItemIndex = -1
FillAndBind()
```

6. Click the **Start** button ▶ to run the project, then click **Edit** beside Inventory ID 1. The item opens for editing, and the *Update* and *Cancel* buttons appear in the first column in the DataGrid control.

7. Click **Cancel**. The item closes, and the *Edit* button appears beside Inventory ID 1.

8. Close Internet Explorer.

## Creating the Update Button Event Handler

Recall that when you created the *Update* button event handler for the DataList control, you first created an OleDbCommand object that the Web server uses to process the UPDATE action query. Then you specified the object's SQL command, executed the command, and added commands to refresh the control display. You use similar commands in the *Update* button event handler for a DataGrid control. Now you will create the event handler template, add the commands to create the OleDbCommand object, and set the object's Connection property to OleDbConnection1, which is the Web form's database connection.

To create the *Update* button event handler template and the OleDbCommand object:

1. In the InventoryDataGridForm.aspx.vb code behind file, open the **Class** list and select **dgInventory**, then open the **Method** list and select **UpdateCommand**. The event handler template appears in the Code editor.

2. Add the following commands to create the OleDbCommand object and assign the form connection to its Connection property:

```
Dim sqlCommand As New OleDb.OleDbCommand()
sqlCommand.Connection = OleDbConnection1
```

3. Save the file.

The next step is to create objects in the event handler to reference the DataGrid columns. You use the following syntax to reference a column in a DataGrid item:

```
e.Item.Cells(cell_number).Controls(item_number)
```

As with the DataList control, `e` returns data for the selected item in the control. `Item.Cells` represents the collection of cells in the selected row. The *cell_number* specifies the column position, where the first column is *cell_number* 0, the second column is *cell_number* 1, and so forth. Controls specifies the Controls collection, which is the

**10**

collection of controls within the cell, and *item_number* specifies the position of the control within the cell. For example, a cell might contain two controls, such as an *Update* button and a *Cancel* button. For DataGrid controls that retrieve values from a relational database, the *item_number* value is usually 0.

The following expression references the Inventory ID value in the DataGrid in Figure 10-29: `e.Item.Cells(2).Controls(0)`. Note in Figure 10-29 that the Inventory ID value is in the third column, so its *item_number* value is 2.

Now you will add the commands to the UpdateCommand event handler to create objects to reference the Inventory ID, Size, Color, and Price column values in the DataGrid control. As with the DataList control, you will create TextBox objects to reference each DataGrid cell and use the DataKeys.Item property to reference the data table's primary key.

To add the commands to create objects to reference the DataGrid column values:

1. Add the following commands just before the **End Sub** command in the UpdateCommand event handler:

```
Dim intInvID As Integer = ↵
dgInventory.DataKeys.Item(e.Item.ItemIndex)
Dim txtSize As TextBox = e.Item.Cells(3).Controls(0)
Dim txtColor As TextBox = e.Item.Cells(4).Controls(0)
Dim txtPrice As TextBox = e.Item.Cells(5).Controls(0)
Dim txtQOH As TextBox = e.Item.Cells(6).Controls(0)
```

2. Save the file.

Now you will add the commands to create the SQL UPDATE action query. You will concatenate the TextBox objects' Text properties to specify the INVENTORY table values and use the selected item's INV_ID column value as the search condition. Recall that in an UPDATE action query, you must separate each column name/value pair with a comma, and you must enclose text values in single quotation marks. You will first add commands that use the Replace function to replace all string single quotation marks with two single quotation marks for the values that the user updates in the ITEM_SIZE and COLOR columns because these columns contain text strings. You will also remove the currency formatting in the INV_PRICE column because the column contains a currency symbol, and you cannot insert a number data value that displays a currency symbol. Then you will create the SQL command.

To create the SQL action query:

1. Add the following commands just before the **End Sub** command in the UpdateCommand event handler:

```
Dim strReplacedColor As String = ↵
Replace(txtColor.Text, "'", "''")
Dim strReplacedSize As String = ↵
Replace(txtSize.Text, "'", "''")
```

```
sqlCommand.CommandText = "UPDATE INVENTORY " & _
"SET INV_SIZE = '" & strReplacedSize & _
"', COLOR = '" & strReplacedColor & _
"', INV_PRICE = " & txtPrice.Text & _
", INV_QOH = " & txtQOH.Text & _
" WHERE INV_ID = " & intInvID
```

2. Select the **InventoryDataGridForm.aspx** tab to open the form in Design view, right-click the **DataGrid** control, then click **Property Builder**.

3. Select the **Columns** tab, select the **Price** column in the *Selected columns* list, delete the value in the *Data formatting expression* field value, then click **OK** to save the change.

4. Save the file.

Now you will finish the *Update* button event handler by creating a Message Label on the Web form that displays a message stating whether or not the query was successful. You will also add the commands to execute the SQL command, close the item that is open for editing, and refresh the DataGrid display. These commands are virtually identical to the commands you used in Figure 10-18 for the DataList UpdateCommand event handler. Then you will test the event handler.

To finish and test the *Update* button event handler:

1. In the **InventoryDataGridForm.aspx** Web form in Design view, open the Toolbox, make sure that the Web Forms tab is selected, select the **Label** tool, then draw a Label control directly under the Inventory Items Label at the top of the form.

2. Right-click the new **Label** control, click **Properties** to open the Properties Window, change the (ID) property value to **lblMessage**, delete the Text property value, select another property to apply the change, then close the Properties Window.

3. Select the **InventoryDataGridForm.aspx.vb** tab to open the code behind file, then add the shaded commands in Figure 10-30 to the *Update* button event handler. Figure 10-30 shows the code for the completed DataGrid control *Update* button event handler.

4. Click the **Start** button ▶ to run the project.

5. Click **Edit** beside Inventory ID 1 to open the item for editing.

6. Change the *Color* field value to **Navy**, the *Price* field value to **269.99**, and the *Quantity on Hand* field value to **20**, then click **Update**. The "Record successfully updated" message appears in the Message Label, and the updated values appear in the DataGrid control.

**10**

```
Private Sub dgInventory_UpdateCommand(ByVal source As Object, ByVal e As
System.Web.UI.WebControls.DataGridCommandEventArgs) Handles
dgInventory.UpdateCommand
        Dim sqlCommand As New OleDb.OleDbCommand()
        sqlCommand.Connection = OleDbConnection1
        Dim intInvID As Integer = dgInventory.DataKeys.Item(e.Item.ItemIndex)
        Dim txtSize As TextBox = e.Item.Cells(3).Controls(0)
        Dim txtColor As TextBox = e.Item.Cells(4).Controls(0)
        Dim txtPrice As TextBox = e.Item.Cells(5).Controls(0)
        Dim txtQOH As TextBox = e.Item.Cells(6).Controls(0)
        Dim strReplacedColor As String = Replace(txtColor.Text, "'", "''")
        Dim strReplacedSize As String = Replace(txtSize.Text, "'", "''")
        sqlCommand.CommandText = "UPDATE INVENTORY " & _
            "SET INV_SIZE = '" & strReplacedSize & _
            "', COLOR = '" & strReplacedColor & _
            "', INV_PRICE = " & txtPrice.Text & _
            ", INV_QOH = " & txtQOH.Text & _
            " WHERE INV_ID = " & intInvID
        sqlCommand.Connection.Open()
        Try
            sqlCommand.ExecuteNonQuery()
            lblMessage.Text = "Record successfully updated"
        Catch
            lblMessage.Text = "Query error: " & Err.Description
        End Try
        sqlCommand.Connection.Close()
        dgInventory.EditItemIndex = -1
        DsCW1.Tables.Remove("INVENTORY")
        OleDbDataAdapter1.Fill(DsCW1, "dsItems")
        FillAndBind()
    End Sub
```

**Figure 10-30**    Code for the completed DataGrid UpdateCommand event handler

If an error message appears, the cause is probably an error in the command that creates the SQL UPDATE action query. Set a breakpoint on the command immediately after the command that creates the SQL query, then run the project. View the value of the sqlCommand.CommandText property, and make sure that the query is structured correctly. If necessary, copy the SQL command and run it in the Query form to help locate the error.

7. Close Internet Explorer.

## Creating the *Delete* Button Event Handler

The *Delete* button event handler is similar to the *Update* button event handler: It contains commands to create an OleDbCommand object and to configure the object's CommandText property as the SQL command that deletes the record, then executes the query and refreshes the DataGrid control.

Recall from Chapter 9 that the general syntax of the DELETE action query is as follows:

```
DELETE FROM tablename
WHERE search_condition
```

You will configure the SQL query in the *Delete* button event handler so *tablename* is the INVENTORY table, and the *search_condition* references the primary key of the selected item using the DataKeys.Item property. Now you will create and test the *Delete* button event handler.

To create and test the *Delete* button event handler:

1. In the InventoryDataGridForm.aspx.vb code behind file, open the **Class** list, and select **dgInventory**, then open the **Method** list and select **DeleteCommand**. The DeleteCommand event handler template appears in the Code editor.

2. Add the shaded commands in Figure 10-31 to the event handler template.

```
Private Sub dgInventory_DeleteCommand(ByVal source As Object, ↵
ByVal e As System.Web.UI.WebControls.DataGridCommandEventArgs) ↵
Handles dgInventory.DeleteCommand
    Dim sqlCommand As New OleDb.OleDbCommand()
    sqlCommand.Connection = OleDbConnection1
    Dim intInv_ID As Integer = dgInventory.DataKeys.Item(e.Item.ItemIndex)
    sqlCommand.CommandText = "DELETE FROM INVENTORY " & _
                             "WHERE INV_ID = " & intInv_ID
    sqlCommand.Connection.Open()
    Try
        sqlCommand.ExecuteNonQuery()
        lblMessage.Text = "Record successfully deleted"
    Catch
        lblMessage.Text = "Query error: " & Err.Description
    End Try
    sqlCommand.Connection.Close()
    dgInventory.EditItemIndex = -1
    DsCW1.Tables.Remove("INVENTORY")
    OleDbDataAdapter1.Fill(DsCW1, "INVENTORY")
    FillAndBind()
End Sub
```

**Figure 10-31** Code for the completed DataGrid DeleteCommand event handler

3. Click the **Start** button ▶ to run the project. Scroll down in the Internet Explorer window, then click **Delete** to delete Inventory ID 30. The message "Record successfully deleted" appears in the Message Label.

4. Scroll down in the Internet Explorer window and confirm that Inventory ID 30 no longer appears in the DataGrid, then close Internet Explorer.

You have seen that you can use either a DataList or a DataGrid control to display database data and allow users to edit and delete data values. With a DataList control, you specify the

**10**

appearance of the data values using HTML tags in a Web server control template. With a DataGrid control, you specify the appearance of the data values using the Property Builder visual configuration tool. The event handler commands for both controls are very similar. The DataList control allows Web developers more flexibility in configuring the data display, whereas the DataGrid control supports faster Web form development.

## VALIDATING USER INPUTS IN DATALIST AND DATAGRID CONTROLS

Users often make errors when they enter and modify data values, so you must include data validation functions to avoid data entry errors in Web forms. You learned how to validate Web form inputs in Chapter 8 using server validation controls. Server validation controls do not work with DataList and DataGrid controls, however, so you must use different data validation techniques. The best way to validate user inputs in a DataGrid or DataList control when a user opens an item for editing is to add a CustomValidator control to the Web form. (Recall from Chapter 8 that you use the CustomValidator validation control to associate your own custom client-side JavaScript validation functions with Web form controls, and that you can create an equivalent server-side validation function that performs server-side validation if the user's browser does not support client-side scripts.) The following subsections describe how to create both client-side and server-side CustomValidator validation controls to validate DataList and DataGrid control inputs.

### Creating a Client-Side CustomValidator to Validate DataList and DataGrid Inputs

Recall from Chapter 8 that to create a client-side CustomValidator, you create the CustomValidator control, configure the CustomValidator, then write a JavaScript function to perform the validation. When you configure a CustomValidator control, you specify the value of the control's ControlToValidate property, which specifies the Web form control that the CustomerValidator validates. However, when you create a CustomValidator to validate DataList or DataGrid inputs, you cannot directly associate the DataList or DataGrid control to the CustomValidator, so you do not specify a value for the ControlToValidate property. Instead, you reference the DataList or DataGrid input values using commands within the JavaScript function.

To perform the validation, the CustomValidator's JavaScript function examines all of the form's elements, then identifies the elements that are associated with the DataGrid or DataList control you are validating. Then, the function validates the individual input values based on the data value positions in the DataGrid.

To perform validation on DataList and DataGrid controls when a user opens an item for editing, you will use an existing JavaScript function named Validate. Figure 10-32 shows the template for the JavaScript Validate function. You do not need to fully understand all of the syntax in this function because the function uses advanced JavaScript programming techniques. You do, however, need to understand how to modify the function so you can use it in Web forms that contain DataList and DataGrid controls.

```javascript
<script language="javascript">
<!--
function Validate(source, args) {
  args.IsValid = true;
  var intCol = 0;
  var strName = new String();
  var curForm = document.Form1;
  for (i=0; i<curForm.elements.length; i++) {
    if (curForm.elements[i].type == "text") {
      strName = curForm.elements[i].name;
      if (strName.substring ↩
        (0, "data_control_id".length) == "data_control_id") {
        intCol += 1;
        // add error checking commands
        switch (intCol) {
        case 1:  // validation for first text input
          if (curForm.elements[i].value ↩
            comparison_operator value) {
            args.IsValid = false;
            alert("error_message");
          }
          break;
        case 2:  // validation for second text input
          if (curForm.elements[i].value ↩
            comparison_operator value) {
            args.IsValid = false;
            alert("error_message");
          }
          break;
        additional_cases
      }
      // return when first error found
      if (args.IsValid == false) {
        curForm.elements[i].select();
        return;
} } } } }
//-->
</script>
```

**Figure 10-32**   Template for the JavaScript Validate function to validate DataGrid or
DataList inputs

To use the Validate function, you modify the shaded commands in Figure 10-32. The first shaded code highlights the command that identifies the *data_control_id*, which is the (ID) property value of the DataList or DataGrid control you are validating. For example, if you are validating the values that the user enters in the dgInventory

DataGrid control when he or she opens an item for editing, you would specify the *data_control_id* value as *dgInventory*.

The function contains a **switch** decision control structure that validates the values in each text input when the user opens the item for editing. The **switch** decision control structure evaluates the text input's position within the form, and the corresponding **if** decision control structure evaluates the user input value in the text input.

Figure 10-33 shows the layout of the Inventory Web form when a user opens an item for editing. The user can edit the selection's Size, Color, Price, and Quantity on Hand field values. In the JavaScript validation function, each case number value in the **switch** decision control structure corresponds to the input's position on the form. The first input is the Size input, so Case 1 validates the Size input value. The second input is the Color input, so Case 2 validates the Color input value. Case 3 validates the Price input, and Case 4 validates the Quantity on Hand input.

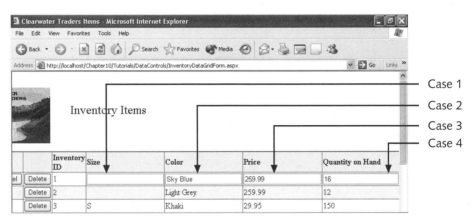

**Figure 10-33**    Inventory Web form with an item opened for editing

In the **if** decision control structure in Figure 10-32, the shaded *comparison_operator* represents the type of validation comparison, such as equals (=), greater than (>), less than (<), and so forth. The *value* specifies the value to which the input is compared. For example, suppose you want to validate that the Price input value is not an empty string literal. You would use the equals sign (=) as the *comparison_operator* and an empty string literal (" ")as the *value*. The *error_message* is the message that appears to the user if he or she enters an invalid input.

You would use the following code to create the case that confirms that the Quantity on Hand value is not an empty string literal in the JavaScript Validate function:

```
Case 4:
  if (curForm.elements[i].value = "") {
    args.IsValid = false;
  alert("Please enter the Quantity on Hand");
  }
break;
```

Note that the case number for the Quantity on Hand input is 4, because the Quantity on Hand input is in the fourth column in the DataGrid. If you want to omit a validation function for a specific item, you simply omit that case number. For example, if you do not need to validate the Size input value, which is form input number 1, the `switch` decision control structure will not contain a section for Case 1.

Now you will create and configure a CustomValidator validation control on the Inventory Web form. You will specify that the validation control's ClientValidationFunction property value is Validate, which is the name of the custom JavaScript function in Figure 10-32.

To add the CustomValidator validation control to the form:

1. Select the **InventoryDataGridForm.aspx** tab to open the form in Design view, then reposition the InventoryItems and lblMessage label controls as shown in Figure 10-34.

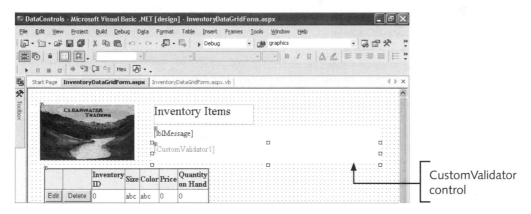

**Figure 10-34**    Creating the CustomValidator control

2. Open the Toolbox, make sure that the Web Forms tab is selected, scroll down in the Toolbox, then select the **CustomValidator** tool. Draw the CustomValidator control on the Web form as shown in Figure 10-34.

3. Right-click the new **CustomValidator** control, click **Properties** to open the Properties window, and change the ClientValidationFunction property value to **Validate**. Delete the ErrorMessage property value, select another property to apply the changes, then close the Properties window.

Now you will add the JavaScript function to your form. You will copy the function template from the ClientValidation.txt file that is in the Chapter10 folder on your Data Disk, then paste the template into the Web form in HTML view. Then you will modify the function so it works correctly in your form. You will validate that the Price text input value is greater than 0 and that the Quantity on Hand input value is not an empty string literal.

To add the JavaScript Validate function to your form:

1. In Visual Studio .NET, click **File** on the menu bar, point to **Open**, click **File**, navigate to the Chapter10 folder on your Data Disk, select **ClientValidation.txt**, then click **Open**. The validation function template appears in the Visual Studio.Net text editor.

2. Copy all of the code in ClientValidation.txt, then close the ClientValidation.txt window.

3. With the InventoryDataGridForm.aspx Web form open in Design view, select the **HTML** tab to open the form in HTML view. Place the insertion point just before the closing **</head>** tag, press **Enter** to create a new blank line, then paste the copied function text onto the new blank line.

4. Modify the function as shown in the shaded commands in Figure 10-35.

```
function Validate(source, args) {
  args.IsValid = true;
  var intCol = 0;
  var strName = new String();
  var curForm = document.Form1;
  for (i=0; i<curForm.elements.length; i++) {
    if (curForm.elements[i].type == "text") {
      strName = curForm.elements[i].name;
      if (strName.substring
        (0, "dgInventory".length) == "dgInventory") {
        intCol += 1;
        // add error checking commands
        switch (intCol) {
        case 3:  // validation for Price text input
           if (curForm.elements[i].value <= 0) {
             args.IsValid = false;
             alert("Please enter a value greater than 0 for price");
           }
           break;
        case 4:  // validation for QOH text input
           if (curForm.elements[i].value == "") {
             args.IsValid = false;
             alert("Please enter a value for quantity on hand");
           }
           break;
        }

        // return when first error found
        if (args.IsValid == false) {
          curForm.elements[i].select();
          return;
        }
} } } } }
```

**Figure 10-35**   Commands to validate Price and Quantity on Hand inputs

5. Click the **Start** button ▶ to run the project. Click **Edit** beside Inventory ID 1, change the *Price* field value to **–3**, then click **Update**. An alert appears advising you to enter a price value greater than 0. Click **OK**.

6. Change the *Price* field value back to **269.99**, delete the *Quantity on Hand* field value, then click **Update**. An alert appears advising you to enter a value for quantity on hand. Click **OK**.

7. Type **16** in the *Quantity on Hand* field, then click **Update**. A message appears stating "Record successfully updated."

8. Close Internet Explorer.

## Creating a Server-Side Validation Function to Validate DataList and DataGrid Inputs

Recall that when you create a CustomValidator control, you should add a server-side validation function as a backup in case the user's browser does not support JavaScript. To implement the server-side validation function, you will create a function named ValidEntries in the form code behind file and add the command to call the function to the UpdateCommand event handler. The function receives as parameters the inputs to validate and evaluates whether the inputs are valid. If the inputs are valid, the function returns the value True to the UpdateCommand event handler, which then executes the UPDATE action query. If the inputs are not valid, the function returns the value False, and the UpdateCommand event handler does not execute the UPDATE action query.

Now you will add the server-side validation function that confirms that the Price value is greater than 0, and that the Quantity on Hand value is not an empty string literal. You will also add to the UpdateCommand event handler the command to call the function. Then you will disable the client-side validation function you created in the preceding set of steps, because the client-side validation takes precedence over the server-side validation. Then you will run the form and test the server-side validation function.

To add and test the server-side validation function:

1. Select the **InventoryDataGridForm.aspx.vb** tab to open the code behind file, and scroll down in the Code editor.

2. Just before the **End Class** command at the end of the file, add the commands shown in Figure 10-36 to create the ValidEntries function.

3. Scroll up to the UpdateCommand event handler, then add the commands to call the ValidEntries function by adding the shaded commands shown in Figure 10-37.

**10**

```
Private Function ValidEntries(ByVal strPrice As String, _
                            ByVal strQOH As String) As Boolean
    ValidEntries = False
    If strPrice <= 0 Then
        lblMessage.Text = "Please enter a price value greater than 0"
    ElseIf strQOH = "" Then
        lblMessage.Text = "Please enter a value for quantity on hand"
    Else
        ValidEntries = True
    End If
End Function
```

**Figure 10-36**    Commands to create the server-side validation function

```
Private Sub dgInventory_UpdateCommand(ByVal source As Object, ⮐
ByVal e As System.Web.UI.WebControls.DataGridCommandEventArgs) ⮐
Handles dgInventory.UpdateCommand
    Dim sqlCommand As New OleDb.OleDbCommand()
    sqlCommand.Connection = OleDbConnection1
    Dim intInvID As Integer = ⮐
        dgInventory.DataKeys.Item(e.Item.ItemIndex)
    Dim txtSize As TextBox = e.Item.Cells(3).Controls(0)
    Dim txtColor As TextBox = e.Item.Cells(4).Controls(0)
    Dim txtPrice As TextBox = e.Item.Cells(5).Controls(0)
    Dim txtQOH As TextBox = e.Item.Cells(6).Controls(0)
    If ValidEntries(txtPrice.Text, txtQOH.Text) = True Then
        Dim strReplacedColor As String = ⮐
            Replace(txtColor.Text, "'", "''")
        Dim strReplacedSize As String = ⮐
            Replace(txtSize.Text, "'", "''")
        sqlCommand.CommandText = "UPDATE INVENTORY " & _
            "SET INV_SIZE = '" & strReplacedSize & _
            "', COLOR = '" & strReplacedColor & _
            "', INV_PRICE = " & txtPrice.Text & _
            ", INV_QOH = " & txtQOH.Text & _
            " WHERE INV_ID = " & intInvID
        sqlCommand.Connection.Open()
        Try
            sqlCommand.ExecuteNonQuery()
            lblMessage.Text = "Record successfully updated"
        Catch
            lblMessage.Text = "Query error: " & Err.Description
        End Try
        sqlCommand.Connection.Close()
        dgInventory.EditItemIndex = -1
        FillAndBind()
    End If
End Sub
```

**Figure 10-37**    Commands to call the server-side validation function

4. Select the **InventoryDataGridForm.aspx** tab, select the **Design** tab to open the form in Design view, right-click the **[CustomValidator1]** control, click **Properties**, set the Enabled property value to **False**, select another property to apply the change, then close the Properties Window.

5. Click the **Start** button ▶ to run the project. Click **Edit** beside Inventory ID 1, change the *Price* field value to **-3**, then click **Update**. The CustomValidator control displays a message advising you to enter a price value greater than 0.

6. Change the *Price* field value back to **269.99**, delete the *Quantity on Hand* field value, then click **Update**. The CustomValidator control displays the message advising you to enter a value for quantity on hand.

7. Type **16** in the *Quantity on Hand* field, then click **Update**. The message "Record successfully updated" appears.

8. Close Internet Explorer. Because you are finished working with the InventoryDataGridForm.aspx Web form, close all open windows in the Browser Window.

---

## CREATING A WEB FORM TO INSERT NEW DATA VALUES

So far, you have learned how to create Web forms to display, update, and delete data values. Another important database-driven Web site task is to allow users to insert new data records. For example, when a Clearwater Traders customer purchases merchandise, a Web form must insert into the CUSTOMER table values that provide personal information about the customer. A different Web form must insert values into the ORDERS and ORDER_LINE tables to provide information about the purchase.

A Web form that inserts data values displays TextBox rich server controls for each table column in which the user enters a data value and a Button control that the user clicks to submit the new values. The Button's click event handler contains the commands that insert the new data values into the database. To learn how to insert new data values, you will use the Clearwater Traders Customer Information Web form shown in Figure 10-38.

This Web form contains TextBox rich server controls in which the user enters personal information that will be stored in the CUSTOMER table in the Clearwater Traders database. The form also contains validation server controls to confirm that the user enters a value in the *Last Name* TextBox and enters his or her birth date using the correct date format. In addition, the form contains a Message Label that displays form status messages. Now you will add this Web form to the DataControls project.

To add the Customer Information form to the project:

1. Switch to Windows Explorer, and copy **CustomerInfoForm.aspx** and **CustomerInfoForm.aspx.vb** from the Chapter10 folder on your Data Disk to the Chapter10\Tutorials\DataControls folder on your Solution Disk.

2. Switch back to Visual Studio .NET, add the **CustomerInfoForm.aspx** and **CustomerInfoForm.aspx.vb** files to the DataControls project, then set the CustomerInfoForm.aspx node as the project Start Page.

3. Make sure that the *CustomerInfoForm.aspx* node is selected in the Solution Explorer project tree, then click the **View Designer** button to open the form in Design view.

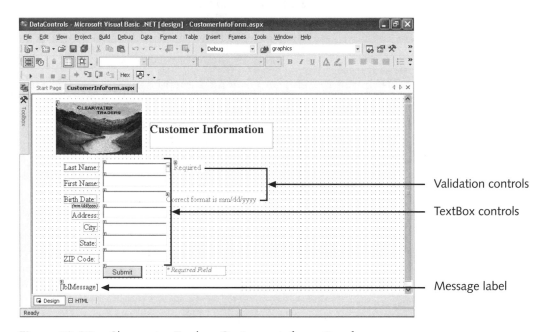

**Figure 10-38**    Clearwater Traders Customer Information form

To insert into the database the data values that the user enters in the form TextBox controls, the Submit button's event handler must contain commands that create a new data connection and an OleDbCommand object. Next, the event handler creates the SQL INSERT action query, which references the TextBox values on the form. Finally, the event handler executes the query. The following subsections describe these steps.

## Creating the Data Connection and OleDbCommand Object

Earlier in the chapter you learned how to write program commands to create and configure a data connection and an OleDbCommand object. You will use the same commands to create a data connection and an OleDbCommand object in the Customer Information form's Submit button event handler. To create the data connection, you will copy the command you used to create the data connection in the ItemsForm.aspx.vb file that you created earlier in the chapter. By copying an existing data connection, you ensure that the connect string parameters are correct.

To create the data connection and OleDbCommand object:

1. In the Solution Explorer, select the **ItemsForm.aspx** node, then click the **View Code** button [≡] to open the form's code behind file.

2. Copy the command in the Declarations block that creates the connCW data connection. (This command begins with the code `Private connCW As New`.) Then close the ItemsForm.aspx.vb window in the Browser Window.

3. In the Solution Explorer, select the **CustomerInfoForm.aspx** node if necessary, then click the **View Code** button [≡] to open this form's code behind file.

4. Place the insertion point at the end of the last command in the Declarations block, press **Enter** to create a new blank line, then paste the copied command onto the new blank line.

5. In the CustomerInfoForm.aspx.vb code behind file, add the following commands to the btnSubmit_Click event handler template to create and configure the new OleDbCommand object:

```
Dim sqlCommand As New OleDb.OleDbCommand()
sqlCommand.Connection = connCW
```

6. Save the file.

## Creating the SQL INSERT Action Query

Recall that the general format of the INSERT action query is as follows:

```
INSERT INTO tablename (column1_name, column2_name, …)
VALUES (column1_value, column2_value, …)
```

In the SQL query that you will create to insert values from the Customer Information form into the CUSTOMER table, you will insert values for the C_ID, C_LAST, C_FIRST, C_BIRTHDATE, C_ADDRESS, C_CITY, C_STATE, and C_ZIP columns. Recall from Chapter 9 that the C_ID field is a surrogate key, so the database will automatically generate the column value. If you are using an Oracle9i database, you will use the C_ID_SEQUENCE sequence you created in Chapter 9 to generate the C_ID value. If you are using an Access database, the C_ID column has the AutoNumber data type, so you will omit the C_ID column in the INSERT action query, and the Access DBMS will automatically insert the value.

All of the column fields except C_ID and C_BIRTHDATE are text strings, so the query will enclose the values in single quotation marks. The C_BIRTHDATE column has the date data type, so Oracle9i users will use the TO_DATE function to convert the text representation of the date to a date data type. Access users will enclose the date value in pound signs (#). Now you will add the command to create the INSERT action query.

10

To add the command to create the INSERT action query:

1. In the CustomerInfoForm.aspx.vb code behind file, add the command to the btnSubmit_Click event handler just before the **End Sub** command.

    *If you are using an Oracle9i database*, add the following command:

    ```
    sqlCommand.CommandText = "INSERT INTO CUSTOMER " & _
    "(C_ID, C_LAST, C_FIRST, C_BIRTHDATE, C_ADDRESS, " & _
    "C_CITY, C_STATE, C_ZIP) VALUES " & _
    "(C_ID_SEQUENCE.NEXTVAL, '" & txtLast.Text & _
    "', '" & txtFirst.Text & "', TO_DATE('" & _
    txtBirthDate.Text & "', 'MM/DD/YYYY'), '" & _
    txtAddress.Text & "', '" & txtCity.Text & _
    "', '" & txtState.Text & "', '" & txtZip.Text & "')"
    ```

    *If you are using an Access database, add the following command:*

    ```
    sqlCommand.CommandText = "INSERT INTO CUSTOMER " & _
    "(C_LAST, C_FIRST, C_BIRTHDATE, C_ADDRESS, " & _
    "C_CITY, C_STATE, C_ZIP) VALUES ('" & txtLast.Text & _
    "', '" & txtFirst.Text & "', #" & txtBirthDate.Text & _
    "#, '" & txtAddress.Text & "', '" & txtCity.Text & _
    "', '" & txtState.Text & "', '" & txtZip.Text & "')"
    ```

2. Save the file.

## Executing the Query

To execute the INSERT query, you will add a command to open the data connection, add commands to call the ExecuteNonQuery method within a **Try/Catch/End Try** block, then display the confirmation or error message in the form's Message Label. You will also add the command to close the data connection. Then you will run the form and test the event handler. To learn how to debug the query using the Query form, you will set a breakpoint on the command that creates the SQL INSERT query and view the command syntax in a watch.

To add the commands to execute the query, debug the query, and then run the form:

1. Add the shaded commands in Figure 10-39 to the btnSubmit_Click event handler.

Figure 10-39 shows the code for the completed btnSubmit_Click event handler for processing an INSERT action query using an Oracle9i database. The Access INSERT action query syntax is similar, except that it does not insert the C_ID column value because Access retrieves the value using an AutoNumber field, and the Access action query inserts the date value by enclosing the date text string in pound signs (#).

```
Private Sub btnSubmit_Click(ByVal sender As System.Object, ↵
ByVal e As System.EventArgs) Handles btnSubmit.Click
   Dim sqlCommand As New OleDb.OleDbCommand()
   sqlCommand.Connection = connCW
   sqlCommand.CommandText = "INSERT INTO CUSTOMER " & _
      "(C_ID, C_LAST, C_FIRST, C_BIRTHDATE, C_ADDRESS, " & _
      "C_CITY, C_STATE, C_ZIP) VALUES " & _
      "(C_ID_SEQUENCE.NEXTVAL, '" & txtLast.Text & _
      "', '" & txtFirst.Text & "', TO_DATE('" & _
      txtBirthDate.Text & "', 'MM/DD/YYYY'), '" & _
      txtAddress.Text & "', '" & txtCity.Text & _
      "', '" & txtState.Text & "', '" & _
      txtZip.Text & "')"
   sqlCommand.Connection.Open()
   Try
      sqlCommand.ExecuteNonQuery()
      lblMessage.Text = "Record successfully inserted"
   Catch
      lblMessage.Text = "Insert error: " & Err.Description
   End Try
   sqlCommand.Connection.Close()
End Sub
```

**Figure 10-39**    Completed code for processing an INSERT action query

2. To view and debug the INSERT action query during form execution, set a breakpoint on the following command:

   `sqlCommand.Connection.Open()`

3. Click the **Start** button ▶ to run the form. The form appears in Internet Explorer.

4. Type **Chen** in the *Last Name* field, **Emily** in the *First Name* field, **05/15/1980** in the *Birth Date* field, **323 Parker Place** in the *Address* field, **Troy** in the *City* field, **NY** in the *State* field, **12234** in the *ZIP Code* field, then click **Submit**.

5. The Debugger window opens, and the execution arrow appears on the command with the breakpoint. To view the value of the INSERT action query, highlight the text `sqlCommand.CommandText` in the command just before the breakpoint, then place the mouse pointer on the highlighted text. The INSERT action query text appears in a ScreenTip. Examine the action query text, and confirm that the query is formed correctly.

6. Click the **Continue** button ▶ to resume execution. The Message Label displays the message "Record successfully inserted."

If an error message appears, close Internet Explorer, set a breakpoint on the command immediately after the command that creates the SQL query, then view the SQL query and determine whether you made a syntax error. If you cannot find the error, create a watch on the sqlCommand.CommandText expression, copy the value of the expression with the data values inserted from the form, run the Query form, then paste the copied query into the *Enter query* TextBox and run the query. Then use the Query form error messages to help debug the query.

 If you are using an Oracle9*i* database and an error message appears stating that the C_ID_SEQUENCE does not exist, close Internet Explorer. In the Visual Studio .NET Solution Explorer, set the QueryForm.aspx node as the project Start Page, run the project, then create the sequence by typing the following command in the *Enter query* field on the Query form: CREATE SEQUENCE C_ID_SEQUENCE START WITH 10.

7. Close Internet Explorer, then clear the breakpoint.

## Creating a Data Bound List Control

Often Web forms that allow users to enter data values provide **pick lists**, which are lists that display allowable values for selections. For example, you often select the abbreviation for your state of residence from a pick list. Using pick lists to allow users to select data entry values ensures that selected values are valid because only valid values appear on the list. In addition, pick lists make data entry easier for users because users may not know the required value.

To create a pick list, you can create a **data bound List control**, which is a rich server control that displays values from a data source, such as a database, in a list format. To create a data bound List control, you create the List control on the Web form using any of the list controls, such as a ListBox, DropDownList, or RadioButtonList. You create a data adapter that retrieves the data values that appear in the list and a data set that stores the retrieved values. Then you add commands that bind the list to the data set.

Now you will add a data bound list to the Customer Information form that allows users to select their state of residence from a list rather than typing the value in the *State* TextBox control. You will create a DropDownList control that will contain values from the STATE table in the Clearwater Traders database (see Figure 9-10). The STATE table stores state names in the S_NAME column and their associated two-character abbreviations in the S_ABBREVIATION column. When the user opens the list, the list will display the state names. When the user selects a state name, the control will display the selection. When the SQL command inserts the values into the database, the SQL command will insert the associated two-character state abbreviation.

First you will delete the existing *State* TextBox control and create the DropDownList control on the Web form in its place. Then you will add the commands to create a new data adapter and data set to retrieve and store the retrieved state names and abbreviations. These commands will appear in the Page_Load procedure in an `If Not IsPostback` decision structure so they execute only for first-time requests.

To create the DropDownList control, data adapter, and data set:

1. Select the **CustomerInfoForm.aspx** tab to view the form in Design view, select the **State** TextBox control, then press **Delete** to delete the *State* TextBox control.

2. Open the Toolbox, make sure that the Web Forms tab is selected, then select the **DropDownList** tool and create a new DropDownList control on the right edge of the State Label, as shown in Figure 10-40.

3. Right-click the new **DropDownList** control, click **Properties** to open the Properties Window, change the (ID) property value to **lstState**, select another property to apply the change, then close the Properties Window. (Note that in the (ID) value, "lst" begins with a lowercase letter *L* and denotes that the control is a list.)

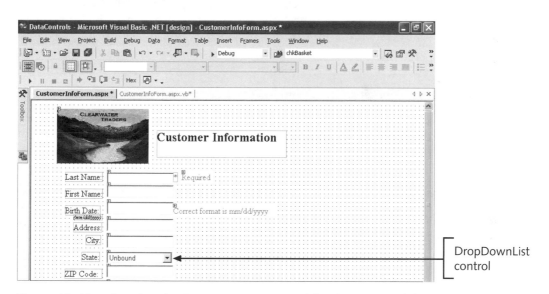

**Figure 10-40**    Creating the DropDownList control for the State pick list

4. Select the **CustomerInfoForm.aspx.vb** tab to open the form's code behind file, then add the following commands to the Page_Load procedure to create a new data adapter and data set, then fill the data set:

```
If Not IsPostBack Then
    Dim daState As New OleDb.OleDbDataAdapter ↵
    ("SELECT S_NAME, S_ABBREVIATION " & _
    "FROM STATE ORDER BY S_NAME", connCW)
    Dim dsState As New DataSet()
    daState.Fill(dsState, "STATE")
End If
```

Currently the btnSubmit_Click event handler references the txtState TextBox control that you deleted, so the reference is flagged as an error. You will change this reference a little later.

5. Save the file.

To bind the data set to the DropDownList control, you assign the data set as the control's DataSource property, and the STATE table within the data set as the control's DataMember property. Recall from Chapter 8 that each item in a DropDownList control has a Text property and a Value property. The Text property defines the value that appears in the list, and the Value property defines an associated value. You will assign the DropDownList control's DataTextField value to the S_NAME column in the data table, so the list displays the state names. You will assign the control's DataValueField value to the S_ABBREVIATION column. And, you will call the DataBind method to bind the retrieved values to the DropDownList control. You will also change the reference to the txtState TextBox in the INSERT action query to the SelectedItem.Value property of the DropDownList control. Then you will run the form, view the pick list values, and insert another record.

To bind the data set to the DropDownList control and run the form:

1. In the CustomerInfoForm.aspx.vb code behind file, add the shaded commands to the Page_Load procedure as shown in Figure 10-41 to bind the data set to the control.

```
Private Sub Page_Load(ByVal sender As System.Object, ↵
ByVal e As System.EventArgs) Handles MyBase.Load
   If Not IsPostBack Then
      Dim daState As New OleDb.OleDbDataAdapter _
      ("SELECT S_NAME, S_ABBREVIATION FROM STATE " & _
      "ORDER BY S_NAME", connCW)
      Dim dsState As New DataSet()
      daState.Fill(dsState, "STATE")
      lstState.DataSource = dsState
      lstState.DataMember = "STATE"
      lstState.DataTextField = "S_NAME"
      lstState.DataValueField = "S_ABBREVIATION"
      lstState.DataBind()
   End If
End Sub
```

**Figure 10-41**   Commands to bind the DropDownList control to the data set

2. In the command that creates the INSERT action query, delete **txtState.Text**, then replace it with **lstState.SelectedItem.Value**.

If you are using an Oracle9*i* database, the reference to txtState.Text will appear in the next-to-last line of the command that creates the INSERT query. If you are using an Access database, the reference will appear in the last line of the command that creates the query.)

3. Click the **Start** button ▶ to run the form.

4. Type **Randall** in the *Last Name* field, **Patrick** in the *First Name* field, **09/01/1975** in the *Birth Date* field, **1444 Timberlake Drive** in the *Address* field, and **Las Cruces** in the *City* field. Select **New Mexico** in the *State* list, type **85778** in the *ZIP Code* field, then click **Submit**.

5. The message "Record successfully inserted" appears in the Message Label. Close Internet Explorer.

6. Because you are finished working with the CustomerInfoForm.aspx form, close all open windows in the Browser Window.

## DISPLAYING MASTER-DETAIL DATA ON A WEB FORM

10

In a database, a record in one table may reference multiple related records in another table using a one-to-many relationship, which is also called a master-detail relationship. In a **master-detail relationship**, a master record in one table has many related detail records in another table. For example, in the Clearwater Traders database, a master record in the CUSTOMER table may have many associated, or detail, order records in the ORDERS table. You can create a Web form that displays master-detail data by displaying the master and detail records in two related lists. When the user selects an item in the master list, the form automatically displays the selected item's detail records in the detail list.

To learn how to display master-detail data on a Web form, you will create the Web form in Figure 10-42. This form allows Clearwater Traders customers to select a merchandise category, such as "Children's Clothing," then view descriptions and photographs of the category's merchandise items. In this form, the CATEGORY table provides the master records, and the ITEM table provides the detail records. A specific category can describe multiple items, and each item belongs to a specific category.

The master values will appear in a data bound DropDownList control that displays the CATEGORY_DESC (category description) column values in the CATEGORY table. The detail values will appear in a DataGrid control, which shows the ITEM table's ITEM_DESC (item description) column value and displays the graphic image file specified by the ITEM_IMAGE column. When the form first opens, the detail list does not appear. The detail list appears only after the user selects an item in the master list.

Now you will create a Web form named MasterDetailForm.aspx that will display the master-detail data. You will copy the connCW data connection from the ItemsForm.aspx Web form and paste it into the new form.

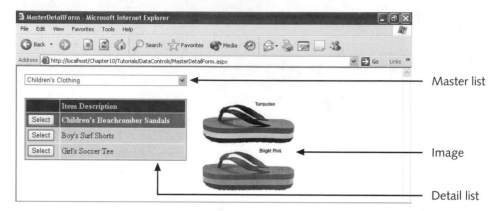

**Figure 10-42** Web form that displays master-detail data

To create the Web form and copy the data connection:

1. Open the Solution Explorer if necessary, right-click the **DataControls** node, point to **Add**, then click **Add Web Form**. Change the *Name* field value to **MasterDetailForm.aspx**, then click **Open**.

2. Right-click the **MasterDetailForm.aspx** node in the project tree, then click **Set As Start Page**.

3. In the Solution Explorer, select the **ItemsForm.aspx** node, then click the **View Code** button 📄 to open the form's code behind file.

4. Copy the command in the Declarations block that creates the connCW data connection. (This command begins with the code `Private connCW As New`.) Then close the ItemsForm.aspx.vb window in the Browser Window.

5. In the Solution Explorer, select the **MasterDetailForm.aspx** node if necessary, then click the **View Code** button 📄 to open the form's code behind file.

6. Place the insertion point at the end of the last command in the Declarations block, press **Enter** to create a new blank line, then paste the copied command onto the new blank line.

7. Save the file.

Next you will create a data bound DropDownList control to display the master items, which are the category description values. Every list control has an **AutoPostBack** property that specifies whether the list raises the postback event when the user selects a list item. By default, the AutoPostBack value is set to False, and the form is not posted back to the Web server when the user selects a list item. However, to display the detail items, a server-side event handler must execute to configure the detail list. Therefore, you will configure the new DropDownList so its AutoPostBack property is True. You will also add commands to the Page_Load procedure to create a data adapter and data set to retrieve and store the list values and to bind the data set to the control. (These are similar to the commands you used earlier to create these data components.) Then you will run the form and test the data bound DropDownList control.

To create and test the data bound DropDownList control:

1. Select the **MasterDetailForm.aspx** tab to view the form in Design view, open the Toolbox, make sure that the Web Forms tab is selected, then select the **DropDownList** tool and create a new DropDownList control to represent the master list shown in Figure 10-42.

2. Right-click the new **DropDownList** control, click **Properties** to open the Properties Window, and change the (ID) property value to **lstCategory**. (Note that the (ID) value begins with a lowercase letter *L*.) Change the AutoPostBack property value to **True**, select another property to apply the changes, then close the Properties Window.

3. Select the **MasterDetailForm.aspx.vb** tab to open the form's code behind file, delete the comment text in the Page_Load procedure, then add the shaded commands in Figure 10-43 to the Page_Load procedure to create the data bound DropDownList control.

```
Private Sub Page_Load(ByVal sender As System.Object,  ↵
ByVal e As System.EventArgs) Handles MyBase.Load
    Dim daCategory As New OleDb.OleDbDataAdapter _
        ("SELECT CAT_ID, CAT_DESC FROM CATEGORY " & _
        "ORDER BY CAT_DESC", connCW)
    Dim dsCategory As New DataSet()
    If Not IsPostBack Then
        daCategory.Fill(dsCategory, "CATEGORY")
        lstCategory.DataSource = dsCategory
        lstCategory.DataMember = "CATEGORY"
        lstCategory.DataTextField = "CAT_DESC"
        lstCategory.DataValueField = "CAT_ID"
        lstCategory.DataBind()
    End If
End Sub
```

**Figure 10-43**    Commands to create the data bound DropDownList control

4. Click the **Start** button ▶ to run the form. When the form appears in Internet Explorer, open the list and confirm that the item description data values appear.

5. Close Internet Explorer.

The next step is to create the DataGrid control that displays the detail data. You must first create the data adapter and data set. Recall that when you display data in a DataGrid control, you use the OleDbDataAdapter Configuration Wizard to create the data adapter. You will specify that the adapter retrieves all of the records in the ITEM table. Then you will generate the data set.

To create the data adapter and generate the data set:

1. Select the **MasterDetailForm.aspx** tab to open the form in Design view, open the Toolbox, select the **Data** tab, then double-click **OleDbDataAdapter**. The OleDbDataAdapter Configuration Wizard opens. Click **Next**.

2. Select the correct data connection, then click **Next**.

   *If you are using an Oracle9i database*, select the **ORCL.CWUSER** connection.

   *If you are using an Access database*, select the **ACCESS.A:\Chapter10\ Tutorials\DataControls\Clearwater.mdb** connection.

3. Make sure that the *Use SQL statements* option button is selected, then click **Next**.

4. Type **SELECT * FROM ITEM** in the *What data should the data adapter load into the dataset* field.

5. Click **Advanced Options**, clear the **Generate Insert, Update and Delete statements** check box, click **OK**, click **Next**, then click **Finish**. The new data adapter and the data connection appear in the component tray.

6. Right-click **OleDbDataAdapter1** in the component tray and click **Properties**. Change the (Name) property value to **daItems**, select another property to apply the change, then close the Properties Window.

7. Right-click **daItems** in the component tray, then click **Generate Dataset**. Select the **New** option button, change the *New* field value to **dsItems**, then click **OK**. The DsItems1 data set appears in the component tray. (Recall that the Generate Dataset dialog box always appends a number after the data set name.)

8. Save the form.

Next you will create and configure the DataGrid control. You will create a new DataGrid on the Web form, then configure its properties. You will set its Visible property to False so the DataGrid does not appear when the form first opens.

To create and configure the DataGrid control:

1. In the MasterDetailForm.aspx form in Design view, open the Toolbox, select the **Web Forms** tab, select the **DataGrid** tool, then draw a DataGrid control to represent the detail list as shown in Figure 10-42.

2. Right-click the new **DataGrid** control, then click **Properties.** Change the (ID) property value to **dgItems**, the Height property value to **55px**, and the Visible property value to **False**. Select another property to apply the changes, then close the Properties Window.

3. Right-click the **DataGrid** control, then click **Property Builder**. Make sure that the General tab is selected, then open the **DataSource** list and select **DsItems1**, open the **DataMember** list and select **ITEM**, and open the **Data key field** list and select **ITEM_ID**.

4. Select the **Columns** tab and clear the **Create columns automatically at run time** check box. Then select **ITEM_DESC** in the *Available columns* list, and click the **Add** button ⟩ to move the ITEM_DESC selection to the *Selected columns* list. Change the *Header* text field value to **Item Description**.

5. Select **ITEM_IMAGE** in the *Available columns* list, then click the **Add** button ⟩ to move the selection to the *Selected columns* list. Because this column will not actually appear in the data grid, but you will reference it to display the image, clear the **Visible** check box. Then click **OK** to close the dgItems Properties dialog box.

6. Save the form.

You have created the master list and the detail list, but they don't yet work together. Currently, the DataGrid displays all of the values in the ITEM table, but it should display only the items for the selected category. To implement the master-detail linkage, you create an event handler for the master list's SelectedIndexChanged event. When the user selects a different list item, the event handler executes and refreshes the values that appear in the detail list.

Now you will create a SelectedIndexChanged event handler for the lstCategory DropDownList control. This event handler will contain a command that modifies the daItems data adapter's SelectCommand.CommandText property. The new command uses the selected category's SelectedItem.Value property, which is the CAT_ID value, as a search value. The remaining event handler commands refill the data adapter, rebind the DataGrid control to the retrieved data values, and set the Visible property of the DataGrid control to True so the DataGrid appears on the Web form. After you create the event handler, you will run the form and test the master-detail link.

To implement and test the master-detail link:

1. In the MasterDetailForm.aspx form in Design view, double-click the **DropDownList** control. The lstCategory_SelectedIndexChanged event handler template appears in the Code editor.

2. Add the shaded commands in Figure 10-44 to implement the master-detail link.

3. Click the **Start** button ▶ to run the form. The Category DropDownList control appears on the Web form.

4. Open the **Category** list and select **Women's Clothing**. The descriptions for the items in the Women's Clothing category appear in the detail DataGrid control.

```
Private Sub lstCategory_SelectedIndexChanged(ByVal sender ↵
As System.Object, ByVal e As System.EventArgs) Handles ↵
lstCategory.SelectedIndexChanged
    daItems.SelectCommand.CommandText = "SELECT * FROM ITEM " & _
        "WHERE CAT_ID = " & lstCategory.SelectedItem.Value
    daItems.Fill(DsItems1, "ITEM")
    dgItems.DataBind()
    dgItems.Visible = True
End Sub
```

**Figure 10-44**    Commands to create the master list's SelectedIndexChanged event handler

5. Open the **Category** list again and select **Children's Clothing**. The descriptions for the items in the Children's Clothing category appear in the detail DataGrid control.

6. Close Internet Explorer.

You now know the basic steps for making a Web form that displays a master-detail data relationship. Next you will enhance the form so it looks like Figure 10-42. You will format the DataGrid control using the AutoFormat feature, which automatically applies a predefined format to the grid headings and rows, and add the Select buttons so the user can select an individual item and display its image in the Image control. You will also add an Image control to the form. The Image control will not appear when the form first opens, so you will set its Visible property to False.

To format the DataGrid control and add the Select buttons and Image control:

1. Select the **MasterDetailForm.aspx** tab to open the Web form in Design view, right-click the **DataGrid** control, then click **Auto Format**. The Auto Format window opens.

2. Select **Professional 3** in the *Select a scheme* list. A template for the formatting scheme appears in the Preview pane, showing the proposed format of the heading, normal rows, a selected row, and the footer. Click **OK** to apply the format.

3. Right-click the **DataGrid** control, then click **Property Builder**. Select the **Columns** tab, scroll down in the *Available columns* list, open the **Button Column** node, click **Select**, then click the **Add** button `>` to add the Select button to the *Selected columns* list.

4. Make sure that *Select* is selected in the *Selected columns* list, then click the **Up arrow** two times to move Select so it is the first list item. Open the **Button type** list, select **PushButton**, then click **OK** to close the dgItems Properties dialog box.

5. Open the Toolbox, make sure that the Web Forms tab is selected, select the **Image** tool, then create the Image control as shown in Figure 10-45.

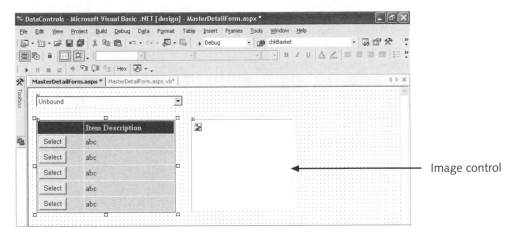

**Figure 10-45** Adding the Image control

6. Right-click the new **Image** control, click **Properties**, change the Image's (ID) property value to **imgItem** and its Visible property to **False**, select another property to apply the changes, then close the Properties Window.

7. Save the form.

To display the image file in the Image control, you will create a SelectedIndexChanged event handler for the DataGrid. This event handler contains a command to assign the Image control's ImageUrl property value as the text that appears in the ITEM_IMAGE column, and contains a second command to set the Image control's Visible property to True. First you will copy the required image files to the Chapter10\Tutorials\ DataControls folder on your Solution Disk. Then you will add a command to the DropDownList's SelectedIndexChanged event handler to set the Image Control's Visible property to False, so that when the user selects a new category during postback processing, an image does not appear until the user selects a specific item within the category. Then you will create the event handler and run the form.

To copy the image files, then create and test the event handler:

1. Switch to Windows Explorer and copy the following seven files from the Chapter10 folder on your Data Disk to the Chapter10\Tutorials\DataControls folder on your Solution Disk: **fleece.jpg**, **girlstee.jpg**, **parka.jpg**, **sandals.jpg**, **shorts**, **jpg**, **surfshorts.jpg**, and **tents.jpg**.

2. Switch back to Visual Studio .NET and select the **MasterDetailForm.aspx.vb** tab to open the code behind file. Scroll down to the lstCategory_SelectedIndex Changed event handler and add the following command as the last command in the event handler, just before the **End Sub** command:

```
imgItem.Visible = False
```

3. Open the **Class** list and select **dgItems**, then open the **Method** list and select **SelectedIndexChanged** to create the SelectedIndexChanged event handler template for the DataGrid. Add the following commands to the event handler to display the image:

```
imgItem.ImageUrl = ⤶
dgItems.Items(dgItems.SelectedIndex).Cells(2).Text
imgItem.Visible = True
```

Recall that to reference an item in a DataGrid control, you reference the Cells collection. Because the ITEM_IMAGE column is the third column in the collection, its index in the Cells collection is 2.

4. Click the **Start** button ▶ to run the form. Open the **Category** list and select **Women's Clothing**. The Women's Clothing item descriptions appear in the DataGrid.

5. Click **Select** beside Women's Hiking Shorts. The item's image appears in the Image control.

6. Click **Select** beside Women's Fleece Pullover. The new image appears in the Image control.

7. Close Internet Explorer, then close Visual Studio .NET and all other open applications.

You have now learned how to retrieve and manipulate data in Web forms. The final task is to create an integrated Web application that links multiple forms to perform complex tasks. You will learn how to do this in Chapter 11.

## CHAPTER SUMMARY

❑ Creating data components using program commands allows you to configure the component properties in the Web form code behind file, set component properties at runtime, and specify relative paths to Access database files.

❑ To display database data on a Web form, you create a data connection, create a data adapter that uses the connection to retrieve the data, create and fill a data set based on the data adapter query, then display the data set values on the Web form.

❑ A data set is a memory structure that stores database data that a data adapter retrieves. A data set contains one or more data tables that contain rows and columns and store related data.

❑ In Web forms, you use data binding to link rich server controls to a data source such as a database. The system queries the database at runtime to determine the data values, then dynamically configures and displays the control on the Web form.

❏ You can use the DataList and DataGrid rich server controls to display multiple columns and multiple rows of retrieved data. You can use any List control, such as a ListBox, DropDownList, or RadioButtonList, to display a single column of retrieved data.

❏ To create a DataList control, you create and configure the control, then create Web server control templates to specify how the control displays the data values on the Web form.

❏ A web server control template consists of HTML elements and other commands. Important templates are the header template, which specifies the appearance of the column headings; the item template, which specifies the appearance of the data values; the alternating item template, which specifies the appearance of every other item in the display; and the edit item template, which specifies the appearance of the list item when a user opens the item for editing.

❏ To implement an *Update* button in a DataList or DataGrid control, you create an UpdateCommand event handler that creates an OleDbCommand object that specifies the UPDATE action query. The event handler then executes the action query and refreshes the control display.

❏ When you create the SQL query for an OleDbCommand object, you must include embedded commas and single quotation marks that enclose text strings so the query is formatted correctly. For text strings that contain single quotation marks, you must replace the single quotation mark with two single quotation marks.

❏ A DataGrid control allows you to display multiple columns and multiple rows of retrieved data and allows users to update and delete data values. To format a DataGrid display, you use the Property Builder visual configuration tool, which requires less custom programming than a DataList control requires.

❏ To validate user inputs in DataList and DataGrid controls, you create a CustomValidator control, then write an associated client-side JavaScript function that evaluates the input values. You should also create a backup server-side validation function that the UpdateCommand event handler calls in case the user's browser does not support JavaScript.

❏ To allow users to use a Web form to insert data values, you create a Web form that contains a TextBox rich server control for each table column, and contains a Button control that the user clicks to submit the values. The Button event handler commands create a new data connection and a new OleDbCommand object, then create and execute the OleDbCommand object's INSERT action query.

❏ You can create data bound List controls to display a single column of retrieved data and to provide pick lists on data entry forms. A pick list allows the user to select a value from a list of allowable values.

❏ In a master-detail relationship, a master record in one table has many related detail records in another table. You can display master-detail data on a Web form by creating a control that displays the master data, then creating a second control that displays the detail data. You then create a SelectedIndexChanged event handler for the master list, so that when the user selects a new master list item, the event handler executes and refreshes the detail list values.

## REVIEW QUESTIONS

1. Write a command to create a connection named connMyConnection to connect to:

    a. An Oracle9*i* database with username "scott," the password "tiger," and the connection string "ORACLE1"

    b. An Access database named Testdata.mdb located in the C:\Databases folder, using an absolute path

    c. An Access database named Testdata.mdb located in the C:\Databases folder, using a relative path

2. Write a command to create a module-level data adapter named daCourses that retrieves all of the records in the COURSE table in the Northwoods University database (see Figure 9-12). Then write commands to create a data set named dsCourses, then fill the COURSE data table in the dsCourses data set using the daCourses data adapter.

3. You use a _____ to retrieve specific data values, and you use a _____ to store the retrieved data values.

    a. Data connection, data adapter

    b. Data adapter, data set

    c. Data connection, data set

    d. Data set, data adapter

4. List the order in which you create the following data components: data adapter, data connection, data set.

5. You use a data adapter's _____ property to dynamically specify the data records that the data adapter retrieves.

6. Describe the similarities and differences between a DataList and a DataGrid control.

7. Write the commands to create a header and item template for a DataList control that displays the S_LAST, S_FIRST, and S_DOB columns from the STUDENT table in the Northwoods University database. Display the items in a table, with the column headings "Last Name," "First Name," and "Date of Birth." Format the S_DOB column using the long date pattern.

8. Usually in a DataList, the *Edit* buttons appear in the _____ template.

   a. Header

   b. Item

   c. Edit item

   d. Footer

   e. Both b and c

9. Write a command to assign an UPDATE action query to an OleDbCommand object named sqlCommand. The action query updates the S_LAST, S_FIRST, and S_DOB fields in the STUDENT table in the Northwoods University database. Assume the data values are stored in TextBox controls named txtLast, txtFirst, and txtDOB, and the S_ID value is stored in a TextBox control named txtSID. The date value in the txtDOB TextBox is formatted using the format "MM/DD/YYYY."

10. Write a command to assign an INSERT action query to an OleDbCommand object named sqlCommand. The action query inserts a record into the LOCATION table in the Northwoods University database, and inserts a value for all table columns. Assume the data values are stored in TextBox controls named txtBldg_Code, txtRoom, and txtCapacity. If you are using an Oracle9*i* database, use a sequence named LOC_ID_SEQUENCE to generate the LOC_ID column value. If you are using an Access database, assume the LOC_ID column has the AutoNumber data type.

11. Write a command to assign a DELETE action query to an OleDbCommand object named sqlCommand. The action query deletes a record from the ENROLLMENT table in the Northwoods University database. The S_ID value is stored in a TextBox control named txtSID, and the C_SEC_ID value is stored in a TextBox control named txtCSecID.

12. When should you use a `Try/Catch/End Try` code block, and why should you use it?

13. Assume you have created a DataGrid control with the (ID) value dgStudents that displays values from the STUDENT table in the Northwoods University database. The DataGrid displays the S_LAST value in the second column and the S_FIRST value in the third column. The S_ID value is the primary key in the data table in the data set. Write commands that appear in the UpdateCommand event handler to create TextBox controls named txtSID, txtSLast, and txtSFirst that reference the current S_ID, S_LAST, and S_FIRST values in the DataGrid control.

14. Why do you need to use a CustomValidator rather than one of the other validation controls to validate DataList and DataGrid inputs?

15. Write the commands to configure a ListBox control named lstF_ID that displays the allowable values for the F_ID column in the STUDENT table in the Northwoods University database. Assume that the F_ID values are stored in a data table named "FACULTY" that is in the dsFaculty data set, and that the data table

**10**

contains columns that represent every column in the FACULTY table in the Northwoods University database in Figure 9-12. Specify that the F_LAST column values appear in the list and that the F_ID column provides the values for the list's DataValueField property.

16. Identify three different master–detail relationships in the Northwoods University database tables.

17. In a Web form that displays master–detail data, why do you need to set the master list's AutoPostBack property to True?

---

## HANDS-ON PROJECTS

To complete the Chapter 10 Hands-on Projects, you first need to create a Web server application named Projects that you associate with the Chapter10\Projects folder on your Solution Disk. Change the Visual Studio .NET projects location to your Chapter10/Projects folder. You will also need to create a Web application project named DataControlProjects whose application root is the Chapter10\Projects application on your Web server. Then you will add the files for each Hands-on project to this Web application project as individual Web forms. These projects use the Northwoods University database tables in Figure 9-12.

*If you are using an Oracle9i database*, start SQL*Plus, log on as User Name *cwuser* and Password *oracle*, and run the Northwoods.sql script in the Chapter10 folder on your Data Disk to create the Northwoods University database.

*If you are using an Access database*, copy the Northwoods.mdb database file from the Chapter10 folder on your Data Disk to the Chapter10\Projects\DataControlProjects folder on your Solution Disk.

### Project 10-1 Creating the Northwoods University Student Information Form

In this project, you will create a DataList control that displays values from the STUDENT table in the Northwoods University database and allows users to edit column values.

1. In the DataControlProjects Web application project you created based on the instructions in the Note at the beginning of the Hands-on projects, create a Web form named StudentForm.aspx that uses a DataList control to display the S_LAST, S_FIRST, S_MI, S_ADDRESS, S_CITY, S_STATE, S_ZIP, S_PHONE, S_CLASS, S_DOB, S_PIN, and F_ID fields for all STUDENT records.

2. Format the DataList control using descriptive column headings, and create an alternating item template so every other row is formatted using a contrasting background color. Display an *Edit* button as the first column in the DataList.

3. When the user clicks *Edit*, display *Update* and *Cancel* buttons for the selection. Create event handlers to allow the user to update all column values.

## Project 10-2 Creating the Northwoods University Faculty Information Form

In this project, you will use a DataGrid control to display data values from the FAC-ULTY table in the Northwoods University database as shown in Figure 10-46.

1. Copy the following files from the Chapter10 folder on your Data Disk to the Chapter10\Projects\DataControlProjects folder on your Solution Disk: blanchard.jpg, brown.jpg, cox.jpg, sheng.jpg, williams.jpg.

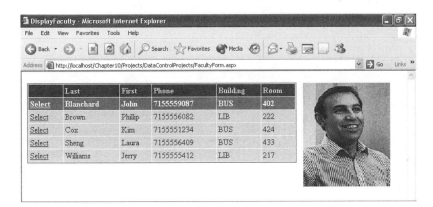

**Figure 10-46**

2. In the DataControlProjects Web application project you created based on the instructions in the Note at the beginning of the Hands-on Projects, create a Web form named FacultyForm.aspx that uses a DataGrid control to display the data shown in Figure 10-46 using data retrieved from the Northwoods University database.

3. Format the DataGrid control using descriptive column headings, and create an alternating item template so every other row is formatted using a contrasting background color.

4. When the user clicks the Select hyperlink for a record, display the faculty member's image as shown, using the image filename retrieved from the FACULTY_IMAGE column in the FACULTY table.

## Project 10-3 Creating the Northwoods University Student Data Entry Form

In this project, you will create the Web form shown in Figure 10-47, which allows users to insert data values into the STUDENT table in the Northwoods University database.

1. In the DataControlProjects Web application project you created based on the instructions in the Note at the beginning of the Hands-on Projects, create a Web form named NewStudent.aspx.

2. Create TextBox, Label, and validation controls as shown in Figure 10-47 to allow users to enter the field values. If you are using an Oracle9*i* database, assign S_ID values using a sequence named S_ID_SEQUENCE. If you are using an Access database, recall that the S_ID field has the AutoNumber data type.

3. Create a data bound list to allow the user to select the S_STATE and F_ID values. Display the state names and faculty member last names in the lists.

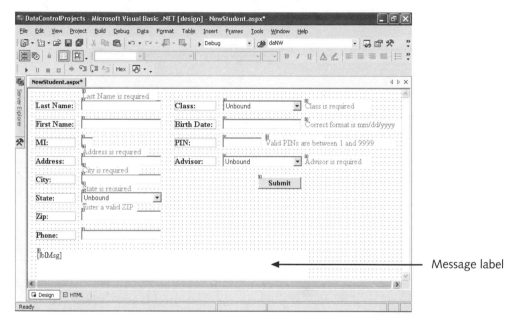

Message label

**Figure 10-47**

4. Create a static DropDownList with values FR, SO, JR, and SR and with displayed text of Freshman, Sophomore, Junior, and Senior to allow the user to select the S_CLASS value. (The static DropDownList does not retrieve these values from the database, but contains the values as static list items when the form first appears. In Chapter 8, you learned how to create a DropDownList control that contains static values.)

5. Create RequiredFieldValidator controls to ensure the *Last Name*, *Address*, *City*, *ZIP*, and *PIN* fields contain values. Create a CompareValidator to ensure that the user selects a value in the *State*, *Advisor*, and *Class* lists. Create a RangeValidator to ensure that the PIN value is between 1 and 9999. Create RegularExpressionValidators to ensure that users enter *Zip* and *Birth Date* values using the specified format.

6. Create an event handler for the *Submit* button that inserts the record into the database and displays a message in the Message Label.

## Project 10-4 Creating the Northwoods University Student Transcript Form

In this project, you will create a form that allows the user to select a Northwoods University student from a data bound list, and then display the student's transcript information, as shown in Figure 10-48.

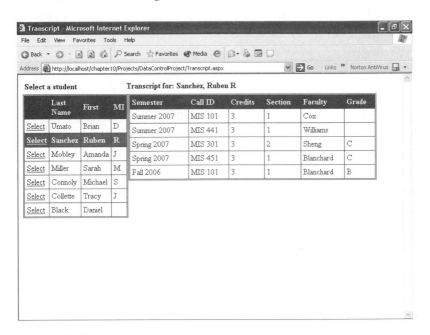

**Figure 10-48**

10

1. In the DataControlProjects Web application project you created based on the instructions in the Note at the beginning of the Hands-on Projects, create a Web form named Transcript.aspx.

2. Create a DataGrid to display the student data as shown in Figure 10-48.

3. Create a DataGrid to display the transcript data. The transcript data will not appear until the user selects a student in the student DataGrid.

At the time of this writing, if you are using an Access database, you cannot generate a data set using a data adapter that contains data that joins more than two tables. This limitation is due to Visual Studio .NET incorrectly generating the Access query syntax. To work around this limitation, you need to create the data adapter first. Before you generate the data set, open the Web Form Designer Generated Code node in the code behind file, find the OleDbSelectCommand2 section, delete the existing query, and replace it with the query you used to create the data adapter.

4. Create a SelectedIndexChanged event handler for the master list that displays the detail DataGrid information for the selected student.

## CASE PROJECTS

To solve the case projects in this chapter, you must first create a new Web server application named Cases that you associate with the Chapter10\Cases folder on your Solution Disk, and you must modify your Visual Studio .NET IDE so it places all project solution files in the Chapter10\Cases folder on your Solution Disk.

### Case Project 10-1 Ashland Valley Soccer League

Create a Web application project named AshlandProject whose application root is the Chapter10/Cases application on your Web server. *If you are using an Oracle9i database*, start SQL*Plus, log on as User Name *cwuser* and Password *oracle*, then run the Ashland.sql script that is in the Chapter10\Cases folder on your Data Disk to refresh the database tables and insert sample data values. *If you are using an Access database*, copy the Ashland.mdb file from the Chapter10\Cases folder on your Data Disk to the Chapter10\Cases\AshlandProject folder on your Solution Disk.

1. Create a Web form named Fields.aspx that displays all of the columns and all of the rows in the FIELDS table in the Ashland database (see Figure 9-26) using a DataList control. Order the output records by FIELD_ID, and format the DataList so every other item appears in a different background color.

2. Create a Web form named Teams.aspx that displays all of the columns and all of the rows in the TEAM table using a DataGrid control. Order the values by team name, and allow the user to edit and delete teams. Do not allow users to update the TEAM_ID value.

3. Create a Web form named Games.aspx that allows users to enter information about new games. Create a TextBox control for each column in the GAME table in Figure 9-26. Allow users to select the HOME_TEAM_ID, VISITING_TEAM_ID, and FIELD_ID values using data bound lists. If you are using an Oracle9i database, create a sequence named GAME_ID_SEQUENCE to generate the value of the GAME_ID column. (You may have already created this sequence in Case 9-1.) If you are using an Access database, recall that the GAME_ID column has the AutoNumber data type.

### Case Project 10-2 Al's Body Shop

Create a Web application project named AlsProject whose application root is the Chapter10/Cases application on your Web server. *If you are using an Oracle9i database*, start SQL*Plus, log on as User Name *cwuser* and Password *oracle*, then run the Als.sql script that is in the Chapter10\Cases folder on your Data Disk to refresh the database tables and insert sample data values. *If you are using an Access database*, copy the Als.mdb file from the Chapter10\Cases folder on your Data Disk to the Chapter10\Cases\AlsProject folder on your Solution Disk.

1. Create a Web form named Customers.aspx that displays all of the columns and all of the rows in the CUSTOMER table in the Als database (see Figure 9-28) using a DataList control. Format the DataList so every other item appears in a different background color.

2. Create a Web form named Services.aspx that displays all of the columns and all of the rows in the SERVICE table using a DataGrid control. Order the values by team name, and allow the user to edit and delete service descriptions and charges. Do not allow users to update the SERVICE_ID value.

3. Create a Web form named Workorder_Services.aspx that displays the master-detail relationship between work orders and services. Create a DataGrid control that displays the columns in the WORKORDER table and displays a *Select* button for each work order. When the user selects a work order, display a description and charge for the work order's services in a second DataGrid control.

## Case Project 10-3 Sun-Ray Videos

Create a Web application project named SunrayProject whose application root is the Chapter10/Cases application on your Web server. *If you are using an Oracle9i database*, start SQL*Plus, log on as User Name *cwuser* and Password *oracle*, then run the Sunray.sql script that is in the Chapter10\Cases folder on your Data Disk to refresh the database tables and insert sample data values. *If you are using an Access database*, copy the Sunray.mdb file from the Chapter10\Cases folder on your Data Disk to the Chapter10\Cases\Sunray folder on your Solution Disk.

1. Create a Web form named Customers.aspx that displays all of the columns and all of the rows in the CUSTOMER table in the Sunray database (see Figure 9-30) using a DataList control. Order the output records by CUSTOMER_ID, and format the DataList so every other item appears in a different background color.

2. Create a Web form named Videos.aspx that displays all of the columns and all of the rows in the VIDEO table using a DataGrid control. Order the values by title, and allow the user to edit and delete videos. Do not allow users to update the VIDEO_ID value.

3. Create a Web form named Video_Formats.aspx that displays video titles in a data bound list. When the user selects a video title, display the associated format descriptions for the video and the cost for each format in a DataGrid control.

4. Create a Web form named Rentals.aspx that allows the user to enter information about a new rental. Create a TextBox control for each column in the RENTAL table (see Figure 9-30). Allow users to select the CUSTOMER_ID from a data bound list that displays the customer name and the VIDEO_FORMAT_ID from a DataGrid that displays video titles and associated format descriptions. If you are using an Oracle9i database, create a sequence named RENTAL_ID_SEQUENCE

to generate the value of the RENTAL_ID column. (You may have already created this sequence in Case 9-3.) If you are using an Access database, recall that the RENTAL_ID column has the AutoNumber data type.

## Case Project 10-4 Learning Technologies, Incorporated

Create a Web application project named LtiProject whose application root is the Chapter10/Cases application on your Web server. *If you are using an Oracle9i database*, start SQL*Plus, log on as User Name *cwuser* and Password *oracle*, then run the Lti.sql script that is in the Chapter10\Cases folder on your Data Disk to refresh the database tables and insert sample data values. *If you are using an Access database*, copy the Lti.mdb file from the Chapter10\Cases folder on your Data Disk to the Chapter10\Cases\Lti folder on your Solution Disk.

1. Create a Web form named Books.aspx that displays all of the columns and all of the rows in the BOOK table in the Lti database (see Figure 9-32) using a DataList control. Order the output records by book title, and format the DataList so every other item appears in a different background color.

2. Create a Web form named Authors.aspx that displays all of the columns and all of the rows in the AUTHOR table using a DataGrid control. Order the values by author last names, and allow the user to edit author values. Do not allow users to update the AUTHOR_ID value.

3. Create a Web form named Book_Authors.aspx that displays book titles in a data bound list. When the user selects a book title, display the name of the book author or authors in a DataGrid control.

# CREATING AN INTEGRATED WEB APPLICATION

**In this chapter, you will:**

♦ Become familiar with an integrated Web application that contains multiple Web forms

♦ Understand how to transfer processing from one Web form to another

♦ Learn how to share data values across multiple Web forms

♦ Learn how to insert records simultaneously in master and detail tables

♦ Learn how to add template columns to a DataGrid control

♦ Implement security using forms-based authentication

♦ Deploy a completed Web application on a production Web server

So far, the database-driven Web forms that you have created work in a stand-alone manner. In this chapter, you will learn how to link related Web forms to create an integrated Web application. Recall that an integrated Web application consists of several Web pages that developers create to solve a problem or provide a service. For example, a software vendor's Web site might use one Web page to display information about its products, a second page to gather inputs about a user's order selections, and a third page to summarize the user's order and provide delivery information. To create an integrated Web application, you will learn how to use program commands to transfer processing from one Web form to another, and how to share data values among Web forms. You will also learn advanced techniques for displaying data in DataGrid controls. Security is a primary concern with Web applications, so the chapter describes how to use forms-based authentication to control access to Web forms. And, you will learn how to move a completed Web application from the development environment to a production Web server.

Before you begin, you will configure your Web server so it contains the applications you need to create and run Web application projects that you will store in the Chapter11\Tutorials folder on your Solution Disk.

> If you are using an Access database, you will have to store your Solution Disk files on a hard drive, instead of floppy disk, because this chapter's tutorial exercises consume about 1.7 MB of disk space. Floppy disks are limited to about 1.4 MB of data. In this chapter, the instructions will show that the tutorial solutions appear in the C:\Chapter11\Tutorials folder on the user's workstation.

To configure your Web server:

1. Start the IIS console, and create an application named Chapter11 that you associate with the Chapter11 folder on your Solution Disk. Configure the application so that users have *Read*, *Run scripts*, and *Browse* privileges.

2. Within the Chapter11 application, create a second application named Tutorials that you associate with the Chapter11\Tutorials folder on your Solution Disk. Configure the application so that users have *Read*, *Run scripts*, and *Browse* privileges.

Next you will refresh your Clearwater Traders database to restore it to its original state as shown in Figure 9-10. If you are using an Oracle9*i* database, you will start SQL*Plus and run the Clearwater.sql script that creates and populates the Clearwater Traders database tables in Figure 9-10. You will also create a sequence named O_ID_SEQUENCE that you will use in the chapter to create new order ID (O_ID) surrogate key values.

> If you are using an Access database, skip these steps. You will copy the database .mdb file to the project folder later.

To refresh your Oracle9*i* database and create the sequence:

1. Click **Start** on the taskbar, point to **All Programs**, point to **Oracle – OraHome92**, point to **Application Development**, and then click **SQL Plus**. The Log On dialog box opens. (Windows 2000 users will click Start, point to Programs, point to Oracle – OraHome92, point to Application Development, and then click SQL Plus.)

2. Type **cwuser** in the *User Name* field, **oracle** in the *Password* field, leave the *Host String* field blank, and then click **OK**. The Oracle SQL*Plus window opens, and the SQL prompt appears. (If you are connecting to an Oracle9*i* Enterprise database, use the connection instructions provided by your instructor or technical support person.)

3. To run the script, type **start A:\Chapter11\Clearwater.sql** at the SQL prompt, and then press **Enter**. (If your Data Disk is stored on a different drive than A or has a different folder path, use that drive or path instead.)

4. Type the following command at the SQL prompt, then press **Enter** to create the sequence:

```
CREATE SEQUENCE O_ID_SEQUENCE START WITH 10;
```

5. Close the Oracle SQL*Plus window to exit SQL*Plus.

## THE CLEARWATER TRADERS INTEGRATED WEB APPLICATION

To learn techniques for creating an integrated Web application, you will work with the Clearwater Traders Web application. Figure 11-1 shows an overview of the Web pages that comprise this Web application.

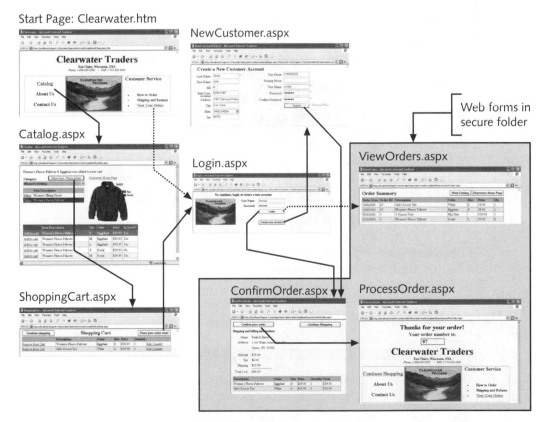

**Figure 11-1**    Clearwater Traders Web application

The Start Page of the Clearwater Traders Web application is the Clearwater.htm static Web page. This Web application supports two primary database-driven processes: allowing customers to place new orders and allowing customers to view their existing orders. The following subsections describe the Web pages that these two processes use.

## The Clearwater Traders New Customer Order Process

The solid lines in Figure 11-1 show the path that the user takes through the new order process. When the user clicks the *Catalog* hyperlink on the Clearwater.htm static Web page in Figure 11-1, the Catalog.aspx Web form, which is shown in Figure 11-2, appears.

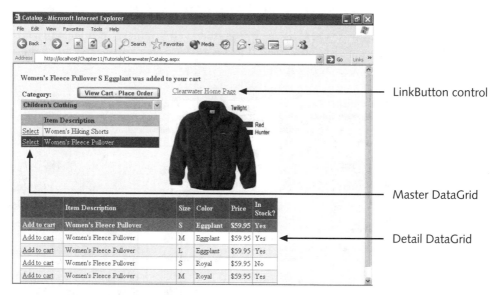

**Figure 11-2** Catalog.aspx Web form

The Catalog.aspx Web form allows the user to view merchandise items, determine whether items are in stock, and select items to order. When the user clicks the *Add to cart* hyperlink beside an item, the item is added to the user's shopping cart. When the user clicks the *View Cart – Place Order* button on the Catalog.aspx Web form, the ShoppingCart.aspx Web form in Figure 11-3 appears.

**Figure 11-3** ShoppingCart.aspx Web form

The ShoppingCart.aspx Web form shows the items in the user's shopping cart, and allows the user to specify the order quantity for each item. When the user clicks the *Remove from Cart* hyperlink, the selection is removed from the shopping cart. When the user clicks the *Edit Quantity* hyperlink for a selection, the item opens for editing, and the user can specify the quantity in the Quantity column. When the user clicks the *Place your order now* button, the Login.aspx Web form, which is shown in Figure 11-4, appears.

**Figure 11-4**    Login.aspx Web form

On the Login.aspx Web form, users who do not yet have Clearwater Traders customer accounts click *Create new account*, which allows users to enter personal information into the NewCustomer.aspx Web form, shown in Figure 11-5, then click *Submit* to create a new customer account. After a user creates a new user account, the ConfirmOrder.aspx Web form in Figure 11-6 appears.

**11**

**Create a New Customer Account**

| | | | |
|---|---|---|---|
| Last Name: | Chen | Day Phone: | 7155559888 |
| First Name: | Emily | Evening Phone: | |
| MI: | M | User Name: | echen |
| Birth Date: (mm/dd/yyyy) | 11/20/1986 | Password: | •••••• |
| Address: | 1154 Broad Street | Confirm Password: | •••••• |
| City: | Wausau | | Submit    * Required Field |
| State: | WISCONSIN | | |
| Zip: | 54688 | | |

**Figure 11-5**    NewCustomer.aspx Web form

A user who already has a Clearwater Traders account types his or her user name and password directly into the Login.aspx Web form TextBox controls. The user then clicks *Login* to log on to the system and display the ConfirmOrder.aspx Web form shown in Figure 11-6. Note that the ConfirmOrder.aspx Web form is in a secure folder (see Figure 11-1), which indicates that a form authentication process has verified that the user has logged on to the system and established his or her identity. You will learn how to create and configure secure folders and form authentication processes later in the chapter.

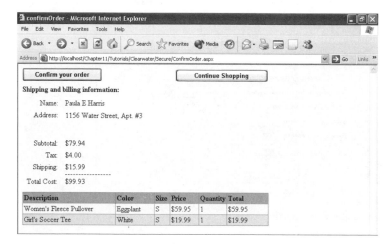

**Figure 11-6**    ConfirmOrder.aspx Web form

The ConfirmOrder.aspx Web form summarizes the order items and displays the total order cost. The user can click *Continue Shopping* to redisplay the Catalog.aspx Web form, or *Confirm your order* to display the ProcessOrder.aspx Web form shown in Figure 11-7, which inserts the order information into the database, thanks the user for the order, and displays the order ID number.

**Figure 11-7**    ProcessOrder.aspx Web form

## The Clearwater Traders View Order Process

The Clearwater Traders Web application also allows returning customers to view information about their past orders. The dashed lines in Figure 11-1 show the path that the user takes through the view order process. When a customer clicks the *View Your Orders* hyperlink on the Clearwater.htm static Web page, the Login.aspx Web page appears if the user has not yet logged on to the system. After the user successfully logs on, the ViewOrders.aspx Web page in Figure 11-8 appears, which summarizes the details of the customer's orders. If a user who has already logged on to the system clicks the *View Your Orders* hyperlink on the Clearwater.htm static Web page or on the ProcessOrder.aspx Web form (see Figure 11-7), the ViewOrders.aspx Web page appears immediately without prompting the user to log on to the system.

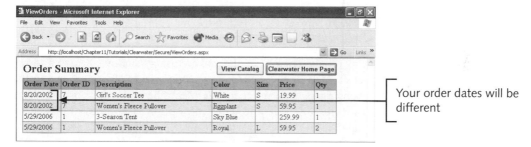

Figure 11-8    ViewOrders.aspx Web form

## Running the Integrated Web Application

Before you create the Clearwater Traders Web application, you will first install a completed version of the application on your Web server and then run the application to become familiar with its operation. To install the completed application on your Web server, you will copy the application's compiled binary files and the .aspx files from your Data Disk to your Solution Disk, and then configure your Web server to run the application.

> You will not copy the Web form code behind files or other project files onto your Web server because the contents of these files have been compiled into a binary format. Later in this chapter, you will learn how to create these compiled files and how to deploy Web application projects on production Web servers.

To install the Clearwater Traders Web application on your Web server:

1. Start Windows Explorer.

   *If you are using an Oracle9i database*, copy the **DemoOracle** folder and its contents from the Chapter11 folder on your Data Disk to the Chapter11\ Tutorials folder on your Solution Disk.

*If you are using an Access database*, copy the **DemoAccess** folder and its contents from the Chapter11 folder on your Data Disk to the Chapter11\ Tutorials folder on your Solution Disk.

2. *If you are using an Access database*, you need to grant Internet users the necessary permissions for the Access database file. In Windows Explorer, navigate to the Chapter11\Tutorials\DemoAccess folder on your Solution Disk, right-click the **DemoAccess** folder, and then click **Properties**. Select the **Security** tab, click **Add**, type **Everyone** in the *Enter the object names to select* field, then click **OK** to close the Select Users or Groups dialog box. In the DemoAccess Properties dialog box, make sure that *Everyone* is selected in the *Group or user names* list, check the **Allow** check box beside *Full Control*, and then click **OK**. (Windows 2000 users should click the Sharing tab, select the *Share this folder* option button, then click the *Permissions* button. On the Permissions dialog box, select *Everyone* from the *Name* pane and check the *Full Control* check box in the Permission pane. Click *OK*, and click *OK* again.)

If the Security tab did not appear and you are using Windows XP, in Windows Explorer, select Tools from the menu, and then select Folder Options. In the Folder Options dialog box select the View tab. Scroll to the bottom of the Advanced settings list box and clear the option Use simple file sharing (Recommended).

3. Switch to the IIS console and open the **Tutorials** application node within the Chapter11 application.

*If you are using an Oracle9i database*, right-click the **DemoOracle** physical directory, then click **Properties**.

*If you are using an Access database*, right-click the **DemoAccess** physical directory, then click **Properties**.

4. Click **Create** to convert the physical directory to an application, and then click **OK**. The new application appears in the IIS console tree.

Now you will start Internet Explorer and run the Web application. Then you will create a new customer order.

To run the Web application using an Oracle9i Enterprise Edition database, the database must have an account with username *cwuser*, password *oracle*, and host string *ORCL*, because the application automatically connects to the database using this account. Your client workstation must be configured so the Oracle9i tnsnames.ora file has an entry that associates the ORCL host string with the Enterprise Edition database. And, the Clearwater.sql SQL script must have previously been run in the *cwuser* user account to create the Clearwater Traders database tables.

To run the Web application and create a customer order:

1. Start Internet Explorer.

   *If you are using an Oracle9i database*, type **http://localhost/Chapter11/ Tutorials/DemoOracle/Clearwater.htm** in the *Address* field, then press **Enter**.

   *If you are using an Access database*, type **http://localhost/Chapter11/ Tutorials/DemoAccess/Clearwater.htm** in the *Address* field, then press **Enter**.

2. The Clearwater.htm static Web page appears. Click the **Catalog** hyperlink.

 If you are unable to view the categories, re-read the Note at the beginning of this exercise and make sure your computer and server are configured correctly.

3. To order an item, open the **Please select a category** list, then select **Women's Clothing**. Click the **Select** hyperlink beside Women's Fleece Pullover to display the item details, then click the **Add to cart** hyperlink beside Women's Fleece Pullover, Size S, Color Eggplant. A message appears on the top of the form to confirm that the item was added to your shopping cart. Figure 11-2 shows how your Web form will appear after you complete this step.

4. To order another item, open the **Please select a category** list, then select **Children's Clothing**. Click the **Select** hyperlink beside Girl's Soccer Tee to display the item details, then click the **Add to cart** hyperlink beside Girl's Soccer Tee, Size S, Color White. A message appears to confirm that the item was added to your shopping cart.

5. Click **View Cart – Place Order**. The ShoppingCart.aspx Web form in Figure 11-3 appears.

6. Click the **Edit Quantity** hyperlink beside Girl's Soccer Tee, change the Quantity value to **2**, and then click **Update Quantity**. The new quantity appears in the Quantity column.

7. Click **Place your order now**. The Login.aspx Web page in Figure 11-4 appears.

8. To log on to the system as a returning user, type **harrispe** in the *User Name* TextBox, **asdfjk** in the *Password* TextBox, then click **Login**. The ConfirmOrder.aspx Web page appears, similar to the ConfirmOrder.aspx Web page shown in Figure 11-6. Note that the secure folder appears in the URL, which indicates that this Web form is in a secure folder.

**11**

9. Click **Confirm your order**. The ProcessOrder.aspx Web form in Figure 11-7 appears. This Web form displays the new order's order number. (Your order number may be different.)

10. Click the **View Your Orders** link. The ViewOrders.aspx Web form appears, similar to the ViewOrders.aspx Web form shown in Figure 11-8. This Web form shows that customer Paula Harris has two orders. One was placed on 5/29/2006, and the second was placed today. (The first order is already stored in the Clearwater Traders database, and you just placed the second order. The order in which your orders appear may be different.) Notice that you did not have to log on to the system again, because you had logged on previously.

Now you will close Internet Explorer and end your shopping session. Then you will start Internet Explorer and open the Clearwater Traders Web application again. This time, you will place an order as a new customer rather than as a returning customer.

To place an order as a new customer:

1. Close Internet Explorer, then restart it.

   *If you are using an Oracle9i database*, type **http://localhost/Chapter11/ Tutorials/DemoOracle/Clearwater.htm** in the *Address* field, then press **Enter**.

   *If you are using an Access database*, type **http://localhost/Chapter11/ Tutorials/DemoAccess/Clearwater.htm** in the *Address* field, then press **Enter**.

2. On the Clearwater.htm static Web page, click the **Catalog** hyperlink, open the **Please select a category** list, then select **Men's Clothing**.

3. Click the **Select** hyperlink beside Men's Expedition Parka, then click the **Add to cart** hyperlink beside Men's Expedition Parka, Size S, Color Spruce. The message appears advising you that the item was added to your shopping cart.

4. Click **View Cart – Place Order** to view the shopping cart, then click **Place your order now** to place the order.

5. To log on as a new customer, click **Create new account** on the Login.aspx Web form. The NewCustomer.aspx Web form in Figure 11-5 appears.

6. Type the data values shown in Figure 11-5 for the new customer. Leave the *Evening Phone* TextBox control blank, and type **emilyc** in the *Password* and *Confirm Password* TextBox controls. Then click **Submit**. The ConfirmOrder.aspx Web page appears, and summarizes the customer and order information.

7. Click **Confirm your order** to place the order. The ProcessOrder.aspx Web form appears.

8. Click the **View Your Orders** hyperlink. The ViewOrders.aspx Web page summarizes the new customer's order.

9. Close Internet Explorer

## Creating and Configuring the Clearwater Traders Tutorial

You have seen that the Clearwater Traders Web application consists of a static Web page and different Web forms that interact with one another and share data values. To make it easier to create the Clearwater Traders Web application, you will base your application on partially completed Web form files that are on your Data Disk. These files contain Web form elements and use Web/database programming concepts that you learned to create in earlier chapters. Throughout this chapter, you will modify these existing files to learn how to create an integrated Web application. Now you will start Visual Studio .NET and create a new Web application project named Clearwater. Then you will add to the project the Web forms on which you will base your integrated application.

To create the new Web application project and add the files to the project:

1. Start Visual Studio .NET. To configure the Visual Studio .NET IDE so it stores the project solution file in the project folder, click **Tools** on the menu bar, click **Options**, make sure the *Environment* folder is selected in the left pane, select **Projects and Solutions**, click **Browse**, navigate to the Chapter11\Tutorials folder on your Solution Disk, click **Open**, and then click **OK**.

2. In Visual Studio .NET, click **File** on the menu bar, point to **New**, click **Project**, make sure the ASP.NET Web Application template is selected, and then type **http://localhost/Chapter11/Tutorials/Clearwater** in the *Location* field to specify the new project name. Click **OK** to create the project. After a few moments, the new project appears in the Solution Explorer.

3. Open the Solution Explorer if necessary, select the **WebForm1.aspx** node, right-click, click **Delete,** then click **OK** to confirm the deletion.

4. Close the Start Page in the Browser Window.

5. Switch to Windows Explorer.

   *If you are using an Oracle9i database*, copy all of the files and folders in the Chapter11\ClearwaterOracle folder on your Data Disk to the Chapter11\Tutorials\Clearwater folder on your Solution Disk.

   *If you are using an Access database*, copy all of the files and folders in the Chapter11\ClearwaterAccess folder on your Data Disk to the Chapter11\Tutorials\Clearwater folder on your Solution Disk.

6. *If you are using an Access database*, grant Internet users the permissions they need to access the Access database file by modifying the security properties of the Chapter11\Tutorials\Clearwater folder on your Solution Disk to allow

**11**

Full Control access to everyone. (You performed a similar operation earlier in the chapter when you installed the demonstration application.)

7. Switch to Visual Studio .NET, then click the **Show All Files** button 🗗 on the Solution Explorer toolbar. The files and folders you copied into the Clearwater folder appear in the project tree. Because the new items have not yet been added to the project, their nodes appear as a File icon 📄.

8. Right-click the **Catalog.aspx** node, which is the first item that has as its node the File icon 📄, then click **Include In Project**. The item's node changes to a Web form icon 📄, which indicates that the item is now included in the project.

9. To add the remaining items to the project, repeat Step 8 for each item in the project tree that has the File icon 📄 beside its name.

10. Right-click the **bin** folder node, then click **Include In Project**.

11. Repeat Step 10 for the Images and Secure folders. Your completed Solution Explorer project tree should look like Figure 11-9.

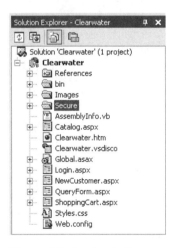

**Figure 11-9**    Project tree showing new project files

12. Right-click the **Clearwater.htm** node, then click **Set As Start Page**.

Before you can run the project, you need to update the data connections in the Web forms and generate the data sets. First you will update the Catalog.aspx Web form.

To update the data connections and generate the data sets in the Catalog.aspx Web form:

1. Select the **Catalog.aspx** node in the Solution Explorer, and then click the **View Designer** button 📄 to open the Web form in Design view.

2. To update the database connection, right-click **OleDbConnection1** in the component tray, then click **Properties** to open the Properties Window.

*If you are using an Oracle9i database*, open the **ConnectionString** property list, select **ORCL.CWUSER** if necessary, then close the Properties Window.

*If you are using an Access database*, open the **ConnectionString** property list, select **<New Connection>**, select the **Provider** tab, select **Microsoft Jet 4.0 OLE DB Provider**, click **Next**, click the **More** button ⌐..⌐, navigate to the Chapter11\Tutorials\Clearwater folder on your Solution Disk, select **Clearwater.mdb**, click **Open**, then click **OK**. Then close the Properties Window.

3. To create the data set that fills the Category list, right-click the **daCategory** component in the component tray, then click **Generate Dataset**. Make sure that the *New* option button is selected, type **dsCW** in the *New* field, make sure that the *CATEGORY (daCategory)* check box is checked, then click **OK** to generate the data set. The DsCW1 data set appears in the component tray.

4. To create the data set that fills the master Items DataGrid, right-click the **daItem** component in the component tray, then click **Generate Dataset**. Make sure that the *Existing* option button is selected, make sure that *Clearwater.dsCW* is selected in the list, make sure that the *ITEM (daItem)* check box is checked, then click **OK** to generate the data set.

5. To create the data set that fills the detail Items DataGrid, right-click the **daDetails** component in the component tray, then click **Generate Dataset**. Make sure that the *Existing* option button is selected, make sure that *Clearwater.dsCW* is selected in the list, make sure that the *INVENTORY (daDetails)* check box is checked, then click **OK** to generate the data set.

6. Click the **Save All** button 🗇 to save all of the project files.

Next you will update data connections and generate required data sets in the other Web forms. You will update the ShoppingCart.aspx, ConfirmOrder.aspx, and ViewOrders.aspx Web forms.

To update the data connections and generate the data sets in the other Web forms:

1. Select the **ShoppingCart.aspx** node in the Solution Explorer, then click the **View Designer** button 🖳 to open the Web form in Design view.

2. To update the database connection, right-click **OleDbConnection1** in the component tray, then click **Properties** to open the Properties Window.

*If you are using an Oracle9i database*, make sure the connection string is set to **ORCL.CWUSER**. *If you are using an Access database*, set the connection string to **ACCESS.Chapter11\Tutorials\Clearwater\ Clearwater.mdb.Admin**.

3. To create the data set that displays the selections in the shopping cart DataGrid control, right-click the **daCart** component in the component tray, then click

**Generate Dataset**. Select the **New** option button, type **dsCart** in the *New* field, then click **OK** to generate the data set. The DsCart1 data set appears in the component tray.

4. Open the **Secure** folder in the Solution Explorer, select the **ConfirmOrder.aspx** node, then click the **View Designer** button ⊞ to open the Web form in Design view.

5. Update **OleDbConnection1** so its connection string property is **ORCL.CWUSER** if you are using an Oracle9*i* database, or **ACCESS.Chapter11\Tutorials\Clearwater\Clearwater.mdb.Admin** if you are using an Access database.

6. To create the data set that displays the order items, right-click the **OleDbDataAdapter1** component in the component tray, then click **Generate Dataset**. Select the **New** option button, type **dsOrder** in the *New* field, then click **OK** to generate the data set. The DsOrder1 data set appears in the component tray.

7. In the Secure folder in the Solution Explorer, select the **ViewOrders.aspx** node, then click the **View Designer** button ⊞ to open the Web form in Design view.

8. Update **OleDbConnection1** so its connection string property is **ORCL.CWUSER** if you are using an Oracle9*i* database, or **ACCESS.Chapter11\Tutorials\Clearwater\Clearwater.mdb.Admin** if you are using an Access database.

9. To create the data set that summarizes the customer orders, right-click the **OleDbDataAdapter1** component in the component tray, then click **Generate Dataset**. Select the **New** option button, type **dsViewOrder** in the *New* field, then click **OK** to generate the data set. The DsViewOrder1 data set appears in the component tray.

10. Close the Properties Window, then click the **Save All** button 🗗 to save the project files.

11. Close the Secure\ConfirmOrder.aspx and Secure\ViewOrders.aspx windows in the Browser Window.

---

## DISPLAYING DIFFERENT WEB FORMS WITHIN AN INTEGRATED WEB APPLICATION

Recall from Figure 11-1 that when the user clicks *View Cart – Place Order* on the Catalog.aspx Web form, a program command executes that displays the ShoppingCart.aspx Web form. Similarly, when the user clicks *Place your order now* on the ShoppingCart.aspx Web form, a command displays the Login.aspx Web form. The solid and dashed lines in

Figure 11-1 indicate when program commands transfer processing to other Web forms in the application.

By default, a Web form always posts back to itself. Therefore it is important to learn how to transfer processing from one Web page or form to another. ASP.NET supports two different methods that transfer application processing from a source Web page or form to a target page or form: the Response.Redirect method and the Server.Transfer method.

## The Response.Redirect Method

In ASP.NET, the **HttpResponse class** stores information about an ASP.NET operation. The **Redirect method** instructs the client browser to display a different Web page. When a command in a Web form code behind file executes the Response.Redirect method, the Web server sends a message to the browser that instructs the browser to request a specified URL. The program containing the command that calls the Response.Redirect method terminates, and the Web server sends the target Web page from the specified URL to the browser. Figure 11-10 illustrates the processing steps for the Response.Redirect method.

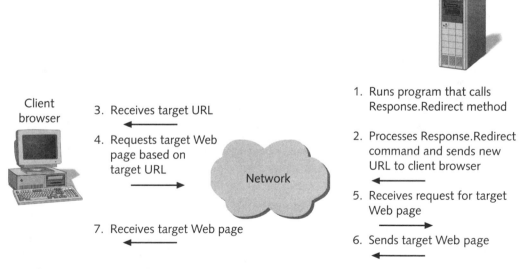

**Figure 11-10**    Response.Redirect method processing steps

The general syntax to call the Response.Redirect method is:

```
Response.Redirect("target_URL")
```

In this syntax, *target_URL* can be any relative or absolute URL. The *target_URL* can contain a parameter list, which you learned about in Chapter 8 in the section titled "Server-Side Processing Using HTML Forms." You would use the following command to redirect processing to the Clearwater.htm static Web page. This command uses a relative URL path, and assumes that the Clearwater.htm file is in the same current working directory as the source Web page.

```
Response.Redirect("Clearwater.htm")
```

## The Server.Transfer Method

In ASP.NET, the **Server object** is a system object that provides access to methods and properties that relate to the Web server. The **Server.Transfer method** transfers processing directly from the current Web form to a target Web form. Both Web forms must be on the same Web server and within the same Web application project. Figure 11-11 illustrates the steps in processing the Server.Transfer method.

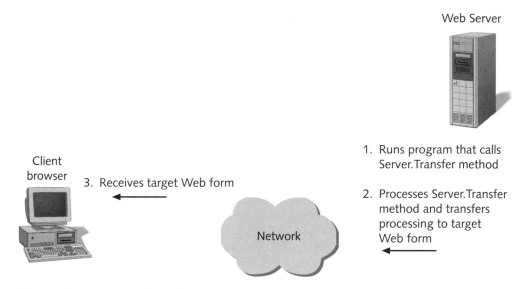

**Figure 11-11**    Server.Transfer method processing steps

Recall that with the Response.Redirect method processing in Figure 11-10, the Web server sends a message to the browser that specifies the URL of the target Web page, the browser requests the target Web page, and then the Web server sends the target Web page back to the browser. This process requires two round trips between the browser and Web server. By transferring processing immediately to the target Web form, the Server.Transfer method avoids these two round trips. As a result, the Server.Transfer method provides faster response to the user and less network traffic than the Response.Redirect method.

The general syntax for calling the Server.Transfer method is:

```
Server.Transfer("target_Web_form_URL")
```

In this syntax, *target_Web_form_URL* is a relative or absolute URL that specifies a Web form .aspx file. You would use the following command to redirect processing to the ShoppingCart.aspx Web form. This command uses a relative URL that assumes that the ShoppingCart.aspx file is in the same current working directory as the current Web page.

```
Server.Transfer("ShoppingCart.aspx")
```

Recall that you can only use the Server.Transfer method to transfer processing from one Web form .aspx file to another. You cannot use the Server.Transfer method to transfer processing to an HTML document with an .htm file extension, or to other types of files that create dynamic Web pages, such as PERL scripts or CGI programs. In addition, the Server.Transfer method bypasses the ASP.NET forms authentication process, so you cannot use Server.Transfer to call Web forms that require authentication. (You will learn more about forms authentication later in this chapter.)

Now you will modify the Web forms in the Clearwater project so the forms call one another using the Response.Redirect and the Server.Transfer methods. First you will create event handlers in the Catalog.aspx and ShoppingCart.aspx Web forms that use the Server.Transfer method. The event handler in the Catalog.aspx Web form will transfer processing to the ShoppingCart.aspx Web form when the user clicks *View Cart – Place Order*. The event handler in the ShoppingCart.aspx Web form will transfer processing back to the Catalog.aspx Web form when the user clicks *Continue shopping*. Then you will run the project and test the event handlers.

To create and test the event handlers that call the Server.Transfer method:

1. Select the **Catalog.aspx** tab in the Browser Window to open the Web form in Design view.

2. Double-click **View Cart – Place Order** to create the btnCheckOut_Click event handler template.

3. To transfer processing to the ShoppingCart.aspx Web form when the user clicks the button, add the following command to the event handler:

```
Server.Transfer("ShoppingCart.aspx")
```

4. Select the **ShoppingCart.aspx** tab in the Browser Window to open the Web form in Design view.

5. Double-click **Continue shopping** to create the btnContinue_Click event handler template, then add the following command to the event handler to transfer processing back to the Catalog.aspx Web form:

```
Server.Transfer("Catalog.aspx")
```

**11**

6. Click the **Start** button ▶ to run the project. The Clearwater Traders home page appears. Click the **Catalog** hyperlink to display the Catalog.aspx Web form, then click **View Cart – Place Order**. The application transfers processing to the ShoppingCart.aspx Web form, which shows that the shopping cart is currently empty.

7. On the ShoppingCart.aspx Web form, click **Continue shopping**. The application transfers processing back to the Catalog.aspx Web form.

8. Close Internet Explorer.

Note that the Catalog.aspx Web form in Figure 11-2 displays a hyperlink with the text *Clearwater Home Page*. This is a **LinkButton rich server control**, which creates a hyperlink on a Web form. To create a LinkButton rich server control, you select the LinkButton tool on the Web Forms tab in the Toolbox, then draw the LinkButton on the Web form. You set the LinkButton's Text property to the hyperlink text. Then you create a Click event handler for the LinkButton that contains a command to call either the Response.Redirect method or the Server.Transfer method.

Now you will create the Clearwater Home Page LinkButton control on the Catalog.aspx Web page. When you create the LinkButton's event handler, you will use a command to call the Response.Redirect method and redirect processing to the Clearwater.htm static home page. Remember that you must use the Response.Redirect method rather than the Server.Transfer method because you cannot use the Server.Transfer method to redirect processing to anything other than a Web form .aspx file.

To create the LinkButton control:

1. Select the **Catalog.aspx** tab in the Browser Window to display the form in Design view. Open the Toolbox, select the Web Forms tab if necessary, select the **LinkButton** tool, then draw the Clearwater Home Page LinkButton control in the position shown in Figure 11-2.

2. Right-click the new **LinkButton**, then click **Properties** to open the Properties Window. Change the (ID) property value to **lnkCW**. (This value begins with a lowercase letter *L*, and stands for *link*.)

3. Change the Text property value to **Clearwater Home Page**, select another property to apply the changes, then close the Properties Window. If necessary, adjust the size of the LinkButton so the text appears on one line.

4. Double-click the new **LinkButton** control to create its event handler template. Add the following command to the lnkCW_Click template:

```
Response.Redirect("Clearwater.htm")
```

5. Click the **Start** button ▶ to run the project. Click the **Catalog** hyperlink to display the Catalog.aspx Web form, then click the **Clearwater Home Page** LinkButton. The Clearwater.htm static Web page appears again.

6. Close Internet Explorer.

In summary, use the Server.Transfer method to transfer processing from a source Web form to a target Web form when the Web forms are in the same Web application and when the target form does not require authentication. Use the Response.Redirect method in all other cases.

# SHARING DATA VALUES ACROSS MULTIPLE WEB FORMS

Web applications that contain multiple Web forms usually need to share data values among the different forms. For example, in the Clearwater Traders Web application, when the user selects an item to place in his or her shopping cart, the item's inventory ID value must transfer from the Catalog.aspx Web form to the ShoppingCart.aspx Web form. The shopping cart inventory ID and quantity values must transfer from the ShoppingCart.aspx Web form to the ConfirmOrder.aspx Web form, which summarizes the order details. And, the user information must transfer from either the Login.aspx or NewCustomer.aspx Web form to the ConfirmOrder.aspx Web form, which summarizes the user's shipping and billing information. You can use three approaches for sharing data values among different forms: server-side cookies, session variables, and application variables.

## Server-Side Cookies

Recall from Chapter 4 that a cookie is a data item about a Web server session that the client computer stores. Different Web pages can retrieve cookie data values, as long as the Web pages originate from the same domain as the Web page that originally created the cookie. In Chapter 4, you learned how to create and process cookies using client-side scripts. You can also create **server-side cookies**, which are cookies that commands in server-side programs create on the client workstation.

To create a server-side cookie, the Web server sends the cookie specification to the browser as a header message in the header section of an HTML document. (Recall that the Web browser uses the information in an HTML document's header section to process the Web page.) In a Web form, you call the **Response.Cookies method** to create a server-side cookie. Recall that a cookie contains data values as variable name/value pairs. You use the following general command to create a new cookie name/value pair:

```
Response.Cookies("variable_name").Value = variable_value
```

In this syntax, *variable_name* is the cookie variable name, and *variable_value* is the associated value. For example, you would use the following command to create a cookie variable named last_name with the associated value "Harris":

```
Response.Cookies("last_name").Value = "Harris"
```

Recall that you can create temporary cookies, which persist only during the current browser session, and persistent cookies, which persist until a specified expiration date. To create a persistent cookie, you set the cookie's Expires property to the desired

11

expiration date. For example, you would use the following command to specify that the last_name value expires on 12/31/2006:

```
Response.Cookies("last_name").Expires = #12/31/2006#
```

 Recall that in VB .NET commands, you enclose date values in pound signs #.

You use the **Request.Cookies method** in a Web form event handler to retrieve the value of a cookie variable. This method has the following general syntax:

```
object = Request.Cookies("variable_name").Value
```

In this syntax, *object* is the object to which you want to assign the cookie value, and might be a VB .NET variable or a Web form property value such as the Text property of a Label control. *Variable_name* is the name of the cookie variable to retrieve. For example, you would use the following command to retrieve the value of the last_name cookie and assign its value to the Text property of a Label control named lblCustLastName:

```
lblCustLastName.Text = Request.Cookies("last_name").Value
```

Although Web developers use cookies extensively, recall that cookies have limitations. Many users are reluctant to allow Web server processes to create cookies on their browsers due to misconceptions about security concerns. Also, recall that browsers limit the maximum size of a cookie and limit the maximum number of cookies that a single Web server can create on a browser: A single cookie can store a maximum of 20 name/value pairs or a maximum of 4,096 characters, and a Web server can create a maximum of 20 cookies on a single workstation. To overcome these limitations, ASP.NET provides session variables, which you will use to share data values among the Web forms in the Clearwater Traders Web application.

## Session Variables

A **session variable** is a value that contains specific information about a browser session. The Web server stores session variable values in the Web server's main memory. Session variables might be used to record information such as the session date and time, the browser software version, which pages the browser requests at the Web site, and the user's preferences and selections. When the browser first requests a Web form (.aspx) page from the Web server, a cookie named SessionID is created on the browser. The **SessionID cookie** stores the browser/Web server session ID, which is a value that uniquely identifies the session. As the user interacts with the Web server, the Web server uses the SessionID cookie value to maintain information about the browser session. When the session ends, the browser discards the SessionID cookie. Note that the Web server stores all of the session information in Web server main memory—only the SessionID value exists as a cookie on the client workstation. This technique overcomes the size and maximum number limitations of cookies. The following sections describe the persistence of session variables and show how to create and use session variables.

## Persistence of Session Variables

Recall that a temporary cookie persists as long as the browser session remains open, and a persistent cookie persists until the cookie's expiration date. Suppose you connect to a Web site that creates cookies. Then, leaving your browser open, you take a coffee break, a lunch break, or a two-week vacation. As long as your browser remains open, you can resume browsing just where you left off, and all of the cookies you created previously will still be available.

Session variables work differently. Because a Web server stores session variables in the Web server's main memory, the server must track the status of browser sessions. When a browser disconnects from the Web server, the Web server reclaims the main memory space occupied by the browser's session variables. Otherwise, the Web server's main memory would become filled with information about disconnected sessions.

Sometimes users do not close their browsers and formally disconnect from Web servers. They take coffee breaks, lunch breaks, or two-week vacations, and leave their browsers open and connected. As a result, Web servers must somehow decide when browser sessions are inactive and automatically disconnect these sessions. To do this, Web servers track the status of browser sessions using a session timeout value. A **session timeout value** is a time interval, measured in minutes, that Web administrators use to identify inactive browser sessions. If a browser session sends no requests to the Web server for the session timeout value interval, the Web server assumes the browser session is inactive, disconnects the session, and reclaims the memory space used by the session's session variables.

The default session timeout value is 20 minutes. You can programmatically reset the session timeout value for a Web application project by setting the Session.Timeout property value in any project form's code behind file. The general syntax for the command to set this property value is as follows:

```
Session.Timeout = timeout_minutes
```

In this syntax, *timeout_minutes* specifies the timeout interval in minutes, and can be any integer value. You would use the following command to change the Session.Timeout property value to 30 minutes:

```
Session.Timeout = 30
```

You can also set the Session.Timeout property for a Web application project in the project's Global.asax.vb file. Recall from Chapter 6 that the Global.asax.vb file contains code to initialize and configure Web applications, and is visible to all Web forms within a project. The Global.asax.vb file contains event handler templates for many different project events, such as when the application starts and ends. Typically, Web developers place the command to set the application's Session.Timeout property in the Application_Start event handler in the Global.asax.vb file.

**11**

You can also specify a Web application project's session timeout value in the project's Web.config file. Recall from Chapter 6 that the Web.config file provides configuration information for the project and project folder. The Web.config file is an XML file that contains data elements that are similar to HTML tags, as well as corresponding element attribute values that are similar to HTML element attributes. To change a project's session timeout value, you modify the `<sessionState>` element, and change its timeout attribute value to the desired session timeout interval. The following code shows an example of the `<sessionState>` element in the Clearwater Traders project's Web.config file:

```
<sessionState
    mode="InProc"
    stateConnectionString="tcpip=127.0.0.1:42424"
    sqlConnectionString="data source=127.0.0.1; ↵
    user id=sa;password="
    cookieless="false"
    timeout="20"
/>
```

By default, the timeout element value is "20," which indicates that the timeout value is 20 minutes. To specify a different number of minutes, you change this value to a different integer value.

So far, all of the approaches for changing the session timeout value apply to a specific Web application project. If you want to change the session timeout value for all applications running on a Web server, you can modify the `<sessionState>` element in the Web server's Machine.config file. A Web server's Machine.config file contains default settings that all ASP.NET Web applications use. This file is in the Windows\Microsoft.NET\ Framework\[*version*]\Config folder on the Web server, and you can modify its settings using any text editor.

You have learned four different ways to specify a Web application project's session timeout value. What if different session timeout values appear in different places? The order of precedence evaluates from most specific, in Web form code behind files, to most general, in the Machine.config file. Session timeout values that you specify in Web form code behind file commands take precedence over all other values. Session timeout values that you specify in the Global.asax.vb file take precedence over values in the Web.config and Machine.config files, and Web.config settings take precedence over Machine.config settings.

## Creating and Using Session Variables

Web servers structure session variables as name/value pairs. You use the following command to create a new session variable:

```
Session("variable_name") = variable_value
```

In this syntax, *variable_name* can be any legal VB .NET variable name. *Variable_value* can be a string, numeric, or date literal value; a variable name; or a control property. For example, the following command creates a session variable named last_name and sets the value to the Text property of a TextBox control named txtLastName:

```
Session("last_name") = txtLastName.Text
```

To retrieve session variable values, you assign the session variable value to an object, such as a variable or control property. You use the following command to assign the value of a session variable to an object:

```
object = Session("variable_name")
```

In this syntax, *object* is the object to which you want to assign the session variable value, and might be a VB .NET variable or a Web form property value such as the Text property of a Label control. *Variable_name* is the name of the session variable to retrieve. For example, you would use the following command to retrieve the value of the last_name session variable and assign its value to the Text property of a Label control named lblCustLastName:

```
lblCustLastName.Text = Session("last_name")
```

When an application no longer needs a session variable, you should remove the variable to release the space it occupies in the Web server's main memory. You use the following command to remove a session variable:

```
Session.Remove("variable_name")
```

You would use the following command to remove the last_name session variable from memory:

```
Session.Remove("last_name")
```

## Creating a Session Variable to Track Shopping Cart Items

When the user clicks the *Add to cart* hyperlink on the Catalog.aspx Web form in Figure 11-2, the Web form adds the inventory ID value of the selected item to the user's shopping cart. To record shopping cart selections, you will create a session variable named ShoppingCartItem. This session variable's value will be the selection's inventory ID (INV_ID) value, which the detail DataGrid at the bottom of the Catalog.aspx Web form in Figure 11-2 provides.

The detail DataGrid in Figure 11-2 has the (ID) value dgDetail. To reference the items in this DataGrid, the event handler that executes when a user makes a selection creates a variable named *row* that references the current DataGrid selection. The following command declares the row variable and sets its value to the current selection:

```
Dim row As Object = dgDetail.Items(dgDetail.SelectedIndex)
```

The code then uses the *row* variable to retrieve the data values stored in individual cells within the DataGrid. For example, the following expression references the current Size value, which is stored in column 2. (Recall that in a DataGrid, the leftmost column number is 0.)

```
row.Cells(2).Text
```

The INV_ID column has been designated as the detail DataGrid's DataKeyField, or primary key. To reference the INV_ID value of the current selection, you use the following expression:

```
dgDetail.DataKeys.Item(row.ItemIndex)
```

Now you will add to the Catalog.aspx Web form the command to create the session variable that stores the INV_ID value of the current detail DataGrid selection in Figure 11-2.

To create the session variable to store the INV_ID value of the current detail DataGrid selection:

1. In the Catalog.aspx.vb code behind file, scroll up to the dgDetail_
   SelectedIndexChanged event handler. Add the shaded commands in
   Figure 11-12 to create a variable named intInvID to reference the
   INV_ID value of the current detail DataGrid selection and create the
   session variable that references the intInvID variable value.

```
Private Sub dgDetail_SelectedIndexChanged↵
(ByVal sender As System.Object, _
ByVal e As System.EventArgs) _
Handles dgDetail.SelectedIndexChanged
    Dim row As Object = dgDetail.Items(dgDetail.SelectedIndex)
    Dim strQOH As String = row.Cells(5).Text
    lblMsg.Visible = True
    If strQOH = "0" Then
        lblMsg.Text = row.Cells(1).Text & " " & row.Cells(2).Text ↵
                    & " " & row.Cells(3).Text & " are out of stock"
        lblMsg.ForeColor = System.Drawing.Color.Red
    Else
        lblMsg.Text = row.Cells(1).Text & " " & row.Cells(2).Text ↵
                    & " " & row.Cells(3).Text & " was added to your cart"
        lblMsg.ForeColor = System.Drawing.Color.Blue
        Dim intInvID As Integer = dgDetail.DataKeys.Item(row.ItemIndex)
        Session("ShoppingCartItem") = intInvID
    End If
    lblMsg.Text = row.Cells(1).Text & " " & row.Cells(2).Text & " " & _
                row.Cells(3).Text & " was added to your cart"
End Sub
```

**Figure 11-12**     Commands to create the session variable to reference the INV_ID value of the detail DataGrid selection

2. Save the file.

Next you will modify the DataGrid on the ShoppingCart.aspx Web form (see Figure 11-3) so the DataGrid displays the selected inventory item's description, color, size, and price, and displays a default order quantity value of 1. To do this, you will modify a procedure named FillTheCart in the ShoppingCart Web form's code behind file. This procedure converts the value of the ShoppingCartItem session variable to a string data type and includes an `If` decision control structure. To determine whether the user has selected an item, the `If` decision control structure condition tests whether the ShoppingCartItem session variable value is an empty string literal `""`. If the user has selected an item, the procedure updates the data adapter and the data set that fill the DataGrid on the ShoppingCart.aspx Web form.

You will write a command that modifies the SelectCommand property of the data adapter's select command. This command will query the database and retrieve from the Clearwater Traders database the information about the selected INV_ID value. The SQL query will use as its search condition the session variable, which stores the current selection's INV_ID value. If the user has not selected an item, a label appears on the ShoppingCart.aspx Web form to advise the user that the shopping cart is empty.

To display the selection information on the ShoppingCart.aspx Web form:

1. Select the **ShoppingCart.aspx** node in the Solution Explorer, then click the **View Code** button 🗏 to open the ShoppingCart.aspx.vb code behind file.

2. Scroll up to the FillTheCart procedure, then add the shaded commands in Figure 11-13 to display the information about the selected item in the DataGrid on the ShoppingCart.aspx Web form.

**11**

```
Private Sub FillTheCart()
   Session("ShoppingCartItem") = Session("ShoppingCartItem").ToString
   If Session("ShoppingCartItem") <> "" Then
       daCW.SelectCommand.CommandText = _
       "SELECT ITEM.ITEM_DESC, INVENTORY.COLOR, " & _
       "INVENTORY.INV_SIZE, INVENTORY.INV_PRICE, " & _
       "INVENTORY.INV_QOH, INVENTORY.INV_ID, " & _
       "ITEM.ITEM_ID, 1 As Qty " & _
       "FROM INVENTORY, ITEM " & _
       "WHERE INVENTORY.ITEM_ID = ITEM.ITEM_ID AND " & _
       "INVENTORY.INV_ID = " & Session("ShoppingCartItem")
       daCW.Fill(dsCart1, "inventory")
       dgCart.DataBind()
   Else
       lblMsg.Text = "<center><b>Your shopping cart is empty↵
                       </b></center>"
   End If
End Sub
```

**Figure 11-13**     Commands to display the selection information on the ShoppingCart.aspx Web form

3. Click the **Start** button ▶ to run the project, then select the **Catalog** hyperlink. Open the **Please select a category** list and select **Children's Clothing**, then click **Select** beside Children's Beachcomber Sandals.

 Currently the Catalog.aspx Web form displays actual inventory item quantities from the INVENTORY table in the Quantity column in the detail DataGrid, rather than the values "Yes" or "No" shown in the In Stock? column in Figure 11-2. Later in the chapter, you will learn how to create a template column to modify these values.

4. Click the **Add to cart** hyperlink beside Children's Beachcomber Sandals, Size 10, Color Turquoise, then click **View Cart – Place Order**. The ShoppingCart.aspx Web form displays the selection.

5. Click **Continue shopping** to redisplay the Catalog.aspx Web page and add another item to the shopping cart. Open the **Please select a category** list and select **Outdoor Gear**, click **Select** beside 3-Season Tent, then click **Add to cart** beside 3-Season Tent, Color Sky Blue.

6. Click **View Cart – Place Order**. The ShoppingCart.aspx Web form displays the most recent selection, which is the 3-Season Tent, but does not display the previous selection (Children's Beachcomber Sandals).

7. Close Internet Explorer.

## Using a Session Variable to Store Multiple Data Values

Currently, the ShoppingCartItem session variable references a single value, which is the most recent selection on the Catalog.aspx Web form. Each time the user selects an item and places it in the shopping cart, the application overwrites the inventory ID value of the current shopping cart item with the inventory ID of the new item. As a result, the application's shopping cart stores only one item. This feature may prevent customers from spending too much money at Clearwater Traders, but the shopping cart really needs to allow users to select multiple items. To allow a user to place multiple items in the shopping cart, you will modify the ShoppingCartItem session variable so it stores multiple inventory ID values. You will structure the ShoppingCartItem session variable as a text string that stores multiple INV_ID values by concatenating them to form a single text string. The session variable will include a colon (:) to separate the individual values. Now you will modify the command in the Catalog.aspx.vb code behind file so the ShoppingCartItem session variable stores multiple inventory ID values separated by colons.

To modify the ShoppingCartItem session variable so it stores multiple inventory ID values:

1. Select the **Catalog.aspx.vb** tab to open the file.

2. In the dgDetail_SelectedIndexChanged event handler, locate the command that assigns the intInvID value to the ShoppingCartItem session variable.

(This command is immediately before the **End If** command in the dgDetail_SelectedIndexChanged event handler.) Modify the command that assigns the intInvID value to the ShoppingCartItem session variable so it appears as follows:

```
Session("ShoppingCartItem") += intInvID.ToString & ":"
```

3. Save the file.

With multiple INV_ID values concatenated in a single text string, you need some way to access individual data values within the session variable so you can display individual items in the ShoppingCart.aspx Web form's DataGrid. For example, suppose the customer selects inventory ID number 1 (3-Season Tent, Color Sky Blue), inventory ID number 3 (Women's Hiking Shorts, Color Khaki, Size S), and inventory ID 5 (Women's Hiking Shorts, Color Khaki, Size L). The session variable value would be 1:3:5. You must write commands to parse the session variable and extract the individual data values 1, 3, and 5.

Now you will modify the ShoppingCart.aspx.vb code behind file so the data adapter and data set that fill the ShoppingCart.aspx Web form's DataGrid retrieve all of the individual INV_ID values in the ShoppingCartItem session variable. To do this, you add commands to parse the concatenated INV_ID values in the ShoppingCartItem session variable, then retrieve the inventory information for each value. This technique involves a complex parsing operation, so rather than writing the code yourself, you will modify the code template in Figure 11-14.

**11**

```
Dim strSessionVar As String = Session("session_variable_name")
Dim intEnd, intStart As Integer
Data_Set.Tables.Remove("table_name")
intStart = 0
intEnd = InStr(strSessionVar, ":")
If intEnd > 0 Then
      While intEnd > 0
         Data_Adapter.SelectCommand.CommandText = _
            SQL_query_with_search_condition_=
            strSessionVar.Substring(intStart, intEnd - intStart - 1)
         Data_Adapter.Fill(Data_Set, "table_name")
         intStart = intEnd
         intEnd = InStr(intEnd + 1, strSessionVar, ":")
      End While
         Data_Grid.DataBind()
   Else
         Data_Grid.Visible = False
         lblMsg.Text = "error_message"
   End If
End Sub
```

**Figure 11-14**   Code template to parse session variable values

This chapter's focus is not on complex parsing techniques, so we do not provide a detailed analysis of the template commands. However, you can use this code to parse any session variable that has multiple values, so long as the session variable values use a colon **:** to separate the individual values.

The code template in Figure 11-14 uses a `While` loop to parse each individual session variable value, retrieve the associated data values using a SQL query, append the new value to the data set, then bind the new value to the DataGrid. (Each time a data adapter fills a data set, the data adapter appends the most recently retrieved data to the data values that are currently in the data set.) To use this code in your program, you must modify the shaded items so they reference the data adapter, data set, DataGrid control, and data set table name in the ShoppingCart.aspx Web form. The (ID) property values for these items are as follows:

| Item | (ID) Value |
| --- | --- |
| Data_Adapter | daCW |
| Data_Set | dsCart1 |
| Data_Grid | dgCart |
| table_name | inventory |

You must also modify the shaded `SQL_query_with_search_condition_=` command so it contains the SQL query that you used in Figure 11-13 to fill the DataGrid. The SQL query search condition in Figure 11-13 uses the current value of the ShoppingCartItem session variable, which is a single value. When you modify the code in the ParseSessionVariableValues template, the SQL query search condition will use the following expression, which represents the current parsed value from the session variable that contains multiple values:

```
strSessionVar.Substring(intStart, intEnd - intStart - 1)
```

For example, if the session variable contains the value 1:3:5, then this expression represents the value 1 the first time it executes, the value 3 the second time it executes, and the value 5 the third time it executes.

Now you will paste the code template commands into the FillTheCart procedure in the ShoppingCart.aspx.vb code behind file. In the code template, you will modify the data adapter, data set, table name, and DataGrid (ID) values, and modify the SQL query so it retrieves the correct values. Then you will run the project and confirm that you can now place multiple items in the shopping cart.

To paste the code to parse session variable values into the ShoppingCart.aspx.vb code behind file, then run the project:

1. In Visual Studio .NET, click **File** on the menu bar, point to **Open**, then click **File**. Navigate to the Chapter11 folder on your Data Disk, select **ParseSessionVariableValues.txt**, then click **Open**.

2. Select all of the commands, click **Edit** on the menu bar, click **Copy**, then close the ParseSessionVariableValues.txt window in the Browser Window.

3. Select the **ShoppingCart.aspx.vb** tab, place the insertion point at the beginning of the first command in the FillTheCart procedure, then press **Enter** to create a new blank line at the beginning of the procedure.

4. Paste the copied commands onto the new blank line, then modify the shaded values as shown in Figure 11-15.

```
Private Sub FillTheCart()
    Dim strSessionVar As String = Session("ShoppingCartItem")
    Dim intEnd, intStart As Integer
    dsCart1.Tables.Remove("inventory")
    intStart = 0
    intEnd = InStr(strSessionVar, ":")
    If intEnd > 0 Then
        While intEnd > 0
            daCW.SelectCommand.CommandText = _
                "SELECT ITEM.ITEM_DESC, INVENTORY.COLOR, " & _
                "INVENTORY.INV_SIZE, INVENTORY.INV_PRICE, " & _
                "INVENTORY.INV_QOH, INVENTORY.INV_ID, " & _
                "ITEM.ITEM_ID, 1 As Qty " & _
                "FROM INVENTORY, ITEM " & _
                "WHERE INVENTORY.ITEM_ID = ITEM.ITEM_ID AND " & _
                "INVENTORY.INV_ID = " & _
                strSessionVar.Substring(intStart, ↵
                intEnd - intStart - 1).ToString()
            daCW.Fill(dsCart1, "inventory")
            intStart = intEnd
            intEnd = InStr(intEnd + 1, strSessionVar, ":")
        End While
        dgCart.DataBind()
    Else
        dgCart.Visible = False
        lblMsg.Text = "<center><b>Your shopping cart is empty</b></center>"
    End If
End Sub
```

**Figure 11-15**    FillTheCart procedure with commands to parse the session variable values

To modify the SQL query, copy the existing SQL query commands from the end of the procedure, then paste them into the template and modify them as necessary.

5. Delete the commands at the end of the procedure so the FillTheCart procedure looks like Figure 11-15.

6. Click the **Start** button ▶ to run the project, then select the **Catalog** hyper-link. Open the **Please select a category** list and select **Children's Clothing**, then click **Select** beside Children's Beachcomber Sandals.

7. Click the **Add to cart** hyperlink beside Children's Beachcomber Sandals, Size 10, Color Turquoise, then click **View Cart – Place Order**. The ShoppingCart.aspx Web form displays the selection.

8. Click **Continue shopping** to redisplay the Catalog.aspx Web page and add another item to the shopping cart. Open the **Please select a category** list and select **Outdoor Gear**, click **Select** beside 3-Season Tent, then click **Add to cart** beside 3-Season Tent, Color Sky Blue.

9. Click **View Cart – Place Order**. Both items now appear in the shopping cart.

10. Close Internet Explorer.

## Using Multiple Session Variables to Store Related Values

Sometimes you need to store multiple related data values in a Web application project. For example, in the shopping cart, you need to store the inventory ID of each selection along with the purchase quantity of each item. To do this, you create another session variable that contains the associated quantity values.

To save the quantity values in a session variable, you will create a second session variable named ShoppingCartQty. This session variable will work in parallel with the ShoppingCartItem session variable: The ShoppingCartItem session variable stores the selected inventory ID values, delimited by colons, and the ShoppingCartQty session variable stores the corresponding quantities of each selection, delimited by colons. Figure 11-16 shows the contents of two sample session variables and shows how the variables contain parallel associated values.

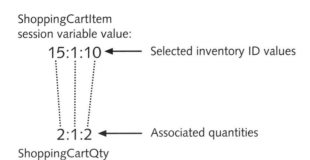

Figure 11-16   Sample contents of parallel ShoppingCartItem and ShoppingCartQty session variables

Figure 11-16 shows that the user has selected inventory ID values 15 (Children's Beachcomber Sandals, Size 10, Color Turquoise), 1 (3-Season Tent, Color Sky Blue), and 10 (Women's Fleece Pullover, Size M, Color Eggplant). The user has specified to order 2 pairs of sandals, 1 tent, and 2 pullovers.

Now you will add the command to the Catalog.aspx.vb code behind file to create the ShoppingCartQty session variable and set the order quantity value to 1 for new selections. To do this, you will add the text string "1:" to the ShoppingCartQty session variable each time the user places a new item in the shopping cart.

To add the command to create and initialize the ShoppingCartQty session variable:

1. Select the **Catalog.aspx.vb** tab to open the file, then add the following command to the dgDetail_SelectedIndexChanged event handler. Add the command just before the **End If** command at the end of the event handler.

   ```
   Session("ShoppingCartQty") += "1:"
   ```

2. Save the file.

When the user clicks the *Edit Quantity* hyperlink on the ShoppingCart.aspx Web page, the selection opens for editing, and the user can change the item quantity, as shown in Figure 11-17.

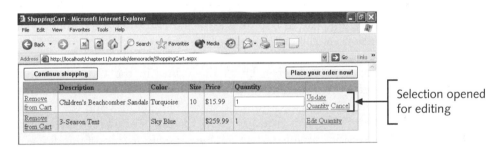

**Figure 11-17**   ShoppingCart.aspx web form with the selection opened for editing

Recall that when a user updates an item in a DataGrid, the DataGrid's UpdateCommand event handler executes. When the user updates the ShoppingCart.aspx DataGrid in Figure 11-17, the event handler needs to update the item quantity in both the DataGrid display and the ShoppingCartQty session variable. This involves some complex parsing operations. To create the UpdateCommand event handler, you will use the code template in Figure 11-18.

```
Dim intPosition As Integer = e.Item.ItemIndex
Dim txtSelection As TextBox = e.Item.Cells(column_number).Controls(0)
Dim strSessionVar As String = Session("session_variable_name")
Dim strNewValue As String
Dim intStart, intEnd, curPosition As Integer
curPosition = 0
intEnd = 0
intStart = InStr(strSessionVar, ":")
While intStart > 0
   If curPosition = intPosition Then
      strNewValue += Trim(txtSelection.Text) & ":"
   Else
      strNewValue += strSessionVar.Substring(intEnd, intStart - intEnd - 1) & ":"
   End If
   intEnd = intStart
   intStart = InStr(intStart + 1, strSessionVar, ":")
   curPosition += 1
End While
Session("session_variable_name") = strNewValue
data_grid_name.EditItemIndex = -1
commands_to_refresh_data_grid
```

**Figure 11-18**    Code template to update a DataGrid and store the updated value in a session variable

This code template steps through each of the values in the Quantity column in the DataGrid and updates the associated quantity in the ShoppingCartQty session variable. Now you will create the UpdateCommand event handler and add the commands from the code template. You will modify the shaded commands to reference the ShoppingCartQty session variable for the *session_variable_name* and the dgCart DataGrid for the *data_grid_name*. The *column_number* value will reference the column number of the Quantity column, which is column number 5 in the DataGrid in Figure 11-17. (Recall that the first column is column 0, the second column is column 1, and so on.)

To create the UpdateCommand event handler to update the selection quantity in the DataGrid and session variable:

1. Select the **ShoppingCart.aspx.vb** tab, open the **Class** list and select **dgCart**, then open the **Method** list and select **UpdateCommand**. The UpdateCommand event handler template appears in the code behind file.

2. Click **File** on the menu bar, point to **Open**, click **File**, then open the **UpdateCommandTemplate.txt** file from the Chapter11 folder on your Data Disk. Copy all of the file commands, then close the file in the Browser Window.

3. Paste the copied template commands into the dgCart_UpdateCommand event handler, then modify the shaded commands in Figure 11-19.

```
Private Sub dgCart_UpdateCommand (ByVal source As Object, ↵
ByVal e As System.Web.UI.WebControls.DataGridCommandEventArgs) ↵
Handles dgCart.UpdateCommand
   Dim intPosition As Integer = e.Item.ItemIndex
   Dim txtSelection As TextBox = e.Item.Cells(5).Controls(0)
   Dim strSessionVar As String = Session("ShoppingCartQty")
   Dim strNewValue As String
   Dim intStart, intEnd, curPosition As Integer
   curPosition = 0
   intEnd = 0
   intStart = InStr(strSessionVar, ":")
   While intStart > 0
      If curPosition = intPosition Then
         strNewValue += Trim(txtSelection.Text) & ":"
      Else
         strNewValue += strSessionVar.Substring↵
         (intEnd, intStart - intEnd - 1) & ":"
      End If
      intEnd = intStart
      intStart = InStr(intStart + 1, strSessionVar, ":")
      curPosition += 1
   End While
   Session("ShoppingCartQty") = strNewValue
   dgCart.EditItemIndex = -1
   FillTheCart()
End Sub
```

**Figure 11-19**     UpdateCommand event handler with commands to update the session variable value

4. Save the file.

Now you will run the project and create a breakpoint on the first line of the procedure that fills the shopping cart. Then you will place some items in the shopping cart, update an item quantity, and step through the commands to view the session variable values.

To run the project and view the session variable values:

1. Scroll up in the ShoppingCart.aspx.vb file, then create a breakpoint on the first command in the FillTheCart procedure. Click the **Start** button ▶ to run the project, and then select the **Catalog** hyperlink. Open the **Please select a category** list and select **Children's Clothing**, then click **Select** beside Children's Beachcomber Sandals. Click **Add to cart** beside Children's Beachcomber Sandals, Size 10, Color Turquoise.

2. Open the **Please select a category** list again, select **Outdoor Gear**, click **Select** beside 3-Season Tent, then click **Add to cart** beside 3-Season Tent, Color Sky Blue.

3. Click **View Cart – Place Order**. Execution pauses on the breakpoint.

11

4. Select **Session("ShoppingCartItem")** in the shaded command, right-click, then click **Add Watch**. The value of the ShoppingCartItem session variable appears as ""15:1:" {String}" in the Watch 1 window, which indicates that the shopping cart contains inventory ID values 15 and 1, and that the session variable value has the String data type.

5. Scroll down in the Code editor to the dgCart_UpdateCommand event handler, select **Session("ShoppingCartQty")** in the third command in the event handler, right-click, then click **Add Watch**. The value of the ShoppingCartQty session variable appears as ""1:1:" {String}" in the Watch 1 window, which indicates that the shopping cart contains one unit of each selection.

6. Click the **Continue** button ▶ to resume execution. The ShoppingCart.aspx Web form appears. Click **Edit Quantity** beside Children's Beachcomber Sandals, click the **Continue** button ▶ to resume execution, change the Quantity value to **2**, then click the **Update Quantity** link. The ShoppingCartQty session variable now appears as ""2:1:" {String}" in the Watch 1 window, which indicates that the UpdateCommand event handler updated the quantity of the first value to 2. Delete the watches.

7. Click the **Stop Debugging** button ■ to halt execution, then clear the breakpoint.

The final task is to modify the FillTheCart procedure that displays the shopping cart items. This procedure must contain commands to parse the ShoppingCartQty session variable, along with the ShoppingCartItem session variable, and display the updated quantity values in the DataGrid. Now you will add these commands to the FillTheCart procedure. Then you will run the project, select some items, update an item quantity, and view the updated quantity in the shopping cart.

To add commands to parse the second session variable and then run the project:

1. In the FillTheCart procedure in the ShoppingCart.aspx.vb code behind file, add or modify the shaded commands in Figure 11-20, which parse the ShoppingCartQty session variable and display the parsed value in the DataGrid.

2. Click the **Start** button ▶ to run the project, and then select the **Catalog** hyperlink. Open the **Please select a category** list and select **Children's Clothing**, then click **Select** beside Children's Beachcomber Sandals. Click **Add to cart** beside Children's Beachcomber Sandals, Size 10, Color Turquoise.

3. Open the **Please select a category** list again, select **Outdoor Gear**, click **Select** beside 3-Season Tent, then click **Add to cart** beside 3-Season Tent, Color Sky Blue.

4. Click **View Cart – Place Order**. The selected items appear in the ShoppingCart.aspx Web form.

```
Private Sub FillTheCart()
    Dim strSessionVar As String = Session("ShoppingCartItem")
    Dim strSessionVar2 As String = Session("ShoppingCartQty")
    Dim intEnd, intStart, intEnd2, intStart2 As Integer
    dsCart1.Tables.Remove("inventory")
    intStart = 0
    intStart2 = 0
    intEnd = InStr(strSessionVar, ":")
    intEnd2 = InStr(strSessionVar2, ":")
    If intEnd > 0 Then
        While intEnd > 0
            daCW.SelectCommand.CommandText = _
                "SELECT ITEM.ITEM_DESC, INVENTORY.COLOR, " & _
                "INVENTORY.INV_SIZE, INVENTORY.INV_PRICE, " & _
                "INVENTORY.INV_QOH, INVENTORY.INV_ID, " & _
                "ITEM.ITEM_ID, " & strSessionVar2.Substring ↵
                (intStart2, intEnd2 - intStart2 - 1) & " As Qty " & _
                "FROM INVENTORY, ITEM " & _
                "WHERE INVENTORY.ITEM_ID = ITEM.ITEM_ID AND " & _
                "INVENTORY.INV_ID = " & _
                strSessionVar.Substring(intStart, intEnd - intStart - 1)
            daCW.Fill(dsCart1, "inventory")
            intStart = intEnd
            intStart2 = intEnd2
            intEnd = InStr(intEnd + 1, strSessionVar, ":")
            intEnd2 = InStr(intEnd2 + 1, strSessionVar2, ":")
        End While
        dgCart.DataBind()
    Else
        dgCart.Visible = False
        lblMsg.Text = "<center><b>Your shopping cart is empty</b></center>"
    End If
End Sub
```

**Figure 11-20**    Commands in FillTheCart procedure to parse the second session variable and display the parsed value in the DataGrid

5. Click **Edit Quantity** beside Children's Beachcomber Sandals, change the Quantity value to **2**, and then click **Update Quantity**. The updated quantity appears in the DataGrid.

6. Close Internet Explorer.

## Removing Values from Session Variables That Store Multiple Values

When a session variable stores multiple data values, you may need to remove selected values from time to time. For example, Clearwater Traders customers will occasionally place an item in their shopping cart, then change their mind about purchasing the item and want to remove it from their shopping cart. Removing an item requires removing the item's INV_ID value from the ShoppingCartItem session variable and removing the item quantity from the ShoppingCartQty session variable. To remove an individual value from a session variable, you will use the RemoveFromSessionVariable function in Figure 11-21.

```
Private Function RemoveFromSessionVariable↵
(ByVal intPosition As Integer, ByVal strSessionVar As String)
   Dim strNewSessionVar As String
   Dim intEnd, intStart, curPosition As Integer
   curPosition = 0
   intStart = 0
   intEnd = InStr(strSessionVar, ":")
   While intEnd > 0
      If curPosition <> intPosition Then
         strNewSessionVar += strSessionVar.Substring↵
         (intStart, intEnd - intStart - 1) & ":"
      End If
      intStart = intEnd
      intEnd = InStr(intEnd + 1, strSessionVar, ":")
      curPosition += 1
   End While
   RemoveFromSessionVariable = strNewSessionVar
End Function
```

**Figure 11-21**    Code to remove a session variable value at a specific position

This function receives as input parameters an integer that represents the position of the data value in the session variable and the session variable name. These input parameters are shaded in Figure 11-21. The function then parses the session variable, removes the value at the specified position, and returns the revised session variable to the calling command.

Now you will add the code for the RemoveFromSessionVariable function to the ShoppingCart.aspx Web form. Then you will create a DeleteCommand event handler, and add commands to the event handler to call the function two times. The first command will specify to remove the current DataGrid selection from the ShoppingCartItem session variable, and the second command will specify to remove the current DataGrid selection from the ShoppingCartQty session variable. (Recall that you use the expression `e.Item.ItemIndex` to reference the current selection in a DataGrid.) Then you will add the command to call the FillTheCart procedure to refresh the shopping cart display. Finally you will run the project, add some items to the shopping cart, and then remove an item.

To add and test the function:

1. In Visual Studio .NET, click **File** on the menu bar, point to **Open**, click **File**, open **RemoveFromSessionVariable.txt** from the Chapter11 folder on your Data Disk, copy all of the file's text, then close the RemoveFromSessionVariable.txt window in the Browser Window.

2. Paste the copied text at the end of the ShoppingCart.aspx.vb code behind file, just before the **End Class** command.

3. In the ShoppingCart.aspx.vb code behind file, open the **Class** list and select **dgCart**, then open the **Method** list and select **DeleteCommand**. The new DeleteCommand event handler template appears in the Code editor.

4. Add the following commands to the dgCart_DeleteCommand event handler to call the function and pass to it the position of the current DataGrid selection and the name of the session variable from which to remove the value associated with the position:

```
Dim i As Integer = e.Item.ItemIndex
Session("ShoppingCartItem") = ↵
RemoveFromSessionVariable(i, Session("ShoppingCartItem"))
Session("ShoppingCartQty") = ↵
RemoveFromSessionVariable(i, Session("ShoppingCartQty"))
FillTheCart()
```

5. Click the **Start** button ▶ to run the project, and then select the **Catalog** hyperlink. Open the **Please select a category** list and select **Children's Clothing**, then click **Select** beside Children's Beachcomber Sandals. Click **Add to cart** beside Children's Beachcomber Sandals, Size 10, Color Turquoise.

6. Open the **Please select a category** list again, select **Outdoor Gear**, click **Select** beside 3-Season Tent, then click **Add to cart** beside 3-Season Tent, Color Sky Blue.

7. Click **View Cart – Place Order**. The selected items appear on the ShoppingCart.aspx Web form.

8. Click the **Remove from Cart** link beside Children's Beachcomber Sandals. The item no longer appears in the shopping cart.

9. Close Internet Explorer.

10. Because you are finished working with the Catalog.aspx and Catalog.aspx.vb files for now, close these windows in the Browser Window.

## Creating Cookieless Web Application Projects

Recall that when a user opens a new browser session, the Web server creates the SessionID cookie on the user's workstation to identify the session. The Web server uses this cookie to track the values of the user's session variables on the Web server. For security or privacy reasons, some users configure their browsers so that Web servers can never create cookies. If a user configures his or her browser this way, applications that use session variables will not work correctly.

To overcome this limitation, ASP.NET allows developers to configure a **cookieless** Web application project, which is a project that stores session ID information without using a cookie. To configure a cookieless Web application project, you open the project's Web.config file, and change the `<sessionState>` variable's cookieless attribute value

**11**

to "true." Figure 11-22 shows the `<sessionState>` variable within the Clearwater Traders project's Web.config file in which the cookieless attribute value has been set to "true."

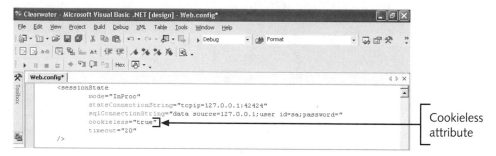

**Figure 11-22** Configuring a Web application project to be cookieless

When a developer configures a project to be cookieless, ASP.NET no longer saves the session ID value in a cookie on the user's workstation. Instead, ASP.NET places the session ID within the URL of the page returned from the Web server, as shown in Figure 11-23.

**Figure 11-23** Session ID value within a URL in a cookieless project

Cookieless Web applications have certain limitations. One limitation is that all hyperlinks in project Web forms must use relative URL paths, because absolute URL paths do not contain the session ID value. If you were to use absolute URL paths, the project would lose its session ID and not work correctly. In addition, if a user saves a URL for a cookieless project in his or her Favorites folder, goes to that favorite URL, and then goes directly to the Clearwater URL without using the browser's back button, the session ID and session variables will be lost.

## Application Variables

Recall that to share data values among Web forms in an integrated Web application, you can use cookies, session variables, or application variables. An **application variable** stores a value on the Web server that is associated with a specific Web application and is accessible to all application users. You would use an application variable to store values that all users may view or change, such as a page hit counter or a voting tally. The commands that create, reference, and remove application variables are very similar to the commands that create, reference, and remove session variables. You use the following syntax to create a session variable:

```
Application("variable_name") = variable_value
```

You use the following syntax to reference a session variable:

```
object = Application("variable_name")
```

You use the following syntax to remove a session variable:

```
Application.Remove("variable_name")
```

For example, you would use the following command to create an application variable named HitCounter and initialize its value as 0:

```
Application("HitCounter") = 0
```

You should use application variables to store values that all application users access, that require small amounts of storage space and quick access times, and that are not critical to the application. If the Web server is shut down for any reason, the application variable values will be lost. If you need to store data values that occupy large amounts of storage space, or that must be retained over time, store the values in a database or in files.

You have learned different ways to share data values among multiple Web forms. You have stored multiple data values in a single session variable and learned how to retrieve and delete multiple data values from a single session variable. In addition, you have learned how to use two related session variables to store associated data values. Finally, you have learned how to create application variables to store values that all project forms can reference.

**11**

## INSERTING MASTER-DETAIL RECORDS SIMULTANEOUSLY

Recall from Chapter 10 that in a database master-detail relationship, a master record in one database table has many related detail records in another table. Often when you insert records in a master table, you must simultaneously insert related records in a detail table. For example, when a Clearwater Traders customer places an order, the system must insert a new record in the ORDERS table. Then, the system must immediately insert one or more records in the ORDER_LINE table to represent each order item.

Figure 11-24 shows the master-detail relationships among the CUSTOMER, ORDERS, and ORDER_LINE tables for this scenario. In the CUSTOMER/ORDERS link, CUSTOMER is the master table and ORDERS is the detail table, indicating that one customer can have many orders. Similarly, in the ORDERS/

ORDER_LINE link, ORDERS is the master table and ORDER_LINE is the detail table, indicating that one record in the ORDERS table can have many associated ORDER_LINE records.

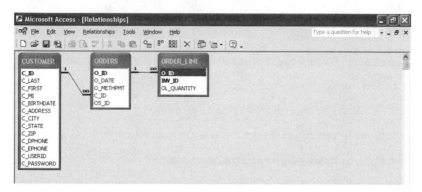

**Figure 11-24**   Master-detail relationships among the CUSTOMER, ORDERS, and ORDER_LINE tables

Inserting master-detail records simultaneously becomes tricky when the DBMS automatically generates a surrogate key value. (If you are using an Oracle9*i* database, a sequence generates the O_ID value. If you are using an Access database, an AutoNumber data column generates the O_ID value.) When you simultaneously insert data values in master-detail tables in which the master table uses a surrogate primary key that the DBMS automatically generates, you need to save the master primary key value as a local variable, then use the local variable value in the INSERT command for the detail records. The following subsections describe the commands to carry out this operation for both an Oracle9*i* and an Access database.

## Retrieving and Storing Oracle9*i* Sequence Values

Recall from Chapter 9 that to use an Oracle9*i* sequence to generate surrogate key values automatically, you use the NEXTVAL sequence pseudocolumn within the SQL INSERT command to retrieve the next sequence value. This command has the following syntax:

```
INSERT INTO tablename (column1_name, column2_name)
VALUES(sequence_name.NEXTVAL, column2_value)
```

Another way to retrieve the next value in an Oracle9*i* sequence is to use a SELECT query that has the following syntax:

```
SELECT sequence_name.NEXTVAL FROM DUAL
```

This query retrieves the next sequence value. Note that the FROM clause references the DUAL database table. DUAL is an Oracle9*i* system table that you use to process commands such as selecting values from pseudocolumns. When you create a Web application that simultaneously inserts a master record along with one or more detail records using an Oracle9*i* database, you retrieve the next sequence value using a SELECT command, then save the value as a local variable before you insert either the master record or the detail records.

To save the next sequence value in a local variable, you create a SQLCommand object in which the CommandText property value is the SQL query that retrieves the next sequence value. Then, you execute the SQLCommand object using the ExecuteScalar method. You use the **ExecuteScalar method** to execute a SELECT command that retrieves a single column of values. The general syntax of the command to call the ExecuteScalar method is:

```
command_object_name.ExecuteScalar()
```

In this syntax, *command_object_name* represents a SQLCommand object. The ExecuteScalar method is similar to the ExecuteNonQuery method you used in Chapter 10, except that you use it only for SELECT queries, because when the method executes the query, it returns only the first value in the first column of the retrieved records.

The following general commands retrieve the next sequence value and then save the value in a local variable:

```
'retrieve next sequence value
SQLCommand.CommandText = ↵
"SELECT sequence_name.NEXTVAL FROM DUAL"
'set retrieved value to local variable
Dim variable_name As Integer = ↵
CInt(SQLCommand.ExecuteScalar())
```

For example, you would use the following commands to retrieve the next value in a sequence named O_ID_SEQUENCE, then save the retrieved value in a variable named intO_ID:

```
SQLCommand.CommandText = ↵
"SELECT O_ID_SEQUENCE.NEXTVAL FROM DUAL"
Dim intO_ID As Integer = CInt(SQLCommand.ExecuteScalar())
```

## Retrieving and Storing Access AutoNumber Values

To insert master-detail records in a Web application project simultaneously using an Access database, you insert the master record as usual. Then you retrieve the last AutoNumber value inserted by your application and assign it to a local variable using the SQL query `SELECT @@IDENTITY`. This query retrieves the AutoNumber value for the INSERT action query most recently executed by the current user within the current browser session.

The `SELECT @@IDENTITY` query will work only if you are using Access versions for Windows 2000 or XP, and if you are using the Jet 4.0 OLE DB provider in your connection.

To store the next AutoNumber value in a local variable, you create a SQLCommand object in which the CommandText property value is the **SELECT @@IDENTITY** SQL query that retrieves the AutoNumber value. Then you execute the SQLCommand object using the ExecuteScalar method. These commands have the following general syntax:

```
SQLCommand.CommandText = "SELECT @@IDENTITY"
Dim variable_name As Integer = ⤶
CInt(SQLCommand.ExecuteScalar())
```

## Simultaneously Inserting the Master and Detail Records

When the user clicks *Confirm your order* on the ConfirmOrder.aspx Web form in Figure 11-6, the button's event handler transfers processing to the ProcessOrder.aspx Web form, which contains commands to insert the new order and order line records into the database. Recall from Figure 9-10 that the customer ID (C_ID) field is a foreign key in the ORDERS table. To insert the new order record in the ORDERS table, the system must determine the C_ID value for the current customer. The system determines the customer's ID value using a query that has a search condition based on the values that the user enters in the *User Name* and *Password* TextBox controls on the Login.aspx Web form in Figure 11-4. Modifying the project to perform this action involves a number of steps. The first step is to add to the *Place your order now* button's event handler on the ShoppingCart.aspx Web form the command to transfer processing to the Login.aspx Web form. You also need to add to the Login button event handler on the Login.aspx Web form the commands that save the values in the *User Name* and *Password* TextBox controls as session variables. These commands store the *User Name* and *Password* values as session variables, and use the UCase function to convert the values to all uppercase letters, so the *User Name* and *Password* values are not case-sensitive. Now you will add comments linking the Login, ConfirmOrder, and ProcessOrder forms. You will also add commands to save the user name and password using session variables.

To add the commands to switch between forms, save the session variable values, and then test the application:

1. Select the **ShoppingCart.aspx** tab in the Browser Window, then double-click **Place your order now** to create a new Click event handler template for the button. Add the following command to the btnOrder_Click event handler template to transfer processing to the Login.aspx Web form:

   **Server.Transfer("Login.aspx")**

2. Select the **Login.aspx** node in the Solution Explorer, then click the **View Code** button ▤ to open the Login.aspx Web form's code behind file. Scroll down to the btnLogin_Click event handler, scroll down in the event handler, then add the following commands to the **If** section of the decision control

structure, immediately after the comment statement ' found the userid and password, continue:

```
Session("UserID") = UCase(txtUsername.Text)
Session("Password") = UCase(txtPassword.Text)
Server.Transfer("Secure/ConfirmOrder.aspx")
```

3. To test the commands, click the **Start** button ▶ to run the project, and then select the **Catalog** hyperlink. Open the **Please select a category** list and select **Children's Clothing**, then click **Select** beside Children's Beachcomber Sandals. Click **Add to cart** beside Children's Beachcomber Sandals, Size 10, Color Turquoise.

4. Click **View Cart – Place Order**. The selected item appears on the ShoppingCart.aspx Web form.

5. Click **Place your order now**. Processing transfers to the Login.aspx Web form.

6. Type **harrispe** in the *User Name* TextBox, **asdfjk** in the *Password* TextBox, then click **Login**. The ConfirmOrder.aspx Web form displays the order summary.

The ConfirmOrder.aspx Web form does not yet display the Total column in the DataGrid, which shows the extended total for each order line. You will learn how to create this column using a template column later in the chapter.

The code that displays the values on the ConfirmOrder.aspx Web form uses techniques that you have already learned, so the code was included in the Web form in the Data Disk file.

7. Close Internet Explorer.

8. Close the ShoppingCart.aspx, ShoppingCart.aspx.vb, and Login.aspx.vb windows in the Browser Window. You should currently have no windows open in the Browser Window.

Recall that when the user clicks *Confirm your order* on the ConfirmOrder.aspx Web form, the application transfers processing to the ProcessOrder.aspx Web form. Commands in the ProcessOrder.aspx Web form's Page_Load procedure insert the order data values into the ORDERS and ORDER_LINE database tables. Next you will add to the ConfirmOrder.aspx Web form's event handler the command to transfer processing to the ProcessOrder.aspx Web form. Then you will begin to add to the ProcessOrder.aspx Web form's Page_Load procedure the commands to insert the data records into the ORDERS and ORDER_LINE tables.

To add the command to transfer processing to the ProcessOrder.aspx Web form:

1. In the Solution Explorer, select the **ConfirmOrder.aspx** node in the Secure folder, then click the **View Designer** button ⊞ to open the Web form in Design view.

2. Double-click **Confirm your order** to create a new Click event handler, then add to the btnOrder_Click event handler the following command to transfer processing to the ProcessOrder.aspx Web form:

```
Server.Transfer("ProcessOrder.aspx")
```

3. Save the file.

## Inserting the Master Record into the ORDERS Table

Next you will add the commands to insert the master record into the ORDERS table. (You will add the commands to insert the records into the ORDER_LINE table a little later.) To insert the master record into the ORDERS table, you must provide values for the O_ID (order ID), O_DATE (order date), O_METHPMT (payment method), C_ID (customer ID), and OS_ID (order source ID) fields (see Figure 11-24).

You will add commands to retrieve the O_ID value from either a sequence or an AutoNumber column, then save the value as a local variable. Another command will use the DateString property to retrieve the current system date for the O_DATE value. (Recall that you used the DateString property to retrieve the current system date in Chapter 6.) When you insert a date value using an Oracle9*i* database, you use the TO_DATE function to convert the date text string expression to a date format, based on a format mask. If you are using an Oracle9*i* database, you must use the VB .NET **Format function** to format the system date value so it matches the Oracle9*i* format mask. The VB .NET Format function has the following general syntax:

```
Format(value, desired_format)
```

Oracle9*i* users will use the following statement to change the format of the current system date to the MM/DD/YYYY format mask:

```
Format(date_value, "MM/dd/yyyy")
```

To simplify the application, you will assume the O_METHPMT value is "CC" (credit card). (In an actual production system, you would allow the customer to specify the payment method.) Also to simplify, you will insert the OS_ID value as NULL. (In a production system, you would allow the user to select these data values from a form control such as a list.)

To determine the C_ID (customer ID) value, you will create a SQLCommand object with a CommandText property that retrieves the C_ID value from the CUSTOMER table, using the UserID and Password session variables as search conditions. If you are using an Oracle9*i* database, you will use the Oracle9*i* UPPER function to translate the retrieved C_USERID and C_PASSWORD values to all uppercase letters to match the session variables. If you are using an Access database, you will use the Access UCase function to translate the retrieved values to uppercase letters. You will use the ExecuteScalar method to execute the query and send the result to a local variable named intCurrentC_ID.

To add and test the commands that insert the master ORDERS record:

1. Select the **ProcessOrder.aspx** node in the Secure folder, then click the **View Code** button ▤ to open the code behind file.

*If you are using an Oracle9i database*, add to the Page_Load procedure the shaded commands in Figure 11-25 that insert the new master record into the ORDERS table.

```
Private Sub Page_Load(ByVal sender As System.Object, ↵
ByVal e As System.EventArgs) Handles MyBase.Load
    connCW.Open()
    SQLCommand.Connection = connCW
    'retrieve and store O_ID value
    SQLCommand.CommandText = "SELECT O_ID_SEQUENCE.NEXTVAL FROM DUAL"
    Dim intO_ID As Integer = CInt(SQLCommand.ExecuteScalar())
    'retrieve current system date
    Dim datOrderDate As Date = DateString
    Dim strOrderDate As String = Format(datOrderDate, ↵
    "MM/dd/yyyy")
    'retrieve C_ID value
    SQLCommand.CommandText = "SELECT CUSTOMER.C_ID " & _
    "FROM CUSTOMER WHERE UPPER(C_USERID) = '" & _
    Session("UserID") & "' AND UPPER(C_PASSWORD) = '" & _
    Session("Password") & "'"
    Dim intC_ID As Integer = CInt(SQLCommand.ExecuteScalar())
    'insert record into ORDERS table
    SQLCommand.CommandText = "INSERT INTO ORDERS (O_ID, " & _
    "O_DATE, O_METHPMT, C_ID) VALUES (" & intO_ID & " , " & _
    "TO_DATE('" & strOrderDate & "','MM/DD/YYYY'), 'CC', " & ↵
    intC_ID & ")"
    Try
        SQLCommand.ExecuteNonQuery()
        lblONum.Text = intO_ID
    Catch
        lblMsg.Text = "Notify the system administrator that an " & _
        "error occurred when inserting into the ORDERS table."
    End Try
    connCW.Close()
End Sub
```

**Figure 11-25**    Commands to insert master record into the ORDERS table using an Oracle9i database

*If you are using an Access database*, add to the Page_Load procedure the shaded commands in Figure 11-26 to insert the new record into the ORDERS table.

11

```
Private Sub Page_Load(ByVal sender As System.Object, ↵
ByVal e As System.EventArgs) Handles MyBase.Load
   connCW.Open()
   SQLCommand.Connection = connCW
   'retrieve current system date
   Dim datOrderDate As Date = DateString
   'retrieve C_ID value
   SQLCommand.CommandText = "SELECT CUSTOMER.C_ID " & _
      "FROM CUSTOMER WHERE UCase(C_USERID) = '" & _
      Session("UserID") & "' AND UCase(C_PASSWORD) = '" & _
      Session("Password") & "'"
   Dim intC_ID As Integer = CInt(SQLCommand.ExecuteScalar())
   'insert record into ORDERS table
   SQLCommand.CommandText = "INSERT INTO ORDERS (O_DATE, " & _
      "O_METHPMT, C_ID) VALUES (#" & datOrderDate & _
      "#, 'CC', " & intC_ID & ")"
   Try
      SQLCommand.ExecuteNonQuery()
      'retrieve O_ID value from Autonumber column
      SQLCommand.CommandText = "SELECT @@IDENTITY"
      Dim intO_ID = CInt(SQLCommand.ExecuteScalar())
      lblONum.Text = intO_ID
   Catch
      lblMsg.Text = "Notify the system administrator that an " & _
         "error occurred when inserting into the ORDERS table."
   End Try
   connCW.Close()
End Sub
```

**Figure 11-26**    Commands to insert the master record into the ORDERS table using an Access database

2. To test the commands, click the **Start** button ▶ to run the project, and then select the **Catalog** hyperlink. Open the **Please select a category** list and select **Children's Clothing**, then click **Select** beside Children's Beachcomber Sandals. Click **Add to cart** beside Children's Beachcomber Sandals, Size 10, Color Turquoise.

3. Click **View Cart – Place Order**, then click **Place your order now**. Processing transfers to the Login.aspx Web form. Type **harrispe** in the *User Name* TextBox, **asdfjk** in the *Password* TextBox, then click **Login**. The ConfirmOrder.aspx Web form displays the order summary.

4. Click **Confirm your order**. If the ORDERS record is successfully inserted into the database, the ProcessOrder.aspx Web form appears and displays the order ID, as shown in Figure 11-7. (Your order ID may be different from the one shown in Figure 11-7.)

If the ProcessOrder.aspx Web form does not appear, confirm that you typed the commands exactly as shown in Figure 11-25 or Figure 11-26. If necessary, set a breakpoint on the first command of the Page_Load procedure in the ProcessOrder.aspx.vb code behind file, then run the project, place an order, and step through the commands to identify the command that is causing the error.

> 5. Close Internet Explorer.

Now you will confirm that the new order record was actually inserted into the ORDERS table. You will set the QueryForm.aspx Web form as the project start page, modify the Query form's data connection so it connects to your database, then query the ORDERS table.

To confirm that the new order record was inserted into the database:

> 1. Right-click the **QueryForm.aspx** node in the Solution Explorer, then click **Set As Start Page**.
>
> 2. To update the QueryForm.aspx data connection, double-click the **QueryForm.aspx** node to open the form in Design view, right-click the **OleDbConnection1** component in the component tray, click **Properties**, then open the ConnectionString list.
>
>    *If you are using an Oracle9i database*, select **ORCL.CWUSER**.
>
>    *If you are using an Access database*, select **ACCESS.C:\Chapter11\Tutorials\ Clearwater\Clearwater.mdb.Admin**.
>
> 3. Close the Properties Window, then close the QueryForm.aspx window in the Browser Window, then click **Yes** to confirm saving your changes in QueryForm.aspx.
>
> 4. Click the **Start** button ▶ to run the project. In the *Enter query* TextBox, type **SELECT * FROM ORDERS**, then click **Run Query** to query the ORDERS table and confirm that the new order record appears in the ORDERS table. The O_DATE should show the current date, and the OS_ID value should appear blank (NULL).
>
> 5. Close Internet Explorer. In Visual Studio .NET, right-click the **Clearwater.htm** node in the Solution Explorer, then click **Set As Start Page**.

## Inserting the Detail Records into the ORDER_LINE Table

The next step is to insert the records to specify the order items and quantities into the ORDER_LINE table. Figure 11-24 shows that the ORDER_LINE table contains the order ID (O_ID), inventory item ID (INV_ID), and item quantity (OL_QUANTITY) values for each order item. Recall that the ShoppingCartItem session variable stores the inventory ID value for each item, and the ShoppingCartQty session variable stores the order quantity for each item. To parse these session variables and insert the associated

**11**

ORDER_LINE records, you will use the code in the AddOrderLineEntries procedure in Figure 11-27.

```
Private Sub AddOrderLineEntries(ByVal intO_ID As Integer)
    Dim strCart As String = Session("ShoppingCartItem")
    Dim strQty As String = Session("ShoppingCartQty")
    Dim strNewCart, strNewQty As String
    Dim sngSubTotal As Single
    Dim endItem, begItem, endQty, begQty As Integer
    begItem = 0
    endItem = InStr(strCart, ":")
    begQty = 0
    endQty = InStr(strQty, ":")
    If endItem > 0 Then
        While endItem > 0
            SQLCommand.CommandText = "INSERT INTO ORDER_LINE " & _
                "(O_ID, INV_ID, OL_QUANTITY) VALUES(" & _
                intO_ID.ToString & ", " & _
                strCart.Substring(begItem, _
                endItem - begItem - 1) & ", " & _
                strQty.Substring(begQty, endQty - begQty - 1) & ")"
            Try
                SQLCommand.ExecuteNonQuery()
            Catch
                lblMsg.Text = "Notify the system administrator " & _
                    "that an error occurred when inserting into " & _
                    "the ORDER_LINE table."
                Exit Sub
            End Try
            ' move to the next cart item
            begItem = endItem
            endItem = InStr(endItem + 1, strCart, ":")
            begQty = endQty
            endQty = InStr(endQty + 1, strQty, ":")
        End While
    Else
        lblMsg.Text = "<center><b>Your shopping cart is empty</b></center>"
    End If
End Sub
```

**Figure 11-27**  Procedure to parse session variables and add associated ORDER_LINE records

This procedure receives the order ID value as an input parameter. It then parses each individual session variable, and forms the INSERT action query to insert the order ID, inventory ID, and order quantity value for each item. Now you will add this code to the ProcessOrder.aspx.vb code behind file. You will also add to the Page_Load procedure the command to call the procedure. Then you will run the project and place an order.

To add the commands to insert the ORDER_LINE records:

1. Click **File** on the menu bar, point to **Open**, then click **File**. Open **AddOrderLineEntries.txt** from the Chapter11 folder on your Data Disk, copy all of the file text, then close the AddOrderLineEntries.txt window in the Browser Window.

2. If necessary, select the Secure\ProcessOrder.aspx.vb tab, then paste the copied text at the end of the code behind file, just before the **End Class** command.

3. In the Secure\ProcessOrder.aspx.vb code behind file's Page_Load procedure, add the following command to call the AddOrderLineEntries procedure. Add the command as the next-to-last command in the **Try** section of the **Try/Catch** block, just before the command that displays the intO_ID value in the lblONum Label control. The final three commands in the **Try** section should appear as follows. (If you are using an Oracle9*i* database, these will be the only commands in the **Try** section.)

```
SQLCommand.ExecuteNonQuery()
AddOrderLineEntries(intO_ID)
lblONum.Text = intO_ID
```

4. To test the commands, click the **Start** button ▶ to run the project, and then select the **Catalog** hyperlink. Open the **Please select a category** list and select **Children's Clothing**, then click **Select** beside Children's Beachcomber Sandals. Click **Add to cart** beside Children's Beachcomber Sandals, Size 10, Color Turquoise.

5. Open the **Please select a category** list again, select **Women's Clothing**, then click **Select** beside Women's Hiking Shorts. Click **Add to cart** beside Women's Hiking Shorts, Size S, Color Khaki.

6. Click **View Cart – Place Order**, then click **Place your order now**. Processing transfers to the Login.aspx Web form. Type **harrispe** in the *User Name* TextBox, **asdfjk** in the *Password* TextBox, then click **Login**. The ConfirmOrder.aspx Web form displays the order summary.

7. Click **Confirm your order**. The ProcessOrder.aspx Web form opens and displays the order ID.

8. Note the order ID value, then close Internet Explorer.

Now you will confirm that the application actually inserted the new records into the ORDERS and ORDER_LINE tables. You will set the QueryForm.aspx Web form as the project Start Page, then query the ORDERS and ORDER_LINE tables.

To confirm that the new order and order line records were inserted into the database:

1. Right-click the **QueryForm.aspx** node in the Solution Explorer, then click **Set As Start Page**.

**11**

2. Click the **Start** button ▶ to run the project. In the *Enter query* TextBox, type **SELECT * FROM ORDERS**, then click **Run Query** to query the ORDERS table. Confirm that the order ID value of the new order appears in the O_ID column.

3. Click **Clear** to clear the Query form, type **SELECT * FROM ORDER_LINE** in the *Enter query* TextBox, then click **Run Query**. The ORDER_LINE records should appear similar to the ones shown in Figure 11-28. Your O_ID value may be different, but will show the O_ID value for the new order that you noted in the previous set of steps.

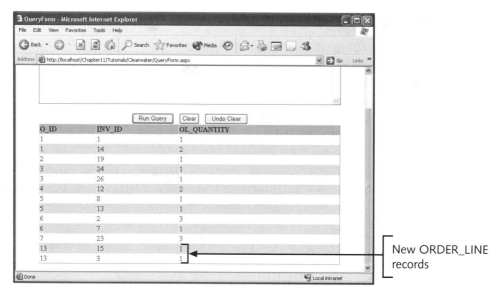

**Figure 11-28**     Viewing the new ORDER_LINE records in the Query form

4. Close Internet Explorer. In Visual Studio .NET, right-click the **Clearwater.htm** node in the Solution Explorer, then click **Set As Start Page**.

5. Because you are finished working with the ConfirmOrder.aspx and ProcessOrder.aspx Web forms, close the Secure\ConfirmOrder.aspx, Secure\ProcessOrder.aspx.vb, and Secure\ConfirmOrder.aspx.vb windows in the Browser Window.

# CREATING TEMPLATE COLUMNS IN A DATAGRID CONTROL

You create a DataGrid **template column** to display calculated values or alternate values from those that the database stores. When you create a template column, you use HTML tags to specify the data that appears in the column. A template column allows you to display almost any values on a DataGrid control flexibly. For example, in the

DataGrid that displays customer order line information in Figure 11-29, a template column displays the extended total of each order line. The template column calculates the extended total by multiplying the item price by the item quantity.

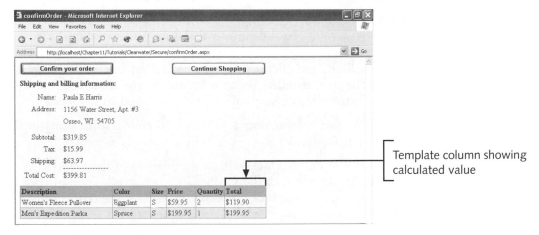

**Figure 11-29**    DataGrid template column showing a calculated data value

In your current Web application project, the ConfirmOrder.aspx Web form does not yet display the extended total value in the Total column as shown in Figure 11-29. Also, the detail DataGrid on the Catalog.aspx Web form currently displays the actual number of items that are in stock for each inventory item, rather than the text stating whether or not the item is in stock, as shown in the In Stock? column in Figure 11-2. Clearwater Traders customers do not need to know how many units of each item are in stock, only whether or not the item is in stock. You will create both of these columns using template columns.

You create a new template column in a DataGrid with the Property Builder visual configuration tool. Then you open the Web form in HTML view, and add HTML tags to define the Web server control template that specifies the values that appear within the template column. The following subsections describe these steps.

## Creating a New Template Column

To create a new template column, you open the Property Builder visual configuration tool, select the Columns page, then add and configure the template column. You can specify the template column's position and other properties within the DataGrid. Now you will create and configure the new template columns in the ConfirmOrder.aspx and Catalog.aspx Web forms.

To create and configure the new template columns:

1. In the Solution Explorer, double-click the **ConfirmOrder.aspx** node in the Secure folder to open the Web form in Design view.

2. Right-click the **DataGrid**, then click **Property Builder**. Select the **Columns** page, scroll down in the *Available columns* list, select **Template Column**, then click the **Add** button  > | to add the template column to the *Selected columns* list. Confirm that the new column is the last item in the list, so it will appear as the last column in the DataGrid.

3. Make sure that the new **Template Column** is selected in the *Selected columns* list, then type **Total** in the *Header text* field to specify the template column heading, and click **OK** to close the Property Builder and save your changes. The new template column appears in the DataGrid. The column is currently blank because you have not yet specified its contents.

4. In the Solution Explorer, double-click the **Catalog.aspx** node to open the Web form in Design view.

5. Right-click the **detail DataGrid** at the bottom of the form, then click **Property Builder**. Select the **Columns** page, scroll down in the *Available columns* list, select **Template Column**, then click the **Add** button  > | to add the template column to the *Selected columns* list. Confirm that the new column is the last column in the list, so it will appear as the last column in the DataGrid.

6. Make sure that the new template column is selected in the *Selected columns* list, then type **In Stock?** in the *Header text* field.

7. Select the **Quantity** column in the *Selected columns* list, clear the **Visible** check box so the quantity on hand values no longer appear on the DataGrid, then click **OK** to close Property Builder and save your changes. The DataGrid displays the template column, and no longer displays the Quantity column.

8. Click the **Save All** button 🖫 to save both forms.

## Defining the Web Server Control Template

In Chapter 10, you created Web server control templates to specify how DataList controls display data. Recall that a Web server control template can contain different templates to specify different regions within the column. You create a header template to specify the appearance of the column header, an item template to specify the appearance of the data items, an alternating item template to display the appearance of every other data item, and so on. You reference data columns using the DataBinder.Eval method, which has the following general syntax:

```
<%# DataBinder.Eval(Container.DataItem, ↵
"column_name") %>
```

Now you will add to the ConfirmOrder.aspx Web form the code to create an item template that displays the product of the Price and Quantity columns in the form DataGrid. In the DataGrid, the Price column derives its values from the INV_PRICE DataGrid column, and the Quantity column derives its values from the QTY DataGrid column.

If you are not sure of a DataGrid column's name, you can view a DataGrid's data set column names in the *Available columns* list in the Property Builder.

You will use the DataBinder.Eval method to reference the INV_PRICE and QTY columns. You will add the formatting expression `"currency"` to the expression to format the template column value using a currency format. This is a new formatting expression that you need to use in template columns to format items as currency.

To create the item template for the template column in the ConfirmOrder.aspx Web form:

1. Select the **Secure\ConfirmOrder.aspx** tab in the Browser Window, then click the **HTML** tab to open the Web form in HTML view.

2. Scroll down to the `<asp:TemplateColumn HeaderText="Total">` tag, place the insertion point after the closing angle bracket (>), then press **Enter** two times to create a new blank line in the file.

3. Starting on the new blank line, add the following commands to create the item template:

```
<ItemTemplate>
<%# Format(DataBinder.Eval(Container.DataItem, "INV_PRICE") ↵
* DataBinder.Eval(Container.DataItem, "QTY"), "currency") %>
</ItemTemplate>
```

4. Save the file.

On the Catalog.aspx Web form, you need to create the template column that displays "Yes" if an item is in stock and "No" if an item is out of stock. To implement this template column, you will display the return value of a function in the template column. You will first create a VB .NET function that receives the quantity on hand value as an input parameter. The function returns the text string "Yes" if the quantity on hand value is greater than zero and the text string "No" if the quantity on hand value is zero. Then you will create the item template for the template column, and call the function from the item template. To call a function from an item template, you use the following general syntax:

```
<ItemTemplate>
   <%# command_to_call_function %>
</ItemTemplate>
```

In the *command_to_call_function*, you can use the DataBinder.Eval method to reference DataGrid column values and pass them as parameters. Now you will add to the Catalog.aspx.vb Web form code behind file the commands to create a function named IsItInStock that performs the required processing. You will also add to the Catalog.aspx Web form the item template that calls the function, passes the quantity on hand value to the function as a parameter, and displays the function return value. Then you will run the project and test your template columns.

11

To add the function and item template to call the function, then run the project:

1. Select the **Catalog.aspx** tab in the Browser Window, then double-click anywhere on the form to open the code behind file.

2. Just before the **End Class** command at the end of the file, add the commands in Figure 11-30 to create the IsItInStock function.

```
Public Function IsItInStock(ByVal strQOH As String) As String
   If CInt(strQOH) > 0 Then
      IsItInStock = "Yes"
   Else
      IsItInStock = "No"
   End If
End Function
```

**Figure 11-30** Function to specify in the template column whether an item is in stock

3. Select the **Catalog.aspx** tab, then click the **HTML** tab to open the form in HTML view.

4. Scroll down to the `<asp:TemplateColumn HeaderText="In Stock?">` tag, place the insertion point after the closing angle bracket, press **Enter** two times to create a new blank line, then type the following commands on the blank line to create the item template and call the function:

```
<ItemTemplate>
   <%# IsItInStock(DataBinder.Eval↵
   (Container.DataItem, "INV_QOH")) %>
</ItemTemplate>
```

5. To test the template columns, click the **Start** button ▶ to run the project, and then select the **Catalog** hyperlink. Open the **Please select a category** list and select **Women's Clothing**, then click **Select** beside Women's Fleece Pullover. Note that the In Stock? column now displays "Yes" for in-stock items and "No" for out-of-stock items.

6. Click **Add to cart** beside Women's Fleece Pullover, Size S, Color Eggplant.

7. Open the **Please select a category** list again, select **Men's Clothing**, then click **Select** beside Men's Expedition Parka. Click **Add to cart** beside Men's Expedition Parka, Size S, Color Spruce.

8. Click **View Cart – Place Order**. Click **Edit Quantity** beside Women's Fleece Pullover, change the Quantity value to **2**, then click **Update Quantity**.

9. Click **Place your order now**. Type **harrispe** in the *User Name* TextBox, **asdfjk** in the *Password* TextBox, then click **Login**. The ConfirmOrder.aspx Web form displays the order summary, which now contains the formatted template column shown in Figure 11-29.

10. Click **Confirm your order**. The ProcessOrder.aspx Web form opens and displays the new order ID.

11. Close Internet Explorer.

12. Close all open windows in the Browser Window.

## IMPLEMENTING FORM SECURITY

Web sites often display information that should be accessible only after a user verifies his or her identity. For example, a Web banking application should display account information only to the account holder, and a travel agency application should display reservation and itinerary information only to the person who created the reservations and itineraries. The Clearwater Traders Web application should display order information on the ViewOrders.aspx Web page in Figure 11-8 only to the person who placed the orders. Today, most Web sites rely on user names and passwords to authenticate user identities. Someday, biological identifiers such as fingerprints, retinal scans, or even DNA analysis may authenticate user identities.

Currently, the *View Your Orders* hyperlink on the Clearwater.htm static Web page references the ViewOrders.aspx Web form in the Secure folder. For security reasons, a user must always log on to the system before he or she can display the ViewOrders.aspx Web form. One way to implement this security measure is to have the *View Your Orders* hyperlink direct users to the Login.aspx Web form, then allow users to access the ViewOrders.aspx Web form from Login.aspx. However, this would be annoying to users who log on to the system and place an order, then immediately want to view their order information. The system would force them to log on a second time to view their order information.

In the Clearwater Traders Web application, the ConfirmOrder.aspx, ProcessOrder.aspx, and ViewOrders.aspx Web forms require **user authentication**, which means that users must identify themselves before the Web form appears. The Clearwater application uses either the Login.aspx Web form or the NewCustomer.aspx Web form to perform user authentication.

ASP.NET supports **forms authentication**, which is a process that allows the system to authenticate user identities once. The system then allows users to access their secure information for the duration of the browser session without having to authenticate their identities again. When you implement forms authentication in a Web application project, you place all Web forms that require user authentication in a secure folder. A **secure folder** is a folder that contains forms that only authenticated users can view. An **anonymous user** is a user who has not yet been authenticated. When an anonymous user connects to the Web application, the user cannot access the Web forms in the secure folder until he or she is authenticated. The user authenticates his or her identify using a **login form**.

Forms authentication secures only Web form .aspx files. If you place static HTML documents and other types of files in a secure folder, anonymous users can access these files.

Figure 11-31 describes the forms authentication process using pseudocode and `If` decision control structures.

```
A user requests a page within a secure folder
If the user is anonymous Then
   The Web server transfers the user to the login form
   The user enters his or her user name and password
   If the system verifies the user name and password Then
      The secure page is sent to the user
   End If
ElseIf the user is authenticated Then
   The secure page is sent to the user
End If
```

**Figure 11-31**   Pseudocode describing the forms authentication process

In the first pseudocode command, the user requests a form in the secure folder. The system checks whether the user is anonymous or authenticated. If the user is anonymous, the system routes the user to the login form, authenticates his or her identity, then displays the secure page. If the user is not successfully authenticated, the authentication process fails, the user is still anonymous, and the user can try to become authenticated again. In the `ElseIf` portion of the command, if the user is initially authenticated, the system displays the secure page without requiring reauthentication.

To enable forms authentication, you must structure your Web application project so the forms that require authentication are in a subfolder within the project folder that will be a secure folder. (In the Clearwater Web application project, these forms are in a subfolder named Secure, but you could name the secure folder any legal folder name.) Then, you configure the Web application project's Web.config file to enable forms authentication, and specify the secure folder location and the name of the Web form that provides user authentication. Finally, you modify the code within the Web forms that transfers processing to forms within the secure folder. The following subsections describe these steps.

## Configuring Forms Authentication in a Web Application Project

To configure a Web application project to use forms authentication, you modify the project's Web.config file. First, you enable forms authentication in the project by modifying the mode attribute of the `<authentication>` element as follows:

```
<authentication mode="Forms">
```

The default authentication mode attribute value is "Windows," and specifies that settings on the Web application's Directory Security properties page in the IIS console establish the project's security. (Recall from Chapter 5 that the Directory Security properties page allows you to specify whether the Web server must verify the identity of the user before allowing the user to access the directory.) Changing the mode attribute value to "Forms" redirects anonymous requests to the login form that authenticates the user's identity. The text within this element is case-sensitive: Note that the "Forms" mode value must begin with an uppercase letter *F*.

To specify the name of the login form, you create a `<forms>` element within the `<authentication>` element, and specify its loginUrl attribute as the URL and filename of the login form. The `<forms>` element uses the following syntax:

```
<forms loginUrl="login_form_url" />
```

The *login_form_url* specifies the URL to the project's login form. You can use either an absolute or relative URL path, and the path is not case-sensitive. The other elements within the element are case-sensitive: Note that `forms` must begin with a lowercase letter *F*, and loginUrl uses mixed-cased letters.

Now you will modify the Web.config file in the Clearwater project to enable forms authentication. You will specify the login form URL as the Login.aspx Web form.

To configure forms authentication in the project Web.config file:

1. Double-click the **Web.config** node in the Solution Explorer, scroll down to the `<authentication>` element, and modify the element so it appears as follows:

```
<authentication mode="Forms">
  <forms loginUrl="Login.aspx" />
</authentication>
```

 The text in these elements is case-sensitive. Type the commands exactly as shown. Also, note that the `<forms>` element must be a separate element within the `<authentication>` element.

2. Save the file.

The next configuration task is to specify the location of the secure folder and the security authorization policies within the secure folder. **Authorization policies** specify the individual users or groups of users who can access the secure folder's contents. To specify the secure folder location, you add a new `<location>` element within the `<configuration>` element that already exists in the Web.config file. To specify the secure folder's authorization policies, you add an `<authorization>` element to the new `<location>` element.

The `<authorization>` element is within the `<system.web>` element in the Web.config file. The `<authorization>` element specifies the users whom the system allows to access project forms. The `<authorization>` element can contain an

`<allow>` element to grant access to specific users explicitly, or a `<deny>` element to deny access to certain users explicitly. These elements have the following general syntax:

```
<allow users="user_IDs" />
<deny users="user_IDs" />
```

In this syntax, *user_IDs* denotes either a list of users, separated by commas, or a wildcard character that specifies the users who are either allowed or denied access to the Web forms. The * wildcard character specifies all users, and the ? character specifies all anonymous users.

By default, the Web.config file contains an `<authorization>` element that specifies the authorization policies of the overall application. By default, this element allows access to all users, so it contains the following `<allow>` element value:

```
<allow users="*" />
```

Clearwater Traders would like to allow anonymous users to connect to their Web site and browse the catalog without having to log on to the system. However, only authenticated users can view the forms in the secure folder. To create a project that has both nonsecure and secure forms, you allow all users to access the project forms, then restrict access in the secure folder to only authenticated users. To restrict access to only authenticated users in the secure folder, you add an <authorization> element to the secure folder that denies access to nonauthenticated (anonymous) users, using the following element syntax:

```
<deny users="?" />
```

In summary, the `<location>` element has the following general syntax to specify the secure folder location and deny access of its contents to nonauthenticated users:

```
<location path="secure_folder_name">
  <system.web>
    <authorization><deny users="?" /></authorization>
  </system.web>
</location>
```

In this syntax, *secure_folder_name* specifies either an absolute or relative path to the project's secure folder. The `<authorization>` element specifies to deny access to anonymous users within the secure folder. Now you will specify that the secure folder location is the secure folder within the project folder. You will specify that only authorized users can access the contents of the secure folder.

To specify the secure folder location and authorization policies:

1. In the Web.config file, scroll to the `<authorization>` element, and confirm that the value is as follows, which allows all users to access all project Web forms:

```
<allow users="*"/>
```

2. Scroll to the top of the Web.config file, place the insertion point after the closing angle bracket in the opening <configuration> tag, press **Enter** two times to create a new blank line in the file, then type the following elements to specify the secure folder and deny access to anonymous users:

```
<location path="Secure">
  <system.web>
    <authorization><deny users="?" /></authorization>
  </system.web>
</location>
```

3. Save the file.

Now you will test forms authentication in the Clearwater Web application. The *View your orders* hyperlink on the Clearwater.htm static page references the ViewOrders.aspx Web form. When you run the project and then immediately select this link, you are an anonymous user who has not yet logged in to the system. Instead of displaying the ViewOrders.aspx Web form, which is in the secure folder, the project will transfer processing to the login form, which is the Login.aspx Web form in Figure 11-4.

To test the project's forms authentication:

1. Click the **Start** button ▶ to run the project. The Clearwater.htm static Web page appears. Move the mouse pointer onto the View your orders link, and note that the hyperlink reference on the browser status bar is *http://localhost/Chapter11/Tutorials/Clearwater/Secure/ViewOrders.aspx*, which is the path to the ViewOrders.aspx Web form.

2. Select the **View your orders** link. The Login.aspx Web form appears, confirming that the project's forms authentication is working correctly.

3. Close Internet Explorer.

4. Close the Web.config window in the Browser Window.

# Modifying Form Commands to Implement Forms Authentication

When you implement forms authentication in a Web application project, you need to modify how the form commands transfer processing to other forms. The following sections describe how to transfer processing from non-secure to secure forms, how to transfer processing from the login form to secure forms, and how to use a form other than the login form to authenticate users.

## Transferring Processing from Nonsecure to Secure Forms

When a project transfers processing from a nonsecure form to a secure form, the nonsecure form transfers processing directly to the secure form. The command that transfers processing does not need to transfer processing to the login form explicitly. For example, Figure 11-1 shows that the event handler in the *Place your order now* button on the ShoppingCart.aspx Web form currently transfers processing to the Login.aspx Web form.

Instead, this event handler should transfer processing directly to the ConfirmOrder.aspx Web form. If the user is not yet authenticated, the system will automatically display the Login.aspx Web form to authenticate the user.

Now you will modify the command in the *Place your order now* button event handler to transfer processing directly to the ConfirmOrder.aspx Web form. You will need to use the Response.Redirect method, because the Server.Transfer method bypasses forms authentication. Then you will run the project and confirm that the Login.aspx Web form opens to authenticate the user.

To modify the event handler that transfers processing to the Web form in the secure folder:

1. Select the **ShoppingCart.aspx** node in the Solution Explorer, then click the **View Code** button ▤ to open the form's code behind file.

2. Scroll down to the btnOrder_Click event handler, then change the command so it appears as follows:

   ```
   Response.Redirect("Secure/ConfirmOrder.aspx")
   ```

3. To test the change, click the **Start** button ▶ to run the project, and then select the **Catalog** hyperlink. Open the **Please select a category** list and select **Women's Clothing**, then click **Select** beside Women's Fleece Pullover.

4. Click **Add to cart** beside Women's Fleece Pullover, Size S, Color Eggplant.

5. Click **View Cart – Place Order**, then click **Place your order now**. The Login.aspx Web form appears, even though the event handler transferred processing directly to the ConfirmOrder.aspx Web form. This confirms that forms authentication is working correctly.

6. Close Internet Explorer, then close the ShoppingCart.aspx.vb window.

## Transferring Processing from the Login Form to the Secure Forms

When you enable forms authentication, you may need to modify the commands that transfer processing from the login form to the secure forms if the login form authenticates multiple secure forms. For example, Figure 11-1 shows that, depending on the user selections, the Login.aspx Web form transfers processing either to the ConfirmOrder.aspx Web form or the ViewOrders.aspx Web form.

In the Clearwater Web application project, the event handler for the *Login* button on the Login.aspx Web form currently always transfers processing to the ConfirmOrders.aspx Web form. This is fine when a user logs on while placing a new order. However, this is not fine when a user clicks the *View your orders* link on the Clearwater.htm static Web page, is routed to the Login.aspx Web form, enters his or her user name and password, and then clicks *login*. The user expects to see his or her order information, and instead sees an error message.

To correct this problem, you need to change the event handler in the *Login* button so it transfers processing to the correct Web form using the RedirectFromLoginPage method. When a project uses forms authentication, the **RedirectFromLoginPage method** automatically redirects processing from the login form back to the form that requires authentication. For example, if a user is placing a new order, this method redirects processing to the ConfirmOrder.aspx Web form after the login page authenticates the user. If the user is trying to view his or her order information, the method redirects processing to the ViewOrders.aspx Web form after the login page authenticates the user.

The general syntax for `FormsAuthentication.RedirectFromLoginPage` is:

```
System.Web.Security.FormsAuthentication. ⤶
RedirectFromLoginPage(userName, createPersistentCookie)
```

The RedirectFromLoginPage method is a method of the System.Web.Security. FormsAuthentication class. The *userName* parameter is a text string that identifies the user. The *createPersistentCookie* parameter is a Boolean value that specifies whether the system will create a persistent cookie to allow the user to bypass the authentication process in subsequent browser sessions. If this parameter value is True, the system will create a persistent cookie that contains the authentication information, so on subsequent visits, the user can bypass the login process. If this parameter value is False, the user will have to enter his or her authentication information during all subsequent visits.

Now you will modify the event handler for the *Login* button in the Login.aspx Web form so it uses the RedirectFromLoginPage method. You will specify that the *userName* parameter is the value that the user types in the *User Name* TextBox on the Login.aspx Web form, and save the value in all uppercase letters so the value is not case-sensitive. You will specify that the *createPersistentCookie* parameter value is False, which requires the user to log on each time he or she connects to the Web site. Then you will run the project and confirm that you can view your customer orders and create a new order.

**11**

To modify the event handler for the *Login* button and then run the project:

1. Select the **Login.aspx** node in the Solution Explorer, then click the **View Code** button ▤ to open the code behind file.

2. Scroll down to the btnLogin_Click event handler. Modify the commands in the `If` decision control structure at the end of the event handler so they appear as follows:

```
If dsCart.Tables("cust").Rows.Count > 0 Then
    ' found the userid and password, continue
    Session("UserID") = UCase(txtUsername.Text)
    Session("Password") = UCase(txtPassword.Text)
    System.Web.Security.FormsAuthentication. ⤶
    RedirectFromLoginPage(UCase(txtUsername.Text), False)
Else
```

3. To test the commands when viewing existing orders, click the **Start** button ▶ to run the project, then select the **View your orders** hyperlink. The Login.aspx Web form appears. Type **harrispe** in the *User Name* TextBox, **asdfjk** in the *Password* TextBox, then click **Login**. The ViewOrders.aspx Web form in Figure 11-8 appears. (Your order information will be different.)

4. Close Internet Explorer.

5. To test the commands when placing a new order, click the **Start** button ▶ to run the project, and then select the **Catalog** hyperlink. Open the **Please select a category** list and select **Women's Clothing**, then click **Select** beside Women's Hiking Shorts. Click **Add to cart** beside Women's Hiking Shorts, Size S, Color Khaki.

6. Click **View Cart – Place Order**, then click **Place your order now**. Processing transfers to the Login.aspx Web form. Type **harrispe** in the *User Name* TextBox, **asdfjk** in the *Password* TextBox, then click **Login**. The ConfirmOrder.aspx Web form displays the order summary.

7. Click **Confirm your order**. The ProcessOrder.aspx Web form opens and displays the order ID.

8. Click the **View your orders** hyperlink. The ViewOrders.aspx Web form appears, and displays information about the new order. Note that you did not need to log on again to view your order information.

9. Close Internet Explorer.

## Using an Alternate Web Form to Authenticate Users

If a user does not yet have an account with Clearwater Traders, he or she clicks *Create new account* on the Login.aspx Web form to display the NewCustomer.aspx Web form. The NewCustomer.aspx Web form allows the user to enter personal information and create a new account, which authenticates the user's identity. When the user clicks *Submit* on the NewCustomer.aspx Web form, the form should transfer processing either to the ConfirmOrder.aspx Web form if the user is placing an order, or to the ViewOrders.aspx Web form if the customer is viewing his or her order information. However, because both of these forms are in the secure folder, the application tries to redirect processing back to the Login.aspx Web form to authenticate the user.

How can you transfer processing to a secure form from a Web form other than the login form? You need to specify manually that the user is authenticated, and then transfer processing to the correct secure form. To transfer processing to the correct secure form, you will use a session variable to save the URL that was redirected to Login.aspx before transferring to NewCustomer.aspx. The application can then use this session variable to redirect processing from NewCustomer.aspx to the correct Web form after the user submits the new account information.

When a project uses forms authentication, you use the GetRedirectUrl method to determine the source URL for a form that is redirected to the login form. The general syntax for a command that assigns this URL to a session variable is:

```
Session("variable_name") = System.↲
Web.Security.FormsAuthentication.GetRedirectUrl↲
(userName, createPersistentCookie)
```

In this command, the *userName* and *createPersistentCookie* parameters are the same as the parameters in the RedirectFromLoginPage method. If the user is not yet authenticated, the *userName* parameter should be an empty string literal (" "). If the user is authenticated, the *userName* parameter should have the same value as is used in the RedirectFromLoginPage method, which is the value the user types in the *User Name* field on the Login.aspx Web form. Another way to make sure that the *userName* parameter has the correct value is to assign its value using the Page object's User.Identity.Name property. When the RedirectFromLoginPage form successfully authenticates a user, this method assigns the *userName* parameter value to the User.Identity.Name object property. You can then use the User.Identity.Name object property in other methods that require the authenticated *userName* parameter. The *createPersistentCookie* parameter can have a value of True or False. Some applications allow users to decide whether or not they want to save their login information for use in future sessions. If they do, use true, otherwise use false. If they save their login information, they won't lose it when they close their browser because it will be stored in a persistent cookie.

Now you will add commands to the event handler for the Create new account button on the Login.aspx Web form. These commands will save the value of the target URL to a session variable named RedirectURL. (The button's event handler already contains the command to call the Server.Transfer method and redirect processing to the NewCustomer.aspx Web form.)

To create the event handler to save the target URL as a session variable:

1. In the Login.aspx.vb code behind file, add as the first command in the btnNew_Click event handler the following command to save the redirected URL as a session variable. (Place this command just before the call to the Server.Transfer method that transfers processing to the NewCustomer.aspx Web form.)

```
Session("RedirectURL") = System.↲
Web.Security.FormsAuthentication.GetRedirectUrl↲
(User.Identity.Name, True)
```

2. Save the file.

The final task is to modify the NewCustomer.aspx Web form. This Web form needs to set the UserID and Password session variables to the *User Name* and *Password* values that the user enters, specify that the user has been authenticated, then transfer processing to the URL stored in the RedirectURL session variable. Normally, the RedirectFromLoginPage method confirms that a user has been authenticated. However, because you want to redirect processing to the URL in the session variable rather than to the form that directed processing to the current form, you will use the **SetAuthCookie method** to specify that the user has been authenticated and you will do the redirection with Response.Redirect. The SetAuthCookie method has the following general syntax:

```
System.Web.Security.FormsAuthentication. ↵
SetAuthCookie(userName, createPersistentCookie)
```

In this code, the *userName* parameter has the Page object's User.Identity.Name property, which is assigned to the *userName* parameter when the form is authenticated. The *createPersistentCookie* parameter can have a value of either True or False, and both work equally well. Now you will add to the NewCustomer.aspx Web form's *Submit* button's event handler commands to set the values of the UserID and Password session variables, confirm that the user is authenticated, then transfer processing to the URL specified in the RedirectURL session variable. Then you will run the project, create a new order, and create a new customer account.

To add the commands to set the session variables, specify that the user is authenticated, transfer processing to the URL specified in the RedirectURL session variable, then run the project:

1. Select the **NewCustomer.aspx** node in the Solution Explorer, then click the **View Code** button 📄 to open the form's code behind file.

2. Scroll down to the btnSubmit_Click event handler, then scroll down in the event handler to the `Try/Catch` block. Add the following commands to the `Try` section, just after the `SQLCommand.ExecuteNonQuery()` command:

```
Session("UserID") = UCase(txtUsername.Text)
Session("Password") = UCase(txtPassword.Text)
System.Web.Security.FormsAuthentication.SetAuthCookie↵
(Session("userid"), False)
Response.Redirect(Session("RedirectURL"))
```

3. Click the **Start** button ▶ to run the project, and then select the **Catalog** hyperlink. Open the **Please select a category** list and select **Women's Clothing**, then click **Select** beside Women's Fleece Pullover.

4. Click **Add to cart** beside Women's Fleece Pullover, Size S, Color Eggplant, click **View Cart – Place Order**, then click **Place your order now**.

5. On the Login.aspx Web form, click **Create new account**. Type **Johnson** in the *Last Name* field, **ajohnson** in the *User Name* field, **jklm** in the *Password* field, and **jklm** in the *Confirm Password* field, then click **Submit**. The ConfirmOrder.aspx Web form appears and displays the new user name in the *Name* field.

6. Close Internet Explorer.

# DEPLOYING A COMPLETED WEB APPLICATION TO A PRODUCTION WEB SERVER

When you **deploy** a Web application, you move the required program files to the production Web site, and then configure the production Web site so it can accept browser requests and return the required application files. Recall that you develop Web programs on a personal Web server, then, after you test and debug the programs, you deploy the programs on a production Web server.

 We can't emphasize enough the importance of thoroughly testing a Web application before deploying it. One bad link or error-generating page can permanently lose a customer or client. Before deploying, check every link and experiment with entering every possible type of allowable entry—including deliberately "bad" entries to test your application's error handling capabilities. If possible, get several people who are not close to the project to do additional testing, because developers are notoriously bad at testing their own projects. To deploy a finished Web application project to a production server, first you create and configure the Web application on the production Web server. Then you compile the project files, and move the required files, which are called the **production application files**, to the correct location on the production server. The following subsections describe these tasks.

## Configuring the Production Web Server

To run ASP.NET Web application projects, your production Web server must have ASP.NET and the .NET common language runtime installed. The Web server must use Internet Explorer Version 5.01 or later, Microsoft Data Access Components Version 2.6 or later, IIS Version 5.0 or later, and Microsoft's latest security updates.

 If you do not want to install all of the Visual Studio .NET software on your Web server, you can install the required components using Microsoft's .NET Framework Redistributable application.

To configure the Web server, you create the **production project folder**, which is the folder on the Web server that contains the production application files. The production project folder can have any legal folder name. (The name does not need to be the same as the project folder name you used while developing the project, because unlike the development environment files, the compiled application does not depend upon absolute path information.) The production project folder can be within an existing Web application, or outside of any existing Web applications on the production Web server. Then you create a new Web application that you associate with the new production project folder. Now you will create the production project folder and the Web application associated with the production project folder.

11

To create the production project folder and associated Web application:

1. Switch to Windows Explorer, and create a new folder named **ClearwaterProduction** in the Chapter11\Tutorials folder on your Solution Disk.

2. *If you are using an Access database*, change the security privileges on the ClearwaterProduction folder so all users have *Full Control* privileges for the folder. Then, copy the **Clearwater.mdb** file from the Chapter11 folder on your Data Disk to the Chapter11\Tutorials\ClearwaterProduction folder on your Solution Disk.

3. Switch to the IIS console, then create a new Web application within the Chapter11/Tutorials application named **ClearwaterProduction** that you associate with the ClearwaterProduction folder in the Chapter11\Tutorials folder on your Solution Disk. Grant the *Read*, *Run scripts*, and *Browse* privileges to the application.

## Moving the Production Application Files to the Web Server

When you deploy a Web application project to a production Web server, you must place the project's compiled (binary) files on the Web server. Visual Studio .NET automatically compiles the project files every time you run the project. You can also explicitly compile the project files by clicking *Build* on the menu bar, then clicking *Build Solution*.

The *Build* menu in Visual Studio .NET contains a *Build Solution* selection, and a *Build project_name* selection, where *project_name* is the name of the project that is currently active. Recall that a solution is a collection of multiple projects. If a solution contains only one project, then clicking *Build Solution* is equivalent to clicking *Build project_name*.

When you compile the project files, Visual Studio .NET places the compiled (binary) files in the bin folder within the project folder. Before you can deploy a Web application project to a production Web server, you must make sure that you have either run the project or explicitly compiled the project files. Now you will explicitly compile the files in the Clearwater Web project.

To compile the project files:

1. In Visual Studio .NET, click **Build** on the menu bar, then click **Build Solution**.

2. A series of messages appears in the Output window, indicating that the project was successfully built.

After compiling the project files, you need to move the production application files to the production project folder. You could manually copy the files using Windows Explorer, but it is easier to use a Visual Studio .NET feature that makes a copy of the production application files. To use this feature, you select *Project* from the menu bar, then select *Copy Project* to display the Copy Project dialog box shown in Figure 11-32.

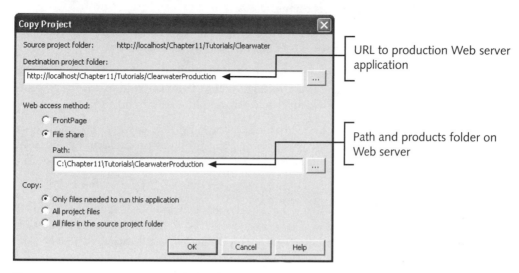

**Figure 11-32**     Copy Project dialog box settings for deploying a project to a production Web server

When you use the Copy Project dialog box to deploy a project to a production Web server, the *Destination project folder* field specifies the URL of the production project folder on the Web server. The *Web access method* option buttons include *FrontPage*, which specifies to use FrontPage extensions to copy the project files, or *File share*, which specifies to copy the project files directly. When you select the *File share* option button, you must specify in the *Path* field the path to the production project folder on the Web server to which the system will copy the project files.

The *Copy* option buttons allow you to copy specific files within the project folder. The *Only files needed to run this application* option button specifies to copy the production application files; the *All project files* option button specifies to copy all of the project files; and the *All files in the source project folder* option button specifies to copy all files in the project folder.

Now you will open the Copy Project dialog box and specify to copy the Clearwater Traders Web application project production files to the ClearwaterProduction Web application you created earlier. You will use the *File share* Web access method, and specify that the path to the project files is the Chapter11\Tutorials\Clearwater folder on your Solution Disk. You will specify to copy only the production application files. Then you will switch to Windows Explorer and examine the copied files.

To copy the production application files to the production Web server application:

1. Click **Project** on the menu bar, and then click **Copy Project**. The Copy Project dialog box opens.

2. Change the *Destination project folder* field value to **http://localhost/ Chapter11/Tutorials/ClearwaterProduction**.

3. Select the **File share** option button, click the **More** button ⌐…⌐ beside the *Path* field, navigate to the Chapter11\Tutorials folder on your Solution Disk, select the **ClearwaterProduction** folder, then click **Open**.

4. Make sure that the *Only files needed to run this application* option button is selected, then click **OK** to copy the project's production application files. Your Copy Project dialog box specifications should look like the ones in Figure 11-32.

 If Visual Studio .NET crashes, it means that you did not configure one of the settings correctly in the Copy Project dialog box. Repeat the previous set of steps, and make sure that the Copy Project dialog box exactly matches Figure 11-32.

When Visual Studio .NET creates a copy of the production application files, it copies the following files:

- All Web form files with .aspx file extensions.

- The bin directory and its contents, which include the project's .dll file and .pdb file. Recall from Chapter 6 that the project .dll file contains the compiled project output file, which is called an assembly. The project .pdb file contains debugging information that the developer uses for debugging the project while it is running on the Web server.

- Web.config, which contains project configuration information.

- Global.asax, which contains event handler commands that are visible to all Web forms in the project. This is an optional file, and is not required unless you modified its commands.

- Styles.css, which defines Cascading Style Sheets (CSSs) within the project. These style sheets enable HTML designers to control the appearance of Web pages. This is another optional file that is not required unless you modified its commands.

Now you will switch to Windows Explorer and examine the files that Visual Studio .NET copied to the production project folder.

To examine the files in the production project folder:

1. Switch to Windows Explorer and navigate to the **Chapter11\Tutorials\ ClearwaterProduction** folder on your Solution Disk. Your project files should look like the ones in Figure 11-33.

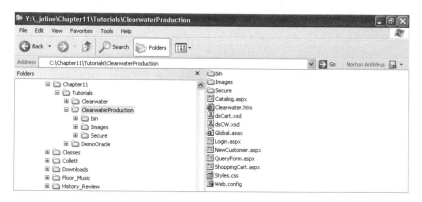

**Figure 11-33**    Production project folder files

Note that the production project folder contains the project .aspx files, the Clearwater.htm static Web page, and the Global.asax, Styles.css, and Web.config files. It also contains the .xsd (XHTML schema definition) files that describe the data set schemas. These files are not required for the production application, so you can delete them if you wish.

2. Open the **bin** folder, and note that it contains the Clearwater.dll and Clearwater.pdb files.

3. Open the **Secure** folder, and note that it contains the .aspx and .xsd files for the Web forms in the secure folder.

The final task is to confirm that the deployed project works correctly. To access the project, you type in a Web browser *Address* field the URL to the project Start Page. For the Clearwater project, this URL is *http://localhost/Chapter11/Tutorials/ClearwaterProduction/ Clearwater.htm*. Now you will test the deployed project.

To test the deployed project:

1. Start Internet Explorer, type **http://localhost/Chapter11/Tutorials/ ClearwaterProduction/Clearwater.htm** in the *Address* field, then press **Enter**. The Clearwater Traders home page appears.

2. Click the **Catalog** hyperlink. The Catalog.aspx Web page opens. Open the **Please select a category** list, then select **Women's Clothing**. Click **Select** beside Women's Fleece Pullover, then click the **Add to cart** hyperlink beside Women's Fleece Pullover, Size S, Color Eggplant. A message appears to confirm that the item was added to your shopping cart.

3. To order another item, open the **Please select a category** list, then select **Children's Clothing**. Click the **Select** hyperlink beside Girl's Soccer Tee to display the item details, then click the **Add to cart** hyperlink beside Girl's Soccer Tee, Size S, Color White. A message appears to confirm that the item was added to your shopping cart.

4. Click **View Cart – Place Order**. The ShoppingCart.aspx Web page in Figure 11-3 appears.

11

5. Click the **Edit Quantity** hyperlink beside Girl's Soccer Tee, change the *Quantity* value to **2**, and then click **Update Quantity**. The new quantity appears in the Quantity column.

6. Click **Place your order now**. The Login.aspx Web page opens. Type **harrispe** in the *User Name* TextBox, **asdfjk** in the *Password* TextBox, then click **Login**. The ConfirmOrder.aspx Web page summarizes the order.

7. Click **Confirm your order**. The ProcessOrder.aspx Web form opens and displays the new order's order number.

8. Click the **View your orders** link. The ViewOrders.aspx Web form summarizes the user's orders.

9. Close Internet Explorer, Visual Studio .NET, and all other open applications.

You have now learned how to create Web application projects, retrieve and manipulate database data using Web forms, then create and deploy an integrated Web application. You have learned how to use a powerful set of tools that make it easy to create and maintain complex Web sites that can support many different business processes.

## Chapter Summary

- To transfer processing to a different Web page in a Web application project, you can use the Response.Redirect method or the Server.Transfer method.

- When a Web server executes the Response.Redirect method, the Web server sends a message to the browser telling the browser to request the specified URL. Then the script that contains the command that calls the Response.Redirect method terminates, and the Web server sends the requested Web page to the browser. When a Web server executes the Server.Transfer method, the Web server immediately transfers processing to the target Web form. The Response.Redirect method requires two round trips between the Web server and the browser, while the Server.Transfer method transfers processing immediately, so the Server.Transfer method provides better system response times.

- You can use the Response.Redirect method to transfer processing to any URL, whereas you can use the Server.Transfer method only to transfer processing to another Web form within the current Web application project.

- You can use server-side cookies and session variables to share data values among different Web forms in a project.

- Server-side cookies are cookies that commands in server-side programs create on the client workstation by sending the cookie specification as a header message in an HTML document's header section. Cookies are limited because many users are reluctant to allow Web servers to create cookies on their workstations and browsers limit the size and number of cookies that a Web server can create.

❐ A session variable is a variable that the Web server stores in its main memory and that contains specific information about each browser session, such as the browser's IP address, the session date and time, and user selections and preferences.

❐ A session variable exists in the main memory of a Web server as long as the browser is actively requesting Web pages. If the Web server does not observe any activity from a browser session for a specific time interval specified by the session timeout value, the Web server classifies the session as inactive and discards the session's session variable values. The default session timeout value is 20 minutes.

❐ You can set the session timeout value in any Web form code behind file, in the project's Global.asax.vb or Web.config file, or in the Web server's Machine.config file.

❐ You can create a session variable that stores multiple data values by concatenating the new values to the existing values along with a delimiter character such as a colon (:). You must then parse the session variable to retrieve the individual values.

❐ To overcome user concerns about the privacy of cookies, you can create a cookieless Web application project, which saves the session ID in the URL. In a cookieless project, you must always use relative URL paths in hyperlinks or commands that transfer processing to different Web pages; otherwise, the session ID value will be lost.

❐ An application variable stores a value on the Web server that is associated with the Web application and is accessible to all application users. Use application variables to store values that all application users access, that require small amounts of storage space and quick access times, and that are not critical to the application.

**11**

❐ To insert a master record and detail records simultaneously when the master record's primary key is a surrogate key that the database generates, you store the surrogate key value as a local variable, then use the local variable value to insert the detail records.

❐ A DataGrid template column creates a column in a DataGrid control in which you use HTML tags to specify the data that appears in the column. You can use a template column to display data values different from the values that appear in the database or to display calculated values.

❐ To create a template column, you create the new column in the Property Builder visual configuration tool, then add to the Web form in HTML view the Web server control template to specify the column's appearance. You can call a VB .NET function from a Web server control template and display the returned value in a template column.

❐ Forms authentication allows the system to authenticate a user's identity once, and then allows the user to access his or her secure information for the duration of the browser session without having to authenticate his or her identity again. To implement forms authentication, you modify the project's Web.config file to enable forms authentication, specify the location of the project's secure folder, and specify the login form.

❐ To deploy a Web application project to a production Web server, you create the production project folder and associated Web application on the Web server. Then you compile the project files and move the required production application files to the production project folder.

## REVIEW QUESTIONS

1. The _____ method switches processing from the current Web form to a different Web page by sending the target Web page's URL to the browser in an HTML document header.

   a. Response.Redirect

   b. Server.Transfer

   c. Response.Cookies

   d. GetRedirectUrl

2. Describe when you use the Server.Transfer method, and when you use the Response.Redirect method.

3. The _____ method bypasses forms authentication when it switches processing from one Web form to another.

   a. Response.Redirect

   b. Server.Transfer

   c. Response.Cookies

   d. GetRedirectUrl

4. Write a command to transfer processing from the StudentForm.aspx Web form to the Northwoods.htm static Web page. Assume both files are stored in the same folder.

5. Write a command that transfers processing from the StudentForm.aspx Web form to the EnrollmentForm.aspx Web form as efficiently as possible. Assume the Web application project does not use forms authentication, and assume that both files are stored in the same folder.

6. A(n) _____ stores data values about a specific browser/Web server session on the client workstation, whereas a(n) _____ stores data values about a specific browser/Web server session in the Web server's main memory.

   a. Server-side cookie, application variable

   b. Session variable, application variable

   c. Server-side cookie, session variable

   d. Application variable, session variable

7. A(n) _____ variable contains data values that are accessible to all browser sessions that connect to a Web server.

8. Write a VB .NET command to create a server-side cookie named StudentNames that contains your first name, then write a command to retrieve the value and assign it to the Text property of a TextBox named txtStudentName.

9. Write the command to create a session variable named StudentNames that contains your first name and the first names of two of your classmates. Delimit the names using a colon (:).

10. List four ways to modify a Web project's session timeout value.

11. Under what circumstances should you change the session timeout value in the Machine.config file?

12. Write the command for changing a Web application's session timeout value in the Global.asax file to 60 minutes.

13. Suppose that the Web.config file specifies that the session timeout value is 20 minutes, and the Global.asax file specifies that the session timeout value is 30 minutes. What is the project's actual session timeout value?

14. What is a cookieless project? How do you configure a project to be cookieless?

15. Describe when you use an application variable in a Web application project.

16. Write the commands to retrieve the next value in an Oracle9*i* sequence named S_ID_SEQUENCE and then store the retrieved value in a variable named intS_ID.

17. Write the commands to retrieve the value that was just inserted into an AutoNumber column in an Access database, then store the retrieved value in a variable named intS_ID.

18. Describe two uses for a template column.

19. The secure folder contains Web forms that can be viewed only by _____.

   a. Web administrators

   b. Authenticated users

   c. Anonymous users

   d. Nonauthenticated users

**11**

20. What is forms authentication?

21. Specify the elements to add to a project's Web.config file to enable forms authentication and specify that the login form is a Web form named NWLogin.aspx.

22. Show the elements to add to a Web project's Web.config file to specify that the secure folder name is NW_Secure_Folder, and to allow only authenticated users to access the secure folder's contents.

23. The Northwoods University Web application uses forms authentication, and the login form is named NWLogin.aspx. Write the command in the *Submit* button on the NWLogin.aspx Web form to transfer processing back to the source form after the NWLogin.aspx Web form authenticates a user's identity. Assume the user's user name value is stored in a session variable named NWUser, and configure the command to save the authentication information in a cookie on the user's workstation.

24. True or false: To deploy a Web application project, you must include the Web form .aspx and .aspx.vb files on the production server.

## HANDS-ON PROJECTS

The Chapter 11 Hands-on Projects create the Northwoods University Web application in Figure 11-34.

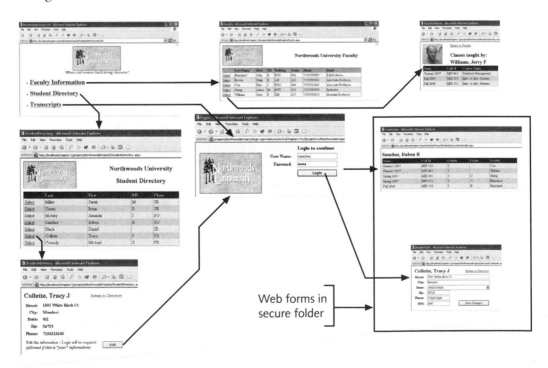

Web forms in secure folder

**Figure 11-34**

To complete the Chapter 11 Hands-on Projects, you need to create a new Web server application named Projects that you associate with the Chapter11\Projects folder on your Solution Disk, and modify your Visual Studio .NET IDE so it places all project solution files in the Chapter11\Projects folder on your Solution Disk. Then create a new Web application project named NorthwoodsProjects whose application root is the Chapter11\ Projects application on your Web server. *If you are using an Oracle9i database*, start SQL*Plus, log on using the *User Name* value *cwuser* and the *Password* value *oracle*, and run the Northwoods.sql script in the Chapter11 folder on your Data Disk. *If you are using an Access database*, copy the Northwoods.mdb database file from the Chapter11 folder on your Data Disk to the Chapter11\Projects\NorthwoodsProjects folder on your Solution Disk. Then copy the files and folders from the Chapter11\Projects folder on your Data Disk to the Chapter11\Projects\NorthwoodsProjects folder on your Solution Disk. Add Northwoods.htm and the Images folder and its contents to the project, and make Northwoods.htm the project's Start Page.

 ## Project 11-1 Creating the Northwoods University Faculty Information Web Forms

In this project, you will create the Faculty and Faculty Classes Web forms in Figure 11–35. The Faculty form displays information about faculty members, and the Faculty Classes form displays information about the courses that a selected faculty member teaches.

11

Faculty.aspx                FacultyClasses.aspx

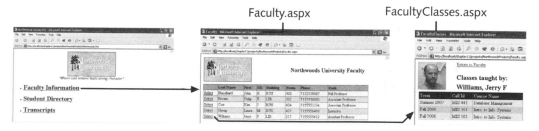

**Figure 11-35**

1. Create new Web forms in the NorthwoodsProject named Faculty.aspx and FacultyClasses.aspx. Create a hyperlink from the Northwoods.htm static Web page to the Faculty.aspx Web form.

2. Create the static Image and Label elements on the Faculty.aspx Web form. Create a LinkButton control with the text "Return to Northwoods Home" that transfers processing back to the Northwoods.htm static Web page.

3. Create a DataGrid control to display the faculty information shown in Figure 11–35. Create a column that retrieves the F_ID column from the FACULTY table, but do not display the F_ID values in the DataGrid. Create a template column to display the faculty F_RANK values using the alternate values as shown. Create a Select

Button hyperlink in the DataGrid. Add commands so that when the user selects a faculty member, the application transfers processing to the FacultyClasses.aspx Web form. (*Hint:* Store the select F_ID value as a session variable.)

4. Create the form elements on the FacultyClasses.aspx Web form as shown. Create a LinkButton control with the text "Return to Faculty" that transfers processing back to the Faculty.aspx Web form.

5. Create a DataGrid control to display the selected faculty member's teaching schedule as shown. Use the F_ID session variable value to query the database and display the information on this form. Sort the information displayed in the DataGrid control by descending TERM_ID value.

## Project 11-2 Creating the Northwoods University Transcript Web Form

In this project, you will create the Login.aspx and Transcripts.aspx Web forms in Figure 11-36. The Transcripts.aspx Web form is in a secure folder, and will appear only after a student has logged on to the Northwoods University Web site.

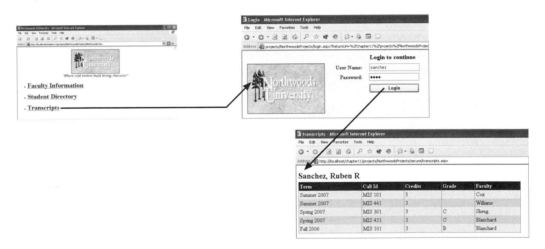

**Figure 11-36**

1. Create a new folder named Secure in the Chapter11\Projects\NorthwoodsProjects folder on your Solution Disk, then add the folder to the project. (This folder will be the project's secure folder, and contain the Web forms that require forms authentication.)

2. Create a new Web form named Login.aspx in the project folder, and create a new Web form named Transcripts.aspx in the secure folder. (*Hint:* To create a Web form in a project subfolder, select the project subfolder, then create the new Web form.) Create a hyperlink from the Northwoods.htm static Web page to the Transcripts.aspx Web form.

3. Configure the project to enable forms authentication. Allow nonauthenticated users to view forms in the project folder, but require user authentication to access forms in the secure folder.

4. Configure the Login.aspx Web form to validate users based on the student's last name and PIN number. (*Hint:* Save the student's S_ID value as a session variable.)

5. Configure the Transcripts.aspx Web form to display the selected student's name in a Label control and the student's course information in a DataGrid control as shown in Figure 11-36. Sort the courses by TERM_ID in descending order.

## Project 11-3 Creating the Northwoods University Student Directory

In this project, you will create the StudentDirectory.aspx, StudentAddress.aspx, Login.aspx, and StudentEdit.aspx Web forms in Figure 11-37 to allow students to view and edit personal information. (You will not need to create the Login.aspx Web form if you already created this Web form in Project 11-2.)

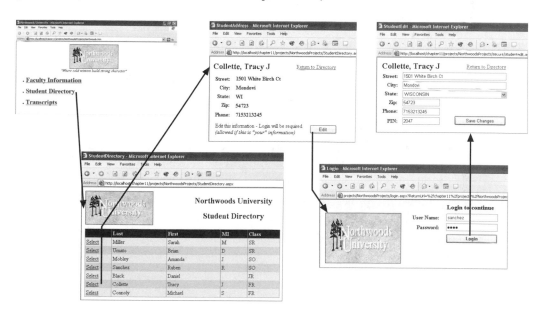

**Figure 11-37**

1. Create a new Web form named StudentDirectory.aspx. Create a DataGrid control on the form as shown in Figure 11-37. Include the S_ID value as a hidden column in the DataGrid. Create a *Select* hyperlink in the DataGrid. Configure the hyperlink's event handler so that when a user selects a student, the system saves the S_ID value in a session variable, then transfers processing to the StudentAddress.aspx form.

2. If necessary, create a subfolder named Secure within the project folder that contains the project Web forms that require user authentication. (You may have already created this folder in Project 11-2.)

3. Configure the project to enable forms authentication. (You may have already done this in Project 11-2.)

4. Create the StudentAddress.aspx and Login.aspx Web forms in the project folder, and the StudentEdit.aspx Web form in the secure folder. (If you already created Login.aspx in Project 11-2, you do not need to create it again.) Create LinkButton controls on the StudentAddress.aspx and StudentEdit.aspx Web forms with the text "Return to Directory." When the user clicks these LinkButton controls, transfer processing back to the StudentDirectory.aspx Web form.

5. When the user clicks *Edit* on the StudentAddress.aspx Web form, transfer processing to the StudentEdit.aspx Web form.

6. Configure the Login.aspx Web form to validate user identities using the student last name and PIN value. (*Hint:* Save the S_ID value as a session variable.)

7. Configure the StudentEdit.aspx Web form as shown in Figure 11-37 to allow students to update their personal information.

 To complete Project 11-4, you must have completed Project 11-1, Project 11-2, or Project 11-3.

## Project 11-4 Deploying the Northwoods Web Application to a Production Web Server

In this project, you will move a completed Web application project to a production server.

1. Create a folder named NorthwoodsProduction in the Chapter11\Projects folder on your Solution Disk, then configure your Web server to use this folder as the production application.

2. Compile the project files if necessary, then copy the production application files to the NorthwoodsProduction folder.

3. Confirm that the production application is working correctly by starting Internet Explorer, then typing *http://localhost/Chapter11/Projects/NorthwoodsProduction/Northwoods.htm* in the *Address* field.

## CASE PROJECTS

 To solve the case projects in this chapter, you must first create a new Web server application named Cases that you associate with the Chapter11\Cases folder on your Solution Disk. Also, modify your Visual Studio .NET IDE so it places all project solution files in the Chapter11\Cases folder on your Solution Disk. Each case will require you to make a separate Web application project.

# Case 11-1 Ashland Valley Soccer League

In this case, you will create an integrated Web application project for the Ashland Valley Soccer League that includes the Web forms shown in Figure 11-38.

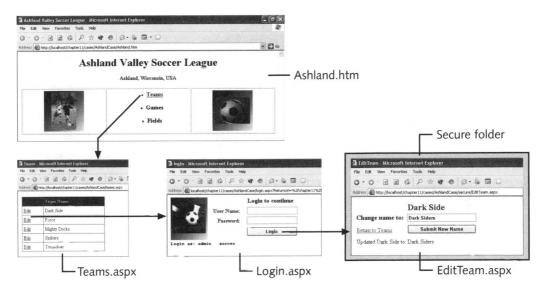

**Figure 11-38**

1. Create a new Web application project named AshlandCase whose application root is the Chapter11\Cases folder on your Solution Disk.

2. Initialize the Ashland database.

   *If you are using an Oracle9i database*, start SQL*Plus, log on using the *User Name* value *cwuser* and *Password* value *oracle*, then run the Ashland.sql script that is in the Chapter11\Cases folder on your Data Disk to refresh the database tables and insert sample data values. *If you are using an Access database*, copy the Ashland.mdb file from the Chapter11\Cases folder on your Data Disk to the Chapter11\Cases\AshlandCase folder on your Solution Disk, and modify the Security properties of the AshlandCase folder so all Internet users have full control.

3. Copy Ashland.htm from the Chapter11\Cases folder on your Data Disk to the Chapter11\Cases\AshlandCase folder on your Solution Disk.

4. Create a new folder named Images in the Chapter11\Cases\AshlandCase folder on your Solution Disk, then copy the following files from the Chapter11\Cases folder on your Data Disk to the new folder: players.jpg, soccerball.jpg, games.jpg, and hands.jpg.

5. Create the Teams.aspx, Login.aspx, and EditTeam.aspx Web forms shown in Figure 11-38. The Teams.aspx Web form displays information about teams, and the EditTeam.aspx Web form allows authenticated users to change the team name.

The Login.aspx Web form authenticates users using the *User Name* value *admin* and the *Password* value *soccer*. The Web form does not retrieve these values from the database; instead the values are hard-coded into the commands in the Login.aspx form. (*Hint:* The column displaying the *Edit* hyperlinks in Teams.aspx is really a Select column.)

## Case Project 11-2 Al's Body Shop

In this case, you will create an integrated Web project for the Al's Body Shop that includes the Web forms shown in Figure 11-39.

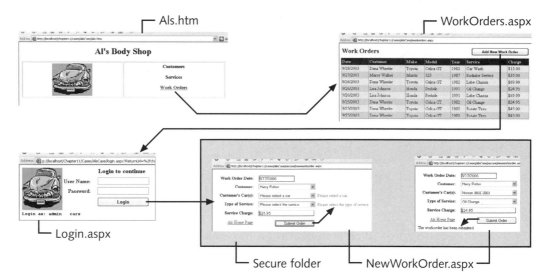

**Figure 11-39**

1. Create a new Web application project named AlsCase whose application root is the Chapter11\Cases folder on your Solution Disk.

2. Initialize the Als database:

   *If you are using an Oracle9i database*, start SQL*Plus, log on using the *User Name* value *cwuser* and the *Password* value *oracle*, then run the Als.sql script that is in the Chapter11\Cases folder on your Data Disk to refresh the database tables and insert sample data values. *If you are using an Access database*, copy the Als.mdb file from the Chapter11\Cases folder on your Data Disk to the Chapter11\Cases\AlsCase folder on your Solution Disk, and modify the Security properties of the AlsCase folder so all Internet users have full control.

3. Copy Als.htm from the Chapter11\Cases folder on your Data Disk to the Chapter11\Cases\AlsCase folder on your Solution Disk.

4. Create a new folder named Images in the Chapter11\Cases\AlsCase folder on your Solution Disk, then copy the car.jpg file from the Chapter11\Cases folder on your Data Disk to the new folder.

5. Create the WorkOrders.aspx, NewWorkOrder.aspx, and Login.aspx Web forms shown in Figure 11-39.

6. The WorkOrders.aspx Web form displays information about work orders in a DataGrid control. Format the date and charge columns using the formats as shown. When the user clicks *Add New Work Order,* the application transfers processing to the NewWorkOrder.aspx Web form, which requires user authentication.

7. The Login.aspx Web form authenticates users using the *User Name* value *admin* and *Password* value *cars.* The Web form does not retrieve these values from the database; instead the values are hard-coded into the commands in the Login.aspx form.

8. The NewWorkOrder.aspx Web form automatically displays the current date in the *Work Order Date* field when the form first opens, and uses data bound DropDownList controls to display selections for customer names, a selected customer's car or cars, and available types of service. (In the *Customer's Car(s)* field, display only the cars associated with the selected customer.) When the user selects a type of service, use a query to display the service charge in a Label control automatically. Add appropriate validation controls to ensure that the user selects a customer, car, and type of service. When the user clicks *Submit Order,* save the work order information in the database. Create a LinkButton control with the text "Als Home Page" to transfer processing back to the Als.htm static Web page. (*Hint:* Set the CausesValidation property of the LinkButton to False. Otherwise, the validation controls will force the user to satisfy the validation controls before transferring back to the home page.)

## Case Project 11-3 Sun-Ray Videos

In this case, you will create an integrated Web application project for Sun-Ray Videos.

1. Create a new Web application project named SunrayCase whose application root is the Chapter11\Cases folder on your Solution Disk.

2. Initialize the Sun Ray database:

   *If you are using an Oracle9i database,* start SQL*Plus, log on using the *User Name* value *cwuser* and the *Password* value *oracle,* then run the Sunray.sql script that is in the Chapter11\Cases folder on your Data Disk to refresh the database tables and insert sample data values. *If you are using an Access database,* copy the Sunray.mdb file from the Chapter11\Cases folder on your Data Disk to the Chapter11\Cases\SunrayCase folder on your Solution Disk, and modify the Security properties of the SunrayCase folder so all Internet users have full control.

3. Create a static Web page named Sunray.htm that displays at least one graphic image. Create hyperlinks on the home page to the following Web forms:

   ❐ A nonsecure Web form that lists all video categories in a DataGrid. When the user selects a category, a detail DataGrid displays all titles within the category and their associated formats.

❐ A secure Web form that displays all active customer rentals. (*Hint:* An active customer rental's DATE_IN value in the SUNRAY_VIDEO table is NULL.) This Web form uses a DataGrid to display customer names, categories of the rentals, titles of the rentals, date rented, and the date the rental is due.

4. Create a login form to authenticate users. This form authenticates users using the *User Name* value *admin* and *Password* value *sunray*. The Web form does not retrieve these values from the database; instead the values are hard-coded into the commands in the login form.

## Case Project 11-4 Learning Technologies, Incorporated

In this case, you will create an integrated Web application project for Learning Technologies, Incorporated.

1. Create a new Web application project named LtiCase whose application root is the Chapter11\Cases folder on your Solution Disk.

2. Initialize the Lti database:

*If you are using an Oracle9i database*, start SQL*Plus, log on using the *User Name* value *cwuser* and the *Password* value *oracle*, then run the Lti.sql script that is in the Chapter11\Cases folder on your Data Disk to refresh the database tables and insert sample data values. *If you are using an Access database*, copy the Lti.mdb file from the Chapter11\Cases folder on your Data Disk to the Chapter11\Cases\ LtiCase folder on your Solution Disk, and modify the Security properties of the LtiCase folder so all Internet users have full control.

3. Create a static Web page that contains hyperlinks to Web forms displaying information about authors and books.

4. Create a secure Web form that displays author information in a DataGrid control. Allow users to edit author information. When the user selects an author, display information about the selected author's book in a detail DataGrid.

5. Create a secure Web form that displays book titles, ISBNs, publication dates, and book prices in a DataGrid. When the user selects a book, display a detail DataGrid that shows the warehouses that store the selection, along with the quantity on hand in each warehouse.

6. Create a login form to authenticate users. This form authenticates users using the *User Name* value *admin* and *Password* value *lti*. The Web form does not retrieve these values from the database; instead the values are hard-coded into the commands in the login form.

# Index